WOMEN OF NORTHERN, WESTERN, AND CENTRAL AFRICA

WOMEN OF NORTHERN, WESTERN, AND CENTRAL AFRICA

A Bibliography, 1976–1985

**Compiled by
Davis A. Bullwinkle**

African Special Bibliographic Series, Number 10

Greenwood Press
New York • Westport, Connecticut • London

Library of Congress Cataloging-in-Publication Data

Bullwinkle, Davis.
    Women of northern, western, and central Africa : a bibliography,
1976-1985 / compiled by Davis A. Bullwinkle.
      p. cm.—(African special bibliographic series, ISSN
0749-2308 ; no. 10)
    Includes index.
    ISBN 0-313-26609-3 (lib. bdg. : alk. paper)
    1. Women—Africa—Bibliography. 2. Women—Africa, North—
Bibliography. 3. Women—Africa, West—Bibliography. 4. Women—
Africa, Central—Bibliography. I. Title. II. Series.
  Z7964.A3B85 1989
  [HQ1787]
  016.3054'096—dc20   89-2160

British Library Cataloguing in Publication Data is available.

Library of Congress Catalog Card Number: 89-2160
ISBN: 0-313-26609-3
ISSN: 0749-2308

First published in 1989

Greenwood Press, Inc.
88 Post Road West, Westport, Connecticut 06881

Printed in the United States of America

For Judy

Who in my middle years I have
found to share my life
And who brings joy and love,
support, kindness and meaning
to my life

And for Carol

Who showed me the true value of loving
another human being and whose
lifetime of love
I shall cherish for all my years

I dedicate this work

Contents

CONTENTS

CONTENTS

CONTENTS

CONTENTS

CONTENTS

CONTENTS

xiii

CONTENTS

CONTENTS

CONTENTS

Foreword

This work is the outgrowth of a paper I wrote a number of years ago that was published by the African Bibliographic Center in Washington, D.C. That paper, a bibliography on women in Africa during the 1970's stimulated my interest in creating a work that would bring together all the English language publications written about women in Africa during the United Nations Decade for Women from 1976-1985.

The work could never have been completed without the tremendous help of two people. During the research phase of this work, I discussed the computer needs of the work with a friend named Vicki Tynan. Over the next five months, Vicki wrote a complete computer program for this project. Due to the size and complexity of a project like this, the program was extremely time consuming to produce. Few works of this scope have ever been attempted and we were soon to learn we were on the fringe of computer technology as it applies to manipulating a large amount of data.

Vicki's son Dylan, already a computer whiz at sixteen, helped get me through my first major computer project and orientation with my computer and the integrated software.

Their help during every conceivable hour of the day made this project a much easier and manageable one. I am very grateful to them both for their time and patience.

Preface

'Women of Northern, Western and Central Africa: A Bibliography, 1976-1985' is the second of a three volume Africana Special Bibliographic Series to be published by Greenwood Press. This second volume includes materials divided into general subjects by regions and subjects by nations of Northern, Western and Central Africa.

Thirty-four subject headings will be utilized over the scope of the entire three volume set. Unique to these last two volumes is the heading of divorce, which was not used in the previous volume. The subject heading of apartheid and race relations, while not unique to South Africa, will only be used in the South Africa bibliography.

The third volume in this series will be called, 'Women of Eastern and Southern Africa: A Bibliography, 1976-1985'. It will include data from two regions and seventeen nations. Countries with fewer than thirty citations will not be divided by subjects. Instead, their data will be alphabetized by author.

The complete three-volume work indexes over 4,100 original English language research works on women in Africa and covers all aspects of their lives. The original citations are cross-referenced by as many subject headings as possible for best coverage. The scope of this work covers all subject areas where materials on or about women might appear. It differs from some previous bibliographic projects that covered very specialized materials.

A follow-up volume of this three-volume work is already being researched. Covering the years from 1986-1990, it will hopefully be published in 1993. I will continue to publish this research in as timely a manner as possible. Those of you completing research that might be relevant to upcoming works and would like to have information about your work disseminated may contact me at 213 Colonial Court, Little Rock, Arkansas, 72201 or by phone at either (501) 682-2867 or (501) 666-9048.

Introduction

In 1945, the nations of the world met in San Francisco to sign the charter of a new international organization to be known as the United Nations. Among its stated goals were the "attainment of world peace, the reaffirmation of faith in human rights, the dignity of worth of the human person as well as the equal rights of men and women of all nations."

Since then, the United Nations has encountered a greater degree of difficulty than anticipated in achieving the goals of its original charter. Nations are constantly warring with each other and the number of repressive governments has increased through the years. Hundreds of thousands of people have been oppressed by their own governments for their actions of speaking out against government policies to quash the goals of human dignity and freedom. Thousands of women, children and men have died of starvation and disease because governments have neither taken the steps needed to prevent the problems nor the steps needed to have the international community involved in the solutions.

Due to the conditions that created these problems, as well as the traditional, social and economic roles played by women in the developing world, the United Nations became alarmed that the goal of equality among the sexes was not being achieved by its members. Two years after the United Nations charter was signed, the organization created its Commission on the Status of Women.

In 1972, twenty-four years after the creation of the U.N., a group of nongovernmental organizations (NGOs) sent a request to the United Nations Commission on the Status of Women to look into the possibility of having the U.N. choose a one-year period to focus attention on the problems faced by women in the world. Egypt, Finland, France, Hungary Romania and the Philippines introduced a resolution to the

U.N. General Assembly which had been previously adopted by
the Commission. The year 1975 was declared International
Women's Year. The goals of this one year period were stated
as being, "to intensify action to promote equality between
women and men and to increase women's contribution to
national and international development." The U.N. delegates
agreed, while approving the Commission's declaration, to add
peace and equality to the already stated goals for the year.

Specific objectives for each of the individual goals
stated in the declaration were established. Among them
were... "to achieve full equality before the law in all
fields where it did not already exist; to meet the health
needs of girls and women equally with those of boys and men;
to promote equality of economic rights; to improve the
quality of rural life; and to eliminate illiteracy and
ensure equality of educational opportunities." Emphasis was
placed on "realizing the principle of the rights of people
to self-determination; combating racism and racial
discrimination wherever it manifests itself; and lending
support to the victims of racism, apartheid and colonialism
as well as supporting women and children in armed struggle."

In May of 1974, the United Nations Economic and Social
Council requested a United Nations conference to scrutinize
U.N. agencies as to how they had carried out the
recommendations for the elimination of discrimination
against women made by the Commission on the Status of Women.
In November of that year, the United Nations chose Mexico as
the site of what would be the first of three world
conferences on the plight of women throughout the world.

In June of 1975, the World Conference of the
International Women's Year convened in Mexico City. United
Nations members from one hundred and thirty-three nations
attended. The African continent was represented by
thirty-nine delegates. Other than United Nations delegates,
representatives from one hundred and fourteen
nongovernmental organizations also attended. Specific
African NGOs attending were the African National Congress
(ANC), the African National Council, and four national
liberation groups.

During the two weeks of meetings, the delegates labored
to create a World Plan of Action that could be used to
implement the stated objectives of the International Women's
Year. The plan was divided into actions that could be taken
by national governments and actions that could be undertaken
by NGOs and other international organizations. Those
actions included social, economic, legal, administrative and
educational proposals. To governments it was suggested that
a "national machinery" be established to manage and promote
efforts in each country to advance the status of women. To
international and regional organizations, particularly the
United Nations and its agencies, it was proposed that they
extend assistance to individual governments and

nongovernmental organizations to support their efforts in
achieving the recommendations.

The conference stressed the objective of achieving a
partial number of the goals from the Plan of Action by 1980.
Among the goals for that-five year period were a decrease in
the illiteracy rate; a concerted effort to create more
employment opportunities; the acknowledgment of the economic
value of women's work in the home, in food production and in
marketing; and the commitment to the development of modern
rural technology. Another important objective of this five
year period was that individual governments undertake the
responsibility to guarantee women equality in the execution
of their civil, social and political rights, especially
those associated with economic, marital and civil matters.

Once the Plan of Action was complete, thirty-five
resolutions attached to the plan were approved by the
conference. These resolutions dealt with such diverse
issues as the integration of women in development; the
establishment of research and training centers for women in
Africa; the status of women under apartheid; the condition
of women in rural areas, and the health needs of Third World
women.

From this two-week conference came the recommendation
that the United Nations proclaim the decade from 1976-1985
as the United Nations Decade for Women and Development. The
delegates believed that this proclamation would guarantee
that national and international activity on the equality of
women would maintain its momentum and continue, and that
agencies of the United Nations would take steps to enact the
Plan of Action and evaluate their previous achievements to
advance the status of women. Support from international and
regional intergovernmental organizations outside the United
Nations would result in the development of programs to carry
out the Plan of Action and achieve the objectives of the
United Nations International Women's Year as well as the
United Nations Decade for Women.

At the end of 1975, the U.N. General Assembly voted to
support the report of the World Plan of Action and its
resolutions. The assembly proclaimed the years 1976-1985 as
"The United Nations Decade for Women, Equality, Development
and Peace." They declared this ten year period to be one in
which a concerted effort would be made by national,
regional, and international organizations to implement the
Plan of Action and related resolutions. Nations were called
upon to act quickly and establish short, medium and long
term goals, including by 1980 the implementation of a
minimum number of the plan's objectives.

As a final action on this issue, the United Nations
announced that a second world conference would be held
in 1980 to evaluate and appraise the accomplishments made by
member nations in achieving the partial goals and

and objectives of the International Women's Year and Decade.
Held in Copenhagen, Denmark in mid-July of 1980, the
conference attracted delegates from one hundred forty-five
nations. This almost ten percent increase in participation
by member nations once again emphasized the growing
importance of women's issues on the international scene.
Among the African NGOs who attended were representatives
from the African National Congress (ANC), the South West
Africa People's Organization (SWAPO), and the Pan African
Congress. Along with the reevaluation of the previous five
years' work and the realization of the objectives drawn in
Mexico City, the important issues of health, education and
employment were added as additional themes of this
conference.

The program of the conference included four important
topics. Among these were the effects of apartheid on women
in Southern Africa and special measures to assist them; a
mid-decade review and evaluation of the successes and
obstacles to achieving the objectives of the decade; the
effects of the Israeli occupation on Palestinian women; and
the study and creation of proposals for advancing the status
of women and reinforcing established strategies to displace
hurdles to full and equal participation in development.

A second Plan of Action for the concluding five years of
the decade (1980-1985) was discussed and promulgated. This
Plan of Action emphasized the achievement of equality,
development and peace with special emphasis on health,
education and employment. The forty-eight resolutions
adopted by the conference were aimed at attaining the goals
of the next five-year period and the decade overall.

On December 11, 1980, the United Nations General
Assembly adopted a resolution supporting the conference's
Plan of Action for the second half of the decade. Also set
in motion was the planning for the end of the decade world
conference to be held in Nairobi, Kenya, in mid-1985.

The last of the three world conferences convened in
Nairobi, July 25, 1985. Representatives from one hundred
forty nations attended. Eighteen thousand women, nearly
three times as many as had attended the first world
conference in Mexico City, arrived in Nairobi. The
conference's theme was the review and appraisal of the
achievements and the failures of the decade. Almost twelve
hundred NGO workshops were conducted in overcrowded
classrooms and outdoor spaces. Oriented around the main
themes of development, equality and peace, the workshops
also dealt with the issues of health, education, and
employment.

The results of the three world conferences and the
United Nations Decade for Women highlighted the wretched
conditions faced by the women of Africa and the Third World.
As a continent, Africa has the highest percent of illiterate
women in the world. It is estimated that under

twenty percent of all African women can read and write and that may be a liberal figure. Children are brought into this world by the fewest number of trained maternity personnel and suffer from the lowest birthrates in the developing world. It is believed that African infant mortality rates in excess of ninety-five per one thousand live births, while being the highest in the world, are also responsible for the low expectation of life in Africa. Female children attend primary schools in smaller numbers than males. Secondary education, while limited to both sexes, is still undertaken by three times as many boys as girls. African women marry at younger ages than their peers throughout the world, usually between fifteen and seventeen years of age. They also produce more children than any group of women on earth, averaging six and a half children for every childbearing woman in Africa. It is no wonder that African women have the lowest life expectancy on earth. That tragic age is just 48.6 years.

Historically, the women of Africa have been the principal contributors for labor needed to produce Africa's food crops. They have suffered from unequal access to extension services and training and have been discriminated against in their efforts to gain credit. It is estimated that African women deliver eighty percent of the labor and organization needed in the production of Africa's food. Women often spend from nine to ten hours a day laboring in the fields, then a sizeable number of hours performing other tasks such as gathering firewood, preserving food, caring for their children and elderly relatives, putting food in storage, making meals and retrieving water. They may also be involved in some form of work that produces saleable commodities such as soap, vegetables and handicrafts that can be traded for necessities such as food and household items.

In the not too distant past, Africa as a continent fulfilled her needs by producing all of the food her people required. By 1980, Africa was forced to import almost fifteen percent of her total food essentials. Africa's inability to produce enough food to feed her people is due to a number of factors, not the least of which were colonial policies and the introduction of cash crop economies by those governments. As a result of these governmental policies, women have found themselves overburdened in their roles as primary food producers. Over the last twenty-five to thirty years, large numbers of African men have left their native land holdings and migrated to Africa's cities looking for work. While African men historically have never had a great penchant for working the land, the loss of their labor has seriously affected Africa's women. The amount of work expected or required of women has increased dramatically.

In Sub-Saharan Africa the rights to land have traditionally belonged to women. Colonial governments, ignoring historic cultural patterns, allocated land

ownership to men. These policies displaced subsistence
agriculture with cash crop commodities such as coffee and
cotton. Development projects instigated by new national
governments also discriminated against women by recognizing
men as the owners of projects. Men have been encouraged to
grow cash crops for the economic rewards available to them
while women have still been responsible for a large part of
the labor required to grow these crops. The rewards of
independence and supposedly egalitarian governments have not
been kind to Africa's women. The benefits still elude them.
     Another of the major problems faced by women throughout
the Third World has been the failure of governments and
development agencies to acknowledge women as a factor in
development projects and in the decision making process.
While women make up over fifty percent of the world's
population, only a small percentage of them hold
administrative careers in Third World governments. As a
result of this, women are not involved in the
decision-making processes and their opinions are often
ignored. A crisis of self image has also hurt African and
Third World women. They themselves do not value their own
labor in food production by the same criteria as men's labor
in agriculture. The same views are prevalent among
agricultural economists and development planners who do not
take into consideration the time women spend planting,
weeding, harvesting and other daily chores previously
mentioned. Acceptance of the facts concerning the role of
women in food production is still slow in coming. Many
research studies support the efforts of women to execute and
oversee agricultural projects successfully. Still,
agricultural development planning continues to ignore their
position of importance and their capabilities. The role of
women as food producers must be recognized before the
problems of food shortages can be eliminated.
     If conditions for women in Africa and the Third World
are to be improved, governments must provide their female
citizens the same opportunities they afford their male
citizens. Equal opportunities in the areas of education and
training, the elimination of illiteracy, and the equal
access to credit sources would provide some solutions to the
problems women face in Third World development. Women must
have equal access to agricultural extension services to help
provide them with the information and technological data
they need to compete and increase crop yields. The
employment of more female agricultural extension
professionals might also be of great help. Between 1977 and
1984 less than one-fifth of all those sent overseas for
professional training programs were women. The introduction
of modern rural technology is a necessity women must have
for them to gain advancements in mechanization, improved
water systems, better methods of food production and
preservation, and greater access to fuel resources.

A special emphasis by African governments is also quickly needed in the field of women's health. Programs begun by the World Health Organization (WHO) in 1980 in a number of African nations have been very successful. Women's volunteer organizations are being trained at the WHO Regional Training Center in Mauritius. There they are instructed in maternal health care, family planning and child health. Promising results have been achieved in West Africa. The vaccination of children against childhood diseases such as tetanus, measles, poliomyelitis, tuberculosis and diphtheria have commenced. Governments throughout the Third World must move quickly and have relative success in dealing with the problems of their female citizens. The health of their nations sit in the balance. Development of any kind cannot succeed without a population free of the worries of catastrophic diseases that plague the African continent and other Third World nations. In Africa, 48.6 years of age certainly cannot be accepted as a fulfilled lifetime.

While the achievements of the United Nations Decade for Women, or the lack of them, will be discussed and debated for years, it is promising to know that the decade forced many governments to take a more objective look at the position women hold and the problems they face in their countries. The world conference and the media forced them to recognize the reality they refused to face. Two-thirds of all illiterates are women and most refugees are women and children. It is they who are facing major health problems that could dramatically alter the history of nations.

Technology, while helping to develop nations and making labor less difficult for men, and therefore more profitable, has actually failed to help women and in many cases has made their lives more demanding. Technology must be shared amongst all people in rural developing countries.

While achievements during the decade were exemplified by dramatic increases in women's and girls' participation in educational programs and small gains in employment opportunities, they have been minimal to say the least. Access to credit through new organizations such as the Women's Bank will be helpful if they continue to receive support from the international financial institutions.

This bibliographic research project was initiated in the anticipation of it becoming a major contribution in the Social Sciences and the field of African Studies. The citations that follow are arranged into five specific groups. They include articles appearing in journals and edited books, as well as Masters theses, Ph.D dissertations, conference papers and individual books on women in Africa and the Third World.

INTRODUCTION

Unlike the two previous world conferences in Mexico City and Copenhagen, a complete bibliography of papers presented at the conference has not and probably will not be published by the NGO committee. Research on this project was delayed for a period of time in the hope that such a list would be forthcoming. A final document for the Nairobi conference was published by the NGO. This document lists titles of some papers by the themes by which they were presented. Access to these papers may be possible through the Economic Commission for Africa's African Training and Research Center for Women in Addis Ababa, Ethiopia, the International Women's Tribunal Center in New York City, or the International Center for Research on Women in Washington, D.C. Addresses for these organizations can be found in Appendix A of this document.

It is unfortunate, to say the least, that a document as comprehensive as this one is not able to contain a list of the papers from the last world conference and the NGO workshops. Their inclusion would have made this a more complete work.

In publishing this comprehensive work on previously written research on African women, I hope that those using this document and contemplating further research on African and Third World women will use it to analyze where future research might best take place. This work is unique. No other book, periodical, or database has in the past brought together the amount of information on African women that this project has. This work is only the beginning of an ongoing project that will disseminate accumulated data on women in Africa. A five-year update of the research covering the post-decade period is forthcoming.

The gains of the decade have been disappointing. That a decade had to be chosen to underscore the injustices and widespread inequalities of women throughout the world is a tragedy in itself. I hope the decade and its poor results will demonstrate to all who care in this world that so much more needs to be done to guarantee that all peoples of this planet have the chance to live fulfilling lives. And, I hope it will inspire further research to help solve the problems of the oppressed and underprivileged.

General Subject Bibliography—
Northern Africa

AGRICULTURE

Cloud, Kathleen
   "Sex Roles in Food Production and Distribution Systems in
   the Sahel." (In) Cowen, Ann B. (ed.). Proceedings and
   Papers of the International Conference on Women and Food:
   Consortium for International Development. Tucson,
   Arizona: University of Arizona. 1978. pp. 62-89.
Cloud, Kathleen
   Sex Roles in Food Production and Food Distribution
   Systems in the Sahel. Washington, D.C.: U.S. Department
   of State. U.S. Agency for International Development.
   Office of Women in Development. 1977. 20p.
Dulansey, Maryanne L.
   Women in Development Program Concerns in Francophone
   Sahel: Report of a Workshop. Washington, D.C.: U.S.
   Department of State. U.S. Agency for International
   Development. Bobo-Dioulasso, Upper Volta. June 5-7,
   1979. 11p.
Hagan, A.L.
   "The Role of Women in Rural Development: Some Critical
   Issues." (In) Mondjanagni, A.C. La Participation
   Populaire an Developpement en Afrique Noire. Paris:
   Karthala; Doula, Institut Pan Africain Pour Le
   Developpement. 1984. pp. 75-87.
Kamba, Kate
   "Fuel Wood and Energy Development for African Women."
   Paper Presented at the Workshop on Women in Agricultural
   Development. Addis Ababa, Ethiopia: United Nations
   Economic Commission for Africa. Awassa, Ethiopia. June
   26, 1983. 13p.
Kizerbo, Joseph
   "Women and the Energy Crisis in the Sahel Africa. From
   the Seminar on Fuel and Energy Development for African
   Women in Rural Areas, Bamako, Mali, December, 1980."
   Unasylva. Volume 33 #133 1981. pp. 5-10.

Roboff, Farron V. and Renwick, Hilary L.
"The Changing Role of Women in the Development of the
Sahel." Paper Presented to the Annual Meeting of the
African Studies Association. Paper #92. Boston,
Massachusetts. 1976. 12p.
U.S. Agency for International Development (U.S. AID)
Examples of Women in Development Programs in Sahel
Francophone West Africa. Washington, D.C.: U.S.
Department of State. U.S. AID. Office of Sahel and
Francophone West Africa, Bureau for Africa. 1979. 27p.
U.S. Agency for International Development (U.S. AID)
Training Women in the Sahel. Washington, D.C.: U.S.
Department of State. U.S. AID. Office of Women in
Development. 1978. 47p.
Youssef, Nadia H.
"Women and Agricultural Production in Muslim Societies."
Studies in Comparative International Development. Volume
12 #1 Spring, 1977. pp. 41-58.

BIBLIOGRAPHIES

Abdel Kader, Soha
"Research on the Status of Women, Development and
Population Trends in Arab States: An Annotated
Bibliography." (In) UNESCO. Bibliographic Guide to
Studies on the Status of Women: Development and
Population. Paris: United Nations Educational,
Scientific and Cultural Organization. 1983. pp. 67-81.
Al-Qazza, Ayad
Women in the Middle East and North Africa: An Annotated
Bibliography. Austin, Texas: University of Texas Press.
Center for Middle Eastern Studies. Middle East Monograph
#2. 1977. 179p.
Fikry, M.
Traditional Maternal and Child Health Care and Related
Problems in the Sahel: A Bibliographic Study.
Washington, D.C.: U.S. Department of State. U.S. Agency
for International Development. Sahel Development
Project. 1977. 123p.
Geletkanycz, Christine and Egan, Susan
Literature Review: The Practice of Female Circumcision.
Washington, D.C.: U.S. Department of Health, Education
and Welfare. Office of International Health. Mimeo.
1979.
Meghdessian, S.R.
The Status of Arab Women: A Select Bibliography.
Westport, Connecticut: Greenwood Press. 1980. 176p.

CULTURAL ROLES

Abu-Lughod, Lila
"A Community of Secrets: The Separate World of Bedouin

2

Women." Signs. Volume 10 #4 Summer, 1985. pp.
637-657.
Accad, Evelyne
"Complex Inter-Relation of Women's Liberation and Arab
Nationalism in North African Novels Written by Women."
Paper Presented at the Annual Meeting of the African
Studies Association. Paper #1. Boston, Massachusetts.
1976. 16p.
Accad, Evelyne
"The Prostitute in Arab and North African Fiction." (In)
Horn, Pierre L. and Pringle, Mary B. (eds.). The Image
of the Prostitute in Modern Literature. New York: Ungar.
1984. pp. 63-75.
Accad, Evelyne
"The Theme of Sexual Oppression in the North African
Novel." (In) Beck, Lois and Keddie, Nikki R. (eds.).
Women in the Muslim World. Cambridge, Massachusetts:
Harvard University Press. 1978. pp. 617-628.
Accad, Evelyne
Veil of Shame: The Role of Women in the Contemporary
Fiction of North Africa and the Arab World. Sherbrooke,
Canada: Editions Naaman. 1978. 182p.
Adamson, Kay
"Approaches to the Study of Women in North Africa: As
Reflected in Research of Various Scholars." Maghreb
Review. Volume 3 #7-8 May-August, 1978. pp. 22-31.
Al-Qazza, Ayad
"Current Status of Research on Women in the Arab World."
Middle Eastern Studies. Volume 14 #3 October, 1978.
pp. 372-384.
Al-Qazza, Ayad
Women in the Middle East and North Africa: An Annotated
Bibliography. Austin, Texas: University of Texas Press.
Center for Middle Eastern Studies. Middle East Monograph
#2. 1977. 179p.
Allman, James
"Family Life, Women's Status, and Fertility: Middle East
and North African Perspectives." (In) Allman, James
(ed.). Women's Studies and Fertility in the Muslim
World. New York: Praeger Publishers. Praeger Special
Studies. 1978. pp. 24-47.
Allman, James
"Family Patterns, Women's Status and Fertility in
Middle-East and North-Africa." International Journal of
Sociology of the Family. Volume 8 #1 1978. pp. 19-35.
Allman, James
"The Demographic Transition in the Middle East and North
Africa." International Journal of Middle East Studies.
Volume 12 #3 November, 1980. pp. 277-301.
Allman, James (ed.)
Women's Status and Fertility in the Muslim World. New
York: Praeger Publishers. Praeger Special Studies.
1978. 378p.

Badran, Margot F.
"Middle East and North Africa: Women." Trends in
History. Volume 1 #1 1979. pp. 123-129.

Baffoun, Alya
"Women and Social Change in the Muslim Arab World."
Women's Studies International Forum. Volume 5 #2 1982.

Caldwell, Pat
"Egypt and the Arab World." (In) Caldwell, John C.
(ed.). The Persistence of High Fertility: Population
Prospects in the Third World. Canberra, Australia:
Australian National University. Department of
Demography. Volume Two. 1977. pp. 593-616.

Casajus, Dominique
"The Wedding Ritual Among the Kel Ferwan Tuaregs."
Journal of the Anthropological Society of Oxford. Volume
14 #2 1983. pp. 227-257.

Chamie, Joseph and Weller, Robert H.
"Levels, Trends and Differentials in Nuptiality in the
Middle East and North Africa." Genus. Volume 39 #1-4
January-December, 1983. pp. 213-231.

Chamie, Joseph and Weller, Robert H.
Levels, Trends and Differentials in Nuptiality in the
Middle East and North Africa. Tallahassee, Florida:
Florida State University. Center for the Study of
Population. College of Social Sciences. Working Paper
#83-02. 1983. 12p.

Chamie, Joseph
Polygamy Among Arabs. New York: United Nations. U.N.
Population Division. 1985.

Cloud, Kathleen
"Sex Roles in Food Production and Distribution Systems in
the Sahel." (In) Cowen, Ann B. (ed.). Proceedings and
Papers of the International Conference on Women and Food:
Consortium for International Development. Tucson,
Arizona: University of Arizona. 1978. pp. 62-89.

Cloud, Kathleen
Sex Roles in Food Production and Food Distribution
Systems in the Sahel. Washington, D.C.: U.S. Department
of State. U.S. Agency for International Development.
Office of Women in Development. 1977. 20p.

Dulansey, Maryanne L.
Women in Development Program Concerns in Francophone
Sahel: Report of a Workshop. Washington, D.C.: U.S.
Department of State. U.S. Agency for International
Development. Bobo-Dioulasso, Upper Volta. June 5-7,
1979. 11p.

Duza, M. Badrud and Sivamurthy, M.
"Household Structure in Selected Urban Areas of Four Arab
and African Cities." (In) Huzayyin, S.A. and Acsadi,
G.T. (eds.). Family and Marriage in Some African and
Asiatic Countries. Cairo: Cairo Demographic Centre.
Research Monograph Series #6. 1976. pp. 267-284.

4

Duza, M. Badrud and Seetharam, K.S. and Sivamurthy, M.
"Patterns of Family Cycles in Selected Areas of Four Arab
and African Cities: Some Demographic Implications." (In)
Huzayyin, S.A. and Acsadi, G.T. (eds.). Family and
Marriage in Some African and Asiatic Countries. Cairo:
Cairo Demographic Centre. CDC Research Monograph Series
#6. 1976. pp. 245-265.

El Sadaawi, Nawal
The Hidden Face of Eve: Women in the Arab World. Boston:
Beacon Press. 1982. 212p.

Esposito, John L.
Women in Muslim Family Law. Syracuse, New York: Syracuse
University Press. Contemporary Issues in the Middle East
Series. 1982. 172p.

Faulkner, Constance
"Women's Studies in the Muslim Middle East." Journal of
Ethnic Studies. Volume 8 #3 Fall, 1980. pp. 67-76.

Fernea, Elizabeth W.
Women and the Family in the Middle East: New Voices of
Change. Austin, Texas: University of Texas Press. 1984.
368p.

Fikry, M.
Traditional Maternal and Child Health Care and Related
Problems in the Sahel: A Bibliographic Study.
Washington, D.C.: U.S. Department of State. U.S. Agency
for International Development. Sahel Development
Project. 1977. 123p.

Gadalla, Saad M.
Population Policy and Family Planning Communication
Strategies in the Arab States Region. Paris: UNESCO.
Volume One: Summaries of Pertinent Literature and
Research Studies. 1978.

Geletkanycz, Christine and Egan, Susan
Literature Review: The Practice of Female Circumcision.
Washington, D.C.: U.S. Department of Health, Education
and Welfare. Office of International Health. Mimeo.
1979.

Ginat, Joseph (ed.)
Women in Muslim Rural Society: Status and Role in Family
Community. New Brunswick, New Jersey: Transition Books.
1981. 268p.

Hayani, Ibrahim
"The Changing Role of Arab Women." Convergence. Volume
13 #1 1980. pp. 136-142.

Hussain, Freda (ed.)
Muslim Women. New York: St. Martin's Press. 1983.
240p.

Huzayyin, S.A.
"Marriage and Remarriage in Islam." (In) Dupaquier, J.
and Helin, E. and Laslett, P. and Livi-Bacci, M. (eds.).
Marriage and Remarriage in Populations of the Past. New
York: Academic Press. Population and Social Structure:
Advances in Historical Demography Series. 1981. pp.
95-109.

International Development Research Centre (IDRC)
    Nutritional Status of the Rural Population of the Sahel:
    Report of a Working Group, Paris, France, April 28-29,
    1980. Ottawa, Canada: IDRC. 1981. 92p.
Joseph, Roger
    "Sexual Dialectics and Strategy in Berber Marriage."
    Journal of Comparative Family Studies. Volume 7 #3
    Autumn, 1976. pp. 471-481.
Joseph, Terri B.
    "Poetry as a Strategy of Power: The Case of Riffian
    Berber Women." Signs. Volume 5 #3 Spring, 1980. pp.
    418-434.
Kamba, Kate
    "Fuel Wood and Energy Development for African Women."
    Paper Presented at the Workshop on Women in Agricultural
    Development. Addis Ababa, Ethiopia: United Nations
    Economic Commission for Africa. Awassa, Ethiopia. June
    26, 1983. 13p.
Keenan, Jeremy
    "Power and Wealth Are Cousins: Descent, Class and Marital
    Strategies Among the Kel Ahaggar." Africa. Volume 47 #3
    1977. pp. 242-252.
Keenan, Jeremy
    "The Tuareg Veil." Middle East Studies. Volume 13 #1
    January, 1977. pp. 3-13.
Kizerbo, Joseph
    "Women and the Energy Crisis in the Sahel Africa. From
    the Seminar on Fuel and Energy Development for African
    Women in Rural Areas, Bamako, Mali, December, 1980."
    Unasylva. Volume 33 #133 1981. pp. 5-10.
Klein, H.
    "Crimes Against Thirty Million." New Statesman. Volume
    98 August 24, 1979. pp. 266-268.
Klein, Martin A.
    "Women in Slavery in the Western Sudan." (In) Robertson,
    Claire C. and Klein, Martin A. (eds.). Women and Slavery
    in Africa. Madison, Wisconsin: University of Wisconsin
    Press. 1983. pp. 67-92.
Koning, Karen L.
    "Revolutionary Potential Among Arab Women Today."
    Mawazo. Volume 4 #4 1976. pp. 48-57.
Mahran, M.
    "Medical Dangers of Female Circumcision." International
    Planned Parenthood Federation (IPPF) Medical Bulletin.
    Volume 15 #2 April, 1981.
McLean, Scilla
    "Female Genital Mutilation." ISIS Women's International
    Bulletin. #25 1982. pp. 26-32.
McLean, Scilla and Graham, Stella E.
    Female Circumcision, Excision and Infibulation: The Fact
    and Proposals for Change. London: Minority Rights Group.
    Report #47. Second Revised Edition. 1985. 21p.

Mernissi, Fatima
    "Women, Saints and Sanctuaries." Signs. Volume 3 #1
    Autumn, 1977. pp. 101-112.
Mernissi, Fatima
    "Women, Saints and Sanctuaries." (In) Wellesley
    Editorial Committee. Women and National Development: The
    Complexities of Change. Chicago: University of Chicago
    Press. 1977. pp. 101-112.
Minces, Juliette
    The House of Obedience: Women in Arab Society. London:
    Zed Press. Westport, Connecticut: Lawrence Hill. 1982.
    114p.
Moen, Elizabeth W.
    Genital Mutilation: Everywoman's Problem. East Lansing,
    Michigan: Michigan State University. Office of Women in
    International Development. Working Paper #22. April,
    1983.
Mukhtar, Behiza
    "A Question of Our Children's Bodies: The Medical Injury
    Caused to a Girl by Circumcision." Paper Presented at
    the Conference on Islam and Family Planning. Sponsored
    by the International Planned Parenthood Federation.
    Banjul, Gambia. October 21-24, 1979. 7p.
Musallam, B.
    Sex and Society in Islam: Birth Control Before the 19th
    Century. Cambridge, New York: Cambridge University
    Press. Cambridge Studies in Islamic Civilization. 1983.
    176p.
Nagi, Mostafa H. and Stockwell, Edward G.
    "Muslim Fertility: Recent Trends and Future Outlook."
    Journal of South Asian and Middle Eastern Studies.
    Volume 6 #2 Winter, 1982. pp. 48-70.
Nagi, Mostafa H.
    "Trends and Differentials in Moslem Fertility." Journal
    of Biosocial Science. Volume 16 #2 April, 1984. pp.
    189-204.
Paraiso, Maitre A.
    "Family Planning Legislation in the Francophone Countries
    of Africa." (In) International Planned Parenthood
    Federation (IPPF). Proceedings of the IPPF Africa
    Regional Conference. London: IPPF. 1977. pp. 247-255.
Peters, Emrys L.
    "The Status of Women in Four Middle East Communities."
    (In) Beck, Lois and Keddie, Nikki R. (eds.). Women in
    the Muslim World. Cambridge, Massachusetts: Harvard
    University Press. 1978. pp. 311-350.
Reyna, Stephen P.
    "Economics and Fertility: Waiting for the Demographic
    Transition in the Dry Zone of Francophone West Africa."
    (In) Caldwell, John C. (ed.). The Persistence of High
    Fertility: Population Prospects in the Third World.

Canberra, Australia: Australian National University.
Department of Demography. Volume One. 1977. pp.
393-426.

Roboff, Farron V. and Renwick, Hilary L.
"The Changing Role of Women in the Development of the
Sahel." Paper Presented to the Annual Meeting of the
African Studies Association. Paper #92. Boston,
Massachusetts. 1976. 12p.

Sadik, Nafis
"Muslim Women Today." Populi. Volume 12 #1 1985. pp.
36-51.

Sanderson, Lilian P.
Against the Mutilation of Women: The Struggle Against
Unnecessary Suffering. London: Ithaca Press. 1981.
117p.

Shaalan, Mohammed
"Clitoris Envy: A Psychdynamic Construct Instrumental in
Female Circumcision." Paper Presented at the Seminar on
Traditional Practices Affecting the Health of Women and
Children: Female Circumcision, Childhood Marriage,
Nutritional Taboos, etc. Alexandria, Egypt: World Health
Organization. Eastern Mediterranean Regional Office.
Khartoum, Sudan. February 10-15, 1979.

Shaalan, Mohammed
"Clitoris Envy: A Psychodynamic Construct Instrumental in
Female Circumcision." Paper Presented at the Seminar on
Traditional Practices Affecting the Health of Women and
Children. World Conference of the United Nations Decade
for Women. New York: United Nations. Copenhagen,
Denmark. July 14-30, 1980.

Sindzingre, N.
"Plus and Minus--Concerning Female Circumcision."
Cahiers d'Etudes Africaines. Volume 17 #1 1977. pp.
65-76.

Smith, Jane I. (ed.)
Women in Contemporary Muslim Societies. Lewisburg,
Pennsylvania: Bucknell University Press. 1980. 264p.

Smith, Janet I.
"The Experience of Muslim Women: Considerations of Power
and Authority." (In) Haddad, Yvonne Y. and Haines, Byron
and Findly, Ellison (eds.). The Islamic Impact.
Syracuse, New York: Syracuse University Press. 1984.
pp. 89-112.

Taba, A.H.
"Female Circumcision." World Health. May, 1979. pp.
8-13.

Taba, A.H.
"Female Circumcision." (In) World Health Organization.
Traditional Practices Affecting the Health of Women and
Children: Female Circumcision, Childhood Marriage,
Nutritional Taboos, etc. Report of a Seminar, Khartoum,
Sudan, February 10-15, 1979. Alexandria, Egypt: WHO/EMRO
Technical Publication #2. 1979. pp. 43-52.

Thiam, Awa
"Women's Fight for the Abolition of Sexual Mutilation."
International Social Science Journal. Volume 35 #4 1983.
pp. 747-756.
Tillion, Germaine
The Republic of Cousins: Women's Oppression in
Mediterranean Society. London: Al Saqi Books.
Translated by Q. Hoare. 1983. 181p.
U.S. Agency for International Development (U.S. AID)
Non-Formal Education--Women in Sahel. Washington, D.C.:
U.S. Deapartment of State. U.S. AID. 1978. 23p.
Waines, D.
"Through a Veil Darkly--The Study of Women in Muslim
Societies." Comparative Studies in Society and History.
Volume 24 #4 1982.
Wegner, J.R.
"The Status of Women in Jewish and Islamic Marriage and
Divorce Law." Harvard Women's Law Journal. Volume 5 #1
1982.
Youssef, Nadia H.
"Women and Agricultural Production in Muslim Societies."
Studies in Comparative International Development. Volume
12 #1 Spring, 1977. pp. 41-58.

DEVELOPMENT AND TECHNOLOGY

Abdel Kader, Soha
"Research on the Status of Women, Development and
Population Trends in Arab States: An Annotated
Bibliography." (In) UNESCO. Bibliographic Guide to
Studies on the Status of Women: Development and
Population. Paris: United Nations Educational,
Scientific and Cultural Organization. 1983. pp. 67-81.
Baffoun, Alya
"Women and Social Change in the Muslim Arab World."
Women's Studies International Forum. Volume 5 #2 1982.
Dulansey, Maryanne L.
Women in Development Program Concerns in Francophone
Sahel: Report of a Workshop. Washington, D.C.: U.S.
Department of State. U.S. Agency for International
Development. Bobo-Dioulasso, Upper Volta. June 5-7,
1979. 11p.
Hagan, A.L.
"The Role of Women in Rural Development: Some Critical
Issues." (In) Mondjanagni, A.C. La Participation
Populaire an Developpement en Afrique Noire. Paris:
Karthala; Doula, Institut Pan Africain Pour Le
Developpement. 1984. pp. 75-87.
Kamba, Kate
"Fuel Wood and Energy Development for African Women."
Paper Presented at the Workshop on Women in Agricultural

Development. Addis Ababa, Ethiopia: United Nations
Economic Commission for Africa. Awassa, Ethiopia. June
26, 1983. 13p.

Kizerbo, Joseph
"Women and the Energy Crisis in the Sahel Africa. From
the Seminar on Fuel and Energy Development for African
Women in Rural Areas, Bamako, Mali, December, 1980."
Unasylva. Volume 33 #133 1981. pp. 5-10.

Marshall, Susan E.
"Politics and Female Status in North Africa: A
Reconsideration of Development Theory." Economic
Development and Cultural Change. Volume 32 #3 April,
1984. pp. 499-524.

Roboff, Farron V. and Renwick, Hilary L.
"The Changing Role of Women in the Development of the
Sahel." Paper Presented to the Annual Meeting of the
African Studies Association. Paper #92. Boston,
Massachusetts. 1976. 12p.

Shaw, R. Paul
"Women's Employment in the Arab World: A Strategy of
Selective Intervention." Development and Change. Volume
12 #2 April, 1981. pp. 237-272.

U.S. Agency for International Development (U.S. AID)
Examples of Women in Development Programs in Sahel
Francophone West Africa. Washington, D.C.: U.S.
Department of State. U.S. AID. Office of Sahel and
Francophone West Africa, Bureau for Africa. 1979. 27p.

U.S. Agency for International Development (U.S. AID)
Training Women in the Sahel. Washington, D.C.: U.S.
Department of State. U.S. AID. Office of Women in
Development. 1978. 47p.

Youssef, Nadia H.
"Women and Agricultural Production in Muslim Societies."
Studies in Comparative International Development. Volume
12 #1 Spring, 1977. pp. 41-58.

DIVORCE

Wegner, J.R.
"The Status of Women in Jewish and Islamic Marriage and
Divorce Law." Harvard Women's Law Journal. Volume 5 #1
1982.

ECONOMICS

Cloud, Kathleen
"Sex Roles in Food Production and Distribution Systems in
the Sahel." (In) Cowen, Ann B. (ed.). Proceedings and
Papers of the International Conference on Women and Food:
Consortium for International Development. Tucson,
Arizona: University of Arizona. 1978. pp. 62-89.

Cloud, Kathleen
   Sex Roles in Food Production and Food Distribution
   Systems in the Sahel. Washington, D.C.: U.S. Department
   of State. U.S. Agency for International Development.
   Office of Women in Development. 1977. 20p.
Dulansey, Maryanne L.
   Women in Development Program Concerns in Francophone
   Sahel: Report of a Workshop. Washington, D.C.: U.S.
   Department of State. U.S. Agency for International
   Development. Bobo-Dioulasso, Upper Volta. June 5-7,
   1979. 11p.
Hagan, A.L.
   "The Role of Women in Rural Development: Some Critical
   Issues." (In) Mondjanagni, A.C. La Participation
   Populaire an Developpement en Afrique Noire. Paris:
   Karthala; Doula, Institut Pan Africain Pour Le
   Developpement. 1984. pp. 75-87.
Kamba, Kate
   "Fuel Wood and Energy Development for African Women."
   Paper Presented at the Workshop on Women in Agricultural
   Development. Addis Ababa, Ethiopia: United Nations
   Economic Commission for Africa. Awassa, Ethiopia. June
   26, 1983. 13p.
Marshall, Susan E.
   "Politics and Female Status in North Africa: A
   Reconsideration of Development Theory." Economic
   Development and Cultural Change. Volume 32 #3 April,
   1984. pp. 499-524.
Reyna, Stephen P.
   "Economics and Fertility: Waiting for the Demographic
   Transition in the Dry Zone of Francophone West Africa."
   (In) Caldwell, John C. (ed.). The Persistence of High
   Fertility: Population Prospects in the Third World.
   Canberra, Australia: Australian National University.
   Department of Demography. Volume One. 1977. pp.
   393-426.
Roboff, Farron V. and Renwick, Hilary L.
   "The Changing Role of Women in the Development of the
   Sahel." Paper Presented to the Annual Meeting of the
   African Studies Association. Paper #92. Boston,
   Massachusetts. 1976. 12p.
Shaw, R. Paul
   "Women's Employment in the Arab World: A Strategy of
   Selective Intervention." Development and Change. Volume
   12 #2 April, 1981. pp. 237-272.
U.S. Agency for International Development (U.S. AID)
   Examples of Women in Development Programs in Sahel
   Francophone West Africa. Washington, D.C.: U.S.
   Department of State. U.S. AID. Office of Sahel and
   Francophone West Africa, Bureau for Africa. 1979. 27p.
Youssef, Nadia H.
   "Women and Agricultural Production in Muslim Societies."
   Studies in Comparative International Development. Volume
   12 #1 Spring, 1977. pp. 41-58.

EDUCATION AND TRAINING

Abdel Kader, Soha
    The Status of Research on Women in the Arab Region,
    1960-1978. Paris: UNESCO. Division of Human Rights and
    Peace. January, 1979.
Al-Qazza, Ayad
    "Current Status of Research on Women in the Arab World."
    Middle Eastern Studies. Volume 14 #3 October, 1978.
    pp. 372-384.
Faulkner, Constance
    "Women's Studies in the Muslim Middle East." Journal of
    Ethnic Studies. Volume 8 #3 Fall, 1980. pp. 67-76.
U.S. Agency for International Development (U.S. AID)
    Non-Formal Education--Women in Sahel. Washington, D.C.:
    U.S. Deapartment of State. U.S. AID. 1978. 23p.
U.S. Agency for International Development (U.S. AID)
    Training Women in the Sahel. Washington, D.C.: U.S.
    Department of State. U.S. AID. Office of Women in
    Development. 1978. 47p.

EMPLOYMENT AND LABOR

Ahdab-Yehia, May
    "Women, Employment and Fertility Trends in the Arab
    Middle East and North Africa." (In) Kupinsky, Stanley
    (ed.). The Fertility of Working Women: A Synthesis of
    International Research. New York: Praeger Publishers.
    Preager Special Studies in International Economics and
    Development. 1977. pp. 172-187.
Hagan, A.L.
    "The Role of Women in Rural Development: Some Critical
    Issues." (In) Mondjanagni, A.C. La Participation
    Populaire an Developpement en Afrique Noire. Paris:
    Karthala; Doula, Institut Pan Africain Pour Le
    Developpement. 1984. pp. 75-87.
Shaw, R. Paul
    "Women's Employment in the Arab World: A Strategy of
    Selective Intervention." Development and Change. Volume
    12 #2 April, 1981. pp. 237-272.

EQUALITY AND LIBERATION

Abdel Kader, Soha
    The Status of Research on Women in the Arab Region,
    1960-1978. Paris: UNESCO. Division of Human Rights and
    Peace. January, 1979.
Accad, Evelyne
    "Complex Inter-Relation of Women's Liberation and Arab
    Nationalism in North African Novels Written by Women."

Paper Presented at the Annual Meeting of the African
Studies Association. Paper #1. Boston, Massachusetts.
1976. 16p.
Accad, Evelyne
"Interrelationship Between Arab Nationalism and Feminist
Consciousness in the North African Novels Written by
Women." Ba Shiru. Volume 8 #2 1977. pp. 3-12.
Koning, Karen L.
"Revolutionary Potential Among Arab Women Today."
Mawazo. Volume 4 #4 1976. pp. 48-57.

FAMILY LIFE

Allman, James
"Family Life, Women's Status, and Fertility: Middle East
and North African Perspectives." (In) Allman, James
(ed.). Women's Studies and Fertility in the Muslim
World. New York: Praeger Publishers. Praeger Special
Studies. 1978. pp. 24-47.
Allman, James
"Family Patterns, Women's Status and Fertility in
Middle-East and North-Africa." International Journal of
Sociology of the Family. Volume 8 #1 1978. pp. 19-35.
Allman, James (ed.)
Women's Status and Fertility in the Muslim World. New
York: Praeger Publishers. Praeger Special Studies.
1978. 378p.
Caldwell, Pat
"Egypt and the Arab World." (In) Caldwell, John C.
(ed.). The Persistence of High Fertility: Population
Prospects in the Third World. Canberra, Australia:
Australian National University. Department of
Demography. Volume Two. 1977. pp. 593-616.
Chamie, Joseph
Polygamy Among Arabs. New York: United Nations. U.N.
Population Division. 1985.
Duza, M. Badrud and Sivamurthy, M.
"Household Structure in Selected Urban Areas of Four Arab
and African Cities." (In) Huzayyin, S.A. and Acsadi,
G.T. (eds.). Family and Marriage in Some African and
Asiatic Countries. Cairo: Cairo Demographic Centre.
Research Monograph Series #6. 1976. pp. 267-284.
Duza, M. Badrud and Seetharam, K.S. and Sivamurthy, M.
"Patterns of Family Cycles in Selected Areas of Four Arab
and African Cities: Some Demographic Implications." (In)
Huzayyin, S.A. and Acsadi, G.T. (eds.). Family and
Marriage in Some African and Asiatic Countries. Cairo:
Cairo Demographic Centre. CDC Research Monograph Series
#6. 1976. pp. 245-265.
El Sadaawi, Nawal
The Hidden Face of Eve: Women in the Arab World. Boston:
Beacon Press. 1982. 212p.
Esposito, John L.
Women in Muslim Family Law. Syracuse, New York: Syracuse

University Press. Contemporary Issues in the Middle East
Series. 1982. 172p.
Fernea, Elizabeth W.
Women and the Family in the Middle East: New Voices of
Change. Austin, Texas: University of Texas Press. 1984.
368p.
Ginat, Joseph (ed.)
Women in Muslim Rural Society: Status and Role in Family
Community. New Brunswick, New Jersey: Transition Books.
1981. 268p.
Hayani, Ibrahim
"The Changing Role of Arab Women." Convergence. Volume
13 #1 1980. pp. 136-142.
Joseph, Roger
"Sexual Dialectics and Strategy in Berber Marriage."
Journal of Comparative Family Studies. Volume 7 #3
Autumn, 1976. pp. 471-481.
Keenan, Jeremy
"Power and Wealth Are Cousins: Descent, Class and Marital
Strategies Among the Kel Ahaggar." Africa. Volume 47 #3
1977. pp. 242-252.
Roboff, Farron V. and Renwick, Hilary L.
"The Changing Role of Women in the Development of the
Sahel." Paper Presented to the Annual Meeting of the
African Studies Association. Paper #92. Boston,
Massachusetts. 1976. 12p.
Smith, Jane I. (ed.)
Women in Contemporary Muslim Societies. Lewisburg,
Pennsylvania: Bucknell University Press. 1980. 264p.
Smith, Janet I.
"The Experience of Muslim Women: Considerations of Power
and Authority." (In) Haddad, Yvonne Y. and Haines, Byron
and Findly, Ellison (eds.). The Islamic Impact.
Syracuse, New York: Syracuse University Press. 1984.
pp. 89-112.
Tillion, Germaine
The Republic of Cousins: Women's Oppression in
Mediterranean Society. London: Al Saqi Books.
Translated by Q. Hoare. 1983. 181p.
Waines, D.
"Through a Veil Darkly--The Study of Women in Muslim
Societies." Comparative Studies in Society and History.
Volume 24 #4 1982.

FAMILY PLANNING AND CONTRACEPTION

Allman, James
"Family Life, Women's Status, and Fertility: Middle East
and North African Perspectives." (In) Allman, James
(ed.). Women's Studies and Fertility in the Muslim
World. New York: Praeger Publishers. Praeger Special
Studies. 1978. pp. 24-47.

Allman, James
  "Family Patterns, Women's Status and Fertility in
  Middle-East and North-Africa." International Journal of
  Sociology of the Family. Volume 8 #1 1978. pp. 19-35.
Allman, James (ed.)
  Women's Status and Fertility in the Muslim World. New
  York: Praeger Publishers. Praeger Special Studies.
  1978. 378p.
Gadalla, Saad M.
  Population Policy and Family Planning Communication
  Strategies in the Arab States Region. Paris: UNESCO.
  Volume One: Summaries of Pertinent Literature and
  Research Studies. 1978.
Musallam, B.
  Sex and Society in Islam: Birth Control Before the 19th
  Century. Cambridge, New York: Cambridge University
  Press. Cambridge Studies in Islamic Civilization. 1983.
  176p.
Nagi, Mostafa H. and Stockwell, Edward G.
  "Muslim Fertility: Recent Trends and Future Outlook."
  Journal of South Asian and Middle Eastern Studies.
  Volume 6 #2 Winter, 1982. pp. 48-70.
Nagi, Mostafa H.
  "Trends and Differentials in Moslem Fertility." Journal
  of Biosocial Science. Volume 16 #2 April, 1984. pp.
  189-204.
Paraiso, Maitre A.
  "Family Planning Legislation in the Francophone Countries
  of Africa." (In) International Planned Parenthood
  Federation (IPPF). Proceedings of the IPPF Africa
  Regional Conference. London: IPPF. 1977. pp. 247-255.

FERTILITY AND INFERTILITY

Ahdab-Yehia, May
  "Women, Employment and Fertility Trends in the Arab
  Middle East and North Africa." (In) Kupinsky, Stanley
  (ed.). The Fertility of Working Women: A Synthesis of
  International Research. New York: Praeger Publishers.
  Preager Special Studies in International Economics and
  Development. 1977. pp. 172-187.
Allman, James
  "Family Life, Women's Status, and Fertility: Middle East
  and North African Perspectives." (In) Allman, James
  (ed.). Women's Studies and Fertility in the Muslim
  World. New York: Praeger Publishers. Praeger Special
  Studies. 1978. pp. 24-47.
Allman, James
  "Family Patterns, Women's Status and Fertility in
  Middle-East and North-Africa." International Journal of
  Sociology of the Family. Volume 8 #1 1978. pp. 19-35.

Allman, James
"Natural Fertility and Associated Intermediate Variables in Some Arab Countries." Egyptian Population and Family Planning Review. Volume 14 #1 June, 1980. pp. 22-70.

Allman, James
"The Demographic Transition in the Middle East and North Africa." International Journal of Middle East Studies. Volume 12 #3 November, 1980. pp. 277-301.

Allman, James
Natural Fertility in North Africa and the Middle-East. New York: Columbia University Press/U.S. AID. 1980.

Allman, James (ed.)
Women's Status and Fertility in the Muslim World. New York: Praeger Publishers. Praeger Special Studies. 1978. 378p.

Caldwell, Pat
"Egypt and the Arab World." (In) Caldwell, John C. (ed.). The Persistence of High Fertility: Population Prospects in the Third World. Canberra, Australia: Australian National University. Department of Demography. Volume Two. 1977. pp. 593-616.

Nagi, Mostafa H. and Stockwell, Edward G.
"Muslim Fertility: Recent Trends and Future Outlook." Journal of South Asian and Middle Eastern Studies. Volume 6 #2 Winter, 1982. pp. 48-70.

Nagi, Mostafa H.
"Trends and Differentials in Moslem Fertility." Journal of Biosocial Science. Volume 16 #2 April, 1984. pp. 189-204.

Reyna, Stephen P.
"Economics and Fertility: Waiting for the Demographic Transition in the Dry Zone of Francophone West Africa." (In) Caldwell, John C. (ed.). The Persistence of High Fertility: Population Prospects in the Third World." Canberra, Australia: Australian National University. Department of Demography. Volume One. 1977. pp. 393-426.

HEALTH, NUTRITION AND MEDICINE

Allman, James
"Natural Fertility and Associated Intermediate Variables in Some Arab Countries." Egyptian Population and Family Planning Review. Volume 14 #1 June, 1980. pp. 22-70.

Fikry, M.
Traditional Maternal and Child Health Care and Related Problems in the Sahel: A Bibliographic Study. Washington, D.C.: U.S. Department of State. U.S. Agency for International Development. Sahel Development Project. 1977. 123p.

Geletkanycz, Christine and Egan, Susan
Literature Review: The Practice of Female Circumcision.

Washington, D.C.: U.S. Department of Health, Education
and Welfare. Office of International Health. Mimeo.
1979.
Hill, Allan G. (ed.)
Population, Health and Nutrition in the Sahel: Issues in
the Welfare of Selected West African Communities.
Boston: KPI. 1985. 399p.
International Development Research Centre (IDRC)
Nutritional Status of the Rural Population of the Sahel:
Report of a Working Group, Paris, France, April 28-29,
1980. Ottawa, Canada: IDRC. 1981. 92p.
Mahran, M.
"Medical Dangers of Female Circumcision." International
Planned Parenthood Federation (IPPF) Medical Bulletin.
Volume 15 #2 April, 1981.
McLean, Scilla
"Female Genital Mutilation." ISIS Women's International
Bulletin. #25 1982. pp. 26-32.
McLean, Scilla and Graham, Stella E.
Female Circumcision, Excision and Infibulation: The Fact
and Proposals for Change. London: Minority Rights Group.
Report #47. Second Revised Edition. 1985. 21p.
Moen, Elizabeth W.
Genital Mutilation: Everywoman's Problem. East Lansing,
Michigan: Michigan State University. Office of Women in
International Development. Working Paper #22. April,
1983.
Mukhtar, Behiza
"A Question of Our Children's Bodies: The Medical Injury
Caused to a Girl by Circumcision." Paper Presented at
the Conference on Islam and Family Planning. Sponsored
by the International Planned Parenthood Federation.
Banjul, Gambia. October 21-24, 1979. 7p.
Sanderson, Lilian P.
Against the Mutilation of Women: The Struggle Against
Unnecessary Suffering. London: Ithaca Press. 1981.
117p.
Shaalan, Mohammed
"Clitoris Envy: A Psychdynamic Construct Instrumental in
Female Circumcision." Paper Presented at the Seminar on
Traditional Practices Affecting the Health of Women and
Children: Female Circumcision, Childhood Marriage,
Nutritional Taboos, etc. Alexandria, Egypt: World Health
Organization. Eastern Mediterranean Regional Office.
Khartoum, Sudan. February 10-15, 1979.
Shaalan, Mohammed
"Clitoris Envy: A Psychodynamic Construct Instrumental in
Female Circumcision." Paper Presented at the Seminar on
Traditional Practices Affecting the Health of Women and
Children. World Conference of the United Nations Decade
for Women. New York: United Nations. Copenhagen,
Denmark. July 14-30, 1980.

Sindzingre, N.
    "Plus and Minus--Concerning Female Circumcision."
    Cahiers d'Etudes Africaines. Volume 17 #1 1977. pp.
    65-76.
Taba, A.H.
    "Female Circumcision." World Health. May, 1979. pp.
    8-13.
Taba, A.H.
    "Female Circumcision." (In) World Health Organization.
    Traditional Practices Affecting the Health of Women and
    Children: Female Circumcision, Childhood Marriage,
    Nutritional Taboos, etc. Report of a Seminar, Khartoum,
    Sudan, February 10-15, 1979. Alexandria, Egypt: WHO/EMRO
    Technical Publication #2. 1979. pp. 43-52.
Thiam, Awa
    "Women's Fight for the Abolition of Sexual Mutilation."
    International Social Science Journal. Volume 35 #4 1983.
    pp. 747-756.

HISTORY

Adamson, Kay
    "Approaches to the Study of Women in North Africa: As
    Reflected in Research of Various Scholars." Maghreb
    Review. Volume 3 #7-8 May-August, 1978. pp. 22-31.
Badran, Margot F.
    "Middle East and North Africa: Women." Trends in
    History. Volume 1 #1 1979. pp. 123-129.
Hall, Richard
    Lovers on the Nile: The Incredible African Journeys of
    Sam and Florence Baker. New York: Random House. 1980.
    254p.
Klein, H.
    "Crimes Against Thirty Million." New Statesman. Volume
    98 August 24, 1979. pp. 266-268.
Klein, Martin A.
    "Women in Slavery in the Western Sudan." (In) Robertson,
    Claire C. and Klein, Martin A. (eds.). Women and Slavery
    in Africa. Madison, Wisconsin: University of Wisconsin
    Press. 1983. pp. 67-92.
Musallam, B.
    Sex and Society in Islam: Birth Control Before the 19th
    Century. Cambridge, New York: Cambridge University
    Press. Cambridge Studies   in Islamic Civilization.
    1983. 176p.

LAW AND LEGAL ISSUES

Esposito, John L.
    Women in Muslim Family Law. Syracuse, New York: Syracuse
    University Press. Contemporary Issues in the Middle East
    Series. 1982. 172p.

Paraiso, Maitre A.
"Family Planning Legislation in the Francophone Countries
of Africa." (In) International Planned Parenthood
Federation (IPPF). Proceedings of the IPPF Africa
Regional Conference. London: IPPF. 1977. pp. 247-255.
Wegner, J.R.
"The Status of Women in Jewish and Islamic Marriage and
Divorce Law." Harvard Women's Law Journal. Volume 5 #1
1982.

LITERATURE

Accad, Evelyne
"Complex Inter-Relation of Women's Liberation and Arab
Nationalism in North African Novels Written by Women."
Paper Presented at the Annual Meeting of the African
Studies Association. Paper #1. Boston, Massachusetts.
1976. 16p.
Accad, Evelyne
"Interrelationship Between Arab Nationalism and Feminist
Consciousness in the North African Novels Written by
Women." Ba Shiru. Volume 8 #2 1977. pp. 3-12.
Accad, Evelyne
"The Prostitute in Arab and North African Fiction." (In)
Horn, Pierre L. and Pringle, Mary B. (eds.). The Image
of the Prostitute in Modern Literature. New York: Ungar.
1984. pp. 63-75.
Accad, Evelyne
"The Theme of Sexual Oppression in the North African
Novel." (In) Beck, Lois and Keddie, Nikki R. (eds.).
Women in the Muslim World. Cambridge, Massachusetts:
Harvard University Press. 1978. pp. 617-628.
Accad, Evelyne
Veil of Shame: The Role of Women in the Contemporary
Fiction of North Africa and the Arab World. Sherbrooke,
Canada: Editions Naaman. 1978. 182p.
Joseph, Terri B.
"Poetry as a Strategy of Power: The Case of Riffian
Berber Women." Signs. Volume 5 #3 Spring, 1980. pp.
418-434.

MARITAL RELATIONS AND NUPTIALITY

Abu-Lughod, Lila
"A Community of Secrets: The Separate World of Bedouin
Women." Signs. Volume 10 #4 Summer, 1985. pp.
637-657.
Caldwell, Pat
"Egypt and the Arab World." (In) Caldwell, John C.
(ed.). The Persistence of High Fertility: Population
Prospects in the Third World. Canberra, Australia:
Australian National University. Department of
Demography. Volume Two. 1977. pp. 593-616.

Casajus, Dominique
    "The Wedding Ritual Among the Kel Ferwan Tuaregs."
    Journal of the Anthropological Society of Oxford. Volume
    14 #2 1983. pp. 227-257.
Chamie, Joseph and Weller, Robert H.
    "Levels, Trends and Differentials in Nuptiality in the
    Middle East and North Africa." Genus. Volume 39 #1-4
    January-December, 1983. pp. 213-231.
Chamie, Joseph and Weller, Robert H.
    Levels, Trends and Differentials in Nuptiality in the
    Middle East and North Africa. Tallahassee, Florida:
    Florida State University. Center for the Study of
    Population. College of Social Sciences. Working Paper
    #83-02. 1983. 12p.
Chamie, Joseph
    Polygamy Among Arabs. New York: United Nations. U.N.
    Population Division. 1985.
Duza, M. Badrud and Sivamurthy, M.
    "Household Structure in Selected Urban Areas of Four Arab
    and African Cities." (In) Huzayyin, S.A. and Acsadi,
    G.T. (eds.). Family and Marriage in Some African and
    Asiatic Countries. Cairo: Cairo Demographic Centre.
    Research Monograph Series #6. 1976. pp. 267-284.
Duza, M. Badrud and Seetharam, K.S. and Sivamurthy, M.
    "Patterns of Family Cycles in Selected Areas of Four Arab
    and African Cities: Some Demographic Implications." (In)
    Huzayyin, S.A. and Acsadi, G.T. (eds.). Family and
    Marriage in Some African and Asiatic Countries. Cairo:
    Cairo Demographic Centre. CDC Research Monograph Series
    #6. 1976. pp. 245-265.
Esposito, John L.
    Women in Muslim Family Law. Syracuse, New York: Syracuse
    University Press. Contemporary Issues in the Middle East
    Series. 1982. 172p.
Fernea, Elizabeth W.
    Women and the Family in the Middle East: New Voices of
    Change. Austin, Texas: University of Texas Press. 1984.
    368p.
Ginat, Joseph (ed.)
    Women in Muslim Rural Society: Status and Role in Family
    Community. New Brunswick, New Jersey: Transition Books.
    1981. 268p.
Hayani, Ibrahim
    "The Changing Role of Arab Women." Convergence. Volume
    13 #1 1980. pp. 136-142.
Huzayyin, S.A.
    "Marriage and Remarriage in Islam." (In) Dupaquier, J.
    and Helin, E. and Laslett, P. and Livi-Bacci, M. (eds.).
    Marriage and Remarriage in Populations of the Past. New
    York: Academic Press. Population and Social Structure:
    Advances in Historical Demography Series. 1981. pp.
    95-109.

Joseph, Roger
"Sexual Dialectics and Strategy in Berber Marriage."
Journal of Comparative Family Studies. Volume 7 #3
Autumn, 1976. pp. 471-481.
Keenan, Jeremy
"Power and Wealth Are Cousins: Descent, Class and Marital
Strategies Among the Kel Ahaggar." Africa. Volume 47 #3
1977. pp. 242-252.
Smith, Janet I.
"The Experience of Muslim Women: Considerations of Power
and Authority." (In) Haddad, Yvonne Y. and Haines, Byron
and Findly, Ellison (eds.). The Islamic Impact.
Syracuse, New York: Syracuse University Press. 1984.
pp. 89-112.
Tillion, Germaine
The Republic of Cousins: Women's Oppression in
Mediterranean Society. London: Al Saqi Books.
Translated by Q. Hoare. 1983. 181p.
Waines, D.
"Through a Veil Darkly--The Study of Women in Muslim
Societies." Comparative Studies in Society and History.
Volume 24 #4 1982.
Wegner, J.R.
"The Status of Women in Jewish and Islamic Marriage and
Divorce Law." Harvard Women's Law Journal. Volume 5 #1
1982.

MISCELLANEOUS

Accad, Evelyne
"The Prostitute in Arab and North African Fiction." (In)
Horn, Pierre L. and Pringle, Mary B. (eds.). The Image
of the Prostitute in Modern Literature. New York: Ungar.
1984. pp. 63-75.
Gadalla, Saad M.
Population Policy and Family Planning Communication
Strategies in the Arab States Region. Paris: UNESCO.
Volume One: Summaries of Pertinent Literature and
Research Studies. 1978.
Hill, Allan G. (ed.)
Population, Health and Nutrition in the Sahel: Issues in
the Welfare of Selected West African Communities.
Boston: KPI. 1985. 399p.

NATIONALISM

Accad, Evelyne
"Complex Inter-Relation of Women's Liberation and Arab
Nationalism in North African Novels Written by Women."

Paper Presented at the Annual Meeting of the African
Studies Association. Paper #1. Boston, Massachusetts.
1976. 16p.
Accad, Evelyne
   "Interrelationship Between Arab Nationalism and Feminist
   Consciousness in the North African Novels Written by
   Women." Ba Shiru. Volume 8 #2 1977. pp. 3-12.

POLITICS AND GOVERNMENT

Koning, Karen L.
   "Revolutionary Potential Among Arab Women Today."
   Mawazo. Volume 4 #4 1976. pp. 48-57.
Marshall, Susan E.
   "Politics and Female Status in North Africa: A
   Reconsideration of Development Theory." Economic
   Development and Cultural Change. Volume 32 #3 April,
   1984. pp. 499-524.

RELIGION AND WITCHCRAFT

Baffoun, Alya
   "Women and Social Change in the Muslim Arab World."
   Women's Studies International Forum. Volume 5 #2 1982.
Esposito, John L.
   Women in Muslim Family Law. Syracuse, New York: Syracuse
   University Press. Contemporary Issues in the Middle East
   Series. 1982. 172p.
Faulkner, Constance
   "Women's Studies in the Muslim Middle East." Journal of
   Ethnic Studies. Volume 8 #3 Fall, 1980. pp. 67-76.
Geletkanycz, Christine and Egan, Susan
   Literature Review: The Practice of Female Circumcision.
   Washington, D.C.: U.S. Department of Health, Education
   and Welfare. Office of International Health. Mimeo.
   1979.
Ginat, Joseph (ed.)
   Women in Muslim Rural Society: Status and Role in Family
   Community. New Brunswick, New Jersey: Transition Books.
   1981. 268p.
Hayani, Ibrahim
   "The Changing Role of Arab Women." Convergence. Volume
   13 #1 1980. pp. 136-142.
Hussain, Freda (ed.)
   Muslim Women. New York: St. Martin's Press. 1983.
   240p.
Huzayyin, S.A.
   "Marriage and Remarriage in Islam." (In) Dupaquier, J.
   and Helin, E. and Laslett, P. and Livi-Bacci, M. (eds.).
   Marriage and Remarriage in Populations of the Past. New

York: Academic Press. Population and Social Structure:
Advances in Historical Demography Series. 1981. pp.
95-109.
Mahran, M.
"Medical Dangers of Female Circumcision." International
Planned Parenthood Federation (IPPF) Medical Bulletin.
Volume 15 #2 April, 1981.
McLean, Scilla
"Female Genital Mutilation." ISIS Women's International
Bulletin. #25 1982. pp. 26-32.
McLean, Scilla and Graham, Stella E.
Female Circumcision, Excision and Infibulation: The Fact
and Proposals for Change. London: Minority Rights Group.
Report #47. Second Revised Edition. 1985. 21p.
Mernissi, Fatima
"Women, Saints and Sanctuaries." Signs. Volume 3 #1
Autumn, 1977. pp. 101-112.
Mernissi, Fatima
"Women, Saints and Sanctuaries." (In) Wellesley
Editorial Committee. Women and National Development: The
Complexities of Change. Chicago: University of Chicago
Press. 1977. pp. 101-112.
Moen, Elizabeth W.
Genital Mutilation: Everywoman's Problem. East Lansing,
Michigan: Michigan State University. Office of Women in
International Development. Working Paper #22. April,
1983.
Mukhtar, Behiza
"A Question of Our Children's Bodies: The Medical Injury
Caused to a Girl by Circumcision." Paper Presented at
the Conference on Islam and Family Planning. Sponsored
by the International Planned Parenthood Federation.
Banjul, Gambia. October 21-24, 1979. 7p.
Musallam, B.
Sex and Society in Islam: Birth Control Before the 19th
Century. Cambridge, New York: Cambridge University
Press. Cambridge Studies in Islamic Civilization. 1983.
176p.
Nagi, Mostafa H. and Stockwell, Edward G.
"Muslim Fertility: Recent Trends and Future Outlook."
Journal of South Asian and Middle Eastern Studies.
Volume 6 #2 Winter, 1982. pp. 48-70.
Nagi, Mostafa H.
"Trends and Differentials in Moslem Fertility." Journal
of Biosocial Science. Volume 16 #2 April, 1984. pp.
189-204.
Sadik, Nafis
"Muslim Women Today." Populi. Volume 12 #1 1985. pp.
36-51.
Smith, Jane I. (ed.)
Women in Contemporary Muslim Societies. Lewisburg,
Pennsylvania: Bucknell University Press. 1980. 264p.

Smith, Janet I.
  "The Experience of Muslim Women: Considerations of Power
  and Authority." (In) Haddad, Yvonne Y. and Haines, Byron
  and Findly, Ellison (eds.). The Islamic Impact.
  Syracuse, New York: Syracuse University Press. 1984.
  pp. 89-112.
Wegner, J.R.
  "The Status of Women in Jewish and Islamic Marriage and
  Divorce Law." Harvard Women's Law Journal. Volume 5 #1
  1982.
Youssef, Nadia H.
  "Women and Agricultural Production in Muslim Societies."
  Studies in Comparative International Development. Volume
  12 #1 Spring, 1977. pp. 41-58.

RESEARCH

Abdel Kader, Soha
  "Research on the Status of Women, Development and
  Population Trends in Arab States: An Annotated
  Bibliography." (In) UNESCO. Bibliographic Guide to
  Studies on the Status of Women: Development and
  Population. Paris: United Nations Educational,
  Scientific and Cultural Organization. 1983. pp. 67-81.
Abdel Kader, Soha
  The Status of Research on Women in the Arab Region,
  1960-1978. Paris: UNESCO. Division of Human Rights and
  Peace. January, 1979.
Adamson, Kay
  "Approaches to the Study of Women in North Africa: As
  Reflected in Research of Various Scholars." Maghreb
  Review. Volume 3 #7-8 May-August, 1978. pp. 22-31.
Al-Qazza, Ayad
  "Current Status of Research on Women in the Arab World."
  Middle Eastern Studies. Volume 14 #3 October, 1978.
  pp. 372-384.
Al-Qazza, Ayad
  Women in the Middle East and North Africa: An Annotated
  Bibliography. Austin, Texas: University of Texas Press.
  Center for Middle Eastern Studies. Middle East Monograph
  #2. 1977. 179p.
Faulkner, Constance
  "Women's Studies in the Muslim Middle East." Journal of
  Ethnic Studies. Volume 8 #3 Fall, 1980. pp. 67-76.
Gadalla, Saad M.
  Population Policy and Family Planning Communication
  Strategies in the Arab States Region. Paris: UNESCO.
  Volume One: Summaries of Pertinent Literature and
  Research Studies. 1978.
Rassam, Amal
  "Towards a Theoretical Framework for the Study of Women
  in the Arab World." Cultures. Volume 8 #3 1982.

SEX ROLES

Abu-Lughod, Lila
   "A Community of Secrets: The Separate World of Bedouin
   Women." Signs. Volume 10 #4 Summer, 1985. pp.
   637-657.
Accad, Evelyne
   "The Theme of Sexual Oppression in the North African
   Novel." (In) Beck, Lois and Keddie, Nikki R. (eds.).
   Women in the Muslim World. Cambridge, Massachusetts:
   Harvard University Press. 1978. pp. 617-628.
Allman, James
   "Family Life, Women's Status, and Fertility: Middle East
   and North African Perspectives." (In) Allman, James
   (ed.). Women's Studies and Fertility in the Muslim
   World. New York: Praeger Publishers. Praeger Special
   Studies. 1978. pp. 24-47.
Allman, James
   "Family Patterns, Women's Status and Fertility in
   Middle-East and North-Africa." International Journal of
   Sociology of the Family. Volume 8 #1 1978. pp. 19-35.
Allman, James (ed.)
   Women's Status and Fertility in the Muslim World. New
   York: Praeger Publishers. Praeger Special Studies.
   1978. 378p.
Casajus, Dominique
   "The Wedding Ritual Among the Kel Ferwan Tuaregs."
   Journal of the Anthropological Society of Oxford. Volume
   14 #2 1983. pp. 227-257.
Chamie, Joseph and Weller, Robert H.
   "Levels, Trends and Differentials in Nuptiality in the
   Middle East and North Africa." Genus. Volume 39 #1-4
   January-December, 1983. pp. 213-231.
Chamie, Joseph and Weller, Robert H.
   Levels, Trends and Differentials in Nuptiality in the
   Middle East and North Africa. Tallahassee, Florida:
   Florida State University. Center for the Study of
   Population. College of Social Sciences. Working Paper
   #83-02. 1983. 12p.
Chamie, Joseph
   Polygamy Among Arabs. New York: United Nations. U.N.
   Population Division. 1985.
Cloud, Kathleen
   "Sex Roles in Food Production and Distribution Systems in
   the Sahel." (In) Cowen, Ann B. (ed.). Proceedings and
   Papers of the International Conference on Women and Food:
   Consortium for International Development. Tucson,
   Arizona: University of Arizona. 1978. pp. 62-89.
Cloud, Kathleen
   Sex Roles in Food Production and Food Distribution
   Systems in the Sahel. Washington, D.C.: U.S. Department
   of State. U.S. Agency for International Development.
   Office of Women in Development. 1977. 20p.

Duza, M. Badrud and Sivamurthy, M.
    "Household Structure in Selected Urban Areas of Four Arab
    and African Cities." (In) Huzayyin, S.A. and Acsadi,
    G.T. (eds.). Family and Marriage in Some African and
    Asiatic Countries. Cairo: Cairo Demographic Centre.
    Research Monograph Series #6. 1976. pp. 267-284.
Duza, M. Badrud and Seetharam, K.S. and Sivamurthy, M.
    "Patterns of Family Cycles in Selected Areas of Four Arab
    and African Cities: Some Demographic Implications." (In)
    Huzayyin, S.A. and Acsadi, G.T. (eds.). Family and
    Marriage in Some African and Asiatic Countries. Cairo:
    Cairo Demographic Centre. CDC Research Monograph Series
    #6. 1976. pp. 245-265.
El Sadaawi, Nawal
    The Hidden Face of Eve: Women in the Arab World. Boston:
    Beacon Press. 1982. 212p.
Esposito, John L.
    Women in Muslim Family Law. Syracuse, New York: Syracuse
    University Press. Contemporary Issues in the Middle East
    Series. 1982. 172p.
Fernea, Elizabeth W.
    Women and the Family in the Middle East: New Voices of
    Change. Austin, Texas: University of Texas Press. 1984.
    368p.
Ginat, Joseph (ed.)
    Women in Muslim Rural Society: Status and Role in Family
    Community. New Brunswick, New Jersey: Transition Books.
    1981. 268p.
Hayani, Ibrahim
    "The Changing Role of Arab Women." Convergence. Volume
    13 #1 1980. pp. 136-142.
Joseph, Roger
    "Sexual Dialectics and Strategy in Berber Marriage."
    Journal of Comparative Family Studies. Volume 7 #3
    Autumn, 1976. pp. 471-481.
Joseph, Terri B.
    Poetry as a Strategy of Power: The Case of Riffian Berber
    Women. Signs. Volume 5 #3 Spring, 1980. pp. 418-434.
Kamba, Kate
    "Fuel Wood and Energy Development for African Women."
    Paper Presented at the Workshop on Women in Agricultural
    Development. Addis Ababa, Ethiopia: United Nations
    Economic Commission for Africa. Awassa, Ethiopia. June
    26, 1983. 13p.
Keenan, Jeremy
    "Power and Wealth Are Cousins: Descent, Class and Marital
    Strategies Among the Kel Ahaggar." Africa. Volume 47 #3
    1977. pp. 242-252.
Keenan, Jeremy
    "The Tuareg Veil." Middle East Studies. Volume 13 #1
    January, 1977. pp. 3-13.

Kizerbo, Joseph
    "Women and the Energy Crisis in the Sahel Africa.   From
    the Seminar on Fuel and Energy Development for African
    Women in Rural Areas, Bamako, Mali, December, 1980."
    Unasylva. Volume 33 #133 1981. pp. 5-10.
Minces, Juliette
    The House of Obedience: Women in Arab Society.   London:
    Zed Press. Westport, Connecticut: Lawrence Hill. 1982.
    114p.
Smith, Jane I. (ed.)
    Women in Contemporary Muslim Societies. Lewisburg,
    Pennsylvania: Bucknell University Press. 1980. 264p.
Smith, Janet I.
    "The Experience of Muslim Women: Considerations of Power
    and Authority." (In) Haddad, Yvonne Y. and Haines, Byron
    and Findly, Ellison (eds.).   The Islamic Impact.
    Syracuse, New York: Syracuse University Press. 1984.
    pp. 89-112.
Tillion, Germaine
    The Republic of Cousins: Women's Oppression in
    Mediterranean Society.   London: Al Saqi Books.
    Translated by Q. Hoare. 1983. 181p.
Waines, D.
    "Through a Veil Darkly--The Study of Women in Muslim
    Societies." Comparative Studies in Society and History.
    Volume 24 #4 1982.
Youssef, Nadia H.
    "Women and Agricultural Production in Muslim Societies."
    Studies in Comparative International Development. Volume
    12 #1 Spring, 1977. pp. 41-58.

SEXUAL MUTILATION/CIRCUMCISION

El Sadaawi, Nawal
    The Hidden Face of Eve: Women in the Arab World.   Boston:
    Beacon Press. 1982. 212p.
Geletkanycz, Christine and Egan, Susan
    Literature Review: The Practice of Female Circumcision.
    Washington, D.C.: U.S. Department of Health, Education
    and Welfare. Office of International Health. Mimeo.
    1979.
Klein, H.
    "Crimes Against Thirty Million." New Statesman. Volume
    98 August 24, 1979. pp. 266-268.
Mahran, M.
    "Medical Dangers of Female Circumcision." International
    Planned Parenthood Federation (IPPF) Medical Bulletin.
    Volume 15 #2 April, 1981.
McLean, Scilla
    "Female Genital Mutilation." ISIS Women's International
    Bulletin. #25 1982. pp. 26-32.

McLean, Scilla and Graham, Stella E.
    Female Circumcision, Excision and Infibulation: The Fact
    and Proposals for Change. London: Minority Rights Group.
    Report #47. Second Revised Edition. 1985. 21p.
Moen, Elizabeth W.
    Genital Mutilation: Everywoman's Problem. East Lansing,
    Michigan: Michigan State University. Office of Women in
    International Development. Working Paper #22. April,
    1983.
Mukhtar, Behiza
    "A Question of Our Children's Bodies: The Medical Injury
    Caused to a Girl by Circumcision." Paper Presented at
    the Conference on Islam and Family Planning. Sponsored
    by the International Planned Parenthood Federation.
    Banjul, Gambia. October 21-24, 1979. 7p.
Sanderson, Lilian P.
    Against the Mutilation of Women: The Struggle Against
    Unnecessary Suffering. London: Ithaca Press. 1981.
    117p.
Shaalan, Mohammed
    "Clitoris Envy: A Psychdynamic Construct Instrumental in
    Female Circumcision." Paper Presented at the Seminar on
    Traditional Practices Affecting the Health of Women and
    Children: Female Circumcision, Childhood Marriage,
    Nutritional Taboos, etc. Alexandria, Egypt: World Health
    Organization. Eastern Mediterranean Regional Office.
    Khartoum, Sudan. February 10-15, 1979.
Shaalan, Mohammed
    "Clitoris Envy: A Psychodynamic Construct Instrumental in
    Female Circumcision." Paper Presented at the Seminar on
    Traditional Practices Affecting the Health of Women and
    Children. World Conference of the United Nations Decade
    for Women. New York: United Nations. Copenhagen,
    Denmark. July 14-30, 1980.
Sindzingre, N.
    "Plus and Minus--Concerning Female Circumcision."
    Cahiers d'Etudes Africaines. Volume 17 #1 1977. pp.
    65-76.
Taba, A.H.
    "Female Circumcision." World Health. May, 1979. pp.
    8-13.
Taba, A.H.
    "Female Circumcision." (In) World Health Organization.
    Traditional Practices Affecting the Health of Women and
    Children: Female Circumcision, Childhood Marriage,
    Nutritional Taboos, etc. Report of a Seminar, Khartoum,
    Sudan, February 10-15, 1979. Alexandria, Egypt: WHO/EMRO
    Technical Publication #2. 1979. pp. 43-52.
Thiam, Awa
    "Women's Fight for the Abolition of Sexual Mutilation."
    International Social Science Journal. Volume 35 #4 1983.
    pp. 747-756.

SLAVERY

Klein, Martin A.
    "Women in Slavery in the Western Sudan." (In) Robertson,
    Claire C. and Klein, Martin A. (eds.). Women and Slavery
    in Africa. Madison, Wisconsin: University of Wisconsin
    Press. 1983. pp. 67-92.

STATUS OF WOMEN

Abdel Kader, Soha
    "Research on the Status of Women, Development and
    Population Trends in Arab States: An Annotated
    Bibliography." (In) UNESCO. Bibliographic Guide to
    Studies on the Status of Women: Development and
    Population. Paris: United Nations Educational,
    Scientific and Cultural Organization. 1983. pp. 67-81.
Abdel Kader, Soha
    The Status of Research on Women in the Arab Region,
    1960-1978. Paris: UNESCO. Division of Human Rights and
    Peace. January, 1979.
Accad, Evelyne
    "Interrelationship Between Arab Nationalism and Feminist
    Consciousness in the North African Novels Written by
    Women." Ba Shiru. Volume 8 #2 1977. pp. 3-12.
Al-Qazza, Ayad
    "Current Status of Research on Women in the Arab World."
    Middle Eastern Studies. Volume 14 #3 October, 1978.
    pp. 372-384.
Allman, James
    "Family Life, Women's Status, and Fertility: Middle East
    and North African Perspectives." (In) Allman, James
    (ed.). Women's Studies and Fertility in the Muslim
    World. New York: Praeger Publishers. Praeger Special
    Studies. 1978. pp. 24-47.
Allman, James
    "Family Patterns, Women's Status and Fertility in
    Middle-East and North-Africa." International Journal of
    Sociology of the Family. Volume 8 #1 1978. pp. 19-35.
Allman, James (ed.)
    Women's Status and Fertility in the Muslim World. New
    York: Praeger Publishers. Praeger Special Studies.
    1978. 378p.
Baffoun, Alya
    "Women and Social Change in the Muslim Arab World."
    Women's Studies International Forum. Volume 5 #2 1982.
Ginat, Joseph (ed.)
    Women in Muslim Rural Society: Status and Role in Family
    Community. New Brunswick, New Jersey: Transition Books.
    1981. 268p.

Koning, Karen L.
    "Revolutionary Potential Among Arab Women Today."
    Mawazo. Volume 4 #4 1976. pp. 48-57.
Marshall, Susan E.
    "Politics and Female Status in North Africa: A
    Reconsideration of Development Theory." Economic
    Development and Cultural Change. Volume 32 #3 April,
    1984. pp. 499-524.
Meghdessian, S.R.
    The Status of Arab Women: A Select Bibliography.
    Westport, Connecticut: Greenwood Press. 1980. 176p.
Minces, Juliette
    The House of Obedience: Women in Arab Society. London:
    Zed Press. Westport, Connecticut: Lawrence Hill. 1982.
    114p.
Peters, Emrys L.
    "The Status of Women in Four Middle East Communities."
    (In) Beck, Lois and Keddie, Nikki R. (eds.). Women in
    the Muslim World. Cambridge, Massachusetts: Harvard
    University Press. 1978. pp. 311-350.
Sadik, Nafis
    "Muslim Women Today." Populi. Volume 12 #1 1985. pp.
    36-51.

WOMEN AND THEIR CHILDREN

Mukhtar, Behiza
    "A Question of Our Children's Bodies: The Medical Injury
    Caused to a Girl by Circumcision." Paper Presented at
    the Conference on Islam and Family Planning. Sponsored
    by the International Planned Parenthood Federation.
    Banjul, Gambia. October 21-24, 1979. 7p.

NATIONS OF NORTHERN AFRICA

Algeria

CULTURAL ROLES

Akeb, Fatiha and Abdelaziz, Malika
"Algerian Women Discuss the Need For Change." (In)
Fernea, Elizabeth W. (ed.). Women and the Family in the
Middle East: New Voices of Change. Austin, Texas:
University of Texas Press. 1985. pp. 8-26.

Anonymous
"Algerian Women: Myths of Liberation." Connexions. #2
Fall, 1981.

Anonymous
"No Easy Exit From Slavery Behind the Veil in Algeria."
(In) Ibrahim, Saad E. and Hopkins, Nicholas S. (eds.).
Arab Society in Transition: A Reader. Cairo, Egypt:
American University Cairo. 1977.

Anonymous
"Women and Work in Constitutions: Algeria." Women at
Work. Volume 2 1977. pp. 7-8.

Benatia, Farouk
"Some Ideas About Women's Work in Algeria."
International Social Science Journal. Volume 32 #3 1980.
pp. 464-478.

Boals, Kay
"The Politics of Cultural Liberation: Male-Female
Relations in Algeria." (In) Carroll, Berenice A. (ed.).
Liberating Women's History. Chicago: University of
Chicago Press. 1976. pp. 194-211.

Bowen, Donna L.
"Attitudes Toward Family and Family Planning in the
Pre-Saharan Maghreb." Maghreb Review. Volume 8 #1-2
January-April, 1983. pp. 8-17.

Danforth, Sandra C.
"The Social and Political Implications of Muslim Middle
Eastern Women's Participation in Violent Political
Conflict." Women and Politics. Volume 4 Spring, 1984.
pp. 35-54.

Grosse, Scott D.
    "The Politics of Family Planning in the Maghreb."
    Studies in Comparative International Development. Volume
    17 #1 Spring, 1982. pp. 22-48.
Hakiki, Fatiha and Talahite, Claude
    "Human Sciences Research on Algerian Women." (In) United
    Nations Educational, Scientific and Cultural
    Organization. Social Science Research and Women in the
    Arab World. Paris: UNESCO. 1984. pp. 82-93.
Hakiki, Fatiha and Talahite, Claude
    "Human Sciences Research on Algerian Women." Paper
    Presented at the Meeting of Arab Women Researchers on the
    Development of Research in the Social Sciences on Women
    in the Arab World. Paris: United Nations Educational,
    Scientific and Cultural Organization. Tunis, Tunisia.
    1982. 13p.
Harrow, K.
    "Not Such a Long Way, Baby--The Situation of the Women
    Today in the Maghreb and its Thematic Representation in
    Literature." Current Bibliography on African Affairs.
    Volume 9 #3 1976. pp. 228-249.
Keenan, Jeremy
    "The Tuareg Veil." Middle East Studies. Volume 13 #1
    1977. pp. 242-252.
Khodja, Souad
    "Women's Work as Viewed in Present-Day Algerian Society."
    International Labour Review. Volume 121 #4 July-August,
    1982. pp. 481-489.
Laws, Sophie
    "New Family Code Deprives Algerian Women of Rights
    (Interview With Nadine Claire)." Off Our Backs. Volume
    15 March, 1985. pp. 5-7+.
Marshall, Susan E.
    "The Power of the Veil: The Politics of Female Status in
    North Africa." Ph.D Dissertation: University of
    Massachusetts. Amherst, Massachusetts. 1980. 274p.
Marshall, Susan E. and Stokes, Randall G.
    "Tradition and the Veil: Female Status in Tunisia and
    Algeria." Journal of Modern African Studies. Volume 19
    #4 December, 1981. pp. 625-646.
Minces, Juliette
    "Women in Algeria." (In) Beck, Lois and Keddie, Nikki R.
    (eds.). Women in the Muslim World. Cambridge,
    Massachusetts: Harvard University Press. 1978. pp.
    159-171.
Mondot-Bernard, Jacqueline M.
    "Fertility and Breast-Feeding in Africa." African
    Environment. #14-16 1981. pp. 131-150.
Oussedik, Fatima
    "Algeria: The Day to Day Struggle." (In) Morgan, Robin
    (ed.). Sisterhood is Global. Garden City, New York:
    Anchor Books. 1984. pp. 45-49.

Parsons, David H.
"Change and Ambiguity in Male-Female Relations in an
Algerian City." Ph.D Dissertation: Northwestern
University. Evanston, Illinois. 1979. 402p.
Ramdane, Babadji
"Sexual Equality, Constitution and Islamic Law in
Algeria." Al-Raida. Volume 6 #26 1983. pp. 3-4.
Stiehm, Judith
"Algerian Women: Honor, Survival and Islamic Socialism."
(In) Iglitzin, Lynn and Ross, Ruth (eds.). Women in the
World: A Comparative Study. Santa Barbara, California:
Clio Press. Studies in Comparative Politics #6. 1976.
pp. 229-241.
Tabutin, Dominique
"Nuptiality and Fertility in Maghreb." (In) Ruzicka,
L.T. (ed.). Nuptiality and Fertility: Proceedings of a
Seminar, January 8-11, 1979. Liege, Netherlands: Union
for the Scientific Study of Population. 1982. pp.
101-122.
United Nations Educational, Scientific and Cultural Organ.
"Social Science Research and Women in the Arab World."
Paris: UNESCO. 1984. 175p.
Vallin, Jacques
"Fertility in Algeria: Trends and Differentials." (In)
Allman, James (ed.). Women's Status and Fertility in the
Muslim World. New York: Praeger Publishers. Praeger
Special Studies. 1978. pp. 131-151.
Wolff, Ursula
"Women in Africa--Maghribian Society in Transition."
Africa Report. Volume 22 #1 January-February, 1977.
pp. 41-43.

DEVELOPMENT AND TECHNOLOGY

Baffoun, Alya
"Some Remarks on Women and Development in the Maghreb."
(In) Rivlin, Helen A. and Helmer, Katherine (eds.). The
Changing Middle Eastern City. Binghamton, New York:
State University of New York. Center for Social
Analysis. 1980. pp. 141-148.
Hakiki, Fatiha and Talahite, Claude
"Human Sciences Research on Algerian Women." (In) United
Nations Educational, Scientific and Cultural
Organization. Social Science Research and Women in the
Arab World. Paris: UNESCO. 1984. pp. 82-93.
Hakiki, Fatiha and Talahite, Claude
"Human Sciences Research on Algerian Women." Paper
Presented at the Meeting of Arab Women Researchers on the
Development of Research in the Social Sciences on Women
in the Arab World. Paris: United Nations Educational,
Scientific and Cultural Organization. Tunis, Tunisia.
1982. 13p.

Minces, Juliette
"Women in Algeria." (In) Beck, Lois and Keddie, Nikki R. (eds.). Women in the Muslim World. Cambridge, Massachusetts: Harvard University Press. 1978. pp. 159-171.

Oussedik, Fatima
"The Conditions Required for Women Themselves to Conduct Research on Women in the Arab World." Paper Presented at the Meeting of Arab Women Researchers on the Development of Research in the Social Sciences Women in the Arab World. Paris: United Nations Educational, Scientific and Cultural Organization. Tunis, Tunisia. 1982. 11p.

Oussedik, Fatima
"The Conditions Required for Women to Conduct Research on Women in the Arab World." (In) United Nations Educational, Scientific and Cultural Organization. Social Science Research and Women in the Arab World. Paris: UNESCO. 1984. pp. 113-121.

United Nations Economic Commission for Africa (UNECA)
National, Sub-Regional and Regional Machineries for Women in Development. Report and Directory. Addis Ababa, Ethiopia: UNECA. November, 1979. 93p.

DIVORCE

Dorph, K.J.
"Islamic Law in Contemporary North Africa: A Study of the Laws of Divorce in the Maghreb." Women's Studies International Forum. Volume 5 #2 1982. pp. 169-182.

ECONOMICS

Baffoun, Alya
"Some Remarks on Women and Development in the Maghreb." (In) Rivlin, Helen A. and Helmer, Katherine (eds.). The Changing Middle Eastern City. Binghamton, New York: State University of New York. Center for Social Analysis. 1980. pp. 141-148.

Khodja, Souad
"Women's Work as Viewed in Present-Day Algerian Society." International Labour Review. Volume 121 #4 July-August, 1982. pp. 481-489.

EDUCATION AND TRAINING

Baffoun, Alya
"Research in the Social Sciences on North African Women: Problems, Trends and Needs." (In) United Nations Educational, Scientific and Cultural Organization.

Social Science Research and Women in the Arab World.
Paris: UNESCO. 1984. pp. 41-58.
Benallegue, Nora
"Algerian Women in the Struggle for Independence and
Reconstruction." International Social Science Journal.
Volume 35 #4 1983. pp. 703-717.
Oussedik, Fatima
"The Conditions Required for Women Themselves to Conduct
Research on Women in the Arab World." Paper Presented at
the Meeting of Arab Women Researchers on the Development
of Research in the Social Sciences Women in the Arab
World. Paris: United Nations Educational, Scientific and
Cultural Organization. Tunis, Tunisia. 1982. 11p.
Oussedik, Fatima
"The Conditions Required for Women to Conduct Research on
Women in the Arab World." (In) United Nations
Educational, Scientific and Cultural Organization.
Social Science Research and Women in the Arab World.
Paris: UNESCO. 1984. pp. 113-121.

EMPLOYMENT AND LABOR

Anonymous
"Women and Work in Constitutions: Algeria." Women at
Work. Volume 2 1977. pp. 7-8.
Baffoun, Alya
"Research in the Social Sciences on North African Women:
Problems, Trends and Needs." (In) United Nations
Educational, Scientific and Cultural Organization.
Social Science Research and Women in the Arab World.
Paris: UNESCO. 1984. pp. 41-58.
Benallegue, Nora
"Algerian Women in the Struggle for Independence and
Reconstruction." International Social Science Journal.
Volume 35 #4 1983. pp. 703-717.
Benatia, Farouk
"Some Ideas About Women's Work in Algeria."
International Social Science Journal. Volume 32 #3 1980.
pp. 464-478.
Khodja, Souad
"Women's Work as Viewed in Present-Day Algerian Society."
International Labour Review. Volume 121 #4 July-August,
1982. pp. 481-489.
Oussedik, Fatima
"The Conditions Required for Women Themselves to Conduct
Research on Women in the Arab World." Paper Presented at
the Meeting of Arab Women Researchers on the Development
of Research in the Social Sciences Women in the Arab
World. Paris: United Nations Educational, Scientific and
Cultural Organization. Tunis, Tunisia. 1982. 11p.
Oussedik, Fatima
"The Conditions Required for Women to Conduct Research on
Women in the Arab World." (In) United Nations

Educational, Scientific and Cultural Organization.
Social Science Research and Women in the Arab World.
Paris: UNESCO. 1984. pp. 113-121.

EQUALITY AND LIBERATION

Ahmed, Leila
   "Feminism and Feminist Movements in the Middle East, A
   Preliminary Exploration: Turkey, Egypt, Algeria, People's
   Democratic Republic of Yemen." Women's Studies
   International. Volume 5 #2 1982. pp. 153-168.
Ahmed, Leila
   "Women's Liberation Movements in 19th and 20th Century
   Middle East." Paper Presented at the Meeting of Experts
   on the Theoretical Frameworks and Methodological
   Approaches to Studies on the Role of Women in History as
   Actors in Economic, Social, Political and Ideological
   Processes. Paris: United Nations Educational, Scientific
   and Cultural Organization. 1984. 24p.
Anonymous
   "Algerian Women: Myths of Liberation." Connexions. #2
   Fall, 1981.
Benallegue, Nora
   "Algerian Women in the Struggle for Independence and
   Reconstruction." International Social Science Journal.
   Volume 35 #4 1983. pp. 703-717.
Benatia, Farouk
   "Some Ideas About Women's Work in Algeria."
   International Social Science Journal. Volume 32 #3 1980.
   pp. 464-478.
Boals, Kay
   "The Politics of Cultural Liberation: Male-Female
   Relations in Algeria." (In) Carroll, Berenice A. (ed.).
   Liberating Women's History. Chicago: University of
   Chicago Press. 1976. pp. 194-211.
Hakiki, Fatiha and Talahite, Claude
   "Human Sciences Research on Algerian Women." (In) United
   Nations Educational, Scientific and Cultural
   Organization. Social Science Research and Women in the
   Arab World. Paris: UNESCO. 1984. pp. 82-93.
Hakiki, Fatiha and Talahite, Claude
   "Human Sciences Research on Algerian Women." Paper
   Presented at the Meeting of Arab Women Researchers on the
   Development of Research in the Social Sciences on Women
   in the Arab World. Paris: United Nations Educational,
   Scientific and Cultural Organization. Tunis, Tunisia.
   1982. 13p.
Laws, Sophie
   "New Family Code Deprives Algerian Women of Rights
   (Interview With Nadine Claire)." Off Our Backs. Volume
   15 March, 1985. pp. 5-7+.

Ramdane, Babadji
"Sexual Equality, Constitution and Islamic Law in Algeria." Al-Raida. Volume 6 #26 1983. pp. 3-4.

FAMILY LIFE

Akeb, Fatiha and Abdelaziz, Malika
"Algerian Women Discuss the Need For Change." (In) Fernea, Elizabeth W. (ed.). Women and the Family in the Middle East: New Voices of Change. Austin, Texas: University of Texas Press. 1985. pp. 8-26.
Bowen, Donna L.
"Attitudes Toward Family and Family Planning in the Pre-Saharan Maghreb." Maghreb Review. Volume 8 #1-2 January-April, 1983. pp. 8-17.
Charrad, Mournira
"Family Policy and Political Development: A Comparison of Tunisia, Algeria and Morocco." Paper Presented at the Annual Meeting of the African Studies Association. Paper #13. Houston, Texas. 1977.

FAMILY PLANNING AND CONTRACEPTION

Anonymous
"An Analysis of Algerian Fertility Using the Correspondance Method." Population. Volume 34 #1 January-February, 1979. pp. 196-203.
Baffoun, Alya
"Research in the Social Sciences on North African Women: Problems, Trends and Needs." (In) United Nations Educational, Scientific and Cultural Organization. Social Science Research and Women in the Arab World. Paris: UNESCO. 1984. pp. 41-58.
Bowen, Donna L.
"Attitudes Toward Family and Family Planning in the Pre-Saharan Maghreb." Maghreb Review. Volume 8 #1-2 January-April, 1983. pp. 8-17.
Grosse, Scott D.
"The Politics of Family Planning in the Maghreb." Studies in Comparative International Development. Volume 17 #1 Spring, 1982. pp. 22-48.
Tabutin, Dominique
"Nuptiality and Fertility in Maghreb." (In) Ruzicka, L.T. (ed.). Nuptiality and Fertility: Proceedings of a Seminar, January 8-11, 1979. Liege, Netherlands: Union for the Scientific Study of Population. 1982. pp. 101-122.
Vallin, Jacques
"Fertility in Algeria: Trends and Differentials." (In) Allman, James (ed.). Women's Status and Fertility in the Muslim World. New York: Praeger Publishers. Praeger Special Studies. 1978. pp. 131-151.

FERTILITY AND INFERTILITY

Anonymous
"An Analysis of Algerian Fertility Using the
Correspondance Method." Population. Volume 34 #1
January-February, 1979. pp. 196-203.
Mondot-Bernard, Jacqueline M.
"Fertility and Breast-Feeding in Africa." African
Environment. #14-16 1981. pp. 131-150.
Tabutin, Dominique
"Nuptiality and Fertility in Maghreb." (In) Ruzicka,
L.T. (ed.). Nuptiality and Fertility: Proceedings of a
Seminar, January 8-11, 1979. Liege, Netherlands: Union
for the Scientific Study of Population. 1982. pp.
101-122.
Vallin, Jacques
"Fertility in Algeria: Trends and Differentials." (In)
Allman, James (ed.). Women's Status and Fertility in the
Muslim World. New York: Praeger Publishers. Praeger
Special Studies. 1978. pp. 131-151.

HEALTH, NUTRITION AND MEDICINE

Mondot-Bernard, Jacqueline M.
"Fertility and Breast-Feeding in Africa." African
Environment. #14-16 1981. pp. 131-150.

HISTORY

Ahmed, Leila
"Women's Liberation Movements in 19th and 20th Century
Middle East." Paper Presented at the Meeting of Experts
on the Theoretical Frameworks and Methodological
Approaches to Studies on the Role of Women in History as
Actors in Economic, Social, Political and Ideological
Processes. Paris: United Nations Educational, Scientific
and Cultural Organization. 1984. 24p.

LAW AND LEGAL ISSUES

Dorph, K.J.
"Islamic Law in Contemporary North Africa: A Study of the
Laws of Divorce in the Maghreb." Women's Studies
International Forum. Volume 5 #2 1982. pp. 169-182.
Laws, Sophie
"New Family Code Deprives Algerian Women of Rights
(Interview With Nadine Claire)." off our backs. Volume
15 March, 1985. pp. 5-7+.

ALGERIA

Ramdane, Babadji
"Sexual Equality, Constitution and Islamic Law in
Algeria." Al-Raida. Volume 6 #26 1983. pp. 3-4.

LITERATURE

Harrow, K.
"Not Such a Long Way, Baby--The Situation of the Women
Today in the Maghreb and its Thematic Representation in
Literature." Current Bibliography on African Affairs.
Volume 9 #3 1976. pp. 228-249.
Lippert, Anne
"The Emerging Woman in Algerian Literature: New Roles or
Old?" Paper Presented at the Annual Meeting of the
African Studies Association. Paper #45. Houston, Texas.
1977. 13p.
Mortimer, Mildred P.
"The Evolution of Assa Djebar's Feminist Conscience."
(In) Wylie, Hal and Julien, Eileen and Linnemann, Russell
J. (eds.). Contemporary African Literature. Washington,
D.C.: Three Continents Press. 1983. pp. 7-14.
Mortimer, Mildred P.
"The Femine Image in the Algerian Novel of French
Expression." Paper Presented at the African Literature
Association Conference. 1977. 22p.
Mortimer, Mildred P.
"The Feminine Image in the Algerian Novel of French
Expression." Ba Shiru. Volume 8 #2 1977. pp. 51-62.
Van Houwelingen
"Francophone Literature in North Africa." (In) Schipper,
Mineke (ed.). Unheard Words: Women and Literature in
Africa, the Arab World, Asia, the Caribbean, and Latin
America. New York: Alliison and Busby. 1985. pp.
102-113.

MARITAL RELATIONS AND NUPTIALITY

Grosse, Scott D.
"The Politics of Family Planning in the Maghreb."
Studies in Comparative International Development. Volume
17 #1 Spring, 1982. pp. 22-48.
Parsons, David H.
"Change and Ambiguity in Male-Female Relations in an
Algerian City." Ph.D Dissertation: Northwestern
University. Evanston, Illinois. 1979. 402p.
Tabutin, Dominique
"Nuptiality and Fertility in Maghreb." (In) Ruzicka,
L.T. (ed.). Nuptiality and Fertility: Proceedings of a
Seminar, January 8-11, 1979. Liege, Netherlands: Union
for the Scientific Study of Population. 1982. pp.
101-122.

NATIONALISM

Benallegue, Nora
  "Algerian Women in the Struggle for Independence and
  Reconstruction." International Social Science Journal.
  Volume 35 #4 1983. pp. 703-717.

ORGANIZATIONS

Danforth, Sandra C.
  "The Social and Political Implications of Muslim Middle
  Eastern Women's Participation in Violent Political
  Conflict." Women and Politics. Volume 4 Spring, 1984.
  pp. 35-54.
United Nations Economic Commission for Africa (UNECA)
  National, Sub-Regional and Regional Machineries for Women
  in Development. Report and Directory. Addis Ababa,
  Ethiopia: UNECA. November, 1979. 93p.

POLITICS AND GOVERNMENT

Ahmed, Leila
  "Feminism and Feminist Movements in the Middle East, A
  Preliminary Exploration: Turkey, Egypt, Algeria, People's
  Democratic Republic of Yemen." Women's Studies
  International. Volume 5 #2 1982. pp. 153-168.
Ahmed, Leila
  "Women's Liberation Movements in 19th and 20th Century
  Middle East." Paper Presented at the Meeting of Experts
  on the Theoretical Frameworks and Methodological
  Approaches to Studies on the Role of Women in History as
  Actors in Economic, Social, Political and Ideological
  Processes. Paris: United Nations Educational, Scientific
  and Cultural Organization. 1984. 24p.
Anonymous
  "Algerian Women: Myths of Liberation." Connexions. #2
  Fall, 1981.
Benallegue, Nora
  "Algerian Women in the Struggle for Independence and
  Reconstruction." International Social Science Journal.
  Volume 35 #4 1983. pp. 703-717.
Boals, Kay
  "The Politics of Cultural Liberation: Male-Female
  Relations in Algeria." (In) Carroll, Berenice A. (ed.).
  Liberating Women's History. Chicago: University of
  Chicago Press. 1976. pp. 194-211.
Charrad, Mournira
  "Family Policy and Political Development: A Comparison of
  Tunisia, Algeria and Morocco." Paper Presented at the
  Annual Meeting of the African Studies Association. Paper
  #13. Houston, Texas. 1977.

Danforth, Sandra C.
    "The Social and Political Implications of Muslim Middle
    Eastern Women's Participation in Violent Political
    Conflict." Women and Politics. Volume 4 Spring, 1984.
    pp. 35-54.
Laws, Sophie
    "New Family Code Deprives Algerian Women of Rights
    (Interview With Nadine Claire)." Off Our Backs. Volume
    15 March, 1985. pp. 5-7+.
Marshall, Susan E.
    "The Power of the Veil: The Politics of Female Status in
    North Africa." Ph.D Dissertation: University of
    Massachusetts. Amherst, Massachusetts. 1980. 274p.
Ramdane, Babadji
    "Sexual Equality, Constitution and Islamic Law in
    Algeria." Al-Raida. Volume 6 #26 1983. pp. 3-4.
Stiehm, Judith
    "Algerian Women: Honor, Survival and Islamic Socialism."
    (In) Iglitzin, Lynn and Ross, Ruth (eds.). Women in the
    World: A Comparative Study. Santa Barbara, California:
    Clio Press. Studies in Comparative Politics #6. 1976.
    pp. 229-241.
United Nations Economic Commission for Africa (UNECA)
    National, Sub-Regional and Regional Machineries for Women
    in Development. Report and Directory. Addis Ababa,
    Ethiopia: UNECA. November, 1979. 93p.

RELIGION AND WITCHCRAFT

Charrad, Mournira
    "Family Policy and Political Development: A Comparison of
    Tunisia, Algeria and Morocco." Paper Presented at the
    Annual Meeting of the African Studies Association. Paper
    #13. Houston, Texas. 1977.
Dorph, K.J.
    "Islamic Law in Contemporary North Africa: A Study of the
    Laws of Divorce in the Maghreb." Women's Studies
    International Forum. Volume 5 #2 1982. pp. 169-182.
Grosse, Scott D.
    "The Politics of Family Planning in the Maghreb."
    Studies in Comparative International Development. Volume
    17 #1 Spring, 1982. pp. 22-48.
Ramdane, Babadji
    "Sexual Equality, Constitution and Islamic Law in
    Algeria." Al-Raida. Volume 6 #26 1983. pp. 3-4.
Stiehm, Judith
    "Algerian Women: Honor, Survival and Islamic Socialism."
    (In) Iglitzin, Lynn and Ross, Ruth (eds.). Women in the
    World: A Comparative Study. Santa Barbara, California:
    Clio Press. Studies in Comparative Politics #6. 1976.
    pp. 229-241.

RESEARCH

Baffoun, Alya
    "Research in the Social Sciences on North African Women:
    Problems, Trends and Needs." (In) United Nations
    Educational, Scientific and Cultural Organization.
    Social Science Research and Women in the Arab World.
    Paris: UNESCO. 1984. pp. 41-58.
Hakiki, Fatiha and Talahite, Claude
    "Human Sciences Research on Algerian Women." (In) United
    Nations Educational, Scientific and Cultural
    Organization. Social Science Research and Women in the
    Arab World. Paris: UNESCO. 1984. pp. 82-93.
Hakiki, Fatiha and Talahite, Claude
    "Human Sciences Research on Algerian Women." Paper
    Presented at the Meeting of Arab Women Researchers on the
    Development of Research in the Social Sciences on Women
    in the Arab World. Paris: United Nations Educational,
    Scientific and Cultural Organization. Tunis, Tunisia.
    1982. 13p.
Oussedik, Fatima
    "The Conditions Required for Women Themselves to Conduct
    Research on Women in the Arab World." Paper Presented at
    the Meeting of Arab Women Researchers on the Development
    of Research in the Social Sciences Women in the Arab
    World. Paris: United Nations Educational, Scientific and
    Cultural Organization. Tunis, Tunisia. 1982. 11p.
Oussedik, Fatima
    "The Conditions Required for Women to Conduct Research on
    Women in the Arab World." (In) United Nations
    Educational, Scientific and Cultural Organization.
    Social Science Research and Women in the Arab World.
    Paris: UNESCO. 1984. pp. 113-121.
United Nations Economic Commission for Africa (UNECA)
    National, Sub-Regional and Regional Machineries for Women
    in Development. Report and Directory. Addis Ababa,
    Ethiopia: UNECA. November, 1979. 93p.
United Nations Educational, Scientific and Cultural Organ.
    Social Science Research and Women in the Arab World.
    Paris: UNESCO. 1984. 175p.

SEX ROLES

Anonymous
    "No Easy Exit From Slavery Behind the Veil in Algeria."
    (In) Ibrahim, Saad E. and Hopkins, Nicholas S. (eds.).
    Arab Society in Transition: A Reader. Cairo: American
    University Cairo. 1977.
Benatia, Farouk
    "Some Ideas About Women's Work in Algeria."
    International Social Science Journal. Volume 32 #3 1980.
    pp. 464-478.

Harrow, K.
    "Not Such a Long Way, Baby--The Situation of the Women
    Today in the Maghreb and its Thematic Representation in
    Literature." Current Bibliography on African Affairs.
    Volume 9 #3 1976. pp. 228-249.
Keenan, Jeremy
    "The Tuareg Veil." Middle East Studies. Volume 13 #1
    1977. pp. 242-252.
Khodja, Souad
    "Women's Work as Viewed in Present-Day Algerian Society."
    International Labour Review. Volume 121 #4 July-August,
    1982. pp. 481-489.
Marshall, Susan E.
    "The Power of the Veil: The Politics of Female Status in
    North Africa." Ph.D Dissertation: University of
    Massachusetts. Amherst, Massachusetts. 1980. 274p.
Marshall, Susan E. and Stokes, Randall G.
    "Tradition and the Veil: Female Status in Tunisia and
    Algeria." Journal of Modern African Studies. Volume 19
    #4 December, 1981. pp. 625-646.
Oussedik, Fatima
    "Algeria: The Day to Day Struggle." (In) Morgan, Robin
    (ed.). Sisterhood is Global. Garden City, New York:
    Anchor Books. 1984. pp. 45-49.
Parsons, David H.
    "Change and Ambiguity in Male-Female Relations in an
    Algerian City." Ph.D Dissertation: Northwestern
    University. Evanston, Illinois. 1979. 402p.
Ramdane, Babadji
    "Sexual Equality, Constitution and Islamic Law in
    Algeria." Al-Raida. Volume 6 #26 1983. pp. 3-4.

STATUS OF WOMEN

Ahmed, Leila
    "Feminism and Feminist Movements in the Middle East, A
    Preliminary Exploration: Turkey, Egypt, Algeria, People's
    Democratic Republic of Yemen." Women's Studies
    International. Volume 5 #2 1982. pp. 153-168.
Ahmed, Leila
    "Women's Liberation Movements in 19th and 20th Century
    Middle East." Paper Presented at the Meeting of Experts
    on the Theoretical Frameworks and Methodological
    Approaches to Studies on the Role of Women in History as
    Actors in Economic, Social, Political and Ideological
    Processes. Paris: United Nations Educational, Scientific
    and Cultural Organization. 1984. 24p.
Akeb, Fatiha and Abdelaziz, Malika
    "Algerian Women Discuss the Need For Change." (In)
    Fernea, Elizabeth W. (ed.). Women and the Family in the
    Middle East: New Voices of Change. Austin, Texas:
    University of Texas Press. 1985. pp. 8-26.

Anonymous
   "Algerian Women: Myths of Liberation." Connexions. #2
   Fall, 1981.
Anonymous
   "No Easy Exit From Slavery Behind the Veil in Algeria."
   (In) Ibrahim, Saad E. and Hopkins, Nicholas S. (eds.).
   Arab Society in Transition: A Reader. Cairo: American
   University Cairo. 1977.
Benallegue, Nora
   "Algerian Women in the Struggle for Independence and
   Reconstruction." International Social Science Journal.
   Volume 35 #4 1983. pp. 703-717.
Harrow, K.
   "Not Such a Long Way, Baby--The Situation of the Women
   Today in the Maghreb and its Thematic Representation in
   Literature." Current Bibliography on African Affairs.
   Volume 9 #3 1976. pp. 228-249.
Marshall, Susan E.
   "The Power of the Veil: The Politics of Female Status in
   North Africa." Ph.D Dissertation: University of
   Massachusetts. Amherst, Massachusetts. 1980. 274p.
Marshall, Susan E. and Stokes, Randall G.
   "Tradition and the Veil: Female Status in Tunisia and
   Algeria." Journal of Modern African Studies. Volume 19
   #4 December, 1981. pp. 625-646.
Minces, Juliette
   "Women in Algeria." (In) Beck, Lois and Keddie, Nikki R.
   (eds.). Women in the Muslim World. Cambridge,
   Massachusetts: Harvard University Press. 1978. pp.
   159-171.
Vallin, Jacques
   "Fertility in Algeria: Trends and Differentials." (In)
   Allman, James (ed.). Women's Status and Fertility in the
   Muslim World. New York: Praeger Publishers. Praeger
   Special Studies. 1978. pp. 131-151.
Wolff, Ursula
   "Women in Africa--Maghribian Society in Transition."
   Africa Report. Volume 22 #1 January-February, 1977.
   pp. 41-43.

Egypt

ABORTION

Toledano, E.R.
   "Slave Dealers, Women, Pregnancy and Abortion: The Study
   of a Circassian Slave Girl in Mid-19th Century Cairo."
   Slavery and Abolition. Volume 2 1981. pp. 53-68.
Toppozada, Hussein K. and Rizk, Mohammed A. and Abul-Einin,
Mostafa A. and Medhat, Ibrahim
   "Epidemiology of Abortion in Alexandria." Alexandria
   Medical Journal. Volume 26 #1/2 1980.

AGRICULTURE

Levy, Victor
   "Cropping Pattern, Mechanization, Child Labor and
   Fertility Behavior in a Farming Economy: Rural Egypt."
   Economic Development and Cultural Change. Volume 33 #4
   July, 1985. pp. 777-791.
Nawar, I.A.
   "Role of Rural Women in Rural Development." Paper
   Presented at the Workshop on the Role of Women and Home
   Economics in Rural Development in Africa. Rome: United
   Nations Food and Agricultural Organization. Alexandria,
   Egypt. October 17, 1983. 5p.
Schutjer, Wayne A. and Stokes, C. Shannon and Poindexter,
John R.
   "Farm Size, Land Ownership and Fertility in Rural Egypt."
   Land Economics. Volume 59 #4 November, 1983. pp.
   393-403.
Shanawany, Haifaa A.
   "Operational Proposals to Reinforce the Role of the Raida
   Rifiaa in Family Development in Egypt." Population
   Studies Quarterly Review. Volume 58 July-September,
   1981. pp. 31-34.

Sonia, Abadir R.
　　Problems Concerning Women and Their Consideration in
　　Development Planning: The Case of Egypt. Paris: United
　　Nations Educational, Scientific and Cultural
　　Organiaztion. Workshop on Women and National
　　Development, Cairo, 1984. 1985. 77p.
Stokes, C. Shannon and Schutjer, Wayne A.
　　"A Cautionary Note on Public Policies in Conflict: Land
　　Reform and Human Fertility in Rural Egypt." Comparative
　　Politics. Volume 16 #1 October, 1983. pp. 97-104.
United Nations Economic Commission for Africa (UNECA)
　　Women and Cooperatives: Egypt, The Libyan Arab Jamahiriya
　　and the Sudan. Addis Ababa, Ethiopia: UNECA. Research
　　Series. 1980.
Weidner-Read, Barbara L.
　　"Water, Women, Health and Housing: A Case Study of Rural
　　Reconstruction in Egypt." Ph.D Dissertation: University
　　of Utah. Salt Lake City, Utah. 1983. 206p.
Zimmerman, Sonja D.
　　The Cheese Makers of Kafr al Bahr: The Role of Egyptian
　　Women in Animal Husbandry and Dairy Production. Leiden,
　　Netherlands: State University of Leiden. Institute for
　　Social and Cultural Studies. Research Center: Women and
　　Development 1982. 55p.
Zimmerman, Sonja D.
　　The Women of Kafr al Bahr: Research Into the Working
　　Conditions of Women in an Egyptian Village. Leiden,
　　Netherlands: State University of Leiden. Institute for
　　Social and Cultural Studies. Research Center: Women and
　　Development. 1982. 149p.

ARTS

Early, Evelyn A.
　　"Catharsis and Creation in Informal Narratives of Baladi
　　Women in Cairo." Anthropological Quarterly. Volume 58
　　#4 1985. pp. 172-189.

CULTURAL ROLES

Abdel-Rahman, Mohamed E.
　　"Effectiveness of Socio-Economic Factors in Determining
　　Levels and Patterns of Fertility: A Demography Study of
　　Egypt(1950-1970)." Population Studies. Volume 9 #63
　　October-December, 1982. pp. 49-58+.
Abou-Gamrah, Hamed
　　"Fertility Levels and Differentials by Mother's Education
　　in Some Countries of the ECWA Region." (In) Cairo
　　Demographic Centre (CDC). Determinants of Fertility in
　　Some African and Asian Countries. Cairo: CDC. 1982.
　　pp. 191-211.

Abou-Gamrah, Hamed and Gheita, Naguib H.
    "Socio-Economic Status and Household Structure Among
    Selected Industrial Workers in Mehalla El-Kubra, Egypt."
    (In) Huzayyin, S.A. and Acsadi, G.T. (eds). Family and
    Marriage in Some African and Asiatic Countries. Cairo:
    Cairo Demographic Centre. Research Monograph Series #6.
    1976. pp. 143-159.
Abu-Lughod, Lila
    "A Community of Secrets: The Separate World of Bedouin
    Women." Signs. Volume 10 #4 Summer, 1985. pp.
    637-657.
Abu-Lughod, Lila
    "Honor, Modesty and Poetry in a Bedouin Society: Ideology
    and Experience Among Awlad Ali of Egypt." Ph.D.
    Dissertation: Harvard University. Cambridge,
    Massachusetts. 1984. 347p.
Acsadi, George T. and Hammam, Nabila M.
    "Marriage and Family Among Selected Female Health
    Personnel in Cairo." (In) Huzayyin, S.A. and Acsadi,
    G.T. (eds.). Family and Marriage in Some African and
    Asiatic Countries. Cairo: Cairo Demographic Centre. CDC
    Research Monograph Series #6. 1976. pp. 115-141.
Afifi, Zeinab E.M.
    "Determinants of Growth of Infants in an Egyptian
    Village: Maternal Anthropometry, Birth Interval, Solid
    Food and Death of Siblings." Human Biology. Volume 57
    #4 1985. pp. 649-658.
Al-Guindi, Fadwa
    "The Angels in the Nile: A Theme in Nubian Ritual." (In)
    Kennedy, John G. (ed.). Nubian Ceremonial Life.
    Berkeley, California: University of California Press.
    1978. pp. 104-113.
Al-Katsha, Samiha
    "Changes in Nubian Wedding Ceremonials." (In) Kennedy,
    John G. (ed.). Nubian Ceremonial Life. Berkeley,
    California: University of California Press. 1978. pp.
    171-202.
Al-Sadawi, Nawal
    "Growing Up Female in Egypt." (In) Fernea, Elizabeth W.
    (ed.). Women and the Family in the Middle East: New
    Voices of Change. Austin, Texas: University of Texas
    Press. 1985. pp. 111-120.
Anonymous
    "Marriage, Fertility and Family Planning: Summary of the
    Major Findings of the Egyptian Rural Fertility Survey,
    1979." Population Studies (Cairo). Volume 9
    January-March, 1982. pp. 37-49.
Aromasodu, M.C.
    "Traditional Practices Affecting the Health of Women in
    Pregnancy and Childbirth." Paper Presented at the
    Seminar on Traditional Practices Affecting the Health of

Women and Children: Female Circumcision, Childhood
Marriage, Nutritional Taboos, etc. Alexandria, Egypt:
World Health Organization. Eastern Mediterranean
Regional Office. Khartoum, Sudan. February 10-15, 1979.
Arthur, Rose H.
  "Feminine Motifs in Eight Nag Hammadi Documents." Th.D
  Dissertation: Graduate Theological Union. Berkeley,
  California. 1979. 298p.
Assaad, Marie B.
  "A Communication Gap Regarding Female Circumcision."
  (In) Blair, Patricia W. (ed.). Health Needs of the
  World's Poor Women. Washington, D.C.: Equity Policy
  Center. 1981. pp. 9-11.
Assaad, Marie B.
  "Female Circumcision in Egypt." Paper Presented at the
  Seminar on Traditional Practices Affecting the Health of
  Women and Children: Female Circumcision, Childhood
  Marriage, Nutritional Taboos, Etc. Alexandria, Egypt:
  World Health Organization. Eastern Mediterranean
  Regional Office. Khartoum, Sudan. February 10-15, 1979.
Assaad, Marie B.
  "Female Circumcision in Egypt: Current Research and
  Social Implications." Paper Presented at the Seminar on
  Traditional Practices Affecting the Health of Women and
  Children. World Conference of the United Nations Decade
  for Women. Copenhagen, Denmark. July 14-30, 1980.
Assaad, Marie B.
  "Female Circumcision in Egypt: Social Implications,
  Current Research and Prospects for Change." Studies in
  Family Planning. Volume 11 #1 January, 1980. pp. 3-16.
Atif, Nadia
  The Context of Women's Work: Employment, Fertility,
  Development and the Seven Roles of Women in Mehalla Al
  Kubr. Cairo: Center for Egyptian Civilzation Studies.
  1981.
Atiya, Nayra (ed.)
  Khul-Khaal: Five Egyptian Women Tell Their Stories.
  Syracuse, New York: Syracuse University Press.
  Contemporary Issues in the Middle East Series. 1982.
  216p.
Aulas, Marie C.
  Egypt's Working Women: Sadat's Strange Peace. Washington
  D.C.: Middle East Research and Information Project.
  MERIP Reports #82. 1979. 26p.
Bach, Rebecca and Gadalla, Saad M. and Khattab, Hind A. and
Gulick, John
  "Mothers' Influence on Daughters' Orientations Toward
  Education: An Egyptian Case Study." Comparative
  Education Review. Volume 29 #3 August, 1985. pp.
  375-384.
Burton, John W.
  "Nilotic Women: A Diachronic Perspective." Journal of
  Modern African Studies. Volume 20 #3 1982. pp. 467-491.

Caldwell, Pat
    "Egypt and the Arab World." (In) Caldwell, John C.
    (ed.). The Persistence of High Fertility: Population
    Prospects in the Third World. Canberra, Australia:
    Australian National University. Department of
    Demography. Volume Two. 1977. pp. 593-616.
Chaudhry, Sayeeda A.
    "Female Labor Force Participation and its Relationship to
    Fertility Rate: Some Policy Implications for Developing
    Countries." Ph.D Dissertation: George Washington
    University. Washington, D.C. 1984. 410p.
Cole, Juan R.
    "Feminism, Class, and Islam in Turn-of-the-Century
    Egypt." International Journal of Middle East Studies.
    Volume 13 #4 November, 1981. pp. 387-407.
Darwish, O.A.
    "Weaning Practices in Urban and Rural Egypt." Food and
    Nutrition Bulletin. Volume 4 #1 January, 1982.
Duza, M. Badrud and Ibrahim, Issa A.
    "Nuptiality and Household Structure in Nubian Villages,
    Egypt." (In) Huzayyin, S.A. and Acsadi, G.T. (eds.).
    Family and Marriage in Some African and Asiatic
    Countries. Cairo: Cairo Demographic Centre. CDC
    Research Monograph Series #6. 1976. pp. 97-113.
Early, Evelyn A.
    "Catharsis and Creation in Informal Narratives of Baladi
    Women in Cairo." Anthropological Quarterly. Volume 58
    #4 1985. pp. 172-189.
Early, Evelyn A.
    "Catharsis and Creation: The Everyday Narratives of
    Baladi Women of Cairo." Anthropological Quarterly.
    Volume 58 #4 October, 1985. pp. 172-181.
Early, Evelyn A.
    "Fatima: A Life History of an Egyptian Woman From Bulaq."
    (In) Fernea, Elizabeth W. (ed.). Women and the Family in
    the Middle East: New Voices of Change. Austin, Texas:
    University of Texas Press. 1985. pp. 76-83.
Early, Evelyn A.
    "Logic of Well Being: Therapeutic Narratives in Cairo,
    Egypt." Social Science and Medicine. Volume 16 #16
    1982. pp. 1491-1497.
Egypt. National Commission for UNESCO
    The Role of Working Mothers in Early Childhood Education:
    Arab Republic of Egypt, 1977. Paris: United Nations
    Educational, Scientific and Cultural Organization.
    January, 1978. 31p.
Egypt. Population and Family Planning Board
    "Marriage, Fertility and Family Planning: Summary of the
    Major Findings of the Egyptian Rural Fertility Survey,
    1979." Population Studies. Volume 9 #60 January-March,
    1982. pp. 37-49.

Egypt. State Information Service
   Egyptian Women: Progress in the Balance. Cairo, Egypt:
   State Information Service. 1980. 55p.
El Baymoumi, Soheir
   "Health and Illness as Indices of Sex Status in an
   Egyptian Village." Paper Presented at the 75th Annual
   Meeting of the American Anthropological Association.
   Washington, D.C. November 17-21, 1976.
El Guindi, Fadwa
   "Veiled Activism: Egyptian Women in the Contemporary
   Islamic Movement." Mediterranean Peoples. Volume 22/23
   January-June, 1983. pp. 79-89.
El Guindi, Fadwa
   "Veiling Infitah With Muslim Ethic: Egypt's Contemporary
   Islamic Movement." Social Problems. Volume 28 #4
   April, 1981. pp. 465-485.
El Hakim, Ahmed S.
   "Female Circumcision in Egypt." Paper Presented at the
   Seminar on Traditional Practices Affecting the Health of
   Women and Children. World Conference of the United
   Nations Decade for Women. New York: United Nations.
   Copenhagen, Denmark. July 14-30, 1980.
El Hakim, Ahmed S.
   "Mental Aspects of Circumcision." Paper Presented at the
   Seminar on Traditional Practices Affecting the Health of
   Women and Children. World Conference of the United
   Nations Decade for Women. New York: United Nations.
   Copenhagen, Denmark. July 14-30, 1980.
El Hakim, Ahmed S.
   "Mental Aspects of Female Circumcision in Egypt." Paper
   Presented at the Seminar on Traditional Practices
   Affecting the Health of Women and Children: Female
   Circumcision, Childhood Marriage, Nutritional Taboos,
   etc. Alexandria, Egypt: World Health Organization.
   Eastern Mediterranean Regional Office. Khartoum, Sudan.
   February 10-15, 1979.
El Saadawi, Nawal
   "Egypt: When a Female Rebels..." (In) Morgan, Robin
   (ed.). Sisterhood is Global. Garden City, New York:
   Anchor Books. 1984. pp. 194-206.
El Sadaawi, Nawal
   "Creative Women in Changing Societies: A Personal
   Reflection." Race and Class. Volume 22 #2 Autumn,
   1980. pp. 159-182.
El-Deeb, Bothaina M.
   "Fertility and Mortality in a Rural Egyptian Community: A
   Case Study in Beshla Village, Daqahliya Governorate,
   Lower Egypt." Population Studies. Volume 7 #53
   April-June, 1980. pp. 87-100.
El-Deeb, Bothaina M.
   The Dynamics of Birth Spacing and Marital Fertility in
   Egypt. Cairo: Cairo Demographic Centre. CDC Research
   Monograph Series #12. 1984. pp. 83-104.

El-Guindy M.
"The Impact of Divorce and Widowhood on Fertility in Egypt." Egyptian Population and Family Planning Review. Volume 13 #1/2 June-December, 1979. pp. 84-94.

El-Karamani, Yussuf I.
"Islam and Family Planning: A Brief Study." Population Studies. Volume 10 #64 January-March, 1983. pp. 31-44.

El-Kharboutly, Maitre A.
"Law and the Status of Women in the Arab Republic of Egypt." (In) Columbia Human Rights Law Review (eds.). Law and the Status of Women: An International Symposium. New York: United Nations. Centre for Social Development and Humanitarian Affairs. 1977. pp. 35-50.

El-Messiri, Sawsan
"Self-Images of Traditional Urban Women in Cairo." (In) Beck, Lois and Keddie, Nikki R. (eds.). Women in the Muslim World. Cambridge, Massachusetts: Harvard University Press. 1978. pp. 522-540.

Fahmy, Hoda Y.
"Changing Women in a Changing Society: A Study of Emergent Consciousness of Young Women in the City of Akhmin in Upper Egypt." M.A. Thesis: American University of Cairo. Department of Sociology/Anthropology/ Psychology. Cairo. 1978.

Farghali, Fathi
Household Characteristics and Rural Out-Migration in Upper Egypt. Cairo: Cairo Demographic Center (CDC). CDC Research Monograph Series #12. 1984. pp. 287-303.

Gadalla, Saad M. and McCarthy, James and Campbell, Oona
"How the Number of Living Sons Influences Contraceptive Use in Menoufia Governorate, Egypt." Studies in Family Planning. Volume 16 #3 May-June, 1985. pp. 164-169.

Gadalla, Saad M.
Is There Hope? Fertility and Family Planning in a Rural Egyptian Community. Chapel Hill, North Carolina: University of North Carolina. Carolina Population Center. 1977. 259p.

Govaerts, K.
"Attachment Behavior of the Egyptian Mother." International Journal of Nursing Studies. Volume 18 #1 1981. pp. 53-60.

Hakem, Ahmed M. and Hrbek, Ivan and Vercoutter, Jean
"The Matriarchs of Meroe: A Powerful Line of Queens Who Ruled the Kushitic Empire." UNESCO Courier. Volume 32 #8/9 August-September, 1979. pp. 58-59.

Hall, Marjorie J.
"The Position of Women in Egypt and the Sudan as Reflected in Feminist Writing Since 1900." Ph.D Dissertation: University of London. London. 1977. 369p.

Hamzawi, Riad
"Factors Affecting Egyptian Rural Women's Fertility: A

Theoretical Explanation." Population Studies. Volume 12
#72 January-March, 1985. pp. 29-43.
Hussein, Aziza
"Recent Amendments to Egypt's Personal Status Law." (In)
Fernea, Elizabeth W. (ed.). Women and the Family in the
Middle East: New Voices of Change. Austin, Texas:
University of Texas Press. 1985. pp. 229-232.
Ibrahim, Barbara L.
"Cairo's Factory Women." (In) Fernea, Elizabeth W.
(ed.). Women and the Family in the Middle East: New
Voices of Change. Austin, Texas: University of Texas
Press. 1985. pp. 293-302.
Ibrahim, Barbara L.
"Social Change and the Industrial Experience: Women as
Production Workers in Urban Egypt." Ph.D Dissertation:
Indiana University. Bloomington, Indiana. 1980. 269p.
Ibrahim, Madlain M.
Has Age at Marriage Increased in Rural Egypt. Cairo:
Cairo Demographic Centre. CDC Research Monograph Series
#12. 1984. pp. 43-61.
Issa, Mahmoud S.
"A Time Series Analysis of Marriage in Egypt, 1962-1973."
(In) Huzayyin, S.A. and Acsadi, G.T. (eds.). Family and
Marriage in Some African and Asiatic Countries. Cairo:
Cairo Demographic Centre. CDC Research Monograph Series
#6. 1976. pp. 373-390.
Jennings, Anne M.
"Power and Influence: Women's Associations in an Egyptian
Nubian Village." Ph.D Dissertation: University of
California, Riverside. Riverside, California. 1985.
215p.
Junsay, Alma T.
"Patterns and Determinants of Female Labor Force
Participation in Developing Nations." Ph.D Dissertation:
Brigham Young University. Provo, Utah. 1985. 205p.
Kafafi, Laila
"Age at Marriage and Cumulative Fertility in Rural
Egypt." Ph.D Dissertation: Duke University. Durham,
North Carolina. 1983. 140p.
Kennedy, John G.
"Circumcision and Excision Ceremonies." (In) Kennedy,
John G. (ed.). Nubian Ceremonial Life. Berkeley,
California: University of California Press. 1978. pp.
151-170.
Kennedy, John G.
"Nubian Death Ceremonies." (In) Kennedy, John G. (ed.).
Nubian Ceremonial Life. Berkeley, California: University
of California Press. 1978. pp. 224-244.
Kennedy, John G.
"Nubian Zar Ceremonies as Psycho-Therapy." (In) Kennedy,
John G. (ed.). Nubian Ceremonial Life. Berkeley,
California: University of California Press. 1978. pp.
203-223.

Khafagy, Fatma
   "Women and Labor Migration: One Village in Egypt."   MERIP
   Reports.   Volume 14 #124   June, 1984.   pp. 17-21.
Khalifa, Atef M. and Way, Ann A.
   Marriage, Fertility and Family Planning: A Study of the
   RFS, 1979.   Cairo: Population and Family Planning Board.
   1981.
Krieger, Laurie E.
   "Body Notions, Gender Roles and Fertility Regulating
   Method Use in Imbaba, Cairo."   Ph.D Dissertation:
   University of North Carolina at Chapel Hill.   Chapel
   Hill, North Carolina.   1984.   285p.
Levy, Victor
   "Cropping Pattern, Mechanization, Child Labor and
   Fertility Behavior in a Farming Economy: Rural Egypt."
   Economic Development and Cultural Change.   Volume 33 #4
   July, 1985.   pp. 777-791.
Lowi, Miriam
   "The Truth Sometimes Shocks."   Index on Censorship.
   Volume 11 #3   June, 1982.   pp. 18-20.
Loza, Sarah F.
   "Differential Age at Marriage and Fertility in Egypt."
   (In) Cairo Demographic Centre (CDC).   Determinants of
   Fertility in Some African and Asian Countries.   Cairo:
   CDC.   CDC Research Monograph Series #10.   1982.   pp.
   51-66.
Loza-Soliman, Sarah F.
   "Roles of Women and Their Impact on Fertility: An
   Egyptian Case Study."   (In) International Union for the
   Scientific Study of Population (IUSSP).   International
   Population Conference: Solicited Papers.   Liege, Belgium:
   IUSSP.   Volume Three.   1981.   pp. 571-584.
Marei, Wafaa A.
   "Female Emancipation and Changing Political Leadership: A
   Study of Five Arab Countries."   Ph.D Dissertation:
   Rutgers University.   New Brunswick, New Jersey.   1978.
   364p.
Marshall, Susan E.
   "The Power of the Veil: The Politics of Female Status in
   North Africa."   Ph.D Dissertation: University of
   Massachusetts.   Amherst, Massachusetts.   1980.   274p.
Marsot, Afaf L.
   "The Revolutionary Gentlewomen in Egypt."   (In) Beck,
   Lois and Keddie, Nikki R. (eds.).   Women in the Muslim
   World.   Cambridge, Massachusetts: Harvard University
   Press.   1978.   pp. 261-276.
Merriam, Kathleen H.
   "The Impact of Educational Experiences Upon the
   Professional and Public Careers of Contemporary Egyptian
   Women."   Paper Presented at the Wellesley Conference on
   Women and Development.   Wellesley, Massachusetts:
   Wellesley College.   June 2-6, 1976.

Merriam, Kathleen H.
   "The Impact of Modern Secular Education Upon Egyptian
   Women's Participation in Public Life." Paper Presented
   at the Annual Meeting of the Middle East Studies
   Association. Los Angeles, California. November 10-13,
   1976.
Mikhail, A.N.
   "Traditional Feeding Practices in Pregnancy and Lactation
   in an Egyptian Community." Paper Presented at the
   Seminar on Traditional Practices Affecting the Health of
   Women and Children. World Conference of the United
   Nations Decade for Women. New York: United Nations.
   Copenhagen, Denmark. July 14-30, 1980.
Mikhail, A.N.
   "Traditional Feeding Practices in Pregnancy." Paper
   Presented at the Seminar on Traditional Practices
   Affecting the Health of Women and Children: Female
   Circumcision, Childhood Marriage, Nutritional Taboos,
   etc. Alexandria Egypt: World Health Organization.
   Eastern Mediterranean Regional Office. Khartoum, Sudan.
   February 10-15, 1979.
Mohsen, Safia K.
   "New Images, Old Reflections: Working Middle Class Women
   in Egypt." (In) Fernea, Elizabeth W. (ed.). Women and
   Family in the Middle East: New Voices of Change. Austin,
   Texas: University of Texas Press. 1985. pp. 56-71.
Morsy, Soheir A.
   "Gender, Power, and Illness in an Egyptian Village."
   Ph.D Dissertation: Michigan State University. East
   Lansing, Michigan. 1978. 450p.
Morsy, Soheir A.
   "Sex Differences and Folk Illness in an Egyptian
   Village." (In) Beck, Lois and Keddie, Nikki R. (eds.).
   Women in the Muslim World. Cambridge, Massachsetts:
   Harvard University Press. 1978. pp. 599-616.
Morsy, Soheir A.
   "Sex Roles, Power and Illness in an Egyptian Village."
   American Ethnologist. Volume 5 #1 1978. pp. 137-150.
Nadim, Nawal
   "Family Relationships in a Harah in Cairo." (In) El-Din
   Ibrahim, Saad and Hopkins, Nicholas (eds.). Arab Society
   in Transition. Cairo: American University in Cairo.
   1977.
Nasr, Z.
   "Islam and the Subordination of Women." Egypte
   Contemporaine. Volume 70 #378 1979. pp. 5-29.
Nawar, I.A.
   "Role of Rural Women in Rural Development." Paper
   Presented at the Workshop on the Role of Women and Home
   Economics in Rural Development in Africa. Rome: United
   Nations Food and Agricultural Organization. Alexandria,
   Egypt. October 17, 1983. 5p.

Nawar, Leila M.
"Household Structure and Age at Marriage in Abbasia,
Cairo." (In) Huzayyin, S.A. and Acsadi, G.T. (eds.).
Family and Marriage in Some African and Asiatic
Countries. Cairo: Cairo Demographic Centre. Research
Monograph Series #6. 1976. pp. 67-96.

Nelson, Cynthia
"Islamic Tradition and Women's Education in Egypt." (In)
Archer, Sandra (ed.). World Yearbook of Education 1984:
Women and Education. New York: Nichols Publishing Co.
1984. pp. 211-226.

Njoki, Margaret
"Female Circumcision in Egypt." Paper Presented at the
Seminar on Traditional Practices Affecting the Health of
Women and Children: Female Circumcision, Childhood
Marriage, Nutritional Taboos, etc. Alexandria, Egypt:
World Health Organization. Eastern Mediterranean
Regional Office. Khartoum, Sudan. February 10-15, 1979.

Nour, S.F.
"Attitudes of Selected Wives Toward Some Homemaking
Tasks." Paper Presented at the Workshop on the Role of
Women and Home Economics in Rural Development in Africa.
Rome: United Nations Food and Agricultural Organization.
Alexandria, Egypt. October 17, 1983. 11p.

Olusanya, P.O.
The Demographic, Health, Economic and Social Impact of
Family Planning in Selected African Countries. Addis
Ababa, Ethiopia: United Nations Economic Commission for
Africa. ECA/PD/1985-9. March, 1985. 97p.

Potts, M. and Stanowitz, B. and Fortney, J.A.
Childbirth in Developing Countries. Hingham,
Massachusetts: MTP Press. 1983. 162p.

Qayyum, Shah A.
"Women in the Muslim World: A Case Study of Egypt." (In)
Phadnis, Urmila and Malani, Indira (eds.). Women of the
World: Illusion and Reality. New Delhi, India: Vikas
Publishing House Ltd. 1978. pp. 150-174.

Raccagni, Michelle
"Origins of Feminism in Egypt and Tunisia." Ph.D
Dissertation: New York University. New York, New York.
1983. 327p.

Royal, Anne M.
"Male/Female Pharyngealization Patterns in Cairo Arabic:
A Socio-Linguistic Study of Two Neighborhoods." Ph.D
Dissertation: University of Texas. Austin, Texas. 1985.
228p.

Rugh, Andrea B.
Family in Contemporary Egypt. Syracuse, New York:
Syracuse University Press. Contemporary Issues in the
Middle East. 1984. 305p.

Rugh, Andrea B.
"Women and Work: Strategies and Choices in a Lower-Class
Quarter in Cairo," (In) Fernea, Elizabeth E. (ed.).

Women and the Family in the Middle East: New Voices of
Change. Austin, Texas: University of Texas Press. 1985.
pp. 273-288.
Salem, Afaf A.
    "Female Circumcision in Egypt." Paper Presented at the
    Seminar on Traditional Practices Affecting the Health of
    Women and Children: Female Circumcision, Childhood
    Marriage, Nutritional Taboos, etc. Alexandria, Egypt:
    World Health Organization. Eastern Mediterranean
    Regional Office. February 10-15, 1979.
Salem, Afaf A.
    "Female Circumcision in Egypt." Paper Presented at the
    Seminar on Tradional Practices Affecting the Health of
    Women and Children. World Conference of the United
    Nations Decade for Women. New York: United Nations.
    Copenhagen, Denmark. July 14-30, 1980.
Salem, Afaf A.
    "The Practice of Circumcision in Egypt." Paper Presented
    at the Seminar on Traditional Practices Affecting the
    Health of Women and Children. World Conference of the
    United Nations Decade for Women. New York: United
    Nations. Copenhagen, Denmark. July 14-30, 1980.
Sallam, Azza M.A.
    "The Return to the Veil Among Undergraduate Females at
    Minya University, Egypt." Ph.D Dissertation: Purdue
    University. West Lafayette, Indiana. 1980. 173p.
Sayed, Hussein A.A.
    "A Model For the Study of Nuptiality." Egyptian
    Population and Family Planning Review. Volume 12 #1/2
    June-December, 1978. pp. 25-39.
Sayed, Hussein A.A.
    "Regional Pattern of Differentials in Contraceptive Use
    in Egypt." (In) Cairo Demographic Centre (CDC).
    Determinants of Fertility in Some African and Asian
    Countries. Cairo: CDC. CDC Research Monograph Series
    #10. 1982. pp. 67-88.
Schutjer, Wayne A. and Stokes, C. Shannon and Poindexter,
John R.
    "Farm Size, Land Ownership and Fertility in Rural Egypt."
    Land Economics. Volume 59 #4 November, 1983. pp.
    393-403.
Schutjer, Wayne A. and Stokes, C. Shannon and Poindexter,
John R.
    Why Not Use Contraception? The Economics of Fertility
    Regulation Among Rural Egyptian Women. University Park,
    Pennsylvania: Pennsylvania State University. Population
    Issues Research Center. 1984.
Smock, Audrey C. and Youssef, Nadia H.
    "Egypt: From Seclusion to Limited Participation." (In)
    Giele, Janet Z. and Smock, Audrey C. (eds.). Women:
    Their Roles and Status in Eight Countries. New York:
    Wiley-Interscience. 1977. pp. 33-79.

Sokona, Ousmane and Casterline, John B.
Socioeconomic Differentials in Age at Marriage in Egypt.
Providence, Rhode Island: Brown University. Population
Studies and Training Center. PSTC Working Paper Series
#WP-85-03. April, 1985. 32p.

Stillman, Yedida K.
"The Importance of the Cairo Geniza Manuscripts for the
History of Medieval Female Attire." International
Journal of Middle East Studies. Volume 7 #4 October,
1976. pp. 579-590.

Stokes, C. Shannon and Schutjer, Wayne A.
"A Cautionary Note on Public Policies in Conflict: Land
Reform and Human Fertility in Rural Egypt." Comparative
Politics. Volume 16 #1 October, 1983. pp. 97-104.

Stokes, C. Shannon and Schutjer, Wayne A. and Poindexter,
John R.
"A Note on Desired Family Size and Contraceptive Use in
Rural Egypt." Journal of Biosocial Science. Volume 15
#1 January, 1983. pp. 59-65.

Stycos, J. Mayone and Bindary, Aziz and Avery, Roger C. and
Khalifa, Atef M. and Sayed, Hussein A.A. and Way, Ann A.
"Contraception and Community in Egypt: A Preliminary
Evaluation of the Population/Development Mix." Studies
in Family Planning. Volume 13 #12 Part One December,
1982. pp. 365-372.

Sukkary-Stolba, S.
"Changing Roles of Women in Egypt's Newly Reclaimed
Lands." Anthropological Quarterly. Volume 58 #4
October, 1985. pp. 182-189.

Sullivan, E.
Women and Work in Egypt. New York: American University
in Cairo. Cairo Papers in Social Sciences. Volume 4.
December, 1981. pp. 1-44.

Tadros, Helmi R.
Social Security and the Family in Egypt. New York:
American University in Cairo. Cairo Papers in Social
Science. Volume 7 #1. March, 1984. 87p.

Taha, Ibrahim K. and Abdelghany, Abdelghany M.
"Recent Socio-Economic Fertility Differentials in Egypt."
(In) Cairo Demographic Center (CDC). Determinants of
Fertility in Some Asian and African Countries. Cairo:
CDC. CDC Research Monograph Series #10. 1982. pp.
89-116.

Taplin, Ruth
"Women and Work in Egypt: An Historical Perspective."
Paper Presented at the Annual Meeting of the Pacific
Sociological Association. 1985. 20p.

Taylor, Elizabeth
"Egyptian Migration and Peasant Wives." MERIP Reports.
Volume 14 #124 June, 1984. pp. 3-10.

Tucker, Judith E.
Women in 19th Century Egypt. New York: Columbia
University Press. 1985. 251p.

United Nations Educational, Scientific and Cultural Organ.
    Social Science Research and Women in the Arab World.
    Paris: UNESCO. 1984. 175p.
Weimer, Joan M.
    "Belly Dancer and the Virgin: Mythic Women in Modern
    Egypt." Southwest Review. Volume 61 #1 Winter, 1976.
    pp. 1-14.
Wikan, Unni
    Life Among the Poor in Cairo. New York: Tavistock
    Publications in Association With Methuen, Inc.
    Translated by Ann Henning. 1980. 173p.
Williams, J.A.
    "Veiling in Egypt as a Political and Social Phenomenon."
    (In) Esposito, John L. (ed.). Islam and Development.
    Syracuse, New York: Syracuse University Press. 1980.
    pp. 71-85.
Younis, M.N. and Abou El-Ela, N.M. and Sultan, M. and
El-Maaddawi, Y. and El-Masry, G.
    "Socio-Medical Factors Affecting the Utilization of
    Different Contraceptive Methods at Al-Azhar Rural Family
    Health Clinic." Population Sciences. #6 1985. pp.
    27-34.
Zimmerman, Sonja D.
    The Cheese Makers of Kafr al Bahr: The Role of Egyptian
    Women in Animal Husbandry and Dairy Production. Leiden,
    Netherlands: State University of Leiden. Institute for
    Social and Cultural Studies. Research Center: Women and
    Development 1982. 55p.
Zimmerman, Sonja D.
    The Women of Kafr al Bahr: Research Into the Working
    Conditions of Women in an Egyptian Village. Leiden,
    Netherlands: State University of Leiden. Institute for
    Social and Cultural Studies. Research Center: Women and
    Development. 1982. 149p.

DEVELOPMENT AND TECHNOLOGY

Atif, Nadia
    The Context of Women's Work: Employment, Fertility,
    Development and the Seven Roles of Women in Mehalla Al
    Kubr. Cairo: Center for Egyptian Civilzation Studies.
    1981.
Chaudhry, Sayeeda A.
    "Female Labor Force Participation and its Relationship to
    Fertility Rate: Some Policy Implications for Developing
    Countries." Ph.D Dissertation: George Washington
    University. Washington, D.C. 1984. 410p.
Duza, A.
    "Women's Involvement in Socioeconomic Projects Related to
    Family Planning." Population Studies. Volume 8 #58
    July-September, 1981. pp. 3-30.

Early, Evelyn A.
    Entrepreneurship Among Lower Class Egyptian Women.
    Chicago: University of Illinois. 1978.
Egypt. State Information Service
    Egyptian Women: Progress in the Balance. Cairo: State
    Information Service. 1980. 55p.
Fahmy, Hoda Y.
    "Building Upon Tradtion: A Women's Handicraft Project in
    Upper Egypt." Assignment Children. Volume 49/50
    Spring, 1980. pp. 197-206.
Field, John O. and Ropes, George
    "Infant Mortality, the Birth Rate and Development in
    Egypt." Egypte Contemporaine. Volume 71 #381 July,
    1980. pp. 213-265.
Graham-Brown, Sarah
    "Home-Grown Graduates." Middle East. #91 May, 1982.
Gran, Judith
    "Impact of the World Market on Egyptian Women." MERIP
    Reports. #58 June, 1977. pp. 3-7.
Hassan, Shafick S.
    "The Role of Economic Development in Controlling
    Fertility in Egypt." (In) Cairo Demographic Centre
    (CDC). Aspects of Population Change and Development in
    Some African and Asian Countries. Cairo: CDC. CDC
    Research Monograph Series #9. 1984. pp. 173-196.
Ibrahim, Barbara L.
    "Social Change and the Industrial Experience: Women as
    Production Workers in Urban Egypt." Ph.D Dissertation:
    Indiana University. Bloomington, Indiana. 1980. 269p.
Ibrahim, Barbara L.
    Women and Factory Work in Egypt: The Intersection of
    Labor Demand and Household Strategies. Cairo: American
    University. 1982.
Issa, Mahmoud S.
    "Modernisation and the Fertility Transition, Egypt:
    1975." Ph.D Dissertation: University of Pennsylvania.
    Philadelphia, Pennsylvania. 1981. 434p.
Issa, Mahmoud S.
    Modernization and the Fertility Transition, Egypt, 1975.
    Philadelphia, Pennsylvania: University of Pennsylvania.
    Population Studies Center. African Demography Program
    Working Paper #3. June, 1980. 49p.
Khalifa, Atef M. and Way, Ann A.
    "An Evaluation of the Impact of the Population and
    Development Program (PDP), Based on Data From the 1980
    Contraceptive Prevalence Survey." (In) Cairo Demographic
    Center (CDC). Determinants of Fertility in Some African
    and Asian Countries. Cairo: CDC. CDC Research Monograph
    Series #10. 1982. pp. 117-153.
Lynch, Patricia D. and Fahmy, Hoda Y.
    Craftswomen in Kerdassa, Egypt: Household Production and
    Reproduction. Geneva: International Labour Organization.

World Employment Programme. Population and Labour
Policies Programme. Working Paper #126. WEP 2-21.
1983. 75p.
Morcos, Widad
"The New Family Law in Egypt." Cemam Reports
(1978-1979). 1981.
Nawar, I.A.
"Role of Rural Women in Rural Development." Paper
Presented at the Workshop on the Role of Women and Home
Economics in Rural Development in Africa. Rome: United
Nations Food and Agricultural Organization. Alexandria,
Egypt. October 17, 1983. 5p.
Poston, Dudley L. and El-Badry, Samia M.
Moderization and Childlessness Among the Governorates of
the Arab Republic of Egypt, 1976. Austin, Texas:
University of Texas Press. Texas Population Research
Center Papers. Series Six. #6.017. 1984. 23p.
Sayed, Hussein A.A. and Stycos, J. Mayone and Khalifa, Atef
M. and Avery, Roger C.
"An Assessment of the Population and Development Program
(PDP) Based on the Results of the Second Rural Fertility
Survey (RFS II)." Population Studies. Volume 10 #65
April-June, 1983. pp. 3-40.
Shanawany, Haifaa A.
"Operational Proposals to Reinforce the Role of the Raida
Rifiaa in Family Development in Egypt." Population
Studies Quarterly Review. Volume 58 July-September,
1981. pp. 31-34.
Smock, Audrey C. and Youssef, Nadia H.
"Egypt: From Seclusion to Limited Participation." (In)
Giele, Janet Z. and Smock, Audrey C. (eds.). Women:
Their Roles and Status in Eight Countries. New York:
Wiley-Interscience. 1977. pp. 33-79.
Sonia, Abadir R.
Problems Concerning Women and Their Consideration in
Development Planning: The Case of Egypt. Paris: United
Nations Educational, Scientific and Cultural
Organiaztion. Workshop on Women and National
Development, Cairo, 1984. 1985. 77p.
Stokes, C. Shannon and Schutjer, Wayne A.
"A Cautionary Note on Public Policies in Conflict: Land
Reform and Human Fertility in Rural Egypt." Comparative
Politics. Volume 16 #1 October, 1983. pp. 97-104.
Sukkary-Stolba, S.
"Changing Roles of Women in Egypt's Newly Reclaimed
Lands." Anthropological Quarterly. Volume 58 #4
October, 1985. pp. 182-189.
United Nations Economic Commission for Africa (UNECA)
Women and Cooperatives: Egypt, The Libyan Arab Jamahiriya
and the Sudan. Addis Ababa, Ethiopia: UNECA. Research
Series. 1980.
Weidner-Read, Barbara L.
"Water, Women, Health and Housing: A Case Study of Rural

Reconstruction in Egypt." Ph.D Dissertation: University
of Utah. Salt Lake City, Utah. 1983. 206p.

Youssef, Nadia H.
A Woman-Specific Strategy Statement: The Case of Egypt.
Washington, D.C.: U.S. Department of State. U.S. Agency
for International Development. Office of Planning and
Budget. 1980.

Zimmerman, Sonja D.
The Cheese Makers of Kafr al Bahr: The Role of Egyptian
Women in Animal Husbandry and Dairy Production. Leiden,
Netherlands: State University of Leiden. Institute for
Social and Cultural Studies. Research Center: Women and
Development 1982. 55p.

Zimmermann, Sonja D.
The Women of Kafr al Bahr: Research Into the Working
Conditions of Women in an Egyptian Village. Leiden,
Netherlands: University of Leiden. Research Center for
Women and Development. 1982. 149p.

DIVORCE

El-Guindy M.
"The Impact of Divorce and Widowhood on Fertility in
Egypt." Egyptian Population and Family Planning Review.
Volume 13 #1/2 June-December, 1979. pp. 84-94.

ECONOMICS

Abdel-Rahman, Mohamed E.
"Effectiveness of Socio-Economic Factors in Determining
Levels and Patterns of Fertility: A Demography Study of
Egypt(1950-1970)." Population Studies. Volume 9 #63
October-December, 1982. pp. 49-58+.

Abou-Gamrah, Hamed and Gheita, Naguib H.
"Socio-Economic Status and Household Structure Among
Selected Industrial Workers in Mehalla El-Kubra, Egypt."
(In) Huzayyin, S.A. and Acsadi, G.T. (eds). Family and
Marriage in Some African and Asiatic Countries. Cairo:
Cairo Demographic Centre. Research Monograph Series #6.
1976. pp. 143-159.

Alli, S.M.
"Women in the Labour Force Data of Egypt." (In) The
Population Council. The Measurement of Women's Economic
Participation: Report of a Study Group. Giza, Egypt: The
Population Council. October, 1979.

Aulas, Marie C.
Egypt's Working Women: Sadat's Strange Peace. Washington
D.C.: Middle East Research and Information Project.
MERIP Reports #82. 1979. 26p.

Brink, Judy H.
"The Effect of Education and Employment on the Status of

Rural Egyptian Women." Ph.D Dissertation: University of
Pittsburgh. Pittsburgh, Pennsylvania. 1985. 217p.

Chaudhry, Sayeeda A.
"Female Labor Force Participation and its Relationship to
Fertility Rate: Some Policy Implications for Developing
Countries." Ph.D Dissertation: George Washington
University. Washington, D.C. 1984. 410p.

Early, Evelyn A.
Entrepreneurship Among Lower Class Egyptian Women.
Chicago: University of Illinois. 1978.

Egyptian Ministry of Information
Women and Work in the Arab Republic of Egypt. Cairo:
Arab Republic of Egypt. Ministry of Information. State
Information Service. 1985. 29p.

Fahmy, Hoda Y.
"Building Upon Tradtion: A Women's Handicraft Project in
Upper Egypt." Assignment Children. Volume 49/50
Spring, 1980. pp. 197-206.

Farghali, Fathi
"Female Labour Force Participation in Greater Cairo."
(In) Cairo Demographic Centre (CDC). Studies in African
and Asian Demography. Cairo: CDC. CDC Research
Monograph Series #11. 1983. pp. 367-380.

Gran, Judith
"Impact of the World Market on Egyptian Women." MERIP
Reports. #58 June, 1977. pp. 3-7.

Hammam, Mona
"Egypt's Working Women: Textile Workers of Chubra
el-Kheima." MERIP Reports. #9 November, 1979.

Hammam, Mona
"Women Workers and the Practice of Freedom as Education:
The Egyptian Experience." Ph.D Dissertation: University
of Kansas. Lawrence, Kansas. 1977. 243p.

Hammam, Mona
"Women and Industrial Work in Egypt: The Chubra
el-Kheima." Arab Studies Quarterly. Volume 2 #1
Winter, 1980. pp. 50-69.

Hassan, Shafick S.
"The Role of Economic Development in Controlling
Fertility in Egypt." (In) Cairo Demographic Centre
(CDC). Aspects of Population Change and Development in
Some African and Asian Countries. Cairo: CDC. CDC
Research Monograph Series #9. 1984. pp. 173-196.

Ibrahim, Barbara L.
"Family Strategies--A Perspective on Women's Entry to the
Labor Force in Egypt." International Journal of
Sociology. Volume 11 #2 July-December, 1981. pp.
235-249.

Ibrahim, Barbara L.
"Social Change and the Industrial Experience: Women as
Production Workers in Urban Egypt." Ph.D Dissertation:
Indiana University. Bloomington, Indiana. 1980. 269p.

Ibrahim, Barbara L.
   Women and Factory Work in Egypt: The Intersection of
   Labor Demand and Household Strategies. Cairo: American
   University. 1982.
Junsay, Alma T.
   "Patterns and Determinants of Female Labor Force
   Participation in Developing Nations." Ph.D Dissertation:
   Brigham Young University. Provo, Utah. 1985. 205p.
Khafagy, Fatma
   "Women and Labor Migration: One Village in Egypt." MERIP
   Reports. Volume 14 #124 June, 1984. pp. 17-21.
Khidr, S.
   "Absenteeism of Working Women and Productivity." M.A.
   Thesis: Ain-Shams University. Cairo, Egypt. 1983.
Lynch, Patricia D.
   Women and Work: Getting From Today to Tomorrow No Matter
   What the Rewards Offered. Cairo, Egypt: Unpublished
   Paper. 1981.
Lynch, Patricia D. and Fahmy, Hoda Y.
   Craftswomen in Kerdassa, Egypt: Household Production and
   Reproduction. Geneva: International Labour Organization.
   World Employment Programme. Population and Labour
   Policies Programme. Working Paper #126. WEP 2-21.
   1983. 75p.
Mohsen, Safia K.
   "New Images, Old Reflections: Working Middle Class Women
   in Egypt." (In) Fernea, Elizabeth W. (ed.). Women and
   Family in the Middle East: New Voices of Change. Austin,
   Texas: University of Texas Press. 1985. pp. 56-71.
Morcos, Widad
   "The New Family Law in Egypt." Cemam Reports
   (1978-1979). 1981.
Nawar, I.A.
   "Role of Rural Women in Rural Development." Paper
   Presented at the Workshop on the Role of Women and Home
   Economics in Rural Development in Africa. Rome: United
   Nations Food and Agricultural Organization. Alexandria,
   Egypt. October 17, 1983. 5p.
Nour, S.F.
   "Attitudes of Selected Wives Toward Some Homemaking
   Tasks." Paper Presented at the Workshop on the Role of
   Women and Home Economics in Rural Development in Africa."
   Rome: United Nations Food and Agricultural Organization.
   Alexandria, Egypt. October 17, 1983. 11p.
Papanek, Hanna
   "Class and Gender in Education-Employment Linkages."
   Comparative Education Review. Volume 29 August, 1985.
   pp. 317-346.
Sonia, Abadir R.
   Problems Concerning Women and Their Consideration in
   Development Planning: The Case of Egypt. Paris: United
   Nations Educational, Scientific and Cultural

Organiaztion. Workshop on Women and National
Development, Cairo, 1984. 1985. 77p.

Sullivan, E.
Women and Work in Egypt. New York: American University
in Cairo. Cairo Papers in Social Sciences. Volume 4.
December, 1981. pp. 1-44.

Tadros, Helmi R.
Social Security and the Family in Egypt. New York:
American University in Cairo. Cairo Papers in Social
Science. Volume 7 #1. March, 1984. 87p.

Taplin, Ruth
"Women and Work in Egypt: An Historical Perspective."
Paper Presented at the Annual Meeting of the Pacific
Sociological Association. 1985. 20p.

United Nations Economic Commission for Africa (UNECA)
Women and Cooperatives: Egypt, The Libyan Arab Jamahiriya
and the Sudan. Addis Ababa, Ethiopia: UNECA. Research
Series. 1980.

Weidner-Read, Barbara L.
"Water, Women, Health and Housing: A Case Study of Rural
Reconstruction in Egypt." Ph.D Dissertation: University
of Utah. Salt Lake City, Utah. 1983. 206p.

EDUCATION AND TRAINING

Abou-Gamrah, Hamed
"Fertility Levels and Differentials by Mother's Education
in Some Countries of the ECWA Region." (In) Cairo
Demographic Centre (CDC). Determinants of Fertility in
Some African and Asian Countries. Cairo: CDC. 1982.
pp. 191-211.

Abou-Gamrah, Hamed
"Fertility and Childhood Mortality by Mother's and
Father's Education in Cairo, 1976." Population Bulletin
of the Economic Commission for Western Asia. #19
December, 1980. pp. 81-92.

Bach, Rebecca and Gadalla, Saad M. and Khattab, Hind A. and
Gulick, John
"Mothers' Influence on Daughters' Orientations Toward
Education: An Egyptian Case Study." Comparative
Education Review. Volume 29 #3 August, 1985. pp.
375-384.

Brink, Judy H.
"The Effect of Education and Employment on the Status of
Rural Egyptian Women." Ph.D Dissertation: University of
Pittsburgh. Pittsburgh, Pennsylvania. 1985. 217p.

Egypt. Centr. Agency for Public Mobilisation and Statistics
1976 Population and Housing Census. Fertility and
Internal Migration and Movement of Workers and Students.
Cairo: Central Agency. December, 1980. 440p.

Egypt. National Commission for UNESCO
    The Role of Working Mothers in Early Childhood Education:
    Arab Republic of Egypt, 1977. Paris: United Nations
    Educational, Scientific and Cultural Organization.
    January, 1978. 31p.
El Sadaawi, Nawal
    "Creative Women in Changing Societies: A Personal
    Reflection." Race and Class. Volume 22 #2 Autumn,
    1980. pp. 159-182.
Fahmy, Hoda Y.
    "Building Upon Tradtion: A Women's Handicraft Project in
    Upper Egypt." Assignment Children. Volume 49/50
    Spring, 1980. pp. 197-206.
Graham-Brown, Sarah
    "Home-Grown Graduates." Middle East. #91 May, 1982.
Howard-Merriam, Kathleen
    "Egypt's Other Political Elite." Western Political
    Quarterly. Volume 34 #1 March, 1981. pp. 174-187.
Howard-Merriam, Kathleen
    "Women, Education and the Professions in Egypt."
    Comparative Education Review. Volume 23 #2 June, 1979.
    pp. 256-270.
Junsay, Alma T.
    "Patterns and Determinants of Female Labor Force
    Participation in Developing Nations." Ph.D Dissertation:
    Brigham Young University. Provo, Utah. 1985. 205p.
Khalifa, Atef M.
    "The Influence of Wife's Education on Fertility in Rural
    Egypt." Journal of Biosocial Science. Volume 8 #1
    January, 1976. pp. 53-60.
Loza, Sarah F.
    "Differential Concern for Children's Education and Its
    Effect on Fertility." Population Studies (Cairo).
    Volume 6 #51 Oct.-Dec., 1979. pp. 9-29.
Mehrez, Zeinab M.
    Femine Education: Egypt's Experience in This Field and
    the Extent to Which this Education is Presently Needed.
    Cairo: Educational Documentation and Information Agency.
    National Center for Educational Research. 1978. 17p.
Merriam, Kathleen H.
    "The Impact of Educational Experiences Upon the
    Professional and Public Careers of Contemporary Egyptian
    Women." Paper Presented at the Wellesley Conference on
    Women and Development. Wellesley, Massachusetts:
    Wellesley College. June 2-6, 1976.
Merriam, Kathleen H.
    "The Impact of Modern Secular Education Upon Egyptian
    Women's Participation in Public Life." Paper Presented
    at the Annual Meeting of the Middle East Studies
    Association. Los Angeles, California. November 10-13,
    1976.

Nelson, Cynthia
   "Islamic Tradition and Women's Education in Egypt." (In)
   Archer, Sandra (ed.). World Yearbook of Education 1984:
   Women and Education. New York: Nichols Publishing Co.
   1984. pp. 211-226.
Papanek, Hanna
   "Class and Gender in Education-Employment Linkages."
   Comparative Education Review. Volume 29 August, 1985.
   pp. 317-346.
Raccagni, Michelle
   "Origins of Feminism in Egypt and Tunisia." Ph.D
   Dissertation: New York University. New York, New York.
   1983. 327p.
Sallam, Azza M.A.
   "The Return to the Veil Among Undergraduate Females at
   Minya University, Egypt." Ph.D Dissertation: Purdue
   University. West Lafayette, Indiana. 1980. 173p.
Sonia, Abadir R.
   Problems Concerning Women and Their Consideration in
   Development Planning: The Case of Egypt. Paris: United
   Nations Educational, Scientific and Cultural
   Organiaztion. Workshop on Women and National
   Development, Cairo, 1984. 1985. 77p.
Sproul, Christine
   "The American College for Girls, Cairo, Egypt: Its
   History and Influence on Egyptian Women. A Study of
   Selected Graduates." Ph.D Dissertation: University of
   Utah. Salt Lake City, Utah. 1982. 209p.
Wahba, Mostafa A.
   Educational Aspects of the Labour Force in Egypt.
   Cairo: Cairo Demographic Centre. CDC Research Monograph
   Series #12. 1984. pp. 155-182.

EMPLOYMENT AND LABOR

Abou-Gamrah, Hamed and Gheita, Naguib H.
   "Socio-Economic Status and Household Structure Among
   Selected Industrial Workers in Mehalla El-Kubra, Egypt."
   (In) Huzayyin, S.A. and Acsadi, G.T. (eds). Family and
   Marriage in Some African and Asiatic Countries. Cairo:
   Cairo Demographic Centre. Research Monograph Series #6.
   1976. pp. 143-159.
Alli, S.M.
   "Women in the Labour Force Data of Egypt." (In) The
   Population Council. The Measurement of Women's Economic
   Participation: Report of a Study Group. Giza, Egypt: The
   Population Council. October, 1979.
Atif, Nadia
   The Context of Women's Work: Employment, Fertility,
   Development and the Seven Roles of Women in Mehalla Al
   Kubr. Cairo: Center for Egyptian Civilzation Studies.
   1981.

Aulas, Marie C.
    Egypt's Working Women: Sadat's Strange Peace. Washington
    D.C.: Middle East Research and Information Project.
    MERIP Reports #82. 1979. 26p.
Brink, Judy H.
    "The Effect of Education and Employment on the Status of
    Rural Egyptian Women." Ph.D Dissertation: University of
    Pittsburgh. Pittsburgh, Pennsylvania. 1985. 217p.
Chaudhry, Sayeeda A.
    "Female Labor Force Participation and its Relationship to
    Fertility Rate: Some Policy Implications for Developing
    Countries." Ph.D Dissertation: George Washington
    University. Washington, D.C. 1984. 410p.
Early, Evelyn A.
    Entrepreneurship Among Lower Class Egyptian Women.
    Chicago: University of Illinois. 1978.
Egypt. Centr. Agency for Public Mobilisation and Statistics
    1976 Population and Housing Census. Fertility and
    Internal Migration and Movement of Workers and Students.
    Cairo, Egypt: Central Agency. December, 1980. 440p.
Egypt. National Commission for UNESCO
    The Role of Working Mothers in Early Childhood Education:
    Arab Republic of Egypt, 1977. Paris: United Nations
    Educational, Scientific and Cultural Organization.
    January, 1978. 31p.
Egyptian Ministry of Information
    Women and Work in the Arab Republic of Egypt. Cairo:
    Arab Republic of Egypt. Ministry of Information. State
    Information Service. 1985. 29p.
Farghali, Fathi
    "Female Labour Force Participation in Greater Cairo."
    (In) Cairo Demographic Centre (CDC). Studies in African
    and Asian Demography. Cairo, Egypt: CDC. CDC Research
    Monograph Series #11. 1983. pp. 367-380.
Graham-Brown, Sarah
    "Home-Grown Graduates." Middle East. #91 May, 1982.
Gran, Judith
    "Impact of the World Market on Egyptian Women." MERIP
    Reports. #58 June, 1977. pp. 3-7.
Hammam, Mona
    "Egypt's Working Women: Textile Workers of Chubra
    el-Kheima." MERIP Reports. #9 November, 1979.
Hammam, Mona
    "Women Workers and the Practice of Freedom as Education:
    The Egyptian Experience." Ph.D Dissertation: University
    of Kansas. Lawrence, Kansas. 1977. 243p.
Hammam, Mona
    "Women and Industrial Work in Egypt: The Chubra
    el-Kheima." Arab Studies Quarterly. Volume 2 #1
    Winter, 1980. pp. 50-69.
Hamzawi, Riad
    "The Relationship Between Female Employment and

Fertility." Ph.D Dissertation: Case Western Reserve
University. Cleveland, Ohio. 1982. 136p.
Hanbel, Ibrahim
"The Effects of Working Mothers." Paper Presented at the
Maternity Seminar. Cairo: Egyptian Ministry of Social
Affairs, Public Administration of Family Childhood.
March, 1982.
Hassan, Shafick S.
"The Role of Economic Development in Controlling
Fertility in Egypt." (In) Cairo Demographic Centre
(CDC). Aspects of Population Change and Development in
Some African and Asian Countries. Cairo: CDC. CDC
Research Monograph Series #9. 1984. pp. 173-196.
Howard-Merriam, Kathleen
"Women, Education and the Professions in Egypt."
Comparative Education Review. Volume 23 #2 June, 1979.
pp. 256-270.
Ibrahim, Barbara L.
"Family Strategies--A Perspective on Women's Entry to the
Labor Force in Egypt." International Journal of
Sociology. Volume 11 #2 July-December, 1981. pp.
235-249.
Ibrahim, Barbara L.
"Social Change and the Industrial Experience: Women as
Production Workers in Urban Egypt." Ph.D Dissertation:
Indiana University. Bloomington, Indiana. 1980. 269p.
Ibrahim, Barbara L.
Women and Factory Work in Egypt: The Intersection of
Labor Demand and Household Strategies. Cairo: American
University. 1982.
Issa, M.
The Egyptian Women's Participation in the Labour Force:
Secular Trends, Age Patterns and Determinants,
1907-1976. Cairo: Central Agency for Public Mobilization
and Statistics. 1979.
Junsay, Alma T.
"Patterns and Determinants of Female Labor Force
Participation in Developing Nations." Ph.D Dissertation:
Brigham Young University. Provo, Utah. 1985. 205p.
Khafagy, Fatma
"Women and Labor Migration: One Village in Egypt." MERIP
Reports. Volume 14 #124 June, 1984. pp. 17-21.
Khidr, S.
"Absenteeism of Working Women and Productivity." M.A.
Thesis: Ain-Shams University. Cairo, Egypt. 1983.
Levy, Victor
"Cropping Pattern, Mechanization, Child Labor and
Fertility Behavior in a Farming Economy: Rural Egypt."
Economic Development and Cultural Change. Volume 33 #4
July, 1985. pp. 777-791.
Loza, Sarah F.
"Employment of Women Action Programme in a Ready Made

Clothes Factory, South Tahrir." Population Studies.
January-March, 1979. pp. 1-19.
Loza-Soliman, Sarah F.
"Roles of Women and Their Impact on Fertility: An
Egyptian Case Study." (In) International Union for the
Scientific Study of Population (IUSSP). International
Population Conference: Solicited Papers. Liege, Belgium:
IUSSP. Volume Three. 1981. pp. 571-584.
Lynch, Patricia D.
Women and Work: Getting From Today to Tomorrow No Matter
What the Rewards Offered. Cairo. Unpublished Paper.
1981.
Lynch, Patricia D. and Fahmy, Hoda Y.
Craftswomen in Kerdassa, Egypt: Household Production and
Reproduction. Geneva: International Labour Organization.
World Employment Programme. Population and Labour
Policies Programme. Working Paper #126. WEP 2-21.
1983. 75p.
Merriam, Kathleen H.
"The Impact of Educational Experiences Upon the
Professional and Public Careers of Contemporary Egyptian
Women." Paper Presented at the Wellesley Conference on
Women and Development. Wellesley, Massachusetts:
Wellesley College. June 2-6, 1976.
Merriam, Kathleen H.
"The Impact of Modern Secular Education Upon Egyptian
Women's Participation in Public Life." Paper Presented
at the Annual Meeting of the Middle East Studies
Association. Los Angeles, California. November 10-13,
1976.
Mohsen, Safia K.
"New Images, Old Reflections: Working Middle Class Women
in Egypt." (In) Fernea, Elizabeth W. (ed.). Women and
Family in the Middle East: New Voices of Change. Austin,
Texas: University of Texas Press. 1985. pp. 56-71.
Moore, C.
"Women Engineers in Egypt: Growing Equality Amidst
Professional Impoverishment." Paper Presented at the
Annual Meeting of the American Political Science
Association. New York. September, 1978.
Omar, Said M.
"Some Demographic Aspects of Labour Force in Sharkia
Governorate, Egypt (1960-1976)." Population Studies.
Volume 11 #71 October-December, 1984. pp. 35-65.
Papanek, Hanna
"Class and Gender in Education-Employment Linkages."
Comparative Education Review. Volume 29 August, 1985.
pp. 317-346.
Rugh, Andrea B.
"Women and Work: Strategies and Choices in a Lower-Class
Quarter in Cairo," (In) Fernea, Elizabeth E. (ed.).
Women and the Family in the Middle East: New Voices of

Change. Austin, Texas: University of Texas Press. 1985.
pp. 273-288.

Sallam, Ihab Z.
Occupational Patterns and Trends in Cairo Governorate.
Cairo: Cairo Demographic Center. CDC Research Monograph
Series #12. 1984. pp. 183-200.

Sullivan, E.
Women and Work in Egypt. New York: American University
in Cairo. Cairo Papers in Social Sciences. Volume 4.
December, 1981. pp. 1-44.

Taplin, Ruth
"Women and Work in Egypt: An Historical Perspective."
Paper Presented at the Annual Meeting of the Pacific
Sociological Association. 1985. 20p.

Taylor, Elizabeth
"Egyptian Migration and Peasant Wives." MERIP Reports.
Volume 14 #124 June, 1984. pp. 3-10.

Wahba, Mostafa A.
Educational Aspects of the Labour Force in Egypt.
Cairo: Cairo Demographic Centre. CDC Research Monograph
Series #12. 1984. pp. 155-182.

Zimmerman, Sonja D.
The Cheese Makers of Kafr al Bahr: The Role of Egyptian
Women in Animal Husbandry and Dairy Production. Leiden,
Netherlands: State University of Leiden. Institute for
Social and Cultural Studies. Research Center: Women and
Development. 1982. 55p.

Zimmerman, Sonja D.
The Women of Kafr al Bahr: Research Into the Working
Conditions of Women in an Egyptian Village. Leiden,
Netherlands: State University of Leiden. Institute for
Social and Cultural Studies. Research Center: Women and
Development. 1982. 149p.

EQUALITY AND LIBERATION

Ahmed, Leila
"Feminism and Feminist Movements in the Middle East, A
Preliminary Exploration: Turkey, Egypt, Algeria, People's
Democratic Republic of Yemen." Women's Studies
International. Volume 5 #2 1982. pp. 153-168.

Ahmed, Leila
"Women's Liberation Movements in 19th and 20th Century
Middle East." Paper Presented at the Meeting of Experts
on the Theoretical Frameworks and Methodological
Approaches to Studies on the Role of Women in History as
Actors in Economic, Social, Political and Ideological
Processes. Paris: United Nations Educational, Scientific
and Cultural Organization. 1984. 24p.

Anonymous
"Egyptian Woman Wins Battle for Equality With Man."

M.E.N. Economic Weekly. Volume 21 #32 August 6, 1982.
pp. 10-12.
Cole, Juan R.
"Feminism, Class, and Islam in Turn-of-the-Century
Egypt." International Journal of Middle East Studies.
Volume 13 #4 November, 1981. pp. 387-407.
El Guindi, Fadwa
"Veiled Activism: Egyptian Women in the Contemporary
Islamic Movement." Mediterranean Peoples. Volume 22/23
January-June, 1983. pp. 79-89.
El Guindi, Fadwa
"Veiling Infitah With Muslim Ethic: Egypt's Contemporary
Islamic Movement." Social Problems. Volume 28 #4
April, 1981. pp. 465-485.
El Saadawi, Nawal
"Egypt: When a Female Rebels..." (In) Morgan, Robin
(ed.). Sisterhood is Global. Garden City, New York:
Anchor Books. 1984. pp. 194-206.
El Sadaawi, Nawal
"Creative Women in Changing Societies: A Personal
Reflection." Race and Class. Volume 22 #2 Autumn,
1980. pp. 159-182.
Eliraz, Giora
"Egyptian Intellectuals and Women's Emancipation,
1919-1939." Asian and African Studies. Volume 16 #1
March, 1982. pp. 95-120.
Fahmy, Hoda Y.
"Changing Women in a Changing Society: A Study of
Emergent Consciousness of Young Women in the City of
Akhmin in Upper Egypt." M.A. Thesis: American University
of Cairo. Department of Sociology/Anthropology/
Psychology. Cairo. 1978.
Graham-Brown, Sarah
"Feminism in Egypt: A Conversation With Nawal Sadawi."
MERIP Reports. #95 March, 1981. pp. 24-27.
Marei, Wafaa A.
"Female Emancipation and Changing Political Leadership: A
Study of Five Arab Countries." Ph.D Dissertation:
Rutgers University. New Brunswick, New Jersey. 1978.
364p.
Moore, C.
"Women Engineers in Egypt: Growing Equality Amidst
Professional Impoverishment." Paper Presented at the
Annual Meeting of the American Political Science
Association. New York. September, 1978.
Phillipp, Thomas
"Feminism and Nationalist Politics in Egypt." (In) Beck,
Lois and Keddie, Nikki R. (eds.). Women in the Muslim
World. Cambridge, Massachusetts: Harvard University
Press. 1978. pp. 277-294.
Raccagni, Michelle
"Origins of Feminism in Egypt and Tunisia." Ph.D

Dissertation: New York University. New York, New York.
1983. 327p.

Steinem, Gloria
"Two Cheers for Egypt: Talks With Jihan Sadat and Other
Daughters of the Nile." MS. Volume 8 June, 1980. pp.
72+.

Tolchin, Susan and Tolchin, Martin
"The Feminist Revolution of Jihan Sadat." New York Times
Magazine. March 16, 1980. pp. 21+.

FAMILY LIFE

Abou-Gamrah, Hamed and Gheita, Naguib H.
"Socio-Economic Status and Household Structure Among
Selected Industrial Workers in Mehalla El-Kubra, Egypt."
(In) Huzayyin, S.A. and Acsadi, G.T. (eds). Family and
Marriage in Some African and Asiatic Countries. Cairo:
Cairo Demographic Centre. Research Monograph Series #6.
1976. pp. 143-159.

Acsadi, George T. and Hammam, Nabila M.
"Marriage and Family Among Selected Female Health
Personnel in Cairo." (In) Huzayyin, S.A. and Acsadi,
G.T. (eds.). Family and Marriage in Some African and
Asiatic Countries. Cairo: Cairo Demographic Centre. CDC
Research Monograph Series #6. 1976. pp. 115-141.

Al-Sadawi, Nawal
"Growing Up Female in Egypt." (In) Fernea, Elizabeth W.
(ed.). Women and the Family in the Midle East: New
Voices of Change. Austin, Texas: University of Texas
Press. 1985. pp. 111-120.

Atiya, Nayra (ed.)
Khul-Khaal: Five Egyptian Women Tell Their Stories.
Syracuse, New York: Syracuse University Press.
Contemporary Issues in the Middle East Series. 1982.
216p.

Caldwell, Pat
"Egypt and the Arab World." (In) Caldwell, John C.
(ed.). The Persistence of High Fertility: Population
Prospects in the Third World. Canberra, Australia:
Australian National University. Department of
Demography. Volume Two. 1977. pp. 593-616.

Duza, M. Badrud and Ibrahim, Issa A.
"Nuptiality and Household Structure in Nubian Villages,
Egypt." (In) Huzayyin, S.A. and Acsadi, G.T. (eds.).
Family and Marriage in Some African and Asiatic
Countries. Cairo: Cairo Demographic Centre. CDC
Research Monograph Series #6. 1976. pp. 97-113.

Early, Evelyn A.
"Catharsis and Creation: The Everyday Narratives of
Baladi Women of Cairo." Anthropological Quarterly.
Volume 58 #4 October, 1985. pp. 172-181.

Early, Evelyn A.
   "Fatima: A Life History of an Egyptian Woman From Bulaq."
   (In) Fernea, Elizabeth W. (ed.). Women and the Family in
   the Middle East: New Voices of Change. Austin, Texas:
   University of Texas Press. 1985. pp. 76-83.
Egypt. Population and Family Planning Board
   "Marriage, Fertility and Family Planning: Summary of the
   Major Findings of the Egyptian Rural Fertility Survey,
   1979." Population Studies. Volume 9 #60 January-March,
   1982. pp. 37-49.
El-Kharboutly, Maitre A.
   "Law and the Status of Women in the Arab Republic of
   Egypt." (In) Columbia Human Rights Law Review (eds.).
   Law and the Status of Women: An International Symposium.
   New York: United Nations. Centre for Social Development
   and Humanitarian Affairs. 1977. pp. 35-50.
Farghali, Fathi
   Household Characteristics and Rural Out-Migration in
   Upper Egypt. Cairo: Cairo Demographic Center (CDC). CDC
   Research Monograph Series #12. 1984. pp. 287-303.
Hanbel, Ibrahim
   "The Effects of Working Mothers." Paper Presented at the
   Maternity Seminar. Cairo: Egyptian Ministry of Social
   Affairs, Public Administration of Family Childhood.
   March, 1982.
Ibrahim, Barbara L.
   "Cairo's Factory Women." (In) Fernea, Elizabeth W.
   (ed.). Women and the Family in the Middle East: New
   Voices of Change. Austin, Texas: University of Texas
   Press. 1985. pp. 293-302.
Ibrahim, Barbara L.
   "Family Strategies--A Perspective on Women's Entry to the
   Labor Force in Egypt." International Journal of
   Sociology. Volume 11 #2 July-December, 1981. pp.
   235-249.
Ibrahim, Barbara L.
   Women and Factory Work in Egypt: The Intersection of
   Labor Demand and Household Strategies. Cairo: American
   University. 1982.
Junsay, Alma T.
   "Patterns and Determinants of Female Labor Force
   Participation in Developing Nations." Ph.D Dissertation:
   Brigham Young University. Provo, Utah. 1985. 205p.
Khafagy, Fatma
   "Women and Labor Migration: One Village in Egypt." MERIP
   Reports. Volume 14 #124 June, 1984. pp. 17-21.
Levy, Victor
   "Cropping Pattern, Mechanization, Child Labor and
   Fertility Behavior in a Farming Economy: Rural Egypt."
   Economic Development and Cultural Change. Volume 33 #4
   July, 1985. pp. 777-791.

Loza-Soliman, Sarah F.
    "Roles of Women and Their Impact on Fertility: An
    Egyptian Case Study." (In) International Union for the
    Scientific Study of Population (IUSSP). International
    Population Conference: Solicited Papers. Liege, Belgium:
    IUSSP. Volume Three. 1981. pp. 571-584.
Lynch, Patricia D. and Fahmy, Hoda Y.
    Craftswomen in Kerdassa, Egypt: Household Production and
    Reproduction. Geneva: International Labour Organization.
    World Employment Programme. Population and Labour
    Policies Programme. Working Paper #126. WEP 2-21.
    1983. 75p.
Morcos, Widad
    "The New Family Law in Egypt." Cemam Reports
    (1978-1979). 1981.
Nadim, Nawal
    "Family Relationships in a Harah in Cairo." (In) El-Din
    Ibrahim, Saad and Hopkins, Nicholas (eds.). Arab Society
    in Transition. Cairo: American University in Cairo.
    1977.
Nawar, Leila M.
    "Household Structure and Age at Marriage in Abbasia,
    Cairo." (In) Huzayyin, S.A. and Acsadi, G.T. (eds.).
    Family and Marriage in Some African and Asiatic
    Countries. Cairo: Cairo Demographic Centre. Research
    Monograph Series #6. 1976. pp. 67-96.
Nour, S.F.
    "Attitudes of Selected Wives Toward Some Homemaking
    Tasks." Paper Presented at the Workshop on the Role of
    Women and Home Economics in Rural Development in Africa.
    Rome: United Nations Food and Agricultural Organization.
    Alexandria, Egypt. October 17, 1983. 11p.
Omran, Abdel R. and Standley, C.C. (eds.)
    "Further Studies on Family Formation Patterns and Health:
    An International Collaborative Study in Columbia, Egypt,
    Pakistan and the Syrian Arab Republic." Geneva: World
    Health Organization. 1981. 464p.
Rugh, Andrea B.
    Family in Contemporary Egypt. Syracuse, New York:
    Syracuse University Press. Contemporary Issues in the
    Middle East. 1984. 305p.
Stokes, C. Shannon and Schutjer, Wayne A. and Poindexter,
John R.
    "A Note on Desired Family Size and Contraceptive Use in
    Rural Egypt." Journal of Biosocial Science. Volume 15
    #1 January, 1983. pp. 59-65.
Sukkary-Stolba, S.
    "Changing Roles of Women in Egypt's Newly Reclaimed
    Lands." Anthropological Quarterly. Volume 58 #4
    October, 1985. pp. 182-189.
Tadros, Helmi R.
    Social Security and the Family in Egypt. New York:

American University in Cairo. Cairo Papers in Social
Science. Volume 7 #1. March, 1984. 87p.
Weimer, Joan M.
"Belly Dancer and the Virgin: Mythic Women in Modern
Egypt." Southwest Review. Volume 61 #1 Winter, 1976.
pp. 1-14.
Wikan, Unni
Life Among the Poor in Cairo. New York: Tavistock
Publications in Association With Methuen, Inc.
Translated by Ann Henning. 1980. 173p.

FAMILY PLANNING AND CONTRACEPTION

Abdel-Rahman, Mohamed E.
"Effectiveness of Socio-Economic Factors in Determining
Levels and Patterns of Fertility: A Demography Study of
Egypt(1950-1970)." Population Studies. Volume 9 #63
October-December, 1982. pp. 49-58+.
Abou-Gamrah, Hamed
"Effects of Nuptiality and Family Planning on Fertility."
Egyptian Population and Family Planning Review. Volume
14 #1 June, 1980. pp. 12-21.
Abou-Gamrah, Hamed
"Fertility Levels and Differentials by Mother's Education
in Some Countries of the ECWA Region." (In) Cairo
Demographic Centre (CDC). Determinants of Fertility in
Some African and Asian Countries. Cairo: CDC. 1982.
pp. 191-211.
Abou-Gamrah, Hamed
Review and Evaluation of Studies on the Determinants of
Fertility in Egypt. Cairo: Supreme Council for
Population and Family Planning. Population and Family
Planning Board. Research Office. Research Monograph #2.
July, 1981. 74p.
Aly, Ferial A. and El-Guenedi, Moushera M. and El-Guenedi,
Mervat M. and Nassar, Madga E. and Rizk, Mohammed A.
"Developing, Implementing and Evaluating a Socio-Economic
Scale to Study Clients Attending Family Planning Clinic
at the Shatby Maternity Hospital." Population Studies.
Volume 10 #6 July-September, 1983. pp. 3-17+.
Aly, Hekmat E. and Dakroury, Ahmed H. and Said, Amin K. and
Hussein, Mohamed A.
"Use of Nutrition Surveys for Family Planning Evaluation:
The Case of the Arab Republic of Egypt Nutrition Status."
Journal of the Egyptian Public Health Association.
Volume 54 #5-6 1979. pp. 290-312.
Anonymous
"Marriage, Fertility and Family Planning: Summary of the
Major Findings of the Egyptian Rural Fertility Survey,
1979." Population Studies (Cairo). Volume 9
January-March, 1982. pp. 37-49.

Boraie, M. Samir and Sarma, R.S.
"Fertility Levels in Egypt in 1960 and 1976: Some Factors
Influencing the Change." (In) Cairo Demographic Centre
(CDC). Determinants of Fertility in Some African and
Asian Countries. Cairo: CDC. CDC Research Monograph
Series #10. 1982. pp. 169-187.

Burkhardt, Robert and Field, John O.
"Family Planning in Rural Egypt: A View From the Health
System." L'Egypte Contemporaine. Volume 71 #379
January, 1980. pp. 41-69.

Chaudhry, Sayeeda A.
"Female Labor Force Participation and its Relationship to
Fertility Rate: Some Policy Implications for Developing
Countries." Ph.D Dissertation: George Washington
University. Washington, D.C. 1984. 410p.

Coale, Ansley J. and El-Atoum, Shafik
"Duration-Specific Marital Fertility in Egypt."
Population Bulletin of ECWA. #22-23 June-December,
1982. pp. 5-30.

Diepenhorst, M.J.
Population Problems and Family Planning in Five
Countries: A Transcultural Reconnaissance. Amsterdam,
Netherlands: Koninklijk Instituut Voor de Tropen. 1982.
228p.

Duza, A.
"Women's Involvement in Socioeconomic Projects Related to
Family Planning." Population Studies. Volume 8 #58
July-September, 1981. pp. 3-30.

Egypt. Population and Family Planning Board
"Some Statistics Concerning Family Planning Services in
Egypt During 1977." Egyptian Population and Family
Planning Review. Volume 11 #1/2 June-December, 1977.
pp. 96-102.

El Baymoumi, Soheir
"Health and Illness as Indices of Sex Status in an
Egyptian Village." Paper Presented at the 75th Annual
Meeting of the American Anthropological Association.
Washington, D.C. November 17-21, 1976.

El Kalla, Hassan H.
"Evaluation of Family Planning Program in Egypt,
1966-1979." M.S. Thesis: University of Texas. Health
Science Center. School of Public Health. Houston,
Texas. 1980. 115p.

El-Deeb, Bothaina M.
"Fertility and Mortality in a Rural Egyptian Community: A
Case Study in Beshla Village, Daqahliya Governorate,
Lower Egypt." Population Studies. Volume 7 #53
April-June, 1980. pp. 87-100.

El-Deeb, Bothaina M.
The Dynamics of Birth Spacing and Marital Fertility in
Egypt. Cairo: Cairo Demographic Centre. CDC Research
Monograph Series #12. 1984. pp. 83-104.

El-Karamani, Yussuf I.
    "Islam and Family Planning: A Brief Study." Population
    Studies. Volume 10 #64 January-March, 1983. pp. 31-44.
El-Rafie, M. and Mourad, I.M.
    "Some Intermediate of Fertility in Egypt." Egyptian
    Population and Family Planning Review. Volume 14 #1
    June, 1980. pp. 1-11.
Farid, Samir
    "Fertility Patterns in the Arab Region." International
    Family Planning Perspectives. Volume 10 #4 December,
    1984. pp. 119-125.
Fortney, Judith A. and Saleh, Saneya and Gadalla, Saad M.
and Rogers, Susan M.
    "Causes of Death to Women of Reproductive Age in Egypt."
    Paper Presented at the 52nd Annual Meeting of the
    Population Association of America. Collected Papers.
    Volume Three. Pittsburgh, Pennsylvania. April 14-16,
    1983. pp. 531-552.
Gadalla, N. Nosseir and Gillespie, D.G.
    "Household Distribution of Contraceptives in Rural
    Egypt." Studies in Family Planning. Volume 11 #3
    March, 1980. pp. 105-113.
Gadalla, Saad M. and McCarthy, James and Campbell, Oona
    "How the Number of Living Sons Influences Contraceptive
    Use in Menoufia Governorate, Egypt." Studies in Family
    Planning. Volume 16 #3 May-June, 1985. pp. 164-169.
Gadalla, Saad M.
    Is There Hope? Fertility and Family Planning in a Rural
    Egyptian Community. Chapel Hill, North Carolina:
    University of North Carolina. Carolina Population
    Center. 1977. 259p.
Gadalla, Saad M.
    "The Influence of Reproduction Norms on Family Size and
    Fertility Behavior in Rural Egypt." (In) Ibrahim, Saad
    E. and Hopkins, Nicholas S. (eds.). Arab Society in
    Transition: A Reader. Cairo: American University in
    Cairo. 1977. pp. 323-342.
Hamzawi, Riad
    "Factors Affecting Egyptian Rural Women's Fertility: A
    Theoretical Explanation." Population Studies. Volume 12
    #72 January-March, 1985. pp. 29-43.
Hassan, Ezzeldin O. and Wahba, Mamdouh
    Fertility Management, 1981: Proceeedings of the 8th
    Annual Conference of the Egyptian Fertility Care Society
    (EFCA). Cairo: EFCA. Shebin el-Koam, Egypt. June
    10-12, 1982. 108p.
Hassan, Shafick S.
    "The Role of Economic Development in Controlling
    Fertility in Egypt." (In) Cairo Demographic Centre
    (CDC). Aspects of Population Change and Development in
    Some African and Asian Countries. Cairo: CDC. CDC
    Research Monograph Series #9. 1984. pp. 173-196.

Hassouna, Mary T.
"Assessment of Family Planning Service Delivery in Egypt." Studies in Family Planning. Volume 11 #5 May, 1980. pp. 159-166.

Hassouna, Mary T.
"Policy Formation and Implementation and the Diffusion of Contraceptive Technology in the Arab Republic of Egypt." Ph.D Dissertation: University of Denver. Denver, Colorado. 1979. 390p.

Hassouna, Mary T.
An Action Research on the Promotion of Conventional Methods of Contraceptives Among Egyptian Married Couples. Cairo: Population and Family Planning Board. Research Office. Research Monograph #3. 1981. 63p.

Hefnawi, F.G. and Younis, N.M. and Nadim, N el-Messiri
"Final Progress Report: Acceptability of a Long Acting Injectable as a Post-Partum Contraceptive in Egypt." Population Sciences. #4 1983. pp. 87-122.

Issa, Mahmoud S.
"Modernisation and the Fertility Transition, Egypt: 1975." Ph.D Dissertation: University of Pennsylvania. Philadelphia, Pennsylvania. 1981. 434p.

Issa, Mahmoud S.
"Modernization and the Fertility Transition, Egypt, 1975." Philadelphia, Pennsylvania: University of Pennsylvania. Population Studies Center. African Demography Program Working Paper #3. June, 1980. 49p.

Khalifa, Atef M. and Way, Ann A.
"An Evaluation of the Impact of the Population and Development Program (PDP), Based on Data From the 1980 Contraceptive Prevalence Survey." (In) Cairo Demographic Center (CDC). Determinants of Fertility in Some African and Asian Countries. Cairo: CDC. CDC Research Monograph Series #10. 1982. pp. 117-153.

Khalifa, Atef M. and Sayed, Hussein A.A. and El-Khorazaty, Mohamed Nabil E. and Way, Ann A.
Family Planning in Rural Egypt, 1980: A Report on the Results of the Egypt Contraceptive Prevalence Survey. Columbia, Maryland: Westinghouse Health Systems. Cairo: Population and Family Planning Board. December, 1982. 221p.

Khalifa, Atef M. and Way, Ann A.
Marriage, Fertility and Family Planning: A Study of the RFS, 1979. Cairo: Population and Family Planning Board. 1981.

Khalifa, Atef M. and Sayed, Hussein A.A. and El-Khorazaty, Mohamed Nabil E. and Way, Ann A.
"Prevalence, Continuation and Availability of Contraceptive Methods." Egyptian Population and Family Planning Review. Volume 16 #2 December, 1982. pp. 1-31.

Khalifa, Atef M.
"Rural-Urban Fertility Differences and Trends in Egypt, 1930-1970." (In) Allman, James (ed.). Women's Status

and Fertility in the Muslim World. New York: Praeger
Publishing. Praeger Special Studies. 1978. pp. 77-94.
Khalifa, Atef M.
    "The Influence of Wife's Education on Fertility in Rural
    Egypt." Journal of Biosocial Science. Volume 8 #1
    January, 1976. pp. 53-60.
Khalifa, Atef M. and Helmy, Hussein A. and El-Khorazaty,
Mohamed Nabil E. and Way, Ann A.
    "The Results of the Egyptian Contraceptive Prevalence
    Survey in Rural Egypt, 1980." Population Studies.
    Volume 9 #63 October-December, 1982. pp. 37-46+.
Krieger, Laurie E.
    "Body Notions, Gender Roles and Fertility Regulating
    Method Use in Imbaba, Cairo." Ph.D Dissertation:
    University of North Carolina at Chapel Hill. Chapel
    Hill, North Carolina. 1984. 285p.
Loza, Sarah F.
    "Determinants of Fertility and the Demand for Family
    Planning: A Review and Assessment of Studies and How They
    Explain the Egyptian Experience." Population Studies.
    Volume 9 #62 July-September, 1982. pp. 3-32.
Loza, Sarah F.
    "Determinants of Fertility and the Demand for Family
    Planning: A Review and Assessment of Studies and How They
    Explain the Egyptian Experience." (In) Cairo Demographic
    Centre (CDC). Studies in African and Asian Demography.
    Cairo: CDC. CDC Research Monograph Series #11. 1983.
    pp. 85-124.
Loza, Sarah F.
    "Differential Concern for Children's Education and Its
    Effect on Fertility." Population Studies (Cairo).
    Volume 6 #51 October-December, 1979. pp. 9-29.
Loza-Soliman, Sarah F. and Khorazaty, N.
    "Causes of Fertility Differences in Egypt: Intermediate
    Variable Analysis." Paper Presented at a Conference at
    the High Institute of Statistical Studies and Research.
    Cairo. 1979.
Nosseir, Nazek
    "Assessment of an Action Program, Menoufia Governorate,
    Egypt." (In) Cairo Demographic Centre (CDC). Studies in
    African and Asian Demography. Cairo: CDC. CDC Research
    Monograph Series #11. 1983. pp. 125-153.
Nosseir, Nazek
    Measurement of Intermediate Variables Affecting Fertility
    in Rural Egypt. Cairo: Institute of Statistical Studies
    and Research. 1979. 22p.
Olusanya, P.O.
    The Demographic, Health, Economic and Social Impact of
    Family Planning in Selected African Countries. Addis
    Ababa, Ethiopia: United Nations Economic Commission for
    Africa. ECA/PD/1985-9. March, 1985. 97p.

Omran, Abdel R. and Standley, C.C. (eds.)
    Further Studies on Family Formation Patterns and Health:
    An International Collaborative Study in Columbia, Egypt,
    Pakistan and the Syrian Arab Republic. Geneva: World
    Health Organization. 1981. 464p.
Poston, Dudley L. and El-Badry, Samia M.
    Moderization and Childlessness Among the Governorates of
    the Arab Republic of Egypt, 1976. Austin, Texas:
    University of Texas Press. Texas Population Research
    Center Papers. Series Six. #6.017. 1984. 23p.
Potts, M. and Stanowitz, B. and Fortney, J.A.
    Childbirth in Developing Countries. Hingham,
    Massachusetts: MTP Press. 1983. 162p.
Ragheb, Seham and Aly, Ferial A. and Nayel, Sayed and
Shoeib, Fatma
    "Women's Acceptability of the Condom and Diaphragm in
    Shatby Family Planning Clinic in Alexandria." Population
    Studies. Volume 9 #63 October-December, 1982. pp.
    17-29+.
Sayed, Hussein A.A. and El-Khorazaty, Mohamed Nabil E. and
Way, Anne A.
    Fertility and Family Planning in Egypt, 1984. Cairo:
    Egypt National Population Council. 1985. 313p.
Sayed, Hussein A.A.
    "Fertility and Family Planning in Rural Egypt (The Second
    Rural Fertility Survey, 1982)." (In) Cairo Demographic
    Centre (CDC). Studies in African and Asian Demography.
    Cairo, Egypt: CDC. CDC Research Monograph Series #11.
    1983. pp. 155-177.
Sayed, Hussein A.A. and Way, Peter O.
    Life-Table Analysis of Contraceptive Continuation in
    Rural Egypt. Cairo: Cairo Demographic Centre. CDC
    Working Paper #12. 1985. 20p.
Sayed, Hussein A.A.
    "Regional Pattern of Differentials in Contraceptive Use
    in Egypt." (In) Cairo Demographic Centre (CDC).
    Determinants of Fertility in Some African and Asian
    Countries. Cairo: CDC. CDC Research Monograph Series
    #10. 1982. pp. 67-88.
Sayed, Hussein A.A.
    "The Population Family Planning Program in Egypt:
    Structure and Performance." Population Studies. Volume
    11 #70 July-September, 1984. pp. 3-38.
Sayed, Hussein A.A.
    Contraceptive Continuation in Rural Egypt. Cairo: Cairo
    Demographic Center. CDC Research Monograph Series #12.
    1984. pp. 63-82.
Schutjer, Wayne A. and Stokes, C. Shannon and Poindexter,
John R.
    "Farm Size, Land Ownership and Fertility in Rural Egypt."
    Land Economics. Volume 59 #4 November, 1983. pp.
    393-403.

Schutjer, Wayne A. and Stokes, C. Shannon and Poindexter,
John R.
   Why Not Use Contraception? The Economics of Fertility
   Regulation Among Rural Egyptian Women. University Park,
   Pennsylvania: Pennsylvania State University. Population
   Issues Research Center. 1984.
Shaaban, M.M.
   "A Prospective Study of Norplant Implants and the
   TCU-38AG IUD in Assiut, Egypt." Studies in Family
   Planning. Volume 14 June-July, 1983. pp. 163-169.
Shanawany, Haifaa A.
   "Operational Proposals to Reinforce the Role of the Raida
   Rifiaa in Family Development in Egypt." Population
   Studies Quarterly Review. Volume 58 July-September,
   1981. pp. 31-34.
Stokes, C. Shannon and Schutjer, Wayne A. and Poindexter,
John R.
   "A Note on Desired Family Size and Contraceptive Use in
   Rural Egypt." Journal of Biosocial Science. Volume 15
   #1 January, 1983. pp. 59-65.
Stycos, J. Mayone and Bindary, Aziz and Avery, Roger C. and
Khalifa, Atef M. and Sayed, Hussein A.A. and Way, Ann A.
   "Contraception and Community in Egypt: A Preliminary
   Evaluation of the Population/Development Mix." Studies
   in Family Planning. Volume 13 #12 Part One December,
   1982. pp. 365-372.
Taha, Ibrahim K. and Abdelghany, Abdelghany M.
   "Recent Socio-Economic Fertility Differentials in Egypt."
   (In) Cairo Demographic Center (CDC). Determinants of
   Fertility in Some Asian and African Countries. Cairo:
   CDC. CDC Research Monograph Series #10. 1982. pp.
   89-116.
Tsui, Amy O. and Declerque, Julie and Abul-Ata, Mohammed F.
   Contraceptive Rumor, Misinformation and Oral
   Contraception Use in Egypt. Chapel Hill, North Carolina:
   University of North Carolina. Carolina Population
   Center. 1985.
Younis, M.N. and Abou El-Ela, N.M. and Sultan, M. and
El-Maaddawi, Y. and El-Masry, G.
   "Socio-Medical Factors Affecting the Utilization of
   Different Contraceptive Methods at Al-Azhar Rural Family
   Health Clinic." Population Sciences. #6 1985. pp.
   27-34.

FERTILITY AND INFERTILITY

Abd-Allah, Abdel-Kawi M.
   Recent Fertility Levels and Differentials in Egypt.
   Cairo: Cairo Demographic Centre. 1981. 235p.
Abdel-Rahman, Mohamed E.
   "Effectiveness of Socio-Economic Factors in Determining
   Levels and Patterns of Fertility: A Demography Study of

Egypt(1950-1970)." Population Studies. Volume 9 #63
October-December, 1982. pp. 49-58+.
Abou-Gamrah, Hamed
"Effects of Nuptiality and Family Planning on Fertility."
Egyptian Population and Family Planning Review. Volume
14 #1 June, 1980. pp. 12-21.
Abou-Gamrah, Hamed
"Fertility Levels and Differentials by Mother's Education
in Some Countries of the ECWA Region." (In) Cairo
Demographic Centre (CDC). Determinants of Fertility in
Some African and Asian Countries. Cairo: CDC. 1982.
pp. 191-211.
Abou-Gamrah, Hamed
"Fertility and Childhood Mortality by Mother's and
Father's Education in Cairo, 1976." Population Bulletin
of the Economic Commission for Western Asia. #19
December, 1980. pp. 81-92.
Abou-Gamrah, Hamed
Review and Evaluation of Studies on the Determinants of
Fertility in Egypt. Cairo: Supreme Council for
Population and Family Planning. Population and Family
Planning Board. Research Office. Research Monograph #2.
July, 1981. 74p.
Atif, Nadia
The Context of Women's Work: Employment, Fertility,
Development and the Seven Roles of Women in Mehalla Al
Kubr. Cairo: Center for Egyptian Civilzation Studies.
1981.
Boraie, M. Samir and Sarma, R.S.
"Fertility Levels in Egypt in 1960 and 1976: Some Factors
Influencing the Change." (In) Cairo Demographic Centre
(CDC). Determinants of Fertility in Some African and
Asian Countries. Cairo: CDC. CDC Research Monograph
Series #10. 1982. pp. 169-187.
Bucht, B. and El-Badry, M.A.
Reflections on Recent Levels and Trends of Fertility and
Mortality in Egypt. Cairo: Cairo Demographic Centre.
CDC Working Paper #9. 1984. 34p.
Caldwell, Pat
"Egypt and the Arab World." (In) Caldwell, John C.
(ed.). The Persistence of High Fertility: Population
Prospects in the Third World. Canberra, Australia:
Australian National University. Department of
Demography. Volume Two. 1977. pp. 593-616.
Chaudhry, Sayeeda A.
"Female Labor Force Participation and its Relationship to
Fertility Rate: Some Policy Implications for Developing
Countries." Ph.D Dissertation: George Washington
University. Washington, D.C. 1984. 410p.
Coale, Ansley J. and El-Atoum, Shafik
"Duration-Specific Marital Fertility in Egypt."
Population Bulletin of ECWA. #22-23 June-December,
1982. pp. 5-30.

Darwish, O.A. and El-Nagar, M. and Eid, E.E. and
El-Sherbini, A.F.
    "Interrelationships Between Anemia and Fertility Patterns
    in Rural Egyptian Women." Egyptian Population and Family
    Planning Review. Volume 13 #1-2 June-December, 1979.
    pp. 1-28.
Diepenhorst, M.J.
    Population Problems and Family Planning in Five
    Countries: A Transcultural Reconnaissance. Amsterdam,
    Netherlands: Koninklijk Instituut Voor de Tropen. 1982.
    228p.
Egypt. Centr. Agency for Public Mobilisation and Statistics
    1976 Population and Housing Census. Fertility and
    Internal Migration and Movement of Workers and Students.
    Cairo: Central Agency. December, 1980. 440p.
Egypt. Population and Family Planning Board
    "Marriage, Fertility and Family Planning: Summary of the
    Major Findings of the Egyptian Rural Fertility Survey,
    1979." Population Studies. Volume 9 #60 January-March,
    1982. pp. 37-49.
El-Deeb, Bothaina M.
    "Fertility and Mortality in a Rural Egyptian Community: A
    Case Study in Beshla Village, Daqahliya Governorate,
    Lower Egypt." Population Studies. Volume 7 #53
    April-June, 1980. pp. 87-100.
El-Deeb, Bothaina M.
    The Dynamics of Birth Spacing and Marital Fertility in
    Egypt. Cairo: Cairo Demographic Centre. CDC Research
    Monograph Series #12. 1984. pp. 83-104.
El-Guindy M.
    "The Impact of Divorce and Widowhood on Fertility in
    Egypt." Egyptian Population and Family Planning Review.
    Volume 13 #1/2 June-December, 1979. pp. 84-94.
El-Nomrosi, M.M.
    "Analytical Study of Fertility and Mortality Tendencies
    in Egypt During the Period 1950-1980." Population
    Studies. Volume 8 #59 October-December, 1981.
El-Rafie, M. and Mourad, I.M.
    "Some Intermediate of Fertility in Egypt." Egyptian
    Population and Family Planning Review. Volume 14 #1
    June, 1980. pp. 1-11.
Farid, Samir
    "Fertility Patterns in the Arab Region." International
    Family Planning Perspectives. Volume 10 #4 December,
    1984. pp. 119-125.
Field, John O. and Ropes, George
    "Infant Mortality, the Birth Rate and Development in
    Egypt." Egypte Contemporaine. Volume 71 #381 July,
    1980. pp. 213-265.
Gadalla, Saad M.
    Is There Hope? Fertility and Family Planning in a Rural
    Egyptian Community. Chapel Hill, North Carolina:

University of North Carolina. Carolina Population
Center. 1977. 259p.
Gadalla, Saad M.
"The Influence of Reproduction Norms on Family Size and
Fertility Behavior in Rural Egypt." (In) Ibrahim, Saad
E. and Hopkins, Nicholas S. (eds.). Arab Society in
Transition: A Reader. Cairo: American University in
Cairo. 1977. pp. 323-342.
Hamzawi, Riad
"Factors Affecting Egyptian Rural Women's Fertility: A
Theoretical Explanation." Population Studies. Volume 12
#72 January-March, 1985. pp. 29-43.
Hamzawi, Riad
"The Relationship Between Female Employment and
Fertility." Ph.D Dissertation: Case Western Reserve
University. Cleveland, Ohio. 1982. 136p.
Hassan, Ezzeldin O. and Wahba, Mamdouh
Fertility Management, 1981: Proceeedings of the 8th
Annual Conference of the Egyptian Fertility Care Society
(EFCA). Cairo: EFCA. Shebin el-Koam, Egypt. June
10-12, 1982. 108p.
Hassan, Shafick S.
The Role of Economic Development in Controlling Fertility
in Egypt. (In) Cairo Demographic Centre (CDC). Aspects
of Population Change and Development in Some African and
Asian Countries. Cairo: CDC. CDC Research Monograph
Series #9. 1984. pp. 173-196.
International Statistical Institute (ISI)
The Egyptian Fertility Survey, 1980: A Summary of
Findings. Voorburg, Netherlands: ISI. World Fertility
Survey Report #42. November, 1983. 33p.
Issa, Mahmoud S.
"Modernisation and the Fertility Transition, Egypt:
1975." Ph.D Dissertation: University of Pennsylvania.
Philadelphia, Pennsylvania. 1981. 434p.
Issa, Mahmoud S.
Modernization and the Fertility Transition, Egypt, 1975.
Philadelphia, Pennsylvania: University of Pennsylvania.
Population Studies Center. African Demography Program
Working Paper #3. June, 1980. 49p.
Kafafi, Laila
"Age at Marriage and Cumulative Fertility in Rural
Egypt." Ph.D Dissertation: Duke University. Durham,
North Carolina. 1983. 140p.
Karmakar, Ratna
"Time Series Causality Between Infant Mortality and
Fertility in Less Developed Countries." Ph.D
Dissertation: City University of New York. New York, New
York. 1982. 158p.
Khalifa, Atef M. and Way, Ann A.
"An Evaluation of the Impact of the Population and
Development Program (PDP), Based on Data From the 1980
Contraceptive Prevalence Survey." (In) Cairo Demographic

Center (CDC). Determinants of Fertility in Some African
and Asian Countries. Cairo: CDC. CDC Research Monograph
Series #10. 1982. pp. 117-153.
Khalifa, Atef M. and Way, Ann A.
Marriage, Fertility and Family Planning: A Study of the
RFS, 1979. Cairo: Population and Family Planning Board.
1981.
Khalifa, Atef M.
"Rural-Urban Fertility Differences and Trends in Egypt,
1930-1970." (In) Allman, James (ed.). Women's Status and
Fertility in the Muslim World. New York: Praeger
Publishing. Praeger Special Studies. 1978. pp. 77-94.
Khalifa, Atef M.
"The Influence of Wife's Education on Fertility in Rural
Egypt." Journal of Biosocial Science. Volume 8 #1
January, 1976. pp. 53-60.
Khalifa, Atef M. and Helmy, Hussein A. and El-Khorazaty,
Mohamed Nabil E. and Way, Ann A.
"The Results of the Egyptian Contraceptive Prevalence
Survey in Rural Egypt, 1980." Population Studies.
Volume 9 #63 October-December, 1982. pp. 37-46+.
Krieger, Laurie E.
"Body Notions, Gender Roles and Fertility Regulating
Method Use in Imbaba, Cairo." Ph.D Dissertation:
University of North Carolina at Chapel Hill. Chapel
Hill, North Carolina. 1984. 285p.
Levy, Victor
"Cropping Pattern, Mechanization, Child Labor and
Fertility Behavior in a Farming Economy: Rural Egypt."
Economic Development and Cultural Change. Volume 33 #4
July, 1985. pp. 777-791.
Loza, Sarah F.
"Determinants of Fertility and the Demand for Family
Planning: A Review and Assessment of Studies and How They
Explain the Egyptian Experience." Population Studies.
Volume 9 #62 July-September, 1982. pp. 3-32.
Loza, Sarah F.
"Determinants of Fertility and the Demand for Family
Planning: A Review and Assessment of Studies and How They
Explain the Egyptian Experience." (In) Cairo Demographic
Centre (CDC). Studies in African and Asian Demography.
Cairo, Egypt: CDC. CDC Research Monograph Series #11.
1983. pp. 85-124.
Loza, Sarah F.
"Differential Age at Marriage and Fertility in Egypt."
(In) Cairo Demographic Centre (CDC). Determinants of
Fertility in Some African and Asian Countries. Cairo,
Egypt: CDC. CDC Research Monograph Series #10. 1982.
pp. 51-66.
Loza, Sarah F.
"Differential Concern for Children's Education and Its
Effect on Fertility." Population Studies (Cairo).
Volume 6 #51 October-December, 1979. pp. 9-29.

Loza-Soliman, Sarah F. and Khorazaty, N.
    "Causes of Fertility Differences in Egypt: Intermediate
    Variable Analysis." Paper Presented at a Conference at
    the High Institute of Statistical Studies and Research.
    Cairo. 1979.
Loza-Soliman, Sarah F.
    Roles of Women and Their Impact on Fertility: An Egyptian
    Case Study. (In) International Union for the Scientific
    Study of Population (IUSSP). International Population
    Conference: Solicited Papers. Liege, Belgium: IUSSP.
    Volume Three. 1981. pp. 571-584.
National Research Council
    The Estimation of Recent Trends in Fertility and
    Mortality in Egypt. Washington, D.C.: National Research
    Council. Assembly of Behavioral and Social Sciences.
    Committee on Population and Demography. Panel on Egypt.
    Report #9. 1982. 144p.
Nosseir, Nazek
    Measurement of Intermediate Variables Affecting Fertility
    in Rural Egypt. Cairo: Institute of Statistical Studies
    and Research. 1979. 22p.
Rizk, Ibrahim A. and Stokes, C. Shannon and Nelson, Merwyn
R.
    "The Influence of Individual and Community-Level Child
    Mortality on Fertility in Egypt." Studies in Family
    Planning. Volume 17 #2 Summer, 1982. pp. 74-86.
Rizk, Ibrahim A.
    "The Influence of Infant and Child Mortality on the
    Reproductive Behavior of Women in Rural Egypt: Combining
    Individual and Community Level Data." Ph.D Dissertation:
    Pennsylvania State University. University Park,
    Pennsylvania. 1979. 158p.
Sayed, Hussein A.A. and Stycos, J. Mayone and Khalifa, Atef
M. and Avery, Roger C.
    "An Assessment of the Population and Development Program
    (PDP) Based on the Results of the Second Rural Fertility
    Survey (RFS II)." Population Studies. Volume 10 #65
    April-June, 1983. pp. 3-40.
Sayed, Hussein A.A. and El-Khorazaty, Mohamed Nabil E. and
Way, Anne A.
    Fertility and Family Planning in Egypt, 1984. Cairo:
    Egypt National Population Council. 1985. 313p.
Sayed, Hussein A.A.
    "Fertility and Family Planning in Rural Egypt (The Second
    Rural Fertility Survey, 1982)." (In) Cairo Demographic
    Centre (CDC). Studies in African and Asian Demography.
    Cairo: CDC. CDC Research Monograph Series #11. 1983.
    pp. 155-177.
Sayed, Hussein A.A. and El-Khorazaty, Mohamed Nabil E.
    "Levels and Differentials of Fertility in Egypt: The
    National Fertility Survey, 1974-1975." Population
    Studies (Cairo). Volume 7 #55 October-December, 1980.
    pp. 11-38.

Sayed, Hussein A.A.
    Contraceptive Continuation in Rural Egypt. Cairo: Cairo
    Demographic Center. CDC Research Monograph Series #12.
    1984. pp. 63-82.
Schutjer, Wayne A. and Stokes, C. Shannon and Poindexter,
John R.
    "Farm Size, Land Ownership and Fertility in Rural Egypt."
    Land Economics. Volume 59 #4 November, 1983. pp.
    393-403.
Schutjer, Wayne A. and Stokes, C. Shannon and Poindexter,
John R.
    Why Not Use Contraception? The Economics of Fertility
    Regulation Among Rural Egyptian Women. University Park,
    Pennsylvania: Pennsylvania State University. Population
    Issues Research Center. 1984.
Stokes, C. Shannon and Schutjer, Wayne A.
    "A Cautionary Note on Public Policies in Conflict: Land
    Reform and Human Fertility in Rural Egypt." Comparative
    Politics. Volume 16 #1 October, 1983. pp. 97-104.
Taha, Ibrahim K. and Abdelghany, Abdelghany M.
    "Recent Socio-Economic Fertility Differentials in Egypt."
    (In) Cairo Demographic Center (CDC). Determinants of
    Fertility in Some Asian and African Countries. Cairo:
    CDC. CDC Research Monograph Series #10. 1982. pp.
    89-116.

HEALTH, NUTRITION AND MEDICINE

Abdel-Kader, Soha and Abdel, Aziz M. and Bahgat, R. and
Hefnawi, F.G. and Fawzig, G. and Badraoui, M.H.
    "Effect of Some Progestational Steroids on Lactation in
    Egyptian Women. II--Chemical Composition of Milk During
    the First Year of Lactation." Journal of Biosocial
    Science. Volume 8 #1 January, 1976. pp. 49-52.
Abou-Gamrah, Hamed
    Review and Evaluation of Studies on the Determinants of
    Fertility in Egypt. Cairo: Supreme Council for
    Population and Family Planning. Population and Family
    Planning Board. Research Office. Research Monograph #2.
    July, 1981. 74p.
Afifi, Zeinab E.M.
    "Determinants of Growth of Infants in an Egyptian
    Village: Maternal Anthropometry, Birth Interval, Solid
    Food and Death of Siblings." Human Biology. Volume 57
    #4 1985. pp. 649-658.
Aly, Ferial A. and El-Guenedi, Moushera M. and El-Guenedi,
Mervat M. and Nassar, Madga E. and Rizk, Mohammed A.
    "Developing, Implementing and Evaluating a Socio-Economic
    Scale to Study Clients Attending Family Planning Clinic
    at the Shatby Maternity Hospital." Population Studies.
    Volume 10 #6 July-September, 1983. pp. 3-17+.

Aly, Hekmat E. and Dakroury, Ahmed H. and Said, Amin K. and
Hussein, Mohamed A.
    "Use of Nutrition Surveys for Family Planning Evaluation:
    The Case of the Arab Republic of Egypt Nutrition Status."
    Journal of the Egyptian Public Health Association.
    Volume 54 #5-6 1979. pp. 290-312.
Aromasodu, M.C.
    "Traditional Practices Affecting the Health of Women in
    Pregnancy and Childbirth." Paper Presented at the
    Seminar on Traditional Practices Affecting the Health of
    Women and Children: Female Circumcision, Childhood
    Marriage, Nutritional Taboos, etc. Alexandria, Egypt:
    World Health Organization. Eastern Mediterranean
    Regional Office. Khartoum, Sudan. February 10-15, 1979.
Assaad, Marie B.
    "A Communication Gap Regarding Female Circumcision."
    (In) Blair, Patricia W. (ed.). Health Needs of the
    World's Poor Women. Washington, D.C.: Equity Policy
    Center. 1981. pp. 9-11.
Assaad, Marie B.
    "Female Circumcision in Egypt." Paper Presented at the
    Seminar on Traditional Practices Affecting the Health of
    Women and Children: Female Circumcision, Childhood
    Marriage, Nutritional Taboos, Etc. Alexandria, Egypt:
    World Health Organization. Eastern Mediterranean
    Regional Office. Khartoum, Sudan. February 10-15, 1979.
Assaad, Marie B.
    "Female Circumcision in Egypt: Current Research and
    Social Implications." Paper Presented at the Seminar on
    Traditional Practices Affecting the Health of Women and
    Children. World Conference of the United Nations Decade
    for Women. Copenhagen, Denmark. July 14-30, 1980.
Assaad, Marie B.
    "Female Circumcision in Egypt: Social Implications,
    Current Research and Prospects for Change." Studies in
    Family Planning. Volume 11 #1 January, 1980. pp. 3-16.
Boraie, M. Samir and Sarma, R.S.
    "Fertility Levels in Egypt in 1960 and 1976: Some Factors
    Influencing the Change." (In) Cairo Demographic Centre
    (CDC). Determinants of Fertility in Some African and
    Asian Countries. Cairo: CDC. CDC Research Monograph
    Series #10. 1982. pp. 169-187.
Burkhardt, Robert and Field, John O.
    "Family Planning in Rural Egypt: A View From the Health
    System." L'Egypte Contemporaine. Volume 71 #379
    January, 1980. pp. 41-69.
Darwish, O.A. and El-Nagar, M. and Eid, E.E. and
El-Sherbini, A.F.
    "Interrelationships Between Anemia and Fertility Patterns
    in Rural Egyptian Women." Egyptian Population and Family
    Planning Review. Volume 13 #1-2 June-December, 1979.
    pp. 1-28.

Darwish, O.A.
   "Weaning Practices in Urban and Rural Egypt." Food and
   Nutrition Bulletin. Volume 4 #1 January, 1982.
Duza, A.
   "Women's Involvement in Socioeconomic Projects Related to
   Family Planning." Population Studies. Volume 8 #58
   July-September, 1981. pp. 3-30.
Early, Evelyn A.
   "Logic of Well Being: Therapeutic Narratives in Cairo,
   Egypt." Social Science and Medicine. Volume 16 #16
   1982. pp. 1491-1497.
Egypt. Centr. Agency for Public Mobilisation and Statistics
   1976 Population and Housing Census. Fertility and
   Internal Migration and Movement of Workers and Students.
   Cairo: Central Agency. December, 1980. 440p.
El Baymoumi, Soheir
   "Health and Illness as Indices of Sex Status in an
   Egyptian Village." Paper Presented at the 75th Annual
   Meeting of the American Anthropological Association.
   Washington, D.C. November 17-21, 1976.
El Hakim, Ahmed S.
   "Female Circumcision in Egypt." Paper Presented at the
   Seminar on Traditional Practices Affecting the Health of
   Women and Children. World Conference of the United
   Nations Decade for Women. New York: United Nations.
   Copenhagen, Denmark. July 14-30, 1980.
El Hakim, Ahmed S.
   "Mental Aspects of Circumcision." Paper Presented at the
   Seminar on Traditional Practices Affecting the Health of
   Women and Children. World Conference of the United
   Nations Decade for Women. New York: United Nations.
   Copenhagen, Denmark. July 14-30, 1980.
El Hakim, Ahmed S.
   "Mental Aspects of Female Circumcision in Egypt." Paper
   Presented at the Seminar on Traditional Practices
   Affecting the Health of Women and Children: Female
   Circumcision, Childhood Marriage, Nutritional Taboos,
   etc. Alexandria, Egypt: World Health Organization.
   Eastern Mediterranean Regional Office. Khartoum, Sudan.
   February 10-15, 1979.
El Kalla, Hassan H.
   "Evaluation of Family Planning Program in Egypt,
   1966-1979." M.S. Thesis: University of Texas. Health
   Science Center. School of Public Health. Houston,
   Texas. 1980. 115p.
El-Rafie, M. and Mourad, I.M.
   "Some Intermediate of Fertility in Egypt." Egyptian
   Population and Family Planning Review. Volume 14 #1
   June, 1980. pp. 1-11.
Fortney, Judith A. and Saleh, Saneya and Gadalla, Saad M.
and Rogers, Susan M.
   "Causes of Death to Women of Reproductive Age in Egypt."
   Paper Presented at the 52nd Annual Meeting of the

Population Association of America. Collected Papers.
Volume Three. Pittsburgh, Pennsylvania. April 14-16,
1983. pp. 531-552.

Gadalla, Saad M.
"The Influence of Reproduction Norms on Family Size and
Fertility Behavior in Rural Egypt." (In) Ibrahim, Saad
E. and Hopkins, Nicholas S. (eds.). Arab Society in
Transition: A Reader. Cairo: American University in
Cairo. 1977. pp. 323-342.

Govaerts, K.
"Attachment Behavior of the Egyptian Mother."
International Journal of Nursing Studies. Volume 18 #1
1981. pp. 53-60.

Hamzawi, Riad
"The Relationship Between Female Employment and
Fertility." Ph.D Dissertation: Case Western Reserve
University. Cleveland, Ohio. 1982. 136p.

Hanbel, Ibrahim
"The Effects of Working Mothers." Paper Presented at the
Maternity Seminar. Cairo: Egyptian Ministry of Social
Affairs, Public Administration of Family Childhood.
March, 1982.

Hassouna, Mary T.
"Assessment of Family Planning Service Delivery in
Egypt." Studies in Family Planning. Volume 11 #5 May,
1980. pp. 159-166.

Hassouna, Mary T.
"Policy Formation and Implementation and the Diffusion of
Contraceptive Technology in the Arab Republic of Egypt."
Ph.D Dissertation: University of Denver. Denver,
Colorado. 1979. 390p.

Hassouna, Mary T.
An Action Research on the Promotion of Conventional
Methods of Contraceptives Among Egyptian Married Couples.
Cairo: Population and Family Planning Board. Research
Office. Research Monograph #3. 1981. 63p.

Hefnawi, F.G.
"Effect of Some Progestational Steroids on Lactation in
Egyptian Women. I--Milk Yield During the First Year of
Lactation." Journal of Biosocial Science. Volume 8 #1
January, 1976. pp. 45-48.

Hefnawi, F.G. and Younis, N.M. and Nadim, N el-Messiri
"Final Progress Report: Acceptability of a Long Acting
Injectable as a Post-Partum Contraceptive in Egypt."
Population Sciences. #4 1983. pp. 87-122.

Issa, Mahmoud S.
"Modernisation and the Fertility Transition, Egypt:
1975." Ph.D Dissertation: University of Pennsylvania.
Philadelphia, Pennsylvania. 1981. 434p.

Issa, Mahmoud S.
Modernization and the Fertility Transition, Egypt, 1975.
Philadelphia, Pennsylvania: University of Pennsylvania.

Population Studies Center. African Demography Program Working Paper #3. June, 1980. 49p.

Janowitz, Barbara and Lewis, Joann H. and Parnell, A. and Hefnawi, F.G.
"Breast-Feeding and Child Survival in Egypt." Journal of Biosocial Science. Volume 13 #3 July, 1981. pp. 287-297.

Kamal, Ibrahim
"Lactation Patterns in the Egyptian Woman." (In) Jelliffe, D.B. and Jelliffe, E.F. and Sai, F.T. and Senanayake, P. (eds.). Lactation, Fertility and the Working Woman. London: International Planned Parenthood Federation. 1979. pp. 87-96.

Karmakar, Ratna
"Time Series Causality Between Infant Mortality and Fertility in Less Developed Countries." Ph.D Dissertation: City University of New York. New York, New York. 1982. 158p.

Kennedy, John G.
"Circumcision and Excision Ceremonies." (In) Kennedy, John G. (ed.). Nubian Ceremonial Life. Berkeley, California: University of California Press. 1978. pp. 151-170.

Kennedy, John G.
"Nubian Zar Ceremonies as Psycho-Therapy." (In) Kennedy, John G. (ed.). Nubian Ceremonial Life. Berkeley, California: University of California Press. 1978. pp. 203-223.

Loza, Sarah F.
"Determinants of Fertility and the Demand for Family Planning: A Review and Assessment of Studies and How They Explain the Egyptian Experience." Population Studies. Volume 9 #62 July-September, 1982. pp. 3-32.

Loza, Sarah F.
"Determinants of Fertility and the Demand for Family Planning: A Review and Assessment of Studies and How They Explain the Egyptian Experience." (In) Cairo Demographic Centre (CDC). Studies in African and Asian Demography. Cairo: CDC. CDC Research Monograph Series #11. 1983. pp. 85-124.

Loza-Soliman, Sarah F. and Khorazaty, N.
"Causes of Fertility Differences in Egypt: Intermediate Variable Analysis." Paper Presented at a Conference at the High Institute of Statistical Studies and Research. Cairo. 1979.

Mikhail, A.N.
"Traditional Feeding Practices in Pregnancy and Lactation in an Egyptian Community." Paper Presented at the Seminar on Traditional Practices Affecting the Health of Women and Children. World Conference of the United Nations Decade for Women. New York: United Nations. Copenhagen, Denmark. July 14-30, 1980.

Mikhail, A.N.
"Traditional Feeding Practices in Pregnancy." Paper
Presented at the Seminar on Traditional Practices
Affecting the Health of Women and Children: Female
Circumcision, Childhood Marriage, Nutritional Taboos,
etc. Alexandria Egypt: World Health Organization.
Eastern Mediterranean Regional Office. Khartoum, Sudan.
February 10-15, 1979.

Morsy, Soheir A.
"Gender, Power, and Illness in an Egyptian Village."
Ph.D Dissertation: Michigan State University. East
Lansing, Michigan. 1978. 450p.

Morsy, Soheir A.
"Sex Differences and Folk Illness in an Egyptian
Village." (In) Beck, Lois and Keddie, Nikki R. (eds.).
Women in the Muslim World. Cambridge, Massachsetts:
Harvard University Press. 1978. pp. 599-616.

Morsy, Soheir A.
"Sex Roles, Power and Illness in an Egyptian Village."
American Ethnologist. Volume 5 #1 1978. pp. 137-150.

National Research Council
The Estimation of Recent Trends in Fertility and
Mortality in Egypt. Washington, D.C.: National Research
Council. Assembly of Behavioral and Social Sciences.
Committee on Population and Demography. Panel on Egypt.
Report #9. 1982. 144p.

Njoki, Margaret
"Female Circumcision in Egypt." Paper Presented at the
Seminar on Traditional Practices Affecting the Health of
Women and Children: Female Circumcision, Childhood
Marriage, Nutritional Taboos, etc. Alexandria, Egypt:
World Health Organization. Eastern Mediterranean
Regional Office. Khartoum, Sudan. February 10-15, 1979.

Nosseir, Nazek
"Assessment of an Action Program, Menoufia Governorate,
Egypt." (In) Cairo Demographic Centre (CDC). Studies in
African and Asian Demography. Cairo: CDC. CDC Research
Monograph Series #11. 1983. pp. 125-153.

Nosseir, Nazek
Measurement of Intermediate Variables Affecting Fertility
in Rural Egypt. Cairo: Institute of Statistical Studies
and Research. 1979. 22p.

Olusanya, P.O.
The Demographic, Health, Economic and Social Impact of
Family Planning in Selected African Countries. Addis
Ababa, Ethiopia: United Nations Economic Commission for
Africa. ECA/PD/1985-9. March, 1985. 97p.

Omran, Abdel R. and Standley, C.C. (eds.)
Further Studies on Family Formation Patterns and Health:
An International Collaborative Study in Columbia, Egypt,
Pakistan and the Syrian Arab Republic. Geneva: World
Health Organization. 1981. 464p.

Poston, Dudley L. and El-Badry, Samia M.
    Moderization and Childlessness Among the Governorates of
    the Arab Republic of Egypt, 1976. Austin, Texas:
    University of Texas Press. Texas Population Research
    Center Papers. Series Six. #6.017. 1984. 23p.
Potts, M. and Stanowitz, B. and Fortney, J.A.
    Childbirth in Developing Countries. Hingham,
    Massachusetts: MTP Press. 1983. 162p.
Rizk, Ibrahim A.
    "The Influence of Infant and Child Mortality on the
    Reproductive Behavior of Women in Rural Egypt: Combining
    Individual and Community Level Data." Ph.D Dissertation:
    Pennsylvania State University. University Park,
    Pennsylvania. 1979. 158p.
Salem, Afaf A.
    "Female Circumcision in Egypt." Paper Presented at the
    Seminar on Traditional Practices Affecting the Health of
    Women and Children: Female Circumcision, Childhood
    Marriage, Nutritional Taboos, etc. Alexandria, Egypt:
    World Health Organization. Eastern Mediterranean
    Regional Office. February 10-15, 1979.
Salem, Afaf A.
    "Female Circumcision in Egypt." Paper Presented at the
    Seminar on Tradional Practices Affecting the Health of
    Women and Children. World Conference of the United
    Nations Decade for Women. New York: United Nations.
    Copenhagen, Denmark. July 14-30, 1980.
Salem, Afaf A.
    "The Practice of Circumcision in Egypt." Paper Presented
    at the Seminar on Traditional Practices Affecting the
    Health of Women and Children. World Conference of the
    United Nations Decade for Women. New York: United
    Nations. Copenhagen, Denmark. July 14-30, 1980.
Sayed, Hussein A.A. and Way, Peter O.
    Life-Table Analysis of Contraceptive Continuation in
    Rural Egypt. Cairo: Cairo Demographic Centre. CDC
    Working Paper #12. 1985. 20p.
Schutjer, Wayne A. and Stokes, C. Shannon and Poindexter,
John R.
    Why Not Use Contraception? The Economics of Fertility
    Regulation Among Rural Egyptian Women. University Park,
    Pennsylvania: Pennsylvania State University. Population
    Issues Research Center. 1984.
Serour, G.I. and Younis, N.M. and Hefnawi, F.G. and El-Bahy,
M. and Dagistany, H.F. and Nawar, M.
    "Perinatal Mortality in an Egyptian Maternity Hospital."
    International Journal of Gynaecology and Obstetrics.
    Volume 19 #6 December, 1981. pp. 447-451.
Shaaban, M.M.
    "A Prospective Study of Norplant Implants and the
    TCU-38AG IUD in Assiut, Egypt." Studies in Family
    Planning. Volume 14 June-July, 1983. pp. 163-169.

Shanawany, Haifaa A.
"Operational Proposals to Reinforce the Role of the Raida
Rifiaa in Family Development in Egypt." Population
Studies Quarterly Review. Volume 58 July-September,
1981. pp. 31-34.

Toledano, E.R.
"Slave Dealers, Women, Pregnancy and Abortion: The Study
of a Circassian Slave Girl in Mid-19th Century Cairo."
Slavery and Abolition. Volume 2 1981. pp. 53-68.

Toppozada, Hussein K. and Rizk, Mohammed A. and Abul-Einin,
Mostafa A. and Medhat, Ibrahim
"Epidemiology of Abortion in Alexandria." Alexandria
Medical Journal. Volume 26 #1/2 1980.

Tsui, Amy O. and Declerque, Julie and Abul-Ata, Mohammed F.
Contraceptive Rumor, Misinformation and Oral
Contraception Use in Egypt. Chapel Hill, North Carolina:
University of North Carolina. Carolina Population
Center. 1985.

Weidner-Read, Barbara L.
"Water, Women, Health and Housing: A Case Study of Rural
Reconstruction in Egypt." Ph.D Dissertation: University
of Utah. Salt Lake City, Utah. 1983. 206p.

Younis, M.N. and Abou El-Ela, N.M. and Sultan, M. and
El-Maaddawi, Y. and El-Masry, G.
"Socio-Medical Factors Affecting the Utilization of
Different Contraceptive Methods at Al-Azhar Rural Family
Health Clinic." Population Sciences. #6 1985. pp.
27-34.

HISTORY

Ahmed, Leila
"Women's Liberation Movements in 19th and 20th Century
Middle East." Paper Presented at the Meeting of Experts
on the Theoretical Frameworks and Methodological
Approaches to Studies on the Role of Women in History as
Actors in Economic, Social, Political and Ideological
Processes. Paris: United Nations Educational, Scientific
and Cultural Organization. 1984. 24p.

Cannon, B.D.
"Nineteenth Century Arabic Writings on Women and Society:
The Interim Role of the Masonic Press in Cairo
(Al-Lataif, 1885-1895)." International Journal of Middle
East Studies. Volume 17 November, 1985. pp. 463-484.

Cole, Juan R.
"Feminism, Class, and Islam in Turn-of-the-Century
Egypt." International Journal of Middle East Studies.
Volume 13 #4 November, 1981. pp. 387-407.

Eliraz, Giora
"Egyptian Intellectuals and Women's Emancipation,
1919-1939." Asian and African Studies. Volume 16 #1
March, 1982. pp. 95-120.

Ghorayeb, Rose
    "Archives: May Ziadeh (1886-1941)." Signs. Volume 5 #2
    Winter, 1979. pp. 375-382.
Hakem, Ahmed M. and Hrbek, Ivan and Vercoutter, Jean
    "The Matriarchs of Meroe: A Powerful Line of Queens Who
    Ruled the Kushitic Empire." UNESCO Courier. Volume 32
    #8/9 August-September, 1979. pp. 58-59.
Issa, M.
    The Egyptian Women's Participation in the Labour Force:
    Secular Trends, Age Patterns and Determinants,
    1907-1976. Cairo: Central Agency for Public Mobilization
    and Statistics. 1979.
Lesko, Barbara S.
    The Remarkable Women of Ancient Egypt. Berkeley,
    Califronia: B.C. Scribe Publications. 1978. 34p.
Macurdy, Grace H.
    Hellenistic Queens: A Study of Woman-Power in Macedonia,
    Seleucid, Syria, and Ptolemaic Egypt. Baltimore,
    Maryland: Johns Hopkins University Press. 1976. 250p.
Patai, R.
    "Maria the Jewess--Founding Mother of Alchemy." Ambix.
    Volume 29 #3 November, 1982. pp. 177-192.
Pomeroy, Sarah B.
    Women in Hellenistic Egypt: From Alexander to Cleopatra.
    New York: Schocken Books. 1984. 224p.
Robins, Gay
    "The God's Wife of Amun in the 18th Dynasty in Egypt."
    (In) Cameron, Averil and Kuhrt, Amelie (eds.). Images of
    Women in Antiquity. London: Croom Helm. 1983. pp.
    65-78.
Stillman, Yedida K.
    "The Importance of the Cairo Geniza Manuscripts for the
    History of Medieval Female Attire." International
    Journal of Middle East Studies. Volume 7 #4 October,
    1976. pp. 579-590.
Taplin, Ruth
    "Women and Work in Egypt: An Historical Perspective."
    Paper Presented at the Annual Meeting of the Pacific
    Sociological Association. 1985. 20p.
Toledano, E.R.
    "Slave Dealers, Women, Pregnancy and Abortion: The Study
    of a Circassian Slave Girl in Mid-19th Century Cairo."
    Slavery and Abolition. Volume 2 1981. pp. 53-68.
Tucker, Judith E.
    "Problems in the Historiography of Women in the Middle
    East: The Case of the 19th Century Egypt." International
    Journal of Middle East Studies. Volume 15 #3 August,
    1983. pp. 321-336.
Tucker, Judith E.
    Women in 19th Century Egypt. New York: Columbia
    University Press. 1985. 251p.
Van Sertima, Ivan
    Black Women in Antiquity. New Brunswick, New Jersey:
    Transaction Books. 1985. 160p.

LAW AND LEGAL ISSUES

Anonymous
    "Egyptian Woman Wins Battle for Equality With Man."
    M.E.N. Economic Weekly. Volume 21 #32 August 6, 1982.
    pp. 10-12.
El Saadawi, Nawal
    "Egypt: When a Female Rebels..." (In) Morgan, Robin
    (ed.). Sisterhood is Global. Garden City, New York:
    Anchor Books. 1984. pp. 194-206.
El-Kharboutly, Maitre A.
    "Law and the Status of Women in the Arab Republic of
    Egypt." (In) Columbia Human Rights Law Review (eds.).
    Law and the Status of Women: An International Symposium.
    New York: United Nations. Centre for Social Development
    and Humanitarian Affairs. 1977. pp. 35-50.
Hussein, Aziza
    "Recent Amendments to Egypt's Personal Status Law." (In)
    Fernea, Elizabeth W. (ed.). Women and the Family in the
    Middle East: New Voices of Change. Austin, Texas:
    University of Texas Press. 1985. pp. 229-232.
Morcos, Widad
    "The New Family Law in Egypt." Cemam Reports
    (1978-1979). 1981.

LITERATURE

Abu-Lughod, Lila
    "Honor, Modesty and Poetry in a Bedouin Society: Ideology
    and Experience Among Awlad Ali of Egypt." Ph.D.
    Dissertation: Harvard University. Cambridge,
    Massachusetts. 1984. 347p.
Cannon, B.D.
    "Nineteenth Century Arabic Writings on Women and Society:
    The Interim Role of the Masonic Press in Cairo
    (Al-Lataif, 1885-1895)." International Journal of Middle
    East Studies. Volume 17 November, 1985. pp. 463-484.
El Saadawi, Nawal
    Woman at Point Zero. London: Zed Books Ltd. 1983.
    106p.
Hall, Marjorie J.
    "The Position of Women in Egypt and the Sudan as
    Reflected in Feminist Writing Since 1900." Ph.D
    Dissertation: University of London. London. 1977.
    369p.
Lowi, Miriam
    "The Truth Sometimes Shocks." Index on Censorship.
    Volume 11 #3 June, 1982. pp. 18-20.

Suleiman, M.W.
  "Changing Attitudes Toward Women in Egypt: The Role of
  Fiction in Women's Magazines." Middle Eastern Studies.
  Volume 14 #3 October, 1978. pp. 352-371.

MARITAL RELATIONS AND NUPTIALITY

Abou-Gamrah, Hamed
  "Effects of Nuptiality and Family Planning on Fertility."
  Egyptian Population and Family Planning Review. Volume
  14 #1 June, 1980. pp. 12-21.
Abou-Gamrah, Hamed and Gheita, Naguib H.
  "Socio-Economic Status and Household Structure Among
  Selected Industrial Workers in Mehalla El-Kubra, Egypt."
  (In) Huzayyin, S.A. and Acsadi, G.T. (eds). Family and
  Marriage in Some African and Asiatic Countries. Cairo:
  Cairo Demographic Centre. Research Monograph Series #6.
  1976. pp. 143-159.
Abu-Lughod, Lila
  "A Community of Secrets: The Separate World of Bedouin
  Women." Signs. Volume 10 #4 Summer, 1985. pp.
  637-657.
Acsadi, George T. and Hammam, Nabila M.
  "Marriage and Family Among Selected Female Health
  Personnel in Cairo." (In) Huzayyin, S.A. and Acsadi,
  G.T. (eds.). Family and Marriage in Some African and
  Asiatic Countries. Cairo: Cairo Demographic Centre. CDC
  Research Monograph Series #6. 1976. pp. 115-141.
Al-Katsha, Samiha
  "Changes in Nubian Wedding Ceremonials." (In) Kennedy,
  John G. (ed.). Nubian Ceremonial Life. Berkeley,
  California: University of California Press. 1978. pp.
  171-202.
Aly, Ferial A. and El-Guenedi, Moushera M. and El-Guenedi,
Mervat M. and Nassar, Madga E. and Rizk, Mohammed A.
  "Developing, Implementing and Evaluating a Socio-Economic
  Scale to Study Clients Attending Family Planning Clinic
  at the Shatby Maternity Hospital." Population Studies.
  Volume 10 #6 July-September, 1983. pp. 3-17+.
Anonymous
  "Marriage, Fertility and Family Planning: Summary of the
  Major Findings of the Egyptian Rural Fertility Survey,
  1979." Population Studies (Cairo). Volume 9
  January-March, 1982. pp. 37-49.
Boraie, M. Samir and Sarma, R.S.
  "Fertility Levels in Egypt in 1960 and 1976: Some Factors
  Influencing the Change." (In) Cairo Demographic Centre
  (CDC). Determinants of Fertility in Some African and
  Asian Countries. Cairo: CDC. CDC Research Monograph
  Series #10. 1982. pp. 169-187.

Burkhardt, Robert and Field, John O.
  "Family Planning in Rural Egypt: A View From the Health
  System." L'Egypte Contemporaine. Volume 71 #379
  January, 1980. pp. 41-69.
Caldwell, Pat
  "Egypt and the Arab World." (In) Caldwell, John C.
  (ed.). The Persistence of High Fertility: Population
  Prospects in the Third World. Canberra, Australia:
  Australian National University. Department of
  Demography. Volume Two. 1977. pp. 593-616.
Chaudhry, Sayeeda A.
  "Female Labor Force Participation and its Relationship to
  Fertility Rate: Some Policy Implications for Developing
  Countries." Ph.D Dissertation: George Washington
  University. Washington, D.C. 1984. 410p.
Coale, Ansley J. and El-Atoum, Shafik
  "Duration-Specific Marital Fertility in Egypt."
  Population Bulletin of ECWA. #22-23 June-December,
  1982. pp. 5-30.
Duza, M. Badrud and Ibrahim, Issa A.
  "Nuptiality and Household Structure in Nubian Villages,
  Egypt." (In) Huzayyin, S.A. and Acsadi, G.T. (eds.).
  Family and Marriage in Some African and Asiatic
  Countries. Cairo: Cairo Demographic Centre. CDC
  Research Monograph Series #6. 1976. pp. 97-113.
El Baymoumi, Soheir
  "Health and Illness as Indices of Sex Status in an
  Egyptian Village." Paper Presented at the 75th Annual
  Meeting of the American Anthropological Association.
  Washington, D.C. November 17-21, 1976.
El-Deeb, Bothaina M.
  The Dynamics of Birth Spacing and Marital Fertility in
  Egypt. Cairo: Cairo Demographic Centre. CDC Research
  Monograph Series #12. 1984. pp. 83-104.
El-Kharboutly, Maitre A.
  "Law and the Status of Women in the Arab Republic of
  Egypt." (In) Columbia Human Rights Law Review (eds.).
  Law and the Status of Women: An International Symposium.
  New York: United Nations. Centre for Social Development
  and Humanitarian Affairs. 1977. pp. 35-50.
El-Rafie, M. and Mourad, I.M.
  "Some Intermediate of Fertility in Egypt." Egyptian
  Population and Family Planning Review. Volume 14 #1
  June, 1980. pp. 1-11.
Farid, Samir
  "Fertility Patterns in the Arab Region." International
  Family Planning Perspectives. Volume 10 #4 December,
  1984. pp. 119-125.
Gadalla, N. Nosseir and Gillespie, D.G.
  "Household Distribution of Contraceptives in Rural
  Egypt." Studies in Family Planning. Volume 11 #3
  March, 1980. pp. 105-113.

Gadalla, Saad M. and McCarthy, James and Campbell, Oona
    "How the Number of Living Sons Influences Contraceptive
    Use in Menoufia Governorate, Egypt." Studies in Family
    Planning. Volume 16 #3 May-June, 1985. pp. 164-169.
Gadalla, Saad M.
    Is There Hope? Fertility and Family Planning in a Rural
    Egyptian Community. Chapel Hill, North Carolina:
    University of North Carolina. Carolina Population
    Center. 1977. 259p.
Hamzawi, Riad
    "Factors Affecting Egyptian Rural Women's Fertility: A
    Theoretical Explanation." Population Studies. Volume 12
    #72 January-March, 1985. pp. 29-43.
Hassouna, Mary T.
    An Action Research on the Promotion of Conventional
    Methods of Contraceptives Among Egyptian Married Couples.
    Cairo: Population and Family Planning Board. Research
    Office. Research Monograph #3. 1981. 63p.
Ibrahim, Barbara L.
    "Cairo's Factory Women." (In) Fernea, Elizabeth W.
    (ed.). Women and the Family in the Middle East: New
    Voices of Change. Austin, Texas: University of Texas
    Press. 1985. pp. 293-302.
Ibrahim, Barbara L.
    "Family Strategies--A Perspective on Women's Entry to the
    Labor Force in Egypt." International Journal of
    Sociology. Volume 11 #2 July-December, 1981. pp.
    235-249.
Ibrahim, Madlain M.
    "Has Age at Marriage Increased in Rural Egypt." Cairo:
    Cairo Demographic Centre. CDC Research Monograph Series
    #12. 1984. pp. 43-61.
Issa, Mahmoud S.
    "A Time Series Analysis of Marriage in Egypt, 1962-1973."
    (In) Huzayyin, S.A. and Acsadi, G.T. (eds.). Family and
    Marriage in Some African and Asiatic Countries. Cairo:
    Cairo Demographic Centre. CDC Research Monograph Series
    #6. 1976. pp. 373-390.
Kafafi, Laila
    "Age at Marriage and Cumulative Fertility in Rural
    Egypt." Ph.D Dissertation: Duke University. Durham,
    North Carolina. 1983. 140p.
Khalifa, Atef M. and Sayed, Hussein A.A. and El-Khorazaty,
Mohamed Nabil E. and Way, Ann A.
    Family Planning in Rural Egypt, 1980: A Report on the
    Results of the Egypt Contraceptive Prevalence Survey.
    Columbia, Maryland: Westinghouse Health Systems. Cairo:
    Population and Family Planning Board. December, 1982.
    221p.
Khalifa, Atef M. and Way, Ann A.
    Marriage, Fertility and Family Planning: A Study of the
    RFS, 1979. Cairo: Population and Family Planning Board.
    1981.

Khalifa, Atef M. and Sayed, Hussein A.A. and El-Khorazaty,
Mohamed Nabil E. and Way, Ann A.
    "Prevalence, Continuation and Availability of
    Contraceptive Methods." Egyptian Population and Family
    Planning Review. Volume 16 #2 December, 1982. pp.
    1-31.
Khalifa, Atef M.
    "The Influence of Wife's Education on Fertility in Rural
    Egypt." Journal of Biosocial Science. Volume 8 #1
    January, 1976. pp. 53-60.
Loza, Sarah F.
    "Determinants of Fertility and the Demand for Family
    Planning: A Review and Assessment of Studies and How They
    Explain the Egyptian Experience." Population Studies.
    Volume 9 #62 July-September, 1982. pp. 3-32.
Loza, Sarah F.
    "Determinants of Fertility and the Demand for Family
    Planning: A Review and Assessment of Studies and How They
    Explain the Egyptian Experience." (In) Cairo Demographic
    Centre (CDC). Studies in African and Asian Demography.
    Cairo: CDC. CDC Research Monograph Series #11. 1983.
    pp. 85-124.
Loza, Sarah F.
    "Differential Age at Marriage and Fertility in Egypt."
    (In) Cairo Demographic Centre (CDC). Determinants of
    Fertility in Some African and Asian Countries. Cairo:
    CDC. CDC Research Monograph Series #10. 1982. pp.
    51-66.
Loza, Sarah F.
    "Differential Concern for Children's Education and Its
    Effect on Fertility." Population Studies (Cairo).
    Volume 6 #51 October-December, 1979. pp. 9-29.
Loza-Soliman, Sarah F. and Khorazaty, N.
    "Causes of Fertility Differences in Egypt: Intermediate
    Variable Analysis." Paper Presented at a Conference at
    the High Institute of Statistical Studies and Research.
    Cairo. 1979.
Nadim, Nawal
    "Family Relationships in a Harah in Cairo." (In) El-Din
    Ibrahim, Saad and Hopkins, Nicholas (eds.). Arab Society
    in Transition. Cairo: American University in Cairo.
    1977.
Nasr, Z.
    "Islam and the Subordination of Women." Egypte
    Contemporaine. Volume 70 #378 1979. pp. 5-29.
Nawar, Leila M.
    "Household Structure and Age at Marriage in Abbasia,
    Cairo." (In) Huzayyin, S.A. and Acsadi, G.T. (eds.).
    Family and Marriage in Some African and Asiatic
    Countries. Cairo: Cairo Demographic Centre. Research
    Monograph Series #6. 1976. pp. 67-96.
Nosseir, Nazek
    Measurement of Intermediate Variables Affecting Fertility

in Rural Egypt. Cairo: Institute of Statistical Studies and Research. 1979. 22p.

Omran, Abdel R. and Standley, C.C. (eds.)
Further Studies on Family Formation Patterns and Health: An International Collaborative Study in Columbia, Egypt, Pakistan and the Syrian Arab Republic. Geneva: World Health Organization. 1981. 464p.

Ragheb, Seham and Aly, Ferial A. and Nayel, Sayed and Shoeib, Fatma
"Women's Acceptability of the Condom and Diaphragm in Shatby Family Planning Clinic in Alexandria." Population Studies. Volume 9 #63 October-December, 1982. pp. 17-29+.

Rizk, Ibrahim A. and Stokes, C. Shannon and Nelson, Merwyn R.
"The Influence of Individual and Community-Level Child Mortality on Fertility in Egypt." Studies in Family Planning. Volume 17 #2 Summer, 1982. pp. 74-86.

Rizk, Ibrahim A.
"The Influence of Infant and Child Mortality on the Reproductive Behavior of Women in Rural Egypt: Combining Individual and Community Level Data." Ph.D Dissertation: Pennsylvania State University. University Park, Pennsylvania. 1979. 158p.

Sayed, Hussein A.A.
"A Model For the Study of Nuptiality." Egyptian Population and Family Planning Review. Volume 12 #1/2 June-December, 1978. pp. 25-39.

Sayed, Hussein A.A. and El-Khorazaty, Mohamed Nabil E. and Way, Anne A.
Fertility and Family Planning in Egypt, 1984. Cairo: Egypt National Population Council. 1985. 313p.

Sayed, Hussein A.A.
"Regional Pattern of Differentials in Contraceptive Use in Egypt." (In) Cairo Demographic Centre (CDC). Determinants of Fertility in Some African and Asian Countries. Cairo: CDC. CDC Research Monograph Series #10. 1982. pp. 67-88.

Sokona, Ousmane and Casterline, John B.
Socioeconomic Differentials in Age at Marriage in Egypt. Providence, Rhode Island: Brown University. Population Studies and Training Center. PSTC Working Paper Series #WP-85-03. April, 1985. 32p.

Stokes, C. Shannon and Schutjer, Wayne A. and Poindexter, John R.
"A Note on Desired Family Size and Contraceptive Use in Rural Egypt." Journal of Biosocial Science. Volume 15 #1 January, 1983. pp. 59-65.

Stycos, J. Mayone and Bindary, Aziz and Avery, Roger C. and Khalifa, Atef M. and Sayed, Hussein A.A. and Way, Ann A.
"Contraception and Community in Egypt: A Preliminary Evaluation of the Population/Development Mix." Studies

in Family Planning.   Volume 13 #12 Part One   December,
    1982.   pp. 365-372.
Taylor, Elizabeth
    "Egyptian Migration and Peasant Wives."   MERIP Reports.
    Volume 14 #124   June, 1984.   pp. 3-10.
Tsui, Amy O. and Declerque, Julie and Abul-Ata, Mohammed F.
    Contraceptive Rumor, Misinformation and Oral
    Contraception Use in Egypt.   Chapel Hill, North Carolina:
    University of North Carolina.   Carolina Population
    Center.   1985.
Weimer, Joan M.
    "Belly Dancer and the Virgin: Mythic Women in Modern
    Egypt."   Southwest Review.   Volume 61 #1   Winter, 1976.
    pp. 1-14.
Younis, M.N. and Abou El-Ela, N.M. and Sultan, M. and
El-Maaddawi, Y. and El-Masry, G.
    "Socio-Medical Factors Affecting the Utilization of
    Different Contraceptive Methods at Al-Azhar Rural Family
    Health Clinic."   Population Sciences.   #6 1985.   pp.
    27-34.

MASS MEDIA

Abdel-Rahman, A.
    Image of the Egyptian Woman in the Mass Media.   Cairo:
    University of Cairo.   1978.
Al-Hadeedy, M.
    Image of Women in the Egyptian Cinema.   Cairo: University
    of Cairo.   1977.
Anani, Elma and Keita, Alkaly M. and Rahman, Awatef A.
    Women and the Mass Media in Africa: Case Studies From
    Sierra Leone, the Niger and Egypt.   Addis Ababa,
    Ethiopia: United Nations Economic Commission for Africa.
    African Training and Research Centre for Women.   1981.
    38p.

MIGRATION

Egypt.   Centr. Agency for Public Mobilisation and Statistics
    1976 Population and Housing Census.   Fertility and
    Internal Migration and Movement of Workers and Students.
    Cairo: Central Agency.   December, 1980.   440p.
Farghali, Fathi
    Household Characteristics and Rural Out-Migration in
    Upper Egypt.   Cairo: Cairo Demographic Center (CDC).   CDC
    Research Monograph Series #12.   1984.   pp. 287-303.
Khafagy, Fatma
    "Women and Labor Migration: One Village in Egypt."   MERIP
    Reports.   Volume 14 #124   June, 1984.   pp. 17-21.

Taylor, Elizabeth
    "Egyptian Migration and Peasant Wives." MERIP Reports.
    Volume 14 #124 June, 1984. pp. 3-10.

NATIONALISM

Marsot, Afaf L.
    "The Revolutionary Gentlewomen in Egypt." (In) Beck,
    Lois and Keddie, Nikki R. (eds.). Women in the Muslim
    World. Cambridge, Massachusetts: Harvard University
    Press. 1978. pp. 261-276.
Phillipp, Thomas
    "Feminism and Nationalist Politics in Egypt." (In) Beck,
    Lois and Keddie, Nikki R. (eds.). Women in the Muslim
    World. Cambridge, Massachusetts: Harvard University
    Press. 1978. pp. 277-294.

ORGANIZATIONS

Anonymous
    "Feminist Organizations in Egypt." M.E.N. Economic
    Weekly. Volume 21 #16 April 16, 1982. pp. 12-13.
Jennings, Anne M.
    "Power and Influence: Women's Associations in an Egyptian
    Nubian Village." Ph.D Dissertation: University of
    California, Riverside. Riverside, California. 1985.
    215p.
United Nations Economic Commission for Africa (UNECA)
    Women and Cooperatives: Egypt, The Libyan Arab Jamahiriya
    and the Sudan. Addis Ababa, Ethiopia: UNECA. Research
    Series. 1980.

POLITICS AND GOVERNMENT

Ahmed, Leila
    "Feminism and Feminist Movements in the Middle East, A
    Preliminary Exploration: Turkey, Egypt, Algeria, People's
    Democratic Republic of Yemen." Women's Studies
    International. Volume 5 #2 1982. pp. 153-168.
Ahmed, Leila
    "Women's Liberation Movements in 19th and 20th Century
    Middle East." Paper Presented at the Meeting of Experts
    on the Theoretical Frameworks and Methodological
    Approaches to Studies on the Role of Women in History as
    Actors in Economic, Social, Political and Ideological
    Processes. Paris: United Nations Educational, Scientific
    and Cultural Organization. 1984. 24p.
Aulas, Marie C.
    Egypt's Working Women: Sadat's Strange Peace. Washington

D.C.: Middle East Research and Information Project.
MERIP Reports #82. 1979. 26p.
Howard-Merriam, Kathleen
"Egypt's Other Political Elite." Western Political
Quarterly. Volume 34 #1 March, 1981. pp. 174-187.
Marei, Wafaa A.
"Female Emancipation and Changing Political Leadership: A
Study of Five Arab Countries." Ph.D Dissertation:
Rutgers University. New Brunswick, New Jersey. 1978.
364p.
Marshall, Susan E.
"The Power of the Veil: The Politics of Female Status in
North Africa." Ph.D Dissertation: University of
Massachusetts. Amherst, Massachusetts. 1980. 274p.
Marsot, Afaf L.
"The Revolutionary Gentlewomen in Egypt." (In) Beck,
Lois and Keddie, Nikki R. (eds.). Women in the Muslim
World. Cambridge, Massachusetts: Harvard University
Press. 1978. pp. 261-276.
Phillipp, Thomas
"Feminism and Nationalist Politics in Egypt." (In) Beck,
Lois and Keddie, Nikki R. (eds.). Women in the Muslim
World. Cambridge, Massachusetts: Harvard University
Press. 1978. pp. 277-294.
Steinem, Gloria
"Two Cheers for Egypt: Talks With Jihan Sadat and Other
Daughters of the Nile." MS. Volume 8 June, 1980. pp.
72+.
Tolchin, Susan and Tolchin, Martin
"The Feminist Revolution of Jihan Sadat." New York Times
Magazine. March 16, 1980. pp. 21+.
Williams, J.A.
"Veiling in Egypt as a Political and Social Phenomenon."
(In) Esposito, John L. (ed.). Islam and Development.
Syracuse, New York: Syracuse University Press. 1980.
pp. 71-85.

RELIGION AND WITCHCRAFT

Al-Guindi, Fadwa
"The Angels in the Nile: A Theme in Nubian Ritual." (In)
Kennedy, John G. (ed.). Nubian Ceremonial Life.
Berkeley, California: University of California Press.
1978. pp. 104-113.
Al-Katsha, Samiha
"Changes in Nubian Wedding Ceremonials." (In) Kennedy,
John G. (ed.). Nubian Ceremonial Life. Berkeley,
California: University of California Press. 1978. pp.
171-202.
Arthur, Rose H.
"Feminine Motifs in Eight Nag Hammadi Documents." Th.D

Dissertation: Graduate Theological Union. Berkeley, California. 1979. 298p.

Cole, Juan R.
"Feminism, Class, and Islam in Turn-of-the-Century Egypt." International Journal of Middle East Studies. Volume 13 #4 November, 1981. pp. 387-407.

El Guindi, Fadwa
"Veiled Activism: Egyptian Women in the Contemporary Islamic Movement." Mediterranean Peoples. Volume 22/23 January-June, 1983. pp. 79-89.

El Guindi, Fadwa
"Veiling Infitah With Muslim Ethic: Egypt's Contemporary Islamic Movement." Social Problems. Volume 28 #4 April, 1981. pp. 465-485.

El-Karamani, Yussuf I.
"Islam and Family Planning: A Brief Study." Population Studies. Volume 10 #64 January-March, 1983. pp. 31-44.

El-Kharboutly, Maitre A.
"Law and the Status of Women in the Arab Republic of Egypt." (In) Columbia Human Rights Law Review (eds.). Law and the Status of Women: An International Symposium. New York: United Nations. Centre for Social Development and Humanitarian Affairs. 1977. pp. 35-50.

Kennedy, John G.
"Nubian Death Ceremonies." (In) Kennedy, John G. (ed.). Nubian Ceremonial Life. Berkeley, California: University of California Press. 1978. pp. 224-244.

Kennedy, John G.
"Nubian Zar Ceremonies as Psycho-Therapy." (In) Kennedy, John G. (ed.). Nubian Ceremonial Life. Berkeley, California: University of California Press. 1978. pp. 203-223.

Merriam, Kathleen H.
"The Impact of Modern Secular Education Upon Egyptian Women's Participation in Public Life." Paper Presented at the Annual Meeting of the Middle East Studies Association. Los Angeles, California. November 10-13, 1976.

Nasr, Z.
"Islam and the Subordination of Women." Egypte Contemporaine. Volume 70 #378 1979. pp. 5-29.

Nelson, Cynthia
"Islamic Tradition and Women's Education in Egypt." (In) Archer, Sandra (ed.). World Yearbook of Education 1984: Women and Education. New York: Nichols Publishing Co. 1984. pp. 211-226.

Qayyum, Shah A.
"Women in the Muslim World: A Case Study of Egypt." (In) Phadnis, Urmila and Malani, Indira (eds.). Women of the World: Illusion and Reality. New Delhi, India: Vikas Publishing House Ltd. 1978. pp. 150-174.

Robins, Gay
  "The God's Wife of Amun in the 18th Dynasty in Egypt."
  (In) Cameron, Averil and Kuhrt, Amelie (eds.). Images of
  Women in Antiquity. London: Croom Helm. 1983. pp.
  65-78.

RESEARCH

Abou-Gamrah, Hamed
  Review and Evaluation of Studies on the Determinants of
  Fertility in Egypt. Cairo: Supreme Council for
  Population and Family Planning. Population and Family
  Planning Board. Research Office. Research Monograph #2.
  July, 1981. 74p.
Assaad, Marie B.
  "Female Circumcision in Egypt: Social Implications,
  Current Research and Prospects for Change." Studies in
  Family Planning. Volume 11 #1 January, 1980. pp. 3-16.
Egypt. Population and Family Planning Board
  "Some Statistics Concerning Family Planning Services in
  Egypt During 1977." Egyptian Population and Family
  Planning Review. Volume 11 #1/2 June-December, 1977.
  pp. 96-102.
Ghorayeb, Rose
  "Archives: May Ziadeh (1886-1941)." Signs. Volume 5 #2
  Winter, 1979. pp. 375-382.
Stillman, Yedida K.
  "The Importance of the Cairo Geniza Manuscripts for the
  History of Medieval Female Attire." International
  Journal of Middle East Studies. Volume 7 #4 October,
  1976. pp. 579-590.
United Nations Educational, Scientific and Cultural Organ.
  Social Science Research and Women in the Arab World.
  Paris: UNESCO. 1984. 175p.
Zimmerman, Sonja D.
  The Women of Kafr al Bahr: Research Into the Working
  Conditions of Women in an Egyptian Village. Leiden,
  Netherlands: State University of Leiden. Institute for
  Social and Cultural Studies. Research Center: Women and
  Development. 1982. 149p.

SEX ROLES

Abu-Lughod, Lila
  "A Community of Secrets: The Separate World of Bedouin
  Women." Signs. Volume 10 #4 Summer, 1985. pp.
  637-657.
Abu-Lughod, Lila
  "Honor, Modesty and Poetry in a Bedouin Society: Ideology
  and Experience Among Awlad Ali of Egypt." Ph.D.

Dissertation: Harvard University. Cambridge,
Massachusetts. 1984. 347p.

Al-Sadawi, Nawal
"Growing Up Female in Egypt." (In) Fernea, Elizabeth W.
(ed.). Women and the Family in the Midle East: New
Voices of Change. Austin, Texas: University of Texas
Press. 1985. pp. 111-120.

Atif, Nadia
The Context of Women's Work: Employment, Fertility,
Development and the Seven Roles of Women in Mehalla Al
Kubr. Cairo: Center for Egyptian Civilzation Studies.
1981.

Early, Evelyn A.
"Catharsis and Creation in Informal Narratives of Baladi
Women in Cairo." Anthropological Quarterly. Volume 58
#4 1985. pp. 172-189.

Egypt. National Commission for UNESCO
The Role of Working Mothers in Early Childhood Education:
Arab Republic of Egypt, 1977. Paris: United Nations
Educational, Scientific and Cultural Organization.
January, 1978. 31p.

Egypt. State Information Service
Egyptian Women: Progress in the Balance. Cairo: State
Information Service. 1980. 55p.

El Guindi, Fadwa
"Veiled Activism: Egyptian Women in the Contemporary
Islamic Movement." Mediterranean Peoples. Volume 22/23
January-June, 1983. pp. 79-89.

El Guindi, Fadwa
"Veiling Infitah With Muslim Ethic: Egypt's Contemporary
Islamic Movement." Social Problems. Volume 28 #4
April, 1981. pp. 465-485.

El Saadawi, Nawal
"Egypt: When a Female Rebels..." (In) Morgan, Robin
(ed.). Sisterhood is Global. Garden City, New York:
Anchor Books. 1984. pp. 194-206.

El Saadawi, Nawal
Woman at Point Zero. London: Zed Books Ltd. 1983.
106p.

Fahmy, Hoda Y.
"Changing Women in a Changing Society: A Study of
Emergent Consciousness of Young Women in the City of
Akhmin in Upper Egypt." M.A. Thesis: American University
of Cairo. Department of Sociology/Anthropology/
Psychology. Cairo. 1978.

Khafagy, Fatma
"Women and Labor Migration: One Village in Egypt." MERIP
Reports. Volume 14 #124 June, 1984. pp. 17-21.

Krieger, Laurie E.
"Body Notions, Gender Roles and Fertility Regulating
Method Use in Imbaba, Cairo." Ph.D Dissertation:
University of North Carolina at Chapel Hill. Chapel
Hill, North Carolina. 1984. 285p.

Loza-Soliman, Sarah F.
   "Roles of Women and Their Impact on Fertility: An
   Egyptian Case Study."   (In) International Union for the
   Scientific Study of Population (IUSSP).   International
   Population Conference: Solicited Papers.   Liege, Belgium:
   IUSSP.   Volume Three.   1981.   pp. 571-584.
Marshall, Susan E.
   "The Power of the Veil: The Politics of Female Status in
   North Africa."   Ph.D Dissertation: University of
   Massachusetts.   Amherst, Massachusetts.   1980.   274p.
Morsy, Soheir A.
   "Gender, Power, and Illness in an Egyptian Village."
   Ph.D Dissertation: Michigan State University.   East
   Lansing, Michigan.   1978.   450p.
Morsy, Soheir A.
   "Sex Differences and Folk Illness in an Egyptian
   Village."   (In) Beck, Lois and Keddie, Nikki R. (eds.).
   Women in the Muslim World.   Cambridge, Massachsetts:
   Harvard University Press.   1978.   pp. 599-616.
Morsy, Soheir A.
   "Sex Roles, Power and Illness in an Egyptian Village."
   American Ethnologist.   Volume 5 #1 1978.   pp. 137-150.
Nasr, Z.
   "Islam and the Subordination of Women."   Egypte
   Contemporaine.   Volume 70 #378 1979.   pp. 5-29.
Nawar, I.A.
   "Role of Rural Women in Rural Development."   Paper
   Presented at the Workshop on the Role of Women and Home
   Economics in Rural Development in Africa.   Rome: United
   Nations Food and Agricultural Organization.   Alexandria,
   Egypt.   October 17, 1983.   5p.
Nelson, Cynthia
   "Islamic Tradition and Women's Education in Egypt."   (In)
   Archer, Sandra (ed.).   World Yearbook of Education 1984:
   Women and Education.   New York: Nichols Publishing Co.
   1984.   pp. 211-226.
Nour, S.F.
   "Attitudes of Selected Wives Toward Some Homemaking
   Tasks."   Paper Presented at the Workshop on the Role of
   Women and Home Economics in Rural Development in Africa.
   Rome: United Nations Food and Agricultural Organization.
   Alexandria, Egypt.   October 17, 1983.   11p.
Qayyum, Shah A.
   "Women in the Muslim World: A Case Study of Egypt."   (In)
   Phadnis, Urmila and Malani, Indira (eds.).   Women of the
   World: Illusion and Reality.   New Delhi, India: Vikas
   Publishing House Ltd.   1978.   pp. 150-174.
Royal, Anne M.
   "Male/Female Pharyngealization Patterns in Cairo Arabic:
   A Socio-Linguistic Study of Two Neighborhoods."   Ph.D
   Dissertation: University of Texas.   Austin, Texas.   1985.
   228p.

Sokona, Ousmane and Casterline, John B.
   "Socioeconomic Differentials in Age at Marriage in
   Egypt." Providence, Rhode Island: Brown University.
   Population Studies and Training Center. PSTC Working
   Paper Series #WP-85-03. April, 1985. 32p.
Sukkary-Stolba, S.
   "Changing Roles of Women in Egypt's Newly Reclaimed
   Lands." Anthropological Quarterly. Volume 58 #4
   October, 1985. pp. 182-189.
Sullivan, E.
   Women and Work in Egypt. New York: American University
   in Cairo. Cairo Papers in Social Sciences. Volume 4.
   December, 1981. pp. 1-44.
Taylor, Elizabeth
   "Egyptian Migration and Peasant Wives." MERIP Reports.
   Volume 14 #124 June, 1984. pp. 3-10.
Tucker, Judith E.
   Women in Nineteenth-Century Egypt. Cambridge, England:
   Cambridge University Press. 1985. 251p.
Williams, J.A.
   "Veiling in Egypt as a Political and Social Phenomenon."
   (In) Esposito, John L. (ed.). Islam and Development.
   Syracuse, New York: Syracuse University Press. 1980.
   pp. 71-85.
Zimmerman, Sonja D.
   The Cheese Makers of Kafr al Bahr: The Role of Egyptian
   Women in Animal Husbandry and Dairy Production. Leiden,
   Netherlands: State University of Leiden. Institute for
   Social and Cultural Studies. Research Center: Women and
   Development 1982. 55p.
Zimmerman, Sonja D.
   The Women of Kafr al Bahr: Research Into the Working
   Conditions of Women in an Egyptian Village. Leiden,
   Netherlands: State University of Leiden. Institute for
   Social and Cultural Studies. Research Center: Women and
   Development. 1982. 149p.

SEXUAL MUTILATION/CIRCUMCISION

Assaad, Marie B.
   "A Communication Gap Regarding Female Circumcision."
   (In) Blair, Patricia W. (ed.). Health Needs of the
   World's Poor Women. Washington, D.C.: Equity Policy
   Center. 1981. pp. 9-11.
Assaad, Marie B.
   "Female Circumcision in Egypt." Paper Presented at the
   Seminar on Traditional Practices Affecting the Health of
   Women and Children: Female Circumcision, Childhood
   Marriage, Nutritional Taboos, Etc. Alexandria, Egypt:
   World Health Organization. Eastern Mediterranean
   Regional Office. Khartoum, Sudan. February 10-15, 1979.

Assaad, Marie B.
   "Female Circumcision in Egypt: Current Research and
   Social Implications." Paper Presented at the Seminar on
   Traditional Practices Affecting the Health of Women and
   Children. World Conference of the United Nations Decade
   for Women. Copenhagen, Denmark. July 14-30, 1980.
Assaad, Marie B.
   "Female Circumcision in Egypt: Social Implications,
   Current Research and Prospects for Change." Studies in
   Family Planning. Volume 11 #1 January, 1980. pp. 3-16.
El Hakim, Ahmed S.
   "Female Circumcision in Egypt." Paper Presented at the
   Seminar on Traditional Practices Affecting the Health of
   Women and Children. World Conference of the United
   Nations Decade for Women. New York: United Nations.
   Copenhagen, Denmark. July 14-30, 1980.
El Hakim, Ahmed S.
   "Mental Aspects of Circumcision." Paper Presented at the
   Seminar on Traditional Practices Affecting the Health of
   Women and Children. World Conference of the United
   Nations Decade for Women. New York: United Nations.
   Copenhagen, Denmark. July 14-30, 1980.
El Hakim, Ahmed S.
   "Mental Aspects of Female Circumcision in Egypt." Paper
   Presented at the Seminar on Traditional Practices
   Affecting the Health of Women and Children: Female
   Circumcision, Childhood Marriage, Nutritional Taboos,
   etc. Alexandria, Egypt: World Health Organization.
   Eastern Mediterranean Regional Office. Khartoum, Sudan.
   February 10-15, 1979.
Kennedy, John G.
   "Circumcision and Excision Ceremonies." (In) Kennedy,
   John G. (ed.). Nubian Ceremonial Life. Berkeley,
   California: University of California Press. 1978. pp.
   151-170.
Njoki, Margaret
   "Female Circumcision in Egypt." Paper Presented at the
   Seminar on Traditional Practices Affecting the Health of
   Women and Children: Female Circumcision, Childhood
   Marriage, Nutritional Taboos, etc. Alexandria, Egypt:
   World Health Organization. Eastern Mediterranean
   Regional Office. Khartoum, Sudan. February 10-15, 1979.
Salem, Afaf A.
   "Female Circumcision in Egypt." Paper Presented at the
   Seminar on Traditional Practices Affecting the Health of
   Women and Children: Female Circumcision, Childhood
   Marriage, Nutritional Taboos, etc. Alexandria, Egypt:
   World Health Organization. Eastern Mediterranean
   Regional Office. February 10-15, 1979.
Salem, Afaf A.
   "Female Circumcision in Egypt." Paper Presented at the
   Seminar on Tradional Practices Affecting the Health of
   Women and Children. World Conference of the United

Nations Decade for Women. New York: United Nations.
Copenhagen, Denmark. July 14-30, 1980.
Salem, Afaf A.
"The Practice of Circumcision in Egypt." Paper Presented
at the Seminar on Traditional Practices Affecting the
Health of Women and Children. World Conference of the
United Nations Decade for Women. New York: United
Nations. Copenhagen, Denmark. July 14-30, 1980.
Weimer, Joan M.
"Belly Dancer and the Virgin: Mythic Women in Modern
Egypt." Southwest Review. Volume 61 #1 Winter, 1976.
pp. 1-14.

SLAVERY

Toledano, E.R.
"Slave Dealers, Women, Pregnancy and Abortion: The Study
of a Circassian Slave Girl in Mid-19th Century Cairo."
Slavery and Abolition. Volume 2 1981. pp. 53-68.

STATUS OF WOMEN

Ahmed, Leila
"Feminism and Feminist Movements in the Middle East, A
Preliminary Exploration: Turkey, Egypt, Algeria, People's
Democratic Republic of Yemen." Women's Studies
International. Volume 5 #2 1982. pp. 153-168.
Ahmed, Leila
"Women's Liberation Movements in 19th and 20th Century
Middle East." Paper Presented at the Meeting of Experts
on the Theoretical Frameworks and Methodological
Approaches to Studies on the Role of Women in History as
Actors in Economic, Social, Political and Ideological
Processes. Paris: United Nations Educational, Scientific
and Cultural Organization. 1984. 24p.
Brink, Judy H.
"The Effect of Education and Employment on the Status of
Rural Egyptian Women." Ph.D Dissertation: University of
Pittsburgh. Pittsburgh, Pennsylvania. 1985. 217p.
Egypt. State Information Service
Egyptian Women: Progress in the Balance. Cairo: State
Information Service. 1980. 55p.
El Baymoumi, Soheir
"Health and Illness as Indices of Sex Status in an
Egyptian Village." Paper Presented at the 75th Annual
Meeting of the American Anthropological Association.
Washington, D.C. November 17-21, 1976.
El Saadawi, Nawal
Woman at Point Zero. London: Zed Books Ltd. 1983.
106p.

El-Kharboutly, Maitre A.
    "Law and the Status of Women in the Arab Republic of
    Egypt." (In) Columbia Human Rights Law Review (eds.).
    Law and the Status of Women: An International Symposium.
    New York: United Nations. Centre for Social Development
    and Humanitarian Affairs. 1977. pp. 35-50.
Eliraz, Giora
    "Egyptian Intellectuals and Women's Emancipation,
    1919-1939." Asian and African Studies. Volume 16 #1
    March, 1982. pp. 95-120.
Graham-Brown, Sarah
    "Feminism in Egypt: A Conversation With Nawal Sadawi."
    MERIP Reports. #95 March, 1981. pp. 24-27.
Howard-Merriam, Kathleen
    "Egypt's Other Political Elite." Western Political
    Quarterly. Volume 34 #1 March, 1981. pp. 174-187.
Marshall, Susan E.
    "The Power of the Veil: The Politics of Female Status in
    North Africa." Ph.D Dissertation: University of
    Massachusetts. Amherst, Massachusetts. 1980. 274p.
Moore, C.
    "Women Engineers in Egypt: Growing Equality Amidst
    Professional Impoverishment." Paper Presented at the
    Annual Meeting of the American Political Science
    Association. New York. September, 1978.
Phillipp, Thomas
    "Feminism and Nationalist Politics in Egypt." (In) Beck,
    Lois and Keddie, Nikki R. (eds.). Women in the Muslim
    World. Cambridge, Massachusetts: Harvard University
    Press. 1978. pp. 277-294.
Smock, Audrey C. and Youssef, Nadia H.
    "Egypt: From Seclusion to Limited Participation." (In)
    Giele, Janet Z. and Smock, Audrey C. (eds.). Women:
    Their Roles and Status in Eight Countries. New York:
    Wiley-Interscience. 1977. pp. 33-79.
Steinem, Gloria
    "Two Cheers for Egypt: Talks With Jihan Sadat and Other
    Daughters of the Nile." MS. Volume 8 June, 1980. pp.
    72+.
Tolchin, Susan and Tolchin, Martin
    "The Feminist Revolution of Jihan Sadat." New York Times
    Magazine. March 16, 1980. pp. 21+.

URBANIZATION

Darwish, O.A.
    "Weaning Practices in Urban and Rural Egypt." Food and
    Nutrition Bulletin. Volume 4 #1 January, 1982.
El-Messiri, Sawsan
    "Self-Images of Traditional Urban Women in Cairo." (In)
    Beck, Lois and Keddie, Nikki R. (eds.). Women in the

Muslim World. Cambridge, Massachusetts: Harvard
University Press. 1978. pp. 522-540.
Ibrahim, Barbara L.
"Social Change and the Industrial Experience: Women as
Production Workers in Urban Egypt." Ph.D Dissertation:
Indiana University. Bloomington, Indiana. 1980. 269p.
Khalifa, Atef M.
"Rural-Urban Fertility Differences and Trends in Egypt,
1930-1970." (In) Allman, James (ed.). Women's Status
and Fertility in the Muslim World. New York: Praeger
Publishing. Praeger Special Studies. 1978. pp. 77-94.

WOMEN AND THEIR CHILDREN

Aromasodu, M.C.
"Traditional Practices Affecting the Health of Women in
Pregnancy and Childbirth." Paper Presented at the
Seminar on Traditional Practices Affecting the Health of
Women and Children: Female Circumcision, Childhood
Marriage, Nutritional Taboos, etc. Alexandria, Egypt:
World Health Organization. Eastern Mediterranean
Regional Office. Khartoum, Sudan. February 10-15, 1979.
Darwish, O.A.
"Weaning Practices in Urban and Rural Egypt." Food and
Nutrition Bulletin. Volume 4 #1 January, 1982.
Egypt. National Commission for UNESCO
The Role of Working Mothers in Early Childhood Education:
Arab Republic of Egypt, 1977. Paris: United Nations
Educational, Scientific and Cultural Organization.
January, 1978. 31p.
Govaerts, K.
"Attachment Behavior of the Egyptian Mother."
International Journal of Nursing Studies. Volume 18 #1
1981. pp. 53-60.
Hanbel, Ibrahim
"The Effects of Working Mothers." Paper Presented at the
Maternity Seminar. Cairo: Egyptian Ministry of Social
Affairs, Public Administration of Family Childhood.
March, 1982.
Janowitz, Barbara and Lewis, Joann H. and Parnell, A. and
Hefnawi, F.G.
"Breast-Feeding and Child Survival in Egypt." Journal of
Biosocial Science. Volume 13 #3 July, 1981. pp.
287-297.
Kamal, Ibrahim
"Lactation Patterns in the Egyptian Woman." (In)
Jelliffe, D.B. and Jelliffe, E.F. and Sai, F.T. and
Senanayake, P. (eds.). Lactation, Fertility and the
Working Woman. London: International Planned Parenthood
Federation. 1979. pp. 87-96.
Mikhail, A.N.
"Traditional Feeding Practices in Pregnancy and Lactation
in an Egyptian Community." Paper Presented at the
Seminar on Traditional Practices Affecting the Health of

Women and Children. World Conference of the United
Nations Decade for Women. New York: United Nations.
Copenhagen, Denmark. July 14-30, 1980.
Mikhail, A.N.
"Traditional Feeding Practices in Pregnancy." Paper
Presented at the Seminar on Traditional Practices
Affecting the Health of Women and Children: Female
Circumcision, Childhood Marriage, Nutritional Taboos,
etc. Alexandria Egypt: World Health Organization.
Eastern Mediterranean Regional Office. Khartoum, Sudan.
February 10-15, 1979.
Wikan, Unni
Life Among the Poor in Cairo. New York: Tavistock
Publications in Association With Methuen, Inc.
Translated by Ann Henning. 1980. 173p.

Libya

Abdalla, S.E. and Gibson, J.T.
"The Relationship of Exposure to American Culture on the
Attitude of Libyan Nationals Toward the Role of Women in
the Workplace." Contemporary Educational Psychology.
Volume 9 #3 1984. pp. 294-302.

Abugeilah, Bashir A.
"Family Patterns and Newly Emerging Attitudes Toward
Marriage and the Status of Women in the South of Libya:
The Case of Murzuk." Ph.D Dissertation: University of
Pittsburgh. Pittsburgh, Pennsylvania. 1984. 220p.

Ahmed, Abdel A.
"Functional Literacy Programmes for Agricultural,
Industrial and Women's Sector: Socialist People's Libyan
Arab Jamahiriya." Paris: United Nations Educational,
Scientific and Cultural Organization. 1981. 21p.

Al-Huni, Ali M.
"Determinants for Female Labour Force Participation: The
Case of Libya." Ph.D Dissertation: University of
Pittsburgh. Pittsburgh, Pennsylvania. 1979.

Al-Nouri, Qais N.
"Changing Marriage Patterns in Libya: Attitudes of
University Students." Journal of Contemporary Family
Studies. Volume 11 Spring, 1980. pp. 219-232.

Al-Rubeai, M.A. and Abdulla, Amina S. and Gray, Elmer
"Analysis of the Human Sex Ratio: Factors Influencing
Family Size in Libya." Journal of Heredity. Volume 74
#1 January-February, 1983. pp. 39-42.

Alfahum, Siba
The Libyan Woman, 1965-1975. Beirut, Lebanon: Women's
International League for Peace and Freedom. Lebanese
Section. 1977.

Allaghi, Farida
"Libya: The Wave of Consciousness Cannot be Reversed."

(In) Morgan, Robin (ed.). Sisterhood is Global. Garden
City, New York: Anchor Books. 1984. pp. 424-435.

Allaghi, Farida A.
"Rural Women and Decision Making: A Case Study in the
Kufra Settlement Project, Libya." Ph.D Dissertation:
Colorado State University. Fort Collins, Colorado.
1981. 258p.

Allaghi, Farida A.
"Rural Women in a Resettlement Project: The Case of the
Libyan Arab Jamahiriya." (In) International Labour
Organization (ILO). Rural Development and Women in
Africa. Geneva: ILO. 1984. pp. 137-145.

Araji, Sharon
"The Influence of Social Structure and the Family on
Women's Roles: The Libyan Case." Ph.D Dissertation:
Washington State University. Pullman, Washington. 1982.

Attir, Mustafa O.
"Ideology, Value Changes, and Women's Social Position in
Libyan Society." (In) Fernea, Elizabeth W. (ed.). Women
and the Family in the Middle East: New Voices of Change.
Austin, Texas: University of Texas Press. 1985. pp.
121-133.

Baffoun, Alya
"Research in the Social Sciences on North African Women:
Problems, Trends and Needs." (In) United Nations
Educational, Scientific and Cultural Organization.
Social Science Research and Women in the Arab World.
Paris: UNESCO. 1984. pp. 41-58.

Baffoun, Alya
"Some Remarks on Women and Development in the Maghreb."
(In) Rivlin, Helen A. and Helmer, Katherine (eds.). The
Changing Middle Eastern City. Binghamton, New York:
State University of New York. Center for Social
Analysis. 1980. pp. 141-148.

Biri, El-Waheshy A. and Pendleton, Brian F. and Garland T.
Neal
"Correlates of Men's Attitudes Toward Women's Roles in
Libya." Paper Presented at the Annual Meetng of the
Society for the Study of Social Programs. Tripoli,
Libya: Al-Fateh University. 1981. 19p.

Biri, El-Waheshy A.
"Men's Attitudes Towards Women's Roles in Libya: An
Indicator of Social Change." Ph.D Dissertation:
University of Akron. Akron, Ohio. 1981. 182p.

Bowen, Donna L.
"Attitudes Toward Family and Family Planning in the
Pre-Saharan Maghreb." Maghreb Review. Volume 8 #1-2
January-April, 1983. pp. 8-17.

Dorph, K.J.
"Islamic Law in Contemporary North Africa: A Study of the
Laws of Divorce in the Maghreb." Women's Studies
International Forum. Volume 5 #2 1982. pp. 169-182.

Ehtewish, Omran S.
    "Fertility Differentials in the Socialist Peoples Libyan
    Arab Jamahiriya." Ph.D Dissertation: Mississippi State
    University. Starkvillle, Mississippi. 1980. 334p.
El-Huni, Ali M.
    "Determinants of Female Labor Force Participation: The
    Case of Libya." Ph.D Dissertation: Oklahoma State
    University. Stillwater, Oklahoma. 1978. 144p.
Grosse, Scott D.
    "The Politics of Family Planning in the Maghreb."
    Studies in Comparative International Development. Volume
    17 #1 Spring, 1982. pp. 22-48.
Harrow, K.
    "Not Such a Long Way, Baby--The Situation of the Women
    Today in the Maghreb and its Thematic Representation in
    Literature." Current Bibliography on African Affairs.
    Volume 9 #3 1976. pp. 228-249.
Marshall, Susan E.
    "The Power of the Veil: The Politics of Female Status in
    North Africa." Ph.D Dissertation: University of
    Massachusetts. Amherst, Massachusetts. 1980. 274p.
Mayer, Ann E.
    "Developments on the Law of Marriage and Divorce in Libya
    Since the 1969 Revolution." Journal of African Law.
    Spring, 1978. pp. 30-49.
Mayer, Ann E.
    "Libyan Legislation in Defense of Arabo-Islamic Sexual
    Mores." American Journal of Comparative Law. Volume 28
    Spring, 1980. pp. 287-314.
Mernissi, Fatima
    Country Reports on Women in North Africa, Libya, Morocco,
    and Tunisia. Addis Ababa, Ethiopia: United Nations
    Economic Commission for Africa. African Training and
    Research Centre for Women. 1978. 42p.
Peters, Emrys L.
    "Aspects of Bedouin Bridewealth Among Camel Herders in
    Cyrenaica." (In) Comaroff, J.L. (ed.). The Meaning of
    Marriage Payments. New York: Academic Press. 1980. pp.
    125-160.
Tabutin, Dominique
    "Nuptiality and Fertility in Maghreb." (In) Ruzicka,
    L.T. (ed.). Nuptiality and Fertility: Proceedings of a
    Seminar, January 8-11, 1979. Liege, Netherlands: Union
    for the Scientific Study of Population. 1982. pp.
    101-122.
United Nations Economic Commission for Africa (UNECA)
    Women and Cooperatives: Egypt, The Libyan Arab Jamahiriya
    and the Sudan. Addis Ababa, Ethiopia: UNECA. Research
    Series. 1980.
United Nations Educational, Scientific and Cultural Organ.
    Social Science Research and Women in the Arab World.
    Paris: UNESCO. 1984. 175p.

Wolff, Ursula
    "Women in Africa--Maghribian Society in Transition."
    Africa Report. Volume 22 #1 January-February, 1977.
    pp. 41-43.
Wright, Claudia
    "A Slower Revolution." Middle East. #87 January, 1982.
    pp. 40-41.
Zagallai, Farida
    "Programs to Improve the Position of Women in a
    Traditional Culture: An Evaluation of a Rural Women's
    Development Center in Libya." Paper Presented at the
    International Sociological Association Meeting. 1978.

Morocco

AGRICULTURE

Beneria, Lourdes
  "Women and Rural Development--Morocco." Cultural
  Survival Quarterly. Volume 8 #2 Summer, 1984. pp.
  30-31.
Boutaout, Anya
  "Rural Development in the Region of Marrakesh."
  Community Development Journal. Volume 14 #1 January,
  1979. pp. 41-47.
Davis, Susan S.
  "Working Women in a Moroccan Village." (In) Beck, Lois
  and Keddie, Nikki (eds.). Women in the Muslim World.
  Cambridge, Massachusetts: Harvard University Press.
  1978. pp. 416-433.
Hirschmann, David and Vaughan, Megan
  "Food Production and Income Generation in a Matrilineal
  Society: Rural Women in Zomba, Malawi." Journal of
  Southern African Studies. Volume 10 #1 October, 1983.
  pp. 86-99.
Maher, Vanessa
  "Work, Consumption and Authority Within the Household: A
  Moroccan Case." (In) Young, Kate and Wolkowitz, Carol
  and McCullagh, Roslyn (eds.). Of Marriage and the
  Market: Women's Subordination in International
  Perspective. London: CSE Books. 1981. pp. 69-87.
Mernissi, Fatima
  "Capitalist Development and Perceptions of Women in
  Arab-Muslim Society: An Illustration of Peasant Women in
  Gharb, Morocco." (In) International Labour Organization
  (ILO). Rural Development and Women in Africa. Geneva:
  ILO. 1984. pp. 123-128.
Vinogradon, Amal R.
  "Cultural Values, Economic Realities and Rural Women in
  Morocco: Contradictions and Accommodations." Paper

Presented at the Wellesley Conference on Women and
National Development. Wellesley, Massachusetts:
Wellesley College. June 2-6, 1976.

CULTURAL ROLES

Ayachesebag, G.
    "Cultural Script of North African Jewish Women: The
    Making of an Eshet-Hayil." Transactional Analysis
    Journal. Volume 13 #4 1983. pp. 231-233.
Belarbi, Aicha
    "Research in the Social Sciences on Women in Morocco."
    (In) UNESCO. Social Science Research and Women in the
    Arab World. Paris: United Nations Educational,
    Scientific and Cultural Organization. 1984. pp. 59-81.
Belarbi, Aicha
    "Research in the Social Sciences on Women in Morocco."
    Paper Presented at the Meeting of Arab Women Researchers
    on the Development of Research in the Social Sciences on
    Women in the Arab World. Paris: UNESCO. Tunis, Tunisia.
    1981. 24p.
Beneria, Lourdes
    "Women and Rural Development--Morocco." Cultural
    Survival Quarterly. Volume 8 #2 Summer, 1984. pp.
    30-31.
Bhattacharyya, Amit K.
    "Role of Rural-Urban Income Inequality in Fertility
    Reductions: Cases in Turkey, Taiwan and Morocco."
    Economic Development and Cultural Change. Volume 26 #1
    October, 1977. pp. 117-138.
Bowen, Donna L.
    "Attitudes Toward Family and Family Planning in the
    Pre-Saharan Maghreb." Maghreb Review. Volume 8 #1-2
    January-April, 1983. pp. 8-17.
Chaudhry, Sayeeda A.
    "Female Labor Force Participation and its Relationship to
    Fertility Rate: Some Policy Implications for Developing
    Countries." Ph.D Dissertation: George Washington
    University. Washington, D.C. 1984. 410p.
Davis, Susan S.
    "Formal and Nonformal Roles of Moraccan Village Women."
    Ph.D Dissertation: University of Michigan. Ann Arbor,
    Michigan. 1978. 391p.
Davis, Susan S.
    Patience and Power: Women's Lives in a Moroccan Village.
    Cambridge, Massachusetts: Schenkman. 1983. 198p.
Davis, Susan S.
    "The Determinants of Social Position Among Rural Moroccan
    Women." (In) Smith, Jane I. (ed.). Women in
    Contemporary Muslim Societies. Lewisburg, Pennsylvania:
    Bucknell University Press. 1980. pp. 87-99.

Davis, Susan S.
"Women, Men and Moraccan Economic Development." Journal
of South Asian and Middle Eastern Studies. Volume 5 #2
1981.
Davis, Susan S.
"Working Women in a Moroccan Village." (In) Beck, Lois
and Keddie, Nikki (eds.). Women in the Muslim World.
Cambridge, Massachusetts: Harvard University Press.
1978. pp. 416-433.
Deshen, Shlomo
"Women in the Jewish Family in Pre-Colonial Morocco."
Anthropological Quarterly. Volume 56 #3 July, 1983.
pp. 134-144.
Dunayevskaya, Raya
"The Break With Kautsky, 1910-1911: From Mass Strike
Theory to Crisis Over Morocco and Hushed-Up 'Woman
Question'." News and Letters. Volume 25 April, 1980.
pp. 5-8.
Dwyer, Daisy H.
"Bridging the Gap Between the Sexes in Moroccan Legal
Practice." (In) Schlegel, Alice E. (ed.). Sexual
Stratification: A Cross-Cultural View. New York:
Columbia University Press. 1977. pp. 41-66.
Dwyer, Daisy H.
Images and Self-Images. Male and Female in Morocco. New
York: Columbia University Press. 1978. 194p.
Dwyer, Daisy H.
"Law Actual and Perceived: The Sexual Politics of Law in
Morocco." Law and Society Review. Volume 13 #3 Spring,
1979. pp. 739-756.
Dwyer, Daisy H.
"Sexual Ideology and Systems of Partial Consciousness:
The Moroccan Case." Paper Presented at the 27th Annual
Meeting of the American Anthropological Association.
Washington, D.C. November 17-21, 1976.
Dwyer, Daisy H.
"Women, Sufism and Decision-Making in Moroccan Islam."
(In) Beck, Lois and Keddie, Nikki R. (eds.). Women in
the Muslim World. Cambridge, Massachusetts: Harvard
University Press. 1978. pp. 585-598.
El Belghiti, Malika
"The Role of Women in Socio-Economic Development:
Indicators as Instruments of Social Analysis; The Case of
Morocco." (In) Buvinic, Mayra and Schumacher, Ilsa.
Women and Development: Indicators of Their Changing Role.
Paris: United Nations Educational, Scientific and
Cultural Organization. 1981. pp. 15-32.
Grosse, Scott D.
"The Politics of Family Planning in the Maghreb."
Studies in Comparative International Development. Volume
17 #1 Spring, 1982. pp. 22-48.

Harfoush, Samira
   "Women and Africa: Nontraditional Training for Women in
   the Arab World." Africa Report. Volume 26 #2
   March-April, 1981. pp. 51-55.
Harrow, K.
   "Not Such a Long Way, Baby--The Situation of the Women
   Today in the Maghreb and its Thematic Representation in
   Literature." Current Bibliography on African Affairs.
   Volume 9 #3 1976. pp. 228-249.
Hirschmann, David and Vaughan, Megan
   "Food Production and Income Generation in a Matrilineal
   Society: Rural Women in Zomba, Malawi." Journal of
   Southern African Studies. Volume 10 #1 October, 1983.
   pp. 86-99.
Joseph, Roger
   "Sexual Dialectics and Strategy in Berber Marriage."
   (In) Kurian, George (ed.). Cross-Cultural Perspectives
   of Mate Selection and Marriage. Westport, Connecticut:
   Greenwood Press. Contributions in Family Studies #3.
   1979. pp. 191-201.
Lecomte, Jean and Marcoux, Alain
   "Contraception and Fertility in Morocco and Tunisia."
   Studies in Family Planning. Volume 7 #7 July, 1976.
   pp. 182-187.
Llewelyn-Davies, Melissa
   Some Women of Marrakech. Newton, Massachusetts: Public
   Broadcasting Associates. 1981. 18p.
Maher, Vanessa
   "Possession and Dispossesion: Maternity and Mortality in
   Morocco." (In) Medick, Hans and Sabean, David W. (eds.).
   Interest and Emotion: Essays on the Study of Family and
   Kinship. Cambridge, New York: Cambridge University
   Press. 1984. pp. 103-128.
Maher, Vanessa
   "Women and Social Change in Morocco." (In) Beck, Lois
   and Keddie, Nikki R. (eds.). Women in the Muslim World.
   Cambridge, Massachusetts: Harvard University Press.
   1978. pp. 100-123.
Maher, Vanessa
   "Work, Consumption and Authority Within the Household: A
   Moroccan Case." (In) Young, Kate and Wolkowitz, Carol
   and McCullagh, Roslyn (eds.). Of Marriage and the
   Market: Women's Subordination in International
   Perspective. London: CSE Books. 1981. pp. 69-87.
Marshall, Susan E.
   "The Power of the Veil: The Politics of Female Status in
   North Africa." Ph.D Dissertation: University of
   Massachusetts. Amherst, Massachusetts. 1980. 274p.
Mernissi, Fatima
   "Capitalist Development and Perceptions of Women in
   Arab-Muslim Society: An Illustration of Peasant Women in
   Gharb, Morocco." (In) International Labour Organization

(ILO). Rural Development and Women in Africa. Geneva:
ILO. 1984. pp. 123-128.
Mernissi, Fatima
Historical Insights for New Population Strategies: Women
in Pre-Colonial Morocco. Paris: United Nations
Educational, Scientific and Cultural Organization.
Division of Applied Social Sciences. 1978.
Mernissi, Fatima
"Morocco: The Merchant's Daughter and the Son of the
Sultan." (In) Morgan, Robin (ed.). Sisterhood is
Global. Garden City, New York: Anchor Books. 1984. pp.
444-453.
Mernissi, Fatima
"Obstacles to Family Planning Practice in Urban Morocco."
Studies in Family Planning. Volume 2 #12 December,
1976.
Mernissi, Fatima
"Peasant Women of Morocco Talk." Ideas and Action
Bulletin. #158 1984.
Mernissi, Fatima
"The Patriarch in the Moroccan Family: Myth or Reality?"
(In) Allman, James (ed.). Women's Status and Fertility
in the Muslim World. New York: Praeger Publishers.
Praeger Special Studies. 1978. pp. 312-332.
Mernissi, Fatima
"Women and the Impact of Capitalist Development in
Morocco (Part Two)." Feminist Issues: A Journal of
Feminist Social and Political Theory. Volume 3 #1
Spring, 1983. p. 61+.
Mernissi, Fatima
Women in Emergent Morocco: Changes and Continuities.
Quantico, Virginia: Flame International. 1982.
Mernissi, Fatima
"Women's Solidarity in the Courtyards of Saints' Tombs:
Morocco." Paper Presented at the Wellesley Conference on
Women and Development. Wellesley, Massachusetts:
Wellesley College. June 2-6, 1976.
Mernissi, Fatima
"Zhor's World: A Moroccan Domestic Worker Speaks Out."
Feminist Issues. Volume 2 #1 Spring, 1982.
Mernissi, Fatima
Country Reports on Women in North Africa, Libya, Morocco,
and Tunisia. Addis Ababa, Ethiopia: United Nations
Economic Commission for Africa. African Training and
Research Centre for Women. 1978. 42p.
Rassam, Amal
"Women and Domestic Power in Morocco." International
Journal of Middle East Studies. Volume 12 #1 August,
1980. pp. 171-180.
Rosen, Lawrence
"The Negotiation of Reality: Male Female Relations in
Sefrou, Morocco." (In) Beck, Lois and Keddie, Nikki R.

(eds.). Women in the Muslim World. Cambridge,
Massachusetts: Harvard University Press. 1978. pp
561-584.
Sabagh, Georges and Yim, Sun B.
"The Relationship Between Migration and Fertility in an
Historical Context: The Case of Morocco in the 1960's."
International Migration Review. Volume 14 #4 Winter,
1980. pp. 525-538.
Stillman, N.A.
"Women on Folk Medicine: Judaeo-Arabic Texts From
Sefrou." Journal of the American Oriental Society.
Volume 103 #3 July-September, 1983. pp. 485-493.
Tabutin, Dominique
"Nuptiality and Fertility in Maghreb." (In) Ruzicka,
L.T. (ed.). Nuptiality and Fertility: Proceedings of a
Seminar, January 8-11, 1979. Liege, Netherlands: Union
for the Scientific Study of Population. 1982. pp.
101-122.
United Nations Educational, Scientific and Cultural Organ.
Social Science Research and Women in the Arab World.
Paris: UNESCO. 1984. 175p.
Vinogradon, Amal R.
"Cultural Values, Economic Realities and Rural Women in
Morocco: Contradictions and Accommodations." Paper
Presented at the Wellesley Conference on Women and
National Development. Wellesley, Massachusetts:
Wellesley College. June 2-6, 1976.
Webster, Sheila K.
"Women, Sex and Marriage in Moroccan Proverbs."
International Journal of Middle East Studies. Volume 14
#2 May, 1982. pp. 173-184.
Wolff, Ursula
"Women in Africa--Maghribian Society in Transition."
Africa Report. Volume 22 #1 January-February, 1977.
pp. 41-43.

DEVELOPMENT AND TECHNOLOGY

Baffoun, Alya
"Some Remarks on Women and Development in the Maghreb."
(In) Rivlin, Helen A. and Helmer, Katherine (eds.). The
Changing Middle Eastern City. Binghamton, New York:
State University of New York. Center for Social
Analysis. 1980. pp. 141-148.
Beneria, Lourdes
"Women and Rural Development--Morocco." Cultural
Survival Quarterly. Volume 8 #2 Summer, 1984. pp.
30-31.
Bhattacharyya, Amit K.
"Role of Rural-Urban Income Inequality in Fertility
Reductions: Cases in Turkey, Taiwan and Morocco."

Economic Development and Cultural Change. Volume 26 #1
October, 1977. pp. 117-138.
Boutaout, Anya
"Rural Development in the Region of Marrakesh."
Community Development Journal. Volume 14 #1 January,
1979. pp. 41-47.
Chaudhry, Sayeeda A.
"Female Labor Force Participation and its Relationship to
Fertility Rate: Some Policy Implications for Developing
Countries." Ph.D Dissertation: George Washington
University. Washington, D.C. 1984. 410p.
Davis, Susan S.
"Women, Men and Moraccan Economic Development." Journal
of South Asian and Middle Eastern Studies. Volume 5 #2
1981.
El Belghiti, Malika
Socio-Economic Indicators of the Participation of Women
in Development in the Arab World: A Critical Approach on
the Basis of the Case of Morocco: Summary. Paris: United
Nations Educational, Scientific and Cultural
Organization. April, 1980. 6p.
El Belghiti, Malika
"The Role of Women in Socio-Economic Development:
Indicators as Instruments of Social Analysis; The Case of
Morocco." (In) Buvinic, Mayra and Schumacher, Ilsa.
Women and Development: Indicators of Their Changing Role.
Paris: United Nations Educational, Scientific and
Cultural Organization. 1981. pp. 15-32.
Hirschmann, David and Vaughan, Megan
"Food Production and Income Generation in a Matrilineal
Society: Rural Women in Zomba, Malawi." Journal of
Southern African Studies. Volume 10 #1 October, 1983.
pp. 86-99.
Howard-Merriam, Kathleen
"Women's Political Participation in Morocco's
Development: How Much and for Whom." Maghreb Review.
Volume 9 #1/2 1984. pp. 12-25.
Maher, Vanessa
"Women and Social Change in Morocco." (In) Beck, Lois
and Keddie, Nikki R. (eds.). Women in the Muslim World.
Cambridge, Massachusetts: Harvard University Press.
1978. pp. 100-123.
Mernissi, Fatima
"Capitalist Development and Perceptions of Women in
Arab-Muslim Society: An Illustration of Peasant Women in
Gharb, Morocco." (In) International Labour Organization
(ILO). Rural Development and Women in Africa. Geneva:
ILO. 1984. pp. 123-128.
Mernissi, Fatima
"Women and the Impact of Capitalist Development in
Morocco (Part One)." Feminist Issues: A Journal of

Feminist Social and Political Theory. Volume 2 #3 Fall, 1982.
Mernissi, Fatima
  "Women and the Impact of Capitalist Development in Morocco (Part Two)." Feminist Issues: A Journal of Feminist Social and Political Theory. Volume 3 #1 Spring, 1983. p. 61+.
Mernissi, Fatima
  Women in Emergent Morocco: Changes and Continuities. Quantico, Virginia: Flame International. 1982.
Mernissi, Fatima
  "Women's Solidarity in the Courtyards of Saints' Tombs: Morocco." Paper Presented at the Wellesley Conference on Women and Development. Wellesley, Massachusetts: Wellesley College. June 2-6, 1976.
Mernissi, Fatima
  Country Reports on Women in North Africa, Libya, Morocco, and Tunisia. Addis Ababa, Ethiopia: United Nations Economic Commission for Africa. African Training and Research Centre for Women. 1978. 42p.
Vinogradon, Amal R.
  "Cultural Values, Economic Realities and Rural Women in Morocco: Contradictions and Accommodations." Paper Presented at the Wellesley Conference on Women and National Development. Wellesley, Massachusetts: Wellesley College. June 2-6, 1976.
Youssef, Nadia H.
  Women and Their Professional Future: An Assessment of Training Needs and Training Programs, Morocco. Washington, D.C.: U.S. Department of State. U.S. Agency for International Development. International Center for Research on Women. 1978. 59p.

DIVORCE

Dorph, K.J.
  "Islamic Law in Contemporary North Africa: A Study of the Laws of Divorce in the Maghreb." Women's Studies International Forum. Volume 5 #2 1982. pp. 169-182.

ECONOMICS

Baffoun, Alya
  "Some Remarks on Women and Development in the Maghreb." (In) Rivlin, Helen A. and Helmer, Katherine (eds.). The Changing Middle Eastern City. Binghamton, New York: State University of New York. Center for Social Analysis. 1980. pp. 141-148.
Bhattacharyya, Amit K.
  "Role of Rural-Urban Income Inequality in Fertility Reductions: Cases in Turkey, Taiwan and Morocco."

Economic Development and Cultural Change. Volume 26 #1
October, 1977. pp. 117-138.
Boutaout, Anya
"Rural Development in the Region of Marrakesh."
Community Development Journal. Volume 14 #1 January,
1979. pp. 41-47.
Chaudhry, Sayeeda A.
"Female Labor Force Participation and its Relationship to
Fertility Rate: Some Policy Implications for Developing
Countries." Ph.D Dissertation: George Washington
University. Washington, D.C. 1984. 410p.
Davis, Susan S.
"Women, Men and Moraccan Economic Development." Journal
of South Asian and Middle Eastern Studies. Volume 5 #2
1981.
El Belghiti, Malika
Socio-Economic Indicators of the Participation of Women
in Development in the Arab World: A Critical Approach on
the Basis of the Case of Morocco: Summary. Paris: United
Nations Educational, Scientific and Cultural
Organization. April, 1980. 6p.
El Belghiti, Malika
"The Role of Women in Socio-Economic Development:
Indicators as Instruments of Social Analysis; The Case of
Morocco." (In) Buvinic, Mayra and Schumacher, Ilsa.
Women and Development: Indicators of Their Changing Role.
Paris: United Nations Educational, Scientific and
Cultural Organization. 1981. pp. 15-32.
Hirschmann, David and Vaughan, Megan
"Food Production and Income Generation in a Matrilineal
Society: Rural Women in Zomba, Malawi." Journal of
Southern African Studies. Volume 10 #1 October, 1983.
pp. 86-99.
Mernissi, Fatima
"Women and the Impact of Capitalist Development in
Morocco (Part One)." Feminist Issues: A Journal of
Feminist Social and Political Theory. Volume 2 #3 Fall,
1982.
Mernissi, Fatima
"Women and the Impact of Capitalist Development in
Morocco (Part Two)." Feminist Issues: A Journal of
Feminist Social and Political Theory. Volume 3 #1
Spring, 1983. p. 61+.
Mernissi, Fatima
Women in Emergent Morocco: Changes and Continuities.
Quantico, Virginia: Flame International. 1982.
Mernissi, Fatima
Country Reports on Women in North Africa, Libya, Morocco,
and Tunisia. Addis Ababa, Ethiopia: United Nations
Economic Commission for Africa. African Training and
Research Centre for Women. 1978. 42p.

Vinogradon, Amal R.
    "Cultural Values, Economic Realities and Rural Women in
    Morocco: Contradictions and Accommodations." Paper
    Presented at the Wellesley Conference on Women and
    National Development. Wellesley, Massachusetts:
    Wellesley College. June 2-6, 1976.

EDUCATION AND TRAINING

Baffoun, Alya
    "Research in the Social Sciences on North African Women:
    Problems, Trends and Needs." (In) United Nations
    Educational, Scientific and Cultural Organization.
    Social Science Research and Women in the Arab World.
    Paris: UNESCO. 1984. pp. 41-58.
Harfoush, Samira
    "Women and Africa: Nontraditional Training for Women in
    the Arab World." Africa Report. Volume 26 #2
    March-April, 1981. pp. 51-55.
U.S. Agency for International Development (U.S. AID)
    Non-Formal Education for Women in Morocco. Washington,
    D.C.: U.S. Department of State. U.S. AID. International
    Center for Research on Women. 1979.
U.S. Agency for International Development (U.S. AID)
    An Evaluation of Non-Formal Education Program for Women
    in Morocco. Washington, D.C.: U.S. Department of State.
    U.S. AID. International Center for Research on Women.
    1979.
Youssef, Nadia H.
    Women and Their Professional Future: An Assessment of
    Training Needs and Training Programs, Morocco.
    Washington, D.C.: U.S. Department of State. U.S. Agency
    for International Development. International Center for
    Research on Women. 1978. 59p.
Youssef, Nadia H. and Sadka, N. and Murphy, E.
    An Evaluation of Non-Formal Educational Programs for
    Women in Morocco. Washington, D.C.: U.S. Department of
    State. U.S. Agency for International Development.
    Near-East Regional Bureau. 1977.

EMPLOYMENT AND LABOR

Baffoun, Alya
    "Research in the Social Sciences on North African Women:
    Problems, Trends and Needs." (In) United Nations
    Educational, Scientific and Cultural Organization.
    Social Science Research and Women in the Arab World.
    Paris: UNESCO. 1984. pp. 41-58.
Beneria, Lourdes
    "Women and Rural Development--Morocco." Cultural

Survival Quarterly. Volume 8 #2 Summer, 1984. pp.
30-31.
Chaudhry, Sayeeda A.
"Female Labor Force Participation and its Relationship to
Fertility Rate: Some Policy Implications for Developing
Countries." Ph.D Dissertation: George Washington
University. Washington, D.C. 1984. 410p.
Davis, Susan S.
"Working Women in a Moroccan Village." (In) Beck, Lois
and Keddie, Nikki (eds.). Women in the Muslim World.
Cambridge, Massachusetts: Harvard University Press.
1978. pp. 416-433.
Dunayevskaya, Raya
"The Break With Kautsky, 1910-1911: From Mass Strike
Theory to Crisis Over Morocco and Hushed-up 'Woman
Question'." News and Letters. Volume 25 April, 1980.
pp. 5-8.
El Belghiti, Malika
Socio-Economic Indicators of the Participation of Women
in Development in the Arab World: A Critical Approach on
the Basis of the Case of Morocco: Summary. Paris: United
Nations Educational, Scientific and Cultural
Organization. April, 1980. 6p.
El Belghiti, Malika
"The Role of Women in Socio-Economic Development:
Indicators as Instruments of Social Analysis; The Case of
Morocco." (In) Buvinic, Mayra and Schumacher, Ilsa.
Women and Development: Indicators of Their Changing Role.
Paris: United Nations Educational, Scientific and
Cultural Organization. 1981. pp. 15-32.
Maher, Vanessa
"Work, Consumption and Authority Within the Household: A
Moroccan Case." (In) Young, Kate and Wolkowitz, Carol
and McCullagh, Roslyn (eds.). Of Marriage and the
Market: Women's Subordination in International
Perspective. London: CSE Books. 1981. pp. 69-87.
Mernissi, Fatima
"Women and the Impact of Capitalist Development in
Morocco (Part One)." Feminist Issues. Volume 2 #3 Fall,
1982.
Mernissi, Fatima
Women in Emergent Morocco: Changes and Continuities.
Quantico, Virginia: Flame International. 1982.
Mernissi, Fatima
"Zhor's World: A Moroccan Domestic Worker Speaks Out."
Feminist Issues. Volume 2 #1 Spring, 1982.

EQUALITY AND LIBERATION

Rassam, Amal
"Women and Domestic Power in Morocco." International
Journal of Middle East Studies. Volume 12 #1 August,
1980. pp. 171-180.

FAMILY LIFE

Belarbi, Aicha
    Research in the Social Sciences on Women in Morocco.
    Paper Presented at the Meeting of Arab Women Researchers
    on the Development of Research in the Social Sciences on
    Women in the Arab World. Paris: UNESCO. Tunis, Tunisia.
    1981. 24p.
Bowen, Donna L.
    "Attitudes Toward Family and Family Planning in the
    Pre-Saharan Maghreb." Maghreb Review. Volume 8 #1-2
    January-April, 1983. pp. 8-17.
Bowen, Donna L.
    "Women and Public Health in Morocco: One Family's
    Experience." (In) Fernea, Elizabeth W. (ed.). Women and
    the Family in the Middle East: New Voices of Change.
    Austin, Texas: University of Texas Press. 1985. pp.
    134-144.
Charrad, Mournira
    "Family Policy and Political Development: A Comparison of
    Tunisia, Algeria and Morocco." Paper Presented at the
    Annual Meeting of the African Studies Association. Paper
    #13. Houston, Texas. 1977.
Davis, Susan S.
    "Formal and Nonformal Roles of Moraccan Village Women."
    Ph.D Dissertation: University of Michigan. Ann Arbor,
    Michigan. 1978. 391p.
Davis, Susan S.
    "Patience and Power: Women's Lives in a Moroccan
    Village." Cambridge, Massachusetts: Schenkman. 1983.
    198p.
Deshen, Shlomo
    "Women in the Jewish Family in Pre-Colonial Morocco."
    Anthropological Quarterly. Volume 56 #3 July, 1983.
    pp. 134-144.
Dwyer, Daisy H.
    Images and Self-Images. Male and Female in Morocco. New
    York: Columbia University Press. 1978. 194p.
Maher, Vanessa
    "Work, Consumption and Authority Within the Household: A
    Moroccan Case." (In) Young, Kate and Wolkowitz, Carol
    and McCullagh, Roslyn (eds.). Of Marriage and the
    Market: Women's Subordination in International
    Perspective. London: CSE Books. 1981. pp. 69-87.
Mernissi, Fatima
    "The Patriarch in the Moroccan Family: Myth or Reality?"
    (In) Allman, James (ed.). Women's Status and Fertility
    in the Muslim World. New York: Praeger Publishers.
    Praeger Special Studies. 1978. pp. 312-332.
Rassam, Amal
    "Women and Domestic Power in Morocco." International
    Journal of Middle East Studies. Volume 12 #1 August,
    1980. pp. 171-180.

FAMILY PLANNING AND CONTRACEPTION

Baffoun, Alya
"Research in the Social Sciences on North African Women:
Problems, Trends and Needs." (In) United Nations
Educational, Scientific and Cultural Organization.
Social Science Research and Women in the Arab World.
Paris: UNESCO. 1984. pp. 41-58.
Belarbi, Aicha
"Research in the Social Sciences on Women in Morocco."
(In) UNESCO. Social Science Research and Women in the
Arab World. Paris: United Nations Educational,
Scientific and Cultural Organization. 1984. pp. 59-81.
Belarbi, Aicha
"Research in the Social Sciences on Women in Morocco."
Paper Presented at the Meeting of Arab Women Researchers
on the Development of Research in the Social Sciences on
Women in the Arab World. Paris: UNESCO. Tunis, Tunisia.
1981. 24p.
Bhattacharyya, Amit K.
"Role of Rural-Urban Income Inequality in Fertility
Reductions: Cases in Turkey, Taiwan and Morocco."
Economic Development and Cultural Change. Volume 26 #1
October, 1977. pp. 117-138.
Bowen, Donna L.
"Attitudes Toward Family and Family Planning in the
Pre-Saharan Maghreb." Maghreb Review. Volume 8 #1-2
January-April, 1983. pp. 8-17.
Chaudhry, Sayeeda A.
"Female Labor Force Participation and its Relationship to
Fertility Rate: Some Policy Implications for Developing
Countries." Ph.D Dissertation: George Washington
University. Washington, D.C. 1984. 410p.
Farid, Samir
"Fertility Patterns in the Arab Region." International
Family Planning Perspectives. Volume 10 #4 December,
1984. pp. 119-125.
Grosse, Scott D.
"The Politics of Family Planning in the Maghreb."
Studies in Comparative International Development. Volume
17 #1 Spring, 1982. pp. 22-48.
Lecomte, Jean and Marcoux, Alain
"Contraception and Fertility in Morocco and Tunisia."
Studies in Family Planning. Volume 7 #7 July, 1976.
pp. 182-187.
Mernissi, Fatima
"Obstacles to Family Planning Practice in Urban Morocco."
Studies in Family Planning. Volume 2 #12 December,
1976.
Tabutin, Dominique
"Nuptiality and Fertility in Maghreb." (In) Ruzicka,

L.T. (ed.). Nuptiality and Fertility: Proceedings of a Seminar, January 8-11, 1979. Liege, Netherlands: Union for the Scientific Study of Population. 1982. pp. 101-122.

FERTILITY AND INFERTILITY

Chaudhry, Sayeeda A.
"Female Labor Force Participation and its Relationship to Fertility Rate: Some Policy Implications for Developing Countries." Ph.D Dissertation: George Washington University. Washington, D.C. 1984. 410p.
Farid, Samir
"Fertility Patterns in the Arab Region." International Family Planning Perspectives. Volume 10 #4 December, 1984. pp. 119-125.
Lecomte, Jean and Marcoux, Alain
"Contraception and Fertility in Morocco and Tunisia." Studies in Family Planning. Volume 7 #7 July, 1976. pp. 182-187.
Sabagh, Georges and Yim, Sun B.
"The Relationship Between Migration and Fertility in an Historical Context: The Case of Morocco in the 1960's." International Migration Review. Volume 14 #4 Winter, 1980. pp. 525-538.
Tabutin, Dominique
"Nuptiality and Fertility in Maghreb." (In) Ruzicka, L.T. (ed.). Nuptiality and Fertility: Proceedings of a Seminar, January 8-11, 1979. Liege, Netherlands: Union for the Scientific Study of Population. 1982. pp. 101-122.

HEALTH, NUTRITION AND MEDICINE

Bowen, Donna L.
"Women and Public Health in Morocco: One Family's Experience." (In) Fernea, Elizabeth W. (ed.). Women and the Family in the Middle East: New Voices of Change. Austin, Texas: University of Texas Press. 1985. pp. 134-144.
Maher, Vanessa
"Possession and Dispossesion: Maternity and Mortality in Morocco." (In) Medick, Hans and Sabean, David W. (eds.). Interest and Emotion: Essays on the Study of Family and Kinship. Cambridge, New York: Cambridge University Press. 1984. pp. 103-128.
Stillman, N.A.
"Women on Folk Medicine: Judaeo-Arabic Texts From Sefrou." Journal of the American Oriental Society. Volume 103 #3 July-September, 1983. pp. 485-493.

HISTORY

Belarbi, Aicha
  "Research in the Social Sciences on Women in Morocco."
  (In) UNESCO. Social Science Research and Women in the
  Arab World. Paris: United Nations Educational,
  Scientific and Cultural Organization. 1984. pp. 59-81.
Belarbi, Aicha
  "Research in the Social Sciences on Women in Morocco."
  Paper Presented at the Meeting of Arab Women Researchers
  on the Development of Research in the Social Sciences on
  Women in the Arab World. Paris: UNESCO. Tunis, Tunisia.
  1981. 24p.
Dunayevskaya, Raya
  "The Break With Kautsky, 1910-1911: From Mass Strike
  Theory to Crisis Over Morocco and Hushed-up 'Woman
  Question'." News and Letters. Volume 25 April, 1980.
  pp. 5-8.
Mernissi, Fatima
  "Historical Insights for New Population Strategies: Women
  in Pre-Colonial Morocco." Paris: United Nations
  Educational, Scientific and Cultural Organization.
  Division of Applied Social Sciences. 1978.

LAW AND LEGAL ISSUES

Dorph, K.J.
  "Islamic Law in Contemporary North Africa: A Study of the
  Laws of Divorce in the Maghreb." Women's Studies
  International Forum. Volume 5 #2 1982. pp. 169-182.
Dwyer, Daisy H.
  "Bridging the Gap Between the Sexes in Moroccan Legal
  Practice." (In) Schlegel, Alice E. (ed.). Sexual
  Stratification: A Cross-Cultural View. New York:
  Columbia University Press. 1977. pp. 41-66.
Dwyer, Daisy H.
  "Law Actual and Perceived: The Sexual Politics of Law in
  Morocco." Law and Society Review. Volume 13 #3 Spring,
  1979. pp. 739-756.

LITERATURE

Harrow, K.
  "Not Such a Long Way, Baby--The Situation of the Women
  Today in the Maghreb and its Thematic Representation in
  Literature." Current Bibliography on African Affairs.
  Volume 9 #3 1976. pp. 228-249.
Van Houwelingen
  "Francophone Literature in North Africa." (In) Schipper,
  Mineke (ed.). Unheard Words: Women and Literature in
  Africa, the Arab World, Asia, the Caribbean, and Latin

America. New York: Alliison and Busby. 1985. pp.
102-113.

MARITAL RELATIONS AND NUPTIALITY

Chaudhry, Sayeeda A.
"Female Labor Force Participation and its Relationship to
Fertility Rate: Some Policy Implications for Developing
Countries." Ph.D Dissertation: George Washington
University. Washington, D.C. 1984. 410p.
Davis, Susan S.
Patience and Power: Women's Lives in a Moroccan Village.
Cambridge, Massachusetts: Schenkman. 1983. 198p.
Farid, Samir
"Fertility Patterns in the Arab Region." International
Family Planning Perspectives. Volume 10 #4 December,
1984. pp. 119-125.
Grosse, Scott D.
"The Politics of Family Planning in the Maghreb."
Studies in Comparative International Development. Volume
17 #1 Spring, 1982. pp. 22-48.
Joseph, Roger
"Sexual Dialectics and Strategy in Berber Marriage."
(In) Kurian, George (ed.). Cross-Cultural Perspectives
of Mate Selection and Marriage. Westport, Connecticut:
Greenwood Press. Contributions in Family Studies #3.
1979. pp. 191-201.
Lecomte, Jean and Marcoux, Alain
"Contraception and Fertility in Morocco and Tunisia."
Studies in Family Planning. Volume 7 #7 July, 1976.
pp. 182-187.
Maher, Vanessa
"Possession and Dispossesion: Maternity and Mortality in
Morocco." (In) Medick, Hans and Sabean, David W. (eds.).
Interest and Emotion: Essays on the Study of Family and
Kinship. Cambridge, New York: Cambridge University
Press. 1984. pp. 103-128.
Maher, Vanessa
"Work, Consumption and Authority Within the Household: A
Moroccan Case." (In) Young, Kate and Wolkowitz, Carol
and McCullagh, Roslyn (eds.). Of Marriage and the
Market: Women's Subordination in International
Perspective. London: CSE Books. 1981. pp. 69-87.
Mernissi, Fatima
"Obstacles to Family Planning Practice in Urban Morocco."
Studies in Family Planning. Volume 2 #12 December,
1976.
Rosen, Lawrence
"The Negotiation of Reality: Male Female Relations in
Sefrou, Morocco." (In) Beck, Lois and Keddie, Nikki R.

(eds.). Women in the Muslim World. Cambridge,
Massachusetts: Harvard University Press. 1978. pp
561-584.
Sabagh, Georges and Yim, Sun B.
"The Relationship Between Migration and Fertility in an
Historical Context: The Case of Morocco in the 1960's."
International Migration Review. Volume 14 #4 Winter,
1980. pp. 525-538.
Tabutin, Dominique
"Nuptiality and Fertility in Maghreb." (In) Ruzicka,
L.T. (ed.). Nuptiality and Fertility: Proceedings of a
Seminar, January 8-11, 1979. Liege, Netherlands: Union
for the Scientific Study of Population. 1982. pp.
101-122.
Webster, Sheila K.
"Women, Sex and Marriage in Moroccan Proverbs."
International Journal of Middle East Studies. Volume 14
#2 May, 1982. pp. 173-184.

MIGRATION

Hirschmann, David and Vaughan, Megan
"Food Production and Income Generation in a Matrilineal
Society: Rural Women in Zomba, Malawi." Journal of
Southern African Studies. Volume 10 #1 October, 1983.
pp. 86-99.
Sabagh, Georges and Yim, Sun B.
"The Relationship Between Migration and Fertility in an
Historical Context: The Case of Morocco in the 1960's."
International Migration Review. Volume 14 #4 Winter,
1980. pp. 525-538.

MISCELLANEOUS

Maher, Vanessa
"Possession and Dispossesion: Maternity and Mortality in
Morocco." (In) Medick, Hans and Sabean, David W. (eds.).
Interest and Emotion: Essays on the Study of Family and
Kinship. Cambridge, New York: Cambridge University
Press. 1984. pp. 103-128.

POLITICS AND GOVERNMENT

Charrad, Mournira
"Family Policy and Political Development: A Comparison of
Tunisia, Algeria and Morocco." Paper Presented at the
Annual Meeting of the African Studies Association. Paper
#13. Houston, Texas. 1977.

Howard-Merriam, Kathleen
   "Women's Political Participation in Morocco's
   Development: How Much and for Whom." Maghreb Review.
   Volume 9 #1/2 1984. pp. 12-25.
Marshall, Susan E.
   "The Power of the Veil: The Politics of Female Status in
   North Africa." Ph.D Dissertation: University of
   Massachusetts. Amherst, Massachusetts. 1980. 274p.

RELIGION AND WITCHCRAFT

Ayachesebag, G.
   "Cultural Script of North African Jewish Women: The
   Making of an Eshet-Hayil." Transactional Analysis
   Journal. Volume 13 #4 1983. pp. 231-233.
Charrad, Mournira
   "Family Policy and Political Development: A Comparison of
   Tunisia, Algeria and Morocco." Paper Presented at the
   Annual Meeting of the African Studies Association. Paper
   #13. Houston, Texas. 1977.
Davis, Susan S.
   Patience and Power: Women's Lives in a Moroccan Village.
   Cambridge, Massachusetts: Schenkman. 1983. 198p.
Davis, Susan S.
   "The Determinants of Social Position Among Rural Moroccan
   Women." (In) Smith, Jane I. (ed.). Women in
   Contemporary Muslim Societies. Lewisburg, Pennsylvania:
   Bucknell University Press. 1980. pp. 87-99.
Deshen, Shlomo
   "Women in the Jewish Family in Pre-Colonial Morocco."
   Anthropological Quarterly. Volume 56 #3 July, 1983.
   pp. 134-144.
Dorph, K.J.
   "Islamic Law in Contemporary North Africa: A Study of the
   Laws of Divorce in the Maghreb." Women's Studies
   International Forum. Volume 5 #2 1982. pp. 169-182.
Dwyer, Daisy H.
   Images and Self-Images. Male and Female in Morocco.
   New York: Columbia University Press. 1978. 194p.
Dwyer, Daisy H.
   "Women, Sufism and Decision-Making in Moroccan Islam."
   (In) Beck, Lois and Keddie, Nikki R. (eds.). Women in
   the Muslim World. Cambridge, Massachusetts: Harvard
   University Press. 1978. pp. 585-598.
Grosse, Scott D.
   "The Politics of Family Planning in the Maghreb."
   Studies in Comparative International Development. Volume
   17 #1 Spring, 1982. pp. 22-48.
Maher, Vanessa
   "Possession and Dispossesion: Maternity and Mortality in
   Morocco." (In) Medick, Hans and Sabean, David W. (eds.).
   Interest and Emotion: Essays on the Study of Family and

Kinship. Cambridge, New York: Cambridge University
    Press. 1984. pp. 103-128.
Mernissi, Fatima
    "Morocco: The Merchant's Daughter and the Son of the
    Sultan." (In) Morgan, Robin (ed.). Sisterhood is
    Global. Garden City, New York: Anchor Books. 1984. pp.
    444-453.
Mernissi, Fatima
    "Obstacles to Family Planning Practice in Urban Morocco."
    Studies in Family Planning. Volume 2 #12 December,
    1976.

RESEARCH

Baffoun, Alya
    "Research in the Social Sciences on North African Women:
    Problems, Trends and Needs." (In) United Nations
    Educational, Scientific and Cultural Organization.
    Social Science Research and Women in the Arab World.
    Paris: UNESCO. 1984. pp. 41-58.
Belarbi, Aicha
    "Research in the Social Sciences on Women in Morocco."
    (In) UNESCO. Social Science Research and Women in the
    Arab World. Paris: United Nations Educational,
    Scientific and Cultural Organization. 1984. pp. 59-81.
Belarbi, Aicha
    "Research in the Social Sciences on Women in Morocco."
    Paper Presented at the Meeting of Arab Women Researchers
    on the Development of Research in the Social Sciences on
    Women in the Arab World. Paris: UNESCO. Tunis, Tunisia.
    1981. 24p.
United Nations Educational, Scientific and Cultural Organ.
    Social Science Research and Women in the Arab World.
    Paris: UNESCO. 1984. 175p.

SEX ROLES

Beneria, Lourdes
    "Women and Rural Development--Morocco." Cultural
    Survival Quarterly. Volume 8 #2 Summer, 1984. pp.
    30-31.
Davis, Susan S.
    "Formal and Nonformal Roles of Moraccan Village Women."
    Ph.D Dissertation: University of Michigan. Ann Arbor,
    Michigan. 1978. 391p.
Davis, Susan S.
    Patience and Power: Women's Lives in a Moroccan Village.
    Cambridge, Massachusetts: Schenkman. 1983. 198p.

Davis, Susan S.
"The Determinants of Social Position Among Rural Moroccan Women." (In) Smith, Jane I. (ed.). Women in Contemporary Muslim Societies. Lewisburg, Pennsylvania: Bucknell University Press. 1980. pp. 87-99.

Dwyer, Daisy H.
"Bridging the Gap Between the Sexes in Moroccan Legal Practice." (In) Schlegel, Alice E. (ed.). Sexual Stratification: A Cross-Cultural View. New York: Columbia University Press. 1977. pp. 41-66.

Dwyer, Daisy H.
"Sexual Ideology and Systems of Partial Consciousness: The Moroccan Case." Paper Presented at the 27th Annual Meeting of the American Anthropological Association. Washington, D.C. November 17-21, 1976.

Dwyer, Daisy H.
"Women, Sufism and Decision-Making in Moroccan Islam." (In) Beck, Lois and Keddie, Nikki R. (eds.). Women in the Muslim World. Cambridge, Massachusetts: Harvard University Press. 1978. pp. 585-598.

El Belghiti, Malika
"The Role of Women in Socio-Economic Development: Indicators as Instruments of Social Analysis; The Case of Morocco." (In) Buvinic, Mayra and Schumacher, Ilsa. Women and Development: Indicators of Their Changing Role. Paris: United Nations Educational, Scientific and Cultural Organization. 1981. pp. 15-32.

Harrow, K.
"Not Such a Long Way, Baby--The Situation of the Women Today in the Maghreb and its Thematic Representation in Literature." Current Bibliography on African Affairs. Volume 9 #3 1976. pp. 228-249.

Hirschmann, David and Vaughan, Megan
"Food Production and Income Generation in a Matrilineal Society: Rural Women in Zomba, Malawi." Journal of Southern African Studies. Volume 10 #1 October, 1983. pp. 86-99.

Joseph, Roger
"Sexual Dialectics and Strategy in Berber Marriage." (In) Kurian, George (ed.). Cross-Cultural Perspectives of Mate Selection and Marriage. Westport, Connecticut: Greenwood Press. Contributions in Family Studies #3. 1979. pp. 191-201.

Maher, Vanessa
"Women and Social Change in Morocco." (In) Beck, Lois and Keddie, Nikki R. (eds.). Women in the Muslim World. Cambridge, Massachusetts: Harvard University Press. 1978. pp. 100-123.

Maher, Vanessa
"Work, Consumption and Authority Within the Household: A Moroccan Case." (In) Young, Kate and Wolkowitz, Carol and McCullagh, Roslyn (eds.). Of Marriage and the

Market: Women's Subordination in International
Perspective. London: CSE Books. 1981. pp. 69-87.
Marshall, Susan E.
    "The Power of the Veil: The Politics of Female Status in
    North Africa." Ph.D Dissertation: University of
    Massachusetts. Amherst, Massachusetts. 1980. 274p.
Mernissi, Fatima
    "Morocco: The Merchant's Daughter and the Son of the
    Sultan." (In) Morgan, Robin (ed.). Sisterhood is
    Global. Garden City, New York: Anchor Books. 1984. pp.
    444-453.
Mernissi, Fatima
    "Peasant Women of Morocco Talk." Ideas and Action
    Bulletin. #158 1984.
Mernissi, Fatima
    Women in Emergent Morocco: Changes and Continuities.
    Quantico, Virginia: Flame International. 1982.
Mernissi, Fatima
    "Zhor's World: A Moroccan Domestic Worker Speaks Out."
    Feminist Issues. Volume 2 #1 Spring, 1982.
Rassam, Amal
    "Women and Domestic Power in Morocco." International
    Journal of Middle East Studies. Volume 12 #1 August,
    1980. pp. 171-180.
Rosen, Lawrence
    "The Negotiation of Reality: Male Female Relations in
    Sefrou, Morocco." (In) Beck, Lois and Keddie, Nikki R.
    (eds.). Women in the Muslim World. Cambridge,
    Massachusetts: Harvard University Press. 1978. pp
    561-584.
Webster, Sheila K.
    "Women, Sex and Marriage in Moroccan Proverbs."
    International Journal of Middle East Studies. Volume 14
    #2 May, 1982. pp. 173-184.

STATUS OF WOMEN

Belarbi, Aicha
    "Research in the Social Sciences on Women in Morocco."
    (In) UNESCO. Social Science Research and Women in the
    Arab World. Paris: United Nations Educational,
    Scientific and Cultural Organization. 1984. pp. 59-81.
Belarbi, Aicha
    "Research in the Social Sciences on Women in Morocco."
    Paper Presented at the Meeting of Arab Women Researchers
    on the Development of Research in the Social Sciences on
    Women in the Arab World. Paris: UNESCO. Tunis, Tunisia.
    1981. 24p.
Harrow, K.
    "Not Such a Long Way, Baby--The Situation of the Women
    Today in the Maghreb and its Thematic Representation in

Literature." Current Bibliography on African Affairs.
Volume 9 #3 1976. pp. 228-249.
Marshall, Susan E.
"The Power of the Veil: The Politics of Female Status in
North Africa." Ph.D Dissertation: University of
Massachusetts. Amherst, Massachusetts. 1980. 274p.
Mernissi, Fatima
"The Patriarch in the Moroccan Family: Myth or Reality?"
(In) Allman, James (ed.). Women's Status and Fertility
in the Muslim World. New York: Praeger Publishers.
Praeger Special Studies. 1978. pp. 312-332.
Wolff, Ursula
"Women in Africa--Maghribian Society in Transition."
Africa Report. Volume 22 #1 January-February, 1977.
pp. 41-43.

URBANIZATION

Bhattacharyya, Amit K.
"Role of Rural-Urban Income Inequality in Fertility
Reductions: Cases in Turkey, Taiwan and Morocco."
Economic Development and Cultural Change. Volume 26 #1
October, 1977. pp. 117-138.
Mernissi, Fatima
"Obstacles to Family Planning Practice in Urban Morocco."
Studies in Family Planning. Volume 2 #12 December,
1976.

Tunisia

ABORTION

Nazer, Isam
    "The Tunisian Experience in Legal Abortion."
    International Journal of Gynaecology and Obstetrics.
    Volume 17 #5 March-April, 1980. pp. 488-492.

AGRICULTURE

Nassif, Hind
    "Women's Economic Roles in Developing Tunisia." Paper
    Presented at the 9th Annual Convention of the Association
    of Arab-American University Graduates/Middle East Studies
    Association. New York City, New York. October 1-3,
    1976.
Sherif-Stanford, Nahla
    "Modernization by Decree: The Role of Tunisian Women in
    Development: Constraints and Prospects." Ph.D
    Dissertation: University of Missouri-Columbia. Columbia,
    Missouri. 1984. 278p.

CULTURAL ROLES

Abed, Bassam K.
    "The Social Organization of Production and Reproduction
    in Rural Tunisia." Ph.D Dissertation: Pennsylvania State
    University. University Park, Pennsylvania. 1979. 263p.
Ali, Badressalam B. and Ahmad, Mahbub
    "Births Averted in Tunisia by Contraception in Recent
    Years." (In) Cairo Demographic Centre (CDC).
    Determinants of Fertility in Some African and Asian
    Countries. Cairo: CDC. CDC Research Monograph Series
    #10. 1982. pp. 263-299.
Almeida Costa, E. and Sanchez de Almeida, M.
    "Psychological Factors Affecting Change in Women's Roles

and Status: A Crosscultural Study." International
Journal of Psychology. Volume 18 #1-2 1983. pp. 3-35.
Anonymous
"Birth Control in Tunisia." Population. Volume 33 #1
January-February, 1978. pp. 194-205.
Arntsen, Andrea
"Women and Social Change in Tunisia." Ph.D Dissertation:
Georgetown University. Washington, D.C. 1977. 554p.
Auerbach, Liesa S.
"Childbirth in Tunisia; Implications of a Decision-Making
Model." Social Science and Medicine. Volume 16 #16
1982. pp. 1499-1506.
Auerbach, Liesa S.
"Women's Domestic Power: A Study of Women's Roles in a
Tunisian Town." Ph.D Dissertation: University of
Illinois at Urbana-Champaign. Urbana, Illinois. 1980.
425p.
Ayad, Mohamed and Jemai, Yolande
"Fertility Declines in Tunisia: Factors Affecting Recent
Trends." (In) Allman, James (ed.). Women's Status and
Fertility in the Muslim World. New York: Praeger
Publishers. Praeger Special Studies. 1978. pp.
152-163.
Beaujot, Roderic
"Cultural Constructions of Demographic Inquiry:
Experiences of an Expatriate Researcher in Tunisia."
Culture. Volume 5 #1 1985. pp. 3-15.
Beaujot, Roderic and Bchir, Mongi
Fertility in Tunisia: Traditional and Modern Contrasts.
Washington, D.C.: Population Reference Bureau. August,
1984. 59p.
Bowen, Donna L.
"Attitudes Toward Family and Family Planning in the
Pre-Saharan Maghreb." Maghreb Review. Volume 8 #1-2
January-April, 1983. pp. 8-17.
Brown, K.L.
"Campaign to Encourage Family Planning in Tunisia and
Some Responses at the Village Level." Middle Eastern
Studies. Volume 17 #1 January, 1981. pp. 64-84.
Durrani, Lorna H.
"Employment of Women and Social Change." (In) Stone,
Russell A. and Simmons, John (eds.). Change in Tunisia:
Studies in the Social Sciences. Albany, New York: State
University of New York Press. 1976. pp. 57-72.
Duza, M. Badrud and Baldwin, C. Stephen
"Nuptiality and Population Policy: An Investigation in
Tunisia, Sri Lanka and Malaysia." New York: Population
Council. 1977. 83p.
Evers, B. and Wagenmans, W.
Jobs and Value: Social Effects of Export-Oriented
Industrialization in Tunisia. Tilburg, Netherlands:
Tilburg Development Research Institute. Research Report
#9. 1977. 80p.

Grosse, Scott D.
    "The Politics of Family Planning in the Maghreb."
    Studies in Comparative International Development.   Volume
    17 #1   Spring, 1982.   pp. 22-48.
Halila, Souad
    "From Koranic Law to Civil Law: Emancipation of Tunisian
    Women Since 1956."   Feminist Issues.   Volume 4   Fall,
    1984.   pp. 23-44.
Harrow, K.
    "Not Such a Long Way, Baby--The Situation of the Women
    Today in the Maghreb and its Thematic Representation in
    Literature."   Current Bibliography on African Affairs.
    Volume 9 #3 1976.   pp. 228-249.
Jemai, Yolande and Jemai, Hedi
    Methods of Measuring the Impact of Family Planning
    Programmes on Fertility: The Case of Tunisia.   Geneva.
    1976.
Jones, Marie T.
    "Educating Girls in Tunisia: Issues Generated by the
    Drive for Universal Enrollment."   (In) Kelly, G.P. and
    Elliott. C.M. (eds.).   Women's Education in the Third
    World: Comparative Perspectives.   Albany, New York: State
    University of New York Press.   1982.   pp. 31-50.
Jones, Marie T.
    "Education of Girls in Tunisia: Policy Implications of
    the Drive for Universal Enrollment."   Comparative
    Education Review.   Volume 24 #2 Part Two   June, 1980.
    pp. S106-S123.
Larson, Barbara K.
    "The Status of Women in a Tunisian Village: Limits to
    Autonomy, Influence and Power."   Signs.   Volume 9 #3
    September, 1984.   pp. 417-433.
Lecomte, Jean and Marcoux, Alain
    "Contraception and Fertility in Morocco and Tunisia."
    Studies in Family Planning.   Volume 7 #7   July, 1976.
    pp. 182-187.
Maguire, Elizabeth S. and Way, Ann A. and Ayad, Mohamed
    "The Delivery and Use of Contraceptive Services in Rural
    Tunisia."   International Family Planning Perspectives.
    Volume 8 #3   September, 1982. pp. 96-101.
Marei, Wafaa A.
    "Female Emancipation and Changing Political Leadership: A
    Study of Five Arab Countries."   Ph.D Dissertation:
    Rutgers University.   New Brunswick, New Jersey.   1978.
    364p.
Marshall, Susan E.
    "The Power of the Veil: The Politics of Female Status in
    North Africa."   Ph.D Dissertation: University of
    Massachusetts.   Amherst, Massachusetts.   1980.   274p.
Marshall, Susan E. and Stokes, Randall G.
    "Tradition and the Veil: Female Status in Tunisia and
    Algeria."   Journal of Modern African Studies.   Volume 19
    #4   December, 1981.   pp. 625-646.

Mernissi, Fatima
    Country Reports on Women in North Africa, Libya, Morocco,
    and Tunisia. Addis Ababa, Ethiopia: United Nations
    Economic Commission for Africa. African Training and
    Research Centre for Women. 1978. 42p.
Miller, Christine D.
    "The Effects of Socioeconomic Development Upon a Model of
    Women's Fertility Decision Making in a Tunisian
    Community." Ph.D Dissertation: University of
    California-Irvine. Irvine, California. 1985. 336p.
Nassif, Hind
    "Marriage Patterns and Social Change in Rural Tunisia."
    Ph.D Dissertation: Catholic University of America.
    Washington, D.C. 1978. 282p.
Nassif, Hind
    "Women's Economic Roles in Developing Tunisia." Paper
    Presented at the 9th Annual Convention of the Association
    of Arab-American University Graduates/Middle East Studies
    Association. New York City, New York. October 1-3,
    1976.
Nazer, Isam
    "The Tunisian Experience in Legal Abortion."
    International Journal of Gynaecology and Obstetrics.
    Volume 17 #5 March-April, 1980. pp. 488-492.
O'Barr, Jean F.
    "A Longitudinal Analysis of Political Efficiency and
    Support Among Women and Men in Tunisia." Paper Presented
    at the Wellesley Conference on Women and Development.
    Wellesley, Massachusetts: Wellsley College. June 2-6,
    1976.
Ouni, Ali B.
    "Divorce in Tunisia, 1963-1972." (In) Huzayyin, S.A. and
    Acsadi, G.T. (eds.). Family and Marriage in Some African
    and Asiatic Countries. Cairo: Cairo Demographic Centre.
    CDC Research Monograph Series #6. 1976. pp. 505-529.
Raccagni, Michelle
    "Origins of Feminism in Egypt and Tunisia." Ph.D
    Dissertation: New York University. New York, New York.
    1983. 327p.
Sherif-Stanford, Nahla
    "Modernization by Decree: The Role of Tunisian Women in
    Development: Constraints and Prospects." Ph.D
    Dissertation: University of Missouri-Columbia. Columbia,
    Missouri. 1984. 278p.
Stroobant, A.
    "A Relation Between Fecundity, Lactation and Infant
    Mortality: Initial Results of a Survey Based on a Sample
    Representative of the Population of Nabeul." Tunisie
    Medicale. Volume 56 1978. pp. 171-178.
Tabutin, Dominique
    "Nuptiality and Fertility in Maghreb." (In) Ruzicka,
    L.T. (ed.). Nuptiality and Fertility: Proceedings of a
    Seminar, January 8-11, 1979. Liege, Netherlands: Union

for the Scientific Study of Population. 1982. pp.
101-122.
Tessler, Mark A.
"Gender and Participant Citizenship in Tunisia." Journal
of Arab Affairs. Volume 2 #1 October, 1982. pp. 47-84.
Tessler, Mark A. and Rogers, Janet M. and Schneider, Daniel
R.
"Tunisian Attitudes Toward Women and Child Rearing."
(In) Allman, James (ed.). Women's Status and Fertility
in the Muslim World. New York: Praeger Publishers.
Praeger Special Studies. 1978. pp. 289-311.
Tessler, Mark A. and Rogers, Janet M. and Schneider, Daniel
R.
"Women's Emancipation in Tunisia." (In) Beck, Lois and
Keddie, Nikki R. (eds.). Women in the Muslim World.
Cambridge, Massachusetts: Harvard University Press.
1978. pp. 141-158.
Thorne, Melvin and Montague, Joel
"Family Planning and the Problems of Development." (In)
Stone, Russell A. and Simmons, John (eds.). Change in
Tunisia. Albany, New York: State University of New York
Press. 1976. pp. 201-215.
United Nations
Socio-Economic Development and Fertility Decline: An
Application of the Eastern Synthesis Approach to World
Survey Data. New York: United Nations. Department of
International Economic and Social Affairs. Population
Division. #IESA/P/WP/88. May, 1985. 115p.
United Nations Educational, Scientific and Cultural Organ.
National Inventory on the Place of Women in Tunisian
Society. Paris: UNESCO. 1976. 80p.
United Nations Educational, Scientific and Cultural Organ.
Social Science Research and Women in the Arab World.
Paris: UNESCO. 1984. 175p.
Waltz, S.E.
"Women's Housing Needs in the Arab Cultural Context of
Tunisia." Ekistics. Volume 52 #1 January-February,
1985. pp. 28-34.
Wolff, Ursula
"Women in Africa--Maghribian Society in Transition."
Africa Report. Volume 22 #1 January-February, 1977.
pp. 41-43.
Zahra, Nadia
"Baraka, Material, Power and Women in Tunisia." Revue
d'Histoire Maghrebine. #10-#11 January, 1978. pp.
5-21.

DEVELOPMENT AND TECHNOLOGY

Baffoun, Alya
"Some Remarks on Women and Development in the Maghreb."
(In) Rivlin, Helen A. and Helmer, Katherine (eds.). The
Changing Middle Eastern City. Binghamton, New York:

State University of New York. Center for Social
Analysis. 1980. pp. 141-148.

Jones, Marie T.
"Public Influence on Government Policy: Family Planning
and Manpower Development in Tunisia." Ph.D Dissertation:
Princeton University. Princeton, New Jersey. 1979.
421p.

Mernissi, Fatima
Country Reports on Women in North Africa, Libya, Morocco,
and Tunisia. Addis Ababa, Ethiopia: United Nations
Economic Commission for Africa. African Training and
Research Centre for Women. 1978. 42p.

Miller, Christine D.
"The Effects of Socioeconomic Development Upon a Model of
Women's Fertility Decision Making in a Tunisian
Community." Ph.D Dissertation: University of
California-Irvine. Irvine, California. 1985. 336p.

Nassif, Hind
"Women's Economic Roles in Developing Tunisia." Paper
Presented at the 9th Annual Convention of the Association
of Arab-American University Graduates/Middle East Studies
Association. New York, New York. October 1-3, 1976.

O'Barr, Jean F.
"A Longitudinal Analysis of Political Efficiency and
Support Among Women and Men in Tunisia." Paper Presented
at the Wellesley Conference on Women and Development.
Wellesley, Massachusetts: Wellsley College. June 2-6,
1976.

Sherif-Stanford, Nahla
"Modernization by Decree: The Role of Tunisian Women in
Development: Constraints and Prospects." Ph.D
Dissertation: University of Missouri-Columbia. Columbia,
Missouri. 1984. 278p.

Thorne, Melvin and Montague, Joel
"Family Planning and the Problems of Development." (In)
Stone, Russell A. and Simmons, John (eds.). Change in
Tunisia. Albany, New York: State University of New York
Press. 1976. pp. 201-215.

United Nations
"Socio-Economic Development and Fertility Decline: An
Application of the Eastern Synthesis Approach to World
Survey Data." New York: United Nations. Department of
International Economic and Social Affairs. Population
Division. #IESA/P/WP/88. May, 1985. 115p.

DIVORCE

Dorph, K.J.
"Islamic Law in Contemporary North Africa: A Study of the
Laws of Divorce in the Maghreb." Women's Studies
International Forum. Volume 5 #2 1982. pp. 169-182.

Ouni, Ali B.
"Divorce in Tunisia, 1963-1972." (In) Huzayyin, S.A. and
Acsadi, G.T. (eds.). Family and Marriage in Some African
and Asiatic Countries. Cairo: Cairo Demographic Centre.
CDC Research Monograph Series #6. 1976. pp. 505-529.

ECONOMICS

Baffoun, Alya
"Some Remarks on Women and Development in the Maghreb."
(In) Rivlin, Helen A. and Helmer, Katherine (eds.). The
Changing Middle Eastern City. Binghamton, New York:
State University of New York. Center for Social
Analysis. 1980. pp. 141-148.
Durrani, Lorna H.
"Employment of Women and Social Change." (In) Stone,
Russell A. and Simmons, John (eds.). Change in Tunisia:
Studies in the Social Sciences. Albany, New York: State
University of New York Press. 1976. pp. 57-72.
Evers, B. and Wagenmans, W.
"Jobs and Value: Social Effects of Export-Oriented
Industrialization in Tunisia." Tilburg, Netherlands:
Tilburg Development Research Institute. Research Report
#9. 1977. 80p.
Jones, Marie T.
"Public Influence on Government Policy: Family Planning
and Manpower Development in Tunisia." Ph.D Dissertation:
Princeton University. Princeton, New Jersey. 1979.
421p.
Mernissi, Fatima
Country Reports on Women in North Africa, Libya, Morocco,
and Tunisia. Addis Ababa, Ethiopia: United Nations
Economic Commission for Africa. African Training and
Research Centre for Women. 1978. 42p.
Nassif, Hind
"Women's Economic Roles in Developing Tunisia." Paper
Presented at the 9th Annual Convention of the Association
of Arab-American University Graduates/Middle East Studies
Association. New York City, New York. October 1-3,
1976.
Sherif-Stanford, Nahla
"Modernization by Decree: The Role of Tunisian Women in
Development: Constraints and Prospects." Ph.D
Dissertation: University of Missouri-Columbia. Columbia,
Missouri. 1984. 278p.
United Nations
Socio-Economic Development and Fertility Decline: An
Application of the Eastern Synthesis Approach to World
Survey Data. New York: United Nations. Department of
International Economic and Social Affairs. Population
Division. #IESA/P/WP/88. May, 1985. 115p.

EDUCATION AND TRAINING

Ahearne, Alice
"Family Planning in Tunisia: An Educational Program and its Implementation." Ph.D Dissertation: Michigan State University. East Lansing, Michigan. 1977. 155p.

Baffoun, Alya
"Research in the Social Sciences on North African Women: Problems, Trends and Needs." (In) United Nations Educational, Scientific and Cultural Organization. Social Science Research and Women in the Arab World. Paris: UNESCO. 1984. pp. 41-58.

Jones, Marie T.
"Educating Girls in Tunisia: Issues Generated by the Drive for Universal Enrollment." (In) Kelly, G.P. and Elliott. C.M. (eds.). Women's Education in the Third World: Comparative Perspectives. Albany, New York: State University of New York Press. 1982. pp. 31-50.

Jones, Marie T.
"Education of Girls in Tunisia: Policy Implications of the Drive for Universal Enrollment." Comparative Education Review. Volume 24 #2 Part Two June, 1980. pp. S106-S123.

Raccagni, Michelle
"Origins of Feminism in Egypt and Tunisia." Ph.D Dissertation: New York University. New York, New York. 1983. 327p.

United Nations Educational, Scientific and Cultural Organ.
"National Inventory on the Place of Women in Tunisian Society." Paris: UNESCO. 1976. 80p.

EMPLOYMENT AND LABOR

Baffoun, Alya
"Research in the Social Sciences on North African Women: Problems, Trends and Needs." (In) United Nations Educational, Scientific and Cultural Organization. Social Science Research and Women in the Arab World. Paris: UNESCO. 1984. pp. 41-58.

Baldwin, C.S.
"Policies and Realities of Delayed Marriage: The Cases of Tunisia, Sri Lanka, Malaysia and Bangladesh." PRB Report. Volume 13 #4 1977.

Durrani, Lorna H.
"Employment of Women and Social Change." (In) Stone, Russell A. and Simmons, John (eds.). Change in Tunisia: Studies in the Social Sciences. Albany, New York: State University of New York Press. 1976. pp. 57-72.

Evers, B. and Wagenmans, W.
    Jobs and Value: Social Effects of Export-Oriented
    Industrialization in Tunisia. Tilburg, Netherlands:
    Tilburg Development Research Institute. Research Report
    #9. 1977. 80p.
Jones, Marie T.
    "Public Influence on Government Policy: Family Planning
    and Manpower Development in Tunisia." Ph.D Dissertation:
    Princeton University. Princeton, New Jersey. 1979.
    421p.
Nassif, Hind
    "Women's Economic Roles in Developing Tunisia." Paper
    Presented at the 9th Annual Convention of the Association
    of Arab-American University Graduates/Middle East Studies
    Association. New York City, New York. October 1-3,
    1976.
Sherif-Stanford, Nahla
    "Modernization by Decree: The Role of Tunisian Women in
    Development: Constraints and Prospects." Ph.D
    Dissertation: University of Missouri-Columbia. Columbia,
    Missouri. 1984. 278p.
United Nations Educational, Scientific and Cultural Organ.
    National Inventory on the Place of Women in Tunisian
    Society. Paris: UNESCO. 1976. 80p.

EQUALITY AND LIBERATION

Arntsen, Andrea
    "Women and Social Change in Tunisia." Ph.D Dissertation:
    Georgetown University. Washington, D.C. 1977. 554p.
Halila, Souad
    "From Koranic Law to Civil Law: Emancipation of Tunisian
    Women Since 1956." Feminist Issues. Volume 4 Fall,
    1984. pp. 23-44.
Marei, Wafaa A.
    "Female Emancipation and Changing Political Leadership: A
    Study of Five Arab Countries." Ph.D Dissertation:
    Rutgers University. New Brunswick, New Jersey. 1978.
    364p.
Raccagni, Michelle
    "Origins of Feminism in Egypt and Tunisia." Ph.D
    Dissertation: New York University. New York. 1983.
    327p.
Tessler, Mark A. and Rogers, Janet M. and Schneider, Daniel
R.
    "Women's Emancipation in Tunisia." (In) Beck, Lois and
    Keddie, Nikki R. (eds.). Women in the Muslim World.
    Cambridge, Massachusetts: Harvard University Press.
    1978. pp. 141-158.

FAMILY LIFE

Arntsen, Andrea
   "Women and Social Change in Tunisia." Ph.D Dissertation:
   Georgetown University. Washington, D.C. 1977. 554p.
Auerbach, Liesa S.
   "Women's Domestic Power: A Study of Women's Roles in a
   Tunisian Town." Ph.D Dissertation: University of
   Illinois at Urbana-Champaign. Urbana, Illinois. 1980.
   425p.
Baldwin, C.S.
   "Policies and Realities of Delayed Marriage: The Cases of
   Tunisia, Sri Lanka, Malaysia and Bangladesh." PRB
   Report. Volume 13 #4 1977.
Bowen, Donna L.
   "Attitudes Toward Family and Family Planning in the
   Pre-Saharan Maghreb." Maghreb Review. Volume 8 #1-2
   January-April, 1983. pp. 8-17.
Charrad, Mournira
   "Family Policy and Political Development: A Comparison of
   Tunisia, Algeria and Morocco." Paper Presented at the
   Annual Meeting of the African Studies Association. Paper
   #13. Houston, Texas. 1977.
Evers, B. and Wagenmans, W.
   Jobs and Value: Social Effects of Export-Oriented
   Industrialization in Tunisia. Tilburg, Netherlands:
   Tilburg Development Research Institute. Research Report
   #9. 1977. 80p.
Larson, Barbara K.
   "The Status of Women in a Tunisian Village: Limits to
   Autonomy, Influence and Power." Signs. Volume 9 #3
   September, 1984. pp. 417-433.
Miller, Christine D.
   "The Effects of Socioeconomic Development Upon a Model of
   Women's Fertility Decision Making in a Tunisian
   Community." Ph.D Dissertation: University of
   California-Irvine. Irvine, California. 1985. 336p.
Ouni, Ali B.
   "Divorce in Tunisia, 1963-1972." (In) Huzayyin, S.A. and
   Acsadi, G.T. (eds.). Family and Marriage in Some African
   and Asiatic Countries. Cairo: Cairo Demographic Centre.
   CDC Research Monograph Series #6. 1976. pp. 505-529.
Sherif-Stanford, Nahla
   "Modernization by Decree: The Role of Tunisian Women in
   Development: Constraints and Prospects." Ph.D
   Dissertation: University of Missouri-Columbia. Columbia,
   Missouri. 1984. 278p.
United Nations Educational, Scientific and Cultural Organ.
   National Inventory on the Place of Women in Tunisian
   Society. Paris: UNESCO. 1976. 80p.

TUNISIA

Waltz, S.E.
   "Women's Housing Needs in the Arab Cultural Context of
   Tunisia." Ekistics. Volume 52 #1 January-February,
   1985. pp. 28-34.

FAMILY PLANNING AND CONTRACEPTION

Ahearne, Alice
   "Family Planning in Tunisia: An Educational Program and
   its Implementation." Ph.D Dissertation: Michigan State
   University. East Lansing, Michigan. 1977. 155p.
Ali, Badressalam B. and Ahmad, Mahbub
   "Births Averted in Tunisia by Contraception in Recent
   Years." (In) Cairo Demographic Centre (CDC).
   Determinants of Fertility in Some African and Asian
   Countries. Cairo: CDC. CDC Research Monograph Series
   #10. 1982. pp. 263-299.
Anonymous
   "Birth Control in Tunisia." Population. Volume 33 #1
   January-February, 1978. pp. 194-205.
Baffoun, Alya
   "Research in the Social Sciences on North African Women:
   Problems, Trends and Needs." (In) United Nations
   Educational, Scientific and Cultural Organization.
   Social Science Research and Women in the Arab World.
   Paris: UNESCO. 1984. pp. 41-58.
Bowen, Donna L.
   "Attitudes Toward Family and Family Planning in the
   Pre-Saharan Maghreb." Maghreb Review. Volume 8 #1-2
   January-April, 1983. pp. 8-17.
Brown, K.L.
   "Campaign to Encourage Family Planning in Tunisia and
   Some Responses at the Village Level." Middle Eastern
   Studies. Volume 17 #1 January, 1981. pp. 64-84.
Farid, Samir
   "Fertility Patterns in the Arab Region." International
   Family Planning Perspectives. Volume 10 #4 December,
   1984. pp. 119-125.
Grosse, Scott D.
   "The Politics of Family Planning in the Maghreb."
   Studies in Comparative International Development. Volume
   17 #1 Spring, 1982. pp. 22-48.
Jemai, Yolande and Jemai, Hedi
   Methods of Measuring the Impact of Family Planning
   Programmes on Fertility: The Case of Tunisia. Geneva.
   1976.
Jones, Marie T.
   "Public Influence on Government Policy: Family Planning
   and Manpower Development in Tunisia." Ph.D Dissertation:
   Princeton University. Princeton, New Jersey. 1979.
   421p.

153

Lecomte, Jean and Marcoux, Alain
    "Contraception and Fertility in Morocco and Tunisia."
    Studies in Family Planning. Volume 7 #7 July, 1976.
    pp. 182-187.
Maguire, Elizabeth S. and Way, Ann A. and Ayad, Mohamed
    "The Delivery and Use of Contraceptive Services in Rural
    Tunisia." International Family Planning Perspectives.
    Volume 8 #3 September, 1982. pp. 96-101.
Miller, Christine D.
    "The Effects of Socioeconomic Development Upon a Model of
    Women's Fertility Decision Making in a Tunisian
    Community." Ph.D Dissertation: University of
    California-Irvine. Irvine, California. 1985. 336p.
Nazer, Isam
    "The Tunisian Experience in Legal Abortion."
    International Journal of Gynaecology and Obstetrics.
    Volume 17 #5 March-April, 1980. pp. 488-492.
Tabutin, Dominique
    "Nuptiality and Fertility in Maghreb." (In) Ruzicka,
    L.T. (ed.). Nuptiality and Fertility: Proceedings of a
    Seminar, January 8-11, 1979. Liege, Netherlands: Union
    for the Scientific Study of Population. 1982. pp.
    101-122.
Tessler, Mark A. and Rogers, Janet M. and Schneider, Daniel
R.
    "Tunisian Attitudes Toward Women and Child Rearing."
    (In) Allman, James (ed.). Women's Status and Fertility
    in the Muslim World. New York: Praeger Publishers.
    Praeger Special Studies. 1978. pp. 289-311.
Thorne, Melvin and Montague, Joel
    "Family Planning and the Problems of Development." (In)
    Stone, Russell A. and Simmons, John (eds.). Change in
    Tunisia. Albany, New York: State University of New York
    Press. 1976. pp. 201-215.
United Nations
    "Socio-Economic Development and Fertility Decline: An
    Application of the Eastern Synthesis Approach to World
    Survey Data." New York: United Nations. Department of
    International Economic and Social Affairs. Population
    Division. #IESA/P/WP/88. May, 1985. 115p.

FERTILITY AND INFERTILITY

Ali, Badressalam B. and Ahmad, Mahbub
    "Births Averted in Tunisia by Contraception in Recent
    Years." (In) Cairo Demographic Centre (CDC).
    Determinants of Fertility in Some African and Asian
    Countries. Cairo: CDC. CDC Research Monograph Series
    #10. 1982. pp. 263-299.
Ayad, Mohamed and Jemai, Yolande
    "Fertility Declines in Tunisia: Factors Affecting Recent
    Trends." (In) Allman, James (ed.). Women's Status and

Fertility in the Muslim World. New York: Praeger
Publishers. Praeger Special Studies. 1978. pp.
152-163.
Beaujot, Roderic
"Cultural Constructions of Demographic Inquiry:
Experiences of an Expatriate Researcher in Tunisia."
Culture. Volume 5 #1 1985. pp. 3-15.
Beaujot, Roderic and Bchir, Mongi
Fertility in Tunisia: Traditional and Modern Contrasts.
Washington, D.C.: Population Reference Bureau. August,
1984. 59p.
Farid, Samir
"Fertility Patterns in the Arab Region." International
Family Planning Perspectives. Volume 10 #4 December,
1984. pp. 119-125.
Hyo-Chai, Lee and Hyoung, Cho and Arowolo, Oladele O. and
Popkin, Barry M.
"Recent Empirical Findings on Fertility: Korea, Nigeria,
Tunisia..." Washington, D.C.: Smithsonian Institution.
Interdisciplinary Communications Program. Occasional
Monograph Series #7. December, 1976. 144p.
Jemai, Yolande and Jemai, Hedi
Methods of Measuring the Impact of Family Planning
Programmes on Fertility: The Case of Tunisia. Geneva.
1976.
Lecomte, Jean and Marcoux, Alain
"Contraception and Fertility in Morocco and Tunisia."
Studies in Family Planning. Volume 7 #7 July, 1976.
pp. 182-187.
Miller, Christine D.
"The Effects of Socioeconomic Development Upon a Model of
Women's Fertility Decision Making in a Tunisian
Community." Ph.D Dissertation: University of
California-Irvine. Irvine, California. 1985. 336p.
Tabutin, Dominique
"Nuptiality and Fertility in Maghreb." (In) Ruzicka,
L.T. (ed.). Nuptiality and Fertility: Proceedings of a
Seminar, January 8-11, 1979. Liege, Netherlands: Union
for the Scientific Study of Population. 1982. pp.
101-122.
Tessler, Mark A. and Rogers, Janet M. and Schneider, Daniel
R.
"Tunisian Attitudes Toward Women and Child Rearing."
(In) Allman, James (ed.). Women's Status and Fertility
in the Muslim World. New York: Praeger Publishers.
Praeger Special Studies. 1978. pp. 289-311.
United Nations
Socio-Economic Development and Fertility Decline: An
Application of the Eastern Synthesis Approach to World
Survey Data. New York: United Nations. Department of
International Economic and Social Affairs. Population
Division. #IESA/P/WP/88. May, 1985. 115p.

HEALTH, NUTRITION AND MEDICINE

Ahearne, Alice
"Family Planning in Tunisia: An Educational Program and
its Implementation." Ph.D Dissertation: Michigan State
University. East Lansing, Michigan. 1977. 155p.
Ali, Badressalam B. and Ahmad, Mahbub
"Births Averted in Tunisia by Contraception in Recent
Years." (In) Cairo Demographic Centre (CDC).
Determinants of Fertility in Some African and Asian
Countries. Cairo: CDC. CDC Research Monograph Series
#10. 1982. pp. 263-299.
Almeida Costa, E. and Sanchez de Almeida, M.
"Psychological Factors Affecting Change in Women's Roles
and Status: A Crosscultural Study." International
Journal of Psychology. Volume 18 #1-2 1983. pp. 3-35.
Anonymous
"Birth Control in Tunisia." Population. Volume 33 #1
January-February, 1978. pp. 194-205.
Auerbach, Liesa S.
"Childbirth in Tunisia; Implications of a Decision-Making
Model." Social Science and Medicine. Volume 16 #16
1982. pp. 1499-1506.
Ayad, Mohamed and Jemai, Yolande
"Fertility Declines in Tunisia: Factors Affecting Recent
Trends." (In) Allman, James (ed.). Women's Status and
Fertility in the Muslim World. New York: Praeger
Publishers. Praeger Special Studies. 1978. pp.
152-163.
Beaujot, Roderic and Bchir, Mongi
Fertility in Tunisia: Traditional and Modern Contrasts.
Washington, D.C.: Population Reference Bureau. August,
1984. 59p.
Brown, K.L.
"Campaign to Encourage Family Planning in Tunisia and
Some Responses at the Village Level." Middle Eastern
Studies. Volume 17 #1 January, 1981. pp. 64-84.
Jemai, Yolande and Jemai, Hedi
"Methods of Measuring the Impact of Family Planning
Programmes on Fertility: The Case of Tunisia." Geneva.
1976.
Maguire, Elizabeth S. and Way, Ann A. and Ayad, Mohamed
"The Delivery and Use of Contraceptive Services in Rural
Tunisia." International Family Planning Perspectives.
Volume 8 #3 September, 1982. pp. 96-101.
Miller, Christine D.
"The Effects of Socioeconomic Development Upon a Model of
Women's Fertility Decision Making in a Tunisian
Community." Ph.D Dissertation: University of
California-Irvine. Irvine, California. 1985. 336p.

Nazer, Isam
"The Tunisian Experience in Legal Abortion."
International Journal of Gynaecology and Obstetrics.
Volume 17 #5 March-April, 1980. pp. 488-492.
Stroobant, A.
"A Relation Between Fecundity, Lactation and Infant
Mortality: Initial Results of a Survey Based on a Sample
Representative of the Population of Nabeul." Tunisie
Medicale. Volume 56 1978. pp. 171-178.

LAW AND LEGAL ISSUES

Dorph, K.J.
"Islamic Law in Contemporary North Africa: A Study of the
Laws of Divorce in the Maghreb." Women's Studies
International Forum. Volume 5 #2 1982. pp. 169-182.
Halila, Souad
"From Koranic Law to Civil Law: Emancipation of Tunisian
Women Since 1956." Feminist Issues. Volume 4 Fall,
1984. pp. 23-44.

LITERATURE

Harrow, K.
"Not Such a Long Way, Baby--The Situation of the Women
Today in the Maghreb and its Thematic Representation in
Literature." Current Bibliography on African Affairs.
Volume 9 #3 1976. pp. 228-249.
Van Houwelingen
"Francophone Literature in North Africa." (In) Schipper,
Mineke (ed.). Unheard Words: Women and Literature in
Africa, the Arab World, Asia, the Caribbean, and Latin
America. New York: Alliison and Busby. 1985. pp.
102-113.

MARITAL RELATIONS AND NUPTIALITY

Abed, Bassam K.
"The Social Organization of Production and Reproduction
in Rural Tunisia." Ph.D Dissertation: Pennsylvania State
University. University Park, Pennsylvania. 1979. 263p.
Auerbach, Liesa S.
"Women's Domestic Power: A Study of Women's Roles in a
Tunisian Town." Ph.D Dissertation: University of
Illinois at Urbana-Champaign. Urbana, Illinois. 1980.
425p.
Baldwin, C.S.
"Policies and Realities of Delayed Marriage: The Cases of
Tunisia, Sri Lanka, Malaysia and Bangladesh." PRB
Report. Volume 13 #4 1977.

Beaujot, Roderic and Bchir, Mongi
    Fertility in Tunisia: Traditional and Modern Contrasts.
    Washington, D.C.: Population Reference Bureau. August,
    1984. 59p.
Duza, M. Badrud and Baldwin, C. Stephen
    Nuptiality and Population Policy: An Investigation in
    Tunisia, Sri Lanka and Malaysia. New York: Population
    Council. 1977. 83p.
Farid, Samir
    "Fertility Patterns in the Arab Region." International
    Family Planning Perspectives. Volume 10 #4 December,
    1984. pp. 119-125.
Grosse, Scott D.
    "The Politics of Family Planning in the Maghreb."
    Studies in Comparative International Development. Volume
    17 #1 Spring, 1982. pp. 22-48.
Larson, Barbara K.
    "The Status of Women in a Tunisian Village: Limits to
    Autonomy, Influence and Power." Signs. Volume 9 #3
    September, 1984. pp. 417-433.
Lecomte, Jean and Marcoux, Alain
    "Contraception and Fertility in Morocco and Tunisia."
    Studies in Family Planning. Volume 7 #7 July, 1976.
    pp. 182-187.
Miller, Christine D.
    "The Effects of Socioeconomic Development Upon a Model of
    Women's Fertility Decision Making in a Tunisian
    Community." Ph.D Dissertation: University of
    California-Irvine. Irvine, California. 1985. 336p.
Nassif, Hind
    "Marriage Patterns and Social Change in Rural Tunisia."
    Ph.D Dissertation: Catholic University of America.
    Washington, D.C. 1978. 282p.
Ouni, Ali B.
    "Divorce in Tunisia, 1963-1972." (In) Huzayyin, S.A. and
    Acsadi, G.T. (eds.). Family and Marriage in Some African
    and Asiatic Countries. Cairo: Cairo Demographic Centre.
    CDC Research Monograph Series #6. 1976. pp. 505-529.
Tabutin, Dominique
    "Nuptiality and Fertility in Maghreb." (In) Ruzicka,
    L.T. (ed.). Nuptiality and Fertility: Proceedings of a
    Seminar, January 8-11, 1979. Liege, Netherlands: Union
    for the Scientific Study of Population. 1982. pp.
    101-122.
Tessler, Mark A. and Rogers, Janet M. and Schneider, Daniel
R.
    "Tunisian Attitudes Toward Women and Child Rearing."
    (In) Allman, James (ed.). Women's Status and Fertility
    in the Muslim World. New York: Praeger Publishers.
    Praeger Special Studies. 1978. pp. 289-311.
Thorne, Melvin and Montague, Joel
    "Family Planning and the Problems of Development." (In)
    Stone, Russell A. and Simmons, John (eds.). Change in

Tunisia. Albany, New York: State University of New York
Press. 1976. pp. 201-215.
United Nations
Socio-Economic Development and Fertility Decline: An
Application of the Eastern Synthesis Approach to World
Survey Data. New York: United Nations. Department of
International Economic and Social Affairs. Population
Division. #IESA/P/WP/88. May, 1985. 115p.
Waltz, S.E.
"Women's Housing Needs in the Arab Cultural Context of
Tunisia." Ekistics. Volume 52 #1 January-February,
1985. pp. 28-34.

POLITICS AND GOVERNMENT

Brown, K.L.
"Campaign to Encourage Family Planning in Tunisia and
Some Responses at the Village Level." Middle Eastern
Studies. Volume 17 #1 January, 1981. pp. 64-84.
Charrad, Mournira
"Family Policy and Political Development: A Comparison of
Tunisia, Algeria and Morocco." Paper Presented at the
Annual Meeting of the African Studies Association. Paper
#13. Houston, Texas. 1977.
Jones, Marie T.
"Public Influence on Government Policy: Family Planning
and Manpower Development in Tunisia." Ph.D Dissertation:
Princeton University. Princeton, New Jersey. 1979.
421p.
Marei, Wafaa A.
"Female Emancipation and Changing Political Leadership: A
Study of Five Arab Countries." Ph.D Dissertation:
Rutgers University. New Brunswick, New Jersey. 1978.
364p.
Marshall, Susan E.
"The Power of the Veil: The Politics of Female Status in
North Africa." Ph.D Dissertation: University of
Massachusetts. Amherst, Massachusetts. 1980. 274p.
O'Barr, Jean F.
"A Longitudinal Analysis of Political Efficiency and
Support Among Women and Men in Tunisia." Paper Presented
at the Wellesley Conference on Women and Development.
Wellesley, Massachusetts: Wellsley College. June 2-6,
1976.
Tessler, Mark A.
"Gender and Participant Citizenship in Tunisia." Journal
of Arab Affairs. Volume 2 #1 October, 1982. pp. 47-84.

RELIGION AND WITCHCRAFT

Charrad, Mournira
"Family Policy and Political Development: A Comparison of
Tunisia, Algeria and Morocco." Paper Presented at the
Annual Meeting of the African Studies Association. Paper
#13. Houston, Texas. 1977.
Dorph, K.J.
"Islamic Law in Contemporary North Africa: A Study of the
Laws of Divorce in the Maghreb." Women's Studies
International Forum. Volume 5 #2 1982. pp. 169-182.
Grosse, Scott D.
"The Politics of Family Planning in the Maghreb."
Studies in Comparative International Development. Volume
17 #1 Spring, 1982. pp. 22-48.

RESEARCH

Baffoun, Alya
"Research in the Social Sciences on North African Women:
Problems, Trends and Needs." (In) United Nations
Educational, Scientific and Cultural Organization.
Social Science Research and Women in the Arab World.
Paris: UNESCO. 1984. pp. 41-58.
Beaujot, Roderic
"Cultural Constructions of Demographic Inquiry:
Experiences of an Expatriate Researcher in Tunisia."
Culture. Volume 5 #1 1985. pp. 3-15.
United Nations Educational, Scientific and Cultural Organ.
"Social Science Research and Women in the Arab World."
Paris: UNESCO. 1984. 175p.

SEX ROLES

Abed, Bassam K.
"The Social Organization of Production and Reproduction
in Rural Tunisia." Ph.D Dissertation: Pennsylvania State
University. University Park, Pennsylvania. 1979. 263p.
Almeida Costa, E. and Sanchez de Almeida, M.
"Psychological Factors Affecting Change in Women's Roles
and Status: A Crosscultural Study." International
Journal of Psychology. Volume 18 #1-2 1983. pp. 3-35.
Arntsen, Andrea
"Women and Social Change in Tunisia." Ph.D Dissertation:
Georgetown University. Washington, D.C. 1977. 554p.
Auerbach, Liesa S.
"Women's Domestic Power: A Study of Women's Roles in a
Tunisian Town." Ph.D Dissertation: University of
Illinois at Urbana-Champaign. Urbana, Illinois. 1980.
425p.

Baldwin, C.S.
   "Policies and Realities of Delayed Marriage: The Cases of
   Tunisia, Sri Lanka, Malaysia and Bangladesh." PRB
   Report. Volume 13 #4 1977.
Duza, M. Badrud and Baldwin, C. Stephen
   Nuptiality and Population Policy: An Investigation in
   Tunisia, Sri Lanka and Malaysia. New York: Population
   Council. 1977. 83p.
Harrow, K.
   "Not Such a Long Way, Baby--The Situation of the Women
   Today in the Maghreb and its Thematic Representation in
   Literature." Current Bibliography on African Affairs.
   Volume 9 #3 1976. pp. 228-249.
Larson, Barbara K.
   "The Status of Women in a Tunisian Village: Limits to
   Autonomy, Influence and Power." Signs. Volume 9 #3
   September, 1984. pp. 417-433.
Marshall, Susan E.
   "The Power of the Veil: The Politics of Female Status in
   North Africa." Ph.D Dissertation: University of
   Massachusetts. Amherst, Massachusetts. 1980. 274p.
Marshall, Susan E. and Stokes, Randall G.
   "Tradition and the Veil: Female Status in Tunisia and
   Algeria." Journal of Modern African Studies. Volume 19
   #4 December, 1981. pp. 625-646.
Nassif, Hind
   "Women's Economic Roles in Developing Tunisia." Paper
   Presented at the 9th Annual Convention of the Association
   of Arab-American University Graduates/Middle East Studies
   Association. New York. October 1-3, 1976.
Sherif-Stanford, Nahla
   "Modernization by Decree: The Role of Tunisian Women in
   Development: Constraints and Prospects." Ph.D
   Dissertation: University of Missouri-Columbia. Columbia,
   Missouri. 1984. 278p.
Tessler, Mark A.
   "Gender and Participant Citizenship in Tunisia." Journal
   of Arab Affairs. Volume 2 #1 October, 1982. pp. 47-84.
Tessler, Mark A. and Rogers, Janet M. and Schneider, Daniel
R.
   "Tunisian Attitudes Toward Women and Child Rearing."
   (In) Allman, James (ed.). Women's Status and Fertility
   in the Muslim World. New York: Praeger Publishers.
   Praeger Special Studies. 1978. pp. 289-311.
Tessler, Mark A. and Rogers, Janet M. and Schneider, Daniel
R.
   "Women's Emancipation in Tunisia." (In) Beck, Lois and
   Keddie, Nikki R. (eds.). Women in the Muslim World.
   Cambridge, Massachusetts: Harvard University Press.
   1978. pp. 141-158.
United Nations
   "Socio-Economic Development and Fertility Decline: An
   Application of the Eastern Synthesis Approach to World

Survey Data." New York: United Nations. Department of
International Economic and Social Affairs. Population
Division. #IESA/P/WP/88. May, 1985. 115p.
United Nations Educational, Scientific and Cultural Organ.
"National Inventory on the Place of Women in Tunisian
Society." Paris: UNESCO. 1976. 80p.
Zahra, Nadia
"Baraka, Material, Power and Women in Tunisia." Revue
d'Histoire Maghrebine. #10-#11 January, 1978. pp.
5-21.

STATUS OF WOMEN

Abed, Bassam K.
"The Social Organization of Production and Reproduction
in Rural Tunisia." Ph.D Dissertation: Pennsylvania State
University. University Park, Pennsylvania. 1979. 263p.
Almeida Costa, E. and Sanchez de Almeida, M.
"Psychological Factors Affecting Change in Women's Roles
and Status: A Crosscultural Study." International
Journal of Psychology. Volume 18 #1-2 1983. pp. 3-35.
Durrani, Lorna H.
"Employment of Women and Social Change." (In) Stone,
Russell A. and Simmons, John (eds.). Change in Tunisia:
Studies in the Social Sciences. Albany, New York: State
University of New York Press. 1976. pp. 57-72.
Harrow, K.
"Not Such a Long Way, Baby--The Situation of the Women
Today in the Maghreb and its Thematic Representation in
Literature." Current Bibliography on African Affairs.
Volume 9 #3 1976. pp. 228-249.
Larson, Barbara K.
"The Status of Women in a Tunisian Village: Limits to
Autonomy, Influence and Power." Signs. Volume 9 #3
September, 1984. pp. 417-433.
Marshall, Susan E.
"The Power of the Veil: The Politics of Female Status in
North Africa." Ph.D Dissertation: University of
Massachusetts. Amherst, Massachusetts. 1980. 274p.
Marshall, Susan E. and Stokes, Randall G.
"Tradition and the Veil: Female Status in Tunisia and
Algeria." Journal of Modern African Studies. Volume 19
#4 December, 1981. pp. 625-646.
Tessler, Mark A. and Rogers, Janet M. and Schneider, Daniel
R.
"Tunisian Attitudes Toward Women and Child Rearing."
(In) Allman, James (ed.). Women's Status and Fertility
in the Muslim World. New York: Praeger Publishers.
Praeger Special Studies. 1978. pp. 289-311.

Tessler, Mark A. and Rogers, Janet M. and Schneider, Daniel R.
"Women's Emancipation in Tunisia." (In) Beck, Lois and Keddie, Nikki R. (eds.). Women in the Muslim World. Cambridge, Massachusetts: Harvard University Press. 1978. pp. 141-158.
United Nations Educational, Scientific and Cultural Organ.
"National Inventory on the Place of Women in Tunisian Society." Paris: UNESCO. 1976. 80p.
Wolff, Ursula
"Women in Africa--Maghribian Society in Transition." Africa Report. Volume 22 #1 January-February, 1977. pp. 41-43.

WOMEN AND THEIR CHILDREN

Tessler, Mark A. and Rogers, Janet M. and Schneider, Daniel R.
"Tunisian Attitudes Toward Women and Child Rearing." (In) Allman, James (ed.). Women's Status and Fertility in the Muslim World. New York: Praeger Publishers. Praeger Special Studies. 1978. pp. 289-311.

Western Sahara

Anonymous
    "West Sahara: Women Fight for Their Freedom." IDOC
    Bulletin. #50-#51 December, 1976.
Balaquer, Soledad
    "Women in Liberation Struggles--Western Sahara." ISIS
    International Bulletin. April, 1977. pp. 11-13.

General Subject Bibliography— Western Africa

AGRICULTURE

Cleveland, David
"Fertility and the Value of Children in Subsistence Agriculture: Savanna West Africa." Paper Presented at the Annual Meeting of the American Anthropological Association. Cincinnati, Ohio. November, 1979.

Cohen, Ronald and Knipp, Maggie
"Women and Change in West Africa: A Synthesis." Paper Presented at the Annual Meeting of the African Studies Association. Paper #16. Philadelphia, Pennsylvania. 1980.

Dulansey, Maryanne L.
Women in Development Program Concerns in Francophone Sahel: Report of a Workshop, Bobo-Dioulasso, Upper Volta, June 5-7, 1979. Washington, D.C.: U.S. Department of State. U.S. Agency for International Development. 1979. 11p.

Fapohunda, Eleanor R.
"Female and Male Work Profiles." (In) Oppong, Christine (ed.). Female and Male in West Africa. London: George Allen and Unwin. 1983. pp. 32-53.

Guyer, Jane I.
Women's Work in the Food Economy of the Cocoa Belt: A Comparison. Brookline, Massachusetts: Boston University. African Studies Center. Working Paper #7. 1978. 34p.

International Labour Office (ILO)
Improved Village Technology for Women's Activities: A Manual for West Africa. London: ILO. 1985.

Kizerbo, Joseph
"Women and the Energy Crisis in the Sahel Africa. From the Seminar on Fuel and Energy Development for African Women in Rural Areas, Bamako, Mali, December, 1980. Unasylva. Volume 33 #133 1981. pp. 5-10.

Okali, Christine
"The Changing Economic Position of Women in Rural Communities in West Africa." Africana Marburgensia. Volume 12 #1/2 1979. pp. 59-93.

Roboff, Farron V. and Renwick, Hilary L.
    "The Changing Role of Women in the Development of the
    Sahel." Paper Presented to the Annual Meeting of the
    African Studies Association. Paper #92. Boston,
    Massachusetts. 1976. 12p.
Spencer, Dunstan S.C.
    Women in a Developing Economy: A West African Case Study.
    East Lansing, Michigan: Michigan State University. 1979.
    134p.
U.S. Agency for International Development (U.S. AID)
    Training Women in the Sahel. Washington, D.C.: U.S.
    Department of State. U.S. AID. Office of Women in
    Development. 1978. 47p.
U.S. Agency for International Development (U.S. AID)
    Examples of Women in Development Programs in Sahel
    Francophone West Africa. Washington, D.C.: U.S.
    Department of State. U.S. AID. Office of Sahel and
    Francophone West Africa, Bureau for Africa. 1979. 27p.
United Nations Economic Commission for Africa (UNECA)
    "Women in African Development." Paper Presented at the
    ACOSCA Bilingual Regional Seminar on Increasing Women's
    Access to Credit Unions in West Africa, Dakar, Senegal,
    March, 1981. Addis Ababa, Ethiopia: UNECA. 1981.

ARTS

Tonkin, Elizabeth
    "Women Excluded? Masking and Masquerading in West
    Africa." (In) Holden, P. (ed.). Women's Religious
    Experience. Totowa, New Jersey: Barnes and Noble. 1983.
    pp. 163-174.

BIBLIOGRAPHIES

Geletkanycz, Christine and Egan, Susan
    Literature Review: The Practice of Female Circumcision.
    Washington, D.C.: U.S. Department of Health, Education
    and Welfare. Office of International Health. Mimeo.
    1979.
Nwanosike, Eugene O.
    Women and Development: A Select Bibliography: A Select
    and Partially Annotated Bibliography. Buea, Cameroon:
    Regional Pan-African Institute for Development/West
    Africa. Bibliographic Series #10. 1980. 63p.

CULTURAL ROLES

Abdalla, Raqiya
    Sisters in Affliction: Circumcision and Infibulation of
    Women in Africa. London: Zed Press. 1982. 122p.
Adepoju, Aderanti
    "Patterns of Migration by Sex." (In) Oppong, Christine

(ed.). Female and Male in West Africa. London: George
Allen and Unwin. 1983. pp. 54-66.
Bates, C.J. and Whitehead, Roger G.
"The Effect of Vitamin C Supplementation on Lactating
Women in Keneba, a West African Rural Community."
International Journal of Vitamin Nutrition Research.
Volume 53 #1 1982. pp. 68-76.
Bates, C.J. and Prentice, Andrew M. and Prentice, Ann and
Whitehead, Roger G.
"Vitamin C Supplementation of Lactating Women in Keneba:
A West African Rural Community." Proceedings of the
Nutrition Society. Volume 41 #3 1982. pp. 124A.
Bisilliat, Jeanne
"The Feminine Sphere in the Institutions of
Songhay-Zarma." (In) Oppong, Christine (ed.). Female
and Male in West Africa. London: George Allen and Unwin.
1983. pp. 99-106.
Campbell, Penelope
"Presbyterian West African Missions: Women as Converts
and Agents of Social Change." Journal of Presbyterian
History. Volume 56 #2 Summer, 1978. pp. 121-132.
Cleveland, David
"Fertility and the Value of Children in Subsistence
Agriculture: Savanna West Africa." Paper Presented at
the Annual Meeting of the American Anthropological
Association. Cincinnati, Ohio. November, 1979.
Davis, W.T.
"Rome and the Ordination of Women." West African
Religion. Volume 17 #2 1978. pp. 3-8.
Di Domenico, Catherine M. and Asuni, Judy and Scott,
Jacqueline
"Family Welfare and Development in Africa." (In)
International Planned Parenthood Federation (IPPF).
Proceedings of the IPPF Africa Regional Conference,
University of Ibadan. London: IPPF. 1976. pp. 283-284.
Dulansey, Maryanne L.
Women in Development Program Concerns in Francophone
Sahel: Report of a Workshop, Bobo-Dioulasso, Upper
Volta, June 5-7, 1979. Washington, D.C.: U.S. Department
of State. U.S. Agency for International Development.
1979. 11p.
Elwert, Georg
"Conflicts Inside and Outside the Household: A West
African Case Study." (In) Smith, Joan (ed.). Households
and the World Economy. Beverly Hills, California: Sage.
1984. pp. 272-296.
Erasto, Muga
Studies in Prostitution: East, West and South Africa,
Zaire and Nevada. Nairobi: Kenya Literature Bureau.
1980.
Fortes, Meyer
"Parenthood, Marriage and Fertility in West Africa."

Journal of Development Studies. Volume 14 #4 July, 1978. pp. 121-149.

Fortes, Meyer
"Family, Marriage and Fertility in West Africa." (In) Oppong, C. and Adaba, G. and Bekombo-Priso, M. and Mogey, J. (eds.). Marriage, Fertility and Parenthood in West Africa. Canberra, Australia: Australian National University Press. 1978. pp. 17-54.

Fraker, Anne and Harrell-Bond, Barbara
"Feminine Influence." West Africa. December 17, 1979. pp. 2182-2186.

Geletkanycz, Christine and Egan, Susan
Literature Review: The Practice of Female Circumcision. Washington, D.C.: U.S. Department of Health, Education and Welfare. Office of International Health. Mimeo. 1979.

Goody, Esther N.
"Some Theoretical and Empirical Aspects of Parenthood in West Africa." (In) Oppong, C. and Adaba, G. and Bekombo-Priso, M. and Mogey, J. (eds.). Marriage, Fertility and Parenthood in West Africa. Canberra, Australia: Australian National University. Department of Demography. Volume One. 1978. pp. 227-272.

Goody, Esther N.
"Parental Strategies: Calculation or Sentiment: Fostering Practices Among West Africans." (In) Medick, Hans and Sabean, David W. (eds.). Interest and Emotion: Essays on the Study of Family and Kinship. Cambridge, New York: Cambridge University Press. 1984. pp. 266-277.

Grandmaison, C. LeCour
"Economic Contracts Between Married People in the West African Area." L'Homme. Volume 19 #3/4 July-December, 1979. pp. 159-170.

Guyer, Jane I.
Women's Work in the Food Economy of the Cocoa Belt: A Comparison. Brookline, Massachusetts: Boston University. African Studies Center. Working Paper #7. 1978. 34p.

Hosken, Fran P.
"Women and Health: Genital And Sexual Mutilation of Females." International Journal of Women's Studies. Volume 3 #3 May-June, 1980. pp. 300-316.

Hosken, Fran P.
"The Violence of Power: The Genital Mutilation of Females." Heresies. Volume 6 #2 Summer, 1978. pp. 28-36.

Hosken, Fran P.
"Female Circumcision in Africa." Victimology. Volume 2 #3/4 1977. pp. 487-498.

Hosken, Fran P.
"Genital Mutilation of Women in Africa." Munger Africana Library Notes. #36 October, 1976. 21p.

Hosken, Fran P.
"Towards an Epidemiology of Genital Mutilation of Females

in Africa." Paper Presented at the Annual Meeting of the
African Studies Association. Paper #43. Baltimore,
Maryland. 1978. 20p.

Hosken, Fran P.
The Hosken Report: Genital and Sexual Mutilation of
Females. Lexington, Massachusetts: Women's International
Network News. 1982. 327p.

Hosken, Fran P.
Female Sexual Mutilations: The Facts and Proposals for
Action. Lexington, Massachusetts: Women's International
Network News. 1980. 102p.

Hosken, Fran P.
"Female Genital Mutilation in the World Today: A Global
Review." International Journal of Health Services.
Volume 11 #3 1981. pp. 415-430.

Hosken, Fran P.
"Female Circumcision and Fertility in Africa." Women and
Health. Volume 1 #6 November-December, 1976. pp. 3-11.

Hosken, Fran P.
"The Epidemiology of Female Genital Mutilation."
Tropical Doctor. July, 1978. pp. 150-156.

Hosken, Fran P.
"Women and Health in East and West Africa: Family
Planning and Female Cicumcision." Paper Presented at the
Seminar on Traditional Practices Affecting the Health of
Women and Children. World Conference of the United
Nations Decade for Women. New York: United Nations.
Copenhagen, Denmark. July 14-30, 1980.

Hosken, Fran P.
"Women and Health in East and West Africa: Family
Planning and Female Circumcision." Paper Presented at
the Seminar on Traditional Practices Affecting the Health
of Women and Children: Female Circumcision, Childhood
Marriage, Nutritional Taboos, etc. Alexandria, Egypt:
World Health Organization. Eastern Mediterranean
Regional Office. Khartoum, Sudan. February 10-15, 1979.

Hosken, Fran P.
"Female Circumcision in the World of Today: A Global
Review." Paper Presented at the Seminar on Traditional
Practices Affecting the Health of Women and Children.
World Conference of the United Nations Decade for Women.
New York: United Nations. Copenhagen, Denmark. July
14-30, 1980.

Hosken, Fran P.
"Female Circumcision in the World of Today: A Global
View." Paper Presented at the Seminar on Traditional
Practices Affecting the Health of Women and Children:
Female Circumcision, Childhood Marriage, Nutritional
Taboos, etc. Alexandria, Egypt: World Health
Organization. Eastern Mediterranean Regional Office.
Khartoum, Sudan. February 10-15, 1979.

Huelsman, Ben R.
"An Anthropological View of Clitoral and Other Female

Genital Mutilations." (In) Lowery, T.P. and Lowery, T.S.
(eds.). The Clitoris. St. Louis, Missouri: Warren H.
Green. 1976. pp. 111-161.

Huzayyin, S.A.
"Marriage and Remarriage in Islam." (In) Dupaquier, J.
and Helin, E. and Laslett, P. and Livi-Bacci, M. (eds.).
Marriage and Remarriage in Populations of the Past. New
York: Academic Press. Population and Social Structure:
Advances in Historical Demography Series. 1981. pp.
95-109.

Igbinovia, Patrick E.
"Prostitution in Black Africa." International Journal of
Women's Studies. Volume 7 #5 November-December, 1984.
pp. 430-449.

International Development Research Centre (IDRC)
Nutritional Status of the Rural Population of the Sahel:
Report of a Working Group, Paris, France, April 28-29,
1980. Ottawa, Canada: IDRC. 1981. 92p.

Jett, Joyce
The Role of Traditional Midwives in the Modern Health
Sector in West and Central Africa. Washington, D.C.:
U.S. Department of State. U.S. Agency for International
Development. January, 1977. 150p.

Jett, Joyce
The Role of Traditional Midwives in the Modern Health
Sector in West and Central Africa. Washington, D.C.:
U.S. Department of State. U.S. Agency for International
Development. January, 1977. 150p.

Karanja, Wambui Wa
"Women and Work: A Study of Female and Male Attitudes in
the Modern Sector of an African Metropolis." (In) Ware,
Helen (ed.). Women, Education and Modernization of the
Family in West Africa. Canberra, Australia: Australian
National University. Department of Demography. Changing
African Family Project Series. Monograph #7. 1978.

Kizerbo, Joseph
"Women and the Energy Crisis in the Sahel Africa. From
the Seminar on Fuel and Energy Development for African
Women in Rural Areas, Bamako, Mali, December, 1980."
Unasylva. Volume 33 #133 1981. pp. 5-10.

Leis, Nancy B.
"West African Women and the Colonial Experience."
Western Canadian Journal of Anthropology. Volume 6 #3
1976. pp. 123-132.

Little, Kenneth L.
"Women's Strategies in Modern Marriage in Anglophone West
Africa: An Ideological and Sociological Appraisal."
Journal of Comparative Family Studies. Volume 8 #3
Autumn, 1977. pp. 341-356.

Little, Kenneth L.
"Women's Strategies in Modern Marriage in Anglophone West
Africa: An Ideological and Sociological Appraisal." (In)

Kurian, George (ed.). Cross-Cultural Perspectives of
Mate Selection and Marriage. Westport, Connecticut:
Greenwood Press. Contributions in Family Studies #3.
1979. pp. 202-217.
Mahran, M.
"Medical Dangers of Female Circumcision." International
Planned Parenthood Federation (IPPF) Medical Bulletin.
Volume 15 #2 April, 1981.
McLean, Scilla
"Female Genital Mutilation." ISIS Women's International
Bulletin. #25 1982. pp. 26-32.
McLean, Scilla and Graham, Stella E.
Female Circumcision, Excision and Infibulation: The Fact
and Proposals for Change. London: Minority Rights Group.
Report #47. Second Revised Edition. 1985. 21p.
Moen, Elizabeth W.
Genital Mutilation: Everywoman's Problem. East Lansing,
Michigan: Michigan State University. Office of Women in
International Development. Working Paper #22. April,
1983.
Mott, Frank L. and Mott, Susan H.
Household Fertility Decision-Making in a West African
Setting: Do Male and Female Surveys Lead to Similar
Interpretations? Worthington, Ohio: Ohio State
University. Center for Human Resource Research. 1984.
Mukhtar, Behiza
"A Question of Our Children's Bodies: The Medical Injury
Caused to a Girl by Circumcision." Paper Presented at
the Conference on Islam and Family Planning. Sponsored
by the International Planned Parenthood Federation.
Banjul, Gambia. October 21-24, 1979. 7p.
Okali, Christine
"The Changing Economic Position of Women in Rural
Communities in West Africa." Africana Marburgensia.
Volume 12 #1/2 1979. pp. 59-93.
Okediji, Frances Olu
"The Limitations of Family Planning Programmes in the
Developing Nations." (In) Oppong, C. and Adaba, G. and
Bekombo-Priso, M. and Mogey, J. (eds.). Marriage,
Fertility and Parenthood in West Africa. Canberra,
Australia: Australian National University. Department of
Demography. Volume Two. 1978. pp. 617-639.
Okediji, Peter A.
"The Status of African Women in Family Planning." (In)
Oppong, C. and Adaba, G. and Bekombo-Priso, M. and Mogey,
J. (eds.). Marriage, Fertility and Parenthood in West
Africa. Canberra, Australia: Australian National
University. Department of Demography. Volume Two.
1978. pp. 673-676.
Oppong, Christine and Adaba, Gemma and Bekomba-Priso, Manga
and Mogey, J. (eds.)
Marriage, Fertility and Parenthood in West Africa.
Canberra, Australia: Australian National University.

Department of Demography. Changing African Family
Project. Monograph #4. Two Volumes. 1978. 848p.
Oppong, Christine (ed.)
   Female and Male in West Africa. Boston: George Allen and
   Unwin. 1983. 402p.
Paraiso, Maitre A.
   "Family Planning Legislation in the Francophone Countries
   of Africa." (In) International Planned Parenthood
   Federation (IPPF). Proceedings of the IPPF Africa
   Regional Conference. London: IPPF. 1977. pp. 247-255.
Reyna, Stephen P.
   "Economics and Fertility: Waiting for the Demographic
   Transition in the Dry Zone of Francophone West Africa."
   (In) Caldwell, John C. (ed.). The Persistence of High
   Fertility: Population Prospects in the Third World.
   Canberra, Australia: Australian National University.
   Department of Demography. Volume One. 1977. pp.
   393-426.
Roboff, Farron V. and Renwick, Hilary L.
   "The Changing Role of Women in the Development of the
   Sahel." Paper Presented to the Annual Meeting of the
   African Studies Association. Paper #92. Boston,
   Massachusetts. 1976. 12p.
Sanderson, Lilian P.
   Against the Mutilation of Women: The Struggle Against
   Unnecessary Suffering. London: Ithaca Press. 1981.
   117p.
Shaalan, Mohammed
   "Clitoris Envy: A Psychodynamic Construct Instrumental in
   Female Circumcision." Paper Presented at the Seminar on
   Traditional Practices Affecting the Health of Women and
   Children. World Conference of the United Nations Decade
   for Women. New York: United Nations. Copenhagen,
   Denmark. July 14-30, 1980.
Shaalan, Mohammed
   "Clitoris Envy: A Psychdynamic Construct Instrumental in
   Female Circumcision." Paper Presented at the Seminar on
   Traditional Practices Affecting the Health of Women and
   Children: Female Circumcision, Childhood Marriage,
   Nutritional Taboos, etc. Alexandria, Egypt: World Health
   Organization. Eastern Mediterranean Regional Office.
   Khartoum, Sudan. February 10-15, 1979.
Sindzingre, N.
   "Plus and Minus--Concerning Female Circumcision."
   Cahiers d'Etudes Africaines. Volume 17 #1 1977. pp.
   65-76.
Soyinka, Susan
   "Family and Fertility in the West African Novel." (In)
   Caldwell, John C. (ed.). The Persistence of High
   Fertility: Population Prospects in the Third World.
   Canberra, Australia: Australian National University.
   Department of Demography. Volume One. 1977. pp.
   427-450.

Strodtbeck, Fred L.
   "Intimacy in Conjugal Interaction and the Capacity to
   Plan." (In) Oppong, C. and Adaba, G. and Bekombo-Priso,
   M. and Mogey, J. (eds.). Marriage, Fertility and
   Parenthood in West Africa. Canberra, Australia:
   Australian National University. Department of
   Demography. Volume Two. 1978. pp. 747-763.
Sudarkasa, Niara
   The Effects of 20th Century Social Change, Especially of
   Migration, on Women of West Africa. Tucson, Arizona:
   University of Arizona. Proceedings of the West Africa
   Conference. 1976. pp. 102-109.
Sudarkasa, Niara
   "Female Employment and Family Organization in West
   Africa." (In) Steady, Filomina C. (ed.). The Black
   Woman Cross-Culturally. Cambridge, Massachusetts:
   Schenkman Publishing. 1981. pp. 49-64.
Taba, A.H.
   "Female Circumcision." World Health. May, 1979. pp.
   8-13.
Taba, A.H.
   "Female Circumcision." (In) World Health Organization.
   Traditional Practices Affecting the Health of Women and
   Children: Female Circumcision, Childhood Marriage,
   Nutritional Taboos, etc. Report of a Seminar, Khartoum,
   Sudan, February 10-15, 1979. Alexandria, Egypt: WHO/EMRO
   Technical Publication #2. 1979. pp. 43-52.
Thiam, Awa
   "Women's Fight for the Abolition of Sexual Mutilation."
   International Social Science Journal. Volume 35 #4 1983.
   pp. 747-756.
Tonkin, Elizabeth
   "Women Excluded? Masking and Masquerading in West
   Africa." (In) Holden, P. (ed.). Women's Religious
   Experience. Totowa, New Jersey: Barnes and Noble. 1983.
   pp. 163-174.
U.S. Agency for International Development (U.S. AID)
   Non-Formal Education--Women in Sahel. Washington, D.C.:
   U.S. Deapartment of State. U.S. AID. 1978. 23p.
Wallace, Karen S.
   "Women and Identity: A Black Francophone Female
   Perspective." Sage: A Scholarly Journal on Black Women.
   Volume 2 #1 1985. pp. 19-23.
Ware, Helen
   "Security in the City: The Role of the Family in Urban
   West Africa." (In) Ruzicka, Lado T. (ed.). The Economic
   and Social Supports for High Fertility: Proceedings of
   the Conference Held in Canberra, November 16-18, 1976.
   Canberra, Australia: Australian National University.
   Development Studies Center. 1977. pp. 385-408.
Ware, Helen
   Women, Education and Modernization of the Family in West
   Africa. Canberra, Australia: Australian National

University. Department of Demography. Changing African
Family Project Series. Monograph #7. 1981. 178p.
Ware, Helen
"Female and Male Life-Cycles." (In) Oppong, Christine
(ed.). Female and Male in West Africa. London: George
Allen and Unwin. 1983. pp. 6-31.
Ware, Helen
"Motivations for the Use of Birth Control: Evidence From
West Africa." Demography. Volume 13 #4 November, 1976.
pp. 479-494.

DEVELOPMENT AND TECHNOLOGY

Cohen, Ronald and Knipp, Maggie
"Women and Change in West Africa: A Synthesis." Paper
Presented at the Annual Meeting of the African Studies
Association. Paper #16. Philadelphia, Pennsylvania.
1980.
DeLancey, Virginia H.
"The Role of Credit Unions in Development for West
African Women." Paper Presented at the Annual Meeting of
the African Studies Association. Paper #29.
Bloomington, Indiana. October 21-24, 1981.
Di Domenico, Catherine M. and Asuni, Judy and Scott,
Jacqueline
"Family Welfare and Development in Africa." (In)
International Planned Parenthood Federation (IPPF).
Proceedings of the IPPF Africa Regional Conference,
University of Ibadan. London: IPPF. 1976. pp. 283-284.
Dulansey, Maryanne L.
Women in Development Program Concerns in Francophone
Sahel: Report of a Workshop, Bobo-Dioulasso, Upper
Volta, June 5-7, 1979. Washington, D.C.: U.S. Department
of State. U.S. Agency for International Development.
1979. 11p.
Fapohunda, Eleanor R.
"Female and Male Work Profiles." (In) Oppong, Christine
(ed.). Female and Male in West Africa. London: George
Allen and Unwin. 1983. pp. 32-53.
Fraker, Anne and Harrell-Bond, Barbara
"Feminine Influence." West Africa. December 17, 1979.
pp. 2182-2186.
Franke, R.
"Mode of Production and Population Patterns: Policy
Implications for West African Development."
International Journal of Health Services. Volume 13
1981. pp. 361-387.
International Labour Office (ILO)
Improved Village Technology for Women's Activities: A
Manual for West Africa. London: ILO. 1985.
Karanja, Wambui Wa
"Women and Work: A Study of Female and Male Attitudes in
the Modern Sector of an African Metropolis." (In) Ware,

Helen (ed.). Women, Education and Modernization of the
Family in West Africa. Canberra, Australia: Australian
National University. Department of Demography. Changing
African Family Project Series. Monograph #7. 1978.
Kizerbo, Joseph
"Women and the Energy Crisis in the Sahel Africa. From
the Seminar on Fuel and Energy Development for African
Women in Rural Areas, Bamako, Mali, December, 1980."
Unasylva. Volume 33 #133 1981. pp. 5-10.
Nwanosike, Eugene O.
Women and Development: A Select Bibliography: A Select
and Partially Annotated Bibliography. Buea, Cameroon:
Regional Pan-African Institute for Development/West
Africa. Bibliographic Series #10. 1980. 63p.
Reno, Barbara M.
Increasing Women's Credit Through Credit Unions in West
Africa. Bilingual Seminar. Nairobi: Africa Co-Operative
Savings and Credit Association. March 2-6, 1981. 43p.
Roboff, Farron V. and Renwick, Hilary L.
"The Changing Role of Women in the Development of the
Sahel." Paper Presented to the Annual Meeting of the
African Studies Association. Paper #92. Boston,
Massachusetts. 1976. 12p.
Spencer, Dunstan S.C.
Women in a Developing Economy: A West African Case Study.
East Lansing, Michigan: Michigan State University. 1979.
134p.
U.S. Agency for International Development (U.S. AID)
Training Women in the Sahel. Washington, D.C.: U.S.
Department of State. U.S. AID. Office of Women in
Development. 1978. 47p.
U.S. Agency for International Development (U.S. AID)
Examples of Women in Development Programs in Sahel
Francophone West Africa. Washington, D.C.: U.S.
Department of State. U.S. AID. Office of Sahel and
Francophone West Africa, Bureau for Africa. 1979. 27p.
United Nations Economic Commission for Africa (UNECA)
"Women in African Development." Paper Presented at the
ACOSCA Bilingual Regional Seminar on Increasing Women's
Access to Credit Unions in West Africa, Dakar, Senegal,
March, 1981. Addis Ababa, Ethiopia: UNECA. 1981.

ECONOMICS

Cohen, Ronald and Knipp, Maggie
"Women and Change in West Africa: A Synthesis." Paper
Presented at the Annual Meeting of the African Studies
Association. Paper #16. Philadelphia, Pennsylvania.
1980.
DeLancey, Virginia H.
"The Role of Credit Unions in Development for West
African Women." Paper Presented at the Annual Meeting of

the African Studies Association. Paper #29.
Bloomington, Indiana. October 21-24, 1981.

Dulansey, Maryanne L.
Women in Development Program Concerns in Francophone
Sahel: Report of a Workshop, Bobo-Dioulasso, Upper
Volta, June 5-7, 1979. Washington, D.C.: U.S. Department
of State. U.S. Agency for International Development.
1979. 11p.

Franke, R.
"Mode of Production and Population Patterns: Policy
Implications for West African Development."
International Journal of Health Services. Volume 13
1981. pp. 361-387.

Grandmaison, C. LeCour
"Economic Contracts Between Married People in the West
African Area." L'Homme. Volume 19 #3/4 July-December,
1979. pp. 159-170.

Guyer, Jane I.
Women's Work in the Food Economy of the Cocoa Belt: A
Comparison. Brookline, Massachusetts: Boston University.
African Studies Center. Working Paper #7. 1978. 34p.

Okali, Christine
"The Changing Economic Position of Women in Rural
Communities in West Africa." Africana Marburgensia.
Volume 12 #1/2 1979. pp. 59-93.

Reno, Barbara M.
Increasing Women's Credit Through Credit Unions in West
Africa. Bilingual Seminar. Nairobi: Africa Co-Operative
Savings and Credit Association. March 2-6, 1981. 43p.

Reyna, Stephen P.
"Economics and Fertility: Waiting for the Demographic
Transition in the Dry Zone of Francophone West Africa."
(In) Caldwell, John C. (ed.). The Persistence of High
Fertility: Population Prospects in the Third World.
Canberra, Australia: Australian National University.
Department of Demography. Volume One. 1977. pp.
393-426.

Roboff, Farron V. and Renwick, Hilary L.
"The Changing Role of Women in the Development of the
Sahel." Paper Presented to the Annual Meeting of the
African Studies Association. Paper #92. Boston,
Massachusetts. 1976. 12p.

Spencer, Dunstan S.C.
Women in a Developing Economy: A West African Case Study.
East Lansing, Michigan: Michigan State University. 1979.
134p.

U.S. Agency for International Development (U.S. AID)
Examples of Women in Development Programs in Sahel
Francophone West Africa. Washington, D.C.: U.S.
Department of State. U.S. AID. Office of Sahel and
Francophone West Africa, Bureau for Africa. 1979. 27p.

United Nations Economic Commission for Africa (UNECA)
     "Women in African Development." Paper Presented at the
     ACOSCA Bilingual Regional Seminar on Increasing Women's
     Access to Credit Unions in West Africa, Dakar, Senegal,
     March, 1981. Addis Ababa, Ethiopia: UNECA. 1981.
Ware, Helen
     "Motivations for the Use of Birth Control: Evidence From
     West Africa." Demography. Volume 13 #4 November, 1976.
     pp. 479-494.

EDUCATION AND TRAINING

Caldwell, Pat and Caldwell, John C.
     "Population Change and Development in the ECWA Region."
     (In) Cairo Demographic Centre (CDC). Aspects of
     Population Change and Development in Some African and
     Asian Countries. Cairo: CDC. CDC Research Monograph
     Series #9. 1984. pp. 43-56.
Cohen, Ronald and Knipp, Maggie
     "Women and Change in West Africa: A Synthesis." Paper
     Presented at the Annual Meeting of the African Studies
     Association. Paper #16. Philadelphia, Pennsylvania.
     1980.
International Labour Office (ILO)
     Improved Village Technology for Women's Activities: A
     Manual for West Africa. London: ILO. 1985.
U.S. Agency for International Development (U.S. AID)
     Non-Formal Education--Women in Sahel. Washington, D.C.:
     U.S. Department of State. U.S. AID. 1978. 23p.
U.S. Agency for International Development (U.S. AID)
     Training Women in the Sahel. Washington, D.C.: U.S.
     Department of State. U.S. AID. Office of Women in
     Development. 1978. 47p.
Ware, Helen
     Women, Education and Modernization of the Family in West
     Africa. Canberra, Australia: Australian National
     University. Department of Demography. Changing African
     Family Project Series. Monograph #7. 1981. 178p.

EMPLOYMENT AND LABOR

Adepoju, Aderanti
     "Patterns of Migration by Sex." (In) Oppong, Christine
     (ed.). Female and Male in West Africa. London: George
     Allen and Unwin. 1983. pp. 54-66.
Caldwell, Pat and Caldwell, John C.
     "Population Change and Development in the ECWA Region."
     (In) Cairo Demographic Centre (CDC). Aspects of
     Population Change and Development in Some African and

Asian Countries. Cairo: CDC. CDC Research Monograph
Series #9. 1984. pp. 43-56.
DeLancey, Virginia H.
"The Role of Credit Unions in Development for West
African Women." Paper Presented at the Annual Meeting of
the African Studies Association. Paper #29. Bloomington,
Indiana. October 21-24, 1981.
Fapohunda, Eleanor R.
"Female and Male Work Profiles." (In) Oppong, Christine
(ed.). Female and Male in West Africa. London: George
Allen and Unwin. 1983. pp. 32-53.
Franke, R.
"Mode of Production and Population Patterns: Policy
Implications for West African Development."
International Journal of Health Services. Volume 13
1981. pp. 361-387.
Guyer, Jane I.
Women's Work in the Food Economy of the Cocoa Belt: A
Comparison. Brookline, Massachusetts: Boston University.
African Studies Center. Working Paper #7. 1978. 34p.
Igbinovia, Patrick E.
"Prostitution in Black Africa." International Journal of
Women's Studies. Volume 7 #5 November-December, 1984.
pp. 430-449.
Karanja, Wambui Wa
"Women and Work: A Study of Female and Male Attitudes in
the Modern Sector of an African Metropolis." (In) Ware,
Helen (ed.). Women, Education and Modernization of the
Family in West Africa. Canberra, Australia: Australian
National University. Department of Demography. Changing
African Family Project Series. Monograph #7. 1978.
Spencer, Dunstan S.C.
Women in a Developing Economy: A West African Case Study.
East Lansing, Michigan: Michigan State University. 1979.
134p.
Sudarkasa, Niara
The Effects of 20th Century Social Change, Especially of
Migration, on Women of West Africa. Tucson, Arizona:
University of Arizona. Proceedings of the West Africa
Conference. 1976. pp. 102-109.
Sudarkasa, Niara
"Female Employment and Family Organization in West
Africa." (In) Steady, Filomina C. (ed.). The Black
Woman Cross-Culturally. Cambridge, Massachusetts:
Schenkman Publishing. 1981. pp. 49-64.

FAMILY LIFE

Bisilliat, Jeanne
"The Feminine Sphere in the Institutions of
Songhay-Zarma." (In) Oppong, Christine (ed.). Female
and Male in West Africa. London: George Allen and Unwin.
1983. pp. 99-106.

Caldwell, Pat and Caldwell, John C.
    "Population Change and Development in the ECWA Region."
    (In) Cairo Demographic Centre (CDC). Aspects of
    Population Change and Development in Some African and
    Asian Countries. Cairo: CDC. CDC Research Monograph
    Series #9. 1984. pp. 43-56.
Di Domenico, Catherine M. and Asuni, Judy and Scott,
Jacqueline
    "Family Welfare and Development in Africa." (In)
    International Planned Parenthood Federation (IPPF).
    Proceedings of the IPPF Africa Regional Conference,
    University of Ibadan. London: IPPF. 1976. pp. 283-284.
Elwert, Georg
    "Conflicts Inside and Outside the Household: A West
    African Case Study." (In) Smith, Joan (ed.). Households
    and the World Economy. Beverly Hills, California: Sage.
    1984. pp. 272-296.
Fortes, Meyer
    "Parenthood, Marriage and Fertility in West Africa."
    Journal of Development Studies. Volume 14 #4 July,
    1978. pp. 121-149.
Fortes, Meyer
    "Family, Marriage and Fertility in West Africa." (In)
    Oppong, C. and Adaba, G. and Bekombo-Priso, M. and Mogey,
    J. (eds.). Marriage, Fertility and Parenthood in West
    Africa. Canberra, Australia: Australian National
    University Press. 1978. pp. 17-54.
Goody, Esther N.
    "Some Theoretical and Empirical Aspects of Parenthood in
    West Africa." (In) Oppong, C. and Adaba, G. and
    Bekombo-Priso, M. and Mogey, J. (eds.). Marriage,
    Fertility and Parenthood in West Africa. Canberra,
    Australia: Australian National University. Department of
    Demography. Volume One. 1978. pp. 227-272.
Goody, Esther N.
    "Parental Strategies: Calculation or Sentiment: Fostering
    Practices Among West Africans." (In) Medick, Hans and
    Sabean, David W. (eds.). Interest and Emotion: Essays on
    the Study of Family and Kinship. Cambridge, New York:
    Cambridge University Press. 1984. pp. 266-277.
Karanja, Wambui Wa
    "Women and Work: A Study of Female and Male Attitudes in
    the Modern Sector of an African Metropolis." (In) Ware,
    Helen (ed.). Women, Education and Modernization of the
    Family in West Africa. Canberra, Australia: Australian
    National University. Department of Demography. Changing
    African Family Project Series. Monograph #7. 1978.
Little, Kenneth L.
    "Women's Strategies in Modern Marriage in Anglophone West
    Africa: An Ideological and Sociological Appraisal."
    Journal of Comparative Family Studies. Volume 8 #3
    Autumn, 1977. pp. 341-356.

Little, Kenneth L.
"Women's Strategies in Modern Marriage in Anglophone West
Africa: An Ideological and Sociological Appraisal." (In)
Kurian, George (ed.). Cross-Cultural Perspectives of
Mate Selection and Marriage. Westport, Connecticut:
Greenwood Press. Contributions in Family Studies #3.
1979. pp. 202-217.
Okediji, Peter A.
"The Status of African Women in Family Planning." (In)
Oppong, C. and Adaba, G. and Bekombo-Priso, M. and Mogey,
J. (eds.). Marriage, Fertility and Parenthood in West
Africa. Canberra, Australia: Australian National
University. Department of Demography. Volume Two.
1978. pp. 673-676.
Oppong, Christine and Adaba, Gemma and Bekomba-Priso, Manga
and Mogey, J. (eds.)
Marriage, Fertility and Parenthood in West Africa.
Canberra, Australia: Australian National University.
Department of Demography. Changing African Family
Project. Monograph #4. Two Volumes. 1978. 848p.
Oppong, Christine (ed.)
Female and Male in West Africa. Boston: George Allen and
Unwin. 1983. 402p.
Roboff, Farron V. and Renwick, Hilary L.
"The Changing Role of Women in the Development of the
Sahel." Paper Presented to the Annual Meeting of the
African Studies Association. Paper #92. Boston,
Massachusetts. 1976. 12p.
Sudarkasa, Niara
The Effects of 20th Century Social Change, Especially of
Migration, on Women of West Africa. Tucson, Arizona:
University of Arizona. Proceedings of the West Africa
Conference. 1976. pp. 102-109.
Sudarkasa, Niara
"Female Employment and Family Organization in West
Africa." (In) Steady, Filomina C. (ed.). The Black
Woman Cross-Culturally. Cambridge, Massachusetts:
Schenkman Publishing. 1981. pp. 49-64.
Ware, Helen
"Security in the City: The Role of the Family in Urban
West Africa." (In) Ruzicka, Lado T. (ed.). The Economic
and Social Supports for High Fertility: Proceedings of
the Conference Held in Canberra, November 16-18, 1976.
Canberra, Australia: Australian National University.
Development Studies Center. 1977. pp. 385-408.
Ware, Helen
Women, Education and Modernization of the Family in West
Africa. Canberra, Australia: Australian National
University. Department of Demography. Changing African
Family Project Series. Monograph #7. 1981. 178p.

FAMILY PLANNING AND CONTRACEPTION

Fortes, Meyer
    "Parenthood, Marriage and Fertility in West Africa."
    Journal of Development Studies. Volume 14 #4 July,
    1978. pp. 121-149.
Fortes, Meyer
    "Family, Marriage and Fertility in West Africa." (In)
    Oppong, C. and Adaba, G. and Bekombo-Priso, M. and Mogey,
    J. (eds.).   Marriage, Fertility and Parenthood in West
    Africa. Canberra, Australia: Australian National
    University Press. 1978. pp. 17-54.
Goody, Esther N.
    "Some Theoretical and Empirical Aspects of Parenthood in
    West Africa." (In) Oppong, C. and Adaba, G. and
    Bekombo-Priso, M. and Mogey, J. (eds.). Marriage,
    Fertility and Parenthood in West Africa. Canberra,
    Australia: Australian National University. Department of
    Demography. Volume One. 1978. pp. 227-272.
Hosken, Fran P.
    "Women and Health in East and West Africa: Family
    Planning and Female Cicumcision." Paper Presented at the
    Seminar on Traditional Practices Affecting the Health of
    Women and Children. World Conference of the United
    Nations Decade for Women. New York: United Nations.
    Copenhagen, Denmark. July 14-30, 1980.
Hosken, Fran P.
    "Women and Health in East and West Africa: Family
    Planning and Female Circumcision." Paper Presented at
    the Seminar on Traditional Practices Affecting the Health
    of Women and Children: Female Circumcision, Childhood
    Marriage, Nutritional Taboos, etc. Alexandria, Egypt:
    World Health Organization. Eastern Mediterranean
    Regional Office. Khartoum, Sudan. February 10-15, 1979.
Little, Kenneth L.
    "Women's Strategies in Modern Marriage in Anglophone West
    Africa: An Ideological and Sociological Appraisal."
    Journal of Comparative Family Studies. Volume 8 #3
    Autumn, 1977. pp. 341-356.
Little, Kenneth L.
    "Women's Strategies in Modern Marriage in Anglophone West
    Africa: An Ideological and Sociological Appraisal." (In)
    Kurian, George (ed.). Cross-Cultural Perspectives of
    Mate Selection and Marriage. Westport, Connecticut:
    Greenwood Press. Contributions in Family Studies #3.
    1979. pp. 202-217.
Meumaun, Alfred K.
    "Integration of Family Planning and Maternal and Child
    Health in Rural West Africa." Journal of Biosocial
    Science. Volume 8 #2 April, 1976. pp. 161-174.
Mott, Frank L. and Mott, Susan H.
    Household Fertility Decision-Making in a West African
    Setting: Do Male and Female Surveys Lead to Similar

Interpretations? Worthington, Ohio: Ohio State
University. Center for Human Resource Research. 1984.
Okediji, Frances Olu
"The Limitations of Family Planning Programmes in the
Developing Nations." (In) Oppong, C. and Adaba, G. and
Bekombo-Priso, M. and Mogey, J. (eds.). Marriage,
Fertility and Parenthood in West Africa. Canberra,
Australia: Australian National University. Department of
Demography. Volume Two. 1978. pp. 617-639.
Okediji, Peter A.
"The Status of African Women in Family Planning." (In)
Oppong, C. and Adaba, G. and Bekombo-Priso, M. and Mogey,
J. (eds.). Marriage, Fertility and Parenthood in West
Africa. Canberra, Australia: Australian National
University. Department of Demography. Volume Two.
1978. pp. 673-676.
Paraiso, Maitre A.
"Family Planning Legislation in the Francophone Countries
of Africa." (In) International Planned Parenthood
Federation (IPPF). Proceedings of the IPPF Africa
Regional Conference. London: IPPF. 1977. pp. 247-255.
Sala-Diakanda, Mpembele
"Problems of Infertility and Sub-Fertility in West and
Central Africa." (In) International Union for the
Scientific Study of Population (IUSSP). International
Population Conference. Papers of the 19th General
Conference. Liege, Belgium: IUSSP. Volume Three. 1981.
pp. 643-666.
Ware, Helen
"Security in the City: The Role of the Family in Urban
West Africa." (In) Ruzicka, Lado T. (ed.). The Economic
and Social Supports for High Fertility: Proceedings of
the Conference Held in Canberra, November 16-18, 1976.
Canberra, Australia: Australian National University.
Development Studies Center. 1977. pp. 385-408.
Ware, Helen
"Motivations for the Use of Birth Control: Evidence From
West Africa." Demography. Volume 13 #4 November, 1976.
pp. 479-494.

FERTILITY AND INFERTILITY

Caldwell, Pat and Caldwell, John C.
"Population Change and Development in the ECWA Region."
(In) Cairo Demographic Centre (CDC). Aspects of
Population Change and Development in Some African and
Asian Countries. Cairo: CDC. CDC Research Monograph
Series #9. 1984. pp. 43-56.
Cleveland, David
"Fertility and the Value of Children in Subsistence
Agriculture: Savanna West Africa." Paper Presented at

the Annual Meeting of the American Anthropological
Association. Cincinnati, Ohio. November, 1979.
Fortes, Meyer
    "Parenthood, Marriage and Fertility in West Africa."
    Journal of Development Studies. Volume 14 #4 July,
    1978. pp. 121-149.
Fortes, Meyer
    "Family, Marriage and Fertility in West Africa." (In)
    Oppong, C. and Adaba, G. and Bekombo-Priso, M. and Mogey,
    J. (eds.). Marriage, Fertility and Parenthood in West
    Africa. Canberra, Australia: Australian National
    University Press. 1978. pp. 17-54.
Hosken, Fran P.
    "Female Circumcision and Fertility in Africa." Women and
    Health. Volume 1 #6 November-December, 1976. pp. 3-11.
Mott, Frank L. and Mott, Susan H.
    Household Fertility Decision-Making in a West African
    Setting: Do Male and Female Surveys Lead to Similar
    Interpretations? Worthington, Ohio: Ohio State
    University. Center for Human Resource Research. 1984.
Oppong, Christine and Adaba, Gemma and Bekomba-Priso, Manga
and Mogey, J. (eds.)
    Marriage, Fertility and Parenthood in West Africa.
    Canberra, Australia: Australian National University.
    Department of Demography. Changing African Family
    Project. Monograph #4. Two Volumes. 1978. 848p.
Reyna, Stephen P.
    "Economics and Fertility: Waiting for the Demographic
    Transition in the Dry Zone of Francophone West Africa."
    (In) Caldwell, John C. (ed.). The Persistence of High
    Fertility: Population Prospects in the Third World.
    Canberra, Australia: Australian National University.
    Department of Demography. Volume One. 1977. pp.
    393-426.
Soyinka, Susan
    "Family and Fertility in the West African Novel." (In)
    Caldwell, John C. (ed.). The Persistence of High
    Fertility: Population Prospects in the Third World.
    Canberra, Australia: Australian National University.
    Department of Demography. Volume One. 1977. pp.
    427-450.
Strodtbeck, Fred L.
    "Intimacy in Conjugal Interaction and the Capacity to
    Plan." (In) Oppong, C. and Adaba, G. and Bekombo-Priso,
    M. and Mogey, J. (eds.). Marriage, Fertility and
    Parenthood in West Africa. Canberra, Australia:
    Australian National University. Department of
    Demography. Volume Two. 1978. pp. 747-763.
Ware, Helen
    "Security in the City: The Role of the Family in Urban
    West Africa." (In) Ruzicka, Lado T. (ed.). The Economic
    and Social Supports for High Fertility: Proceedings of

the Conference Held in Canberra, November 16-18, 1976.
Canberra, Australia: Australian National University.
Development Studies Center. 1977. pp. 385-408.

HEALTH, NUTRITION AND MEDICINE

Abdalla, Raqiya
    Sisters in Affliction: Circumcision and Infibulation of
    Women in Africa. London: Zed Press. 1982. 122p.
Bates, C.J. and Whitehead, Roger G.
    "The Effect of Vitamin C Supplementation on Lactating
    Women in Keneba, a West African Rural Community."
    International Journal of Vitamin Nutrition Research.
    Volume 53 #1 1982. pp. 68-76.
Bates, C.J. and Prentice, Andrew M. and Prentice, Ann and
Whitehead, Roger G.
    "Vitamin C Supplementation of Lactating Women in Keneba:
    A West African Rural Community." Proceedings of the
    Nutrition Society. Volume 41 #3 1982. pp. 124A.
Di Domenico, Catherine M. and Asuni, Judy and Scott,
Jacqueline
    "Family Welfare and Development in Africa." (In)
    International Planned Parenthood Federation (IPPF).
    Proceedings of the IPPF Africa Regional Conference,
    University of Ibadan. London: IPPF. 1976. pp. 283-284.
Farmer, A.E. and Falkowski, W.F. (eds.)
    "Maggot in the Salt: The Snake Factor and the Treatment
    of a Typical Psychosis in West African Women." British
    Journal of Psychiatry. Volume 146 April, 1985. pp.
    446-447.
Franke, R.
    "Mode of Production and Population Patterns: Policy
    Implications for West African Development."
    International Journal of Health Services. Volume 13
    1981. pp. 361-387.
Geletkanycz, Christine and Egan, Susan
    Literature Review: The Practice of Female Circumcision.
    Washington, D.C.: U.S. Department of Health, Education
    and Welfare. Office of International Health. Mimeo.
    1979.
Gordon, Gill
    "Important Issues for Feminist Nutrition Research: A Case
    Study From the Savanna of West Africa." IDS Bulletin.
    Volume 15 #1 1984. pp. 38-44.
Hill, Allan G (ed.).
    Population, Health and Nutrition in the Sahel: Issues in
    the Welfare of Selected West African Communities.
    Boston: KPI. 1985. 399p.
Hosken, Fran P.
    "Women and Health: Genital And Sexual Mutilation of
    Females." International Journal of Women's Studies.
    Volume 3 #3 May-June, 1980. pp. 300-316.

Hosken, Fran P.
    "The Violence of Power: The Genital Mutilation of
    Females." Heresies. Volume 6 #2 Summer, 1978. pp.
    28-36.
Hosken, Fran P.
    "Female Circumcision in Africa." Victimology. Volume 2
    #3/4 1977. pp. 487-498.
Hosken, Fran P.
    "Genital Mutilation of Women in Africa." Munger Africana
    Library Notes. #36 October, 1976. 21p.
Hosken, Fran P.
    "Towards an Epidemiology of Genital Mutilation of Females
    in Africa." Paper Presented at the Annual Meeting of the
    African Studies Association. Paper #43. Baltimore,
    Maryland. 1978. 20p.
Hosken, Fran P.
    The Hosken Report: Genital and Sexual Mutilation of
    Females. Lexington, Massachusetts: Women's International
    Network News. 1982. 327p.
Hosken, Fran P.
    Female Sexual Mutilations: The Facts and Proposals for
    Action. Lexington, Massachusetts: Women's International
    Network News. 1980. 102p.
Hosken, Fran P.
    "Female Genital Mutilation in the World Today: A Global
    Review." International Journal of Health Services.
    Volume 11 #3 1981. pp. 415-430.
Hosken, Fran P.
    "Female Circumcision and Fertility in Africa." Women and
    Health. Volume 1 #6 November-December, 1976. pp. 3-11.
Hosken, Fran P.
    "The Epidemiology of Female Genital Mutilation."
    Tropical Doctor. July, 1978. pp. 150-156.
Hosken, Fran P.
    "Women and Health in East and West Africa: Family
    Planning and Female Cicumcision." Paper Presented at the
    Seminar on Traditional Practices Affecting the Health of
    Women and Children. World Conference of the United
    Nations Decade for Women. New York: United Nations.
    Copenhagen, Denmark. July 14-30, 1980.
Hosken, Fran P.
    "Women and Health in East and West Africa: Family
    Planning and Female Circumcision." Paper Presented at
    the Seminar on Traditional Practices Affecting the Health
    of Women and Children: Female Circumcision, Childhood
    Marriage, Nutritional Taboos, etc. Alexandria, Egypt:
    World Health Organization. Eastern Mediterranean
    Regional Office. Khartoum, Sudan. February 10-15, 1979.
Hosken, Fran P.
    "Female Circumcision in the World of Today: A Global
    Review." Paper Presented at the Seminar on Traditional
    Practices Affecting the Health of Women and Children.

World Conference of the United Nations Decade for Women,
Copenhagen, Denmark, July 14-30, 1980. New York: United
Nations.
Hosken, Fran P.
    "Female Circumcision in the World of Today: A Global
    View." Paper Presented at the Seminar on Traditional
    Practices Affecting the Health of Women and Children:
    Female Circumcision, Childhood Marriage, Nutritional
    Taboos, etc. Alexandria, Egypt: World Health
    Organization. Eastern Mediterranean Regional Office.
    Khartoum, Sudan. February 10-15, 1979.
Huelsman, Ben R.
    "An Anthropological View of Clitoral and Other Female
    Genital Mutilations." (In) Lowery, T.P. and Lowery, T.S.
    (eds.). The Clitoris. St. Louis, Missouri: Warren H.
    Green. 1976. pp. 111-161.
International Development Research Centre (IDRC)
    Nutritional Status of the Rural Population of the Sahel:
    Report of a Working Group, Paris, France, April 28-29,
    1980. Ottawa, Canada: IDRC. 1981. 92p.
Jett, Joyce
    The Role of Traditional Midwives in the Modern Health
    Sector in West and Central Africa. Washington, D.C.:
    U.S. Department of State. U.S. Agency for International
    Development. January, 1977. 150p.
Jett, Joyce
    The Role of Traditional Midwives in the Modern Health
    Sector in West and Central Africa. Washington, D.C.:
    U.S. Department of State. U.S. Agency for International
    Development. January, 1977. 150p.
Mahran, M.
    "Medical Dangers of Female Circumcision." International
    Planned Parenthood Federation (IPPF) Medical Bulletin.
    Volume 15 #2 April, 1981.
McLean, Scilla
    "Female Genital Mutilation." ISIS Women's International
    Bulletin. #25 1982. pp. 26-32.
McLean, Scilla and Graham, Stella E.
    Female Circumcision, Excision and Infibulation: The Fact
    and Proposals for Change. London: Minority Rights Group.
    Report #47. Second Revised Edition. 1985. 21p.
Meumaun, Alfred K.
    "Integration of Family Planning and Maternal and Child
    Health in Rural West Africa." Journal of Biosocial
    Science. Volume 8 #2 April, 1976. pp. 161-174.
Moen, Elizabeth W.
    Genital Mutilation: Everywoman's Problem. East Lansing,
    Michigan: Michigan State University. Office of Women in
    International Development. Working Paper #22. April,
    1983.
Mukhtar, Behiza
    "A Question of Our Children's Bodies: The Medical Injury
    Caused to a Girl by Circumcision." Paper Presented at

the Conference on Islam and Family Planning. Sponsored
by the International Planned Parenthood Federation.
Banjul, Gambia. October 21-24, 1979. 7p.
Sala-Diakanda, Mpembele
"Problems of Infertility and Sub-Fertility in West and
Central Africa." (In) International Union for the
Scientific Study of Population (IUSSP). International
Population Conference. Papers of the 19th General
Conference. Liege, Belgium: IUSSP. Volume Three. 1981.
pp. 643-666.
Sanderson, Lilian P.
Against the Mutilation of Women: The Struggle Against
Unnecessary Suffering. London: Ithaca Press. 1981.
117p.
Shaalan, Mohammed
"Clitoris Envy: A Psychodynamic Construct Instrumental in
Female Circumcision." Paper Presented at the Seminar on
Traditional Practices Affecting the Health of Women and
Children. World Conference of the United Nations Decade
for Women, Copenhagen, Denmark, July 14-30, 1980. New
York: United Nations. 1980.
Shaalan, Mohammed
"Clitoris Envy: A Psychdynamic Construct Instrumental in
Female Circumcision." Paper Presented at the Seminar on
Traditional Practices Affecting the Health of Women and
Children: Female Circumcision, Childhood Marriage,
Nutritional Taboos, etc. Alexandria, Egypt: World Health
Organization. Eastern Mediterranean Regional Office.
Khartoum, Sudan. February 10-15, 1979.
Sindzingre, N.
"Plus and Minus--Concerning Female Circumcision."
Cahiers d'Etudes Africaines. Volume 17 #1 1977. pp.
65-76.
Taba, A.H.
"Female Circumcision." World Health. May, 1979. pp.
8-13.
Taba, A.H.
"Female Circumcision." (In) World Health Organization.
Traditional Practices Affecting the Health of Women and
Children: Female Circumcision, Childhood Marriage,
Nutritional Taboos, etc. Report of a Seminar, Khartoum,
Sudan, February 10-15, 1979. Alexandria, Egypt: WHO/EMRO
Technical Publication #2. 1979. pp. 43-52.
Thiam, Awa
"Women's Fight for the Abolition of Sexual Mutilation."
International Social Science Journal. Volume 35 #4 1983.
pp. 747-756.
Watkinson, M. and Rushton, D.I.
"Plasmodial Pigmentation of Placenta and Outcome of
Pregnancy in West African Mothers." British Medical
Journal. Volume 287 #6387 July 23, 1983. pp. 251-254.

HISTORY

Bisilliat, Jeanne
"The Feminine Sphere in the Institutions of
Songhay-Zarma." (In) Oppong, Christine (ed.). Female
and Male in West Africa. London: George Allen and Unwin.
1983. pp. 99-106.

Campbell, Penelope
"Presbyterian West African Missions: Women as Converts
and Agents of Social Change." Journal of Presbyterian
History. Volume 56 #2 Summer, 1978. pp. 121-132.

Denzer, LaRay
"Women in the West African Nationalist Movement From
1939-1950." Africana Research Review. Volume 7 #4
July, 1976. pp. 65-85.

Leis, Nancy B.
"West African Women and the Colonial Experience."
Western Canadian Journal of Anthropology. Volume 6 #3
1976. pp. 123-132.

LAW AND LEGAL ISSUES

Paraiso, Maitre A.
"Family Planning Legislation in the Francophone Countries
of Africa." (In) International Planned Parenthood
Federation (IPPF). Proceedings of the IPPF Africa
Regional Conference. London: IPPF. 1977. pp. 247-255.

LITERATURE

Smith, Pamela J.
"An Image of Women in Anglophone West African
Literature." Paper Presented at the African Literature
Association Conference. 1976. 11p.

Soyinka, Susan
"Family and Fertility in the West African Novel." (In)
Caldwell, John C. (ed.). The Persistence of High
Fertility: Population Prospects in the Third World.
Canberra, Australia: Australian National University.
Department of Demography. Volume One. 1977. pp.
427-450.

Wallace, Karen S.
"Women and Identity: A Black Francophone Female
Perspective." Sage: A Scholarly Journal on Black Women.
Volume 2 #1 1985. pp. 19-23.

Wilson, Elizabeth A.
"The Portrayal of Woman in the Works of Francophone Women
Writers From West Africa and the French Caribbean." Ph.D
Dissertation: Michigan State University. East Lansing,
Michigan. 1985. 205p.

MARITAL RELATIONS AND NUPTIALITY

Elwert, Georg
  "Conflicts Inside and Outside the Household: A West
  African Case Study." (In) Smith, Joan (ed.). Households
  and the World Economy. Beverly Hills, California: Sage.
  1984. pp. 272-296.
Fortes, Meyer
  "Parenthood, Marriage and Fertility in West Africa."
  Journal of Development Studies. Volume 14 #4 July,
  1978. pp. 121-149.
Fortes, Meyer
  "Family, Marriage and Fertility in West Africa." (In)
  Oppong, C. and Adaba, G. and Bekombo-Priso, M. and Mogey,
  J. (eds.). Marriage, Fertility and Parenthood in West
  Africa. Canberra, Australia: Australian National
  University Press. 1978. pp. 17-54.
Goody, Esther N.
  "Some Theoretical and Empirical Aspects of Parenthood in
  West Africa." (In) Oppong, C. and Adaba, G. and
  Bekombo-Priso, M. and Mogey, J. (eds.). Marriage,
  Fertility and Parenthood in West Africa. Canberra,
  Australia: Australian National University. Department of
  Demography. Volume One. 1978. pp. 227-272.
Goody, Esther N.
  "Parental Strategies: Calculation or Sentiment: Fostering
  Practices Among West Africans." (In) Medick, Hans and
  Sabean, David W. (eds.). Interest and Emotion: Essays on
  the Study of Family and Kinship. Cambridge, New York:
  Cambridge University Press. 1984. pp. 266-277.
Grandmaison, C. LeCour
  "Economic Contracts Between Married People in the West
  African Area." L'Homme. Volume 19 #3/4 July-December,
  1979. pp. 159-170.
Huzayyin, S.A.
  "Marriage and Remarriage in Islam." (In) Dupaquier, J.
  and Helin, E. and Laslett, P. and Livi-Bacci, M. (eds.).
  Marriage and Remarriage in Populations of the Past. New
  York: Academic Press. Population and Social Structure:
  Advances in Historical Demography Series. 1981. pp.
  95-109.
Little, Kenneth L.
  "Women's Strategies in Modern Marriage in Anglophone West
  Africa: An Ideological and Sociological Appraisal."
  Journal of Comparative Family Studies. Volume 8 #3
  Autumn, 1977. pp. 341-356.
Little, Kenneth L.
  "Women's Strategies in Modern Marriage in Anglophone West
  Africa: An Ideological and Sociological Appraisal." (In)
  Kurian, George (ed.). Cross-Cultural Perspectives of
  Mate Selection and Marriage. Westport, Connecticut:
  Greenwood Press. Contributions in Family Studies #3.
  1979. pp. 202-217.

Mott, Frank L. and Mott, Susan H.
    Household Fertility Decision-Making in a West African
    Setting: Do Male and Female Surveys Lead to Similar
    Interpretations? Worthington, Ohio: Ohio State
    University. Center for Human Resource Research. 1984.
Okediji, Frances Olu
    "The Limitations of Family Planning Programmes in the
    Developing Nations." (In) Oppong, C. and Adaba, G. and
    Bekombo-Priso, M. and Mogey, J. (eds.). Marriage,
    Fertility and Parenthood in West Africa. Canberra,
    Australia: Australian National University. Department of
    Demography. Volume Two. 1978. pp. 617-639.
Okediji, Peter A.
    "The Status of African Women in Family Planning." (In)
    Oppong, C. and Adaba, G. and Bekombo-Priso, M. and Mogey,
    J. (eds.). Marriage, Fertility and Parenthood in West
    Africa. Canberra, Australia: Australian National
    University. Department of Demography. Volume Two.
    1978. pp. 673-676.
Oppong, Christine and Adaba, Gemma and Bekomba-Priso, Manga
and Mogey, J. (eds.)
    Marriage, Fertility and Parenthood in West Africa.
    Canberra, Australia: Australian National University.
    Department of Demography. Changing African Family
    Project. Monograph #4. Two Volumes. 1978. 848p.
Oppong, Christine (ed.)
    Female and Male in West Africa. Boston: George Allen and
    Unwin. 1983. 402p.
Strodtbeck, Fred L.
    "Intimacy in Conjugal Interaction and the Capacity to
    Plan." (In) Oppong, C. and Adaba, G. and Bekombo-Priso,
    M. and Mogey, J. (eds.). Marriage, Fertility and
    Parenthood in West Africa. Canberra, Australia:
    Australian National University. Department of
    Demography. Volume Two. 1978. pp. 747-763.
Sudarkasa, Niara
    "Female Employment and Family Organization in West
    Africa." (In) Steady, Filomina C. (ed.). The Black
    Woman Cross-Culturally. Cambridge, Massachusetts:
    Schenkman Publishing. 1981. pp. 49-64.
Ware, Helen
    Women, Education and Modernization of the Family in West
    Africa. Canberra, Australia: Australian National
    University. Department of Demography. Changing African
    Family Project Series. Monograph #7. 1981. 178p.
Ware, Helen
    "Motivations for the Use of Birth Control: Evidence From
    West Africa." Demography. Volume 13 #4 November, 1976.
    pp. 479-494.

MIGRATION

Adepoju, Aderanti
   "Patterns of Migration by Sex." (In) Oppong, Christine
   (ed.). Female and Male in West Africa. London: George
   Allen and Unwin. 1983. pp. 54-66.
Sudarkasa, Niara
   The Effects of 20th Century Social Change, Especially of
   Migration, on Women of West Africa. Tucson, Arizona:
   University of Arizona. Proceedings of the West Africa
   Conference. 1976. pp. 102-109.

MISCELLANEOUS

Caldwell, Pat and Caldwell, John C.
   "Population Change and Development in the ECWA Region."
   (In) Cairo Demographic Centre (CDC). Aspects of
   Population Change and Development in Some African and
   Asian Countries. Cairo: CDC. CDC Research Monograph
   Series #9. 1984. pp. 43-56.
Erasto, Muga
   Studies in Prostitution: East, West and South Africa,
   Zaire and Nevada. Nairobi: Kenya Literature Bureau.
   1980.
Hill, Allan G (ed.).
   Population, Health and Nutrition in the Sahel: Issues in
   the Welfare of Selected West African Communities.
   Boston: KPI. 1985. 399p.
Igbinovia, Patrick E.
   "Prostitution in Black Africa." International Journal of
   Women's Studies. Volume 7 #5 November-December, 1984.
   pp. 430-449.
Ware, Helen
   "Female and Male Life-Cycles." (In) Oppong, Christine
   (ed.). Female and Male in West Africa. London: George
   Allen and Unwin. 1983. pp. 6-31.

NATIONALISM

Denzer, LaRay
   "Women in the West African Nationalist Movement From
   1939-1950." Africana Research Review. Volume 7 #4
   July, 1976. pp. 65-85.

ORGANIZATIONS

DeLancey, Virginia H.
   "The Role of Credit Unions in Development for West
   African Women." Paper Presented at the Annual Meeting of

the African Studies Association. Paper #29. Bloomington, Indiana. October 21-24, 1981.

Reno, Barbara M.
Increasing Women's Credit Through Credit Unions in West Africa. Bilingual Seminar. Nairobi: Africa Co-Operative Savings and Credit Association. March 2-6, 1981. 43p.

POLITICS AND GOVERNMENT

Denzer, LaRay
"Women in the West African Nationalist Movement From 1939-1950." Africana Research Review. Volume 7 #4 July, 1976. pp. 65-85.

Fraker, Anne and Harrell-Bond, Barbara
"Feminine Influence." West Africa. December 17, 1979. pp. 2182-2186.

Leis, Nancy B.
"West African Women and the Colonial Experience." Western Canadian Journal of Anthropology. Volume 6 #3 1976. pp. 123-132.

RELIGION AND WITCHCRAFT

Campbell, Penelope
"Presbyterian West African Missions: Women as Converts and Agents of Social Change." Journal of Presbyterian History. Volume 56 #2 Summer, 1978. pp. 121-132.

Davis, W.T.
"Rome and the Ordination of Women." West African Religion. Volume 17 #2 1978. pp. 3-8.

Elwert, Georg
"Conflicts Inside and Outside the Household: A West African Case Study." (In) Smith, Joan (ed.). Households and the World Economy. Beverly Hills, California: Sage. 1984. pp. 272-296.

Geletkanycz, Christine and Egan, Susan
Literature Review: The Practice of Female Circumcision. Washington, D.C.: U.S. Department of Health, Education and Welfare. Office of International Health. Mimeo. 1979.

Huzayyin, S.A.
"Marriage and Remarriage in Islam." (In) Dupaquier, J. and Helin, E. and Laslett, P. and Livi-Bacci, M. (eds.). Marriage and Remarriage in Populations of the Past. New York: Academic Press. Population and Social Structure: Advances in Historical Demography Series. 1981. pp. 95-109.

Mahran, M.
"Medical Dangers of Female Circumcision." International Planned Parenthood Federation (IPPF) Medical Bulletin. Volume 15 #2 April, 1981.

McLean, Scilla
  "Female Genital Mutilation." ISIS Women's International
  Bulletin. #25 1982. pp. 26-32.
McLean, Scilla and Graham, Stella E.
  Female Circumcision, Excision and Infibulation: The Fact
  and Proposals for Change. London: Minority Rights Group.
  Report #47. Second Revised Edition. 1985. 21p.
Moen, Elizabeth W.
  Genital Mutilation: Everywoman's Problem. East Lansing,
  Michigan: Michigan State University. Office of Women in
  International Development. Working Paper #22. April,
  1983.
Mukhtar, Behiza
  "A Question of Our Children's Bodies: The Medical Injury
  Caused to a Girl by Circumcision." Paper Presented at
  the Conference on Islam and Family Planning. Sponsored
  by the International Planned Parenthood Federation.
  Banjul, Gambia. October 21-24, 1979. 7p.
Tonkin, Elizabeth
  "Women Excluded? Masking and Masquerading in West
  Africa." (In) Holden, P. (ed.). Women's Religious
  Experience. Totowa, New Jersey: Barnes and Noble. 1983.
  pp. 163-174.

RESEARCH

Gordon, Gill
  "Important Issues for Feminist Nutrition Research: A Case
  Study From the Savanna of West Africa." IDS Bulletin.
  Volume 15 #1 1984. pp. 38-44.
Nwanosike, Eugene O.
  Women and Development: A Select Bibliography: A Select
  and Partially Annotated Bibliography. Buea, Cameroon:
  Regional Pan-African Institute for Development/West
  Africa. Bibliographic Series #10. 1980. 63p.

SEX ROLES

Bisilliat, Jeanne
  "The Feminine Sphere in the Institutions of
  Songhay-Zarma." (In) Oppong, Christine (ed.). Female
  and Male in West Africa. London: George Allen and Unwin.
  1983. pp. 99-106.
Di Domenico, Catherine M. and Asuni, Judy and Scott,
Jacqueline
  "Family Welfare and Development in Africa." (In)
  International Planned Parenthood Federation (IPPF).
  Proceedings of the IPPF Africa Regional Conference,
  University of Ibadan. London: IPPF. 1976. pp. 283-284.
Elwert, Georg
  "Conflicts Inside and Outside the Household: A West

African Case Study." (In) Smith, Joan (ed.). Households
and the World Economy. Beverly Hills, California: Sage.
1984. pp. 272-296.

Fortes, Meyer
"Parenthood, Marriage and Fertility in West Africa."
Journal of Development Studies. Volume 14 #4 July,
1978. pp. 121-149.

Fortes, Meyer
"Family, Marriage and Fertility in West Africa." (In)
Oppong, C. and Adaba, G. and Bekombo-Priso, M. and Mogey,
J. (eds.). Marriage, Fertility and Parenthood in West
Africa. Canberra, Australia: Australian National
University Press. 1978. pp. 17-54.

Franke, R.
"Mode of Production and Population Patterns: Policy
Implications for West African Development."
International Journal of Health Services. Volume 13
1981. pp. 361-387.

Grandmaison, C. LeCour
"Economic Contracts Between Married People in the West
African Area." L'Homme. Volume 19 #3/4 July-December,
1979. pp. 159-170.

Guyer, Jane I.
Women's Work in the Food Economy of the Cocoa Belt: A
Comparison. Brookline, Massachusetts: Boston University.
African Studies Center. Working Paper #7. 1978. 34p.

Igbinovia, Patrick E.
"Prostitution in Black Africa." International Journal of
Women's Studies. Volume 7 #5 November-December, 1984.
pp. 430-449.

Jett, Joyce
The Role of Traditional Midwives in the Modern Health
Sector in West and Central Africa. Washington, D.C.:
U.S. Department of State. U.S. Agency for International
Development. January, 1977. 150p.

Karanja, Wambui Wa
"Women and Work: A Study of Female and Male Attitudes in
the Modern Sector of an African Metropolis." (In) Ware,
Helen (ed.). Women, Education and Modernization of the
Family in West Africa. Canberra, Australia: Australian
National University. Department of Demography. Changing
African Family Project Series. Monograph #7. 1978.

Kizerbo, Joseph
"Women and the Energy Crisis in the Sahel Africa. From
the Seminar on Fuel and Energy Development for African
Women in Rural Areas, Bamako, Mali, December, 1980."
Unasylva. Volume 33 #133 1981. pp. 5-10.

Little, Kenneth L.
"Women's Strategies in Modern Marriage in Anglophone West
Africa: An Ideological and Sociological Appraisal."
Journal of Comparative Family Studies. Volume 8 #3
Autumn, 1977. pp. 341-356.

Little, Kenneth L.
    "Women's Strategies in Modern Marriage in Anglophone West
    Africa: An Ideological and Sociological Appraisal." (In)
    Kurian, George (ed.). Cross-Cultural Perspectives of
    Mate Selection and Marriage. Westport, Connecticut:
    Greenwood Press. Contributions in Family Studies #3.
    1979. pp. 202-217.
Oppong, Christine and Adaba, Gemma and Bekomba-Priso, Manga
and Mogey, J. (eds.)
    Marriage, Fertility and Parenthood in West Africa.
    Canberra, Australia: Australian National University.
    Department of Demography. Changing African Family
    Project. Monograph #4. Two Volumes. 1978. 848p.
Oppong, Christine (ed.)
    Female and Male in West Africa. Boston: George Allen and
    Unwin. 1983. 402p.
Wallace, Karen S.
    "Women and Identity: A Black Francophone Female
    Perspective." Sage: A Scholarly Journal on Black Women.
    Volume 2 #1 1985. pp. 19-23.

SEXUAL MUTILATION/CIRCUMCISION

Abdalla, Raqiya
    Sisters in Affliction: Circumcision and Infibulation of
    Women in Africa. London: Zed Press. 1982. 122p.
Geletkanycz, Christine and Egan, Susan
    Literature Review: The Practice of Female Circumcision.
    Washington, D.C.: U.S. Department of Health, Education
    and Welfare. Office of International Health. Mimeo.
    1979.
Hosken, Fran P.
    "Women and Health: Genital And Sexual Mutilation of
    Females." International Journal of Women's Studies.
    Volume 3 #3 May-June, 1980. pp. 300-316.
Hosken, Fran P.
    "The Violence of Power: The Genital Mutilation of
    Females." Heresies. Volume 6 #2 Summer, 1978. pp.
    28-36.
Hosken, Fran P.
    "Female Circumcision in Africa." Victimology. Volume 2
    #3/4 1977. pp. 487-498.
Hosken, Fran P.
    "Genital Mutilation of Women in Africa." Munger Africana
    Library Notes. #36 October, 1976. 21p.
Hosken, Fran P.
    "Towards an Epidemiology of Genital Mutilation of Females
    in Africa." Paper Presented at the Annual Meeting of the
    African Studies Association. Paper #43. Baltimore,
    Maryland. 1978. 20p.
Hosken, Fran P.
    The Hosken Report: Genital and Sexual Mutilation of

Females. Lexington, Massachusetts: Women's International
Network News. 1982. 327p.
Hosken, Fran P.
Female Sexual Mutilations: The Facts and Proposals for
Action. Lexington, Massachusetts: Women's International
Network News. 1980. 102p.
Hosken, Fran P.
"Female Genital Mutilation in the World Today: A Global
Review." International Journal of Health Services.
Volume 11 #3 1981. pp. 415-430.
Hosken, Fran P.
"Female Circumcision and Fertility in Africa." Women and
Health. Volume 1 #6 November-December, 1976. pp. 3-11.
Hosken, Fran P.
"The Epidemiology of Female Genital Mutilation."
Tropical Doctor. July, 1978. pp. 150-156.
Hosken, Fran P.
"Women and Health in East and West Africa: Family
Planning and Female Cicumcision." Paper Presented at the
Seminar on Traditional Practices Affecting the Health of
Women and Children. World Conference of the United
Nations Decade for Women. New York: United Nations.
Copenhagen, Denmark. July 14-30, 1980.
Hosken, Fran P.
"Women and Health in East and West Africa: Family
Planning and Female Circumcision." Paper Presented at
the Seminar on Traditional Practices Affecting the Health
of Women and Children: Female Circumcision, Childhood
Marriage, Nutritional Taboos, etc. Alexandria, Egypt:
World Health Organization. Eastern Mediterranean
Regional Office. Khartoum, Sudan. February 10-15, 1979.
Hosken, Fran P.
"Female Circumcision in the World of Today: A Global
Review." Paper Presented at the Seminar on Traditional
Practices Affecting the Health of Women and Children.
World Conference of the United Nations Decade for Women.
New York: United Nations. Copenhagen, Denmark. July
14-30, 1980.
Hosken, Fran P.
"Female Circumcision in the World of Today: A Global
View." Paper Presented at the Seminar on Traditional
Practices Affecting the Health of Women and Children:
Female Circumcision, Childhood Marriage, Nutritional
Taboos, etc. Alexandria, Egypt: World Health
Organization. Eastern Mediterranean Regional Office.
Khartoum, Sudan. February 10-15, 1979.
Huelsman, Ben R.
"An Anthropological View of Clitoral and Other Female
Genital Mutilations." (In) Lowery, T.P. and Lowery, T.S.
(eds.). The Clitoris. St. Louis, Missouri: Warren H.
Green. 1976. pp. 111-161.
Mahran, M.
"Medical Dangers of Female Circumcision." International

Planned Parenthood Federation (IPPF) Medical Bulletin.
Volume 15 #2 April, 1981.
McLean, Scilla
    "Female Genital Mutilation." ISIS Women's International
    Bulletin. #25 1982. pp. 26-32.
McLean, Scilla and Graham, Stella E.
    Female Circumcision, Excision and Infibulation: The Fact
    and Proposals for Change. London: Minority Rights Group.
    Report #47. Second Revised Edition. 1985. 21p.
Moen, Elizabeth W.
    Genital Mutilation: Everywoman's Problem. East Lansing,
    Michigan: Michigan State University. Office of Women in
    International Development. Working Paper #22. April,
    1983.
Mukhtar, Behiza
    "A Question of Our Children's Bodies: The Medical Injury
    Caused to a Girl by Circumcision." Paper Presented at
    the Conference on Islam and Family Planning. Sponsored
    by the International Planned Parenthood Federation.
    Banjul, Gambia. October 21-24, 1979. 7p.
Sanderson, Lilian P.
    Against the Mutilation of Women: The Struggle Against
    Unnecessary Suffering. London: Ithaca Press. 1981.
    117p.
Shaalan, Mohammed
    "Clitoris Envy: A Psychodynamic Construct Instrumental in
    Female Circumcision." Paper Presented at the Seminar on
    Traditional Practices Affecting the Health of Women and
    Children. World Conference of the United Nations Decade
    for Women. New York: United Nations. Copenhagen,
    Denmark. July 14-30, 1980.
Shaalan, Mohammed
    "Clitoris Envy: A Psychdynamic Construct Instrumental in
    Female Circumcision." Paper Presented at the Seminar on
    Traditional Practices Affecting the Health of Women and
    Children: Female Circumcision, Childhood Marriage,
    Nutritional Taboos, etc. Alexandria, Egypt: World Health
    Organization. Eastern Mediterranean Regional Office.
    Khartoum, Sudan. February 10-15, 1979.
Sindzingre, N.
    "Plus and Minus--Concerning Female Circumcision."
    Cahiers d'Etudes Africaines. Volume 17 #1 1977. pp.
    65-76.
Taba, A.H.
    "Female Circumcision." World Health. May, 1979. pp.
    8-13.
Taba, A.H.
    "Female Circumcision." (In) World Health Organization.
    Traditional Practices Affecting the Health of Women and
    Children: Female Circumcision, Childhood Marriage,
    Nutritional Taboos, etc. Report of a Seminar, Khartoum,
    Sudan, February 10-15, 1979. Alexandria, Egypt: WHO/EMRO
    Technical Publication #2. 1979. pp. 43-52.

Thiam, Awa
"Women's Fight for the Abolition of Sexual Mutilation."
International Social Science Journal. Volume 35 #4 1983.
pp. 747-756.

STATUS OF WOMEN

Fraker, Anne and Harrell-Bond, Barbara
"Feminine Influence." West Africa. December 17, 1979.
pp. 2182-2186.

URBANIZATION

Ware, Helen
"Security in the City: The Role of the Family in Urban
West Africa." (In) Ruzicka, Lado T. (ed.). The Economic
and Social Supports for High Fertility: Proceedings of
the Conference Held in Canberra, November 16-18, 1976.
Canberra, Australia: Australian National University.
Development Studies Center. 1977. pp. 385-408.

WOMEN AND THEIR CHILDREN

Cleveland, David
"Fertility and the Value of Children in Subsistence
Agriculture: Savanna West Africa." Paper Presented at
the Annual Meeting of the American Anthropological
Association. Cincinnati, Ohio. November, 1979.
Goody, Esther N.
"Parental Strategies: Calculation or Sentiment: Fostering
Practices Among West Africans." (In) Medick, Hans and
Sabean, David W. (eds.). Interest and Emotion: Essays on
the Study of Family and Kinship. Cambridge, New York:
Cambridge University Press. 1984. pp. 266-277.
Mukhtar, Behiza
"A Question of Our Children's Bodies: The Medical Injury
Caused to a Girl by Circumcision." Paper Presented at
the Conference on Islam and Family Planning. Sponsored
by the International Planned Parenthood Federation.
Banjul, Gambia. October 21-24, 1979. 7p.
Oppong, Christine and Adaba, Gemma and Bekomba-Priso, Manga
and Mogey, J. (eds.)
Marriage, Fertility and Parenthood in West Africa.
Canberra, Australia: Australian National University.
Department of Demography. Changing African Family
Project. Monograph #4. Two Volumes. 1978. 848p.

NATIONS OF WESTERN AFRICA

Benin

Bay, Edna G.
   "Servitude and Worldly Success in the Palace of Dahomey."
   (In) Robertson, Claire C. and Klein, Martin A. (eds.).
   Women and Slavery in Africa. Madison, Wisconsin:
   University of Wisconsin Press. 1983. pp. 340-367.
Bay, Edna G.
   "The Royal Women of Abomey." Ph.D Dissertation: Boston
   University. Boston, Massachusetts. 1977. 279p.
Eelens, Frank and Donne, L.
   The Proximate Determinants of Fertility in Sub-Saharan
   Africa: A Factbook Based on the Results of the World
   Fertility Survey. Brussels, Belgium: Vrije Universiteit
   Brussel. Interuniversity Programme in Demography. IDP
   Working Paper #1985-3. 1985. 122p.
Franks, James A. and Minnis, Robert L. and Wilson, Paul E.
   Maternal and Child Health/Family Planning Project for the
   Republic of the Gambia and the People's Republic of
   Benin, West Africa. Final Report. Santa Cruz,
   California: University of California--Santa Cruz.
   February, 1980. 514p.
Houeto, Colette S.
   Women and Development: The Case of Benin. Dakar,
   Senegal: UNESCO. Regional Office for Education in
   Africa. 1982.
Kerina, Jane M.
   "Women in Africa: A Select Bibliography." Africa Report.
   Volume 22 #1 January-February, 1977. pp. 44-50.
Lesthaeghe, Ron J. and Eelens, Frank
   Social Organization and Reproductive Regimes: Lessons
   From Sub-Saharan Africa and Historical Western Europe.
   Brussels, Belgium: Vrije Universiteit Brussel.
   Interuniversity Programme in Demography. IDP Working
   Paper #1985-1. 1985. 64p.

Sargent, C.
    "Obstetrical Choice Among Urban Women in Benin." Social
    Science and Medicine. Volume 20 #3 1985. pp. 287-292.
Sargent, Carolyn F.
    "Between Death and Shame: Dimensions of Pain in Bariba
    Culture." Social Science and Medicine. Volume 19 #2
    1984. pp. 1299-1304.
Sargent, Carolyn F.
    "Factors Influencing Women's Choices of Obstetrical Care
    in a Northern District in the People's Republic of
    Benin." Ph.D Dissertation: Michigan State University.
    East Lansing, Michigan. 1979. 395p.
Sargent, Carolyn F.
    "Implications of Role Expectations for Birth Assistance
    Among Bariba Women." Social Science and Medicine.
    Volume 16 #16 1982. pp. 1483-1489.
Sargent, Carolyn F.
    "Utilization of National Health Maternity Services in a
    Northern District of the People's Republic of Benin."
    Rural Africana. Volume 8/9 Fall/Winter, 1980. pp.
    77-89.
Sargent, Carolyn F.
    Cultural Context of Therapeutic Choice: Obstetrical Care
    Decisions Among the Bariba of Benin. Boston: Kluwer
    Boston Inc. 1982. 192p.

Burkina Faso

AGRICULTURE

Barnes, Carolyn
    "Strengthening Voltaic Women's Roles in Development."
    (In) Proceedings and Papers of the International
    Conference on Women and Food: Consortium for
    International Development. Tucson, Arizona: University
    of Arizona. 1978. pp. 71-74.
Blain, Daniele
    "Burkina Faso: Village Women, Development Projects and
    Extension Workers." Ideas and Action Bulletin. #158
    1984. pp. 4-5.
Bleiberg, Fanny M. and Brun, Thierry A. and Goihman, Samuel
and Gouba, Emile
    "Duration of Activities and Energy Expenditure of Female
    Farmers in Dry and Rainy Seasons in Upper Volta."
    British Journal of Nutrition. Volume 43 1980. pp.
    71-82.
Conti, Anna
    "Capitalist Organization of Production Through
    Non-Capitalist Relations: Women's Role in a Pilot
    Resettlement in Upper Volta." Review of African
    Political Economy. #15/16 May-December, 1979. pp.
    75-92.
Conti, Anna
    "Women on 'Schemes' in Upper Volta." Review of African
    Political Economy. #15/16 1979.
Development Alternatives Inc.
    Strengthening Women's Roles on Development (Upper
    Volta). Washington, D.C.: U.S. Department of State.
    U.S. Agency for International Development. Office of
    Women in Development. 1976. 89p.
Dinnerstein, Myra and Cloud, Kathleen
    Report of a Fact-Finding Trip to Niger, Mali, Senegal and

Upper Volta. Washington, D.C.: U.S. Department of State.
U.S. Agency for International Development. 1976. 10p.
Hemmings-Gapihan, Grace S.
"International Development and the Evolution of Women's
Economic Roles: A Case Study From Northern Gulma, Upper
Volta." (In) Bay, Edna G. (ed.). Women and Work in
Africa. Boulder, Colorado: Westview Press. Westview
Special Studies in Africa. 1982. pp. 171-189.
Hemmings-Gapihan, Grace S.
"Women and Economy in Gourma, 1919-1978: A Study of
Economic Change in Burkina Faso." Ph.D Dissertation:
Yale University. New Haven, Connecticut. 1985. 389p.
Henderson, Helen K.
"The Role of Women in Livestock Production: Some
Preliminary Findings." (In) Vengroff, Richard (ed.).
Upper Volta: Environmental Uncertainty and Livestock
Production. Lubbock, Texas: International Center for the
Study of Arid and Semi-Arid Lands. 1980.
Hoskins, Marilyn W. and Guissou, Josephine
Social and Economic Development in Upper Volta: Women's
Perspective. Paris: Societe Africaine d'Etudes et de
Development/U.S. AID Regional Economic Development
Services Office West Africa. 1978. 36p.
Jeffalyn Johnson and Associates Inc.
African Women in Development. Falls Church, Virginia:
Jeffalyn Johnson and Associates Inc. 1980. 125p.
Mitchnik, David A.
The Role of Women in Rural Zaire and Upper Volta:
Improving Methods of Skill Acquisition. Oxford, England:
OXFAM. OXFAM Working Paper #2. 1978. 36p.
Saul, Mahir
"Beer, Sorghum and Women: Production for the Market in
Rural Upper Volta." Africa. Volume 51 #3 1981. pp.
746-764.
Taylor, Ellen
Women Paraprofessionals in Upper Volta's Rural
Development. Ithaca, New York: Cornell University.
Center for International Development. Rural Development
Committee. Special Series on Paraprofessionals. #3.
1981. 56p.
U.S. Agency for International Development (U.S. AID)
Social and Economic Development in Upper Volta: Women's
Perspective. Washington D.C.: U.S. Department of State.
U.S. AID. Regional Economic Development Services
Office/West Africa. 1978. 36p.
U.S. Agency for International Development (U.S. AID)
Strengthening Women's Roles in Development. Ouagadougou,
Upper Volta: U.S. AID Mission. 1977. 114p.

CULTURAL ROLES

Bleiberg, Fanny M. and Brun, Thierry A. and Goihman, Samuel
and Gouba, Emile
    "Duration of Activities and Energy Expenditure of Female
    Farmers in Dry and Rainy Seasons in Upper Volta."
    British Journal of Nutrition. Volume 43 1980. pp.
    71-82.
Bohmer, C.
    "Modernization, Divorce and the Status of Women; le
    tribunal coutumierin Bobodioulasso." African Studies
    Review. Volume 23 #2 September, 1980. pp. 81-90.
Coulibaly, Sidiki P.
    "Religion, Philosphy and Fertility: The Case of Upper
    Volta." (In) Pool, D. Ian and Coulibaly, Sidiki P.
    (eds.). Demographic Transition and Cultural Continuity
    in the Sahel: Aspects of the Social Demography of Upper
    Volta. Ithaca, New York: Cornell University.
    International Population Program. 1977. pp. 98-126.
Hemmings-Gapihan, Grace S.
    "International Development and the Evolution of Women's
    Economic Roles: A Case Study From Northern Gulma, Upper
    Volta." (In) Bay, Edna G. (ed.). Women and Work in
    Africa. Boulder, Colorado: Westview Press. Westview
    Special Studies in Africa. 1982. pp. 171-189.
Hemmings-Gapihan, Grace S.
    "Women and Economy in Gourma, 1919-1978: A Study of
    Economic Change in Burkina Faso." Ph.D Dissertation:
    Yale University. New Haven, Connecticut. 1985. 389p.
Henderson, Helen K.
    "The Role of Women in Livestock Production: Some
    Preliminary Findings." (In) Vengroff, Richard (ed.).
    Upper Volta: Environmental Uncertainty and Livestock
    Production. Lubbock, Texas: International Center for the
    Study of Arid and Semi-Arid Lands. 1980.
Hoskins, Marilyn W. and Guissou, Josephine
    Social and Economic Development in Upper Volta: Women's
    Perspective. Paris: Societe Africaine d'Etudes et de
    Development/U.S. AID Regional Economic Development
    Services Office West Africa. 1978. 36p.
McSweeney, Brenda G. and Freedman, Marion
    "Lack of Time as an Obstacle to Women's Education: The
    Case of Upper Volta." Comparative Education Review.
    Volume 24 #2 Part Two June, 1980. pp. S124-S139.
McSweeney, Brenda G. and Freedman, Marion
    "Lack of Time as an Obstacle to Women's Education: The
    Case of Upper Volta." (In) Kelly, G.P. and Elliott, C.M.
    (eds.). Women's Education in the Third World:
    Comparative Perspectives. Albany, New York: State
    University of New York Press. 1982. pp. 88-103.
McSweeney, Brenda G.
    An Approach to Collecting and Examining Data on Rural
    Women's Time Use and Some Tentative Findings: The Case of

Upper Volta. New York: Population Council. Working
Paper Prepared for the Seminar on Rural Women and the
Sexual Division. March 30, 1979.

Mitchnik, David A.
The Role of Women in Rural Zaire and Upper Volta:
Improving Methods of Skill Acquisition. Oxford, England:
OXFAM. OXFAM Working Paper #2. 1978. 36p.

Pool, Janet S.
"Conjugal Patterns in Upper Volta." (In) Pool, D. Ian
and Coulibaly, Sidiki P. (eds.). Demographic Transition
and Cultural Continuity in the Sahel: Aspects of the
Social Demography of Upper Volta. Ithaca, New York:
Cornell University. International Population Program.
1977. pp. 38-97.

Saul, Mahir
"Beer, Sorghum and Women: Production for the Market in
Rural Upper Volta." Africa. Volume 51 #3 1981. pp.
746-764.

Triendregeogon, Alice
"Female Circumcision in Upper Volta." Paper Presented at
the Seminar on Traditional Practices Affecting the Health
of Women and Children. World Conference of the United
Nations Decade for Women. New York: United Nations.
Copenhagen, Denmark. July 14-30, 1980.

Triendregeogon, Alice
"Female Circumcision in Upper Volta." Paper Presented at
the Seminar on Traditional Practices Affecting the Health
of Women and Children: Female Circumcision, Childhood
Marriage, Nutritional Taboos, etc. Alexandria, Egypt:
World Health Organization. Eastern Mediterranean
Regional Office.(May be in French). Khartoum, Sudan.
1979.

Vad de Walle, Francine and Ouaidou, Nassour
"Status and Fertility Among Urban Blacks in Burkina
Faso." International Family Planning Perspectives.
Volume 11 #2 June, 1985. pp. 60-64.

Walle, Francine V. and Ougidou, Nassour
Women's Status and Childbearing on the Eve of a Fertility
Transition: Upper Volta, 1983. Philadelphia,
Pennsylvania: University of Pennsylvania. Population
Studies Center. 1984.

DEVELOPMENT AND TECHNOLOGY

Barnes, Carolyn
"Strengthening Voltaic Women's Roles in Development."
(In) Proceedings and Papers of the International
Conference on Women and Food: Consortium for
International Development. Tucson, Arizona: University
of Arizona. 1978. pp. 71-74.

Blain, Daniele
"Burkina Faso: Village Women, Development Projects and

Extension Workers." Ideas and Action Bulletin. #158
1984. pp. 4-5.
Bleiberg, Fanny M. and Brun, Thierry A. and Goihman, Samuel
and Gouba, Emile
"Duration of Activities and Energy Expenditure of Female
Farmers in Dry and Rainy Seasons in Upper Volta."
British Journal of Nutrition. Volume 43 1980. pp.
71-82.
Bohmer, C.
"Modernization, Divorce and the Status of Women; le
tribunal coutumierin Bobodioulasso." African Studies
Review. Volume 23 #2 September, 1980. pp. 81-90.
Conti, Anna
"Capitalist Organization of Production Through
Non-Capitalist Relations: Women's Role in a Pilot
Resettlement in Upper Volta." Review of African
Political Economy. #15/16 May-December, 1979. pp.
75-92.
Conti, Anna
"Capitalist Organization of Production Through
Non-Capitalist Relations: Women's Role in a Pilot
Resettlement in Upper Volta." Review of African
Political Economy. #15/16 1979. pp. 75-92.
Conti, Anna
"Women on 'Schemes' in Upper Volta." Review of African
Political Economy. #15/16 1979.
Development Alternatives Inc.
Strengthening Women's Roles on Development (Upper
Volta). Washington, D.C.: U.S. Department of State.
U.S. Agency for International Development. Office of
Women in Development. 1976. 89p.
Dinnerstein, Myra and Cloud, Kathleen
Report of a Fact-Finding Trip to Niger, Mali, Senegal and
Upper Volta. Washington, D.C.: U.S. Department of State.
U.S. Agency for International Development. 1976. 10p.
Hemmings-Gapihan, Grace S.
"International Development and the Evolution of Women's
Economic Roles: A Case Study From Northern Gulma, Upper
Volta." (In) Bay, Edna G. (ed.). Women and Work in
Africa. Boulder, Colorado: Westview Press. Westview
Special Studies in Africa. 1982. pp. 171-189.
Hoskins, Marilyn W. and Guissou, Josephine
Social and Economic Development in Upper Volta: Women's
Perspective. Paris: Societe Africaine d'Etudes et de
Development/U.S. AID Regional Economic Development
Services Office West Africa. 1978. 36p.
Jeffalyn Johnson and Associates Inc.
African Women in Development. Falls Church, Virginia:
Jeffalyn Johnson and Associates Inc. 1980. 125p.
McSweeney, Brenda G. and Freedman, Marion
"Lack of Time as an Obstacle to Women's Education: The
Case of Upper Volta." Comparative Education Review.
Volume 24 #2 Part Two June, 1980. pp. S124-S139.

McSweeney, Brenda G. and Freedman, Marion
"Lack of Time as an Obstacle to Women's Education: The
Case of Upper Volta." (In) Kelly, G.P. and Elliott, C.M.
(eds.). Women's Education in the Third World:
Comparative Perspectives. Albany, New York: State
University of New York Press. 1982. pp. 88-103.

McSweeney, Brenda G.
"The Negative Impact of Development on Women
Reconsidered: A Study of the Women's Education Project in
Upper Volta." Ph.D Dissertation: Tufts University.
Fletcher School of Law and Diplomacy. Boston,
Massachusetts. 1979.

McSweeney, Brenda G.
"Time to Learn, Time for a Better Life. The Women's
Education Project in Upper Volta." Assignment Children.
Volume 49/50 Spring, 1980. pp. 109-126.

McSweeney, Brenda G.
An Approach to Collecting and Examining Data on Rural
Women's Time Use and Some Tentative Findings: The Case of
Upper Volta. New York: Population Council. Working
Paper Prepared for the Seminar on Rural Women and the
Sexual Division. March 30, 1979.

Mitchnik, David A.
The Role of Women in Rural Zaire and Upper Volta:
Improving Methods of Skill Acquisition. Oxford, England:
OXFAM. OXFAM Working Paper #2. 1978. 36p.

Quimby, Lucy
"Islam, Sex Roles and Modernization in Bobo-Dioulasso."
(In) Jules-Rosette, Bennetta (ed.). The New Religions of
Africa. Norwood, New Jersey: Ablex Publishing Co. 1979.
pp. 203-218.

Taylor, Ellen
Women Paraprofessionals in Upper Volta's Rural
Development. Ithaca, New York: Cornell University.
Center for International Development. Rural Development
Committee. Special Series on Paraprofessionals. #3.
1981. 56p.

U.S. Agency for International Development (U.S. AID)
Social and Economic Development in Upper Volta: Women's
Perspective. Washington D.C.: U.S. Department of State.
U.S. AID. Regional Economic Development Services
Office/West Africa. 1978. 36p.

U.S. Agency for International Development (U.S. AID)
Strengthening Women's Roles in Development. Ouagadougou,
Upper Volta: U.S. AID Mission. 1977. 114p.

DIVORCE

Bohmer, C.
"Modernization, Divorce and the Status of Women; le
tribunal coutumierin Bobodioulasso." African Studies
Review. Volume 23 #2 September, 1980. pp. 81-90.

ECONOMICS

Barnes, Carolyn
    "Strengthening Voltaic Women's Roles in Development."
    (In) Proceedings and Papers of the International
    Conference on Women and Food: Consortium for
    International Development. Tucson, Arizona: University
    of Arizona. 1978. pp. 71-74.
Blain, Daniele
    "Burkina Faso: Village Women, Development Projects and
    Extension Workers." Ideas and Action Bulletin. #158
    1984. pp. 4-5.
Conti, Anna
    "Capitalist Organization of Production Through
    Non-Capitalist Relations: Women's Role in a Pilot
    Resettlement in Upper Volta." Review of African
    Political Economy. #15/16 1979. pp. 75-92.
Conti, Anna
    "Women on 'Schemes' in Upper Volta." Review of African
    Political Economy. #15/16 1979.
Development Alternatives Inc.
    Strengthening Women's Roles on Development (Upper
    Volta). Washington, D.C.: U.S. Department of State.
    U.S. Agency for International Development. Office of
    Women in Development. 1976. 89p.
Hemmings-Gapihan, Grace S.
    "International Development and the Evolution of Women's
    Economic Roles: A Case Study From Northern Gulma, Upper
    Volta." (In) Bay, Edna G. (ed.). Women and Work in
    Africa. Boulder, Colorado: Westview Press. Westview
    Special Studies in Africa. 1982. pp. 171-189.
Hemmings-Gapihan, Grace S.
    "Women and Economy in Gourma, 1919-1978: A Study of
    Economic Change in Burkina Faso." Ph.D Dissertation:
    Yale University. New Haven, Connecticut. 1985. 389p.
Hoskins, Marilyn W. and Guissou, Josephine
    Social and Economic Development in Upper Volta: Women's
    Perspective. Paris: Societe Africaine d'Etudes et de
    Development/U.S. AID Regional Economic Development
    Services Office West Africa. 1978. 36p.
Jeffalyn Johnson and Associates Inc.
    African Women in Development. Falls Church, Virginia:
    Jeffalyn Johnson and Associates Inc. 1980. 125p.
McSweeney, Brenda G.
    An Approach to Collecting and Examining Data on Rural
    Women's Time Use and Some Tentative Findings: The Case of
    Upper Volta. New York: Population Council. Working
    Paper Prepared for the Seminar on Rural Women and the
    Sexual Division. March 30, 1979.
Saul, Mahir
    "Beer, Sorghum and Women: Production for the Market in
    Rural Upper Volta." Africa. Volume 51 #3 1981. pp.
    746-764.

Taylor, Ellen
    Women Paraprofessionals in Upper Volta's Rural
    Development. Ithaca, New York: Cornell University.
    Center for International Development. Rural Development
    Committee. Special Series on Paraprofessionals. #3.
    1981. 56p.
U.S. Agency for International Development (U.S. AID)
    Social and Economic Development in Upper Volta: Women's
    Perspective. Washington D.C.: U.S. Department of State.
    U.S. AID. Regional Economic Development Services
    Office/West Africa. 1978. 36p.
U.S. Agency for International Development (U.S. AID)
    Strengthening Women's Roles in Development. Ouagadougou,
    Upper Volta: U.S. AID Mission. 1977. 114p.

EDUCATION AND TRAINING

Barnes, Carolyn
    "Strengthening Voltaic Women's Roles in Development."
    (In) Proceedings and Papers of the International
    Conference on Women and Food: Consortium for
    International Development. Tucson, Arizona: University
    of Arizona. 1978. pp. 71-74.
Clearing House on Development Communications (CDC)
    Project for Equality of Access to Education for Women and
    Young Girls, Upper Volta. Washington, D.C.: CDC.
    Project Profile. January, 1978. 2p.
Development Alternatives Inc.
    Strengthening Women's Roles on Development (Upper Volta).
    Washington, D.C.: U.S. Department of State. U.S. Agency
    for International Development. Office of Women in
    Development. 1976. 89p.
Kwende, Tieba G.
    The Organization of Productive Work in Technical and
    Vocational Schools in Upper Volta: The Experience of the
    Centre for Women's Occupations and Handicrafts,
    Ouagadougou. Dakar, Senegal: UNESCO Regional Office for
    Education in Africa. 1984.
McSweeney, Brenda G. and Freedman, Marion
    "Lack of Time as an Obstacle to Women's Education: The
    Case of Upper Volta." Comparative Education Review.
    Volume 24 #2 Part Two June, 1980. pp. S124-S139.
McSweeney, Brenda G. and Freedman, Marion
    "Lack of Time as an Obstacle to Women's Education: The
    Case of Upper Volta." (In) Kelly, G.P. and Elliott, C.M.
    (eds.). Women's Education in the Third World:
    Comparative Perspectives. Albany, New York: State
    University of New York Press. 1982. pp. 88-103.
McSweeney, Brenda G.
    "The Negative Impact of Development on Women
    Reconsidered: A Study of the Women's Education Project in
    Upper Volta." Ph.D Dissertation: Tufts University.

Fletcher School of Law and Diplomacy. Boston,
Massachusetts. 1979.
McSweeney, Brenda G.
  "Time to Learn, Time for a Better Life. The Women's
  Education Project in Upper Volta." Assignment Children.
  Volume 49/50 Spring, 1980. pp. 109-126.
Mitchnik, David A.
  The Role of Women in Rural Zaire and Upper Volta:
  Improving Methods of Skill Acquisition. Oxford, England:
  OXFAM. OXFAM Working Paper #2. 1978. 36p.
Munson, Martha L.
  "Fertility and Education in Upper Volta." (In) Pool, D.
  Ian and Coulibaly, Sidiki, P. (eds.). Demographic
  Trans-tion and Cultural Continuity in the Sahel: Aspects
  of the Social Demography of Upper Volta. Ithaca, New
  York: Cornell University. International Population
  Program. 1977. pp. 149-171.

EMPLOYMENT AND LABOR

Conti, Anna
  "Capitalist Organization of Production Through
  Non-Capitalist Relations: Women's Role in a Pilot
  Resettlement in Upper Volta." Review of African
  Political Economy. #15/16 1979. pp. 75-92.
Conti, Anna
  "Women on 'Schemes' in Upper Volta." Review of African
  Political Economy. #15/16 1979.
Hemmings-Gapihan, Grace S.
  "International Development and the Evolution of Women's
  Economic Roles: A Case Study From Northern Gulma, Upper
  Volta." (In) Bay, Edna G. (ed.). Women and Work in
  Africa. Boulder, Colorado: Westview Press. Westview
  Special Studies in Africa. 1982. pp. 171-189.
Hemmings-Gapihan, Grace S.
  "Women and Economy in Gourma, 1919-1978: A Study of
  Economic Change in Burkina Faso." Ph.D Dissertation:
  Yale University. New Haven, Connecticut. 1985. 389p.
Kwende, Tieba G.
  The Organization of Productive Work in Technical and
  Vocational Schools in Upper Volta: The Experience of the
  Centre for Women's Occupations and Handicrafts,
  Ouagadougou. Dakar, Senegal: UNESCO Regional Office for
  Education in Africa. 1984.

EQUALITY AND LIBERATION

Clearing House on Development Communications (CDC)
  Project for Equality of Access to Education for Women and
  Young Girls, Upper Volta. Washington, D.C.: CDC.
  Project Profile. January, 1978. 2p.

BURKINA FASO

FAMILY LIFE

Hemmings-Gapihan, Grace S.
"Women and Economy in Gourma, 1919-1978: A Study of
Economic Change in Burkina Faso." Ph.D Dissertation:
Yale University. New Haven, Connecticut. 1985. 389p.

FAMILY PLANNING AND CONTRACEPTION

Armagnac, Catherine and Retel-Laurentin, Anne
"Relations Between Fertility, Birth Intervals, Foetal
Mortality and Maternal Health in Upper Volta."
Population Studies. Volume 35 #2 July, 1981. pp.
217-234.
Coulibaly, Sidiki P.
"Religion, Philosphy and Fertility: The Case of Upper
Volta." (In) Pool, D. Ian and Coulibaly, Sidiki P.
(eds.). Demographic Transition and Cultural Continuity
in the Sahel: Aspects of the Social Demography of Upper
Volta. Ithaca, New York: Cornell University.
International Population Program. 1977. pp. 98-126.
Munson, Martha L.
"Fertility and Education in Upper Volta." (In) Pool, D.
Ian and Coulibaly, Sidiki, P. (eds.). Demographic
Trans-tion and Cultural Continuity in the Sahel: Aspects
of the Social Demography of Upper Volta. Ithaca, New
York: Cornell University. International Population
Program. 1977. pp. 149-171.
Pool, D. Ian
"The Growth of the City of Ouagadougou and Fertility
Trends." (In) Pool, D. Ian and Coulibaly, Sidiki P.
(eds.). Demographic Transition and Cultural Continuity
in the Sahel: Aspects of the Social Demography of Upper
Volta. Ithaca, New York: Cornell University.
International Population Program. 1977. pp. 127-148.

FERTILITY AND INFERTILITY

Armagnac, Catherine and Retel-Laurentin, Anne
"Relations Between Fertility, Birth Intervals, Foetal
Mortality and Maternal Health in Upper Volta."
Population Studies. Volume 35 #2 July, 1981. pp.
217-234.
Benoit, Daniel and Lacombe, Bernard and Levi, Pierre and
Livenais, Patrick and Sodter, Francois
"Main Results of a Survey Based on the Parish Registers
of Kongoussi-Tikare (Mossi Country, Upper Volta, 1978)."
(In) African Historical Demography: Proceedings of a
Seminar Held in the Centre of African Studies.
Edinburgh, Scotland: University of Edinburgh. Center of
African Studies. April 24-25, 1981. pp. 33-44.

Coulibaly, Sidiki P.
"Religion, Philosphy and Fertility: The Case of Upper
Volta." (In) Pool, D. Ian and Coulibaly, Sidiki P.
(eds.). Demographic Transition and Cultural Continuity
in the Sahel: Aspects of the Social Demography of Upper
Volta. Ithaca, New York: Cornell University.
International Population Program. 1977. pp. 98-126.
Lunganga, Layembe
"Pathological Factors Associated With Infertility: The
Case of Upper Volta, 1971." (In) Cairo Demographic
Centre (CDC). Studies in African and Asian Demography.
Cairo: CDC. CDC Research Monograph Series #11. 1983.
pp. 259-285.
Munson, Martha L.
"Fertility and Education in Upper Volta." (In) Pool, D.
Ian and Coulibaly, Sidiki, P. (eds.). Demographic
Trans-tion and Cultural Continuity in the Sahel: Aspects
of the Social Demography of Upper Volta. Ithaca, New
York: Cornell University. International Population
Program. 1977. pp. 149-171.
Munson, Martha L. and Bumpass, Larry L. and Pool, D. Ian
Determinants of Cumulative Fertility in Urban Upper
Volta. Washington, D.C.: National Institute of Mental
Health. 1979.
Pool, D. Ian
"The 1969 Survey on Fertility in Upper Volta." (In)
Pool, D. Ian and Coulibaly, Sidiki P. (eds.).
Demographic Transition and Cultural Transition and
Cultural Continuity in the Sahel: Aspects of the Social
Demography of Upper Volta. Ithaca, New York: Cornell
University. International Population Program. 1977. pp.
267-287.
Pool, D. Ian
"The Growth of the City of Ouagadougou and Fertility
Trends." (In) Pool, D. Ian and Coulibaly, Sidiki P.
(eds.). Demographic Transition and Cultural Continuity
in the Sahel: Aspects of the Social Demography of Upper
Volta. Ithaca, New York: Cornell University.
International Population Program. 1977. pp. 127-148.
Vad de Walle, Francine and Ouaidou, Nassour
"Status and Fertility Among Urban Blacks in Burkina
Faso." International Family Planning Perspectives.
Volume 11 #2 June, 1985. pp. 60-64.
Walle, Francine V. and Ougidou, Nassour
Women's Status and Childbearing on the Eve of a Fertility
Transition: Upper Volta, 1983. Philadelphia,
Pennsylvania: University of Pennsylvania. Population
Studies Center. 1984.

HEALTH, NUTRITION AND MEDICINE

Armagnac, Catherine and Retel-Laurentin, Anne
"Relations Between Fertility, Birth Intervals, Foetal
Mortality and Maternal Health in Upper Volta."
Population Studies. Volume 35 #2 July, 1981. pp.
217-234.
Bleiberg, Fanny M. and Brun, Thierry A. and Goihman, Samuel
and Gouba, Emile
"Duration of Activities and Energy Expenditure of Female
Farmers in Dry and Rainy Seasons in Upper Volta."
British Journal of Nutrition. Volume 43 1980. pp.
71-82.
Lunganga, Layembe
"Pathological Factors Associated With Infertility: The
Case of Upper Volta, 1971." (In) Cairo Demographic
Centre (CDC). Studies in African and Asian Demography.
Cairo: CDC. CDC Research Monograph Series #11. 1983.
pp. 259-285.
Triendregeogon, Alice
"Female Circumcision in Upper Volta." Paper Presented at
the Seminar on Traditional Practices Affecting the Health
of Women and Children. World Conference of the United
Nations Decade for Women. New York: United Nations.
Copenhagen, Denmark. July 14-30, 1980.
Triendregeogon, Alice
"Female Circumcision in Upper Volta." Paper Presented at
the Seminar on Traditional Practices Affecting the Health
of Women and Children: Female Circumcision, Childhood
Marriage, Nutritional Taboos, etc. Alexandria, Egypt:
World Health Organization. Eastern Mediterranean
Regional Office. (May be in French) Khartoum, Sudan.
1979.
Vad de Walle, Francine and Ouaidou, Nassour
"Status and Fertility Among Urban Blacks in Burkina
Faso." International Family Planning Perspectives.
Volume 11 #2 June, 1985. pp. 60-64.
Walle, Francine V. and Ougidou, Nassour
Women's Status and Childbearing on the Eve of a Fertility
Transition: Upper Volta, 1983. Philadelphia,
Pennsylvania: University of Pennsylvania. Population
Studies Center. 1984.

MARITAL RELATIONS AND NUPTIALITY

Armagnac, Catherine and Retel-Laurentin, Anne
"Relations Between Fertility, Birth Intervals, Foetal
Mortality and Maternal Health in Upper Volta."
Population Studies. Volume 35 #2 July, 1981. pp.
217-234.
Pool, Janet S.
"Conjugal Patterns in Upper Volta." (In) Pool, D. Ian

and Coulibaly, Sidiki P. (eds.). Demographic Transition
and Cultural Continuity in the Sahel: Aspects of the
Social Demography of Upper Volta. Ithaca, New York:
Cornell University. International Population Program.
1977. pp. 38-97.
Quimby, Lucy
    "Islam, Sex Roles and Modernization in Bobo-Dioulasso."
    (In) Jules-Rosette, Bennetta (ed.). The New Religions of
    Africa. Norwood, New Jersey: Ablex Publishing Co. 1979.
    pp. 203-218.

ORGANIZATIONS

Kwende, Tieba G.
    The Organization of Productive Work in Technical and
    Vocational Schools in Upper Volta: The Experience of the
    Centre for Women's Occupations and Handicrafts,
    Ouagadougou. Dakar, Senegal: UNESCO Regional Office for
    Education in Africa. 1984.

RELIGION AND WITCHCRAFT

Coulibaly, Sidiki P.
    "Religion, Philosphy and Fertility: The Case of Upper
    Volta." (In) Pool, D. Ian and Coulibaly, Sidiki P.
    (eds.). Demographic Transition and Cultural Continuity
    in the Sahel: Aspects of the Social Demography of Upper
    Volta. Ithaca, New York: Cornell University.
    International Population Program. 1977. pp. 98-126.
Quimby, Lucy
    "Islam, Sex Roles and Modernization in Bobo-Dioulasso."
    (In) Jules-Rosette, Bennetta (ed.). The New Religions of
    Africa. Norwood, New Jersey: Ablex Publishing Co. 1979.
    pp. 203-218.

SEX ROLES

Hemmings-Gapihan, Grace S.
    "Women and Economy in Gourma, 1919-1978: A Study of
    Economic Change in Burkina Faso." Ph.D Dissertation:
    Yale University. New Haven, Connecticut. 1985. 389p.
Henderson, Helen K.
    "The Role of Women in Livestock Production: Some
    Preliminary Findings." (In) Vengroff, Richard (ed.).
    Upper Volta: Environmental Uncertainty and Livestock
    Production. Lubbock, Texas: International Center for the
    Study of Arid and Semi-Arid Lands. 1980.
Mitchnik, David A.
    The Role of Women in Rural Zaire and Upper Volta:
    Improving Methods of Skill Acquisition. Oxford, England:
    OXFAM. OXFAM Working Paper #2. 1978. 36p.

Pool, Janet S.
  "Conjugal Patterns in Upper Volta." (In) Pool, D. Ian
  and Coulibaly, Sidiki P. (eds.). Demographic Transition
  and Cultural Continuity in the Sahel: Aspects of the
  Social Demography of Upper Volta. Ithaca, New York:
  Cornell University. International Population Program.
  1977. pp. 38-97.
Quimby, Lucy
  "Islam, Sex Roles and Modernization in Bobo-Dioulasso."
  (In) Jules-Rosette, Bennetta (ed.). The New Religions of
  Africa. Norwood, New Jersey: Ablex Publishing Co. 1979.
  pp. 203-218.

SEXUAL MUTILATION/CIRCUMCISION

Triendregeogon, Alice
  "Female Circumcision in Upper Volta." Paper Presented at
  the Seminar on Traditional Practices Affecting the Health
  of Women and Children. World Conference of the United
  Nations Decade for Women. New York: United Nations.
  Copenhagen, Denmark. July 14-30, 1980.
Triendregeogon, Alice
  "Female Circumcision in Upper Volta." Paper Presented at
  the Seminar on Traditional Practices Affecting the Health
  of Women and Children: Female Circumcision, Childhood
  Marriage, Nutritional Taboos, etc. Alexandria, Egypt:
  World Health Organization. Eastern Mediterranean
  Regional Office. (May be in French) Khartoum, Sudan.
  1979.

STATUS OF WOMEN

Bohmer, C.
  "Modernization, Divorce and the Status of Women; le
  tribunal coutumierin Bobodioulasso." African Studies
  Review. Volume 23 #2 September, 1980. pp. 81-90.
Vad de Walle, Francine and Ouaidou, Nassour
  "Status and Fertility Among Urban Blacks in Burkina
  Faso." International Family Planning Perspectives.
  Volume 11 #2 June, 1985. pp. 60-64.
Walle, Francine V. and Ougidou, Nassour
  Women's Status and Childbearing on the Eve of a Fertility
  Transition: Upper Volta, 1983. Philadelphia,
  Pennsylvania: University of Pennsylvania. Population
  Studies Center. 1984.

URBANIZATION

Munson, Martha L. and Bumpass, Larry L. and Pool, D. Ian
  Determinants of Cumulative Fertility in Urban Upper

BURKINA FASO

Volta. Washington, D.C.: National Institute of Mental
    Health. 1979.
Vad de Walle, Francine and Ouaidou, Nassour
    "Status and Fertility Among Urban Blacks in Burkina
    Faso." International Family Planning Perspectives.
    Volume 11 #2 June, 1985. pp. 60-64.

Cape Verde Islands

Silva, Andrade E.
    "Women in the Cape Verde Islands: The National Liberation
    Struggle, National Reconstruction and Prospects." Paper
    Presented at the Meeting of Experts on the History of
    Women's Contribution to National Liberation Struggles and
    Their Roles and Needs During Reconstruction in Newly
    Independent Countries in Africa. Paris: United Nations
    Educational, Scientific and Cultural Organization.
    Bissau, Guinea-Bissau. 1983. 21p.

Chad

Conte, Edouard
   Marriage Patterns, Political Change and the Perpetuation
   of Social Inequality in South Karem, Chad. Paris: Office
   de Recherche Scientifique et Technique d'Outre-Mer
   (OSTROM). 1983. 545p.
Conte, Edouard
   "Politics and Marriage in South Kanem (Chad): A
   Statistical Presentation of Endogamy From 1895-1975."
   Cahiers ORSTROM, Serie Sciences Humaines. Volume 16 #4
   1979. pp. 275-297.
Crognier, E.
   "Marriages, Migrations and the Biological Population in a
   Sara Tribe From Chad." Journal of Human Organization.
   Volume 6 #2 February, 1977. pp. 159-168.
LeVine, Robert A.
   "Influences of Women's Schooling on Maternal Behavior in
   the Third World." (In) Kelly, Gail P. and Elliott,
   Carolyn M. (eds.). Women's Education in the Third World:
   Comparative Perspectives. Albany, New York: State
   University of New York Press. 1982. pp. 283-310.
Reyna, Stephen P.
   "Barma Bridewealth: Socialization and the Reproduction of
   Labour in a Domestic African Economy." Africa. Volume
   54 #4 1984. pp. 59-72.
Reyna, Stephen P.
   "Marriage Payments, Household Structure and Domestic
   Labour Supply Among the Barma of Chad." Africa. Volume
   47 #1 1977. pp. 81-88.
Reyna, Stephen P.
   "The Rationality of Divorce: Marital Instability Among
   the Barma of Chad." Journal of Comparative Family
   Studies. Volume 8 #2 Summer, 1977. pp. 269-288.
Reyna, Stephen P.
   "The Rationality of Divorce: Marital Instability Among
   the Barma of Chad." (In) Kurian, George (ed.).
   Cross-Cultural Perspectives of Mate-Selection and

Marriage. Westport, Connecticut: Greenwood Press. Contributions in Family Studies #3. 1979. pp. 313-321.

Rogers, Susan G.
"Anti-Colonial Protest in Africa: A Female Strategy Reconsidered." Heresies. Volume 3 #1 1980. pp. 22-27.

Topping-Bazin, Nancy
"Feminist Perspectives in African Fiction: Bessie Head and Buchi Emecheta." Paper Presented at the Annual Meeting of the African Literature Association. Baltimore, Maryland: University of Maryland. African-American Studies Association. April, 1984.

United States Agency for International Development (US.AID)
Project Paper: Training of Farmer Women for Increased Agricultural Production. N'djamena, Chad: US.AID/Chad. 1978.

Gambia

Bates, C.J.
   "Efficacy of a Riboflavin Supplement Given at Fortnightly
   Intervals to Pregnant and Lactating Women in Rural
   Gambia." Human Nutrition. Clinical Nutrition. Volume
   37 #6 December, 1983. pp. 427-432.
Bates, C.J.
   "Riboflavin Requirements of Lactating Gambian Women: A
   Controlled Supplementation Trial." American Journal of
   Clinical Nutrition. Volume 35 #4 April, 1982. pp.
   701-709.
Bates, C.J.
   "Riboflavin Status in Gambian Pregnant and Lactating
   Women and its Implications for Recommended Dietary
   Allowances." American Journal of Clinical Nutrition.
   Volume 34 #5 May, 1981. pp. 928-935.
Bates, C.J.
   "The Effect of Vitamin C Supplementation on Lactating
   Women in Keneba, a West African Rural Community."
   International Journal of Vitamin Nutrition Research.
   Volume 53 #1 1983. pp. 68-76.
Ceesay-Marenah, Coumba
   "Women's Cooperative Thrift and Credit Societies: An
   Element of Women's Programme in the Gambia." (In) Bay,
   Edna G. (ed.). Women and Work in Africa. Boulder,
   Colorado: Westview Press. Westview Special Studies in
   Africa." 1982. pp. 289-295.
Colvin, Lucie G.
   "The Uprooted in the Western Sahel: Migrants' Quest for
   Cash in the Senegambia: Final Report of the Senegambia
   Migration Study." Washington, D.C.: U.S. Department of
   State. U.S. Agency for International Development. 1980.
   307p.
Colvin, Lucie G.
   "The Uprooted of the Western Sahel: Migrants' Quest for
   Cash in Senegambia." New York: Praeger Publishers.
   1981. 385p.

Dey, Jennie M.
    "Gambian Women: Unequal Partners in Rice Development
    Projects?" (In) Nelson, Nici (ed.). African Women in
    the Development Process. London: Cass. pp. 109-122.
    1981.
Dey, Jennie M.
    "Gambian Women; Unequal Partners in Rice Development
    Projects?" Journal of Development Studies. Volume 17 #3
    April, 1981. pp. 109-122.
Dey, Jennie M.
    "Women Farmers in the Gambia: The Effects of Irrigated
    Rice Development Programmes on Their Role in Rice
    Production." Oxford, England: Oxford University.
    Unpublished Mimeo. 1979.
Dey, Jennie M.
    "Women and Rice in Gambia: The Impact of Irrigated Rice
    Development Projects on the Farming System." Ph.D
    Dissertation: University of Reading. Reading, England.
    1980.
Franks, James A. and Minnis, Robert L. and Wilson, Paul E.
    "Maternal and Child Health/Family Planning Project for
    the Republic of the Gambia and the People's Republic of
    Benin, West Africa. Final Report." Santa Cruz,
    California: University of California--Santa Cruz.
    February, 1980. 514p.
Hamer, Alice J.
    "Diola Women and Migration: A Case Study." (In) Colvin,
    Lucie G. The Uprooted in the Sahel: Migrant's Quest for
    Cash in the Senegambia. Final Report on the Senegambia
    Migration Study. Washington, D.C.: U.S. Department of
    State. U.S. Agency for International Development. 1979.
Lamb, W.H. and Foord, Frances A. and Lamb, Colette M. and
Whitehead, Roger G.
    "Changes in Maternal and Child Mortality Rates in Three
    Isolated Gambian Villages Over Ten Years." Lancet.
    #8408 October 20, 1984. pp. 912-914.
Lamb, W.H. and Lawrence, F. and Whitehead, Roger G.
    "Maintenance Energy-Cost of Pregnancy in Rural Gambian
    Women and Influence of Dietary Status." Lancet. Volume
    2 #8399 1984. pp. 363-365.
Lunn, P.G.
    "The Effect of Improved Nutrition on Plasma Prolactin
    Concentrations and Postpartum Infertility in Lactating
    Gambian Women." American Journal of Clinical Nutrition.
    Volume 39 #2 February, 1984. pp. 227-235.
Mabey, D.C.
    "Tubal Infertility in the Gambia: Chlamydial and
    Gonococcal Serology in Women With Tubal Occlusion
    Compared With Pregnant Controls." Bulletin of the World
    Health Organization. Volume 63 #6 1985. pp. 1107-1113.
National Asso. of Negro Business and Prof. Women's Clubs
    African Women Small Entrepreneurs in Senegal, The Gambia,
    Sierra Leone, Cameroon and Malawi: Prefeasibility Study
    for Providing Assistance. Washington, D.C.: NANBPA.
    1977. 82p.

Paul, Alison A. and Muller, Elisabeth M.
    "Seasonal Variations in Dietary Intake in Pregnant and
    Lactating Women in a Rural Gambian Village." (In) Abei,
    H. and Whitehead, R.G. (eds.). Maternal Nutrition in
    Pregnancy and Lactation. Berne, Switzerland: Han Huber.
    1979.
Paul, Alison A. and Muller, Elizabeth M. and Whitehead,
Roger G.
    "Seasonal Variations in Energy Intake, Body-Weight and
    Skinfold Thickness in Pregnant and Lactating Women in
    Rural Gambia." Proceedings of the Nutrition Society.
    Volume 38 #2 1979. pp. 28A.
Paul, Alison A. and Muller, Elisabeth M. and Whitehead,
Roger G.
    "The Quantitative Effects of Maternal Dietary Energy
    Intake on Pregnancy and Lactation in Rural Gambian
    Women." Transactions of the Royal Society of Tropical
    Medicine and Hygiene. Volume 73 1979. pp. 686-692.
Peil, Margaret
    "Urban Contacts: A Comparison of Women and Men." (In)
    Oppong, Christine (ed.). Female and Male in West Africa.
    London: George Allen and Unwin. 1983. pp. 275-282.
Powers, H.J.
    "Haematological Response to Supplements of Iron and
    Riboflavin to Pregnant and Lactating Women in Rural
    Gambia." Human Nutrition. Clinical Nutrition. Volume
    39 #2 March, 1985. pp.117-129.
Prentice, A.
    "Breast-Milk Antimicrobial Factors of Rural Gambian
    Mothers. I. Influence of Stage of Lactation and
    Maternal Plane of Nutrition." ACTA Paediatrica
    Scandinavica. Volume 73 #6 November, 1984. pp.
    796-802.
Prentice, A.
    "Breastmilk Antimicrobial Factors in Rural Gambian
    Mothers. II. Influence of Season and Prevalence of
    Infection." ACTA Paediatrica Scandinavica. Volume 73 #6
    November, 1984. pp. 803-809.
Prentice, A.
    "Long-Term Energy Balance in Chld-Bearing Gambian Women."
    American Journal of Clinical Nutrition. Volume 34 #12
    December, 1981. pp. 2790-2799.
Prentice, A.M.
    "Dietary Supplementation of Lactating Gambian Women. II.
    Effect of Maternal Health, Nutritional Status and
    Biochemistry." Human Nutrition. Clinical Nutrition.
    Volume 37 #1 January, 1983. pp. 65-74.
Prentice, Andrew M.
    "Dietary Intake and Weight Changes During Pregnancy:
    Birthweight and Lactation Capacity in the Gambia." (In)
    Abei, H. and Whitehead, R.G. (eds.). Maternal Nutrition
    in Pregnancy and Lactation. Berne, Switzerland: Hans
    Huber. 1979.
Prentice, Andrew M. and Roberts, Susan B. and Watkinson, M.
and Whitehead, Roger G. and Paul, Alison A. and Prentice,

Ann and Watkinson, Anne A.
   "Dietary Supplementation of Gambian Nursing Mothers and
   Lactational Performance." Lancet. Volume 2 October 25,
   1980. pp. 886-888.
Prentice, Andrew M.
   "Dietary Supplementation of Lactating Gambian Women..."
   Human Nutrition.   Clinical Nurtrition. Volume 37C #1
   1983. pp. 53-74.
Prentice, Ann and Prentice, Andrew M. and Whitehead, Roger
G.
   "Breast Milk Fat Concentrations of Rural African Women,
   The Gambia: Part One: Short Term Variations Within
   Individuals." British Journal of Nutrition. Volume 45
   #3 May, 1981. pp. 483-494.
Prentice, Ann and Prentice, Andrew M. and Whitehead, Roger
G.
   "Breast Milk Fat Concentrations of Rural African Women:
   Part Two: Long Term Variations Within a Community. The
   Gambia." British Journal of Nutrition. Volume 45 #3
   May, 1981. pp. 495-503.
Swindell, K.
   "Family Farms and Migrant Labour: Strange Farmers of
   Gambia." Canadian Journal of African Studies. Volume 12
   #1 1978. pp. 3-18.
Watkinson, M.
   "Subjective Assessment of Lactational Performance in
   Gambian Mothers." Journal of Tropical Pediatrics.
   Volume 31 #3 June, 1985. pp. 150-152.
Weil, Peter M.
   "The Staff of Life: Food and Female Fertility in a West
   African Society." Africa. Volume 46 #2 1976. pp.
   182-195.
Whitehead, Roger G.
   "Factors Influencing Lactation Performance in Rural
   Gambian Mothers." Lancet. #8082 July 22, 1978. pp.
   178-181.

Ghana

ABORTION

Bleek, Wolf
    "Avoiding Shame: The Ethical Context of Abortion in
    Ghana." Anthropological Quarterly. Volume 54 #4
    October, 1981. pp. 203-209.
Bleek, Wolf
    "Induced Abortion in a Ghanaian Family." African Studies
    Review. Volume 21 #1 April, 1978. pp. 103-120.
Lamptey, Peter and Janowitz, Barbara and Smith, Jason B. and
Klufio, Cecil
    "Abortion Experience Among Obstetric Patients at Korle-Bu
    Hospital, Accra, Ghana." Journal of Biosocial Science.
    Volume 17 #2 April, 1985. pp. 195-203.
Makinwa, P. Kofo
    "The National Cost of Illegal Abortion: A Case for Family
    Planning Programme." Aman. Volume 1 #1 1981. pp.
    36-50.
Pappoe, Matilda E.
    "Women and Abortion." Paper Presented at the National
    Council on Women and Development (NCWD) Seminar on Women
    and Development. Accra, Ghana: NCWD. July, 1978.

AGRICULTURE

African Regional Agricultural Credit Association
    "Women's Programme in Agricultural Credit and Banking.
    Report." Presented at the Policy Maker's Workshop on
    Women's Agricultural Credit and Banking Programmes for
    Selected Eastern and Southern African Countries.
    Nairobi, Kenya. March 14, 1983. 94p.
Breebaart, Gera
    "Women and Extension in the Upper Region of Ghana."
    Approach. Volume 8 1979. pp. 33-41.

Bukh, Jette
    The Village Women of Ghana. Uppsala, Sweden:
    Scandinavian Institute of African Studies. Centre for
    Development Research. Publication #1. 1979. 118p.
Campbell-Platt, Kiran
    "The Impact of Mechanization on the Employment of Women
    in Traditional Sectors." Paper Presented at the National
    Council on Women and Development (NCWD) Seminar on Women
    and Development. Accra, Ghana: NCWD. September, 1978.
Dadson, J.A.
    "Women and Farm Credit in Ghanaian Agriculture: A
    Preliminary Exploration." Paper Presented at the
    Workshop on Women's Contribution to Food Production and
    Rural Development in Africa. Lome, Togo. June, 1981.
Date-Bah, Eugenia
    "Rural Women, Their Activities and Technology in Ghana:
    An Overview." (In) International Labour Organization
    (ILO). Rural Development and Women in Africa. Geneva:
    ILO. 1984. pp. 89-98.
Date-Bah, Eugenia and Brown, C. and Gyeke, L.
    "Ghanaian Women and Cooperatives." Paper Presented at
    the National Council on Women and Development (NCWD)
    Seminar on Women and Development. Accra, Ghana: NCWD.
    September, 1978. 26p.
Date-Bah, Eugenia
    "Technologies for Rural Women in Ghana: Role of
    Socio-Cultural Factors." (In) Ahmed, Iftikhar (ed.).
    Technology and Rural Women: Conceptual and Empirical
    Issues. Boston: George Allen and Unwin. 1985. pp.
    211-251.
Dugbaza, Tetteh
    "Women and Integration in Rural Development." Ghana
    Journal of Sociology. Volume 14 #1 1981. pp. 73-94.
Dumor, Ernest K.
    "Women in Rural Development in Ghana." Rural Africana.
    #17 Fall, 1983. 57-68.
Gbedemah, Charles
    "The Role of Women in the Production of Rice in Northern
    Ghana." Paper Presented at the National Council on Women
    and Development (NCWD) Seminar on Women and Development.
    Legon, Ghana: NCWD. September, 1978.
Greenstreet, Miranda
    "Various Salient Features Concerning the Employment of
    Women Workers in Ghana." Paper Presented at the National
    Council on Women and Development (NCWD) Seminar on Women
    and Development. Accra, Ghana: NCWD. July, 1978.
Greenstreet, Miranda
    Females in the Agricultural Labour Force and Non-Formal
    Education for Rural Development in Ghana. Hague,
    Netherlands: Institute of Social Studies. ISS Occasional
    Paper #90. August, 1981. 23p.
Guyer, Jane I.
    "Women in the Rural Economy: Contemporary Variations."
    (In) Hay, Margaret J. and Stichter, Sharon (eds.).

African Women South of the Sahara. New York: Longman.
1984. pp. 19-32.
Jeffalyn Johnson and Associates Inc.
African Women in Development. Falls Church, Virginia:
Jeffalyn Johnson and Associates Inc. 1980. 125p.
Klingshirn, A.
Investment of Women in Co-Operatives in Zaire and Ghana.
Rome: United Nations Food and Agriculture Organization.
UNFPA/FAO Study. 1978.
Mickelwait, Donald R. and Riegelman, Mary Ann and Sweet,
Charles F.
Women in Rural Development: A Survey of the Roles of
Women in Ghana, Lesotho, Kenya, Nigeria... Boulder,
Colorado: Westview Press. 1976. 224p.
Mikell, Gwendolyn
"Expansion and Contraction in Economic Access for Rural
Women in Ghana." Rural Africana. #21 Winter, 1985.
pp. 13-31.
Mikell, Gwendolyn
"Expansion and Contracting in Economic Access for Rural
Women in Ghana." Paper Presented at the Annual Meeting
of the African Studies Association. Paper #63.
Washington, D.C. November 4-7, 1982.
Okali, Christine
Cocoa and Kinship in Ghana: The Matrilineal Akan of
Ghana. London: Kegan Paul International for the
International African Institute. 1983. 179p.
Okali, Christine
"Kinship and Cocoa Farming in Ghana." (In) Oppong,
Christine (ed.). Female and Male in West Africa.
London: George Allen and Unwin. 1983. pp. 169-178.
Robertson, Claire C.
"The Death of Makola and Other Tragedies: Accra
Agricultural Markets, Rural Women, Ghana." Canadian
Journal of African Studies. Volume 17 #3 1983. pp.
469-496.
Tamakloe, Martha A.
Women in Agriculture: A Study of Mixed Crop Farmers in
Nkwaie-Toase Area. Kumasi, Ghana: Department of Housing
and Planning Research. U.S.T. 1978. 26p.
Tamakloe, Martha A.
"Women in Agriculture: A Study of Mixed Crop Farmers in
Nkawie-Toase Area." Paper Presented at the National
Council on Women and Development (NCWD) Conference on
Women in Development. Legon, Ghana: NCWD. September,
1978.
United Nations Food and Agriculture Organization (FAO)
Market Women in West Africa. Report of the Seminar on
the Role of Women in Marketing Local Farm and Marine
Produce, Accra, Ghana, December 12-16, 1977. Rome: FAO.
1977. 29p.
Vellenga, Dorothy D.
"Matriliny, Patriliny and Class Formation Among Women

Cocoa Farmers in Two Rural Areas of Ghana." Paper
Presented at the Annual Meeting of the African Studies
Association. Paper #126. Bloomington, Indiana. October
21-24, 1981.
Vellenga, Dorothy D.
"Differentiation Among Women Farmers in Two Rural Areas
in Ghana." Labour and Society. Volume 2 #2 April,
1977. pp. 197-208.
Vellenga, Dorothy D.
"Women, Households, and Food Commodity Chains in Southern
Ghana: Contradictions Between Search for Profits and the
Search for Survival." Research Review. Volume 8 #3
1985. pp. 293-318.
Vellenga, Dorothy D.
"Food as a Cash Crop for Women Farmers in Ghana: The
Persistent Search for Profit." Paper Presented at the
Annual Meeting of the Association for Women in
Development. Washington, D.C. October, 1983.

ARTS

Akuffo, F.O.
"High Wastage in Women's Education: The Case of the Rural
Elementary School Girls." Paper Presented at the
National Council on Women and Development (NCWD)
Conference on Women and Development. Accra, Ghana: NCWD
September 3-8, 1978.

CULTURAL ROLES

Abu, Katharine
"The Separateness of Spouses: Conjugal Resources in an
Ashanti Town." (In) Oppong, Christine (ed.). Female and
Male in West Africa. London: George Allen and Unwin.
1983. pp. 156-168.
Adinko, V.
Salt Mining by Women in the Keta Area. Legon, Ghana:
University of Ghana. Department of Sociology. 1980.
Aidoo, Agnes A.
"Asante Queen Mothers in Government and Politics in the
Nineteenth Century." Journal of the Historical Society
of Nigeria. Volume 9 #1 December, 1977. pp. 1-13.
Aidoo, Agnes A.
"Asante Queen Mothers in Government and Politics in the
Nineteenth Century." (In) Steady, Filomina C. (ed.).
The Black Woman Cross-Culturally. Cambridge,
Massachusetts: Schenkman Publishing. 1981. pp. 65-78.
Aidoo, Ama Ata
"Ghana: To Be a Woman." (In) Morgan, Robin (ed.).
Sisterhood is Global. Garden City, New York: Anchor
Books. 1984. pp. 255-265.

Akuffo, F.O.
"High Wastage in Women's Education: The Case of the Rural Elementary School Girls." Paper Presented at the National Council on Women and Development (NCWD) Conference on Women and Development. Accra, Ghana: NCWD September 3-8, 1978.

Ampofo, Daniel A.
"The Danfa Family Planning Program in Rural Ghana." Studies in Family Planning. Volume 7 #10 October, 1976. 266-274.

Ankrah, Kwaku T.
"Assimilation or Selectivity: A Test of Competing Theses on the Relationship Between Rural-Urban Migration and Fertility in Ghana." Ph.D Dissertation: University of Cincinnati. Cincinnati, Ohio. 1979. 178p.

Arhin, Kwame
"The Political and Military Roles of Akan Women." (In) Oppong, Christine (ed.). Female and Male in West Africa. London: George Allen and Unwin. 1983. pp. 91-98.

Armar, A.A. and David, A.S.
"Implementing an Integrative Population Program in Ghana." Paper Presented at the Annual Conference of the International Committee on the Management of Population Programmes. Bali, Indonesia. July 12-14, 1976. pp. 60-69.

Aryee, A.F.
"Urbanization and the Incidence of Plural Marriage: Some Theoretical Perspectives." (In) Oppong, C. and Adaba, G. and Bekombo-Priso, M. and Mogey, J. (eds.). Marriage, Fertility and Parenthood in West Africa. Canberra, Australia: Australian National University. Department of Demography. Volume One. 1978. pp. 367-379.

Aryee, A.F. and Gaisie, Samuel K.
"Fertility Implications of Contemporary Patterns of Nuptiality in Ghana." (In) Ruzicka, L.T. (ed.). Nuptiality and Fertility: Proceedings of a Seminar. Liege, Belgium: International Union for the Scientific Study of Population. January 8-11, 1979. Bruges, Belgium. 1982. pp. 287-304.

Asante-Darko, Nimrod and Van Der Geest, Sjaak
"Male Chauvinism: Men and Women in Ghanaian Highlife Songs." (In) Oppong, Christine (ed.). Female and Male in West Africa. London: George Allen and Unwin. 1983. pp. 242-255.

Asomani, Carolann G.
"A Descriptive Survey of the University Women of Ghana and Their Attitudes Toward the Women's Movement." Ed.D Dissertation: George Washington University. Washington D.C. 1977. 191p.

Assimeng, Max
"The Witchcraft Scene in Ghana: A Sociological Comment." Ghana Social Science Journal. Volume 4 #1 May, 1977. pp. 54-78.

Azu, Gladys D.
    "Women and Contraception." Paper Presented at the
    National Council on Women and Development (NCWD)
    Conference on Women and Development. Accra, Ghana: NCWD
    July, 1978.
Bame, K.N.
    "Some Traditional and Modern Media for Generating Social
    Change in Rural Africa: A Study of Some Traditional and
    Modern Media for Communicating Family Planning in Ghana."
    Paper Prepared for the Fourth World Congress of Rural
    Sociology. 1976. 46p.
Bartel, Philip F.
    "Conjugal Roles and Fertility in Old Country Ghana."
    Paper Presented at the 15th International Seminar on
    Family Research. Lome, Togo. 1976.
Bartle, Philip F.
    "Modernization and the Decline in Women's Status: An
    Example From Matrilineal Akan Community." Paper
    Presented at the National Council on Women and
    Development (NCWD) Seminar on Women and Development.
    Accra, Ghana: NCWD. Accra, Ghana. September, 1978.
Bartle, Philip F.
    "Conjugal Relations, Migration, and Fertility in an Akan
    Community, Obo, Ghana." (In) Oppong, C. and Adaba, G.
    and Bekombo-Priso, M. and Mogey, J. (eds.). Marriage,
    Fertility and Parenthood in West Africa. Canberra,
    Australia: Australian National University. Department of
    Demography. Volume Two. 1978. pp. 521-532.
Belcher, D.W.
    "Attitudes Towards Family Size and Family Planning in
    Rural Ghana Danfa Project: 1972 Survey Findings."
    Journal of Biosocial Science. Volume 10 #1 January,
    1978. pp. 59-79.
Berrian, Brenda F.
    "African Women as Seen in the Works of Flora Nwapa and
    Ama Ata Aidoo." CLA Journal. Volume 25 #3 March, 1982.
    pp. 331-339.
Bhatia, Jagdish C.
    "Correlates of Husband-Wife Attitudes Towards Family
    Planning in Rural Ghana." Health and Population:
    Perspectives and Issues. Volume 5 #2 April-June, 1982.
    pp. 97-107.
Bhatia, Jagdish C.
    "Determinants of Desired Family Size in Rural Ghana: A
    Multivariate Analysis." Demography India. Volume 11 #2
    July-December, 1982. pp. 221-243.
Bhatia, Jagdish C.
    "Age at Marriage Differentials in Ghana: A Multivariate
    Analysis." Demography India. Volume 13 #1-2
    January-December, 1984. pp. 54-69.
Bhatia, Jagdish C.
    "Age at Marriage and Fertility in Ghana." Demography
    India. Volume 12 #2 July-December, 1983. pp. 185-193.

Bhatia, Jagdish C.
"Polygamy-Fertility Inter-Relationship: The Case of
Ghana." Journal of Family Welfare. Volume 31 #4 June,
1985. pp. 46-55.

Bhatia, Jagdish C.
"A Multivariate Analysis of Family Planning Knowledge
Differentials in Rural Ghana." Journal of Family
Welfare. Volume 30 #4 June, 1984. pp. 47-60.

Bleek, Wolf
Birth Control and Sexual Relations in Ghana: A Case Study
of a Rural Town. Amsterdam, Netherlands:
Antropologisch-Sociologisch Centrum. 1976.

Bleek, Wolf
"The Value of Children to Parents in Kwahu, Ghana." (In)
Oppong, C. and Adaba, G. and Bekombo-Priso, M. and Mogey,
J. (eds.). Marriage, Fertility and Parenthood in West
Africa. Canberra, Australia: Australian National
University. Department of Demography. Volume One.
1978. pp. 307-323.

Bleek, Wolf
"The Impossible Decision: Having Children in Kwahu,
Ghana." Paper Presented at the International Union for
the Scientific Study of Population Conference. Liege,
Belgium: IUSSP. Helsinki, Finland. 1978. 51p.

Bleek, Wolf
"Witchcraft, Gossip and Death: A Social Drama." Man.
New Series Volume 11 #4 December, 1976. pp. 526-541.

Bleek, Wolf
"Spacing of Children, Sexual Abstinence and Breast
Feeding in Rural Ghana." Social Science and Medicine.
Volume 10 #5 1976. pp. 225-230.

Bleek, Wolf
"Avoiding Shame: The Ethical Context of Abortion in
Ghana." Anthropological Quarterly. Volume 54 #4
October, 1981. pp. 203-209.

Bleek, Wolf
"Family Planning or Birth Control: The Ghanaian
Contradiction." Cultures et Developpement. Volume 9 #1
1977. pp. 64-81.

Bleek, Wolf
"The Unexpected Repression: How Family Planning
Discriminates Against Women in Ghana." Review of
Ethnology. Volume 7 #25 1981. pp. 193-198.

Bleek, Wolf
"Induced Abortion in a Ghanaian Family." African Studies
Review. Volume 21 #1 April, 1978. pp. 103-120.

Bleek, Wolf
Sexual Relations and Birth Control in Ghana: A Case Study
of a Rural Town. Amsterdam, Netherlands: University of
Amsterdam. Antropologisch-Sociologisch Centrum. Uitgave
#10. 1976. 352p.

Bleek, Wolf
"Marriage in Kwahu, Ghana." (In) Roberts, Simon (ed.).

Law and the Family in Africa. Hague, Netherlands:
Mouton. 1977. pp. 183-204.
Breebaart, Gera
"Women and Extension in the Upper Region of Ghana."
Approach. Volume 8 1979. pp. 33-41.
Breidenbach, Paul
"The Woman on the Beach and the Man in the Bush:
Leadership and Adepthood in the Twelve Apostles Movement
in Ghana." (In) Jules-Rosette, Bennetta (ed.). The New
Religions of Africa. Norwood, New Jersey: Ablex
Publishing Corp. 1979. pp. 99-115.
Brown, Edward K.
"Patterns of Internal Migration in Ghana With Special
Emphasis on the Determinants of Female Migration." Ph.D
Dissertation: University of Pennsylvania. Philadelphia,
Pennsylvania. 1983. 295p.
Brydon, Lynne
"Women at Work: Some Changes in Family Structure in
Amedzofe-Avatime, Ghana." Africa. Volume 49 #2 1979.
pp. 97-110.
Brydon, Lynne
"Avatime Women and Men, 1900-1980." (In) Oppong,
Christine (ed.). Female and Male in Africa. London:
George Allen and Unwin. 1983. pp. 320-329.
Brydon, Lynne
"Status Ambiguity in Amedzofe-Avatime: Women and Men in a
Changing Patrilineal Society." Ph.D Dissertation:
University of Cambridge. Cambridge, England. 1976.
Brydon, Lynne
"The Dimensions of Subordination: A Case Study From
Avatime, Ghana." (In) Afshar, H. (ed.). Women, Work and
Ideology in the Third World. London: Tavistock. 1985.
pp. 109-127.
Bukh, Jette
The Village Women of Ghana. Uppsala, Sweden:
Scandinavian Institute of African Studies. Centre for
Development Research. Publication #1. 1979. 118p.
Caldwell, John C.
"Marriage, the Family and Fertility in Sub-Saharan Africa
With Special Reference to Research Programmes in Ghana
and Nigeria." (In) Huzayyin, S.A. and Acsadi, G.T.
(eds.). Family and Marriage in Some African and Asian
Countries. Cairo: Cairo Demographic Centre. CDC
Research Monograph #6. 1976. pp. 359-371.
Caldwell, John C.
"The Economic Rationality of High Fertility: An
Investigation Illustrated With Nigerian Survey Data.
Population Studies (London). Volume 31 #1 March, 1977.
pp. 5-27.
Caldwell, John C.
Population Growth and Family Change in Africa: The New
Urban Elite in Ghana. London: C. Hurst. 1977. 22p.

Callaway, Barbara J.
    "Women in Ghana." (In) Iglitzin, Lynne B. and Ross, Ruth
    (eds.). Women in the World. Santa Barbara, California:
    Clio Books. 1976. pp. 189-201.
Chinnery-Hesse, Mary
    "Some Comments on the Ghanaian Situation." (In) Boserup,
    Ester (ed.). The Traditional Division of Work Between
    the Sexes, a Source of Inequality. Geneva: International
    Institute for Labour Studies. Research Series #21. 1976.
Chinnery-Hesse, Mary
    "Women and Decision Making--Some Comments on the Themes
    With Special Reference to the Ghanaian Situation."
    Labour and Society. Volume 1 #2 1976. pp. 35-36.
Chukwukere, I.
    "Akan Theory of Conception: Are the Fante Really
    Aberrant?" Africa. Volume 48 #2 1978. pp. 135-147.
Chukwukere, I.
    "Agnatic and Uterine Relations Among the Fante:
    Male/Female Dualism." Africa. Volume 52 #1 1982. pp.
    61-64.
Church, K.V.
    "Women and Family Life in an Ashanti Town." M.A. Thesis:
    University of Ghana. Legon, Ghana. 1978.
Daniels, W.C.
    "The Effect of Marriage on the Status of Children in
    Ghana." (In) Roberts, Simon (ed.). Law and the Family
    in Africa. Hague, Netherlands: Mouton. 1977. pp.
    159-168.
Date-Bah, Eugenia
    The Changing Work Roles of Ghanaian Women. Accra, Ghana:
    National Council on Women and Development. 1980.
Date-Bah, Eugenia
    "Women in an Urban Setting for Ghana: Ghanaian Women in
    Factory Employment." Greenhill Journal of
    Administration. Volume 4 #1/2 April-September, 1977.
    pp. 76-94.
Date-Bah, Eugenia
    "Technologies for Rural Women in Ghana: Role of
    Socio-Cultural Factors." (In) Ahmed, Iftikhar (ed.).
    Technology and Rural Women: Conceptual and Empirical
    Issues. Boston: George Allen and Unwin. 1985. pp.
    211-251.
Dinan, Carmel
    "Work, Marriage and Autonomy." (In) Allen, C. and
    Williams, G. (eds.). Subsaharan Africa. London:
    Macmillan. Sociology of Developing Societies Series.
    1982. pp. 52-57.
Dugbaza, Tetteh
    "Women and Integration in Rural Development." Ghana
    Journal of Sociology. Volume 14 #1 1981. pp. 73-94.
Dumor, Ernest K.
    "Commodity Queens and the Distributive Trade in Ghana: A

Socio-Historical Analysis." African Urban Studies.
Volume 12 1982. pp. 27-45.
Dumor, Ernest K.
"Commodity Queens and the Distributive Trade in Ghana."
Paper Presented at the Annual Meeting of the African
Studies Association. Paper #23. Baltimore, Maryland.
1978. 25p.
Dzidzienyo, Stella
"Housemaids: A Case Study of Domestic Helpers in Ghanaian
Homes." Paper Presented at the National Council on Women
and Development (NCWD) Seminar on Women and Development.
Accra, Ghana: NCWD. September, 1978.
Ebin, Victoria
"Interpretations of Infertility: The Aowin People of
Southwest Ghana." (In) MacCormack, C.P. (ed.).
Ethnography of Fertility and Birth. London: Academic
Press. 1982. pp. 141-159.
Fogelberg, Teresa
Nanumba Women: Working Bees or Idle Bums? Sexual Division
of Labour, Ideology of Work, and Power Relations Between
Women and Men in Gole, A Village in Nanumba District,
Northern Region, Ghana. Leiden, Netherlands: Institute
of Cultural and Social Studies. 1981. 83p.
Fosu, Gabriel B.
"Interrelations Among Health Attitudes, Fertility, and
Mortality in Accra." Ph.D Dissertation: Brown
University. Providence, Rhode Island. 1984. 406p.
Franklin, Jopseph
African: A Photographic Essay on Black Women of Ghana and
Nigeria. Sebastopol, California: Wallingford Books,
Chulainn Press. 1977. 137p.
Gaisie, Samuel K.
The Proximate Determinants of Fertility in Ghana.
Voorburg, Netherlands: International Statistical
Institute. WFS Scientific Report #53. March, 1984.
63p.
Gaisie, Samuel K.
"Child-Spacing Patterns and Fertility Differentials in
Ghana." (In) Page, Hilary J. and Lesthaeghe, Ron (eds.).
Child-Spacing in Tropical Africa: Traditions and Change.
New York: Academic Press. 1981. pp. 237-253.
Gaisie, Samuel K.
"Mediating Mechanisms of Fertility Change in Africa--The
Role of Post-Partum Variables in the Process of Change:
The Case of Ghana." (In) International Union for the
Scientific Study of Population (IUSSP). International
Population Conference: Solicited Papers. Liege,
Netherlands: IUSSP. Volume One. 1981. pp. 95-114.
Goody, Esther N.
Parenthood and Social Reproduction: Fostering and
Occupational Roles in West Africa. Cambridge, New York:
Cambridge University Press. Cambridge Studies In Social
Anthropology #35. 1982. 348p.

Goody, Jack and Duly, Colin and Beeson, Ian and Harrison, Graham
    "On the Absence of Implicit Sex-Preference in Ghana."
    Journal of Biosocial Science. Volume 13 #1 January,
    1981. pp. 87-96.
Hagaman, Barbara L.
    "Beer and Matriliny: The Power of Women in Lobir, Ghana."
    Ph.D Dissertation: Northeastern University. Boston,
    Massachusetts. 1977. 365p.
Hagan, George P.
    "Divorce, Polygyny and Family Welfare." Ghana Journal of
    Sociology. Volume 10 #1 1976. pp. 67-84.
Hagan, George P.
    "Marriage, Divorce and Polygyny in Winneba." (In)
    Oppong, Christine (ed.). Female and Male in West Africa.
    London: George Allen and Unwin. 1983. pp. 192-203.
Hershman, Paul
    "A Comparison of Punjabi and Tallensi Marriage Systems."
    Eastern Anthropologist. Volume 33 #4 October-December,
    1980. pp. 299-334.
Hevi-Yiboe, L.A.
    Smoke in Rural Ghanaian Kitchens. Accra, Ghana: Arakan
    Press. 1979.
Kalu, Wilhemina J.
    "Modern Ga Family Life Patterns: A Look at Changing
    Marriage Structure in Africa." Journal of Black Studies.
    Volume 11 #3 March, 1981. pp. 349-359.
Kilson, Marion
    "Ritual Portrait of a Ga Medium." (In) Jules-Rosette,
    Bennetta (ed.). The New Religions of Africa. Norwood,
    New Jersey: Ablex Publishing Corp. 1979. pp. 67-79.
Lesthaeghe, Ron J. and Eelens, Frank
    Social Organization and Reproductive Regimes: Lessons
    From Sub-Saharan Africa and Historical Western Europe.
    Brussels, Belgium: Vrije Universiteit Brussel.
    Interuniversity Programme in Demography. IDP Working
    Paper #1985-1. 1985. 64p.
Lewis, Mary A.
    "Female Entrepreneural Styles: An Examination of Coastal
    Fante Businesswomen." Ph.D Dissertation: University of
    Washington. Seattle, Washington. 1977. 255p.
Little, Kenneth L.
    "A Question of Matrimonial Strategy? A Comparison of
    Attitudes Between Ghanaian and British University
    Students." Journal of Comparative Family Studies.
    Volume 7 #1 Spring, 1976. pp. 5-22.
Lowy, Michael J.
    "Establishing Paternity and Demanding Child Support in a
    Ghanaian Town." (In) Roberts, Simon (ed.). Law and
    Family in Africa. Hague, Netherlands: Mouton. 1977.
    pp. 15-38.
Luckham, Yaa
    "Law and the Status of Women in Ghana." (In) Columbia

Human Rights Law Review (eds.). Law and the Status of
Women: An International Symposium. New York: United
Nations. Centre for Social Development and Humanitarian
Affairs. 1977. pp. 69-94.
Makinwa, P. Kofo
"The National Cost of Illegal Abortion: A Case for Family
Planning Programme." Aman. Volume 1 #1 1981. pp.
36-50.
McCaffrey, Kathleen M.
Images of Women in the Literatures of Selected Developing
Countries. Washington, D.C.: U.S. Department of State.
U.S. Agency for International Development. Office of
Women in Development. 1981. 229p.
McCaskie, T.C.
"Anti-Witchcraft Cults in Asante..." History in Africa.
Volume 8 1981. pp. 125-154.
McCaskie, T.C.
"State and Society, Marriage and Adultery: Some
Considerations From the Social History of Pre-Colonial
Asante." Journal of African History. Volume 22 #4 1981.
pp. 477-494.
Mendonsa, Eugene L.
"Aspects of Sisala Marriage Prestations." Research
Review. Volume 9 #3 1976.
Mendonsa, Eugene L.
"Status of Women in Sisala Society." Sex Roles. Volume
7 #6 June, 1981. pp. 607-625.
Mendonsa, Eugene L.
"The Position of Women in the Sisala Divination Cult."
(In) Jules-Rosette, Bennetta (ed.). The New Religions of
Africa. Norwood, New Jersey: Ablex Publishing Corp.
1979. pp. 57-66.
Mendonsa, Eugene L.
"The Explanation of High Fertility Among the Sisala of
Northern Ghana." (In) Caldwell, John C. (ed.). The
Persistence of High Fertility: Population Prospects in
the Third World. Canberra, Australia: Australian
National University. Volume One. 1977. pp. 223-258.
Mikell, Gwendolyn
"Expansion and Contraction in Economic Access for Rural
Women in Ghana." Rural Africana. #21 Winter, 1985.
pp. 13-31.
Mikell, Gwendolyn
"Filiation, Economic Crisis and the Status of Women in
Ghana." Canadian Journal of African Studies." Volume 18
#1 1984. pp. 195-218.
Mikell, Gwendolyn
"Expansion and Contracting in Economic Access for Rural
Women in Ghana." Paper Presented at the Annual Meeting
of the African Studies Association. Paper #63.
Washington, D.C. November 4-7, 1982.
Nicholas, D.D.
"Attitudes and Practices of Traditional Birth Attendents

in Ghana: Implications for Training in Africa." Bulletin of the World Health Organization. Volume 54 #3 1976.

Nukunya, Godwin K.
"Women and Marriage." Paper Presented at the National Council on Women and Development (NCWD) Seminar on Women and Development. Accra, Ghana: NCWD. September, 1978.

Odouyoye, Mercy A.
"Namimg the Woman: The Words of the Akan and the Words of the Bible." Bulletin de Theologie Africaine. Volume 3 #5 January-June, 1981. pp. 81-97.

Oduyoye, Mercy A.
"The Asante Woman: Socialization Through Proverbs." African Notes. Volume 8 #1 1979. pp. 5-11.

Oduyoye, Mercy A.
"Female Authority in Asante Law and Constitution." African Notes. Volume 8 #2 1981. pp. 9-14.

Okali, Christine
Cocoa and Kinship in Ghana: The Matrilineal Akan of Ghana. London: Kegan Paul International for the International African Institute. 1983. 179p.

Okali, Christine
"Kinship and Cocoa Farming in Ghana." (In) Oppong, Christine (ed.). Female and Male in West Africa. London: George Allen and Unwin. 1983. pp. 169-178.

Opoku, Kwame
Law of Marriage in Ghana: a Study in Legal Pluralism. Frankfort, Germany: A. Metzner. 1976. 134p.

Oppong, Christine
"Ghanaian Women Teachers as Workers, Kin, Wives and Mothers: A Study of Conjugal Family Solidarity--Norms, Reality and Stress." Paper Presented at the Conference on Women and Development. Wellesley, Massachusetts: Wellesley College. June 2-6, 1976. 25p.

Oppong, Christine
"Motherhood in a Changing World: The Case of Ghana." UNICEF News. Volume 89 #3 1976. pp. 32+.

Oppong, Christine and Bleek, Wolf
"Economic Models and Having Children: Some Evidence From Kwahu, Ghana." Africa. Volume 52 #4 1982. pp. 15-33.

Oppong, Christine
Middle Class African Marriage: A Family Study of Ghanaian Senior Civil Servants. London: George Allen and Unwin. 1981. 190p.

Oppong, Christine
"From Love to Institution: Indications of Change in Akan Marriage." Journal of Family History. Volume 5 #2 1980. pp. 197-209.

Oppong, Christine
"Property, Power and Time: A Reassessment of Ghanaian Student Norms." (In) Oppong, C. and Adaba, G. and Bekombo-Priso, M. and Mogey, J. (eds.). Marriage, Fertility and Parenthood in West Africa. Canberra,

Australia: Australian National University. Department of
Demography. Volume Two. 1978. pp. 601-614.
Oppong, Christine
   "Women's Role and Conjugal Family Systems in Ghana."
   (In) Lupri, E. (ed.). The Changing Position of Women in
   Family and Society. Lieden, Netherlands: Brill. 1983.
   pp. 331-343.
Pappoe, Matilda E.
   "Women and Abortion." Paper Presented at the National
   Council on Women and Development (NCWD) Seminar on Women
   and Development. Accra, Ghana: NCWD. July, 1978.
Pellow, Deborah
   "Work and Autonomy; Women in Accra." American
   Ethnologist. Volume 5 #4 November, 1978. pp. 770-785.
Pellow, Deborah
   Women in Accra: Options for Autonomy. Algonac, Michigan:
   Reference Publications. 1977. 272p.
Peterson, K.J.
   "Brong Midwives and Women in Childbirth: Management of
   Uncertainty in a Division of Labor." Human Organization.
   Volume 41 #4 Winter, 1982. pp. 291-298.
Pine, F.
   "Family Structure and the Division of Labour: Female
   Roles in Urban Ghana." (In) Alavi, H. and Shanin, T.
   (eds.). Introduction to the Sociology of Developing
   Societies. New York: MacMillan. 1982. pp. 387-405.
Roach, Penelope M.
   "Career and Family: Expectations and Realities--A
   Preliminary Report on Ghanaian Secondary School
   Students." Paper Presented at the Women and Work in
   Africa Symposium. Urbana, Illinois: University of
   Illinois-Urbana. April-May, 1979.
Robertson, Claire C.
   "The Impact of Formal Education on Marketing Skills Among
   Central Accra Girls." Paper Presented at the 'Women and
   Work in Africa' Symposium. Urbana, Illinois: University
   of Illinois-Urbana. April-May, 1979.
Robertson, Claire C.
   "Ga Women and Socioeconomic Change in Accra, Ghana."
   (In) Hafkin, N.J. and Bay, E.G. (eds.). Women in Africa:
   Studies in Social and Economic Change. Stanford,
   California: Stanford University Press. 1976. pp.
   111-133.
Robertson, Claire C.
   Sharing the Same Bowl?: A Socioeconomic History of Women
   and Class in Accra, Ghana. Bloomington, Indiana: Indiana
   University Press. 1984. 299p.
Robertson, Claire C.
   "Post-Proclamation Slavery in Accra: a Female Affair?"
   (In) Robertson, Claire C. and Klein, Martin A. (eds.).
   Women and Slavery in Africa. Madison, Wisconsin:
   University of Wisconsin Press. 1983. pp. 220-245.

Robertson, Claire C.
    "In Pursuit of Life Histories: The Problem of Bias."
    Frontiers. Volume 7 #2 1983. pp. 63-69.
Robertson, Claire C.
    "The Death of Makola and Other Tragedies: Accra
    Agricultural Markets, Rural Women, Ghana." Canadian
    Journal of African Studies. Volume 17 #3 1983. pp.
    469-496.
Sanjek, Roger and Sanjek, Lani
    "Notes on Women and Work in Adabraka." African Urban
    Notes. Volume 2 #2 Spring, 1976. pp. 1-26.
Sanjek, Roger
    "Female and Male Domestic Cycles in Urban Africa: The
    Adabraka Case." (In) Oppong, Christine (ed.). Female
    and Male in West Africa. London: George Allen and Unwin.
    1983. pp. 330-343.
Sarpong, Peter
    Girl's Nubility Rites in Ashanti. Tema, Ghana: Ghana
    Publishing Corp. 1977. 103p.
Smock, Audrey C.
    "Ghana: From Autonomy to Subordination." (In) Giele,
    Janet Z. and Smock, Audrey C. (eds.). Women: Roles and
    Status in Eight Countries. New York: Wiley-Interscience.
    1977. pp. 173-216.
Smock, Audrey C.
    "The Impact of Modernization on Women's Position in the
    Family in Ghana." (In) Schlegel, Alice E. (ed.). Sexual
    Stratification: A Cross-Cultural View. New York:
    Columbia University Press. 1977. pp. 192-214.
Sudarkasa, Niara
    "Women and Migration in Contemporary West Africa." (In)
    Wellesley Editorial Committee. Women and National
    Development: The Complexities of Change. Chicago:
    University of Chicago Press. 1977. pp. 178-189.
Sudarkasa, Niara
    "Women and Migration in Contemporary West Africa."
    Signs. Volume 3 #1 Autumn, 1977. pp. 178-189.
Tamakloe, Martha A.
    Women in Agriculture: A Study of Mixed Crop Farmers in
    Nkwaie-Toase Area. Kumasi, Ghana: Department of Housing
    and Planning Research. U.S.T. 1978. 26p.
Tamakloe, Martha A.
    "Women in Agriculture: A Study of Mixed Crop Farmers in
    Nkawie-Toase Area." Paper Presented at the National
    Council on Women and Development (NCWD) Conference on
    Women in Development. Legon, Ghana: NCWD. September,
    1978.
Tawiah, E.O.
    "Determinants of Cumulative Fertility in Ghana."
    Demography. Volume 21 #1 February, 1984. pp. 1-8.
Van Der Geest, Sjaak
    "Role Relationships Between Husband and Wife in Rural

Ghana." Journal of Marriage and the Family. Volume 38 #3 August, 1976. pp. 572-579.

Vellenga, Dorothy D.
"Matriliny, Patriliny and Class Formation Among Women Cocoa Farmers in Two Rural Areas of Ghana." Paper Presented at the Annual Meeting of the African Studies Association. Paper #126. Bloomington, Indiana. October 21-24, 1981.

Vellenga, Dorothy D.
"Attempts to Change the Marriage Laws in Ghana and the Ivory Coast." (In) Foster, P. and Zolberg, A. (eds.). Ghana and the Ivory Coast: Perspectives on Modernisation. Chicago: University of Chicago Press. 1977.

Vellenga, Dorothy D.
"Who is a Wife? Legal Expressions of Heterosexual Conflicts in Ghana." (In) Oppong, Christine (ed.). Female and Male in West Africa. London: George Allen and Unwin. 1983. pp. 144-155.

Vellenga, Dorothy D.
"Differentiation Among Women Farmers in Two Rural Areas in Ghana." Labour and Society. Volume 2 #2 April, 1977. pp. 197-208.

Vellenga, Dorothy D.
"Women, Households, and Food Commodity Chains in Southern Ghana: Contradictions Between Search for Profits and the Search for Survival." Research Review. Volume 8 #3 1985. pp. 293-318.

Vellenga, Dorothy D.
"Food as a Cash Crop for Women Farmers in Ghana: The Persistent Search for Profit." Paper Presented at the Annual Meeting of the Association for Women in Development. Washington, D.C. October, 1983.

Vercruijsse, Emile V.W.
"Fishmongers, Big Dealers and Fishermen: Co-Operation and Conflict Between the Sexes in Ghanaian Canoe Fishing." (In) Oppong, Christine (ed.). Female and Male in West Africa. London: George Allen and Unwin. 1983. pp. 179-191.

Verdon, Michel
"Divorce in Abutia." Africa. Volume 52 #4 1982. pp. 48-65.

Verdon, Michel
"Sleeping Together: The Dynamics of Residence Among the Abutia Ewe." Journal of Anthropological Research. Volume 35 #4 Winter, 1979. pp. 401-425.

Whithead, A.
Women and the Household: Themes Arising From a North-East Ghana Example. Sussex, England: University of Sussex. Institute of Development Studies. Draft Paper Presented at the Conference on Continuing Subordination of Women and the Development Process. 1978.

DEVELOPMENT AND TECHNOLOGY

Adinko, V.
   Salt Mining by Women in the Keta Area. Legon, Ghana:
   University of Ghana. Department of Sociology. 1980.
Afful, K.N. and Steel, William F.
   "Women in the Urban Economy of Ghana: Comment." Paper.
   1978.
African Regional Agricultural Credit Association
   "Women's Programme in Agricultural Credit and Banking.
   Report." Presented at the Policy Maker's Workshop on
   Women's Agricultural Credit and Banking Programmes for
   Selected Eastern and Southern African Countries.
   Nairobi, Kenya. March 14, 1983. 94p.
Akerele, Olubanke
   Women Workers in Ghana, Kenya, Zambia: A Comparative
   Analysis of Women's Employment in the Modern Wage
   Sector. Addis Ababa, Ethiopia: United Nations Economic
   Commission for Africa. African Training and Research
   Center for Women. 1979. 109p.
Bartle, Philip F.
   "Modernization and the Decline in Women's Status: An
   Example From Matrilineal Akan Community." Paper
   Presented at the National Council on Women and
   Development (NCWD) Seminar on Women and Development.
   Accra, Ghana: NCWD. Accra, Ghana. September, 1978.
Breebaart, Gera
   "Women and Extension in the Upper Region of Ghana."
   Approach. Volume 8 1979. pp. 33-41.
Bryson, Judy C.
   "Women in Ghanaian Development Projects." (In)
   University of Arizona. International Conference on Women
   and Food. Volume Three. Tucson, Arizona. January 8-11,
   1978. pp. B21-26.
Bukh, Jette
   The Village Women of Ghana. Uppsala, Sweden:
   Scandinavian Institute of African Studies. Centre for
   Development Research. Publication #1. 1979. 118p.
Callaway, Barbara J.
   "Women in Ghana." (In) Iglitzin, Lynne B. and Ross, Ruth
   (eds.). Women in the World. Santa Barbara, California:
   Clio Books. 1976. pp. 189-201.
Campbell, Claudia R.
   "Women's Employment and Incomes Under Industrialization:
   A Case Study of Ghana." M.A. Thesis: Vanderbilt
   University. Nashville, Tennessee. 1977. 161p.
Campbell, Claudia R. and Steel, William F.
   "The Impact of Industrialization Policies on Women's
   Employment in Ghana Since 1960." Paper Presented at the
   Annual Meeting of the African Studies Association. Paper
   #12. Baltimore, Maryland. 1978. 28p.
Campbell-Platt, Kiran
   "The Impact of Mechanization on the Employment of Women
240

in Traditional Sectors." Paper Presented at the National
Council on Women and Development (NCWD) Seminar on Women
and Development. Accra, Ghana: NCWD. September, 1978.

Chinnery-Hesse, Mary
"Women and Decision Making--Some Comments on the Themes
With Special Reference to the Ghanaian Situation."
Labour and Society. Volume 1 #2 1976. pp. 35-36.

Church, K.V.
"A Study of Socio-Economic Status and Child Care
Arrangements of Women in Madina." Paper Presented at the
National Council on Women and Development (NCWD) Seminar
on Women and Development. Accra, Ghana: NCWD.
September, 1978.

Cole, Jane J.
National Council on Women and Development (NCWD):
Policies and Actions. Accra, Ghana: NCWD 1980.

Cole, Jane J.
"Providing Access to New Skills and Modern
Technologies--The Ghana National Council on Women and
Development." Assignment Children. #38 April-June,
1977. pp. 71-79.

Dadson, J.A.
"Women and Farm Credit in Ghanaian Agriculture: A
Preliminary Exploration." Paper Presented at the
Workshop on Women's Contribution to Food Production and
Rural Development in Africa. Lome, Togo. June, 1981.

Date-Bah, Eugenia
Ghanaian Women in Factory Employment: A Case Study.
Geneva: Institute for Labour Studies. 1978. 9p.

Date-Bah, Eugenia
"Rural Women, Their Activities and Technology in Ghana:
An Overview." (In) International Labour Organization
(ILO). Rural Development and Women in Africa. Geneva:
ILO. 1984. pp. 89-98.

Date-Bah, Eugenia
"Female and Male Factory Workers in Accra." (In) Oppong,
Christine (ed.). Female and Male in Africa. London:
George Allen and Unwin. 1983. pp. 266-274.

Date-Bah, Eugenia and Brown, C. and Gyeke, L.
"Ghanaian Women and Cooperatives." Paper Presented at
the National Council on Women and Development (NCWD)
Seminar on Women and Development. Accra, Ghana: NCWD.
September, 1978. 26p.

Date-Bah, Eugenia
"Women in an Urban Setting for Ghana: Ghanaian Women in
Factory Employment." Greenhill Journal of
Administration. Volume 4 #1/2 April-September, 1977.
pp. 76-94.

Date-Bah, Eugenia
"Technologies for Rural Women in Ghana: Role of
Socio-Cultural Factors." (In) Ahmed, Iftikhar (ed.).
Technology and Rural Women: Conceptual and Empirical
Issues. Boston: George Allen and Unwin. 1985. pp.
211-251.

Dugbaza, Tetteh
  "Women and Integration in Rural Development." Ghana
  Journal of Sociology. Volume 14 #1 1981. pp. 73-94.
Dumor, Ernest K.
  "Women in Rural Development in Ghana." Rural Africana.
  #17 Fall, 1983. 57-68.
Ewusi, Kodwo
  "Women in Occupations in Ghana." Paper Presented at the
  National Council on Women and Development (NCWD) Seminar
  on Women and Development. Accra, Ghana: NCWD.
  September, 1978.
Gbedemah, Charles
  "The Role of Women in the Production of Rice in Northern
  Ghana." Paper Presented at the National Council on Women
  and Development (NCWD) Seminar on Women and Development.
  Legon, Ghana: NCWD. September, 1978.
Ghana National Council on Women and Development (NCWD)
  The First Women's Co-Operative Gari Factory. Accra,
  Ghana: NCWD. 1980.
Greenstreet, Miranda
  "Various Salient Features Concerning the Employment of
  Women Workers in Ghana." Paper Presented at the National
  Council on Women and Development (NCWD) Seminar on Women
  and Development." Accra, Ghana: NCWD. July, 1978.
Greenstreet, Miranda
  Females in the Agricultural Labour Force and Non-Formal
  Education for Rural Development in Ghana. Hague,
  Netherlands: Institute of Social Studies. ISS Occasional
  Paper #90. August, 1981. 23p.
Guyer, Jane I.
  "Women in the Rural Economy: Contemporary Variations."
  (In) Hay, Margaret J. and Stichter, Sharon (eds.).
  African Women South of the Sahara. New York: Longman.
  1984. pp. 19-32.
Jeffalyn Johnson and Associates Inc.
  African Women in Development. Falls Church, Virginia:
  Jeffalyn Johnson and Associates Inc. 1980. 125p.
Kleinkowski, H.
  "Women's Organizations and Their Contribution to
  Development in Ghana: With Special Reference to the
  Christian Mothers Association." M.A. Thesis: Reading
  University. Reading, England. 1976.
Klingshirn, A.
  Investment of Women in Co-Operatives in Zaire and Ghana.
  Rome: United Nations Food and Agriculture Organization.
  UNFPA/FAO Study. 1978.
Mickelwait, Donald R. and Riegelman, Mary Ann and Sweet,
Charles F.
  Women in Rural Development: A Survey of the Roles of
  Women in Ghana, Lesotho, Kenya, Nigeria... Boulder,
  Colorado: Westview Press. 1976. 224p.
Mikell, Gwendolyn
  "African Women Within Nations of Crisis." Transafrica
  Forum. Volume 2 #1 1983. pp. 31-34.

Mikell, Gwendolyn
"Expansion and Contraction in Economic Access for Rural
Women in Ghana." Rural Africana. #21 Winter, 1985.
pp. 13-31.
Mikell, Gwendolyn
"Expansion and Contracting in Economic Access for Rural
Women in Ghana." Paper Presented at the Annual Meeting
of the African Studies Association. Paper #63.
Washington, D.C. November 4-7, 1982.
Nantogmah, Matilda A.
"Active Participation of Ghanaian Women in Integrated
Rural Development." Paper Presented at the Annual
Meeting of the Canadian Association of African Studies.
1978. 27p.
Oppong, Christine
"Issues Concerning the Changing Status of African Women:
Some Lessons From the Ghanaian Experience." (In)
International Planned Parenthood Federation (IPPF).
Proceedings of the IPPF Africa Regional Conference.
London: IPPF. Aug. 3-Sept. 3, 1976. pp. 263-282.
Pappoe, Matilda E.
"Women and Abortion." Paper Presented at the National
Council on Women and Development (NCWD) Seminar on Women
and Development. Accra, Ghana: NCWD. July, 1978.
Pellow, Deborah
Women in Accra: Options for Autonomy. Algonac, Michigan:
Reference Publications. 1977. 272p.
Petritsch, Mechtild
"Women and Development in Ghana." Paper Presented at the
Meeting on Women and International Development Strategy.
Vienna, Austria: United Nations. December 7-11, 1981.
55p.
Robertson, Claire C.
"Formal or Nonformal Education? Entrepreneurial Women in
Ghana." Comparative Education Review. Volume 28
November, 1984. pp. 639-658.
Robertson, Claire C.
"The Impact of Formal Education on Marketing Skills Among
Central Accra Girls." Paper Presented at the 'Women and
Work in Africa' Symposium. Urbana, Illinois: University
of Illinois-Urbana. April-May, 1979.
Smock, Audrey C.
"Ghana: From Autonomy to Subordination." (In) Giele,
Janet Z. and Smock, Audrey C. (eds.). Women: Roles and
Status in Eight Countries. New York: Wiley-Interscience.
1977. pp. 173-216.
Smock, Audrey C.
"The Impact of Modernization on Women's Position in the
Family in Ghana." (In) Schlegel, Alice E. (ed.). Sexual
Stratification: A Cross-Cultural View. New York:
Columbia University Press. 1977. pp. 192-214.
Steel, William F.
"Female and Small-Scale Employment Under Moderization in

Ghana." Economic Development and Cultural Change.
Volume 30 #1 October, 1981. pp.153-168.
Steel, William F.
Data on Labor Force Size, Growth, Composition and
Underutilization by Sex, Firm Size, Sector and
Occupation, Ghana, 1960-1970. Washington, D.C.: World
Bank. 1978. 67p.
Steel, William F.
"Women's Employment and Development: A Conceptual
Framework Applied to Ghana." (In) Bay, Edna G. (ed.).
Women and Work in Africa. Boulder, Colorado: Westview
Press. Westview Special Studies in Africa. 1982. pp.
225-248.
Steel, William F.
Report on Research Program for Ghana National Council of
Women and Development (NCWD). Nashville, Tennessee:
Vanderbilt University. 1976. 39p.
Sudarkasa, Niara
"Women and Migration in Contemporary West Africa." (In)
Wellesley Editorial Committee. Women and National
Development: The Complexities of Change. Chicago:
University of Chicago Press. 1977. pp. 178-189.
Sudarkasa, Niara
"Women and Migration in Contemporary West Africa."
Signs. Volume 3 #1 Autumn, 1977. pp. 178-189.
U.S. Department of Commerce. Bureau of the Census
Illustrative Statistics on Women in Development in
Selected Developing Countries. Washington, D.C.: U.S.
Department of Commerce. 1982. 24p.
United Nations Food and Agriculture Organization (FAO)
Market Women in West Africa. Report of the Seminar on
the Role of Women in Marketing Local Farm and Marine
Produce, Accra, Ghana, December 12-16, 1977. Rome: FAO.
1977. 29p.
Vellenga, Dorothy D.
"Non-Formal Education of Ghanaian Women Into Economic
Roles." Paper Presented at the Annual Meeting of the
African Studies Association. Paper #121. Boston,
Massachusetts. 1976. 13p.
Vellenga, Dorothy D.
"Differentiation Among Women Farmers in Two Rural Areas
in Ghana." Labour and Society. Volume 2 #2 April,
1977. pp. 197-208.
Vellenga, Dorothy D.
"Food as a Cash Crop for Women Farmers in Ghana: The
Persistent Search for Profit." Paper Presented at the
Annual Meeting of the Association for Women in
Development. Washington, D.C. October, 1983.
Whithead, A.
"Women and the Household: Themes Arising From a
North-East Ghana Example." Sussex, England: University
of Sussex. Institute of Development Studies. Draft
Paper Presented at the Conference on Continuing

Subordination of Women and the Development Process.
1978.

DIVORCE

Hagan, George P.
    "Divorce, Polygyny and Family Welfare." Ghana Journal of
    Sociology. Volume 10 #1 1976. pp. 67-84.
Hagan, George P.
    "Marriage, Divorce and Polygyny in Winneba." (In)
    Oppong, Christine (ed.). Female and Male in West Africa.
    London: George Allen and Unwin. 1983. pp. 192-203.
Verdon, Michel
    "Divorce in Abutia." Africa. Volume 52 #4 1982. pp.
    48-65.

ECONOMICS

Adinko, V.
    Salt Mining by Women in the Keta Area. Legon, Ghana:
    University of Ghana. Department of Sociology. 1980.
Afful, K.N. and Steel, William F.
    "Women in the Urban Economy of Ghana: Comment." Paper.
    1978.
African Regional Agricultural Credit Association
    "Women's Programme in Agricultural Credit and Banking.
    Report." Presented at the Policy Maker's Workshop on
    Women's Agricultural Credit and Banking Programmes for
    Selected Eastern and Southern African Countries.
    Nairobi, Kenya. March 14, 1983. 94p.
Akerele, Olubanke
    Women Workers in Ghana, Kenya, Zambia: A Comparative
    Analysis of Women's Employment in the Modern Wage
    Sector. Addis Ababa, Ethiopia: United Nations Economic
    Commission for Africa. African Training and Research
    Center for Women. 1979. 109p.
Breebaart, Gera
    "Women and Extension in the Upper Region of Ghana."
    Approach. Volume 8 1979. pp. 33-41.
Brown, Edward K.
    "Patterns of Internal Migration in Ghana With Special
    Emphasis on the Determinants of Female Migration." Ph.D
    Dissertation: University of Pennsylvania. Philadelphia,
    Pennsylvania. 1983. 295p.
Brydon, Lynne
    "Women at Work: Some Changes in Family Structure in
    Amedzofe-Avatime, Ghana." Africa. Volume 49 #2 1979.
    pp. 97-110.
Bryson, Judy C.
    "Women in Ghanaian Development Projects." (In)
    University of Arizona. International Conference on Women

and Food. Volume Three. Tucson, Arizona. January 8-11,
1978. pp. B21-26.

Caldwell, John C.
"The Economic Rationality of High Fertility: An
Investigation Illustrated With Nigerian Survey Data.
Population Studies (London). Volume 31 #1 March, 1977.
pp. 5-27.

Campbell, Claudia R.
"Women's Employment and Incomes Under Industrialization:
A Case Study of Ghana." M.A. Thesis: Vanderbilt
University. Nashville, Tennessee. 1977. 161p.

Campbell, Claudia R. and Steel, William F.
"The Impact of Industrialization Policies on Women's
Employment in Ghana Since 1960." Paper Presented at the
Annual Meeting of the African Studies Association. Paper
#12. Baltimore, Maryland. 1978. 28p.

Church, K.V.
"A Study of Socio-Economic Status and Child Care
Arrangements of Women in Madina." Paper Presented at the
National Council on Women and Development (NCWD) Seminar
on Women and Development. Accra, Ghana: NCWD.
September, 1978.

Cole, Jane J.
National Council on Women and Development (NCWD):
Policies and Actions. Accra, Ghana: NCWD. 1980.

Dadson, J.A.
"Women and Farm Credit in Ghanaian Agriculture: A
Preliminary Exploration." Paper Presented at the
Workshop on Women's Contribution to Food Production and
Rural Development in Africa. Lome, Togo. June, 1981.

Date-Bah, Eugenia
The Changing Work Roles of Ghanaian Women. Accra, Ghana:
National Council on Women and Development. 1980.

Date-Bah, Eugenia
Ghanaian Women in Factory Employment: A Case Study.
Geneva: Institute for Labour Studies. 1978. 9p.

Date-Bah, Eugenia
"Female and Male Factory Workers in Accra." (In) Oppong,
Christine (ed.). Female and Male in Africa. London:
George Allen and Unwin. 1983. pp. 266-274.

Date-Bah, Eugenia and Brown, C. and Gyeke, L.
"Ghanaian Women and Cooperatives." Paper Presented at
the National Council on Women and Development (NCWD)
Seminar on Women and Development. Accra, Ghana: NCWD.
September, 1978. 26p.

Date-Bah, Eugenia
"Women in an Urban Setting for Ghana: Ghanaian Women in
Factory Employment." Greenhill Journal of
Administration. Volume 4 #1/2 April-September, 1977.
pp. 76-94.

Date-Bah, Eugenia
"Technologies for Rural Women in Ghana: Role of
Socio-Cultural Factors." (In) Ahmed, Iftikhar (ed.).

246

Technology and Rural Women: Conceptual and Empirical
Issues. Boston: George Allen and Unwin. 1985. pp.
211-251.
Dinan, Carmel
"Sugar Daddies and Gold Diggers: The White-Collar Single
Women in Accra." (In) Oppong, Christine (ed.). Female
and Male in West Africa. London: George Allen and Unwin.
1983. pp. 344-366.
Dinan, Carmel
"Pragmatists or Feminists? The Professional 'Single'
Women in Accra, Ghana." Cahiers d'Etudes Africaines.
Volume 17 #1 1977. pp. 15-176.
Dugbaza, Tetteh
"Women and Integration in Rural Development." Ghana
Journal of Sociology. Volume 14 #1 1981. pp. 73-94.
Dumor, Ernest K.
"Women in Rural Development in Ghana." Rural Africana.
#17 Fall, 1983. 57-68.
Dumor, Ernest K.
"Commodity Queens and the Distributive Trade in Ghana: A
Socio-Historical Analysis." African Urban Studies.
Volume 12 1982. pp. 27-45.
Dumor, Ernest K.
"Commodity Queens and the Distributive Trade in Ghana."
Paper Presented at the Annual Meeting of the African
Studies Association. Paper #23. Baltimore, Maryland.
1978. 25p.
Ewusi, Kodwo
"Women in Occupations in Ghana." Paper Presented at the
National Council on Women and Development (NCWD) Seminar
on Women and Development. Accra, Ghana: NCWD.
September, 1978.
Feyisetan, Bamikale J.
"The Determinants of Female Labor Force Participation:
The Effects of the Sectoral Composition of Labor
Markets." Ph.D Dissertation: University of Pennsylvania.
Philadelphia, Pennsylvania. 1982. 235p.
Fogelberg, Teresa
Nanumba Women: Working Bees or Idle Bums? Sexual Division
of Labour, Ideology of Work, and Power Relations Between
Women and Men in Gole, A Village in Nanumba District,
Northern Region, Ghana. Leiden, Netherlands: Institute
of Cultural and Social Studies. 1981. 83p.
Gbedemah, Charles
"The Role of Women in the Production of Rice in Northern
Ghana." Paper Presented at the National Council on Women
and Development (NCWD) Seminar on Women and Development.
Legon, Ghana: NCWD. September, 1978.
Ghana National Council on Women and Development (NCWD)
The First Women's Co-Operative Gari Factory. Accra,
Ghana: NCWD. 1980.
Greenstreet, Miranda
"Various Salient Features Concerning the Employment of

Women Workers in Ghana." Paper Presented at the National
Council on Women and Development (NCWD) Seminar on Women
and Development. Accra, Ghana: NCWD. July, 1978.

Greenstreet, Miranda
Females in the Agricultural Labour Force and Non-Formal
Education for Rural Development in Ghana. Hague,
Netherlands: Institute of Social Studies. ISS Occasional
Paper #90. August, 1981. 23p.

Guyer, Jane I.
"Women in the Rural Economy: Contemporary Variations."
(In) Hay, Margaret J. and Stichter, Sharon (eds.).
African Women South of the Sahara. New York: Longman.
1984. pp. 19-32.

Hagaman, Barbara L.
"Beer and Matriliny: The Power of Women in Lobir, Ghana."
Ph.D Dissertation: Northeastern University. Boston,
Massachusetts. 1977. 365p.

Harrell-Bond, Barbara E.
Women and the 1979 Ghana Revolution. Hanover, New
Hampshire: American University Field Staff. Report #4.
1980. 10p.

Jeffalyn Johnson and Associates Inc.
African Women in Development. Falls Church, Virginia:
Jeffalyn Johnson and Associates Inc. 1980. 125p.

Kleinkowski, H.
"Women's Organizations and Their Contribution to
Development in Ghana: With Special Reference to the
Christian Mothers Association." M.A. Thesis: Reading
University. Reading, England. 1976.

Klingshirn, A.
Investment of Women in Co-Operatives in Zaire and Ghana.
Rome: United Nations Food and Agriculture Organization.
UNFPA/FAO Study. 1978.

Lewis, Mary A.
"Female Entrepreneural Styles: An Examination of Coastal
Fante Businesswomen." Ph.D Dissertation: University of
Washington. Seattle, Washington. 1977. 255p.

Mickelwait, Donald R. and Riegelman, Mary Ann and Sweet,
Charles F.
Women in Rural Development: A Survey of the Roles of
Women in Ghana, Lesotho, Kenya, Nigeria... Boulder,
Colorado: Westview Press. 1976. 224p.

Mikell, Gwendolyn
"African Women Within Nations of Crisis." Transafrica
Forum. Volume 2 #1 1983. pp. 31-34.

Mikell, Gwendolyn
"Expansion and Contraction in Economic Access for Rural
Women in Ghana." Rural Africana. #21 Winter, 1985.
pp. 13-31.

Mikell, Gwendolyn
"Filiation, Economic Crisis and the Status of Women in
Ghana." Canadian Journal of African Studies. Volume 18
#1 1984. pp. 195-218.

Mikell, Gwendolyn
   "Expansion and Contracting in Economic Access for Rural
   Women in Ghana." Paper Presented at the Annual Meeting
   of the African Studies Association. Paper #63.
   Washington, D.C. November 4-7, 1982.
Nantogmah, Matilda A.
   "Active Participation of Ghanaian Women in Integrated
   Rural Development." Paper Presented at the Annual
   Meeting of the Canadian Association of African Studies.
   1978. 27p.
Nantogmah, Matilda A.
   "The Image of Women as Workers With Special Emphasis on
   Ghanaian Women Workers." Paper Presented for the
   Conference on Women and Work in Africa. Urbana,
   Illinois: University of Illinois-Urbana-Champaign. April
   28-May 1, 1979.
Okali, Christine
   Cocoa and Kinship in Ghana: The Matrilineal Akan of
   Ghana. London: Kegan Paul International for the
   International African Institute. 1983. 179p.
Okali, Christine
   "Kinship and Cocoa Farming in Ghana." (In) Oppong,
   Christine (ed.). Female and Male in West Africa.
   London: George Allen and Unwin. 1983. pp. 169-178.
Oppong, Christine
   "Issues Concerning the Changing Status of African Women:
   Some Lessons From the Ghanaian Experience." (In)
   International Planned Parenthood Federation (IPPF).
   Proceedings of the IPPF Africa Regional Conference.
   London: IPPF. Aug. 3-Sept. 3, 1976. pp. 263-282.
Oppong, Christine and Abu, Katharine
   The Changing Maternal Role of Ghanaian Women: Impacts of
   Education, Migration and Employment. Geneva:
   International Labour Organization. Population and Labour
   Policies Programme. Working Paper #143. February, 1984.
   190p.
Oppong, Christine and Bleek, Wolf
   "Economic Models and Having Children: Some Evidence From
   Kwahu, Ghana." Africa. Volume 52 #4 1982. pp. 15-33.
Pellow, Deborah
   "Work and Autonomy; Women in Accra." American
   Ethnologist. Volume 5 #4 November, 1978. pp. 770-785.
Petritsch, Mechtild
   "Women and Development in Ghana." Paper Presented at the
   Meeting on Women and International Development Strategy.
   Vienna, Austria: United Nations. December 7-11, 1981.
   55p.
Robertson, Claire C.
   "Change in the Organization of the Fish Trade in 20th
   Century Accra." African Urban Notes. Volume 2 #2
   Spring, 1976. pp. 43-58.
Robertson, Claire C.
   "The Impact of Formal Education on Marketing Skills Among

Central Accra Girls." Paper Presented at the 'Women and Work in Africa' Symposium. Urbana, Illinois: University of Illinois-Urbana. April-May, 1979.

Robertson, Claire C.
"Ga Women and Socioeconomic Change in Accra, Ghana." (In) Hafkin, N.J. and Bay, E.G. (eds.). Women in Africa: Studies in Social and Economic Change. Stanford, California: Stanford University Press. 1976. pp. 111-133.

Robertson, Claire C.
Sharing the Same Bowl?: A Socioeconomic History of Women and Class in Accra, Ghana. Bloomington, Indiana: Indiana University Press. 1984. 299p.

Robertson, Claire C.
"In Pursuit of Life Histories: The Problem of Bias." Frontiers. Volume 7 #2 1983. pp. 63-69.

Robertson, Claire C.
"The Death of Makola and Other Tragedies: Accra Agricultural Markets, Rural Women, Ghana." Canadian Journal of African Studies. Volume 17 #3 1983. pp. 469-496.

Sagoe, Aba
"Ghana's Market Women." Africa Women. #5 1976.

Sai, Florence A.
"Women Traders." Paper Presented at the National Council on Women and Development (NCWD) Seminar on Women and Development. Accra, Ghana: NCWD. July, 1978.

Sanjek, Roger and Sanjek, Lani
"Notes on Women and Work in Adabraka." African Urban Notes. Volume 2 #2 Spring, 1976. pp. 1-26.

Simms, Ruth and Dumor, Ernest K.
"Women in the Urban Economy of Ghana: Associational Activity and the Enclave Economy." African Urban Notes. Volume 2 #3 Fall/Winter, 1976. pp. 43-64.

Smock, Audrey C.
"Ghana: From Autonomy to Subordination." (In) Giele, Janet Z. and Smock, Audrey C. (eds.). Women: Roles and Status in Eight Countries. New York: Wiley-Interscience. 1977. pp. 173-216.

Steel, William F.
"Female and Small-Scale Employment Under Moderization in Ghana." Economic Development and Cultural Change. Volume 30 #1 October, 1981. pp.153-168.

Steel, William F.
Data on Labor Force Size, Growth, Composition and Underutilization by Sex, Firm Size, Sector and Occupation, Ghana, 1960-1970. Washington, D.C.: World Bank. 1978. 67p.

Sudarkasa, Niara
"Women and Migration in Contemporary West Africa." (In) Wellesley Editorial Committee. Women and National Development: The Complexities of Change. Chicago: University of Chicago Press. 1977. pp. 178-189.

Sudarkasa, Niara
   "Women and Migration in Contemporary West Africa."
   Signs. Volume 3 #1 Autumn, 1977. pp. 178-189.
United Nations Economic Commission for Africa (UNECA)
   Women Workers in Ghana-Kenya-Zambia: A Comparative
   Analysis of Women's Employment in the Modern Wage
   Sector. Addis Ababa, Ethiopia: UNECA. 1979.
United Nations Food and Agriculture Organization (FAO)
   Market Women in West Africa. Report of the Seminar on
   the Role of Women in Marketing Local Farm and Marine
   Produce, Accra, Ghana, December 12-16, 1977. Rome: FAO.
   1977. 29p.
Vellenga, Dorothy D.
   "Non-Formal Education of Ghanaian Women Into Economic
   Roles." Paper Presented at the Annual Meeting of the
   African Studies Association. Paper #121. Boston,
   Massachusetts. 1976. 13p.
Vellenga, Dorothy D.
   "Differentiation Among Women Farmers in Two Rural Areas
   in Ghana." Labour and Society. Volume 2 #2 April,
   1977. pp. 197-208.
Vellenga, Dorothy D.
   "Women, Households, and Food Commodity Chains in Southern
   Ghana: Contradictions Between Search for Profits and the
   Search for Survival." Research Review. Volume 8 #3
   1985. pp. 293-318.
Vellenga, Dorothy D.
   "Food as a Cash Crop for Women Farmers in Ghana: The
   Persistent Search for Profit." Paper Presented at the
   Annual Meeting of the Association for Women in
   Development. Washington, D.C. October, 1983.
Vercruijsse, Emile V.W.
   "Fishmongers, Big Dealers and Fishermen: Co-Operation and
   Conflict Between the Sexes in Ghanaian Canoe Fishing."
   (In) Oppong, Christine (ed.). Female and Male in West
   Africa. London: George Allen and Unwin. 1983. pp.
   179-191.

EDUCATION AND TRAINING

Akuffo, F.O.
   "High Wastage in Women's Education: The Case of the Rural
   Elementary School Girls." Paper Presented at the
   National Council on Women and Development (NCWD)
   Conference on Women and Development. Accra, Ghana: NCWD
   September 3-8, 1978.
Asiedu-Akrofi, F. and Atakpa, S.K.
   Practices Regarding Allocation of Places to Women in
   Schools and Colleges. Research Report for U.S. AID/Ghana
   National Council on Women and Development, Research
   Project. Accra, Ghana: National Council on Women and
   Development. May, 1978.

Cole, Jane J.
   National Council on Women and Development (NCWD):
   Policies and Actions. Accra, Ghana: NCWD. 1980.
Date-Bah, Eugenia
   "Ghanaian Women in Academia: African Women in a New
   Occupational Role." Ghana Journal of Sociology. Volume
   12 #1 1978. pp. 44-71.
Greenstreet, Miranda
   Females in the Agricultural Labour Force and Non-Formal
   Education for Rural Development in Ghana. Hague,
   Netherlands: Institute of Social Studies. ISS Occasional
   Paper #90. August, 1981. 23p.
Houghton, B.D.
   "Women in Education in Ghana." Paper Presented at the
   National Council on Women and Development (NCWD) Seminar
   on Women and Development. Accra, Ghana: NCWD.
   September, 1978.
Nantogmah, Matilda A.
   "Active Participation of Ghanaian Women in Integrated
   Rural Development." Paper Presented at the Annual
   Meeting of the Canadian Association of African Studies.
   1978. 27p.
Oppong, Christine
   "Issues Concerning the Changing Status of African Women:
   Some Lessons From the Ghanaian Experience." (In)
   International Planned Parenthood Federation (IPPF).
   Proceedings of the IPPF Africa Regional Conference.
   London: IPPF. Aug. 3-Sept. 3, 1976. pp. 263-282.
Oppong, Christine
   "Ghanaian Women Teachers as Workers, Kin, Wives and
   Mothers: A Study of Conjugal Family Solidarity--Norms,
   Reality and Stress." Paper Presented at the Conference
   on Women and Development. Wellesley, Massachusetts:
   Wellesley College. June 2-6, 1976. 25p.
Oppong, Christine and Abu, Katharine
   The Changing Maternal Role of Ghanaian Women: Impacts of
   Education, Migration and Employment. Geneva:
   International Labour Organization. Population and Labour
   Policies Programme. Working Paper #143. February, 1984.
   190p.
Pellow, Deborah
   "Work and Autonomy; Women in Accra." American
   Ethnologist. Volume 5 #4 November, 1978. pp. 770-785.
Pellow, Deborah
   Women in Accra: Options for Autonomy. Algonac, Michigan:
   Reference Publications. 1977. 272p.
Roach, Penelope M.
   "Educational Expansion in Ghana, 1952-1975: Some
   Sociological Perspectives on Coeducation and the
   Education of Women." Paper Presented at the Annual
   Meeting of the African Studies Association. Boston,
   Massachusetts. 1976. 18p.

Roach, Penelope M.
    "Career and Family: Expectations and Realities--A
    Preliminary Report on Ghanaian Secondary School
    Students." Paper Presented at the Women and Work in
    Africa Symposium. Urbana, Illinois: University of
    Illinois-Urbana. April-May, 1979.
Robertson, Claire C.
    "Formal or Nonformal Education? Entrepreneurial Women in
    Ghana." Comparative Education Review. Volume 28
    November, 1984. pp. 639-658.
Robertson, Claire C.
    "The Impact of Formal Education on Marketing Skills Among
    Central Accra Girls." Paper Presented at the 'Women and
    Work in Africa' Symposium. Urbana, Illinois: University
    of Illinois-Urbana. April-May, 1979.
Vellenga, Dorothy D.
    "Non-Formal Education of Ghanaian Women Into Economic
    Roles." Paper Presented at the Annual Meeting of the
    African Studies Association. Paper #121. Boston,
    Massachusetts. 1976. 13p.
Weis, Lois
    "Education and the Reproduction of Inequality: The Case
    of Ghana." Comparative Education Review. Volume 23 #1
    February, 1979. pp. 41-51.
Weis, Lois
    "Women and Education in Ghana: Some Problems in Assessing
    Change." International Journal of Women's Studies.
    Volume 3 #5 September-October, 1980. pp. 431-453.

EMPLOYMENT AND LABOR

Adinko, V.
    Salt Mining by Women in the Keta Area. Legon, Ghana:
    University of Ghana. Department of Sociology. 1980.
Afful, K.N. and Steel, William F.
    "Women in the Urban Economy of Ghana: Comment." Paper.
    1978.
African Regional Agricultural Credit Association
    "Women's Programme in Agricultural Credit and Banking.
    Report." Presented at the Policy Maker's Workshop on
    Women's Agricultural Credit and Banking Programmes for
    Selected Eastern and Southern African Countries.
    Nairobi, Kenya. March 14, 1983. 94p.
Akerele, Olubanke
    Women Workers in Ghana, Kenya, Zambia: A Comparative
    Analysis of Women's Employment in the Modern Wage
    Sector. Addis Ababa, Ethiopia: United Nations Economic
    Commission for Africa. African Training and Research
    Center for Women. 1979. 109p.
Brown, Edward K.
    "Patterns of Internal Migration in Ghana With Special
    Emphasis on the Determinants of Female Migration." Ph.D

Dissertation: University of Pennsylvania. Philadelphia,
Pennsylvania. 1983. 295p.
Brydon, Lynne
"Women at Work: Some Changes in Family Structure in
Amedzofe-Avatime, Ghana." Africa. Volume 49 #2 1979.
pp. 97-110.
Brydon, Lynne
"The Dimensions of Subordination: A Case Study From
Avatime, Ghana." (In) Afshar, H. (ed.). Women, Work and
Ideology in the Third World. London: Tavistock. 1985.
pp. 109-127.
Bryson, Judy C.
"Women in Ghanaian Development Projects." (In)
University of Arizona. International Conference on Women
and Food. Volume Three. Tucson, Arizona. January 8-11,
1978. pp. B21-26.
Callaway, Barbara J.
"Women in Ghana." (In) Iglitzin, Lynne B. and Ross, Ruth
(eds.). Women in the World. Santa Barbara, California:
Clio Books. 1976. pp. 189-201.
Campbell, Claudia R.
"Women's Employment and Incomes Under Industrialization:
A Case Study of Ghana." M.A. Thesis: Vanderbilt
University. Nashville, Tennessee. 1977. 161p.
Campbell, Claudia R. and Steel, William F.
"The Impact of Industrialization Policies on Women's
Employment in Ghana Since 1960." Paper Presented at the
Annual Meeting of the African Studies Association. Paper
#12. Baltimore, Maryland. 1978. 28p.
Campbell-Platt, Kiran
"The Impact of Mechanization on the Employment of Women
in Traditional Sectors." Paper Presented at the National
Council on Women and Development (NCWD) Seminar on Women
and Development. Accra, Ghana: NCWD. September, 1978.
Chinnery-Hesse, Mary
"Some Comments on the Ghanaian Situation." (In) Boserup,
Ester (ed.). The Traditional Division of Work Between
the Sexes, a Source of Inequality. Geneva: International
Institute for Labour Studies. Research Series #21.
1976.
Chinnery-Hesse, Mary
"Women and Decision Making--Some Comments on the Themes
With Special Reference to the Ghanaian Situation."
Labour and Society. Volume 1 #2 1976. pp. 35-36.
Church, K.V.
"A Study of Socio-Economic Status and Child Care
Arrangements of Women in Madina." Paper Presented at the
National Council on Women and Development (NCWD) Seminar
on Women and Development. Accra, Ghana: NCWD.
September, 1978.
Cole, Jane J.
National Council on Women and Development (NCWD):
Policies and Actions. Accra, Ghana: NCWD 1980.

Cole, Jane J.
    "Providing Access to New Skills and Modern
    Technologies--The Ghana National Council on Women and
    Development." Assignment Children. #38 April-June,
    1977. pp. 71-79.
Date-Bah, Eugenia
    The Changing Work Roles of Ghanaian Women. Accra, Ghana:
    National Council on Women and Development. 1980.
Date-Bah, Eugenia
    "Ghanaian Women in Academia: African Women in a New
    Occupational Role." Ghana Journal of Sociology. Volume
    12 #1 1978. pp. 44-71.
Date-Bah, Eugenia
    Ghanaian Women in Factory Employment: A Case Study.
    Geneva: Institute for Labour Studies. 1978. 9p.
Date-Bah, Eugenia
    "Rural Women, Their Activities and Technology in Ghana:
    An Overview." (In) International Labour Organization
    (ILO). Rural Development and Women in Africa. Geneva:
    ILO. 1984. pp. 89-98.
Date-Bah, Eugenia
    "Female and Male Factory Workers in Accra." (In) Oppong,
    Christine (ed.). Female and Male in Africa. London:
    George Allen and Unwin. 1983. pp. 266-274.
Date-Bah, Eugenia
    "Women in an Urban Setting for Ghana: Ghanaian Women in
    Factory Employment." Greenhill Journal of
    Administration. Volume 4 #1/2 April-September, 1977.
    pp. 76-94.
Dinan, Carmel
    "Sugar Daddies and Gold Diggers: The White-Collar Single
    Women in Accra." (In) Oppong, Christine (ed.). Female
    and Male in West Africa. London: George Allen and Unwin.
    1983. pp. 344-366.
Dinan, Carmel
    "Pragmatists or Feminists? The Professional 'Single'
    Women in Accra, Ghana." Cahiers d'Etudes Africaines.
    Volume 17 #1 1977. pp. 15-176.
Dinan, Carmel
    "Work, Marriage and Autonomy." (In) Allen, C. and
    Williams, G. (eds.). Subsaharan Africa. London:
    Macmillan. Sociology of Developing Societies Series.
    1982. pp. 52-57.
Dumor, Ernest K.
    "Women in Rural Development in Ghana." Rural Africana.
    #17 Fall, 1983. 57-68.
Dumor, Ernest K.
    "Commodity Queens and the Distributive Trade in Ghana: A
    Socio-Historical Analysis." African Urban Studies.
    Volume 12 1982. pp. 27-45.
Dumor, Ernest K.
    "Commodity Queens and the Distributive Trade in Ghana."
    Paper Presented at the Annual Meeting of the African

Studies Association. Paper #23. Baltimore, Maryland.
1978. 25p.
Dzidzienyo, Stella
"Housemaids: A Case Study of Domestic Helpers in Ghanaian
Homes." Paper Presented at the National Council on Women
and Development (NCWD) Seminar on Women and Development.
Accra, Ghana: NCWD. September, 1978.
Ewusi, Kodwo
"Women in Occupations in Ghana." Paper Presented at the
National Council on Women and Development (NCWD) Seminar
on Women and Development. Accra, Ghana: NCWD.
September, 1978.
Feyisetan, Bamikale J.
"The Determinants of Female Labor Force Participation:
The Effects of the Sectoral Composition of Labor
Markets." Ph.D Dissertation: University of Pennsylvania.
Philadelphia, Pennsylvania. 1982. 235p.
Fogelberg, Teresa
Nanumba Women: Working Bees or Idle Bums? Sexual
Division of Labour, Ideology of Work, and Power Relations
Between Women and Men in Gole, A Village in Nanumba
District, Northern Region, Ghana. Leiden, Netherlands:
Institute of Cultural and Social Studies. 1981. 83p.
Gbedemah, Charles
"The Role of Women in the Production of Rice in Northern
Ghana." Paper Presented at the National Council on Women
and Development (NCWD) Seminar on Women and Development.
Legon, Ghana: NCWD. September, 1978.
Ghana National Council on Women and Development (NCWD)
The First Women's Co-Operative Gari Factory. Accra,
Ghana: NCWD. 1980.
Ghana Trades Union Congress (GTUC)
Position of Women in the Ghana Trades Union Congress.
Accra, Ghana: GTUC. Mimeograph. 1977.
Goody, Esther N.
Parenthood and Social Reproduction: Fostering and
Occupational Roles in West Africa. Cambridge, New York:
Cambridge University Press. Cambridge Studies In Social
Anthropology #35. 1982. 348p.
Greenstreet, Miranda
"Various Salient Features Concerning the Employment of
Women Workers in Ghana." Paper Presented at the National
Council on Women and Development (NCWD) Seminar on Women
and Development. Accra, Ghana: NCWD. July, 1978.
Greenstreet, Miranda
Females in the Agricultural Labour Force and Non-Formal
Education for Rural Development in Ghana. Hague,
Netherlands: Institute of Social Studies. ISS Occasional
Paper #90. August, 1981. 23p.
Guyer, Jane I.
"Women in the Rural Economy: Contemporary Variations."
(In) Hay, Margaret J. and Stichter, Sharon (eds.).

African Women South of the Sahara. New York: Longman.
1984. pp. 19-32.
Klingshirn, A.
    Investment of Women in Co-Operatives in Zaire and Ghana.
    Rome: United Nations Food and Agriculture Organization.
    UNFPA/FAO Study. 1978.
Lewis, Mary A.
    "Female Entrepreneural Styles: An Examination of Coastal
    Fante Businesswomen." Ph.D Dissertation: University of
    Washington. Seattle, Washington. 1977. 255p.
Mickelwait, Donald R. and Riegelman, Mary Ann and Sweet,
Charles F.
    Women in Rural Development: A Survey of the Roles of
    Women in Ghana, Lesotho, Kenya, Nigeria... Boulder,
    Colorado: Westview Press. 1976. 224p.
Nantogmah, Matilda A.
    "Active Participation of Ghanaian Women in Integrated
    Rural Development." Paper Presented at the Annual
    Meeting of the Canadian Association of African Studies.
    1978. 27p.
Nantogmah, Matilda A.
    "The Image of Women as Workers With Special Emphasis on
    Ghanaian Women Workers." Paper Presented for the
    Conference on Women and Work in Africa. Urbana,
    Illinois: University of Illinois-Urbana-Champaign. April
    28-May 1, 1979.
Okali, Christine
    Cocoa and Kinship in Ghana: The Matrilineal Akan of
    Ghana. London: Kegan Paul International for the
    International African Institute. 1983. 179p.
Okali, Christine
    "Kinship and Cocoa Farming in Ghana." (In) Oppong,
    Christine (ed.). Female and Male in West Africa.
    London: George Allen and Unwin. 1983. pp. 169-178.
Oppong, Christine
    "Issues Concerning the Changing Status of African Women:
    Some Lessons From the Ghanaian Experience." (In)
    International Planned Parenthood Federation (IPPF).
    Proceedings of the IPPF Africa Regional Conference.
    London: IPPF. Aug. 3-Sept. 3, 1976. pp. 263-282.
Oppong, Christine and Abu, Katharine
    The Changing Maternal Role of Ghanaian Women: Impacts of
    Education, Migration and Employment. Geneva:
    International Labour Organization. Population and Labour
    Policies Programme. Working Paper #143. February, 1984.
    190p.
Pappoe, Matilda E.
    "Ghana." (In) Jelliffe, D.B. and Jelliffe, E.F.P. and
    Sai, F.T. and Senanayake, P. (eds.). Lactation,
    Fertility and the Working Woman. London: International
    Planned Parenthood Federation. 1979. pp. 97-106.
Pellow, Deborah
    "Work and Autonomy; Women in Accra." American
    Ethnologist. Volume 5 #4 November, 1978. pp. 770-785.

GHANA

Pellow, Deborah
    Women in Accra: Options for Autonomy. Algonac, Michigan:
    Reference Publications. 1977. 272p.
Pine, Frances
    "Family Structure and the Division of Labour: Female
    Roles in Urban Ghana." (In) Alavi, H. and Shanin, T.
    (eds.). Introduction to the Sociology of 'Developing
    Societies'. London: MacMillan. 1982. pp. 387-405.
Roach, Penelope M.
    "Career and Family: Expectations and Realities--A
    Preliminary Report on Ghanaian Secondary School
    Students." Paper Presented at the Women and Work in
    Africa Symposium. Urbana, Illinois: University of
    Illinois-Urbana. April-May, 1979.
Robertson, Claire C.
    "Change in the Organization of the Fish Trade in 20th
    Century Accra." African Urban Notes. Volume 2 #2
    Spring, 1976. pp. 43-58.
Robertson, Claire C.
    "Formal or Nonformal Education? Entrepreneurial Women in
    Ghana." Comparative Education Review. Volume 28
    November, 1984. pp. 639-658.
Robertson, Claire C.
    "The Impact of Formal Education on Marketing Skills Among
    Central Accra Girls." Paper Presented at the 'Women and
    Work in Africa' Symposium. Urbana, Illinois: University
    of Illinois-Urbana. April-May, 1979.
Robertson, Claire C.
    "Ga Women and Socioeconomic Change in Accra, Ghana."
    (In) Hafkin, N.J. and Bay, E.G. (eds.). Women in Africa:
    Studies in Social and Economic Change. Stanford,
    California: Stanford University Press. 1976. pp.
    111-133.
Robertson, Claire C.
    "In Pursuit of Life Histories: The Problem of Bias."
    Frontiers. Volume 7 #2 1983. pp. 63-69.
Robertson, Claire C.
    "The Death of Makola and Other Tragedies: Accra
    Agricultural Markets, Rural Women, Ghana." Canadian
    Journal of African Studies. Volume 17 #3 1983. pp.
    469-496.
Sagoe, Aba
    "Ghana's Market Women." Africa Women. #5 1976.
Sai, Florence A.
    "Women Traders." Paper Presented at the National Council
    on Women and Development (NCWD) Seminar on Women and
    Development. Accra, Ghana: NCWD. July, 1978.
Sanjek, Roger and Sanjek, Lani
    "Notes on Women and Work in Adabraka." African Urban
    Notes. Volume 2 #2 Spring, 1976. pp. 1-26.
Simms, Ruth and Dumor, Ernest K.
    "Women in the Urban Economy of Ghana: Associational

Activity and the Enclave Economy." African Urban Notes.
Volume 2 #3 Fall/Winter, 1976. pp. 43-64.

Steel, William F.
"Female and Small-Scale Employment Under Moderization in
Ghana." Economic Development and Cultural Change.
Volume 30 #1 October, 1981. pp.153-168.

Steel, William F.
Data on Labor Force Size, Growth, Composition and
Underutilization by Sex, Firm Size, Sector and
Occupation, Ghana, 1960-1970. Washington, D.C.: World
Bank. 1978. 67p.

Steel, William F.
"Women's Employment and Development: A Conceptual
Framework Applied to Ghana." (In) Bay, Edna G. (ed.).
Women and Work in Africa. Boulder, Colorado: Westview
Press. Westview Special Studies in Africa. 1982. pp.
225-248.

Steel, William F.
Report on Research Program for Ghana National Council of
Women and Development (NCWD). Nashville, Tennessee:
Vanderbilt University. 1976. 39p.

Sudarkasa, Niara
"Women and Migration in Contemporary West Africa." (In)
Wellesley Editorial Committee. Women and National
Development: The Complexities of Change. Chicago:
University of Chicago Press. 1977. pp. 178-189.

Sudarkasa, Niara
"Women and Migration in Contemporary West Africa."
Signs. Volume 3 #1 Autumn, 1977. pp. 178-189.

Tamakloe, Martha A.
Women in Agriculture: A Study of Mixed Crop Farmers in
Nkwaie-Toase Area. Kumasi, Ghana: Department of Housing
and Planning Research. U.S.T. 1978. 26p.

Tamakloe, Martha A.
"Women in Agriculture: A Study of Mixed Crop Farmers in
Nkawie-Toase Area." Paper Presented at the National
Council on Women and Development (NCWD) Conference on
Women in Development. Legon, Ghana: NCWD. September,
1978.

United Nations Economic Commission for Africa (UNECA)
Women Workers in Ghana-Kenya-Zambia: A Comparative
Analysis of Women's Employment in the Modern Wage
Sector. Addis Ababa, Ethiopia: UNECA. 1979.

United Nations Food and Agriculture Organization (FAO)
Market Women in West Africa. Report of the Seminar on
the Role of Women in Marketing Local Farm and Marine
Produce, Accra, Ghana, December 12-16, 1977. Rome: FAO.
1977. 29p.

Vellenga, Dorothy D.
"Differentiation Among Women Farmers in Two Rural Areas
in Ghana." Labour and Society. Volume 2 #2 April,
1977. pp. 197-208.

Vellenga, Dorothy D.
"Women, Households, and Food Commodity Chains in Southern Ghana: Contradictions Between Search for Profits and the Search for Survival." Research Review. Volume 8 #3 1985. pp. 293-318.
Vercruijsse, Emile V.W.
"Fishmongers, Big Dealers and Fishermen: Co-Operation and Conflict Between the Sexes in Ghanaian Canoe Fishing." (In) Oppong, Christine (ed.). Female and Male in West Africa. London: George Allen and Unwin. 1983. pp. 179-191.
Weis, Lois
"Women and Education in Ghana: Some Problems in Assessing Change." International Journal of Women's Studies. Volume 3 #5 September-October, 1980. pp. 431-453.

EQUALITY AND LIBERATION

Asomani, Carolann G.
"A Descriptive Survey of the University Women of Ghana and Their Attitudes Toward the Women's Movement." Ed.D Dissertation: George Washington University. Washington D.C. 1977. 191p.
Okonkwo, Rina
"Adelaide Casely Hayford: Cultural Nationalist and Feminist." Phylon. Volume 42 #1 1981. pp. 41-51.

FAMILY LIFE

Aryee, A.F.
"Urbanization and the Incidence of Plural Marriage: Some Theoretical Perspectives." (In) Oppong, C. and Adaba, G. and Bekombo-Priso, M. and Mogey, J. (eds.). Marriage, Fertility and Parenthood in West Africa. Canberra, Australia: Australian National University. Department of Demography. Volume One. 1978. pp. 367-379.
Bhatia, Jagdish C.
"Correlates of Husband-Wife Attitudes Towards Family Planning in Rural Ghana." Health and Population: Perspectives and Issues. Volume 5 #2 April-June, 1982. pp. 97-107.
Bhatia, Jagdish C.
"Polygamy-Fertility Inter-Relationship: The Case of Ghana." Journal of Family Welfare. Volume 31 #4 June, 1985. pp. 46-55.
Bleek, Wolf
"The Value of Children to Parents in Kwahu, Ghana." (In) Oppong, C. and Adaba, G. and Bekombo-Priso, M. and Mogey, J. (eds.). Marriage, Fertility and Parenthood in West Africa. Canberra, Australia: Australian National University. Department of Demography. Volume One. 1978. pp. 307-323.

Bleek, Wolf
    Sexual Relations and Birth Control in Ghana: A Case Study
    of a Rural Town. Amsterdam, Netherlands: University of
    Amsterdam. Antropologisch-Sociologisch Centrum. Uitgave
    #10. 1976. 352p.
Brown, Edward K.
    "Patterns of Internal Migration in Ghana With Special
    Emphasis on the Determinants of Female Migration." Ph.D
    Dissertation: University of Pennsylvania. Philadelphia,
    Pennsylvania. 1983. 295p.
Brydon, Lynne
    "Women at Work: Some Changes in Family Structure in
    Amedzofe-Avatime, Ghana." Africa. Volume 49 #2 1979.
    pp. 97-110.
Bukh, Jette
    The Village Women of Ghana. Uppsala, Sweden:
    Scandinavian Institute of African Studies. Centre for
    Development Research. Publication #1. 1979. 118p.
Caldwell, John C.
    "Marriage, the Family and Fertility in Sub-Saharan Africa
    With Special Reference to Research Programmes in Ghana
    and Nigeria." (In) Huzayyin, S.A. and Acsadi, G.T.
    (eds.). Family and Marriage in Some African and Asian
    Countries. Cairo: Cairo Demographic Centre. CDC
    Research Monograph #6. 1976. pp. 359-371.
Caldwell, John C.
    Population Growth and Family Change in Africa: The New
    Urban Elite in Ghana. London: C. Hurst. 1977. 22p.
Church, K.V.
    "Women and Family Life in an Ashanti Town." M.A. Thesis:
    University of Ghana. Legon, Ghana. 1978.
Church, K.V.
    "A Study of Socio-Economic Status and Child Care
    Arrangements of Women in Madina." Paper Presented at the
    National Council on Women and Development (NCWD) Seminar
    on Women and Development. Accra, Ghana: NCWD.
    September, 1978.
Daniels, W.C.
    "The Effect of Marriage on the Status of Children in
    Ghana." (In) Roberts, Simon (ed.). Law and the Family
    in Africa. Hague, Netherlands: Mouton. 1977. pp.
    159-168.
Date-Bah, Eugenia
    The Changing Work Roles of Ghanaian Women. Accra, Ghana:
    National Council on Women and Development. 1980.
Fiawoo, D.K.
    "Some Fertility Patterns of Foster Care in Ghana." (In)
    Oppong, C. (ed.). Marriage, Fertility and Parenthood in
    West Africa. Canberra, Australia: Australian National
    University. Department of Demography. Changing African
    Family Project Monograph #4. 1978.
Gaisie, Samuel K.
    "Child-Spacing Patterns and Fertility Differentials in

Ghana." (In) Page, Hilary J. and Lesthaeghe, Ron (eds.).
Child-Spacing in Tropical Africa: Traditions and Change.
New York: Academic Press. 1981. pp. 237-253.
Goody, Esther N.
Parenthood and Social Reproduction: Fostering and
Occupational Roles in West Africa. Cambridge, New York:
Cambridge University Press. Cambridge Studies In Social
Anthropology #35. 1982. 348p.
Hagaman, Barbara L.
"Beer and Matriliny: The Power of Women in Lobir, Ghana."
Ph.D Dissertation: Northeastern University. Boston,
Massachusetts. 1977. 365p.
Hagan, George P.
"Divorce, Polygyny and Family Welfare." Ghana Journal of
Sociology. Volume 10 #1 1976. pp. 67-84.
Hagan, George P.
"Marriage, Divorce and Polygyny in Winneba." (In)
Oppong, Christine (ed.). Female and Male in West Africa.
London: George Allen and Unwin. 1983. pp. 192-203.
Hevi-Yiboe, L.A.
Smoke in Rural Ghanaian Kitchens. Accra, Ghana: Arakan
Press. 1979.
Kalu, Wilhemina J.
"Modern Ga Family Life Patterns: A Look at Changing
Marriage Structure in Africa." Journal of Black Studies.
Volume 11 #3 March, 1981. pp. 349-359.
Lowy, Michael J.
"Establishing Paternity and Demanding Child Support in a
Ghanaian Town." (In) Roberts, Simon (ed.). Law and
Family in Africa. Hague, Netherlands: Mouton. 1977.
pp. 15-38.
Luckham, Yaa
"Law and the Status of Women in Ghana." (In) Columbia
Human Rights Law Review (eds.). Law and the Status of
Women: An International Symposium. New York: United
Nations. Centre for Social Development and Humanitarian
Affairs. 1977. pp. 69-94.
Oppong, Christine
"Ghanaian Women Teachers as Workers, Kin, Wives and
Mothers: A Study of Conjugal Family Solidarity--Norms,
Reality and Stress." Paper Presented at the Conference
on Women and Development. Wellesley, Massachusetts:
Wellesley College. June 2-6, 1976. 25p.
Oppong, Christine and Abu, Katharine
The Changing Maternal Role of Ghanaian Women: Impacts of
Education, Migration and Employment. Geneva:
International Labour Organization. Population and Labour
Policies Programme. Working Paper #143. February, 1984.
190p.
Oppong, Christine
"Motherhood in a Changing World: The Case of Ghana."
UNICEF News. Volume 89 #3 1976. pp. 32+.

Oppong, Christine
    "A Note From Ghana on Chains of Change in Family Systems
    and Family Size." Journal of Marriage and Family.
    Volume 39 #3 August, 1977. pp. 615-621.
Oppong, Christine
    Middle Class African Marriage: A Family Study of Ghanaian
    Senior Civil Servants. London: George Allen and Unwin.
    1981. 190p.
Oppong, Christine
    "From Love to Institution: Indications of Change in Akan
    Marriage." Journal of Family History. Volume 5 #2 1980.
    pp. 197-209.
Oppong, Christine
    "Property, Power and Time: A Reassessment of Ghanaian
    Student Norms." (In) Oppong, C. and Adaba, G. and
    Bekombo-Priso, M. and Mogey, J. (eds.). Marriage,
    Fertility and Parenthood in West Africa. Canberra,
    Australia: Australian National University. Department of
    Demography. Volume Two. 1978. pp. 601-614.
Oppong, Christine
    "Norms Reality and Stress: Aspects of Conjugal Family
    Solidarity Among Ghanaian Women Teachers." Paper
    Presented at Wellesley Conference on Women and
    Development. Wellesley, Massachusetts: Wellesley
    College. June, 1976.
Oppong, Christine
    "Women's Role and Conjugal Family Systems in Ghana."
    (In) Lupri, E. (ed.). The Changing Position of Women in
    Family and Society. Lieden, Netherlands: Brill. 1983.
    pp. 331-343.
Pine, Frances
    "Family Structure and the Division of Labour: Female
    Roles in Urban Ghana." (In) Alavi, H. and Shanin, T.
    (eds.). Introduction to the Sociology of 'Developing
    Societies'. London: MacMillan. 1982. pp. 387-405.
Roach, Penelope M.
    "Career and Family: Expectations and Realities--A
    Preliminary Report on Ghanaian Secondary School
    Students." Paper Presented at the Women and Work in
    Africa Symposium. Urbana, Illinois: University of
    Illinois-Urbana. April-May, 1979.
Sanjek, Roger
    "Female and Male Domestic Cycles in Urban Africa: The
    Adabraka Case." (In) Oppong, Christine (ed.). Female
    and Male in West Africa. London: George Allen and Unwin.
    1983. pp. 330-343.
Smock, Audrey C.
    "The Impact of Modernization on Women's Position in the
    Family in Ghana." (In) Schlegel, Alice E. (ed.). Sexual
    Stratification: A Cross-Cultural View. New York:
    Columbia University Press. 1977. pp. 192-214.
Sudarkasa, Niara
    "Women and Migration in Contemporary West Africa." (In)

Wellesley Editorial Committee. Women and National
Development: The Complexities of Change. Chicago:
University of Chicago Press. 1977. pp. 178-189.
Sudarkasa, Niara
"Women and Migration in Contemporary West Africa."
Signs. Volume 3 #1 Autumn, 1977. pp. 178-189.
Vellenga, Dorothy D.
"Matriliny, Patriliny and Class Formation Among Women
Cocoa Farmers in Two Rural Areas of Ghana." Paper
Presented at the Annual Meeting of the African Studies
Association. Paper #126. Bloomington, Indiana. October
21-24, 1981.
Vellenga, Dorothy D.
"Women, Households, and Food Commodity Chains in Southern
Ghana: Contradictions Between Search for Profits and the
Search for Survival." Research Review. Volume 8 #3
1985. pp. 293-318.
Whitehead, A.
Women and the Household: Themes Arising From a North-East
Ghana Example. Sussex, England: University of Sussex.
Institute of Development Studies. Draft Paper Presented
at the Conference on Continuing Subordination of Women
and the Development Process. 1978.

FAMILY PLANNING AND CONTRACEPTION

Ampofo, Daniel A.
"The Danfa Family Planning Program in Rural Ghana."
Studies in Family Planning. Volume 7 #10 October, 1976.
266-274.
Armar, A.A. and David, A.S.
"Implementing an Integrative Population Program in
Ghana." Paper Presented at the Annual Conference of the
International Committee on the Management of Population
Programmes. Bali, Indonesia. July 12-14, 1976. pp.
60-69.
Aryee, A.F. and Gaisie, Samuel K.
"Fertility Implications of Contemporary Patterns of
Nuptiality in Ghana." (In) Ruzicka, L.T. (ed.).
Nuptiality and Fertility: Proceedings of a Seminar.
Liege, Belgium: International Union for the Scientific
Study of Population. January 8-11, 1979. Bruges,
Belgium. 1982. pp. 287-304.
Azu, Gladys D.
"Women and Contraception." Paper Presented at the
National Council on Women and Development (NCWD)
Conference on Women and Development. Accra, Ghana: NCWD
July, 1978.
Bame, K.N.
"Some Traditional and Modern Media for Generating Social
Change in Rural Africa: A Study of Some Traditional and
Modern Media for Communicating Family Planning in Ghana."

Paper Prepared for the Fourth World Congress of Rural
Sociology. 1976. 46p.
Bartel, Philip F.
"Conjugal Roles and Fertility in Old Country Ghana."
Paper Presented at the 15th International Seminar on
Family Research. Lome, Togo. 1976.
Bartle, Philip F.
"Conjugal Relations, Migration, and Fertility in an Akan
Community, Obo, Ghana." (In) Oppong, C. and Adaba, G.
and Bekombo-Priso, M. and Mogey, J. (eds.). Marriage,
Fertility and Parenthood in West Africa. Canberra,
Australia: Australian National University. Department of
Demography. Volume Two. 1978. pp. 521-532.
Belcher, D.W.
"Attitudes Towards Family Size and Family Planning in
Rural Ghana Danfa Project: 1972 Survey Findings."
Journal of Biosocial Science. Volume 10 #1 January,
1978. pp. 59-79.
Bhatia, Jagdish C.
"Determinants of Desired Family Size in Rural Ghana: A
Multivariate Analysis." Demography India. Volume 11 #2
July-December, 1982. pp. 221-243.
Bhatia, Jagdish C.
"Age at Marriage and Fertility in Ghana." Demography
India. Volume 12 #2 July-December, 1983. pp. 185-193.
Bhatia, Jagdish C.
"A Multivariate Analysis of Family Planning Knowledge
Differentials in Rural Ghana." Journal of Family
Welfare. Volume 30 #4 June, 1984. pp. 47-60.
Bleek, Wolf
Birth Control and Sexual Relations in Ghana: A Case Study
of a Rural Town. Amsterdam, Netherlands:
Antropologisch-Sociologisch Centrum. 1976.
Bleek, Wolf
"The Impossible Decision: Having Children in Kwahu,
Ghana." Paper Presented at the International Union for
the Scientific Study of Population Conference. Liege,
Belgium: IUSSP. Helsinki, Finland. 1978. 51p.
Bleek, Wolf
"Spacing of Children, Sexual Abstinence and Breast
Feeding in Rural Ghana." Social Science and Medicine.
Volume 10 #5 1976. pp. 225-230.
Bleek, Wolf
"Family Planning or Birth Control: The Ghanaian
Contradiction." Cultures et Developpement. Volume 9 #1
1977. pp. 64-81.
Bleek, Wolf
"The Unexpected Repression: How Family Planning
Discriminates Against Women in Ghana." Review of
Ethnology. Volume 7 #25 1981. pp. 193-198.
Caldwell, John C.
"Marriage, the Family and Fertility in Sub-Saharan Africa
With Special Reference to Research Programmes in Ghana

and Nigeria." (In) Huzayyin, S.A. and Acsadi, G.T.
(eds.). Family and Marriage in Some African and Asian
Countries. Cairo: Cairo Demographic Centre. CDC
Research Monograph #6. 1976. pp. 359-371.
Caldwell, John C.
"The Economic Rationality of High Fertility: An
Investigation Illustrated With Nigerian Survey Data."
Population Studies (London). Volume 31 #1 March, 1977.
pp. 5-27.
Gaisie, Samuel K.
The Proximate Determinants of Fertility in Ghana.
Voorburg, Netherlands: International Statistical
Institute. WFS Scientific Report #53. March, 1984.
63p.
Gaisie, Samuel K.
"Child-Spacing Patterns and Fertility Differentials in
Ghana." (In) Page, Hilary J. and Lesthaeghe, Ron (eds.).
Child-Spacing in Tropical Africa: Traditions and Change.
New York: Academic Press. 1981. pp. 237-253.
Gaisie, Samuel K.
"Mediating Mechanisms of Fertility Change in Africa--The
Role of Post-Partum Variables in the Process of Change:
The Case of Ghana." (In) International Union for the
Scientific Study of Population (IUSSP). International
Population Conference: Solicited Papers. Liege,
Netherlands: IUSSP. Volume One. 1981. pp. 95-114.
Gaisie, Samuel K. and Nabila, J.
Determinants of Fertility and Their Implications for the
Ghana Population Policy. Accra, Ghana: University of
Ghana. International Union for the Scientific Study of
Population. Case Studies of Population Policies in
Developing Countries. 1978.
Lesthaeghe, Ron J. and Eelens, Frank
Social Organization and Reproductive Regimes: Lessons
From Sub-Saharan Africa and Historical Western Europe.
Brussels, Belgium: Vrije Universiteit Brussel.
Interuniversity Programme in Demography. IDP Working
Paper #1985-1. 1985. 64p.
Makinwa, P. Kofo
"The National Cost of Illegal Abortion: A Case for Family
Planning Programme." Aman. Volume 1 #1 1981. pp.
36-50.
Mendonsa, Eugene L.
"The Explanation of High Fertility Among the Sisala of
Northern Ghana." (In) Caldwell, John C. (ed.). The
Persistence of High Fertility: Population Prospects in
the Third World. Canberra, Australia: Australian
National University. Volume One. 1977. pp. 223-258.
Oppong, Christine
"A Note From Ghana on Chains of Change in Family Systems
and Family Size." Journal of Marriage and Family.
Volume 39 #3 August, 1977. pp. 615-621.

Oppong, Christine and Bleek, Wolf
    "Economic Models and Having Children: Some Evidence From
    Kwahu, Ghana."   Africa.   Volume 52 #4 1982.   pp. 15-33.
Oppong, Christine
    "The Crumbling of High Fertility Supports: Data From a
    Study of Ghanaian Primary School Teachers."   (In)
    Caldwell, John C. (ed.).   The Persistence of High
    Fertility: Population Prospects in the Third World.
    Canberra, Australia: Australian National University.
    Volume One.   1977.   pp. 331-360.
Pappoe, Matilda E.
    "Ghana."   (In) Jelliffe, D.B. and Jelliffe, E.F.P. and
    Sai, F.T. and Senanayake, P. (eds.).   Lactation,
    Fertility and the Working Woman.   London: International
    Planned Parenthood Federation.   1979.   pp. 97-106.
Tawiah, E.O.
    "Determinants of Cumulative Fertility in Ghana."
    Demography.   Volume 21 #1   February, 1984.   pp. 1-8.
Ward, W.B. and Sam, M. and Nicholas, D.D. and Pappoe,
Matilda E.
    "Impact of Family Planning Information on Acceptance at a
    Ghanaian Rural Health Post."   International Journal of
    Health Education.   Volume 21 #4 1978.   pp. 273-281.
Wilder, Frank
    New Directions in Population Communications in Three
    Developing Countries.   Washington, D.C.: American Public
    Health Association.   1977.   64p.

FERTILITY AND INFERTILITY

Ampofo, Daniel A.
    "Socio-Cultural and Medical Perspectives in Infertility
    in Ghana: Epidemiological Characteristics of 202 Cases."
    (In) International Planned Parenthood Federation (IPPF).
    Proceedings of the IPPF Africa Regional Conference.
    London: IPPF.   1977.   pp. 96-102.
Ankrah, Kwaku T.
    "Assimilation or Selectivity: A Test of Competing Theses
    on the Relationship Between Rural-Urban Migration and
    Fertility in Ghana."   Ph.D Dissertation: University of
    Cincinnati.   Cincinnati, Ohio.   1979.   178p.
Aryee, A.F. and Gaisie, Samuel K.
    "Fertility Implications of Contemporary Patterns of
    Nuptiality in Ghana."   (In) Ruzicka, L.T. (ed.).
    Nuptiality and Fertility: Proceedings of a Seminar.
    Liege, Belgium: International Union for the Scientific
    Study of Population.   January 8-11, 1979.   Bruges,
    Belgium.   1982.   pp. 287-304.
Bartel, Philip F.
    "Conjugal Roles and Fertility in Old Country Ghana."
    Paper Presented at the 15th International Seminar on
    Family Research.   Lome, Togo.   1976.

Bartle, Philip F.
"Conjugal Relations, Migration, and Fertility in an Akan Community, Obo, Ghana." (In) Oppong, C. and Adaba, G. and Bekombo-Priso, M. and Mogey, J. (eds.). Marriage, Fertility and Parenthood in West Africa. Canberra, Australia: Australian National University. Department of Demography. Volume Two. 1978. pp. 521-532.

Bhatia, Jagdish C.
"Age at Marriage and Fertility in Ghana." Demography India. Volume 12 #2 July-December, 1983. pp. 185-193.

Bhatia, Jagdish C.
"Polygamy-Fertility Inter-Relationship: The Case of Ghana." Journal of Family Welfare. Volume 31 #4 June, 1985. pp. 46-55.

Bleek, Wolf
"The Impossible Decision: Having Children in Kwahu, Ghana." Paper Presented at the International Union for the Scientific Study of Population Conference. Liege, Belgium: IUSSP. Helsinki, Finland. 1978. 51p.

Caldwell, John C.
"Marriage, the Family and Fertility in Sub-Saharan Africa With Special Reference to Research Programmes in Ghana and Nigeria." (In) Huzayyin, S.A. and Acsadi, G.T. (eds.). Family and Marriage in Some African and Asian Countries. Cairo: Cairo Demographic Centre. CDC Research Monograph #6. 1976. pp. 359-371.

Caldwell, John C.
"The Economic Rationality of High Fertility: An Investigation Illustrated With Nigerian Survey Data. Population Studies (London). Volume 31 #1 March, 1977. pp. 5-27.

Dzegede, Sylvi A.
"Urbanization and Fertility Decline in West Africa: Ghana, Sierra Leone and Liberia." Journal of Comparative Family Studies. Volume 12 #2 Spring, 1981. pp. 233-244.

Ebin, Victoria
"Interpretations of Infertility: The Aowin People of Southwest Ghana." (In) MacCormack, C.P. (ed.). Ethnography of Fertility and Birth. London: Academic Press. 1982. pp. 141-159.

Eelens, Frank and Donne, L.
The Proximate Determinants of Fertility in Sub-Saharan Africa: A Factbook Based on the Results of the World Fertility Survey. Brussels, Belgium: Vrije Universiteit Brussel. Interuniversity Programme in Demography. IDP Working Paper #1985-3. 1985. 122p.

Fiawoo, D.K.
"Some Fertility Patterns of Foster Care in Ghana." (In) Oppong, C. (ed.). Marriage, Fertility and Parenthood in West Africa. Canberra, Australia: Australian National University. Department of Demography. Changing African Family Project Monograph #4. 1978.

Fosu, Gabriel B.
   "Interrelations Among Health Attitudes, Fertility, and
   Mortality in Accra." Ph.D Dissertation: Brown
   University. Providence, Rhode Island. 1984. 406p.
Gaisie, Samuel K.
   The Proximate Determinants of Fertility in Ghana.
   Voorburg, Netherlands: International Statistical
   Institute. WFS Scientific Report #53. March, 1984.
   63p.
Gaisie, Samuel K.
   "Child-Spacing Patterns and Fertility Differentials in
   Ghana." (In) Page, Hilary J. and Lesthaeghe, Ron (eds.).
   Child-Spacing in Tropical Africa: Traditions and Change.
   New York: Academic Press. 1981. pp. 237-253.
Gaisie, Samuel K.
   "Mediating Mechanisms of Fertility Change in Africa--The
   Role of Post-Partum Variables in the Process of Change:
   The Case of Ghana." (In) International Union for the
   Scientific Study of Population (IUSSP). International
   Population Conference: Solicited Papers. Liege,
   Netherlands: IUSSP. Volume One. 1981. pp. 95-114.
Gaisie, Samuel K.
   Estimating Ghanaian Fertility, Mortality and Age
   Structure. Chapel Hill, North Carolina: University of
   North Carolina. University of Ghana Population Studies
   #5. Carolina Population Center. 1976.
Gaisie, Samuel K. and Nabila, J.
   Determinants of Fertility and Their Implications for the
   Ghana Population Policy. Accra, Ghana: University of
   Ghana. International Union for the Scientific Study of
   Population. Case Studies of Population Policies in
   Developing Countries. 1978.
Ghana. Central Bureau of Statistics (CBS)
   Ghana Fertility Survey, 1979-1980: First Report. Accra,
   Ghana: CBS. 1983. 187p.
International Statistical Institute (ISI)
   The Ghana Fertility Survey, 1979-80: A Summary of
   Findings. Voorburg, Netherlands: ISI. World Fertility
   Survey Report #39. July, 1983. 16p.
Jain, S.K.
   The Longitudinal Mortality and Fertility Survey in the
   Western Region of Ghana: Analytical Report. Canberra,
   Australia: Australian National University. Department of
   Demography. Research School of Social Sciences. 1981.
   230p.
Lesthaeghe, Ron J. and Eelens, Frank
   Social Organization and Reproductive Regimes: Lessons
   From Sub-Saharan Africa and Historical Western Europe.
   Brussels, Belgium: Vrije Universiteit Brussel.
   Interuniversity Programme in Demography. IDP Working
   Paper #1985-1. 1985. 64p.
Mendonsa, Eugene L.
   "The Explanation of High Fertility Among the Sisala of

Northern Ghana." (In) Caldwell, John C. (ed.). The
Persistence of High Fertility: Population Prospects in
the Third World. Canberra, Australia: Australian
National University. Volume One. 1977. pp. 223-258.
Oppong, Christine
"The Crumbling of High Fertility Supports: Data From a
Study of Ghanaian Primary School Teachers." (In)
Caldwell, John C. (ed.). The Persistence of High
Fertility: Population Prospects in the Third World.
Canberra, Australia: Australian National University.
Volume One. 1977. pp. 331-360.
Owusu, John Y.
Evaluation of the Ghana Fertility Survey, 1979-80.
London: International Statistical Institute. World
Fertility Survey Scientific Report #69. December, 1984.
44p.
Pappoe, Matilda E.
"Ghana." (In) Jelliffe, D.B. and Jelliffe, E.F.P. and
Sai, F.T. and Senanayake, P. (eds.). Lactation,
Fertility and the Working Woman. London: International
Planned Parenthood Federation. 1979. pp. 97-106.
Pool, D. Ian
"Empirical Evidence on Levels and Differentials of
National Fertility in Ghana." Paper Presented at the
International Population Conference. Mexico City,
Mexico. August, 1977.
Tawiah, E.O.
"Determinants of Cumulative Fertility in Ghana."
Demography. Volume 21 #1 February, 1984. pp. 1-8.

HEALTH, NUTRITION AND MEDICINE

Ampofo, Daniel A.
"Socio-Cultural and Medical Perspectives in Infertility
in Ghana: Epidemiological Characteristics of 202 Cases."
(In) International Planned Parenthood Federation (IPPF).
Proceedings of the IPPF Africa Regional Conference.
London: IPPF. 1977. pp. 96-102.
Azu, Gladys D.
"Women and Contraception." Paper Presented at the
National Council on Women and Development (NCWD)
Conference on Women and Development. Accra, Ghana: NCWD
July, 1978.
Bame, K.N.
"Some Traditional and Modern Media for Generating Social
Change in Rural Africa: A Study of Some Traditional and
Modern Media for Communicating Family Planning in Ghana."
Paper Prepared for the Fourth World Congress of Rural
Sociology. 1976. 46p.
Bentsi, C.
"Genital Infections With Chlamydia Trachomatis and

Neisseria Gonorrhoeae in Ghanian Women." Genitourinary
Medicine. Volume 61 #1 February, 1985. pp. 48-50.
Bhatia, Jagdish C.
"Determinants of Desired Family Size in Rural Ghana: A
Multivariate Analysis." Demography India. Volume 11 #2
July-December, 1982. pp. 221-243.
Bleek, Wolf
"Spacing of Children, Sexual Abstinence and Breast
Feeding in Rural Ghana." Social Science and Medicine.
Volume 10 #5 1976. pp. 225-230.
Bleek, Wolf
"Avoiding Shame: The Ethical Context of Abortion in
Ghana." Anthropological Quarterly. Volume 54 #4
October, 1981. pp. 203-209.
Bleek, Wolf
"Family Planning or Birth Control: The Ghanaian
Contradiction." Cultures et Developpement. Volume 9 #1
1977. pp. 64-81.
Bleek, Wolf
"The Unexpected Repression: How Family Planning
Discriminates Against Women in Ghana." Review of
Ethnology. Volume 7 #25 1981. pp. 193-198.
Bleek, Wolf
"Induced Abortion in a Ghanaian Family." African Studies
Review. Volume 21 #1 April, 1978. pp. 103-120.
Cole, Jane J.
"Providing Access to New Skills and Modern
Technologies--The Ghana National Council on Women and
Development." Assignment Children. #38 April-June,
1977. pp. 71-79.
Ebin, Victoria
"Interpretations of Infertility: The Aowin People of
Southwest Ghana." (In) MacCormack, C.P. (ed.).
Ethnography of Fertility and Birth. London: Academic
Press. 1982. pp. 141-159.
Elkins, T.E.
"Routine Gynaecological Clinic in Northern Ghana."
Journal of Tropical Medicine and Hygiene. Volume 87 #5
October, 1984. pp. 193-196.
Fiawoo, D.K.
"Some Fertility Patterns of Foster Care in Ghana." (In)
Oppong, C. (ed.). Marriage, Fertility and Parenthood in
West Africa. Canberra, Australia: Australian National
University. Department of Demography. Changing African
Family Project Monograph #4. 1978.
Fosu, Gabriel B.
"Interrelations Among Health Attitudes, Fertility, and
Mortality in Accra." Ph.D Dissertation: Brown
University. Providence, Rhode Island. 1984. 406p.
Gaisie, Samuel K.
The Proximate Determinants of Fertility in Ghana.
Voorburg, Netherlands: International Statistical
Institute. WFS Scientific Report #53. March, 1984.
63p.

Gaisie, Samuel K.
    "Mediating Mechanisms of Fertility Change in Africa--The
    Role of Post-Partum Variables in the Process of Change:
    The Case of Ghana." (In) International Union for the
    Scientific Study of Population (IUSSP). International
    Population Conference: Solicited Papers. Liege,
    Netherlands: IUSSP. Volume One. 1981. pp. 95-114.
Gaisie, Samuel K.
    Estimating Ghanaian Fertility, Mortality and Age
    Structure. Chapel Hill, North Carolina: University of
    North Carolina. University of Ghana Population Studies
    #5. Carolina Population Center. 1976.
Gaisie, Samuel K. and Nabila, J.
    Determinants of Fertility and Their Implications for the
    Ghana Population Policy. Accra, Ghana: University of
    Ghana. International Union for the Scientific Study of
    Population. Case Studies of Population Policies in
    Developing Countries. 1978.
Lamptey, Peter and Janowitz, Barbara and Smith, Jason B. and
Klufio, Cecil
    "Abortion Experience Among Obstetric Patients at Korle-Bu
    Hospital, Accra, Ghana." Journal of Biosocial Science.
    Volume 17 #2 April, 1985. pp. 195-203.
Nicholas D.D.
    "Attitudes and Practices of Traditional Birth Attendents
    in Ghana: Implications for Training in Africa." Bulletin
    of the World Health Organization. Volume 54 #3 1976.
Odouyoye, Mercy A.
    "Namimg the Woman: The Words of the Akan and the Words of
    the Bible." Bulletin de Theologie Africaine. Volume 3
    #5 January-June, 1981. pp. 81-97.
Ofosu-Amaah, S.
    "The Maternal and Child Health Services in Ghana."
    Journal of Tropical Medicine and Hygiene. Volume 84 #6
    December, 1981. pp. 265-269.
Oppong, Christine
    "Norms Reality and Stress: Aspects of Conjugal Family
    Solidarity Among Ghanaian Women Teachers." Paper
    Presented at Wellesley Conference on Women and
    Development. Wellesley, Massachusetts: Wellesley
    College. June, 1976.
Pappoe, Matilda E.
    "Ghana." (In) Jelliffe, D.B. and Jelliffe, E.F.P. and
    Sai, F.T. and Senanayake, P. (eds.). Lactation,
    Fertility and the Working Woman. London: International
    Planned Parenthood Federation. 1979. pp. 97-106.
Peterson, K.J.
    "Brong Midwives and Women in Childbirth: Management of
    Uncertainty in a Division of Labor." Human Organization.
    Volume 41 #4 Winter, 1982. pp. 291-298.
Shaw-Taylor, Ruth
    "Signs of Mental Stress in Ghana." (In) Blair, Patricia
    W. (ed.). Health Needs of the World's Poor Women.

Washington, D.C.: Equity Policy Center. 1981. pp.
18-21.
Tawiah, E.O.
"Determinants of Cumulative Fertility in Ghana."
Demography. Volume 21 #1 February, 1984. pp. 1-8.
Ward, W.B. and Sam, M. and Nicholas, D.D. and Pappoe,
Matilda E.
"Impact of Family Planning Information on Acceptance at a
Ghanaian Rural Health Post." International Journal of
Health Education. Volume 21 #4 1978. pp. 273-281.
Wilder, Frank
New Directions in Population Communications in Three
Developing Countries. Washington, D.C.: American Public
Health Association. 1977. 64p.

HISTORY

Aidoo, Agnes A.
"Asante Queen Mothers in Government and Politics in the
Nineteenth Century." Journal of the Historical Society
of Nigeria. Volume 9 #1 December, 1977. pp. 1-13.
Aidoo, Agnes A.
"Asante Queen Mothers in Government and Politics in the
Nineteenth Century." (In) Steady, Filomina C. (ed.).
The Black Woman Cross-Culturally. Cambridge,
Massachusetts: Schenkman Publishing. 1981. pp. 65-78.
Arhin, Kwame
"The Political and Military Roles of Akan Women." (In)
Oppong, Christine (ed.). Female and Male in West Africa.
London: George Allen and Unwin. 1983. pp. 91-98.
Brydon, Lynne
"Avatime Women and Men, 1900-1980." (In) Oppong,
Christine (ed.). Female and Male in Africa. London:
George Allen and Unwin. 1983. pp. 320-329.
Harrell-Bond, Barbara E.
Women and the 1979 Ghana Revolution. Hanover, New
Hampshire: American University Field Staff. Report #4.
1980. 10p.
McCaskie, T.C.
"State and Society, Marriage and Adultery: Some
Considerations From the Social History of Pre-Colonial
Asante." Journal of African History. Volume 22 #4 1981.
pp. 477-494.
Okonkwo, Rina
"Adelaide Casely Hayford: Cultural Nationalist and
Feminist." Phylon. Volume 42 #1 1981. pp. 41-51.
Robertson, Claire C.
"Post-Proclamation Slavery in Accra: a Female Affair?"
(In) Robertson, Claire C. and Klein, Martin A. (eds.).
Women and Slavery in Africa. Madison, Wisconsin:
University of Wisconsin Press. 1983. pp. 220-245.

LAW AND LEGAL ISSUES

Daniels, W.C.
"The Effect of Marriage on the Status of Children in Ghana." (In) Roberts, Simon (ed.). Law and the Family in Africa. Hague, Netherlands: Mouton. 1977. pp. 159-168.

Lowy, Michael J.
"Establishing Paternity and Demanding Child Support in a Ghanaian Town." (In) Roberts, Simon (ed.). Law and Family in Africa. Hague, Netherlands: Mouton. 1977. pp. 15-38.

Luckham, Yaa
"Law and the Status of Women in Ghana." (In) Columbia Human Rights Law Review (eds.). Law and the Status of Women: An International Symposium. New York: United Nations. Centre for Social Development and Humanitarian Affairs. 1977. pp. 69-94.

Mendonsa, Eugene L.
"Aspects of Sisala Marriage Prestations." Research Review. Volume 9 #3 1976.

Oduyoye, Mercy Amba
"Female Authority in Asante Law and Constitution." African Notes. Volume 8 #2 1981. pp. 9-14.

Opoku, Kwame
Law of Marriage in Ghana: a Study in Legal Pluralism. Frankfort, Germany: A. Metzner. 1976. 134p.

Vellenga, Dorothy D.
"Attempts to Change the Marriage Laws in Ghana and the Ivory Coast." (In) Foster, P. and Zolberg, A. (eds.). Ghana and the Ivory Coast: Perspectives on Modernisation. Chicago: University of Chicago Press. 1977.

Vellenga, Dorothy D.
"Who is a Wife? Legal Expressions of Heterosexual Conflicts in Ghana." (In) Oppong, Christine (ed.). Female and Male in West Africa. London: George Allen and Unwin. 1983. pp. 144-155.

LITERATURE

Berrian, Brenda F.
"African Women as Seen in the Works of Flora Nwapa and Ama Ata Aidoo." CLA Journal. Volume 25 #3 March, 1982. pp. 331-339.

Bruner, Charlotte H.
"Child Africa as Depicted by Bessie Head and Ama Ata Aidoo." Studies in the Humanities. Volume 7 #2 1979. pp. 5-11.

Hammond, Thomas N.
"Bebey's Courageous Market Women." CLA Journal. Volume 27 #3 1984. pp. 332-342.

McCaffrey, Kathleen M.
  Images of Women in the Literatures of Selected Developing
  Countries. Washington, D.C.: U.S. Department of State.
  U.S. Agency for International Development. Office of
  Women in Development. 1981. 229p.
Staudt, Kathleen A.
  "The Characterization of Women in Soyinka and Armah." Ba
  Shiru. Volume 8 #2 1977. pp. 63-69.

MARITAL RELATIONS AND NUPTIALITY

Abu, Katharine
  "The Separateness of Spouses: Conjugal Resources in an
  Ashanti Town." (In) Oppong, Christine (ed.). Female and
  Male in West Africa. London: George Allen and Unwin.
  1983. pp. 156-168.
Aryee, A.F.
  "Urbanization and the Incidence of Plural Marriage: Some
  Theoretical Perspectives." (In) Oppong, C. and Adaba, G.
  and Bekombo-Priso, M. and Mogey, J. (eds.). Marriage,
  Fertility and Parenthood in West Africa. Canberra,
  Australia: Australian National University. Department of
  Demography. Volume One. 1978. pp. 367-379.
Aryee, A.F. and Gaisie, Samuel K.
  "Fertility Implications of Contemporary Patterns of
  Nuptiality in Ghana." (In) Ruzicka, L.T. (ed.).
  Nuptiality and Fertility: Proceedings of a Seminar.
  Liege, Belgium: International Union for the Scientific
  Study of Population. January 8-11, 1979. Bruges,
  Belgium. 1982. pp. 287-304.
Asante-Darko, Nimrod and Van Der Geest, Sjaak
  "Male Chauvinism: Men and Women in Ghanaian Highlife
  Songs." (In) Oppong, Christine (ed.). Female and Male
  in West Africa. London: George Allen and Unwin. 1983.
  pp. 242-255.
Azu, Gladys D.
  "Women and Contraception." Paper Presented at the
  National Council on Women and Development (NCWD)
  Conference on Women and Development. Accra, Ghana: NCWD
  July, 1978.
Bartel, Philip F.
  "Conjugal Roles and Fertility in Old Country Ghana."
  Paper Presented at the 15th International Seminar on
  Family Research. Lome, Togo. 1976.
Bartle, Philip F.
  "Conjugal Relations, Migration, and Fertility in an Akan
  Community, Obo, Ghana." (In) Oppong, C. and Adaba, G.
  and Bekombo-Priso, M. and Mogey, J. (eds.). Marriage,
  Fertility and Parenthood in West Africa. Canberra,
  Australia: Australian National University. Department of
  Demography. Volume Two. 1978. pp. 521-532.

Belcher, D.W.
    "Attitudes Towards Family Size and Family Planning in
    Rural Ghana Danfa Project: 1972 Survey Findings."
    Journal of Biosocial Science. Volume 10 #1 January,
    1978. pp. 59-79.
Bhatia, Jagdish C.
    "Correlates of Husband-Wife Attitudes Towards Family
    Planning in Rural Ghana." Health and Population:
    Perspectives and Issues. Volume 5 #2 April-June, 1982.
    pp. 97-107.
Bhatia, Jagdish C.
    "Determinants of Desired Family Size in Rural Ghana: A
    Multivariate Analysis." Demography India. Volume 11 #2
    July-December, 1982. pp. 221-243.
Bhatia, Jagdish C.
    "Age at Marriage Differentials in Ghana: A Multivariate
    Analysis." Demography India. Volume 13 #1-2
    January-December, 1984. pp. 54-69.
Bhatia, Jagdish C.
    "Polygamy-Fertility Inter-Relationship: The Case of
    Ghana." Journal of Family Welfare. Volume 31 #4 June,
    1985. pp. 46-55.
Bhatia, Jagdish C.
    "A Multivariate Analysis of Family Planning Knowledge
    Differentials in Rural Ghana." Journal of Family
    Welfare. Volume 30 #4 June, 1984. pp. 47-60.
Bleek, Wolf
    Birth Control and Sexual Relations in Ghana: A Case Study
    of a Rural Town. Amsterdam, Netherlands:
    Antropologisch-Sociologisch Centrum. 1976.
Bleek, Wolf
    "Spacing of Children, Sexual Abstinence and Breast
    Feeding in Rural Ghana." Social Science and Medicine.
    Volume 10 #5 1976. pp. 225-230.
Bleek, Wolf
    Sexual Relations and Birth Control in Ghana: A Case Study
    of a Rural Town. Amsterdam, Netherlands: University of
    Amsterdam. Antropologisch-Sociologisch Centrum. Uitgave
    #10. 1976. 352p.
Bleek, Wolf
    "Marriage in Kwahu, Ghana." (In) Roberts, Simon (ed.).
    Law and the Family in Africa. Hague, Netherlands:
    Mouton. 1977. pp. 183-204.
Caldwell, John C.
    "Marriage, the Family and Fertility in Sub-Saharan Africa
    With Special Reference to Research Programmes in Ghana
    and Nigeria." (In) Huzayyin, S.A. and Acsadi, G.T.
    (eds.). Family and Marriage in Some African and Asian
    Countries. Cairo: Cairo Demographic Centre. CDC
    Research Monograph #6. 1976. pp. 359-371.
Caldwell, John C.
    Population Growth and Family Change in Africa: The New
    Urban Elite in Ghana. London: C. Hurst. 1977. 22p.

276

Church, K.V.
"Women and Family Life in an Ashanti Town." M.A. Thesis: University of Ghana. Legon, Ghana. 1978.

Daniels, W.C.
"The Effect of Marriage on the Status of Children in Ghana." (In) Roberts, Simon (ed.). Law and the Family in Africa. Hague, Netherlands: Mouton. 1977. pp. 159-168.

Dinan, Carmel
"Work, Marriage and Autonomy." (In) Allen, C. and Williams, G. (eds.). Subsaharan Africa. London: Macmillan. Sociology of Developing Societies Series. 1982. pp. 52-57.

Dzegede, Sylvi A.
"Urbanization and Fertility Decline in West Africa: Ghana, Sierra Leone and Liberia." Journal of Comparative Family Studies. Volume 12 #2 Spring, 1981. pp. 233-244.

Gaisie, Samuel K.
"Child-Spacing Patterns and Fertility Differentials in Ghana." (In) Page, Hilary J. and Lesthaeghe, Ron (eds.). Child-Spacing in Tropical Africa: Traditions and Change. New York: Academic Press. 1981. pp. 237-253.

Goody, Esther N.
Parenthood and Social Reproduction: Fostering and Occupational Roles in West Africa. Cambridge, New York: Cambridge University Press. Cambridge Studies In Social Anthropology #35. 1982. 348p.

Goody, Jack and Duly, Colin and Beeson, Ian and Harrison, Graham
"On the Absence of Implicit Sex-Preference in Ghana." Journal of Biosocial Science. Volume 13 #1 January, 1981. pp. 87-96.

Hagaman, Barbara L.
"Beer and Matriliny: The Power of Women in Lobir, Ghana." Ph.D Dissertation: Northeastern University. Boston, Massachusetts. 1977. 365p.

Hagan, George P.
"Divorce, Polygyny and Family Welfare." Ghana Journal of Sociology. Volume 10 #1 1976. pp. 67-84.

Hagan, George P.
"Marriage, Divorce and Polygyny in Winneba." (In) Oppong, Christine (ed.). Female and Male in West Africa. London: George Allen and Unwin. 1983. pp. 192-203.

Hershman, Paul
"A Comparison of Punjabi and Tallensi Marriage Systems." Eastern Anthropologist. Volume 33 #4 October-December, 1980. pp. 299-334.

Hevi-Yiboe, L.A.
Smoke in Rural Ghanaian Kitchens. Accra, Ghana: Arakan Press. 1979.

Kalu, Wilhemina J.
"Modern Ga Family Life Patterns: A Look at Changing

Marriage Structure in Africa." Journal of Black Studies.
Volume 11 #3 March, 1981. pp. 349-359.

Little, Kenneth L.
"A Question of Matrimonial Strategy? A Comparison of
Attitudes Between Ghanaian and British University
Students." Journal of Comparative Family Studies.
Volume 7 #1 Spring, 1976. pp. 5-22.

Lowy, Michael J.
"Establishing Paternity and Demanding Child Support in a
Ghanaian Town." (In) Roberts, Simon (ed.). Law and
Family in Africa. Hague, Netherlands: Mouton. 1977.
pp. 15-38.

Luckham, Yaa
"Law and the Status of Women in Ghana." (In) Columbia
Human Rights Law Review (eds.). Law and the Status of
Women: An International Symposium. New York: United
Nations. Centre for Social Development and Humanitarian
Affairs. 1977. pp. 69-94.

McCaskie, T.C.
"State and Society, Marriage and Adultery: Some
Considerations From the Social History of Pre-Colonial
Asante." Journal of African History. Volume 22 #4 1981.
pp. 477-494.

Mendonsa, Eugene L.
"Aspects of Sisala Marriage Prestations." Research
Review. Volume 9 #3 1976.

Nukunya, Godwin K.
"Women and Marriage." Paper Presented at the National
Council on Women and Development (NCWD) Seminar on Women
and Development. Accra, Ghana: NCWD. September, 1978.

Odouyoye, Mercy A.
"Namimg the Woman: The Words of the Akan and the Words of
the Bible." Bulletin de Theologie Africaine. Volume 3
#5 January-June, 1981. pp. 81-97.

Opoku, Kwame
Law of Marriage in Ghana: a Study in Legal Pluralism.
Frankfort, Germany: A. Metzner. 1976. 134p.

Oppong, Christine
"Ghanaian Women Teachers as Workers, Kin, Wives and
Mothers: A Study of Conjugal Family Solidarity--Norms,
Reality and Stress." Paper Presented at the Conference
on Women and Development. Wellesley, Massachusetts:
Wellesley College. June 2-6, 1976. 25p.

Oppong, Christine
Middle Class African Marriage: A Family Study of Ghanaian
Senior Civil Servants. London: George Allen and Unwin.
1981. 190p.

Oppong, Christine
"From Love to Institution: Indications of Change in Akan
Marriage." Journal of Family History. Volume 5 #2 1980.
pp. 197-209.

Oppong, Christine
"Norms Reality and Stress: Aspects of Conjugal Family
Solidarity Among Ghanaian Women Teachers." Paper

Presented at Wellesley Conference on Women and
Development. Wellesley, Massachusetts: Wellesley
College. June, 1976.

Oppong, Christine
"Women's Role and Conjugal Family Systems in Ghana."
(In) Lupri, E. (ed.). The Changing Position of Women in
Family and Society. Lieden, Netherlands: Brill. 1983.
pp. 331-343.

Pappoe, Matilda E.
"Women and Abortion." Paper Presented at the National
Council on Women and Development (NCWD) Seminar on Women
and Development. Accra, Ghana: NCWD. July, 1978.

Pine, Frances
"Family Structure and the Division of Labour: Female
Roles in Urban Ghana." (In) Alavi, H. and Shanin, T.
(eds.). Introduction to the Sociology of 'Developing
Societies'. London: MacMillan. 1982. pp. 387-405.

Sanjek, Roger
"Female and Male Domestic Cycles in Urban Africa: The
Adabraka Case." (In) Oppong, Christine (ed.). Female
and Male in West Africa. London: George Allen and Unwin.
1983. pp. 330-343.

Smock, Audrey C.
"The Impact of Modernization on Women's Position in the
Family in Ghana." (In) Schlegel, Alice E. (ed.). Sexual
Stratification: A Cross-Cultural View. New York:
Columbia University Press. 1977. pp. 192-214.

Van Der Geest, Sjaak
"Role Relationships Between Husband and Wife in Rural
Ghana." Journal of Marriage and the Family. Volume 38
#3 August, 1976. pp. 572-579.

Vellenga, Dorothy D.
"Matriliny, Patriliny and Class Formation Among Women
Cocoa Farmers in Two Rural Areas of Ghana." Paper
Presented at the Annual Meeting of the African Studies
Association. Paper #126. Bloomington, Indiana. October
21-24, 1981.

Vellenga, Dorothy D.
"Attempts to Change the Marriage Laws in Ghana and the
Ivory Coast." (In) Foster, P. and Zolberg, A. (eds.).
Ghana and the Ivory Coast: Perspectives on Modernisation.
Chicago: University of Chicago Press. 1977.

Vellenga, Dorothy D.
"Who is a Wife? Legal Expressions of Heterosexual
Conflicts in Ghana." (In) Oppong, Christine (ed.).
Female and Male in West Africa. London: George Allen and
Unwin. 1983. pp. 144-155.

Verdon, Michel
"Divorce in Abutia." Africa. Volume 52 #4 1982. pp.
48-65.

Verdon, Michel
"Sleeping Together: The Dynamics of Residence Among the

Abutia Ewe." Journal of Anthropological Research.
Volume 35 #4 Winter, 1979. pp. 401-425.
Whithead, A.
"Women and the Household: Themes Arising From a
North-East Ghana Example." Sussex, England: University
of Sussex. Institute of Development Studies. Draft
Paper Presented at the Conference on Continuing
Subordination of Women and the Development Process.
1978.

MASS MEDIA

Bame, K.N.
"Some Traditional and Modern Media for Generating Social
Change in Rural Africa: A Study of Some Traditional and
Modern Media for Communicating Family Planning in Ghana."
Paper Prepared for the Fourth World Congress of Rural
Sociology. 1976. 46p.

MIGRATION

Ankrah, Kwaku T.
"Assimilation or Selectivity: A Test of Competing Theses
on the Relationship Between Rural-Urban Migration and
Fertility in Ghana." Ph.D Dissertation: University of
Cincinnati. Cincinnati, Ohio. 1979. 178p.
Bartle, Philip F.
"Conjugal Relations, Migration, and Fertility in an Akan
Community, Obo, Ghana." (In) Oppong, C. and Adaba, G.
and Bekombo-Priso, M. and Mogey, J. (eds.). Marriage,
Fertility and Parenthood in West Africa. Canberra,
Australia: Australian National University. Department of
Demography. Volume Two. 1978. pp. 521-532.
Brown, Edward K.
"Patterns of Internal Migration in Ghana With Special
Emphasis on the Determinants of Female Migration." Ph.D
Dissertation: University of Pennsylvania. Philadelphia,
Pennsylvania. 1983. 295p.
Brydon, Lynne
"Women at Work: Some Changes in Family Structure in
Amedzofe-Avatime, Ghana." Africa. Volume 49 #2 1979.
pp. 97-110.
Dzegede, Sylvi A.
"Urbanization and Fertility Decline in West Africa:
Ghana, Sierra Leone and Liberia." Journal of Comparative
Family Studies. Volume 12 #2 Spring, 1981. pp.
233-244.
Oppong, Christine and Abu, Katharine
The Changing Maternal Role of Ghanaian Women: Impacts of
Education, Migration and Employment. Geneva:
International Labour Organization. Population and Labour

Policies Programme. Working Paper #143. February, 1984.
190p.
Sudarkasa, Niara
"Women and Migration in Contemporary West Africa." (In)
Wellesley Editorial Committee. Women and National
Development: The Complexities of Change. Chicago:
University of Chicago Press. 1977. pp. 178-189.
Sudarkasa, Niara
"Women and Migration in Contemporary West Africa."
Signs. Volume 3 #1 Autumn, 1977. pp. 178-189.

NATIONALISM

Harrell-Bond, Barbara E.
Women and the 1979 Ghana Revolution. Hanover, New
Hampshire: American University Field Staff. Report #4.
1980. 10p.
Okonkwo, Rina
"Adelaide Casely Hayford: Cultural Nationalist and
Feminist." Phylon. Volume 42 #1 1981. pp. 41-51.

ORGANIZATIONS

Breebaart, Gera
"Women and Extension in the Upper Region of Ghana."
Approach. Volume 8 1979. pp. 33-41.
Date-Bah, Eugenia and Brown, C. and Gyeke, L.
"Ghanaian Women and Cooperatives." Paper Presented at
the National Council on Women and Development (NCWD)
Seminar on Women and Development. Accra, Ghana: NCWD.
September, 1978. 26p.
Ghana National Council on Women and Development (NCWD)
The First Women's Co-Operative Gari Factory. Accra,
Ghana: NCWD. 1980.
Ghana Trades Union Congress (GTUC)
Position of Women in the Ghana Trades Union Congress.
Accra, Ghana: GTUC. Mimeograph. 1977.
Kleinkowski, H.
"Women's Organizations and Their Contribution to
Development in Ghana: With Special Reference to the
Christian Mothers Association." M.A. Thesis: Reading
University. Reading, England. 1976.
Klingshirn, A.
Investment of Women in Co-Operatives in Zaire and Ghana.
Rome: United Nations Food and Agriculture Organization.
UNFPA/FAO Study. 1978.
Okonkwo, Rina
"Adelaide Casely Hayford: Cultural Nationalist and
Feminist." Phylon. Volume 42 #1 1981. pp. 41-51.
Simms, Ruth and Dumor, Ernest K.
"Women in the Urban Economy of Ghana: Associational

Activity and the Enclave Economy." African Urban Notes.
Volume 2 #3 Fall/Winter, 1976. pp. 43-64.
Steel, William F.
Report on Research Program for Ghana National Council of
Women and Development (NCWD). Nashville, Tennessee:
Vanderbilt University. 1976. 39p.

POLITICS AND GOVERNMENT

Ghana National Council on Women and Development (NCWD)
Participation of Women in Policy-Making Positions at the
Local, National and International Levels. Accra, Ghana:
NCWD. 1980.
Hagaman, Barbara L.
"Beer and Matriliny: The Power of Women in Lobir, Ghana."
Ph.D Dissertation: Northeastern University. Boston,
Massachusetts. 1977. 365p.
Harrell-Bond, Barbara E.
Women and the 1979 Ghana Revolution. Hanover, New
Hampshire: American University Field Staff. Report #4.
1980. 10p.
Makinwa, P. Kofo
"The National Cost of Illegal Abortion: A Case for Family
Planning Programme." Aman. Volume 1 #1 1981. pp.
36-50.
Mikell, Gwendolyn
"African Women Within Nations of Crisis." Transafrica
Forum. Volume 2 #1 1983. pp. 31-34.
Robertson, Claire C.
"Post-Proclamation Slavery in Accra: a Female Affair?"
(In) Robertson, Claire C. and Klein, Martin A. (eds.).
Women and Slavery in Africa. Madison, Wisconsin:
University of Wisconsin Press. 1983. pp. 220-245.

RELIGION AND WITCHCRAFT

Assimeng, Max
"The Witchcraft Scene in Ghana: A Sociological Comment."
Ghana Social Science Journal. Volume 4 #1 May, 1977.
pp. 54-78.
Bleek, Wolf
"Witchcraft, Gossip and Death: A Social Drama." Man.
New Series Volume 11 #4 December, 1976. pp. 526-541.
Breidenbach, Paul
"The Woman on the Beach and the Man in the Bush:
Leadership and Adepthood in the Twelve Apostles Movement
in Ghana." (In) Jules-Rosette, Bennetta (ed.). The New
Religions of Africa. Norwood, New Jersey: Ablex
Publishing Corp. 1979. pp. 99-115.
Kilson, Marion
"Ritual Portrait of a Ga Medium." (In) Jules-Rosette,

Bennetta (ed.). The New Religions of Africa. Norwood,
New Jersey: Ablex Publishing Corp. 1979. pp. 67-79.
Kleinkowski, H.
"Women's Organizations and Their Contribution to
Development in Ghana: With Special Reference to the
Christian Mothers Association." M.A. Thesis: Reading
University. Reading, England. 1976.
McCaskie, T.C.
"Anti-Witchcraft Cults in Asante..." History in Africa.
Volume 8 1981. pp. 125-154.
Mendonsa, Eugene L.
"The Position of Women in the Sisala Divination Cult."
(In) Jules-Rosette, Bennetta (ed.). The New Religions of
Africa. Norwood, New Jersey: Ablex Publishing Corp.
1979. pp. 57-66.
Mendonsa, Eugene L.
"The Explanation of High Fertility Among the Sisala of
Northern Ghana." (In) Caldwell, John C. (ed.). The
Persistence of High Fertility: Population Prospects in
the Third World. Canberra, Australia: Australian
National University. Volume One. 1977. pp. 223-258.
Odouyoye, Mercy A.
"Namimg the Woman: The Words of the Akan and the Words of
the Bible." Bulletin de Theologie Africaine. Volume 3
#5 January-June, 1981. pp. 81-97.
Sarpong, Peter
Girl's Nubility Rites in Ashanti. Tema, Ghana: Ghana
Publishing Corp. 1977. 103p.

RESEARCH

Steel, William F.
Report on Research Program for Ghana National Council of
Women and Development (NCWD). Nashville, Tennessee:
Vanderbilt University. 1976. 39p.
U.S. Department of Commerce. Bureau of the Census
Illustrative Statistics on Women in Development in
Selected Developing Countries. Washington, D.C.: U.S.
Department of Commerce. 1982. 24p.

SEX ROLES

Abu, Katharine
"The Separateness of Spouses: Conjugal Resources in an
Ashanti Town." (In) Oppong, Christine (ed.). Female and
Male in West Africa. London: George Allen and Unwin.
1983. pp. 156-168.
Aidoo, Ama Ata
"Ghana: To Be a Woman." (In) Morgan, Robin (ed.).
Sisterhood is Global. Garden City, New York: Anchor
Books. 1984. pp. 255-265.

Arhin, Kwame
  "The Political and Military Roles of Akan Women." (In)
  Oppong, Christine (ed.). Female and Male in West Africa.
  London: George Allen and Unwin. 1983. pp. 91-98.
Asante-Darko, Nimrod and Van Der Geest, Sjaak
  "Male Chauvinism: Men and Women in Ghanaian Highlife
  Songs." (In) Oppong, Christine (ed.). Female and Male
  in West Africa. London: George Allen and Unwin. 1983.
  pp. 242-255.
Bleek, Wolf
  Sexual Relations and Birth Control in Ghana: A Case Study
  of a Rural Town. Amsterdam, Netherlands: University of
  Amsterdam. Antropologisch-Sociologisch Centrum. Uitgave
  #10. 1976. 352p.
Bleek, Wolf
  "Marriage in Kwahu, Ghana." (In) Roberts, Simon (ed.).
  Law and the Family in Africa. Hague, Netherlands:
  Mouton. 1977. pp. 183-204.
Brydon, Lynne
  "Women at Work: Some Changes in Family Structure in
  Amedzofe-Avatime, Ghana." Africa. Volume 49 #2 1979.
  pp. 97-110.
Brydon, Lynne
  "Status Ambiguity in Amedzofe-Avatime: Women and Men in a
  Changing Patrilineal Society." Ph.D Dissertation:
  University of Cambridge. Cambridge, England. 1976.
Brydon, Lynne
  "The Dimensions of Subordination: A Case Study From
  Avatime, Ghana." (In) Afshar, H. (ed.). Women, Work and
  Ideology in the Third World. London: Tavistock. 1985.
  pp. 109-127.
Bukh, Jette
  The Village Women of Ghana. Uppsala, Sweden:
  Scandinavian Institute of African Studies. Centre for
  Development Research. Publication #1. 1979. 118p.
Campbell-Platt, Kiran
  "The Impact of Mechanization on the Employment of Women
  in Traditional Sectors." Paper Presented at the National
  Council on Women and Development (NCWD) Seminar on Women
  and Development. Accra, Ghana: NCWD. September, 1978.
Chinnery-Hesse, Mary
  "Some Comments on the Ghanaian Situation." (In) Boserup,
  Ester (ed.). The Traditional Division of Work Between
  the Sexes, a Source of Inequality. Geneva: International
  Institute for Labour Studies. Research Series #21.
  1976.
Chinnery-Hesse, Mary
  "Women and Decision Making--Some Comments on the Themes
  With Special Reference to the Ghanaian Situation."
  Labour and Society. Volume 1 #2 1976. pp. 35-36.
Chukwukere, I.
  "Agnatic and Uterine Relations Among the Fante:
  Male/Female Dualism." Africa. Volume 52 #1 1982. pp.
  61-64.

Date-Bah, Eugenia
"Technologies for Rural Women in Ghana: Role of
Socio-Cultural Factors." (In) Ahmed, Iftikhar (ed.).
Technology and Rural Women: Conceptual and Empirical
Issues. Boston: George Allen and Unwin. 1985. pp.
211-251.
Dinan, Carmel
"Sugar Daddies and Gold Diggers: The White-Collar Single
Women in Accra." (In) Oppong, Christine (ed.). Female
and Male in West Africa. London: George Allen and Unwin.
1983. pp. 344-366.
Dugbaza, Tetteh
"Women and Integration in Rural Development." Ghana
Journal of Sociology. Volume 14 #1 1981. pp. 73-94.
Dzidzienyo, Stella
"Housemaids: A Case Study of Domestic Helpers in Ghanaian
Homes." Paper Presented at the National Council on Women
and Development (NCWD) Seminar on Women and Development.
Accra, Ghana: NCWD. September, 1978.
Fogelberg, Teresa
Nanumba Women: Working Bees or Idle Bums? Sexual
Division of Labour, Ideology of Work, and Power Relations
Between Women and Men in Gole, A Village in Nanumba
District, Northern Region, Ghana. Leiden, Netherlands:
Institute of Cultural and Social Studies. 1981. 83p.
Hagaman, Barbara L.
"Beer and Matriliny: The Power of Women in Lobir, Ghana."
Ph.D Dissertation: Northeastern University. Boston,
Massachusetts. 1977. 365p.
Hershman, Paul
"A Comparison of Punjabi and Tallensi Marriage Systems."
Eastern Anthropologist. Volume 33 #4 October-December,
1980. pp. 299-334.
Hevi-Yiboe, L.A.
Smoke in Rural Ghanaian Kitchens. Accra, Ghana: Arakan
Press. 1979.
Lowy, Michael J.
"Establishing Paternity and Demanding Child Support in a
Ghanaian Town." (In) Roberts, Simon (ed.). Law and
Family in Africa. Hague, Netherlands: Mouton. 1977.
pp. 15-38.
McCaskie, T.C.
"State and Society, Marriage and Adultery: Some
Considerations From the Social History of Pre-Colonial
Asante." Journal of African History. Volume 22 #4 1981.
pp. 477-494.
Mendonsa, Eugene L.
"Status of Women in Sisala Society." Sex Roles. Volume
7 #6 June, 1981. pp. 607-625.
Mendonsa, Eugene L.
"The Position of Women in the Sisala Divination Cult."
(In) Jules-Rosette, Bennetta (ed.). The New Religions of
Africa. Norwood, New Jersey: Ablex Publishing Corp.
1979. pp. 57-66.

Nicholas D.D.
"Attitudes and Practices of Traditional Birth Attendents
in Ghana: Implications for Training in Africa." Bulletin
of the World Health Organization. Volume 54 #3 1976.
Nukunya, Godwin K.
"Women and Marriage." Paper Presented at the National
Council on Women and Development (NCWD) Seminar on Women
and Development. Accra, Ghana: NCWD. September, 1978.
Oduyoye, Mercy Amba
"The Asante Woman: Socialization Through Proverbs."
African Notes. Volume 8 #1 1979. pp. 5-11.
Oduyoye, Mercy Amba
"Female Authority in Asante Law and Constitution."
African Notes. Volume 8 #2 1981. pp. 9-14.
Oppong, Christine
"Women's Role and Conjugal Family Systems in Ghana."
(In) Lupri, E. (ed.). The Changing Position of Women in
Family and Society. Lieden, Netherlands: Brill. 1983.
pp. 331-343.
Peterson, K.J.
"Brong Midwives and Women in Childbirth: Management of
Uncertainty in a Division of Labor." Human Organization.
Volume 41 #4 Winter, 1982. pp. 291-298.
Pine, F.
"Family Structure and the Division of Labour: Female
Roles in Urban Ghana." (In) Alavi, H. and Shanin, T.
(eds.). Introduction to the Sociology of Developing
Societies. New York: MacMillan. 1982. pp. 387-405.
Pine, Frances
"Family Structure and the Division of Labour: Female
Roles in Urban Ghana." (In) Alavi, H. and Shanin, T.
(eds.). Introduction to the Sociology of 'Developing
Societies'. London: MacMillan. 1982. pp. 387-405.
Sanjek, Roger and Sanjek, Lani
"Notes on Women and Work in Adabraka." African Urban
Notes. Volume 2 #2 Spring, 1976. pp. 1-26.
Sanjek, Roger
"Female and Male Domestic Cycles in Urban Africa: The
Adabraka Case." (In) Oppong, Christine (ed.). Female
and Male in West Africa. London: George Allen and Unwin.
1983. pp. 330-343.
Smock, Audrey C.
"The Impact of Modernization on Women's Position in the
Family in Ghana." (In) Schlegel, Alice E. (ed.). Sexual
Stratification: A Cross-Cultural View. New York:
Columbia University Press. 1977. pp. 192-214.
Van Der Geest, Sjaak
"Role Relationships Between Husband and Wife in Rural
Ghana." Journal of Marriage and the Family. Volume 38
#3 August, 1976. pp. 572-579.
Vellenga, Dorothy D.
"Who is a Wife? Legal Expressions of Heterosexual
Conflicts in Ghana." (In) Oppong, Christine (ed.).

Female and Male in West Africa. London: George Allen and Unwin. 1983. pp. 144-155.

Vellenga, Dorothy D.
"Women, Households, and Food Commodity Chains in Southern Ghana: Contradictions Between Search for Profits and the Search for Survival." Research Review. Volume 8 #3 1985. pp. 293-318.

Vellenga, Dorothy D.
"Food as a Cash Crop for Women Farmers in Ghana: The Persistent Search for Profit." Paper Presented at the Annual Meeting of the Association for Women in Development. Washington, D.C. October, 1983.

Vercruijsse, Emile V.W.
"Fishmongers, Big Dealers and Fishermen: Co-Operation and Conflict Between the Sexes in Ghanaian Canoe Fishing." (In) Oppong, Christine (ed.). Female and Male in West Africa. London: George Allen and Unwin. 1983. pp. 179-191.

Verdon, Michel
"Sleeping Together: The Dynamics of Residence Among the Abutia Ewe." Journal of Anthropological Research. Volume 35 #4 Winter, 1979. pp. 401-425.

Whithead, A.
Women and the Household: Themes Arising From a North-East Ghana Example. Sussex, England: University of Sussex. Institute of Development Studies. Draft Paper Presented at the Conference on Continuing Subordination of Women and the Development Process. 1978.

SLAVERY

Robertson, Claire C.
"Post-Proclamation Slavery in Accra: a Female Affair?" (In) Robertson, Claire C. and Klein, Martin A. (eds.). Women and Slavery in Africa. Madison, Wisconsin: University of Wisconsin Press. 1983. pp. 220-245.

STATUS OF WOMEN

Bartle, Philip F.
"Modernization and the Decline in Women's Status: An Example From Matrilineal Akan Community." Paper Presented at the National Council on Women and Development (NCWD) Seminar on Women and Development. Accra, Ghana: NCWD. Accra, Ghana. September, 1978.

Luckham, Yaa
"Law and the Status of Women in Ghana." (In) Columbia Human Rights Law Review (eds.). Law and the Status of Women: An International Symposium. New York: United Nations. Centre for Social Development and Humanitarian Affairs. 1977. pp. 69-94.

Mendonsa, Eugene L.
"Status of Women in Sisala Society." Sex Roles. Volume 7 #6 June, 1981. pp. 607-625.

Mikell, Gwendolyn
"Filiation, Economic Crisis and the Status of Women in Ghana." Canadian Journal of African Studies. Volume 18 #1 1984. pp. 195-218.

Oppong, Christine
"Issues Concerning the Changing Status of African Women: Some Lessons From the Ghanaian Experience." (In) International Planned Parenthood Federation (IPPF). Proceedings of the IPPF Africa Regional Conference. London: IPPF. Aug. 3-Sept. 3, 1976. pp. 263-282.

Pellow, Deborah
"Work and Autonomy; Women in Accra." American Ethnologist. Volume 5 #4 November, 1978. pp. 770-785.

Pellow, Deborah
Women in Accra: Options for Autonomy. Algonac, Michigan: Reference Publications. 1977. 272p.

Smock, Audrey C.
"Ghana: From Autonomy to Subordination." (In) Giele, Janet Z. and Smock, Audrey C. (eds.). Women: Roles and Status in Eight Countries. New York: Wiley-Interscience. 1977. pp. 173-216.

URBANIZATION

Afful, K.N. and Steel, William F.
"Women in the Urban Economy of Ghana: Comment." Paper. 1978.

Ankrah, Kwaku T.
"Assimilation or Selectivity: A Test of Competing Theses on the Relationship Between Rural-Urban Migration and Fertility in Ghana." Ph.D Dissertation: University of Cincinnati. Cincinnati, Ohio. 1979. 178p.

Aryee, A.F.
"Urbanization and the Incidence of Plural Marriage: Some Theoretical Perspectives." (In) Oppong, C. and Adaba, G. and Bekombo-Priso, M. and Mogey, J. (eds.). Marriage, Fertility and Parenthood in West Africa. Canberra, Australia: Australian National University. Department of Demography. Volume One. 1978. pp. 367-379.

Caldwell, John C.
Population Growth and Family Change in Africa: The New Urban Elite in Ghana. London: C. Hurst. 1977. 22p.

Dzegede, Sylvi A.
"Urbanization and Fertility Decline in West Africa: Ghana, Sierra Leone and Liberia." Journal of Comparative Family Studies. Volume 12 #2 Spring, 1981. pp. 233-244.

Pine, F.
"Family Structure and the Division of Labour: Female

Roles in Urban Ghana." (In) Alavi, H. and Shanin, T.
(eds.). Introduction to the Sociology of Developing
Societies. New York: MacMillan. 1982. pp. 387-405.
Sanjek, Roger
"Female and Male Domestic Cycles in Urban Africa: The
Adabraka Case." (In) Oppong, Christine (ed.). Female
and Male in West Africa. London: George Allen and Unwin.
1983. pp. 330-343.
Simms, Ruth and Dumor, Ernest K.
"Women in the Urban Economy of Ghana: Associational
Activity and the Enclave Economy." African Urban Notes.
Volume 2 #3 Fall/Winter, 1976. pp. 43-64.

WOMEN AND THEIR CHILDREN

Bleek, Wolf
"The Value of Children to Parents in Kwahu, Ghana." (In)
Oppong, C. and Adaba, G. and Bekombo-Priso, M. and Mogey,
J. (eds.). Marriage, Fertility and Parenthood in West
Africa. Canberra, Australia: Australian National
University. Department of Demography. Volume One.
1978. pp. 307-323.
Church, K.V.
"A Study of Socio-Economic Status and Child Care
Arrangements of Women in Madina." Paper Presented at the
National Council on Women and Development (NCWD) Seminar
on Women and Development. Accra, Ghana: NCWD.
September, 1978.
Mikell, Gwendolyn
"Filiation, Economic Crisis and the Status of Women in
Ghana." Canadian Journal of African Studies. Volume 18
#1 1984. pp. 195-218.
Oppong, Christine
"Motherhood in a Changing World: The Case of Ghana."
UNICEF News. Volume 89 #3 1976. pp. 32+.

Guinea

Bledsoe, Caroline H.
   "The Political Use of Sande Ideology and Symbolism."
   American Ethnologist. Volume 11 #3 August, 1984. pp.
   455-472.
Mouser, Bruce L.
   "Women Slavers in Guinea-Conakry." (In) Robertson,
   Claire C. and Klein, Martin A. (eds.). Women and Slavery
   in Africa. Madison, Wisconsin: University of Wisconsin
   Press. 1983. pp. 320-339.
Renzetti, Claire M. and Curran, Daniel J.
   Socialism and Feminism in Guinea. Newark, Delaware:
   University of Delaware-Newark. 1980.
Ssekamatte-Ssebuliba, John B. and Duza, M. Badrud
   "Dynamics of Nuptiality in East Africa: A Study of Kenya
   and Tanzania." (In) Cairo Demographic Centre (CDC).
   Determinants of Fertility in Some African and Asian
   Countries. Cairo: CDC. CDC Research Monograph Series
   #10. 1982. pp. 351-373.

Guinea-Bissau

Anonymous
"Guinea-Bissau: A Revolution Within a Revolution." IDOC
Bulletin. #50/51 December, 1976.
Brooks, George E.
"A Nhara of the Guinea-Bissau Region: Mae Aurelia
Correia." (In) Robertson, Claire C. and Klein, Martin A.
(eds.). Women and Slavery in Africa. Madison,
Wisconsin: University of Wisconsin Press. 1983. pp.
295-319.
Duquette, D.G.
"Women Power and Initiation in the Bissagos Islands."
African Arts. Volume 12 #5 May, 1979. pp. 31-35.
Handem, Diana
"A History of Women's Contribution to the Struggle for
National Liberation and Reconstruction in Guinea-Bissau."
Paper Presented at the Meeting of Experts on the History
of Women's Contribution to National Liberation Struggles
and Their Roles and Needs During Reconstruction in Newly
Independent Countries of Africa. Paris: United Nations
Educational, Scientific andCultural Organization.
Bissau, Guinea-Bissau. 1983. 19p.
Mundondo, Mabel
"Women Militants in the PAIGC." Africa Women. #6 1976.
United Nations Educational, Scientific, and Cultural Organ.
Final Report: Meeting of Experts on the History of
Women's Contribution to National Liberation Struggles and
Their Roles and Needs During Reconstruction in Newly
Independent Countries of Africa. Paris: UNESCO. Bissau,
Guinea-Bissau. 1983. 14p.
Urdang, Stephanie
"Against Two Foes: The Portuguese and the Men." New
Internationalist. Volume 56 October, 1977. pp. 14-15.
Urdang, Stephanie
Fighting Two Colonialisms: Women in Guinea-Bissau. New
York: Monthly Review. 1979. 320p.

Urdang, Stephanie
    "Precondition for Victory: Women's Liberation in
    Mozambique and Guinea-Bissau." Issue. Volume 8 #1
    Spring, 1978. pp 25-31.
Urdang, Stephanie
    The Liberation of Women as a Necessity for the Successful
    Revolution in Guinea-Bissau, Mozambique and Angola.
    Waltham, Massachusetts: Brandeis University. African
    Studies Association. 1977.
Urdang, Stephanie
    "The Role of Women in the Revolution in Guinea-Bissau."
    (In) Steady, Filomina C. (ed.) The Black Woman
    Cross-Culturally. Cambridge, Massachusetts: Schenkman
    Publishing. 1981. pp. 119-140.
Urdang, Stephanie
    "Women in Liberation Struggles--Guinea-Bissau." ISIS
    International Bulletin. April, 1977. pp. 6-7.
Urdang, Stephanie
    "Women in the Continuing Revolution in Guinea-Bissau."
    Paper Presented at the Annual Meeting of the African
    Studies Association. Paper #119. Boston, Massachusetts.
    1976. 21p.
Urdang, Stephanie
    "Women in the Guinea-Bissau Revolution." Quest. Volume
    4 #2 Winter, 1978. pp. 33-42.

Ivory Coast

AGRICULTURE

Guyer, Jane I.
   "Women in the Rural Economy: Contemporary Variations."
   (In) Hay, Margaret J. and Stichter, Sharon (eds.).
   African Women South of the Sahara. New York: Longman.
   1984. pp. 19-32.
King-Akerele, Olubanke
   Traditional Palm Oil Processing: Women's Role and the
   Applications of Appropriate Technology: Ivory Coast,
   Sierra Leone, Cameroons. Addis Ababa, Ethiopia: United
   Nations Economic Commission for Africa. African Training
   and Research Center for Women. 1983. 52p.
Traore, Aminata
   "Agro-Business and Female Employment in the Ivory Coast."
   Paper Presented at the AAWORD Conference on Women and
   Rural Development. Algiers, Algeria. September, 1982.
Traore, Aminata
   "Women's Access to Resources in the Ivory Coast: Women
   and Land in Adioukrou District." (In) International
   Labour Organization (ILO). Rural Development and Women
   in Africa. Geneva: ILO. 1984. pp. 99-106.

CULTURAL ROLES

Clignet, Remi
   "Social Change and Sexual Differentiation in the Cameroon
   and the Ivory Coast." Signs. Volume 3 #1 Autumn, 1977.
   pp. 244-266.
Clignet, Remi
   "Social Change and Sexual Differentiation in the Cameroon
   and the Ivory Coast." (In) Wellesley Editorial
   Committee. Women in National Development. Chicago:
   University of Chicago Press. 1977. pp. 244-260.
Ellovich, Risa S.
   "Adaptations to the Urban Setting: Dioula Women in

Gagnoa, Ivory Coast." Ph.D Dissertation: Indiana
University. Bloomington, Indiana. 1979. 189p.
Ellovich, Risa S.
"Dioula Women in Town: A View of Intra-Ethnic Variation."
(In) Bourguignon, Erika (ed.). A World of Women.
Anthropological Studies of Women in the Societies of the
World. New York: Praeger Publishers. Praeger Special
Studies. 1980. pp. 87-103.
Ellovich, Risa S.
"Ivorian Women and the Law: A Dioula-Bete Comparison."
Paper Presented at the Annual Meeting of the African
Studies Association. Paper #27. Philadelphia,
Pennsylvania. 1980.
Ellovich, Risa S.
"The Law and Ivorian Women." Anthropos. Volume 80 #1-3
1985. pp. 185-197.
Etienne, Mona
"Gender Relations and Conjugality Among the Baule." (In)
Oppong, Christine (ed.). Female and Male in West Africa.
London: George Allen and Unwin. 1983. pp. 303-319.
Etienne, Mona
"Gender Relations and Conjugality Among the Baule."
Culture. Volume 1 #1 1981. pp. 21-30.
Etienne, Mona
"Social Maternity, Adoptive Relations and the Power of
Women Among the Baule." L'Homme. Volume 19 #3/4
July-December, 1979. pp. 63-108.
Etienne, Mona
"The Case for Social Maternity: Adoption of Children by
Urban Baule Women." Dialectical Anthropology. Volume 4
#3 October, 1979. pp. 237-242.
Etienne, Mona
"Women and Men, Cloth and Colonization: The
Transformation of Product-Distribution Relations Among
the Baule." Cahiers d'Etudes Africaines. Volume 17 #1
1977. pp. 41-64.
Etienne, Mona
"Women and Men, Cloth and Colonization: The
Transformation of Production-Distribution Relations Among
the Baule." (In) Etienne, Mona and Leacock, E. (eds.).
Women and Colonization: Anthropological Perspectives.
New York: Praeger Publishers. 1980. pp. 214-238.
Etienne, Mona
"Women and Slaves: Stratification in an African Society:
The Baule, Ivory Coast." Paper Presented at the 75th
Annual Meeting of the American Anthropological
Association. Washington, D.C. 1976.
Gerstner, G.J. and Leodolter, S. and Matznetter, T.
"Breast Feeding in Industrialized and Agricultural
Countries." Clinical and Experimental Obstetrics and
Gynecology. Volume 9 #3 1982. pp. 193-198.
Gottlieb, Alma
"Beng Baby Decoration: The Efficacy of Symbols and the

Power of Women." Paper Presented at the Annual Meeting
of the African Studies Association. Paper #43.
Bloomington, Indiana. October 21-24, 1981.
Gottlieb, Alma
    "Pregnant Sex, Menstrual Sex and the Cuisine of
    Menstruation: The Beng Case." Paper Presented at the
    22nd Annual Meeting of the Northeastern Anthropological
    Association. Princeton, New Jersey. March, 1982.
Gottlieb, Alma
    "Sex, Fertility and Menstruation Among the Beng of the
    Ivory Coast: A Symbolic Analysis." Africa. Volume 52 #4
    1982. pp. 34-47.
Gottlieb, Alma
    "Village Kapok, Forest Kapok: Notions of Separation,
    Identity and Gender Among the Beng of Ivory Coast." Ph.D
    Dissertation: University of Virginia, Charlottesville.
    Charlottesville, Virginia. 1983. 295p.
Gottlieb, Alma
    "Witches, Kings and the Sacrifice of Identity: The Power
    of Paradox and the Paradox of Power Among the Beng of
    Ivory Coast." Paper Presented at the Annual Meeting of
    the African Studies Association. Paper #33. Washington,
    D.C. November 4-7, 1982.
King-Akerele, Olubanke
    Traditional Palm Oil Processing: Women's Role and the
    Applications of Appropriate Technology: Ivory Coast,
    Sierra Leone, Cameroons. Addis Ababa, Ethiopia: United
    Nations Economic Commission for Africa. African Training
    and Research Center for Women. 1983. 52p.
Lesthaeghe, Ron J. and Eelens, Frank
    Social Organization and Reproductive Regimes: Lessons
    From Sub-Saharan Africa and Historical Western Europe.
    Brussels, Belgium: Vrije Universiteit Brussel.
    Interuniversity Programme in Demography. IDP Working
    Paper #1985-1. 1985. 64p.
Lewis, Barbara C.
    "Economic Activity and Marriage Among Ivorian Urban
    Women." (In) Schlegel, Alice E. (ed.). Sexual
    Stratification: A Cross-Cultural View. New York:
    Columbia University Press. 1977. pp. 161-191.
Lingo, Celestin
    "Profession: Menagere." Agripromo. Volume 27 October,
    1979.
Montgomery, Barbara
    The Economic Role of the Ivorian Women. Ann Arbor,
    Michigan: University of Michigan. Center for Research on
    Economic Development. Discussion Paper #61. 1977. 50p.
Peterson, K.J.
    "Brong Midwives and Women in Childbirth: Management of
    Uncertainty in a Division of Labor." Human Organization.
    Volume 41 #4 Winter, 1982. pp. 291-298.
Vellenga, Dorothy D.
    "Attempts to Change the Marriage Laws in Ghana and the

Ivory Coast." (In) Foster, P. and Zolberg, A. (eds.).
Ghana and the Ivory Coast: Perspectives on Modernisation.
Chicago: University of Chicago Press. 1977.

Vidal, C.
"Sex War in Abidjan--Male, Female Money." Cahiers
d'Etudes Africaines. Volume 17 #1 1977. pp. 121-154.

Walker, Sheila S.
"Witchcraft and Healing in an African Church." Journal
of Religions in Africa. Volume 10 #2 1979. pp. 127-138.

Walker, Sheila S.
"Women in the Harrist Movement." (In) Jules-Rosette,
Bennatta (ed.). The New Religions of Africa. Norwood,
New Jersey: Ablex Publishing Co. 1979. pp. 87-97.

Walker, Sheila S.
"Young Men, Old Men, and Devils in Aeroplanes: The
Harrist Church, The Witchcraft Complex and Social Change
in the Ivory Coast." Journal of Religion in Africa.
Volume 11 #2 1980. pp. 106-123.

Yacoob, May
Ahmadiyya and Urbanization: Migrant Women in Abidjan.
Boston: Boston University. African Studies Center.
Working Papers in African Studies #75. 1983.

DEVELOPMENT AND TECHNOLOGY

Guyer, Jane I.
"Women in the Rural Economy: Contemporary Variations."
(In) Hay, Margaret J. and Stichter, Sharon (eds.).
African Women South of the Sahara. New York: Longman.
1984. pp. 19-32.

King-Akerele, Olubanke
Traditional Palm Oil Processing: Women's Role and the
Applications of Appropriate Technology: Ivory Coast,
Sierra Leone, Cameroons. Addis Ababa, Ethiopia: United
Nations Economic Commission for Africa. African Training
and Research Center for Women. 1983. 52p.

Lewis, Barbara C.
"Female Strategies and Public Goods: Market Women of the
Ivory Coast." Paper Presented at the Conference on Women
and Development. Wellesley, Massachusetts: Wellesley
College. June, 1976.

Lewis, Barbara C.
"The Limitations of Group Action Among Entrepreneurs: The
Market Women of Abidjan, Ivory Coast." (In) Hafkin, N.J.
and Bay, Edna (eds.). Women in Africa: Studies in Social
and Economic Change. Stanford, California: Stanford
University Press. 1976. pp. 135-156.

Montgomery, Barbara
The Economic Role of the Ivorian Women. Ann Arbor,
Michigan: University of Michigan. Center for Research on
Economic Development. Discussion Paper #61. 1977. 50p.

Palmer, Ingrid
    "New Official Ideas on Women and Development." Institute
    for Development Studies. Volume 10 #3 1979. pp. 42-53.
Vidal, C.
    "Sex War in Abidjan--Male, Female Money." Cahiers
    d'Etudes Africaines. Volume 17 #1 1977. pp. 121-154.

ECONOMICS

Etienne, Mona
    "Women and Men, Cloth and Colonization: The
    Transformation of Product-Distribution Relations Among
    the Baule." Cahiers d'Etudes Africaines. Volume 17 #1
    1977. pp. 41-64.
Etienne, Mona
    "Women and Men, Cloth and Colonization: The
    Transformation of Production-Distribution Relations Among
    the Baule." (In) Etienne, Mona and Leacock, E. (eds.).
    Women and Colonization: Anthropological Perspectives.
    New York: Praeger Publishers. 1980. pp. 214-238.
Guyer, Jane I.
    "Women in the Rural Economy: Contemporary Variations."
    (In) Hay, Margaret J. and Stichter, Sharon (eds.).
    African Women South of the Sahara. New York: Longman.
    1984. pp. 19-32.
Lewis, Barbara C.
    "Economic Activity and Marriage Among Ivorian Urban
    Women." (In) Schlegel, Alice E. (ed.). Sexual
    Stratification: A Cross-Cultural View. New York:
    Columbia University Press. 1977. pp. 161-191.
Lewis, Barbara C.
    "Female Strategies and Public Goods: Market Women of the
    Ivory Coast." Paper Presented at the Conference on Women
    and Development. Wellesley, Massachusetts: Wellesley
    College. June, 1976.
Lewis, Barbara C.
    "The Limitations of Group Action Among Entrepreneurs: The
    Market Women of Abidjan, Ivory Coast." (In) Hafkin, N.J.
    and Bay, Edna (eds.). Women in Africa: Studies in Social
    and Economic Change. Stanford, California: Stanford
    University Press. 1976. pp. 135-156.
Montgomery, Barbara
    The Economic Role of the Ivorian Women. Ann Arbor,
    Michigan: University of Michigan. Center for Research on
    Economic Development. Discussion Paper #61. 1977. 50p.
Palmer, Ingrid
    "New Official Ideas on Women and Development." Institute
    for Development Studies. Volume 10 #3 1979. pp. 42-53.
Traore, Aminata
    "Agro-Business and Female Employment in the Ivory Coast."
    Paper Presented at the AAWORD Conference on Women and
    Rural Development. Algiers, Algeria. September, 1982.

Traore, Aminata
 "Women's Access to Resources in the Ivory Coast: Women
 and Land in Adioukrou District." (In) International
 Labour Organization (ILO). Rural Development and Women
 in Africa. Geneva: ILO. 1984. pp. 99-106.
Vidal, C.
 "Sex War in Abidjan--Male, Female Money." Cahiers
 d'Etudes Africaines. Volume 17 #1 1977. pp. 121-154.
Yacoob, May
 Ahmadiyya and Urbanization: Migrant Women in Abidjan.
 Boston: Boston University. African Studies Center.
 Working Papers in African Studies #75. 1983.

EMPLOYMENT AND LABOR

Etienne, Mona
 "Women and Men, Cloth and Colonization: The
 Transformation of Product-Distribution Relations Among
 the Baule." Cahiers d'Etudes Africaines. Volume 17 #1
 1977. pp. 41-64.
Etienne, Mona
 "Women and Men, Cloth and Colonization: The
 Transformation of Production-Distribution Relations Among
 the Baule." (In) Etienne, Mona and Leacock, E. (eds.).
 Women and Colonization: Anthropological Perspectives.
 New York: Praeger Publishers. 1980. pp. 214-238.
Guyer, Jane I.
 "Women in the Rural Economy: Contemporary Variations."
 (In) Hay, Margaret J. and Stichter, Sharon (eds.).
 African Women South of the Sahara. New York: Longman.
 1984. pp. 19-32.
King-Akerele, Olubanke
 Traditional Palm Oil Processing: Women's Role and the
 Applications of Appropriate Technology: Ivory Coast,
 Sierra Leone, Cameroons. Addis Ababa, Ethiopia: United
 Nations Economic Commission for Africa. African Training
 and Research Center for Women. 1983. 52p.
Lewis, Barbara C.
 "Economic Activity and Marriage Among Ivorian Urban
 Women." (In) Schlegel, Alice E. (ed.). Sexual
 Stratification: A Cross-Cultural View. New York:
 Columbia University Press. 1977. pp. 161-191.
Montgomery, Barbara
 The Economic Role of the Ivorian Women. Ann Arbor,
 Michigan: University of Michigan. Center for Research on
 Economic Development. Discussion Paper #61. 1977. 50p.
Palmer, Ingrid
 "New Official Ideas on Women and Development." Institute
 for Development Studies. Volume 10 #3 1979. pp. 42-53.
Traore, Aminata
 "Agro-Business and Female Employment in the Ivory Coast."
 Paper Presented at the AAWORD Conference on Women and
 Rural Development. Algiers, Algeria. September, 1982.

Traore, Aminata
    "Women's Access to Resources in the Ivory Coast: Women
    and Land in Adioukrou District." (In) International
    Labour Organization (ILO). Rural Development and Women
    in Africa. Geneva: ILO. 1984. pp. 99-106.
Vidal, C.
    "Sex War in Abidjan--Male, Female Money." Cahiers
    d'Etudes Africaines. Volume 17 #1 1977. pp. 121-154.
Yacoob, May
    Ahmadiyya and Urbanization: Migrant Women in Abidjan.
    Boston: Boston University. African Studies Center.
    Working Papers in African Studies #75. 1983.

FAMILY LIFE

Etienne, Mona
    "Social Maternity, Adoptive Relations and the Power of
    Women Among the Baule." L'Homme. Volume 19 #3/4
    July-December, 1979. pp. 63-108.
Etienne, Mona
    "The Case for Social Maternity: Adoption of Children by
    Urban Baule Women." Dialectical Anthropology. Volume 4
    #3 October, 1979. pp. 237-242.
Lewis, Barbara C.
    "Female Strategies and Public Goods: Market Women of the
    Ivory Coast." Paper Presented at the Conference on Women
    and Development. Wellesley, Massachusetts: Wellesley
    College. June, 1976.
Lingo, Celestin
    "Profession: Menagere." Agripromo. Volume 27 October,
    1979.
Yacoob, May
    Ahmadiyya and Urbanization: Migrant Women in Abidjan.
    Boston: Boston University. African Studies Center.
    Working Papers in African Studies #75. 1983.

FAMILY PLANNING AND CONTRACEPTION

Gottlieb, Alma
    "Sex, Fertility and Menstruation Among the Beng of the
    Ivory Coast: A Symbolic Analysis." Africa. Volume 52 #4
    1982. pp. 34-47.
Lesthaeghe, Ron J. and Eelens, Frank
    Social Organization and Reproductive Regimes: Lessons
    From Sub-Saharan Africa and Historical Western Europe.
    Brussels, Belgium: Vrije Universiteit Brussel.
    Interuniversity Programme in Demography. IDP Working
    Paper #1985-1. 1985. 64p.

FERTILITY AND INFERTILITY

Eelens, Frank and Donne, L.
  The Proximate Determinants of Fertility in Sub-Saharan
  Africa: A Factbook Based on the Results of the World
  Fertility Survey. Brussels, Belgium: Vrije Universiteit
  Brussel. Interuniversity Programme in Demography. IDP
  Working Paper #1985-3. 1985. 122p.
Gottlieb, Alma
  "Sex, Fertility and Menstruation Among the Beng of the
  Ivory Coast: A Symbolic Analysis." Africa. Volume 52 #4
  1982. pp. 34-47.
Lesthaeghe, Ron J. and Eelens, Frank
  Social Organization and Reproductive Regimes: Lessons
  From Sub-Saharan Africa and Historical Western Europe.
  Brussels, Belgium: Vrije Universiteit Brussel.
  Interuniversity Programme in Demography. IDP Working
  Paper #1985-1. 1985. 64p.

HEALTH, NUTRITION AND MEDICINE

Gerstner, G.J. and Leodolter, S. and Matznetter, T.
  "Breast Feeding in Industrialized and Agricultural
  Countries." Clinical and Experimental Obstetrics and
  Gynecology. Volume 9 #3 1982. pp. 193-198.
Gottlieb, Alma
  "Pregnant Sex, Menstrual Sex and the Cuisine of
  Menstruation: The Beng Case." Paper Presented at the
  22nd Annual Meeting of the Northeastern Anthropological
  Association. Princeton, New Jersey. March, 1982.
Gottlieb, Alma
  "Sex, Fertility and Menstruation Among the Beng of the
  Ivory Coast: A Symbolic Analysis." Africa. Volume 52 #4
  1982. pp. 34-47.
Lauber, E.
  "Prolonged Lactation Performance in a Rural Community of
  the Ivory Coast." Journal of Tropical Pediatrics.
  Volume 27 #2 April, 1981. pp. 74-77.
Lauber, Edgar and Reinhardt, Michael C.
  "Studies on the Quality of Breast Milk During 23 Months
  of Lactation in a Rural Community of the Ivory Coast."
  American Journal of Clinical Nutrition. Volume 32 #5
  May, 1979. pp. 1159-1179.
Peterson, K.J.
  "Brong Midwives and Women in Childbirth: Management of
  Uncertainty in a Division of Labor." Human Organization.
  Volume 41 #4 Winter, 1982. pp. 291-298.
Reinhardt, Michael C.
  "Maternal Anaemia in Abidjan: Its Influence on Placenta
  and Newborns." Helvetica Paediatricia Acta. Volume 33
  Supp. #41 1978. pp. 43-63.

HISTORY

Etienne, Mona
"Women and Slaves: Stratification in an African Society:
The Baule, Ivory Coast." Paper Presented at the 75th
Annual Meeting of the American Anthropological
Association. Washington, D.C. 1976.

LAW AND LEGAL ISSUES

Ellovich, Risa S.
"Ivorian Women and the Law: A Dioula-Bete Comparison."
Paper Presented at the Annual Meeting of the African
Studies Association. Paper #27. Philadelphia,
Pennsylvania. 1980.
Ellovich, Risa S.
"The Law and Ivorian Women." Anthropos. Volume 80 #1-3
1985. pp. 185-197.
Vellenga, Dorothy D.
"Attempts to Change the Marriage Laws in Ghana and the
Ivory Coast." (In) Foster, P. and Zolberg, A. (eds.).
Ghana and the Ivory Coast: Perspectives on Modernisation.
Chicago: University of Chicago Press. 1977.

MARITAL RELATIONS AND NUPTIALITY

Etienne, Mona
"Gender Relations and Conjugality Among the Baule." (In)
Oppong, Christine (ed.). Female and Male in West Africa.
London: George Allen and Unwin. 1983. pp. 303-319.
Etienne, Mona
"Gender Relations and Conjugality Among the Baule."
Culture. Volume 1 #1 1981. pp. 21-30.
Etienne, Mona
"Social Maternity, Adoptive Relations and the Power of
Women Among the Baule." L'Homme. Volume 19 #3/4
July-December, 1979. pp. 63-108.
Etienne, Mona
"The Case for Social Maternity: Adoption of Children by
Urban Baule Women." Dialectical Anthropology. Volume 4
#3 October, 1979. pp. 237-242.
Gottlieb, Alma
"Pregnant Sex, Menstrual Sex and the Cuisine of
Menstruation: The Beng Case." Paper Presented at the
22nd Annual Meeting of the Northeastern Anthropological
Association. Princeton, New Jersey. March, 1982.
Lewis, Barbara C.
"Economic Activity and Marriage Among Ivorian Urban
Women." (In) Schlegel, Alice E. (ed.). Sexual
Stratification: A Cross-Cultural View. New York:
Columbia University Press. 1977. pp. 161-191.

Vellenga, Dorothy D.
"Attempts to Change the Marriage Laws in Ghana and the
Ivory Coast." (In) Foster, P. and Zolberg, A. (eds.).
Ghana and the Ivory Coast: Perspectives on Modernisation.
Chicago: University of Chicago Press. 1977.

MIGRATION

Yacoob, May
Ahmadiyya and Urbanization: Migrant Women in Abidjan.
Boston: Boston University. African Studies Center.
Working Papers in African Studies #75. 1983.

ORGANIZATIONS

Dei, Carleene H.
"Political Activity Among Urban African Women: Le Groupe
D' Animation Culturel De Cocody." Ph.D Dissertation:
Columbia University. New York, New York. 1985. 431p.
Lewis, Barbara C.
"The Limitations of Group Action Among Entrepreneurs: The
Market Women of Abidjan, Ivory Coast." (In) Hafkin, N.J.
and Bay, Edna (eds.). Women in Africa: Studies in Social
and Economic Change. Stanford, California: Stanford
University Press. 1976. pp. 135-156.

POLITICS AND GOVERNMENT

Dei, Carleene H.
"Political Activity Among Urban African Women: Le Groupe
D' Animation Culturel De Cocody." Ph.D Dissertation:
Columbia University. New York, New York. 1985. 431p.
Palmer, Ingrid
"New Official Ideas on Women and Development." Institute
for Development Studies. Volume 10 #3 1979. pp. 42-53.

RELIGION AND WITCHCRAFT

Gottlieb, Alma
"Witches, Kings and the Sacrifice of Identity: The Power
of Paradox and the Paradox of Power Among the Beng of
Ivory Coast." Paper Presented at the Annual Meeting of
the African Studies Association. Paper #33. Washington,
D.C. November 4-7, 1982.
Walker, Sheila S.
"Witchcraft and Healing in an African Church." Journal
of Religions in Africa. Volume 10 #2 1979. pp. 127-138.
Walker, Sheila S.
"Women in the Harrist Movement." (In) Jules-Rosette,

Bennatta (ed.). The New Religions of Africa. Norwood,
New Jersey: Ablex Publishing Co. 1979. pp. 87-97.

SEX ROLES

Clignet, Remi
  "Social Change and Sexual Differentiation in the Cameroon
  and the Ivory Coast." Signs. Volume 3 #1 Autumn, 1977.
  pp. 244-266.
Clignet, Remi
  "Social Change and Sexual Differentiation in the Cameroon
  and the Ivory Coast." (In) Wellesley Editorial
  Committee. Women in National Development. Chicago:
  University of Chicago Press. 1977. pp. 244-260.
Etienne, Mona
  "Gender Relations and Conjugality Among the Baule." (In)
  Oppong, Christine (ed.). Female and Male in West Africa.
  London: George Allen and Unwin. 1983. pp. 303-319.
Etienne, Mona
  "Gender Relations and Conjugality Among the Baule."
  Culture. Volume 1 #1 1981. pp. 21-30.
Gottlieb, Alma
  "Beng Baby Decoration: The Efficacy of Symbols and the
  Power of Women." Paper Presented at the Annual Meeting
  of the African Studies Association. Paper #43.
  Bloomington, Indiana. October 21-24, 1981.
Gottlieb, Alma
  "Village Kapok, Forest Kapok: Notions of Separation,
  Identity and Gender Among the Beng of Ivory Coast." Ph.D
  Dissertation: University of Virginia, Charlottesville.
  Charlottesville, Virginia. 1983. 295p.
Lewis, Barbara C.
  "Female Strategies and Public Goods: Market Women of the
  Ivory Coast." Paper Presented at the Conference on Women
  and Development. Wellesley, Massachusetts: Wellesley
  College. June, 1976.
Peterson, K.J.
  "Brong Midwives and Women in Childbirth: Management of
  Uncertainty in a Division of Labor." Human Organization.
  Volume 41 #4 Winter, 1982. pp. 291-298.
Traore, Aminata
  "Agro-Business and Female Employment in the Ivory Coast."
  Paper Presented at the AAWORD Conference on Women and
  Rural Development. Algiers, Algeria. September, 1982.
Vidal, C.
  "Sex War in Abidjan--Male, Female Money." Cahiers
  d'Etudes Africaines. Volume 17 #1 1977. pp. 121-154.

SLAVERY

Etienne, Mona
  "Women and Slaves: Stratification in an African Society:
  The Baule, Ivory Coast." Paper Presented at the 75th

Annual Meeting of the American Anthropological
Association. Washington, D.C. 1976.

STATUS OF WOMEN

Clignet, Remi
"Social Change and Sexual Differentiation in the Cameroon
and the Ivory Coast." Signs. Volume 3 #1 Autumn, 1977.
pp. 244-266.

URBANIZATION

Dei, Carleene H.
"Political Activity Among Urban African Women: Le Groupe
D' Animation Culturel De Cocody." Ph.D Dissertation:
Columbia University. New York, New York. 1985. 431p.
Ellovich, Risa S.
"Adaptations to the Urban Setting: Dioula Women in
Gagnoa, Ivory Coast." Ph.D Dissertation: Indiana
University. Bloomington, Indiana. 1979. 189p.
Lewis, Barbara C.
"Economic Activity and Marriage Among Ivorian Urban
Women." (In) Schlegel, Alice E. (ed.). Sexual
Stratification: A Cross-Cultural View. New York:
Columbia University Press. 1977. pp. 161-191.
Yacoob, May
Ahmadiyya and Urbanization: Migrant Women in Abidjan.
Boston: Boston University. African Studies Center.
Working Papers in African Studies #75. 1983.

WOMEN AND THEIR CHILDREN

Ellovich, Risa S.
"Ivorian Women and the Law: A Dioula-Bete Comparison."
Paper Presented at the Annual Meeting of the African
Studies Association. Paper #27. Philadelphia,
Pennsylvania. 1980.
Ellovich, Risa S.
"The Law and Ivorian Women." Anthropos. Volume 80 #1-3
1985. pp. 185-197.
Etienne, Mona
"Social Maternity, Adoptive Relations and the Power of
Women Among the Baule." L'Homme. Volume 19 #3/4
July-December, 1979. pp. 63-108.
Etienne, Mona
"The Case for Social Maternity: Adoption of Children by
Urban Baule Women." Dialectical Anthropology. Volume 4
#3 October, 1979. pp. 237-242.
Gottlieb, Alma
"Beng Baby Decoration: The Efficacy of Symbols and the
Power of Women." Paper Presented at the Annual Meeting
of the African Studies Association. Paper #43.

IVORY COAST

Bloomington, Indiana. October 21-24, 1981.

Liberia

Abu, Katie
   "Women's Participation in Rice Farming in Liberia."
   Rome: United Nations Food and Agriculture Organization
   (FAO). 1984.
Akerele, Olunanke
   "Women and the Fishing Industry in Liberia: Measures of
   Women's Participation." Addis Ababa, Ethiopia: United
   Nations Economic Commission for Africa. African Training
   and Research Center for Women. 1979. 82p.
Bellman, Beryl L.
   "The Social Organization of Knowledge in Kpelle Ritual."
   (In) Jules-Rosette, Bennetta (ed.). The New Religions of
   Africa. Norwood, New Jersey: Ablex Publishing Corp.
   1979. pp. 39-56.
Bledsoe, Caroline H.
   "Women's Marital Strategies Among the Kpelle of Liberia."
   Journal of Anthropological Research. Volume 32 #4
   Winter, 1976. pp. 372-389.
Bledsoe, Caroline H.
   "The Political Use of Sande Ideology and Symbolism."
   American Ethnologist. Volume 11 #3 August, 1984. pp.
   455-472.
Bledsoe, Caroline H.
   "Women and Marriage in Kpelle Society." Stanford,
   California: Stanford University Press. 1980. 217p.
Bledsoe, Caroline H.
   "Women and Marriage in Kpelle Society." Ph.D
   Dissertation: Stanford University. Stanford, California.
   1976. 148p.
Carter, Jeanette and Mends-Cole, Joyce
   "Liberian Women: Their Role in Food Production and Their
   Educational and Legal Status." Monrovia, Liberia:

University of Liberia. Washington, D.C.: U.S. Department
of State. U.S. Agency for International Development.
1982.

Currens, Gerald E.
"Women, Men and Rice: Agricultural Innovation in
Northwestern Liberia." Human Organization. Volume 35 #4
Winter, 1976. pp. 355-366.

Dzegede, Sylvi A.
"Urbanization and Fertility Decline in West Africa:
Ghana, Sierra Leone and Liberia." Journal of Comparative
Family Studies. Volume 12 #2 Spring, 1981. pp.
233-244.

Getaweh, S. Momolu
"The Conceptualization of Family-Size Goals Among the
Mende in Sierra Leone and the Vai in Liberia." Ph.D
Dissertation: Boston University. Graduate School.
Boston, Massachusetts. 1984. 419p.

Gyepi-Garbrah, Benjamin
Adolescent Fertility in Liberia. Boston: Pathfinder
Fund. 1985. 55p.

Handwerker, W. Penn
"Reproductive Choices and Behavior: A Test of Two
Theories of Fertility Variation With Data From Monrovia,
Liberia." Medical Anthropology. Volume 5 #3 1981. pp.
262-293.

Handwerker, W. Penn
"Family, Fertility and Economics." Current Anthropology.
Volume 18 #2 June, 1977. pp. 259-287.

Jackson, L.C.
"Malaria in Liberian Children and Mothers: Biocultural
Perceptions of Illness vs. Clinical Evidence of Disease."
Social Science and Medicine. Volume #12 1985. pp.
1281-1287.

Jackson, Robert T. and Latham Michael C.
"Anemia of Pregnancy in Liberia, West Africa: A
Therapeutic Trial." American Journal of Clinical
Nutrition. Volume 35 #4 April, 1982. pp. 710-714.

Kaba, Brahima D.
"Relationships Between Women's Economic Activities and
Their Family Behavior and Expectations in Liberia."
Monrovia, Liberia: University of Liberia. 1978.

Kaba, Brahima D.
"Profile of Liberian Women in Marketing." Monrovia,
Liberia: University of Liberia. Institute of Research.
Profile of Liberian Women in Development Series. 1982.
231p.

Kollehlon, Konia T.
"Residence Background, Internal Migration and Fertility
in Liberia." Ph.D Dissertation: University of Maryland.
College Park, Maryland. 1982. 196p.

Kollehlon, Konia T.
"Women's Work Role and Fertility in Liberia." Africa.
Volume 54 #4 1984. pp. 31-45.

Mehrotra, Gopal K.
   "A Study of Liberia's Population With Special Emphasis on
   Ethnic and Fertility Variations." Ph.D Disseration:
   University of Pennsylvania. Philadelphia, Pennsylvania.
   1980. 283p.
Mikell, Gwendolyn
   "African Women Within Nations of Crisis." Transafrica
   Forum. Volume 2 #1 1983. pp. 31-34.
Monts, Lester P.
   "Dance in the Nai Sande Society." African Arts. Volume
   17 #4 1984. pp. 53-59+.
Saha, S.C.
   "Roles and Statuses of Women in a Traditional African
   Setting: A Study of Women in Liberia." Africa Quarterly.
   Volume 22 #1 1982. pp. 25-33.
Sevareid, Peter
   "My Head Wife to Me: The Law of Evidence in the Rural
   Courts of Liberia." Paper Presented at the Annual
   Meeting of the African Studies Association. Paper #98.
   Philadelphia, Pennsylvania. 1980.

Mali

Ben-Barka, Lalla A.
    "Training of Malian Rural Women: Its Impact on Cash
    Income and on Improvement in Standard of Living: The CMDT
    Case." Ph.D Dissertation: University of Southern
    California. Los Angeles, California. 1985.
Bingen, R. James
    Food Production and Rural Development in the Sahel:
    Lesson From Mali's Operation Riz-Segou. Boulder,
    Colorado: Westview Press. Westview Special Studies in
    Social, Political and Economic Development. 1985. 167p.
Binkin, Nancy J. and Burton, Nadine N. and Toure, Attaher H.
and Traore, M. Lamine and Rochat, Roger W.
    "Women Hospitalized for Abortion Complications in Mali."
    International Family Planning Perspectives. Volume 10 #1
    March, 1984. pp. 8-12.
Caughman, Susan H. and Thiam, Mariam N.
    The Markala Cooperative: A New Approach to Traditional
    Economic Roles. New York: Carnegie Foundation. Seeds
    #5. 1982. 20p.
Caughman, Susan H.
    Women and Development in Mali: An Annotated
    Bibliography. Addis Ababa, Ethiopia: United Nations
    Economic Commission for Africa. African Training and
    Research Centre for Women. Bibliography Series #6.
    1982. 34p.
Caughman, Susan H.
    Women at Work in Mali: The Case of the Markala
    Cooperative. Boston: Boston University. African Studies
    Center. Working Papers in African Studies #50. 1981.
    72p.
Caughman, Susan L.
    New Skills for Rural Women: Report of a Training Program
    for Twelve Malian Community Development Workers Held in

Banjul, The Gambia. Philadelphia, Pennsylvania: American
Friends Service Committee. Women and Development
Program, International Division. 1977.

Cazes, M.H.
"Mating Structure in the Dogon Population in the Tabi
Massif." Social Biology. Volume 28 #3-4 Fall-Winter,
1981. pp. 281-292.

Dettwyler, Katherine A.
"Breastfeeding, Weaning, and Other Infant Feeding
Practices in Mali and Their Effects on Growth and
Development." Ph.D Dissertation: Indiana University.
Bloomington, Indiana. 1985. 397p.

Dinnerstein, Myra and Cloud, Kathleen
Report of a Fact-Finding Trip to Niger, Mali, Senegal and
Upper Volta. Washington, D.C.: U.S. Department of State.
U.S. Agency for International Development. 1976. 10p.

Fleming, Martha D.
"Household Behavior in the Region of Kita and its
Relationship to Agricultural Change." Paper Presented at
the Second Workshop on Sahelian Agriculture. West
Lafayette, Indiana: Purdue University. Department of
Agricultural Economics. 1980.

Fleming, Martha D.
"Social Stratification and Women's Work in the Rural
Malian Household." Paper Presented at the Annual Meeting
of the American Anthropological Association. Washington,
D.C. 1982.

Fleming, Martha D.
Women's Activities in the Kita Zone, Republic of Mali.
Final Report, West Africa Projects. West Lafayette,
Indiana: Purdue University. Department of Agricultural
Economics. 1979.

Hill, Allan G. and Randall S.C. and Sullivan, O.
The Mortality and Fertility of Farmers and Pastoralists
in Central Mali, 1950-1981. London: University of
London. London School of Hygiene and Tropical Medicine.
Centre for Population Studies. CPS Research Paper #82-4.
May, 1982. 54p.

Imperato, P.J.
"The Role of Women in Traditional Healing Among the
Bambara of Mali." Transactions of the Royal Society of
Tropical Medicine and Hygiene. Volume 75 #6 1981. pp.
766-770.

Koenig, D.
"Labor Allocation, Women's Work and Social Stratification
in the Rural Malian Household." Paper Presented at the
Annual Meeting of the American Anthropological
Association. Washington, D.C. December, 1982.

Lewis, John V.
"Descendants and Crops: Two Poles of Production in a
Malian Peasant Village." Ph.D Dissertation: Yale
University. New Haven, Connecticut. 1979. 487p.

Lewis, John V.
    "Domestic Labour Intensity and the Incorporation of
    Malian Peasant Farmers into Localized Descent Groups."
    American Ethnologist. Volume 8 #2 1981. pp. 52-73.
Mathu, Njambi
    "Mali Women Conquer Poverty." International Review of
    Missions. Volume 73 July, 1984. pp. 352-353.
McNeil, Leslie
    "Women of Mali: A Study in Sexual Stratification." B.A.
    Thesis: Harvard University. Department of Anthropology.
    Cambridge, Massachusetts. 1979.
Obichere, B.I.
    "Women and Slavery in the Kingdom of Dahomey." Revue
    Francaise d'Histoire d'Outre-Mer. Voume 65 #1 1978. pp.
    5-20.
Roberts, Richard.
    "Women's Work and Women's Property: Household Social
    Relations in the Maraka Textile Industry of the 19th
    Century." Comparative Studies in Society and History.
    Volume 26 #2 April, 1984. pp. 229-250.
Siby, Mariko F.
    "African Traditions and the Mali Woman." Impact of
    Science on Society. Volume 30 #1 January-March, 1980.
    pp. 11-13.

Mauritania

Abeille, Barbara
   A Study of Female Life in Mauritania. Washington, D.C.:
   U.S. Agency for International Development. Office of
   Women in Development. July, 1979. 55p.
Farid, Samir
   "Fertility Patterns in the Arab Region." International
   Family Planning Perspectives. Volume 10 #4 December,
   1984. pp. 119-125.
Quet, D.
   "Mauritian Voices--A Panorama of Contemporary
   Creative-Writing in English." World Literature Written
   in English. Volume 23 #2 1984. pp. 303-312.
Smale, Melinda S.
   Women in Mauritania: The Effect of Drought and Migration
   on Their Economic Status and Implications for Development
   Programs. Washington, D.C.: U.S. Department of State.
   U.S. Agency for International Development. Office of
   Women in Development. October, 1978. 163p.

Niger

Anani, Elma and Keita, Alkaly M. and Rahman, Awatef A.
    Women and the Mass Media in Africa: Case Studies From
    Sierra Leone, the Niger and Egypt. Addis Ababa,
    Ethiopia: United Nations Economic Commission for Africa.
    African Training and Research Centre for Women. 1981.
    38p.
Barres, Victoria and Brigatti, Pierra and Correze, Annette
and Debourg, Madeleine and Doucet, Marie-Jo and Gentil,
Veronique and Malachowski, Sylvia and Pieressa, Franca and
Snoy, Odette
    The Participation of Rural Women in Development: A
    Project of Rural Women's Animation in Niger, 1966-1975.
    Paris: Institut de Recherche et Application des Methods
    de Developpment (IRAM). 1976. 83p.
Correze, Annette
    The Participation of Rural Women in Development: A
    Project of Rural Women's Animation in Niger, 1966-1977.
    Paris: Institut de Recherche et Application des Methods
    de Developpment (IRAM). April, 1976. 83p.
Dinnerstein, Myra and Cloud, Kathleen
    Report of a Fact-Finding Trip to Niger, Mali, Senegal and
    Upper Volta. Washington, D.C.: U.S. Department of State.
    U.S. Agency for International Development. 1976. 10p.
Faulkingham, Ralph H.
    "Fertility in Tudu: An Analysis of Constraints on
    Fertility in a Village in Niger." (In) Caldwell, John C.
    (ed.). The Persistence of High Fertility: Population
    Prospects in the Third World. Canberra, Australia:
    Australian National University. Volume One. 1977. pp.
    153-188.
Nelson, Nici
    "Mobilising Village Women: Some Organization and
    Management Considerations." Journal of Development
    Studies. Volume 17 #3 April, 1981. pp. 47-58
Roberts, Pepe
    "Integration of Women in the Development Process: Some

Conceptual Problems." Bulletin of the Institute for
Development Studies. Volume 10 #3 April, 1979. pp.
60-66.

Saunders, Margaret O.
"Marriage and Divorce in a Muslim Hausa Town (Mirra,
Niger Republic)." Ph.D Dissertation: Indiana University.
Bloomington, Indiana. 1978. 379p.

Saunders, Margaret O.
"Women's Divorce Strategies in Mirria County, Niger
Republic: Cases From the 'Tribunal de Premier Instance'."
Paper Presented at the Annual Meeting of the African
Studies Association. Paper #86. Los Angeles,
California. 1979. 16p.

Saunders, Margaret O.
"Women's Role in a Muslim Hausa Town (Mirra, Republic of
Niger)." (In) Bourguignon, Erika A. (ed.). A World of
Women: Anthropological Studies of Women in the Societies
of the World. New York: Praeger Publishers. 1980. pp.
57-86.

Smale, Melinda S.
"Women in Development Issues in Niger." (In) U.S. Agency
for International Development/Niamey. Niger Agricultural
Sector Assessment. Niamey, Niger: U.S. AID. Volume Two
Part E. 1979.

Nigeria

ABORTION

Acsadi, Gyorgy
   "Traditional Birth Control Methods in Yorubaland." (In)
   Marshall, John F. and Polgar, Steven (eds.). Culture,
   Natality, and Family Planning. Chapel Hill, North
   Carolina: University of North Carolina. Carolina
   Population Center. 1976. pp. 126-155.
Ajobor, L.N.
   "Contraceptives and Abortions in Nigeria." Nigerian
   Medical Journal. Volume 6 July, 1976. pp. 367+.
Akingba, J.B.
   "Abortion, Maternity and the Other Health Problems in
   Nigeria." Nigerian Medical Journal. Volume 7 #4
   October, 1977. pp. 465-471.
Bakare, Christopher G.
   "Medical and Parmedical Opinion in Nigeria." (In) David,
   Henry P. and Friedman, Herbert L. and Van Der Tak, Jean
   and Sevilla, Marylis J. (eds.). Abortion in
   Psychological Research. New York: Springer Publishing.
   Transnational Family Research Institute Monographs.
   1978. pp. 259-283.
Edeh, J.
   "Abortion and the Law in Nigeria: A Psychiatrists View."
   Nigerian Medical Journal. Volume 9 #5/6 1979. pp.
   631-634.
Okojie, S.E.
   "Induced Illegal Abortions in Benin City, Nigeria."
   International Journal of Gynaecology and Obstetrics.
   Volume 14 #6 1976. pp. 517-521.
Omu, A.E. and Oronsaye, A.U. and Faal, M.K. and Asuquo, E.E.
   "Adolescent Induced Abortion in Benin City, Nigeria."
   International Journal of Gynaecology and Obstetrics.
   Volume 19 #6 December, 1981. pp. 495-499.

Onwuazor, Sammy N.
"Continuity and Change: Abortion and Family Size in a Nigerian Village." (In) Epstein, T. Scarlett and Jackson, Darrell (eds.). The Feasibility of Fertility Planning: Micro Perspectives. Oxford, England: Pergamon Press. 1977. pp. 67-96.

Oronsaye, A.U. and Odiase, G.I.
"Attitudes Toward Abortion and Contraception Among Nigerian Secondary School Girls." International Journal of Gynaecology and Obstetrics. Volume 21 #5 October, 1983. pp. 423-426.

AGRICULTURE

Adekanye, Tomilayo O.
"Innovation and Rural Women in Nigeria: Cassava Processing and Food Production." (In) Ahmed, Iftikhar (ed.). Technology and Rural Women: Conceptual and Empirical Issues. Boston: George Allen and Unwin. 1985. pp. 252-283.

Adekanye, Tomilayo O.
"Women in Agriculture in Nigeria: Problems and Policies for Development." Women's Studies International. Volume 7 #6 1984. pp. 423-431.

Adekanye-Adeyokunnu, T.
Women in Nigerian Agriculture. Ibadan, Nigeria: University of Ibadan. Department of Agricultural Economics. 1982.

Adeyemo, Remi
"Women in Rural Areas: A Case Study of Southwestern Nigeria." Canadian Journal of African Studies. Volume 18 #3 1984. pp. 563-572.

Adeyeye, V.A.
"Women in Traditional Agriculture: Oyo State of Nigeria Experience." MSc Thesis: University of Ibadan. Department of Agricultural Economics. Ibadan, Nigeria. 1977.

Adeyokunnu (Adekanye), Tomilayo O.
Women and Agriculture in Nigeria. Addis Ababa, Ethiopia: United Nations Economic Commission for Africa. African Training and Research Centre for Women. 1980.

Adeyokunnu, Tomilayo O.
"Rural Development and the Position of Women in Africa: Problems and Policies." Paper Presented at the Meeting of the Experts on Research on the Status of Women, Development and Population Trends: Evaluation and Prospects. Paris: United Nations Educational, Scientific and Cultural Organization. 1980. 32p.

Afonja, Simi A.
"Changing Modes of Production and the Sexual Division of Labor Among the Yoruba." Signs. Volume 7 #2 Winter, 1981. pp. 299-313.

Akande, Jadesola O.
"Participation of Women in Rural Development." (In)
International Labour Organization (ILO). Rural
Development and Women in Africa. Geneva: ILO. 1984.
pp. 129-135.

Brown, C.K.
The Participation of Women in Rural Development in Kaduna
State of Nigeria. Zaria, Nigeria: Centre for Social and
Economic Research. ABU Research Paper #5. 1979. 20p.

Burfisher, Mary E. and Horenstein, Nadine R.
"Sex Roles and Development Effects on the Nigerian Tiv
Farm Household." Rural Africana. #21 Winter, 1985.
pp. 31-50.

Burfisher, Mary E. and Horenstein, Nadine R.
Sex Roles in the Nigerian Tiv Farm Household and the
Differential Impacts of Development Projects. Washington
D.C.: U.S. Department of Agriculture. International
Economics Division. 1982.

Burfisher, Mary E. and Horenstein, Nadine R.
Sex Roles in the Nigerian Tiv Farm Household. West
Hartford, Connecticut: Kumarian Press. Women's Roles and
Gender Differences in Development, Cases for Planners.
Volume 2. 1985. 62p.

DeLargy, Pamela and Bilsborrow, Richard E.
A Comparative Assessment of the Fertility Impact of Rural
Development Projects. Chapel Hill, North Carolina:
University of North Carolina. Carolina Population
Center. 1983.

Emeagwali, G.T.
"Women in Pre-Capitalistic Socio-Economic Formations in
Nigeria." (In) Women in Nigeria. London: Zed Press.
1985. pp. 52-55.

Favi, F.
Women's Role in Economic Development: A Case Study of
Villages in Oyo State. Ibadan, Nigeria: University of
Ibadan. Department of Agricultural Extension. Ibadan,
Nigeria. 1977.

Greene, P.A.
Innovative Approaches in Rural Women's Programmes in
Three African Countries: Kenya, Nigeria, Sierra Leone:
Case Studies. Rome: United Nations Food and Agriculture
Organization. 1985. 148p.

Guyer, Jane I.
"Food, Cocoa, and the Division of Labour by Sex in Two
West African Societies." Comparative Studies in Society
and History. Volume 22 #3 July, 1980. pp. 355-370.

Jackson, C.
"Hausa Women and Agricultural Change on the Kano River
Project, Nigeria." (In) Adams, W.M. and Grove, A.T.
(eds.). Irrigation in Tropical Africa: Problems and
Problem Solving. Cambridge, England: Cambridge
University. African Studies Center. 1984. pp. 67-74.

Ladipo, Patricia A. and Adegoke, M.O.
"An Assessment of Rural Women's Agricultural Roles and
Needs: Implications for Home Economics Extension
Curriculum." Paper Presented at the Workshop on the Role
of Women and Home Economics in Rural Development in
Africa. Rome: United Nations Food and Agricultural
Organization. Alexandria, Egypt. October 17, 1983.
12p.

Ladipo, Patricia A.
"Developing Women's Cooperatives: An Experiment in Rural
Nigeria." Journal of Development Studies. Volume 17 #3
April, 1981. pp. 123-136.

Ladipo, Patricia A.
Developing Women's Cooperatives: An Experiment in Rural
Nigeria. Totowa, New Jersey: Frank Cass. 1981. pp.
123-136.

Longhurst, Richard
"Resource Allocation and the Sexual Division of Labor: A
Case Study of a Moslem Hausa Village in Northern
Nigeria." (In) Beneria, Lourdes (ed.). Women and
Development: The Sexual Division of Labor in Rural
Societies: A Study. New York: Praeger Publishers.
Praeger Special Studies. 1982. pp. 95-117.

Longhurst, Richard
"Rural Development Planning and the Sexual Division of
Labour: A Case Study of a Moslem Hausa Village in
Northern Nigeria." (In) International Labour
Organization (ILO). Rural Development and Women in
Africa. Geneva: ILO. 1984. pp. 117-122.

Longhurst, Richard
Rural Development Planning and the Sexual Division of
Labour: A Case Study of a Moslem Village in Northern
Nigeria. Geneva: International Labour Organization.
World Employment Programme Research Working Paper.
Mimeograph #10. 1980.

Martin, S.
"Gender and Innovation--Farming, Cooking and Palm
Processing in the Ngwa Region, Southeastern Nigeria,
1900-1930." Journal of African History. Volume 25 #4
1984. pp. 411-427.

Mickelwait, Donald R. and Riegelman, Mary Ann and Sweet,
Charles F.
Women in Rural Development: A Survey of the Roles of
Women in Ghana, Lesotho, Kenya, Nigeria... Boulder,
Colorado: Westview Press. 1976. 224p.

Ogunsheye, F. Aetowun and Awosika, Keziah and Dennis,
Carolyn and Didomenko, Catherine and Akinkoye, O.
Nigerian Women and Development. Ibadan, Nigeria:
University of Nigeria. 1982.

Okonjo, K.
"Rural Women's Credit Systems: A Nigerian Example."
Studies in Family Planning. Volume 10 #11/12.
November-December, 1979. pp. 326-331.

Okonjo, Kamene
"Rural Women's Credit Systems: A Nigerian Example."
Studies in Family Planning. Volume 10 #11/12
November-December, 1979. pp. 326-331.
Omu, Fred I.A. and Makinwa, P. and Ozo, A.O.
Proceedings of the National Conference on Integrated
Rural Development and Women in Development. Benin City,
Nigeria: University of Benin. Center for Social,
Cultural and Environmental Research. September 22-26,
1980.
Osuntogun, A.
"Rural Women in Agricultural Development: A Nigerian Case
Study." Paper Presented at the Conference on Nigerian
Women and Development in Relation to Changing Family
Structure. Ibadan, Nigeria: University of Ibadan. 1976.
Palmer, Ingrid
Impact of Male Out-Migration on Women in Farming. West
Hartford, Connecticut: Kumarian Press. Women's Roles and
Gender Differences in Development. Volume Seven. Cases
for Planners. 1985. 89p.
Palmer, Ingrid
The Impact of Agrarian Reform on Women. West Hartford,
Connecticut: Kumarian Press. Women's Roles and Gender
Differences in Development. Volume Six. Cases for
Planners. 1985. 89p.
Perchonock, N.
"Double Oppression: Women and Land Matters in Kaduna
State." (In) Women in Nigeria Today. London: Zed Press.
1985. pp. 82-103.
Pittin, Renee
"Documentation and Analysis of the Invisible Work of
Invisible Women: A Nigerian Case Study." International
Labour Review. Volume 123 #4 July-August, 1984. pp.
473-490.
Remy, Dorothy
"Underdevelopment and the Experience of Women: A Nigerian
Case Study." (In) Williams, Gavin (ed.). Nigeria:
Economy and Society. London: Collings. 1976. pp.
123-134.
Sharpe, B.
"Social Knowledge and Farming Systems Research:
Ethnicity, Power and the Invisible Farmers of North
Central Nigeria." African Social Research. #38 1985.
Spaulding, J.
"The Misfortunes of Some: The Advantages of Others: Land
Sales by Women in Sinnar." (In) Hay, M.J. and Wright, M.
(eds.). African Women and the Law: Historical
Perspectives. Boston: Boston University. African
Studies Center. 1978. pp. 3-18.
Spiro, Heather M.
The Fifth World: Women's Rural Activities and Time
Budgets in Nigeria. London: University of London. Queen
Mary College. Department of Geography. Occasional Paper
#19. 1981. 59p.

Spiro, Heather M.
    The Ilora Farm Settlement in Nigeria. West Hartford,
    Connecticut: Kumarian Press. Women's Roles and Gender
    Differences in Development. Cases for Planners. Volume
    Five. 1985. 89p.
Spiro, Heather M.
    The Role of Women in Farming in Oyo State, Nigeria: A
    Case Study in Two Rural Communities. Ibadan, Nigeria:
    International Institute of Tropical Agriculture.
    Agricultural Economics Discussion Paper #7. 1980. 36p.
United Nations Economic Commission for Africa (UNECA)
    Women and Agriculture in Nigeria. Addis Ababa, Ethiopia:
    UNECA. Research Series. 1981.
Watts, Susan J.
    "Rural Women as Food Processors and Traders: Eko Making
    in the Ilorin Area of Nigeria." Journal of Developing
    Areas. Volume 19 October, 1984. pp. 71-82.
Zack-Williams, A.B.
    "Female Labour and Exploitation Within African Social
    Formations." (In) Women in Nigeria Today. London: Zed
    Press. 1985. pp. 61-67.

ARTS

Ames, D.W. and Gourlay, K.A.
    "Kimkim: A Women's Musical Pot." African Arts. Volume
    11 #2 January, 1978. pp. 56-64+.
Borgatti, Jean
    "Songs of Ritual License From Midwestern Nigeria."
    Alcheringa. New Series Volume 2 1976. pp. 66-71.
Boyd, J.
    "The Role of Women as Agents Religieux in Sokoto,"
    Canadian Journal of African Studies. Volume 19 #2 1985.
Drewal, Henry J.
    "Art and Perception of Women in Yoruba Culture." Cahiers
    d'Etudes Africaines. Volume 17 #4 1977. pp. 545-567.
Drewal, Henry J. and Drewal, Margaret T.
    G.EL.ED.E: Art and Female Power Among the Yoruba.
    Bloomington, Indiana: Indiana University Press.
    Traditional Arts of Africa Series. 1983. 306p.
Foss, Susan M.
    "She Who Sits as King: Celebrations for Young Urhobo
    Women." African Arts. Volume 12 #2 February, 1979.
    pp. 44-50.
Okeke, Chukwuanugo S.
    "Wrapper Designs for the Nigerian Market: Design Features
    of Igbo Women's Wrapper." Nigeria Magazine. #142 1982.
    pp. 29-43.
Prewal, Henry
    "Art and the Perception of Women in Yoruba Culture."
    Cahiers d'Etudes Africaines. Volume 17 #4 1977. pp.
    545-568.

NIGERIA

Scott, Victoria
   "Nike Olaniyi, Nigeria's Foremost Female Artist." Paper
   Presented at the Annual Meeting of the African Studies
   Association. Paper #117. Bloomington, Indiana. October
   21-24, 1981.

BIBLIOGRAPHIES

Cobbald, Elizabeth
   "Muslim Hausa Women in Northern Nigeria: An Annotated
   Bibliography." African Research and Documentation.
   Volume 32 1983. pp. 22-29.
Fieloux, M.
   "Bibliographic Chronicle: Invisible and Mute
   Women--Concerning Ibo Riots of 1929." Cahiers d'Etudes
   Africaines. Volume 17 #1 1977. pp. 189+.
Hill, Polly
   "Women's House Trade." (In) Hill, Polly. Population,
   Prosperity and Poverty: Rural Kano, 1900 and 1970.
   Cambridge, New York: Cambridge University Press. 1977.
   240p.
Kisekka, Mere N.
   Women and Development in Nigeria: A Bibliography. Addis
   Ababa, Ethiopia: United Nations Economic Commission for
   Africa. African Training and Research Centre for Women.
   Bibliography Series #4. 1981. 122p.

CULTURAL ROLES

Aborampah, Osei-Mensah
   "Determinants of Breast-Feeding and Post-Partum Sexual
   Abstinence: Analysis of a Sample of Yoruba Women, Western
   Nigeria." Journal of Biosocial Science. Volume 17 #4
   October, 1985. pp. 461-469.
Aborampah, Osei-Mensah
   "Plural Marriage, Post-Partum Abstinence and Fertility
   Among the Yoruba of Western Nigeria." Ph.D Dissertation:
   University of Wisconsin-Madison. Madison, Wisconsin.
   1981. 214p.
Abu Manga, Al-Amin
   "The Concept of 'Woman' in Fulani Narratives." Nigeria
   Magazine. Volume 150 1984. pp. 52-58.
Achebe, Christie C.
   "Continuities, Changes and Challenges: Women's Roles in
   Nigerian Society." Presence Africaine. # 120 1981. pp.
   3-16.
Achebe, Christie C.
   "Social Limitations of the Academic Woman to the Pursuit
   of Education." Nigerian Journal of Education. Volume 2
   #1 1979.

Achike, Okay
    "Problems of Creation and Dissolution of Customary
    Marriages in Nigeria." (In) Roberts, Simon (ed.). Law
    and the Family in Nigeria. Hague, Netherlands: Mouton.
    1977. pp. 145-158.
Acsadi, Gyorgy
    "Traditional Birth Control Methods in Yorubaland." (In)
    Marshall, John F. and Polgar, Steven (eds.). Culture,
    Natality, and Family Planning. Chapel Hill, North
    Carolina: University of North Carolina. Carolina
    Population Center. 1976. pp. 126-155.
Adaba, Gemma
    "Rationality and Responsibility in Family Planning in
    Traditional African Society." (In) Oppong, C. and Adaba,
    G. and Bekombo-Priso, M. and Mogey, J. (eds.). Marriage,
    Fertility and Parenthood in West Africa. Canberra,
    Australia: Australian National University. Department of
    Demography. Volume Two. 1978. pp. 655-672.
Adedeji, John A.
    "The Acceptance of Nigerian Women in Sport."
    International Review of Sport Sociology. Volume 13 #1
    1978. pp. 39-47.
Adegbola, O. and Page, Hilary J.
    "Nuptiality and Fertility in Metropolitan Lagos:
    Components and Compensating Mechanisms." (In) Ruzicka,
    L.T. (ed.). Nuptiality and Fertility: Proceedings of a
    Seminar. Liege, Belgium: International Union for the
    Scientific Study of Population. Bruges, Belgium.
    January 8-11, 1982. pp. 337-362.
Adegbola, O. and Page, Hilary J. and Lesthaeghe, Ron J.
    Breast-Feeding and Post-Partum Abstinence in Metropolitan
    Lagos. Lagos, Nigeria: University of Lagos. Human
    Resources Research Unit. Faculty of Social Sciences.
    Research Bulletin. #80-3. 1980. 38p.
Adekanye, Tomilayo O.
    "Innovation and Rural Women in Nigeria: Cassava
    Processing and Food Production." (In) Ahmed, Iftikhar
    (ed.). Technology and Rural Women: Conceptual and
    Empirical Issues. Boston: George Allen and Unwin. 1985.
    pp. 252-283.
Adekanye, Tomilayo O.
    "Women in Agriculture in Nigeria: Problems and Policies
    for Development." Women's Studies International. Volume
    7 #6 1984. pp. 423-431.
Adekoya, M.A.
    "Barriers to an Effective Organization of Women's Work.
    The Women's Programme Section in Nigeria." Assignment
    Children. Volume 38 #2 April-June, 1977. pp. 80-83.
Adeleye, J.A.
    "Contraceptives and the Female Undergraduates in Ibadan,
    Nigeria." East Africa Medical Journal. Volume 58 #8
    August, 1981. pp. 616-621.
Adelowo, E.D.
    "Islamic Marriage System and the Extents of its Adoption

by Yoruba Muslims of Nigeria." Orita. Volume 14 #1
June, 1982. pp. 16-33.
Ademola, Ade
"Changes in the Patterns of Marriage and Divorce in a
Yoruba Town." Rural Africana. #14 Fall, 1982. pp.
1-24.
Adeney, Miriam
"A Woman Liberated--For What?" Christianity Today.
Volume 28 January 13, 1984. pp. 28-30.
Adeniyi, E.O.
"Population Growth and Fertility Among the Nupe of
Nigeria." (In) Oppong, C. and Adaba, G. and
Bekombo-Priso, M. and Mogey, J. (eds.). Marriage,
Fertility and Parenthood in West Africa. Canberra,
Australia: Australian National University. Department of
Demography. Volume Two. 1978. pp. 435-451.
Adeokun, Lawrence A.
"Family Planning in Southwest Nigeria: Levels and
Determinants of 'KAP'." (In) Adeokun, L.A. (ed.).
1971-1975 National Survey of Fertility, Family and Family
Planning, Phase I: Southwest Nigeria. Ife, Nigeria:
University of Ife. Department of Demography and Social
Statistics. Monograph #1. 1979. pp. 62-104.
Adeokun, Lawrence A.
"Fertility Inhibiting Effects of the Intermediate
Fertility Variables in Two Nigerian Sub-Groups." Genus.
Volume 41 #3-4 July-December, 1984. pp. 89-106.
Adeokun, Lawrence A.
"Lactation Abstinence in Family Building Among the Ekitis
of South-West Nigeria." Paper Presented at the National
Workshop on Population and Economic Development in
Nigeria in the 1980's. Lagos, Nigeria: University of
Lagos. Human Resource Unit. September 12-14, 1979.
Adeokun, Lawrence A.
"Lactation Abstinence in Family Building Among the Ekitis
of Southwest Nigeria." (In) Chojnacka, H. and Olusanya,
P.O. and Folayan, Ojo (eds.). Population and Economic
Development in Nigeria in the 1980's. New York: United
Nations. 1981. pp. 41-57.
Adeokun, Lawrence A.
"Marital Sexual Relationships and Birth Spacing Among Two
Yoruba Sub-Groups." Africa. Volume 52 #4 1982. pp.
1-14.
Adeokun, Lawrence A.
"Marital Sexuality and Birth Spacing Among the Yoruba."
(In) Oppong, Christine (ed.). Female and Male in West
Africa. London: George Allen and Unwin. 1983. pp.
127-137.
Adeokun, Lawrence A.
The Next Child: Spacing Strategies in Yorubaland.
Philadelphia, Pennsylvania: University of Pennsylvania.
Population Studies Center. African Demography Program.
Working Paper #8. September, 1981. 81p.

NIGERIA

Adepoju, Aderanti
"Migration and Fertility: A Case Study in South-West
Nigeria." (In) Oppong, C. and Adaba, G. and
Bekombo-Priso, M. and Mogey, J. (eds.). Marriage,
Fertility and Parenthood in West Africa. Canberra,
Australia: Australian National University. Department of
Demography. Volume Two. 1978. pp. 491-506.
Adepoju, Aderanti
"Migration, Employment and Fertility: A Case Study in
South-West Nigeria." Paper Presented to the 15th
International Seminar on Family Research. Lome, Togo.
1976.
Adepoju, Aderanti
"Rationality and Fertility in the Traditional Yoruba
Society, Southwest, Nigeria." (In) Caldwell, J.C. (ed.).
The Persistence of High Fertility: Population Prospects
in the Third World. Canberra, Australia: Australian
National University. Volume One. 1977. pp. 123-151.
Adeyemo, Remi
"Women in Rural Areas: A Case Study of Southwestern
Nigeria." Canadian Journal of African Studies. Volume
18 #3 1984. pp. 563-572.
Adeyeye, V.A.
"Women in Traditional Agriculture: Oyo State of Nigeria
Experience." MSc Thesis: University of Ibadan.
Department of Agricultural Economics. Ibadan, Nigeria.
1977.
Adeyokunnu (Adekanye), Tomilayo O.
Women and Agriculture in Nigeria. Addis Ababa, Ethiopia:
United Nations Economic Commission for Africa. African
Training and Research Centre for Women. 1980.
Adeyokunnu, Tomilayo O.
"Rural Development and the Position of Women in Africa:
Problems and Policies." Paper Presented at the Meeting
of the Experts on Research on the Status of Women,
Development and Population Trends: Evaluation and
Prospects. Paris: United Nations Educational, Scientific
and Cultural Organization. 1980. 32p.
Afigbo, A.E. and Nwabara, S.N.
"Black Civilization and the 'Population Crisis': A
Cultural Approach." Civilizations. Volume 26 #1-2 1976.
pp. 15-35.
Afonja, Simi A.
"Changing Modes of Production and the Sexual Division of
Labor Among the Yoruba." Signs. Volume 7 #2 Winter,
1981. pp. 299-313.
Afonja, Simi A.
"Current Explanations of Sex-Inequality: A
Reconsideration." Nigerian Journal of Economic and
Social Studies. Volume 21 #2 1981.
Afonja, Simi A.
"The Historical Evolution of the Sexual Division of Labor
in Nigeria." Paper Presented at the Meeting of Experts
on the Theoretical Frameworks and Methodological

324

Approaches to Studies on the Role of Women in History as Actors in Economic, Social, Political and Ideological Processes. Paris: United Nations Educational, Scientific and Cultural Organization. 1984. 20p.

Afonja, Simi A.
"Women, Power and Authority in Traditional Yoruba Society." (In) Dupe, Leela and Leacock, Eleanor and Ardener, Shirley (eds.). Viaibility and Power: Essays on Women in Society and Development. Delhi, India: Oxford University Press. 1983.

Agbamuche, Josephine N.
Customary Marriage in Akwukwu-Igbo. Lagos, Nigeria: Unicorn Enterprises. 1981. 14p.

Akande, Jadesola O.
Law and the Status of Women in Nigeria. Addis Ababa, Ethiopia: United Nations Economic Commission for Africa. African Training and Research Centre for Women. 1979. 77p.

Akingba, J.B.
"Abortion, Maternity and the Other Health Problems in Nigeria." Nigerian Medical Journal. Volume 7 #4 October, 1977. pp. 465-471.

Akinkoye, Olu
"Attitude to Child-Bearing by Single Nigerian Women." Nigerian Journal of Economic and Social Studies. Volume 26 #1 March, 1984.

Aluko, G.B. and Alfa, M.O.
"Marriage and Family." (In) Women in Nigeria Today. London: Zed Press. 1985. pp. 163-173.

Amechi, E.E.
"Woman-to-Woman Marriage: Its Legal Significance." Aman. Volume 1 #1 1981. pp. 20-35.

Ames, D.W. and Gourlay, K.A.
"Kimkim: A Women's Musical Pot." African Arts. Volume 11 #2 January, 1978. pp. 56-64+.

Anyanwu, S.U.
"Issues in and Patterns of Women's Participation of Sports in Nigeria." International Review of Sport Sociology. Volume 15 #1 1980. pp. 85-95.

Arinola, O.A.N.
"The Implications of Female Labour Force Participation on the Family: A Case Study of Some Factory Workers." B.Sc Dissertation: University of Ibadan. Department of Sociology. Ibadan, Nigeria. 1978.

Arowolo, Oladele O.
"Determinants of Fertility Among Yorubas of Nigeria." (In) Hyo-Chai, Lee. Recent Empirical Findings on Fertility: Korea, Nigeria, Tunisia, Venezuala, Philippines. Washington, D.C.: Smithsonian Institution. Interdisciplinary Communications Program. Occasional Monograph #7. 1976. pp. 27-45.

Arowolo, Oladele O.
"Female Labour Force Participation and Fertility: The

Case of Ibadan City in the Western State of Nigeria."
(In) Oppong, C. and Adaba, G. and Bekombo-Priso, M. and
Mogey, J. (eds.). Marriage, Fertility and Parenthood in
West Africa. Canberra, Australia: Australian National
University. Department of Demography. Volume Two.
1978. pp. 533-564.

Arowolo, Oladele O.
"Female Labour Force Participation and Fertility: The
Case of Ibadan City in the Western State of Nigeria."
Paper Presented at the Conference on Marriage, Parenthood
and Fertility in West Africa. 25th International Seminar
of the International Sociological Association. Lome,
Togo. January 3-9, 1976.

Arowolo, Oladele O.
"Fertility of Urban Yoruba Working Women: A Case Study of
Ibadan City." Nigerian Journal of Economic and Social
Studies. Volume 19 #1 March, 1977. pp. 37-66.

Awe, B.
"The Iyalode in the Traditional Yoruba Political System."
(In) Schlegel, Alice E. (ed.). Sexual Stratification: A
Cross-Cultural View. New York: Columbia University
Press. 1977. pp. 144-160.

Awosika, K.
"Women's Education and Participation in the Labour Force:
The Case of Nigeria." (In) Rendel, M. (ed.). Women,
Power and Political Systems. London: Croom Helm. 1981.
262p.

Ayangade, Okun
"Characteristics of Contraceptive Acceptors in an Urban
Nigerian Setting." International Journal of Gynaecology
and Obstetrics. Volume 22 1984. pp. 59-66.

Azuonye, Chukwma
"Women's Folklore in the Novels of Flora Nwapa: Its
Relevance to the Realistic Portrayal of the Igbo Woman."
Paper Presented at the 1981 African Literature
Association Conference. Baltimore, Maryland: University
of Maryland. African-American Studies Department. 1981.

Babatunde, E.D.
"Ketu Myths and the Status of Women: A Structural
Interpretation of Some Yoruba Myths of Origin." Journal
of the Anthropological Society of Oxford. Volume 14 #3
1983. pp. 301-306.

Ballay, Ute B.
"Women in Nigeria: Aspects of Social Transformation."
Africana Marburgensia. Volume 16 #2 1983. pp. 33-59.

Bamisaiye, Anne and Oyediran, M.A.
"Breast-Feeding Among Female Employees at a Major Health
Institution in Lagos, Nigeria." Social Science and
Medicine. Volume 17 #23 1983. pp. 1867-1871.

Bamisaiye, Anne and De Sweemer, Cecile and Ransome-Kuti,
Olikoye
"Developing a Clinic Strategy Appropriate to Community
Family Planning Needs and Practices." Studies in Family

Planning. Volume 9 #2-3 February-March, 1978. pp. 44-48.

Beckett, Paul A. and O'Connell, James O.
"Education and the Situation of Women: Background and Atttitudes of Christian and Muslim Female Students at a Nigerian University." Cultures et Developpement. Volume 8 #2 1976. pp. 242-265.

Benson, Susan and Duffield, Mark
"Women's Work and Economic Change: The Hausa in Sudan and in Nigeria." I.D.S. Bulletin. Volume 10 #9 June, 1979. pp. 13-19.

Berrian, Brenda F.
"African Women as Seen in the Works of Flora Nwapa and Ama Ata Aidoo." CLA Journal. Volume 25 #3 March, 1982. pp. 331-339.

Bongaarts, John
The Fertility Impact of Traditional and Changing Childspacing Practices in Tropical Africa. New York: Population Council. Center for Policy Studies. Working Paper #42. May, 1979. 27p.

Borgatti, Jean
"Songs of Ritual License From Midwestern Nigeria." Alcheringa. New Series Volume 2 1976. pp. 66-71.

Boyd, J.
"The Role of Women as Agents Religieux in Sokoto," Canadian Journal of African Studies. Volume 19 #2 1985.

Burfisher, Mary E. and Horenstein, Nadine R.
"Sex Roles and Development Effects on the Nigerian Tiv Farm Household." Rural Africana. #21 Winter, 1985. pp. 31-50.

Burfisher, Mary E. and Horenstein, Nadine R.
Sex Roles in the Nigerian Tiv Farm Household and the Differential Impacts of Development Projects. Washington D.C.: U.S. Department of Agriculture. International Economics Division. 1982.

Burfisher, Mary E. and Horenstein, Nadine R.
Sex Roles in the Nigerian Tiv Farm Household. West Hartford, Connecticut: Kumarian Press. Women's Roles and Gender Differences in Development, Cases for Planners. Volume 2. 1985. 62p.

Caldwell, John C. and Caldwell, Pat
"Cause and Sequence in the Reduction of Postnatal Abstinence in Ibadan City, Nigeria." (In) Page, Hilary J. and Lesthaeghe, Ron (eds.). Child-Spacing in Tropical Africa: Traditions and Change. New York: Acadenmic Press. 1981. pp. 181-199.

Caldwell, John C.
"Education as a Factor in Mortality Decline: An Examination of Nigerian Data." Population Studies. Volume 33 #3 November, 1979. pp. 395-413.

Caldwell, John C.
Fertility and Household Economy in Nigeria. Calgary, Canada: University of Calgary. 1976. 77p.

Caldwell, John C.
   "Fertility and the Household Economy in Nigeria."
   Journal of Comparative Family Studies. Volume 7 #2
   Summer, 1976. pp. 193-253.
Caldwell, John C.
   "Marriage, the Family and Fertility in Sub-Saharan Africa
   With Special Reference to Research Programmes in Ghana
   and Nigeria." (In) Huzayyin, S.A. and Acsadi, G.T.
   (eds.). Family and Marriage in Some African and Asian
   Countries. Cairo: Cairo Demographic Centre. CDC
   Research Monograph #6. 1976. pp. 359-371.
Caldwell, John C.
   "The Changing African Family Project: A Report With
   Special Reference to the Nigerian Segment." Canberra,
   Australia: Australian National University. 1976. 26p.
Caldwell, John C.
   "The Economic Rationality of High Fertility: An
   Investigation Illustrated With Nigerian Survey Data.
   Population Studies (London). Volume 31 #1 March, 1977.
   pp. 5-27.
Caldwell, John C. and Ware, Helen
   "The Evolution of Family Planning in an African City:
   Ibadan, Nigeria." Population Studies. Volume 31 #3
   November, 1977. pp. 487-508.
Caldwell, John C. and Caldwell, Pat
   "The Role of Marital Sexual Abstinence in Determining
   Fertility: A Study of the Yoruba of Nigeria." Population
   Studies. Volume 31 #2 July, 1977. pp. 193-217.
Caldwell, John C.
   "The Socio-Economic Explanation of High Fertility: Papers
   on the Yoruba Society of Nigeria." Canberra, Australia:
   Australian National University. Department of
   Demography. Changing African Family Project. Series #1.
   1976.
Caldwell, John C.
   Theory of Fertility Decline. New York: Academic Press.
   1982. 385p.
Caldwell, John C.
   "Variations in the Incidence of Sexual Abstinence and the
   Duration of Postnatal Abstinence Among the Yoruba of
   Nigeria." (In) Leridon, Henri and Menken, Jane (eds.).
   Natural Fertility. Patterns and Determinants of Natural
   Fertility: Proceedings of a Seminar on Natural Fertility.
   Liege, Belgium: International Union for the Scientific
   Study of Population. 1979. pp. 397-407.
Callaway, Barbara J.
   "Ambiguous Consequences of the Socialization and
   Seclusion of Hausa Women." Journal of Modern African
   Studies. Volume 22 #3 September, 1984. pp. 429-450.
Callaway, Barbara J. and Kleeman, Katherine E.
   "Women in Nigeria: Three Women of Kano: Modern Women and
   Traditional Life." Africa Report. Volume 30 #2
   March-April, 1985. pp. 26-29.

Callaway, Helen
"Women in Yoruba Tradition and in the Cherubim and
Seraphim Society." (In) Kalu, O.U. (ed.). The History
of Christianity in West Africa. New York: Longman.
1980. pp. 321-332.

Chalifoux, Jean-Jacques
"Secondary Marriage and Levels of Seniority Among the
Abisi (Pitti) Nigeria." Journal of Comparative Family
Studies. Volume 11 #3 Special Issue 1980. pp. 325-334.

Clarke, Peter
"Birom Women Evangelist, Vo Gyang of Forum (FL.
1927-1929)." (In) Isichei, Elizabeth (ed.). Varieties
of Chrisitan Experience in Nigeria. London: MacMillan
Press Ltd. 1982. pp. 163-176.

Cobbald, Elizabeth
"Muslim Hausa Women in Northern Nigeria: An Annotated
Bibliography." African Research and Documentation.
Volume 32 1983. pp. 22-29.

Cohen, Ronald
"How to Grow Feet Out of Your Ears When You Land on Your
Head: Validity in African Survey." (In) Marshall, John
F. and Polgar, Steven (eds.). Culture, Natality and
Family Planning. Chapel Hill, North Carolina: University
of North Carolina. Carolina Population Center. 1976.
pp. 288-301.

Coles, Catherine M.
"Muslim Women in Town: Social Change Among the Hausa of
Northern Nigeria." Ph.D Dissertation: University of
Wisconsin-Madison. Madison, Wisconsin. 1983. 556p.

Coles, Catherine M.
"Urban Muslim Women and Social Change in Northern
Nigeria." Paper Presented at the Annual Meeting of the
African Studies Association. Paper #20. Washington,
D.C. November 4-7, 1982.

Coles, Catherine M.
Urban Muslim Women and Social Change in Northern
Nigeria. East Lansing, Michigan: Michigan State
University. Office of Women in International
Development. Working Paper #19. March, 1983. 28p.

Copley, Anthony
"The Debate on Widow Remarriage and Polygamy: Aspects of
Moral Change in 19th Century Bengal and Yorubaland."
Journal of Imperial and Commonwealth History. Volume 7
#2 January, 1979. pp. 128-148.

Csapo, Marg
"Religious, Social and Economic Factors Hindering the
Education of Girls in Northern Nigeria." Comparative
Education. Volume 17 #3 1981. pp. 311-319.

Daly, Catherine
"On Display: Prescribed Aesthetics Among Kalabari
Females." Paper Presented at the Annual Meeting of the
African Studies Association. Paper #28. Bloomington,
Indiana. October 21-24, 1981.

Daly, Mary C.
"Kalabari Female Appearance and the Tradition of Iria."
Ph.D Dissertation: University of Minnesota. Minneapolis,
Minnesota. 1984. 204p.

Demehin, Ade O.
"Sexual Attitudes in Traditional and Modern Yoruba
Society." International Quarterly of Community Health
and Education. Volume 4 #3 1983. pp. 231-238.

Denga, Daniel I.
"Childlessness and Marital Adjustment in Northern
Nigeria." Journal of Marriage and Family. Volume 44 #3
August, 1979. pp. 799-802.

Dennis, Carolyne
"Women and Development: What Kind of Development?" Paper
Presented at the National Conference on Nigerian Women
and Development in Relation to Changing Family Structure.
Ibadan, Nigeria. University of Ibadan. 1976.

Di Domenico, Catherine M. and Burdin, J.M.
"Breastfeeding Practices Among Urban Women in Ibadan,
Nigeria." (In) Raphael, D. (ed.). Breastfeeding and
Food Policy in a Hungry World. New York: Academic Press.
1979.

Di Domenico, Catherine M. and Asuni, Judy and Scott,
Jacqueline
"Changing Status of African Women: An Exploratory Study
of Working Mothers in Ibadan, Nigeria." (In)
International Planned Parenthood Federation (IPPF).
Proceedings of the IPPF Africa Regional Conference.
London: IPPF. 1977. pp. 283-284.

Di Domenico, Catherine M. and Majuetan, L. Lacey
"Female Industrial Recruits: Women Workers at the
Nigerian Tobacco Company Factory at Ibadan." Paper
Presented at the National Conference on Nigerian Women
and Development in Relation to Changing Family Structure.
Ibadan, Nigeria: University of Ibadan. April 26-30,
1976.

Di Domenico, Catherine M. and Lacey-Mojuetan, Linda
"Occupational Status of Women in Nigeria: A Comparison of
Two Urban Centres." Paper Presented at the Conference on
Nigerian Women and Development in Relation to Changing
Family Structure. Ibadan, Nigeria: University of Ibadan.
Department of Sociology. April 26-30, 1976. 13p.

Di Domenico, Catherine M. and Lacey-Mojuetan, Linda
"Occupational Status of Women in Nigeria: A Comparison of
Two Urban Centres." Africana Marburgensia. Volume 10 #2
1977. pp. 62-79.

Dow, Thomas E.
"Breast Feeding and Abstinence Among the Yoruba."
Studies in Family Planning. Volume 8 #8 August, 1977.
pp. 208-214.

Dow, Thomas E.
  Breast-Feeding, Abstinence, and Family Planning Among the
  Yoruba and Other Sub-Saharan Groups: Patterns and Policy
  Implications. Purchase, New York: State University of
  New York. Department of Sociology. 1978.
Doyle, Pat and Morley, David and Woodland, Margaret and
Cole, Jane J.
  "Birth Intervals, Survival and Growth in a Nigerian
  Village." Journal of Biosocial Science. Volume 10 #1
  January, 1978. pp. 81-94.
Drewal, Henry J.
  "Art and Perception of Women in Yoruba Culture." Cahiers
  d'Etudes Africaines. Volume 17 #4 1977. pp. 545-567.
Drewal, Henry J. and Drewal, Margaret T.
  G.EL.ED.E: Art and Female Power Among the Yoruba.
  Bloomington, Indiana: Indiana University Press.
  Traditional Arts of Africa Series. 1983. 306p.
Durojaiye, Michael O.
  "The Changing Family in the Nigerian Context." Paper
  Presented at the Seminar on the Changing Family in the
  African Context. Paris: United Nations Educational,
  Scientific and Cultural Organization. Maseru, Lesotho.
  1984. 7p.
Edeh, J.
  "Abortion and the Law in Nigeria: A Psychiatrists View."
  Nigerian Medical Journal. Volume 9 #5/6 1979. pp.
  631-634.
Edigbo, P.O. and Chukudebelu, W.O.
  "Child Spacing and Child Mortality Among Nigerian Ibos."
  International Journal of Gynaecology and Obstetrics.
  Volume 18 #5 1980. pp. 372-374.
Ekanem, Ita I. and Uche, Chukwudum
  "Knowledge, Attitude and Practice of Family Planning in
  Eastern Nigeria: Implications and Prospects." Odu.
  Volume 17 #1 1978. pp. 36-63.
Ekanem, Ita I. and Farooq, Ghazi M.
  "The Dynamics of Population Change in Southern Nigeria."
  Genus. Volume 33 #1/2 1977. pp. 119-140.
Ekanem, Ita I.
  "Ways of Controlling Family Size: A Case Study of Eastern
  Nigeria." (In) Oppong, C. and Adaba, G. and
  Bekombo-Priso, M. and Mogey, J. (eds.). Marriage,
  Fertility and Parenthood in West Africa. Canberra,
  Australia: Australian National University. Department of
  Demography. Volume Two. 1978. pp. 691-715.
Ekejiuba, Felicia
  "Contemporary Households and Major Socioeconomic
  Transitions in Eastern Nigeria: Towards a
  Reconceptualization of the Household." Paper Presented
  at the Conferemce on Conceptualizing the Household.
  Cambridge, Massachusetts: Harvard University. November,
  1984.

Ekpere, J.A. and Oyedipe, F.P. and Adegboye, R.O.
"Family Role Differentiation Within the Kwara Nomadic
Fulani." (In) Oppong, C. and Adaba, G. and
Bekombo-Priso, M. and Mogey, J. (eds.). Marriage,
Fertility and Parenthood in West Africa. Canberra,
Australia: Australian National University. Department of
Demography. Volume One. 1978. pp. 55-67.

Elegbe, Isaac A. and Elegbe, Iyabode
"Quantitive Relationships of Candida Albicans Infections
and Dressing Patterns in Nigerian Women." American
Journal of Public Health. Volume 73 April, 1983. pp.
450-452.

Emeagwali, G.T.
"Women in Pre-Capitalistic Socio-Economic Formations in
Nigeria." (In) Women in Nigeria. London: Zed Press.
1985. pp. 52-55.

Erekosima, Tonye V.
"The 'Tartans' of Buguma Women: Cultural Authentication."
Paper Presented at the Annual Meeting of the African
Studies Association. Paper #39. Los Angeles,
California. 1979. 24p.

Essien, Ruth A.
"Perceptions of Nigerian College Students Toward the Role
of Women in Nigerian Development." Ph.D Dissertation:
University of Southern California. Los Angeles,
California. 1981. 214p.

Fadayomi, T.O. and Adelola, I.O. and Oni, B. and Omogbehin,
V.A. and Egbunike, N.A.
The Role of Working Mothers in Early Childhood Education:
A Nigerian Case Study. Paris: UNESCO. Nigerian
Institute of Social and Economic Research. February,
1978. 68p.

Fagbemi, S.
"Occupational and Familial Role Conflicts of Working
Women: A Case Study of the Lafia Canning Factory,
Ibadan." BSc Dissertation: University of Ibadan,
Department of Sociology. Ibadan, Nigeria. 1978.

Fapohunda, Eleanor R.
"Women at Work in Nigeria: Factors Affecting Modern
Sector Employment." (In) Damachi, U.G. and Diejomaoh,
V.P. (eds.). Human Resources and African Development.
New York: Praeger Publishers. 1978. pp. 225-238.

Fapohunda, Olanrewaju J. and Fapohunda, Eleanor R.
The Working Mothers of Lagos. Washington, D.C.:
Smithsonian Institution. Interdisciplinary
Communications Committee. Report of a Study. 1976.

Fardon, Richard
"Sisters, Wives, Wards and Daughters: A Transformational
Analysis of the Political Organization of the Tiv and
Their Neighbors." Part One. Africa. Volume 54 #4 1984.
pp. 2-21.

Fardon, Richard
"Sisters, Wives, Wards and Daughters: A Transformational
Analysis of the Political Organization of the Tiv and
Their Neighbors." Part Two. Africa. Volume 55 #1 1985.
pp. 77-91.
Farooq, Ghazi M. and Ekanem, Ita I. and Ojelade, M.A.
Family Size Preferences and Fertility in South-Western
Nigeria. Geneva: International Labour Office. World
Employment Programme Research. Population and Employment
Working Paper #54. May, 1977. 33p.
Farooq, Ghazi M. and Ojelade, Mukaila A. and Ekanem, Ita I.
"Family Size Preferences and Fertility in Southern
Nigeria." Pula. Volume 2 #2 February, 1983. pp.
83-111.
Farooq, Ghazi M.
Household Fertility Decision-Making in Nigeria. Geneva:
International Labour Organization. Population and Labour
Policies Branch. Employment and Development Working
Paper #75A. 1980.
Farooq, Ghazi M.
"Household Fertility Decision-Making in Nigeria." (In)
Farooq, Ghazi M. and Simmons, George B. (eds.).
Fertility in Developing Countries: An Economic
Perspective on Research and Policy Issues. New York: St.
Martin's Press. 1985. pp. 312-350.
Farooq, Ghazi M. and Adeokun, Lawrence A.
"Impact of Rural Family Planning Program in Ishan,
Nigeria, 1969-1972." Studies in Family Planning. Volume
7 #6 June, 1976. pp. 158-169.
Favi, F.
Women's Role in Economic Development: A Case Study of
Villages in Oyo State. Ibadan, Nigeria: University of
Ibadan. Department of Agricultural Extension. Ibadan,
Nigeria. 1977.
Foss, Susan M.
"She Who Sits as King: Celebrations for Young Urhobo
Women." African Arts. Volume 12 #2 February, 1979.
pp. 44-50.
Franklin, Jopseph
African: A Photographic Essay on Black Women of Ghana and
Nigeria. Sebastopol, California: Wallingford Books,
Chulainn Press. 1977. 137p.
Grossbard, Amyra
"An Economic Analysis of Polygyny: The Case of
Maiduguri." Current Anthropology. Volume 17 #4
December, 1976. pp. 701-707.
Guyer, Jane I.
"Food, Cocoa, and the Division of Labour by Sex in Two
West African Societies." Comparative Studies in Society
and History. Volume 22 #3 July, 1980. pp. 355-370.
Harrington, Judith A.
"Education, Female Status and Fertility in Nigeria."

Paper Presented to the Population Association of America.
Atlanta, Georgia. 1978.

Harrington, Judith A.
"Nutritional Stress and Economic Responsibility: A Study
of Nigerian Women." (In) Buvinic, Mayra and Lycette,
Margaret A. and McGreevey, William P. (eds.). Women and
Poverty in the Third World. Baltimore, Maryland: Johns
Hopkins University. 1983. pp. 130-156.

Harrington, Judith A.
"Some Micro-Socioeconomics of Female Status in Nigeria."
Paper Presented at the Conference: Women in Poverty: What
do We Know?. Washington, D.C.: International Centre for
Research on Women. 1978.

Harrington, Judith A.
Education, Female Status and Fertility in Nigeria. Ann
Arbor, Michigan: University of Michigan. School of
Public Health. Department of Population Planning. 1978.

Haynes, J.
"Some Notes on the Image of 'Women' in Some African
Poems." (In) Women in Nigeria Today. London: Zed Press.
1985. pp. 217-225.

Hendrixson, Joyce
"Islam and the Changing Position of Women in Sokoto:
Appearance and Reality." Paper Presented at the Annual
Meeting of the African Studies Association. Paper #42.
Philadelphia, Pennsylvania. 1980.

Hendrixson, Joyce
"Women and Class Structures in Sokoto." Paper Presented
at the Annual Meeting of the African Studies Association.
Paper #51. Bloomington, Indiana. October 21-24, 1981.

Hill, Polly
"Women's House Trade." (In) Hill, Polly. Population,
Prosperity and Poverty: Rural Kano, 1900 and 1970.
Cambridge, New York: Cambridge University Press. 1977.
240p.

Hoch-Smith, Judith
"Radical Yoruba Female Sexuality: The Witch and the
Prostitute." (In) Hoch-Smith, Judith and Spring, Anita
(eds.). Women in Ritual and Symbolic Roles. New York:
Plenum Press. 1978. pp. 245-267.

Hundung, Martha and Igoche, George
"Integrating Conscientization Into a Program for
Illiteracy, Women in Nigeria." Convergence. Volume 13
#1/2 January-February, 1980. pp. 110-117.

Ifeka-Moller, Caroline
"Female Militancy and Colonial Revolt: The Women's War of
1929, Eastern Nigeria." (In) Ardener, S. (ed.).
Perceiving Women. New York: Halsted Press. 1977. pp.
127-157.

Ifeka-Moller, Caroline
"Racial Categories and Sexual Images in Colonial

Nigeria." Paper Presented at the Meeting of the African
Studies Association of the United Kingdom. 1978. 16p.
Ikonne, Chidi
"Women in Igbo Folktales." Paper Presented at the 1982
African Literature Association Conference. Baltimore,
Maryland: Univerisity of Maryland. African-American
Studies Department. 1982.
Ilori, Felicia
Factors Determining Rural-Urban Fertility Differentials
in Western Nigeria: A Case Study of Ife, Ilesha and
Selected Rural Areas in Oyo Province. Ife, Nigeria:
University of Ife. 1976.
Ipaye, Babatunde
"A Psycho-Demographic View of the Changing Family Within
the African Context." Paper Presented at the Seminar on
the Changing Family in the African Context, 1983. Paris:
United Nations Educational, Scientific and Cultural
Organization. Maseru, Lesotho. 1984. 26p.
Iro, M.I.
"Social Correlates of Divorce Among Lagos Elites Who
Married in Nigeria." (In) Oppong, C. and Adaba, G. and
Bekombo-Priso, M. and Mogey, J. (eds.). Marriage,
Fertility and Parenthood in West Africa. Canberra,
Australia: Australian National University. Department of
Demography. Volume One. 1978. pp. 399-406.
Iro, M.I.
"The Pattern of Elite Divorce in Lagos: 1961-1973."
Journal of Marriage and the Family. Volume 38 #1
February, 1976. pp. 177-182.
Ityavar, Dennis A.
"A Traditional Midwife Practice, Sokoto State, Nigeria."
Social Science and Medicine. Volume 18 #6 1984. pp.
497-501.
Jackson, C.
"Hausa Women and Agricultural Change on the Kano River
Project, Nigeria." (In) Adams, W.M. and Grove, A.T.
(eds.). Irrigation in Tropical Africa: Problems and
Problem Solving. Cambridge, England: Cambridge
University. African Studies Center. 1984. pp. 67-74.
Jackson, S.
"Hausa Women on Strike." Review of African Political
Economy. #13 1978. pp. 21-36.
Johnson, B.C.
"Female Circumcision in Nigeria." Paper Presented at the
Seminar on Traditional Practices Affecting the Health of
Women and Children: Female Circumcision, Childhood
Marriage, Nutritional Taboos, etc. Alexandria, Egypt:
World Health Organization. Eastern Mediterranean
Regional Office. Khartoum, Sudan. February 10-15, 1979.
Jones, Gavin and Lucas, David W.
"Some Sociocultural Factors Affecting Female Labour Force
Participation in Jakarta and Lagos." Labour Capital and
Society. Volume 12 #2 November, 1979. pp. 19-52.

Karanja, Wambui W.
    "Conjugal Decision-Making: Some Data From Lagos." (In)
    Oppong, Christine (ed.). Female and Male in West Africa.
    London: George Allen and Unwin. 1983. pp. 236-241.
Kasunmu, A.B.
    "Economic Consequences of Divorce: A Case Study of Some
    Judicial Decisions in Lagos." (In) Roberts, Simon (ed.).
    Law and the Family in Africa. Hague, Netherlands:
    Mouton. 1977. pp. 129-143.
Knowles, C.
    "Women Under Development: Some Preliminary Remarks."
    (In) Women in Nigeria Today. London: Zed Press. 1985.
    pp. 68-81.
Ladipo, Patricia A. and Adegoke, M.O.
    "An Assessment of Rural Women's Agricultural Roles and
    Needs: Implications for Home Economics Extension
    Curriculum." Paper Presented at the Workshop on the Role
    of Women and Home Economics in Rural Development in
    Africa. Rome: United Nations Food and Agricultural
    Organization. Alexandria, Egypt. October 17, 1983.
    12p.
LeVine, Robert A.
    "Influences of Women's Schooling on Maternal Behavior in
    the Third World." Comparative Education Review. Volume
    24 #2 Part Two June, 1980. pp. S78-S105.
Lesthaeghe, Ron J. and Page, Hilary J. and Adegbola, O.
    "Child-Spacing and Fertility in Lagos." (In) Page,
    Hilary J. and Lesthaeghe, Ron (eds.). Child-Spacing in
    Tropical Africa: Traditions and Change. New York:
    Academic Press. 1981. pp. 147-179.
Longhurst, Richard
    "Resource Allocation and the Sexual Division of Labor: A
    Case Study of a Moslem Hausa Village in Northern
    Nigeria." (In) Beneria, Lourdes (ed.). Women and
    Development: The Sexual Division of Labor in Rural
    Societies: A Study. New York: Praeger Publishers.
    Praeger Special Studies. 1982. pp. 95-117.
Longhurst, Richard
    "Rural Development Planning and the Sexual Division of
    Labour: A Case Study of a Moslem Hausa Village in
    Northern Nigeria." (In) International Labour
    Organization (ILO). Rural Development and Women in
    Africa. Geneva: ILO. 1984. pp. 117-122.
Longhurst, Richard
    Rural Development Planning and the Sexual Division of
    Labour: A Case Study of a Moslem Village in Northern
    Nigeria. Geneva: International Labour Organization.
    World Employment Programme Research Working Paper.
    Mimeograph #10. 1980.
Longhurst, Richard
    The Provision of Basic Needs for Women: A Case Study of a
    Hausa Village in Nigeria. Geneva: International Labour
    Organization. Draft Report. 1977.

Lucas, David W. and Ukaegbu, Alfred O.
"Other Limits of Acceptable Family Size in Southern
Nigeria." Journal of Biosocial Science. Volume 9 #1
January, 1977. pp. 73-82.

Lucas, David W.
"Urban and Rural Fertility in Southern Nigeria." (In)
Ruzicka, Lado T. (ed.). The Economic and Social Supports
for High Fertility: Proceedings of the Conference. 1976.
Canberra, Australia: Australian National University.
Development Studies Center. Canberra, Australia.
November 16-19, 1977. pp. 409-435.

MacLean, Una
"Folk Medicine and Fertility: Aspects of Yoruba Medical
Practice Affecting Women." (In) MacCormack, C.P. (ed.).
Ethnography of Fertility and Birth. London: Academic
Press. 1982. pp. 161-179.

Mack, Beverly B.
"'Waka Daya Ba Ta Kare Nika' One Song Will Not Finish the
Grinding: Hausa Women's Oral Literature." Paper
Presented at the 1981 African Literature Association
Conference. Baltimore, Maryland: University of Maryland.
African-American Studies Department. 1981.

Mack, Beverly B.
"Waka Daya Ba Ta Kare Nika'--One Song Will Not Finish the
Grinding: Hausa Women's Oral Literature." (In) Wylie,
Hal (ed.). Contemporary African Literature. Washington,
D.C.: Three Continents. 1983. pp. 15-46.

Mack, Beverly B.
"Wakokin Mata: Huasa Women's Oral Poetry." Ph.D
Dissertation: University of Wisconsin-Madison. Madison,
Wisconsin. 1981. 328p.

Mack, Delores E.
"Husbands and Wives in Lagos: The Effects of
Socioeconomic Status on the Patterns of Family Living."
Journal of Marriage and the Family. Volume 40 #4
November, 1978. pp. 807-816.

Madunagu, B.E.
"Contemporary Positions and Experiences of Women." (In)
Women in Nigeria Today. London: Zed Press. 1985. pp.
132-137.

Mangvwat, Joyce A.
"Home Economics in Northern Nigeria: An Historical Study,
1842-1980." Ph.D Dissertation: University of
Wisconsin-Madison. Madison, Wisconsin. 1981. 150p.

Mann, Kristin
"Marriage Choices Among the Educated African Elite in
Lagos Colony, 1880-1915." International Journal of
African Historical Studies. Volume 14 #2 1981. pp.
210-228.

Mann, Kristin
Marrying Well: Status and Social Change Among the
Educated Elite in Colonial Lagos. Cambridge, England:

Cambridge University Press. African Studies Series #47.
1985. 194p.

Mann, Kristin
"The Dangers of Dependence: Chrisitian Marriage Among the
Elite Women in Lagos Colony, 1880-1915." Journal of
African History. Volume 24 #1 1983. pp. 37-56.

Mann, Kristin
"The Dangers of Dependence: The Response of Educated
Christian Women in Lagos Colony to Western Marriage."
Paper Presented at the Annual Meeting of the African
Studies Association. Los Angeles, California. October,
1979.

Mann, Kristin
"Women's Rights in Law and Practice: Marriage and Dispute
Settlement in Colonial Lagos." (In) Hay, Margaret J. and
Wright, Marcia (eds.). African Women and the Law:
Historical Perspectives. Boston: Boston University.
African Studies Center. Boston University Papers on
Africa. Volume 7. 1982. pp. 151-171.

Martin, S.
"Gender and Innovation--Farming, Cooking and Palm
Processing in the Ngwa Region, Southeastern Nigeria,
1900-1930." Journal of African History. Volume 25 #4
1984. pp. 411-427.

Mba, Nina E.
"Funmilayo Ransome-Kuti: Continuity and Change in Yoruba
Women's Political Action." Paper Presented at the Annual
Meeting of the African Studies Association. Paper #56.
Washington, D.C. November 4-7, 1982.

Mba, Nina E.
Nigerian Women Mobilized: Women's Political Activity in
Southern Nigeria, 1900-1965. Berkeley, California:
University of California. Institute of International
Studies. Research Series #48. 1982. 348p.

Mba, Nina E.
"Women and Work in Nigeria: An Historical Perspective."
(In) Sanabary, Nagat E. (ed.). Women and World in the
Third World: The Impact of Industrialization and Global
Economic Interdependence. Berkeley, California:
University of California. Center for the Study,
Education and Advancement of Women. 1983.

Mba, Nina E.
"Women in Southern Nigerian Political History,
1900-1965." Ph.D. Dissertation: University of Ibadan.
Ibadan, Nigeria. 1978.

Megafu, U.
"Female Ritual Circumcision in Africa: An Investigation
of the Presumed Benefits Among the Ibos of Nigeria."
East African Medical Journal. Volume 60 #11 1983. pp.
793-800.

Meldrum, Brenda and Di Domenico, Catherine M.
"Production and Reproduction: Women and Breastfeeding:

Some Nigerian Examples." Social Science and Medicine.
Volume 16 #13 1982. pp. 1247-1251.

Meldrum, Brenda
"Traditional Child-Rearing Practices of the Oje Market
Women of Ibadan." (In) Curran, H. Valerie (ed.).
Nigerian Children: Developmental Perspectives. Boston:
Routledge and Kegan Paul. 1984. pp. 174-196.

Mohammed, A.
'Home Outside the Home' (A Sociological Conception of
Prostitution Among the Hausa). Kano, Nigeria: Bayero
University. Department of Sociology. Seminar Paper.
1980.

Mohammed, H.D.
"Women in Nigerian History: Examples From Borno Empire,
Nupeland, and Igboland." (In) Women in Nigeria Today.
London: Zed Press. 1985. pp. 45-51.

Morgan, Robert W.
"Yoruban Modernization and Fertility in Lagos." (In)
Morgan, Robert W. New Perspectives on the Demographic
Transition. Washington, D.C.: Smithsonian Institution.
Interdisciplinary Communications Program. Occasional
Monograph #4. 1976. pp. 1-51.

Morton-Williams, Peter
"Family Structures in an Egbado Yoruba Community." (In)
Oppong, C. and Adaba, G. and Bekombo-Priso, M. and Mogey,
J. (eds.). Marriage, Fertility and Parenthood in West
Africa. Canberra, Australia: Australian National
University. Department of Demography. Volume One.
1978. pp. 69-102.

Mott, Frank L. and Mott, Susan H. (eds.)
"Household Fertility Decisions in West Africa--A
Comparison of Male and Female Survey Results." Studies
in Family Planning. Volume 16 #2 March-April, 1985.
pp. 88-99.

Mudambi, Sumati
"Interrelationships Between Family Structure and Family
Resources in Eastern Nigeria." Journal of Family
Welfare. Volume 26 #3 March, 1980. pp. 13-26.

Muller, Jean-Claude
"On Bridewealth and Meaning Among the Rukuba, Plateau
State, Nigeria." Africa. Volume 48 #2 1978. pp.
161-175.

Muller, Jean-Claude
"On the Relevance of Having Two Husbands: Contribution to
the Study of Polygynous/Polyandrous Marital Forms of the
Jos Plateau." Journal of Comparative Family Studies.
Volume 11 #3 Special Issue. Summer, 1980. pp. 359-369.

Musa, Ayuba Z.
"Assessment of Societal Perceptions and Attitudes Toward
Marriage and Educated Hausa Women in the Northern States
of Nigeria." Ph.D Dissertation: Ohio State University.
Columbus, Ohio. 1981. 178p.

Mustapha, A.R.
   "On Combating Women's Exploitation and Oppression in
   Nigeria." (In) Women in Nigeria Today. London: Zed
   Press. 1985. pp. 241-246.
Myers, Robert A.
   "Circumcision: Its Nature and Practice Among Some Ethnic
   Groups in Southern Nigeria." Social Science and
   Medicine. Volume 21 #5 1985. pp. 581-588.
Naghma, E. Rehan and McFarlane, Hildegarde P. and Sani, Sule
   "Profile of Contraceptive Clients in Katsina, Northern
   Nigeria." Journal of Biosocial Science. Volume 16 #4
   October, 1984. pp. 427-436.
Nevadomsky, J.
   "Motivations of Married Women to Higher Education in
   Nigeria." International Journal of Women's Studies.
   Volume 4 #5 1981.
Nwankwo, Joyce N.
   "A Comparison of Responses of Unmarried Nigerian Final
   Year University Male and Female Students to Factors That
   Affect Mate Selection." Ph.D Dissertation: University of
   Iowa. Iowa City, Iowa. 1981. 139p.
Obadina, E.
   "How Relevant is the Western Women's Liberation Movement
   for Nigeria?" (In) Women in Nigeria Today. London: Zed
   Press. 1985. pp. 138-142.
Oduyoye, Mercy A.
   "Standing on Both Feet: Education and Leadership Training
   of Women in the Methodist Church, Nigeria." Ecumenical
   Review. Volume 33 #1 January, 1981. pp. 60-71.
Offiong, Daniel A.
   "Social Relations and Witch Beliefs Among the Ibibio of
   Nigeria." Journal of Anthropological Research. Volume
   39 #1 1983. pp. 81-95.
Offiong, Daniel A.
   "Social Relations and Witch Beliefs Among the Ibibio."
   Africa. Volume 53 #3 1983. pp. 73-82.
Offiong, Daniel A.
   "The 1978-79 Akpan Ekwong Anti-Witchcraft Crusade in
   Nigeria." Anthropologica. Volume 24 #1 1982. pp.
   27-42.
Offiong, Daniel A.
   "Witchcraft Among the Ibibio of Nigeria." African
   Studies Review. Volume 26 #1 March, 1983. pp. 91-106.
Ogbeide, D.O. and Edebiri, A.A.
   "A Two Year Study of Organised Family Planning Services
   in a Developing Country: Experiences in Bendel State of
   Nigeria." East African Medical Journal. Volume 61 #6
   June, 1984. pp. 470-476.
Ogum, G.E.O.
   "Fertility Differentials in Nigeria." Genus. Volume 36
   #3/4 July-December, 1980. pp. 203-213.
Ogum, G.E.O. and Okorafor, A.E.
   "Seasonality of Births in South-Eastern Nigeria."

Journal of Biosocial Science. Volume 11 #2 April, 1979. pp. 209-218.

Ogundipe-Leslie, Molara
"Nigeria: Not Spinning on the Axis." (In) Morgan, Robin (ed.). Sisterhood is Global. Garden City, New York: Anchor Books. 1984. pp. 494-504.

Ogundipe-Leslie, Molara
"Women in Nigeria." (In) Women in Nigeria Today. London: Zed Press. 1985. pp. 119-131.

Ogunsheye, F. Aetowun and Awosika, Keziah and Dennis, Carolyn and Didomenko, Catherine and Akinkoye, O.
Nigerian Women and Development. Ibadan, Nigeria: University of Nigeria. 1982.

Ojelade, Mukaila A.
"The Socioeconomic Determinants of Fertility Behavior and Attitude in Southwest Nigeria, 1971-1973." Ph.D Dissertation: University of Pennsylvania. Philadelphia, Pennsylvania. 1982. 273p.

Ojoade, J.O.
"African Sexual Proverbs--Some Yoruba Examples." Folklore. Volume 94 #2 1983. pp. 201-213.

Okediji, Frances O. and Caldwell, John C. and Caldwell, Pat and Ware, Helen
"The Changing African Family Project: A Report With Special Reference to the Nigerian Segment." Studies in Family Planning. Volume 7 #5 May, 1976. pp. 126-136.

Okediji, Francis O. and Caldwell, John C. and Caldwell, Pat and Ware, Helen
"The Changing African Family Project: A Report With Special Reference to the Nigerian Segment." (In) Oppong, C. and Adaba, G. and Bekombo-Priso, M. and Mogey, J. (eds.). Marriage, Fertility and Parenthood in West Africa. Canberra, Australia: Australian National University. Department of Demography. 1978. pp. 717-746.

Okeke, Chukwuanugo S.
"Wrapper Designs for the Nigerian Market: Design Features of Igbo Women's Wrapper." Nigeria Magazine. #142 1982. pp. 29-43.

Okojie, Christiana E.E.
"Determinants of Labour Force Participation of Urban Women in Nigeria: A Case Study of Benin City." Nigerian Journal of Economic and Social Studies. Volume 25 #1 1983. pp. 39-59.

Okojie, S.E.
"Induced Illegal Abortions in Benin City, Nigeria." International Journal of Gynaecology and Obstetrics. Volume 14 #6 1976. pp. 517-521.

Okonjo, Isabel K.
"The Role of Women in Social Change Among The Igbo of Southeastern Nigeria Living West of the River Niger."

Ph.D Dissertation: Boston University. Boston,
Massachusetts. 1976. 220p.
Okonjo, Kamene
   "Sex Roles in Nigerian Politics." (In) Oppong, Christine
   (ed.). Female and Male in West Africa. London: George
   Allen and Unwin. 1983. pp. 211-222.
Okonjo, Kamene
   "The Dual-Sex Political System in Operation: Igbo Women
   and Community Politics in Midwestern Nigeria." (In)
   Hafkin, N.J. and Bay, Edna G. (eds.). Women in Africa:
   Studies in Social and Economic Change. Stanford,
   California: Stanford University Press. 1976. pp. 45-58.
Okonjo, Kamene
   "Women's Political Participation in Nigeria." (In)
   Steady, Filomina C. (ed.). The Black Woman
   Cross-Culturally. Cambridge, Massachusetts: Schenkman
   Publishing. 1981. pp. 79-106.
Okore, Augustine O.
   "Rural-Urban Fertility Differentials in Southern Nigeria:
   An Assessment of Some Available Evidence." Population
   Studies. Volume 34 #1 March, 1980. pp. 171-179.
Okore, Augustine O.
   "The Ibos of Arochukwu in the Imo State, Nigeria." (In)
   Caldwell, John C. (ed.). The Persistence of High
   Fertility: Population Prospects in the Third World.
   Canberra, Australia: Australian National University.
   Volume One. 1977. pp. 313-330.
Okore, Augustine O.
   "The Rationale of High Fertility in Rural Nigeria: The
   Case of Ibos in Arochukwu in Iwo State." (In) Ruzicka,
   Lado T. (ed.). The Economic and Social Supports for High
   Fertility: Proceedings of the Conference. Canberra,
   Australia: Australian National University. Development
   Studies Center. November 16-18, 1977. pp. 253-274.
Omideyi, Adekunbi K.
   "Age at Marriage and Marital Fertility in Eastern
   Nigeria." Genus. Volume 39 #1-4 January-December,
   1983. pp. 141-154.
Omideyi, Adekunbi K.
   "The Persistence of High Fertility in Eastern Nigeria: An
   Analysis Based Upon a Sample Survey of Married Women in
   1971-72." Ph.D Dissertation: University of London.
   London School of Economics. London, England. 1983.
   403p.
Omojayowo, Akin
   "Mother in Israel: Chridtianah Olatunrinle in Ondo (c.
   1855-1941)." (In) Isichei, Elizabeth (ed.). Varieties
   of Christian Experience in Nigeria. London: MacMillan
   Press Ltd. 1982. pp. 141-148.
Omu, A.E. and Oronsaye, A.U. and Faal, M.K. and Asuquo, E.E.
   "Adolescent Induced Abortion in Benin City, Nigeria."

International Journal of Gynaecology and Obstetrics.
Volume 19 #6   December, 1981.   pp. 495-499.
Onadeko, M.O.
"Female Circumcision in Nigeria: A Fact or a Farce?"
Journal of Tropical Pediatrics.   Volume 31 #4   August,
1981.   pp. 180-184.
Oni, Gbolahan A.
"Effects of Women's Education on Postpartum Practices and
Fertility in Urban Nigeria."   Studies in Family Planning.
Volume 16 #6 Part One   November-December, 1985.   pp.
321-331.
Onwuazor, Sammy N.
"Continuity and Change: Abortion and Family Size in a
Nigerian Village."   (In) Epstein, T. Scarlett and
Jackson, Darrell (eds.).   The Feasibility of Fertility
Planning: Micro Perspectives.   Oxford, England: Pergamon
Press. 1977.   pp. 67-96.
Oronsaye, A.U. and Odiase, G.I.
"Attitudes Toward Abortion and Contraception Among
Nigerian Secondary School Girls."   International Journal
of Gynaecology and Obstetrics.   Volume 21 #5   October,
1983.   pp. 423-426.
Orubbuloye, Tunji
"High Fertility and the Rural Economy: A Study of Yoruba
Society in Western Nigeria."   (In) Caldwell, John C.
(ed.).   The Persistence of High Fertility: Population
Prospects in the Third World.   Canberra, Australia:
Australian National University.   Department of
Demography.   Volume One.   1977.   pp. 361-392.
Orubuloye, I.O.
"Child-Spacing Among Rural Yoruba Women: Ekiti and Ibadan
Divisions in Nigeria."   (In) Page, Hilary J. and
Lesthaeghe, Ron (eds.).   Child-Spacing in Tropical
Africa: Traditions and Change.   New York: Academic Press.
1981.   pp. 225-236.
Orubuloye, I.O.
"Family Obligations and Fertility in Nigeria: The Case of
the Yoruba of Western Nigeria."   (In) Ruzicka, Lado T.
(ed.).   The Economic and Social Supports for High
Fertility: Proceedings of the Conference.   Canberra,
Australia: Australian National University.   Development
Studies Center.   November 16-18, 1977.   pp. 203-217.
Orubuloye, I.O.
"Fertility, Sexual Abstinence and Contraception Among the
Yoruba of Western Nigeria: A Study of Selected Rural
Communities in Ekiti and Ibadan Divisions."   Ph.D
Dissertation: Australian National University.   Department
of Demography.   Canberra, Australia.   1977.
Orubuloye, I.O.
"Sexual Abstinence Patterns in Rural Western Nigeria:
Evidence From a Survey of Yoruba Women."   Social Science
and Medicine.   Volume 13A #6   November, 1979.   pp.
667-672.

Orubuloye, I.O.
"Sexual Abstinence Patterns in Rural Western Nigeria:
Evidence From a Survey of Yoruba Women." Social Science
and Medicine. Volume 13a #6 November, 1979. pp.
667-672.
Orubuloye, I.O.
Abstinence as a Method of Birth Control: Fertility and
Child-Spacing Practice Amid Rural Yoruba Women in
Nigeria. Canberra, Australia: Australian National
University. Department of Demography. Changing African
Family Project. Monograph #8. 1981. 116p.
Osuhor, P.C.
"Stillbirths in a Savannah District of Northern Nigeria:
The Socio-Economic Socio-Cultural Factors." Nigerian
Medical Journal. Volume 9 #4 April, 1979. pp. 481-485.
Osuntogun, A.
"Rural Women in Agricultural Development: A Nigerian Case
Study." Paper Presented at the Conference on Nigerian
Women and Development in Relation to Changing Family
Structure. Ibadan, Nigeria: University of Ibadan. 1976.
Ottong, Joseph G.
"Population Dynamics, Fertility and Family Planning in a
Rural Community: A Study in Manchol, Southern Nigeria."
(In) Oppong, C. and Adaba, G. and Bekomba-Priso, M. and
Mogey, J. (eds.). Marriage, Fertility and Parenthood in
West Africa. Canberra, Australia: Australian National
University. Department of Demography. Volume Two.
1978.
Owie, Ikponmwosa
"Religious Identity and Attitudes Toward Contraceptives
Among University Students in Nigeria." Social Biology.
Volume 30 #1 Spring, 1983. pp. 101-105.
Owuamanam, Donatus O.
"Marriage and Aspiration to Professional Leadership of
Women Student Teachers in Nigeria." Journal of
Psychology. Volume 115 #1 September, 1983. pp.
103-106.
Oyemade, Adefunke and Ogunmuyiwa, Taiwo A.
"Sociocultural Factors and Fertility in A Rural Nigerian
Community." Studies in Family Planning. Volume 12 #3
March, 1981. pp. 109-111.
Oysakin, Ade
"The Image of Women in Ifa Literary Corpus." Nigeria
Magazine. #141 1982. pp. 16-23.
Page, Hilary J. and Lesthaeghe, Ron J. and Adegbola, O.
Breast-Feeding and Abstinence: Socioeconomic
Differentials in Metropolitan Lagos. Brussels, Belgium:
Vrije Universiteit Brussel. Centrum Sociologie. 1977.
Palmer, Ingrid
Impact of Male Out-Migration on Women in Farming. West

Hartford, Connecticut: Kumarian Press. Women's Roles and
Gender Differences in Development. Volume Seven. Cases
for Planners. 1985. 89p.

Palmer, Ingrid
The Impact of Agrarian Reform on Women. West Hartford,
Connecticut: Kumarian Press. Women's Roles and Gender
Differences in Development. Volume Six. Cases for
Planners. 1985. 89p.

Peil, Margaret
"Urban Contacts: A Comparison of Women and Men." (In)
Oppong, Christine (ed.). Female and Male in West Africa.
London: George Allen and Unwin. 1983. pp. 275-282.

Perchonock, N.
"Double Oppression: Women and Land Matters in Kaduna
State." (In) Women in Nigeria Today. London: Zed Press.
1985. pp. 82-103.

Pittin, Rene
"Gender and Class in Nigeria." Review of African
Political Economy. #31 December, 1984. pp. 71-81.

Pittin, Rene
"Organizing for the Future." (In) Women in Nigeria
Today. London: Zed Press. 1985. pp. 231-240.

Pittin, Renee
"Documentation and Analysis of the Invisible Work of
Invisible Women: A Nigerian Case Study." International
Labour Review. Volume 123 #4 July-August, 1984. pp.
473-490.

Pittin, Renee
"Hausa Women and Islamic Law: Is Reform Necessary."
Paper Presented at the Annual Meeting of the African
Studies Association. Paper #75. 1979. 19p.

Pittin, Renee
"Houses of Women: A Focus on Alternate Life Styles in
Katsina City." (In) Oppong, Christine (ed.). Female and
Male in West Africa. London: George Allen and Unwin.
1983. pp. 291-302.

Pittin, Renee
"Marriage and Alternative Strategies: Career Patterns of
Hausa Women in Katsina City." Ph.D Dissertation:
University of London. School of Oriental and African
Studies. London, England. 1979.

Pittin, Renee
"Migration of Women in Nigeria: The Hausa Case."
International Migration Review. Volume 18 #4 Winter,
1984. pp. 1293-1314.

Pittin, Renee
"Organizing for the Future." (In) Women in Nigeria
Today. London: Zed Press. 1985. pp. 231-240.

Pittin, Renee
Documentation of Women's Work in Nigeria: Problems and
Solutions. Geneva: International Labour Organization.

World Employment Programme Research Working Papers, #125. Restricted Mimeograph. 1982. 49p.

Prewal, Henry
"Art and the Perception of Women in Yoruba Culture." Cahiers d'Etudes Africaines. Volume 17 #4 1977. pp. 545-568.

Rehan, Naghma E. and Abashiya, Aubu K.
"Breastfeeding and Abstinence Among Hausa Women." Studies in Family Planning. Volume 12 #5 May, 1981. pp. 233-237.

Rehan, Naghma E.
"Knowledge, Attitude and Practice of Family Planning in Hausa Women." Social Sciences and Medicine. Volume 18 #10 October, 1984. pp. 839-844.

Rehan, Naghma E.
"Profile of Contraceptive Clients in Katsina, Northern Nigeria." Journal of Biosocial Science. Volume 16 #4 1984. pp. 427-436.

Remy, Dorothy
"Underdevelopment and the Experience of Women: A Nigerian Case Study." (In) Williams, Gavin (ed.). Nigeria: Economy and Society. London: Collings. 1976. pp. 123-134.

Roberts, G.B.
"Parental Attitude Towards Education of Female Children: A Survey of Gokana in Borno Local Government Area." Paper Presented at the Third Annual Conference of Women in Nigeria. Port Harcourt, Nigeria: University of Port Harcourt. April, 1984.

Salamone, Frank A.
"Levirate, Widows and Types of Marriage Among the Dukawa of Northern Nigeria." Afrika und Ubersee. Volume 64 #1 1981. pp. 129-136.

Salamone, Frank A.
"The Arrow and the Bird: Proverbs in the Solution of Hausa Conjugal Conflicts." Journal of Anthropological Research. Volume 32 #4 Winter, 1976. pp. 358-371.

Sangree, Walter H.
"Going Home to Mother: Traditional Marriage Among the Irigwe of Benue-Plateau State, Nigeria." (In) Tiffany, Sharon W. (ed.). Women and Society: An Anthropological Reader. St. Albans, Vermont: Eden Press. 1979. pp. 189-207.

Sangree, Walter H.
"The Persistence of Polyandry in Irigwe, Nigeria." Journal of Comparative Family Studies. Volume 11 #3 Special Issue. Summer, 1980. pp. 335-343.

Sangree, Walter H.
"Traditional Coalitions Among Women of Irigwe, Nigeria: From Co-Wife to Possession Cult Ties." Paper Presented at the Annual Meeting of the African Studies Association. Paper #112. Bloomington, Indiana. October 21-24, 1981.

Santow, G. and Bracher, M.
    "Patterns of Postpartum Sexual Abstinence and Their
    Implications for Fertility in Ibadan, Nigeria." (In)
    Page, Hilary J. and Lesthaeghe, Ron (eds.).
    Child-Spacing in Tropical Africa: Traditions and Change.
    New York: Academic Press. 1981. pp. 201-223.
Schildkrout, Enid
    "Age and Gender in Hausa Society: Socio-Economic Roles of
    Children in Urban Kano." (In) LaFontaine, J.S. (ed.).
    Sex and Age as Principles of Social Differentiation. New
    York: Academic Press. 1978. pp. 109-137.
Schildkrout, Enid
    "Dependence and Autonomy: The Economic Activities of
    Secluded Hausa Women in Kano, Nigeria." (In) Bay, Edna
    G. (ed.). Women and Work in Africa. Boulder, Colorado:
    Westview Press. Westview Special Studies in Africa.
    1982. pp. 55-81.
Schildkrout, Enid
    "Dependence and Autonomy: The Economic Activities of
    Secluded Hausa Women in Kano." (In) Oppong, Christine
    (ed.). Female and Male in West Africa. London: George
    Allen and Unwin. 1983. pp. 107-126.
Schildkrout, Enid
    "Schooling or Seclusion: Choices for Northern Nigerian
    Women." Cultural Survival Quarterly. Volume 8 #2
    Summer, 1984. pp. 46-48.
Schildkrout, Enid
    "Women's Work and Children's Work: Variations Among
    Moslems of Kano." (In) Wallman, S. (ed.). Social
    Anthropology of Work. New York: Academic Press. ASA
    Monograph #19. 1979. pp. 69-85.
Scott, Victoria
    "Nike Olaniyi, Nigeria's Foremost Female Artist." Paper
    Presented at the Annual Meeting of the African Studies
    Association. Paper #117. Bloomington, Indiana. October
    21-24, 1981.
Sembajwe, I.S.L.
    "Religious Fertility Differentials Among the Yoruba of
    Western Nigeria." Journal of Biosocial Science. Volume
    12 #2 April, 1980. pp. 153-164.
Sembajwe, Israel S.
    "Effect of Age at First Marriage, Number of Wives, and
    Type of Marital Union on Fertility." Journal of
    Biosocial Science. Volume 11 #3 July, 1979. pp.
    341-351.
Sembajwe, Israel S.
    "Religious Fertility Differentials Among the Yoruba of
    Western Nigeria." Journal of Biosocial Science. Volume
    12 #2 April, 1980. pp. 153-164.
Sharpe, B.
    "Social Knowledge and Farming Systems Research:

Ethnicity, Power and the Invisible Farmers of North
Central Nigeria." African Social Research. #38 1985.

Smedley, Audrey
"The Implications of Birom Cicisbeism." Journal of
Comparative Family Studies. Volume 11 #3 Special Issue.
Summer, 1980. pp. 345-357.

Smith, Mary F.
Baba of Karo: A Woman of the Muslim Hausa. New Haven,
Connecticut: Yale University Press. 1981. 304p.

Soyinka, Femi
"Sexual Behavior Among University Students in Nigeria."
Archives of Sexual Behavior. Volume 8 January, 1979.
pp. 15-26.

Spaulding, J.
"The Misfortunes of Some: The Advantages of Others: Land
Sales by Women in Sinnar." (In) Hay, M.J. and Wright, M.
(eds.). African Women and the Law: Historical
Perspectives. Boston: Boston University. African
Studies Center. 1978. pp. 3-18.

Spiro, Heather M.
The Ilora Farm Settlement in Nigeria. West Hartford,
Connecticut: Kumarian Press. Women's Roles and Gender
Differences in Development. Cases for Planners. Volume
Five. 1985. 89p.

Spiro, Heather M.
The Role of Women in Farming in Oyo State, Nigeria: A
Case Study in Two Rural Communities. Ibadan, Nigeria:
International Institute of Tropical Agriculture:
Agricultural Economics Discussion Paper #7. 1980. 36p.

St. Peter, Christine
"Changing Worlds: The Nigerian Novels of Buchi Emecheta."
Atlantis. Volume 11 Fall, 1985. pp. 134-146.

Sudarkasa, Niara
"Women and Migration in Contemporary West Africa." (In)
Wellesley Editorial Committee. Women and National
Development: The Complexities of Change. Chicago:
University of Chicago Press. 1977. pp. 178-189.

Sudarkasa, Niara
"Women and Migration in Contemporary West Africa."
Signs. Volume 3 #1 Autumn, 1977. pp. 178-189.

Temuru, S.
"Mother and Child in the Lagos Metropolis." Nigeria
Magazine. #132/133 1980. pp. 3-22.

Uche, Chukwudum and Ekanem, Ita I.
"Knowledge, Attitude and Practice of Family Planning in
Eastern Nigeria: Implications, Prospects and
Suggestions." Sociologus. Volume 32 #2 1982. pp.
97-126.

Uche, Chukwudum
The Environment of Infant and Child Mortality: The Case

of Nigerian Villages. Providence, Rhode Island: Brown
University. Population Studies Center. 1985.
Uchendu, Patrick K.
"The Changing Cultural Role of Igbo Women in Nigeria,
1914-1975." Ph.D Dissertation: New York University. New
York, New York. 1980. 339p.
Udjo, E.O.
"Obstacles to Successful Fertility Control in Nigeria."
Social Science and Medicine. Volume 19 #11 1984. pp.
1167-1171.
Ugwuegbu, D.C.E.
"Educational Orientation and Nigerian Students' Attitudes
to Husband-Wife Relations." Journal of Social
Psychology. Volume 106 October, 1978. pp. 121-122.
Ukaegbu, Alfred O.
"Family Planning Attitudes and Practices in Rural Eastern
Nigeria." Studies in Family Planning. Volume 8 #7
July, 1977. pp. 177-183.
Ukaegbu, Alfred O.
"Family Size Preference of Spouses in Rural Eastern
Nigeria." Journal of Development Studies. Volume 14 #4
July, 1978. pp. 150-164.
Ukaegbu, Alfred O.
"Fertility of Women in Polynous Unions in Rural Eastern
Nigeria." Journal of Marriage and Family. Volume 39 #2
May, 1977. pp. 397-404.
Ukaegbu, Alfred O.
"Socio-Cultural Determination of Fertility: A Case Study
of Rural Eastern Nigeria." Journal of Comparative Family
Studies. Volume 8 #1 Spring, 1977. pp. 99-115.
Ukaegbu, Alfred O.
"The Role of Traditional Marriage Habits in Population
Growth: The Case of Rural Eastern Nigeria." Africa.
Volume 46 #4 1976. pp. 390-398.
United Nations Economic Commission for Africa (UNECA)
Law and the Status of Women in Nigeria. Addis Ababa,
Ethiopia: UNECA. 1979.
United Nations Economic Commission for Africa (UNECA)
Women and Agriculture in Nigeria. Addis Ababa, Ethiopia:
UNECA. Research Series. 1981.
United Nations Educational, Scientific and Cultural Organ.
Women and Development: Indicators of Their Changing
Role. Paris: UNESCO. Socio-Economic Studies #3. 1981.
112p.
Uyanga, Joseph T.
"Child Mortality and Contraception Usage: A Study of
Rural Acceptors in Nigeria." Rural Africana. #14 Fall,
1982. pp. 61-68.
Uyanga, Joseph T.
"Correlates of Population Pressure on Rural Households: A
Nigerian Case Study." Journal of Comparative Family
Studies. Volume 12 #2 Spring, 1981. pp. 219-232.

Uyanga, Joseph T.
"Family Size and the Participation of Women in the Labor Force: A Nigerian Case Study." African Urban Notes. Volume 2 #2 Spring, 1976. pp. 59-72.

Uyanga, Joseph T.
"Family Size, Family Income and Working Mothers in the Jos Plateau Area." Savanna. Volume 6 #1 June, 1977. pp. 25-29.

Uyanga, Joseph T.
"Is Overcrowded Urban Living a Factor in Fertility Decisions? A Case Study of Metropolitan Calabar." Social Action. Volume 29 #2 April-June, 1979. pp. 150-162.

Uyanga, Joseph T.
"Rural-Urban Differences in Child Care and Breastfeeding Behavior in South Eastern Nigeria." Social Science and Medicine. Volume 14D #1 March, 1980. pp. 23-29.

Uyanga, Joseph T.
"Socio-Economic Values in the Fertility Behavior of Nigerians." Social Action. #4 October-December, 1977. pp. 379-398.

Uyanga, Joseph T.
"The Value of Children and Childbearing in Rural Southeastern Nigeria." Rural Africana. #7 Spring, 1980. pp. 37-53.

Van Allen, Judith
"'Aba Riots' or Igbo 'Women's Work'? Ideology, Stratification and the Invisibility of Women." (In) Hafkin, N.J. and Bay, E.G. (eds.). Women in Africa. Stanford, California: Stanford University Press. 1976. pp. 59-85.

Van Allen, Judith
"'Sitting on a Man': Colonialism and the Lost Political Institutions of Igbo Women." (In) Tiffany, Sharon W. (ed.). Women and Society: An Anthropological Reader. St. Albans, Vermont: Eden Press. 1979. pp. 163-187.

Van Allen, Judith
"Aba Riots or Igbo Women's War." Ufahamu. Volume 6 #1 1976.

Verma, O.P. and Singha, P.
"Fertility Pattern of Muslim Hausa Women in Northern Nigeria." Nigerian Journal of Economic and Social Studies. Volume 24 #2 July, 1982. pp. 185-198.

Ware, Helen
"Polygyny: Women's Views in a Transitional Society, Nigeria, 1975." Journal of Marriage and Family. Volume 41 #1 February, 1979. pp. 185-195.

Watts, Susan J.
"Marriage, Migration, A Neglected Form of Long-Term Mobility: A Case Study From Iborin, Nigeria." International Migration Review. Volume 17 #4 Winter, 1983. pp. 682-698.

Watts, Susan J.
    "Rural Women as Food Processors and Traders: Eko Making
    in the Ilorin Area of Nigeria." Journal of Developing
    Areas. Volume 19 October, 1984. pp. 71-82.
Weidemann, Wesley C.
    "Attitudes Toward Family Planning in Southern Nigeria."
    (In) International Planned Parenthood Federation (IPPF).
    Proceedings of the IPPF Africa Regional Conference.
    London: IPPF. 1977. pp. 66-73.
Weiss, Eugene and Udo, A.A.
    The Calabar Rural MCH/FP Project: What We Have Learned
    About Family Planning. New York: Population Council.
    1980.
Weiss, Eugene and Udo, A.A.
    "The Calabar Rural Maternal and Child Health/Family
    Planning Project." Studies in Family Planning. Volume
    12 #2 February, 1981. pp. 47-57.
Weiss, Eugene and Ayeni, Olasola and Ladipo, O.A.
    The Role of Modern Family Planning on Southwestern Rural
    Nigeria. New York: Columbia University. Center for
    Population and Family Health. 1985.
Yusuf, B.
    "Nigerian Women in Politics: Problems and Prospects."
    (In) Women in Nigeria Today. London: Zed Press. 1985.
    pp. 212-216.
Zack-Williams, A.B.
    "Female Labour and Exploitation Within African Social
    Formations." (In) Women in Nigeria Today. London: Zed
    Press. 1985. pp. 61-67.
Zaidi, S.M.H.
    "Perception of Parental Sex Preference by Nigerian
    Children." Journal of Social Psychology. Volume 108 2nd
    Half August, 1979. pp. 267-268.

DEVELOPMENT AND TECHNOLOGY

Adekanye, Tomilayo O.
    "Innovation and Rural Women in Nigeria: Cassava
    Processing and Food Production." (In) Ahmed, Iftikhar
    (ed.). Technology and Rural Women: Conceptual and
    Empirical Issues. Boston: George Allen and Unwin. 1985.
    pp. 252-283.
Adekanye, Tomilayo O.
    "Rural Fish Marketing in Africa: Some Empirical
    Considerations From Nigeria." Journal of Rural
    Development. Volume 6 #1 June, 1983. pp. 77-85.
Adekanye, Tomilayo O.
    "Women in Agriculture in Nigeria: Problems and Policies
    for Development." Women's Studies International. Volume
    7 #6 1984. pp. 423-431.

Adeyemo, Remi
"Women in Rural Areas: A Case Study of Southwestern
Nigeria." Canadian Journal of African Studies. Volume
18 #3 1984. pp. 563-572.
Adeyeye, V.A.
"Women in Traditional Agriculture: Oyo State of Nigeria
Experience." MSc Thesis: University of Ibadan.
Department of Agricultural Economics. Ibadan, Nigeria.
1977.
Adeyokunnu (Adekanye), Tomilayo O.
Women and Agriculture in Nigeria. Addis Ababa, Ethiopia:
United Nations Economic Commission for Africa. African
Training and Research Centre for Women. 1980.
Adeyokunnu, Tomilayo O.
"Rural Development and the Position of Women in Africa:
Problems and Policies." Paper Presented at the Meeting
of the Experts on Research on the Status of Women,
Development and Population Trends: Evaluation and
Prospects. Paris: United Nations Educational, Scientific
and Cultural Organization. 1980. 32p.
Afonja, Simi A.
"Changing Modes of Production and the Sexual Division of
Labor Among the Yoruba." Signs. Volume 7 #2 Winter,
1981. pp. 299-313.
Afonja, Simi A.
"The Historical Evolution of the Sexual Division of Labor
in Nigeria." Paper Presented at the Meeting of Experts
on the Theoretical Frameworks and Methodological
Approaches to Studies on the Role of Women in History as
Actors in Economic, Social, Political and Ideological
Processes. Paris: United Nations Educational, Scientific
and Cultural Organization. 1984. 20p.
Akande, Jadesola O.
"Participation of Women in Rural Development." (In)
International Labour Organization (ILO). Rural
Development and Women in Africa. Geneva: ILO. 1984.
pp. 129-135.
Awosika, K.
"Nigerian Women in the Informal Labour Market." Paper
Presented at the Wellesley Conference on Women and
Development. Wellesley, Massachusetts: Wellesley
College. Wellesley Center for Research on Women. June,
1976.
Awosika, K.
"Women's Education and Participation in the Labour Force:
The Case of Nigeria." (In) Rendel, M. (ed.). Women,
Power and Political Systems. London: Croom Helm. 1981.
262p.
Brown, C.K.
The Participation of Women in Rural Development in Kaduna
State of Nigeria. Zaria, Nigeria: Centre for Social and
Economic Research. ABU Research Paper #5. 1979. 20p.

Burfisher, Mary E. and Horenstein, Nadine R.
"Sex Roles and Development Effects on the Nigerian Tiv
Farm Household." Rural Africana. #21 Winter, 1985.
pp. 31-50.
Burfisher, Mary E. and Horenstein, Nadine R.
Sex Roles in the Nigerian Tiv Farm Household and the
Differential Impacts of Development Projects. Washington
D.C.: U.S. Department of Agriculture. International
Economics Division. 1982.
Burfisher, Mary E. and Horenstein, Nadine R.
Sex Roles in the Nigerian Tiv Farm Household. West
Hartford, Connecticut: Kumarian Press. Women's Roles and
Gender Differences in Development, Cases for Planners.
Volume 2. 1985. 62p.
Coker, E. Joyce
"Training Women for Scientific and Technical Careers."
Paper Presented at the National Workshop on Women in the
Modern Sector Labour Force in Nigeria. Lagos, Nigeria:
University of Lagos. March, 1985.
Dangugo, H.S.
"Women in Electronic Media." (In) Women in Nigeria
Today. London: Zed Press. 1985. pp. 208-211.
David, Sarah
"Women and Industrial Training: Personal Experiences."
Paper Presented at the Third Annual Conference on Women
in Nigeria. Port Harcourt, Nigeria: University of Port
Harcourt. April, 1984.
DeLargy, Pamela and Bilsborrow, Richard E.
A Comparative Assessment of the Fertility Impact of Rural
Development Projects. Chapel Hill, North Carolina:
University of North Carolina. Carolina Population
Center. 1983.
Dennis, Carolyne
"Capitalist Development and Women's Work: A Nigerian Case
Study." Review of African Political Economy. #27/28
1983. pp. 103-119.
Dennis, Carolyne
"Women and Development: What Kind of Development?" Paper
Presented at the National Conference on Nigerian Women
and Development in Relation to Changing Family Structure.
Ibadan, Nigeria. University of Ibadan. 1976.
Enabulele, A.B.
"The Role of Women's Associations in Nigeria's
Development: Social Welfare Aspect." (In) Women in
Nigeria Today. London: Zed Press. 1985. pp. 187-194.
Enahoro, Diane S.
"Constraints to Women Entering Mid-Level Technical
Occupations in Nigeria." Paper Presented at the Third
Annual Women in Nigeria Conference. Port Harcourt,
Nigeria: University of Port Harcourt. April, 1984.
Essien, Ruth A.
"Perceptions of Nigerian College Students Toward the Role
of Women in Nigerian Development." Ph.D Dissertation:

University of Southern California. Los Angeles,
California. 1981. 214p.

Fapohunda, Eleanor R.
"Women at Work in Nigeria: Factors Affecting Modern
Sector Employment." (In) Damachi, U.G. and Diejomaoh,
V.P. (eds.). Human Resources and African Development.
New York: Praeger Publishers. 1978. pp. 225-238.

Favi, F.
Women's Role in Economic Development: A Case Study of
Villages in Oyo State. Ibadan, Nigeria: University of
Ibadan. Department of Agricultural Extension. Ibadan,
Nigeria. 1977.

Greene, P.A.
Innovative Approaches in Rural Women's Programmes in
Three African Countries: Kenya, Nigeria, Sierra Leone:
Case Studies. Rome: United Nations Food and Agriculture
Organization. 1985. 148p.

Iweriebor, Ifeyinwa
"On Becoming a Person--Proposals for Using Education for
the Humanisation of Womankind." Paper Presented at the
Third Annual Conference on Women in Nigeria. Port
Harcourt, Nigeria: University of Port Harcourt. April,
1984.

Jackson, C.
"Hausa Women and Agricultural Change on the Kano River
Project, Nigeria." (In) Adams, W.M. and Grove, A.T.
(eds.). Irrigation in Tropical Africa: Problems and
Problem Solving. Cambridge, England: Cambridge
University. African Studies Center. 1984. pp. 67-74.

Kisekka, Mere N.
"The Identification and Use of Indicators of Women's
Participation in Socio-Economic Development in the
Context of Nigeria and Uganda." Paper Presented at the
Meeting of Experts on the Indicators of Women's
Participation in Socio-Economic Development. Paris:
United Nations Educational, Scientific and Cultural
Organization. 1980. 52p.

Kisekka, Mere N.
Women and Development in Nigeria: A Bibliography. Addis
Ababa, Ethiopia: United Nations Economic Commission for
Africa. African Training and Research Centre for Women.
Bibliography Series #4. 1981. 122p.

Knowles, C.
"Women Under Development: Some Preliminary Remarks."
(In) Women in Nigeria Today. London: Zed Press. 1985.
pp. 68-81.

Longhurst, Richard
"Rural Development Planning and the Sexual Division of
Labour: A Case Study of a Moslem Hausa Village in
Northern Nigeria." (In) International Labour
Organization (ILO). Rural Development and Women in
Africa. Geneva: ILO. 1984. pp. 117-122.

Longhurst, Richard
"Rural Development Planning and the Sexual Division of
Labour: A Case Study of a Moslem Village in Northern
Nigeria." Geneva: International Labour Organization.
World Employment Programme Research Working Paper.
Mimeograph #10. 1980.
Madunagu, B.E.
"Contemporary Positions and Experiences of Women." (In)
Women in Nigeria Today. London: Zed Press. 1985. pp.
132-137.
Mickelwait, Donald R. and Riegelman, Mary Ann and Sweet,
Charles F.
Women in Rural Development: A Survey of the Roles of
Women in Ghana, Lesotho, Kenya, Nigeria... Boulder,
Colorado: Westview Press. 1976. 224p.
Morgan, Robert W.
"Yoruban Modernization and Fertility in Lagos." (In)
Morgan, Robert W. New Perspectives on the Demographic
Transition. Washington, D.C.: Smithsonian Institution.
Interdisciplinary Communications Program. Occasional
Monograph #4. 1976. pp. 1-51.
Nweke, T.
"The Role of Women in Nigerian Society: The Media." (In)
Women in Nigeria Today. London: Zed Press. 1985. pp.
210-207.
Ogundipe-Leslie, Molara
"Women in Nigeria." (In) Women in Nigeria Today.
London: Zed Press. 1985. pp. 119-131.
Ogunsheye, F. Aetowun and Awosika, Keziah and Dennis,
Carolyn and Di Domenico, Catherine and Akinkoye, O.
Nigerian Women and Development. Ibadan, Nigeria:
University of Nigeria. 1982.
Okojie, Christiana E.E.
"Determinants of Labour Force Participation of Urban
Women in Nigeria: A Case Study of Benin City." Nigerian
Journal of Economic and Social Studies. Volume 25 #1
1983. pp. 39-59.
Okonjo, K.
"Rural Women's Credit Systems: A Nigerian Example."
Studies in Family Planning. Volume 10 #11/12.
November-December, 1979. pp. 326-331.
Okonjo, Kamene
"Rural Women's Credit Systems: A Nigerian Example."
Studies in Family Planning. Volume 10 #11/12
November-December, 1979. pp. 326-331.
Okpala, Amon O.
"Female Labor Force Participation and Fertility in
Nigeria: A Study of Lagos." Ph.D Dissertation: Louisiana
State University and Agricultural and Mechanical College.
Baton Rouge, Louisiana. 1984. 158p.
Omu, Fred I.A. and Makinwa, P. and Ozo, A.O.
Proceedings of the National Conference on Integrated
Rural Development and Women in Development. Benin City,

Nigeria: University of Benin. Center for Social,
Cultural and Environmental Research. September 22-26,
1980.
Onibokun, O.
    "Female Labour-Force Participation in Nigeria." (In)
    Ogbue, R.M. Experiments in Integration: The Nigerian
    Experience. Paris: UNESCO. Educafrica Special Issue,
    1981. Regional Office for Education in Africa. 1981.
    pp. 161-167.
Osuntogun, A.
    "Rural Women in Agricultural Development: A Nigerian Case
    Study." Paper Presented at the Conference on Nigerian
    Women and Development in Relation to Changing Family
    Structure. Ibadan, Nigeria: University of Ibadan. 1976.
Palmer, Ingrid
    The Impact of Agrarian Reform on Women. West Hartford,
    Connecticut: Kumarian Press. Women's Roles and Gender
    Differences in Development. Volume Six. Cases for
    Planners. 1985. 89p.
Pittin, Rene
    "Organizing for the Future." (In) Women in Nigeria
    Today. London: Zed Press. 1985. pp. 231-240.
Remy, Dorothy
    "Underdevelopment and the Experience of Women: A Nigerian
    Case Study." (In) Williams, Gavin (ed.). Nigeria:
    Economy and Society. London: Collings. 1976. pp.
    123-134.
Sheehan, Glen and Standing, Guy
    "A Note on Economic Activity of Women in Nigeria."
    Pakistan Development Review. Volume 17 #2 Summer, 1978.
    pp. 253-261.
Simmons, Emmy
    Economic Research on Women in Rural Development in
    Northern Nigeria. Washington, D.C.: American Council on
    Education. Overseas Liaison Committee. OLC Paper #10.
    September, 1976. 26p.
Spaulding, J.
    "The Misfortunes of Some: The Advantages of Others: Land
    Sales by Women in Sinnar." (In) Hay, M.J. and Wright, M.
    (eds.). African Women and the Law: Historical
    Perspectives. Boston: Boston University. African
    Studies Center. 1978. pp. 3-18.
Spiro, Heather M.
    The Fifth World: Women's Rural Activities and Time
    Budgets in Nigeria. London: University of London. Queen
    Mary College. Department of Geography. Occasional Paper
    #19. 1981. 59p.
Spiro, Heather M.
    The Ilora Farm Settlement in Nigeria. West Hartford,
    Connecticut: Kumarian Press. Women's Roles and Gender
    Differences in Development. Cases for Planners. Volume
    Five. 1985. 89p.

Spiro, Heather M.
    The Role of Women in Farming in Oyo State, Nigeria: A
    Case Study in Two Rural Communities. Ibadan, Nigeria:
    International Institute of Tropical Agriculture:
    Agricultural Economics Discussion Paper #7. 1980. 36p.
Standing, Guy and Sheehan, Glen (eds.)
    "Economic Activity of Women in Nigeria." (In) Standing,
    G. and Sheehan, G. (eds.). Labour Force Participation in
    Low Income Countries. Geneva: International Labour
    Organization. 1978. pp. 129-136.
Sudarkasa, Niara
    "Women and Migration in Contemporary West Africa." (In)
    Wellesley Editorial Committee. Women and National
    Development: The Complexities of Change. Chicago:
    University of Chicago Press. 1977. pp. 178-189.
Sudarkasa, Niara
    "Women and Migration in Contemporary West Africa."
    Signs. Volume 3 #1 Autumn, 1977. pp. 178-189.
Trager, Lillian
    "New Economic Structures and Women's Trade Activities:
    Ilesa, Nigeria." Paper Presented at the Annual Meeting
    of the African Studies Association. Paper #117. Boston,
    Massachusetts. 1976. 12p.
United Nations Economic Commission for Africa (UNECA)
    Women and Agriculture in Nigeria. Addis Ababa, Ethiopia:
    UNECA. Research Series. 1981.
United Nations Educational, Scientific and Cultural Organ.
    Women and Development: Indicators of Their Changing
    Role. Paris: UNESCO. Socio-Economic Studies #3. 1981.
    112p.
Zack-Williams, A.B.
    "Female Labour and Exploitation Within African Social
    Formations." (In) Women in Nigeria Today. London: Zed
    Press. 1985. pp. 61-67.

DIVORCE

Aborampah, Osei-Mensah
    "Plural Marriage, Post-Partum Abstinence and Fertility
    Among the Yoruba of Western Nigeria." Ph.D Dissertation:
    University of Wisconsin-Madison. Madison, Wisconsin.
    1981. 214p.
Ademola, Ade
    "Changes in the Patterns of Marriage and Divorce in a
    Yoruba Town." Rural Africana. #14 Fall, 1982. pp.
    1-24.
Cohen, Ronald
    "How to Grow Feet Out of Your Ears When You Land on Your
    Head: Validity in African Survey." (In) Marshall, John
    F. and Polgar, Steven (eds.). Culture, Natality and
    Family Planning. Chapel Hill, North Carolina: University
    of North Carolina. Carolina Population Center. 1976.
    pp. 288-301.

Iro, M.I.
  "Social Correlates of Divorce Among Lagos Elites Who
  Married in Nigeria." (In) Oppong, C. and Adaba, G. and
  Bekombo-Priso, M. and Mogey, J. (eds.). Marriage,
  Fertility and Parenthood in West Africa. Canberra,
  Australia: Australian National University. Department of
  Demography. Volume One. 1978. pp. 399-406.
Iro, M.I.
  "The Pattern of Elite Divorce in Lagos: 1961-1973."
  Journal of Marriage and the Family. Volume 38 #1
  February, 1976. pp. 177-182.
Kasunmu, A.B.
  "Economic Consequences of Divorce: A Case Study of Some
  Judicial Decisions in Lagos." (In) Roberts, Simon (ed.).
  Law and the Family in Africa. Hague, Netherlands:
  Mouton. 1977. pp. 129-143.

ECONOMICS

Adekanye, Tomilayo O.
  "Rural Fish Marketing in Africa: Some Empirical
  Considerations From Nigeria." Journal of Rural
  Development. Volume 6 #1 June, 1983. pp. 77-85.
Adekanye, Tomilayo O.
  "Women in Agriculture in Nigeria: Problems and Policies
  for Development." Women's Studies International. Volume
  7 #6 1984. pp. 423-431.
Adekanye-Adeyokunnu, T.
  Women in Nigerian Agriculture. Ibadan, Nigeria:
  University of Ibadan. Department of Agricultural
  Economics. 1982.
Adepoju, Aderanti
  "Migration and Fertility: A Case Study in South-West
  Nigeria." (In) Oppong, C. and Adaba, G. and
  Bekombo-Priso, M. and Mogey, J. (eds.). Marriage,
  Fertility and Parenthood in West Africa. Canberra,
  Australia: Australian National University. Department of
  Demography. Volume Two. 1978. pp. 491-506.
Adepoju, Aderanti
  "Migration, Employment and Fertility: A Case Study in
  South-West Nigeria." Paper Presented to the 15th
  International Seminar on Family Research. Lome, Togo.
  1976.
Adeyokunnu (Adekanye), Tomilayo O.
  Women and Agriculture in Nigeria. Addis Ababa, Ethiopia:
  United Nations Economic Commission for Africa. African
  Training and Research Centre for Women. 1980.
Agheyisi, R.U.
  "The Labour Market Implications of the Access of Women to
  Higher Education in Nigeria." (In) Women in Nigeria
  Today. London: Zed Press. 1985. pp. 143-156.
Akande, Jadesola O.
  "Participation of Women in Rural Development." (In)

International Labour Organization (ILO). Rural
Development and Women in Africa. Geneva: ILO. 1984.
pp. 129-135.

Arinola, O.A.N.
"The Implications of Female Labour Force Participation on
the Family: A Case Study of Some Factory Workers." B.Sc
Dissertation: University of Ibadan. Department of
Sociology. Ibadan, Nigeria. 1978.

Awosika, K.
"Nigerian Women in the Informal Labour Market." Paper
Presented at the Wellesley Conference on Women and
Development. Wellesley, Massachusetts: Wellesley
College. Wellesley Center for Research on Women. June,
1976.

Awosika, K.
"Women's Education and Participation in the Labour Force:
The Case of Nigeria." (In) Rendel, M. (ed.). Women,
Power and Political Systems. London: Croom Helm. 1981.
262p.

Benson, Susan and Duffield, Mark
"Women's Work and Economic Change: The Hausa in Sudan and
in Nigeria." I.D.S. Bulletin. Volume 10 #9 June, 1979.
pp. 13-19.

Brown, C.K.
The Participation of Women in Rural Development in Kaduna
State of Nigeria, Zaria, Nigeria: Centre for Social and
Economic Research. ABU Research Paper #5. 1979. 20p.

Caldwell, John C.
"The Economic Rationality of High Fertility: An
Investigation Illustrated With Nigerian Survey Data.
Population Studies (London). Volume 31 #1 March, 1977.
pp. 5-27.

Dennis, Carolyne
"Capitalist Development and Women's Work: A Nigerian Case
Study." Review of African Political Economy. #27/28
1983. pp. 103-119.

Dennis, Carolyne
"Women and Development: What Kind of Development?" Paper
Presented at the National Conference on Nigerian Women
and Development in Relation to Changing Family Structure.
Ibadan, Nigeria. University of Ibadan. 1976.

Di Domenico, Catherine M.
"Male and Female Factory Workers in Ibadan." (In)
Oppong, Christine (ed.). Female and Male in West Africa.
London: George Allen and Unwin. 1983. pp. 256-265.

Emeagwali, G.T.
"Women in Pre-Capitalistic Socio-Economic Formations in
Nigeria." (In) Women in Nigeria. London: Zed Press.
1985. pp. 52-55.

Essien, Ruth A.
"Perceptions of Nigerian College Students Toward the Role
of Women in Nigerian Development." Ph.D Dissertation:

University of Southern California. Los Angeles,
California. 1981. 214p.

Fapohunda, Eleanor R.
"Characteristics of Women Workers in Lagos: Data for
Reconsideration by Labour Market Theorists." Labour and
Society. Volume 3 #2 April, 1978. pp. 158-171.

Fapohunda, Eleanor R.
"Characteristics of Women Workers in Lagos: Data for
Reconsideration by Labour Market Theorists." Paper
Presented at the Annual Conference of the Western
Economic Association. Anaheim, California. June 20-30,
1977.

Fapohunda, Eleanor R.
Urban Women's Labour Force Participation Rate Patterns in
Nigeria. Lagos, Nigeria: University of Lagos. 1976.

Fapohunda, Eleanor R.
"Women at Work in Nigeria: Factors Affecting Modern
Sector Employment." (In) Damachi, U.G. and Diejomaoh,
V.P. (eds.). Human Resources and African Development.
New York: Praeger Publishers. 1978. pp. 225-238.

Fapohunda, Olanrewaju J. and Fapohunda, Eleanor R.
The Working Mothers of Lagos. Washington, D.C.:
Smithsonian Institution. Interdisciplinary
Communications Committee. Report of a Study. 1976.

Favi, F.
Women's Role in Economic Development: A Case Study of
Villages in Oyo State. Ibadan, Nigeria: University of
Ibadan. Department of Agricultural Extension. Ibadan,
Nigeria. 1977.

Greene, P.A.
Innovative Approaches in Rural Women's Programmes in
Three African Countries: Kenya, Nigeria, Sierra Leone:
Case Studies. Rome: United Nations Food and Agriculture
Organization. 1985. 148p.

Guyer, Jane I.
"Food, Cocoa, and the Division of Labour by Sex in Two
West African Societies." Comparative Studies in Society
and History. Volume 22 #3 July, 1980. pp. 355-370.

Jackson, S.
"Hausa Women on Strike." Review of African Political
Economy. #13 1978. pp. 21-36.

Johnson, Cheryl J.
"Madam Alimotu Pelewuru and the Lagos Market Women."
Tarikh. Volume 7 #1 1981. pp. 1-10.

Jones, Gavin and Lucas, David W.
"Some Sociocultural Factors Affecting Female Labour Force
Participation in Jakarta and Lagos." Labour Capital and
Society. Volume 12 #2 November, 1979. pp. 19-52.

Lacey, Linda
"Interurban Flows of Population and Occupational Skills
to Three Cities in Nigeria." International Migration
Review. Volume 19 #4 Winter, 1985. pp. 686-707.

Lacey, Linda and Di Domenico, Catherine M.
    Occupational Status of Women in Nigeria: A Comparison of
    Two Urban Centres. Ithaca, New York: Cornell University.
    Department of City and Regional Planning and the Program
    in Urban and Regional Studies. Working Papers in
    Planning #27. 1979. 17p.

Ladipo, Patricia A. and Adegoke, M.O.
    "An Assessment of Rural Women's Agricultural Roles and
    Needs: Implications for Home Economics Extension
    Curriculum." Paper Presented at the Workshop on the Role
    of Women and Home Economics in Rural Development in
    Africa. Rome: United Nations Food and Agricultural
    Organization. Alexandria, Egypt. October 17, 1983.
    12p.

Ladipo, Patricia A.
    "Developing Women's Cooperatives: An Experiment in Rural
    Nigeria." Journal of Development Studies. Volume 17 #3
    April, 1981. pp. 123-136.

Ladipo, Patricia A.
    Developing Women's Cooperatives: An Experiment in Rural
    Nigeria. Totowa, New Jersey: Frank Cass. 1981. pp.
    123-136.

Longhurst, Richard
    "Resource Allocation and the Sexual Division of Labor: A
    Case Study of a Moslem Hausa Village in Northern
    Nigeria." (In) Beneria, Lourdes (ed.). Women and
    Development: The Sexual Division of Labor in Rural
    Societies: A Study. New York: Praeger Publishers.
    Praeger Special Studies. 1982. pp. 95-117.

Longhurst, Richard
    Rural Development Planning and the Sexual Division of
    Labour: A Case Study of a Moslem Village in Northern
    Nigeria. Geneva: International Labour Organization.
    World Employment Programme Research Working Paper.
    Mimeograph #10. 1980.

Lucas, David W. and Ukaegbu, Alfred O.
    "Other Limits of Acceptable Family Size in Southern
    Nigeria." Journal of Biosocial Science. Volume 9 #1
    January, 1977. pp. 73-82.

Madunagu, B.E.
    "Contemporary Positions and Experiences of Women." (In)
    Women in Nigeria Today. London: Zed Press. 1985. pp.
    132-137.

Martin, Carol M.
    "Skill-Building or Unskilled Labour for Female Youth: A
    Bauchi Case." (In) Oppong, Christine (ed.). Female and
    Male in West Africa. London: George Allen and Unwin.
    1983. pp. 223-235.

Martin, Carol M.
    "Women Job Seekers in Bauchi State, Nigeria: Policy
    Options for Employment and Training." Ed.D Thesis:
    University of Massachusetts. Amherst, Massachusetts.
    1981. 312p.

Martin, Carol M.
   "Women Job Seekers--Unskilled Labor or Skill-Building
   Alternatives? Case of Bauchi State, Nigeria." Paper
   Presented at the Annual Meeting of the African Studies
   Association. Paper #81. Bloomington, Indiana. October
   21-24, 1981.
Mba, Nina E.
   "Women and Work in Nigeria: An Historical Perspective."
   (In) Sanabary, Nagat E. (ed.). Women and World in the
   Third World: The Impact of Industrialization and Global
   Economic Interdependence. Berkeley, California:
   University of California. Center for the Study,
   Education and Advancement of Women. 1983.
Meldrum, Brenda and Di Domenico, Catherine M.
   "Production and Reproduction: Women and Breastfeeding:
   Some Nigerian Examples." Social Science and Medicine.
   Volume 16 #13 1982. pp. 1247-1251.
Meldrum, Brenda
   "Traditional Child-Rearing Practices of the Oje Market
   Women of Ibadan." (In) Curran, H. Valerie (ed.).
   Nigerian Children: Developmental Perspectives. Boston:
   Routledge and Kegan Paul. 1984. pp. 174-196.
Mickelwait, Donald R. and Riegelman, Mary Ann and Sweet,
Charles F.
   Women in Rural Development: A Survey of the Roles of
   Women in Ghana, Lesotho, Kenya, Nigeria... Boulder,
   Colorado: Westview Press. 1976. 224p.
Morgan, Robert W.
   "Yoruban Modernization and Fertility in Lagos." (In)
   Morgan, Robert W. New Perspectives on the Demographic
   Transition. Washington, D.C.: Smithsonian Institution.
   Interdisciplinary Communications Program. Occasional
   Monograph #4. 1976. pp. 1-51.
Mustapha, A.R.
   "On Combating Women's Exploitation and Oppression in
   Nigeria." (In) Women in Nigeria Today. London: Zed
   Press. 1985. pp. 241-246.
Ntamere, C.C.
   "Choice of Career and the Effect on Income Differences
   Between Men and Women." Paper Presented at the Third
   Annual Conference on Women in Nigeria. Port Harcourt,
   Nigeria: University of Port Harcourt. April, 1984.
Ogunsheye, F. Aetowun and Awosika, Keziah and Dennis,
Carolyn and Didomenko, Catherine and Akinkoye, O.
   Nigerian Women and Development. Ibadan, Nigeria:
   University of Nigeria. 1982.
Okojie, Christiana E.E.
   "An Economic Analysis of Labour Supply of Women in Benin
   City." Ph.D. Dissertation: University of Ibadan.
   Ibadan, Nigeria. 1981.
Okojie, Christiana E.E.
   "Determinants of Labour Force Participation of Urban
   Women in Nigeria: A Case Study of Benin City." Nigerian

Journal of Economic and Social Studies. Volume 25 #1
1983. pp. 39-59.
Okojie, Christiana E.E.
"Female Migrants in the Urban Labour Market: Benin City,
Nigeria." Canadian Journal of African Studies. Volume
18 #3 1984. pp. 547-562.
Okonjo, K.
"Rural Women's Credit Systems: A Nigerian Example."
Studies in Family Planning. Volume 10 #11/12.
November-December, 1979. pp. 326-331.
Okonjo, Kamene
"Rural Women's Credit Systems: A Nigerian Example."
Studies in Family Planning. Volume 10 #11/12
November-December, 1979. pp. 326-331.
Okpala, Amon O.
"Female Labor Force Participation and Fertility in
Nigeria: A Study of Lagos." Ph.D Dissertation: Louisiana
State University and Agricultural and Mechanical College.
Baton Rouge, Louisiana. 1984. 158p.
Omu, Fred I.A. and Makinwa, P. and Ozo, A.O.
Proceedings of the National Conference on Integrated
Rural Development and Women in Development. Benin City,
Nigeria: University of Benin. Center for Social,
Cultural and Environmental Research. September 22-26,
1980.
Onibokun, O.
"Female Labour-Force Participation in Nigeria." (In)
Ogbue, R.M. Experiments in Integration: The Nigerian
Experience. Paris: UNESCO. Educafrica Special Issue,
1981. Regional Office for Education in Africa. 1981.
pp. 161-167.
Orubbuloye, Tunji
"High Fertility and the Rural Economy: A Study of Yoruba
Society in Western Nigeria." (In) Caldwell, John C.
(ed.). The Persistence of High Fertility: Population
Prospects in the Third World. Canberra, Australia:
Australian National University. Department of
Demography. Volume One. 1977. pp. 361-392.
Osuntogun, A.
"Rural Women in Agricultural Development: A Nigerian Case
Study." Paper Presented at the Conference on Nigerian
Women and Development in Relation to Changing Family
Structure. Ibadan, Nigeria: University of Ibadan. 1976.
Palmer, Ingrid
Impact of Male Out-Migration on Women in Farming. West
Hartford, Connecticut: Kumarian Press. Women's Roles and
Gender Differences in Development. Volume Seven. Cases
for Planners. 1985. 89p.
Palmer, Ingrid
The Impact of Agrarian Reform on Women. West Hartford,
Connecticut: Kumarian Press. Women's Roles and Gender
Differences in Development. Volume Six. Cases for
Planners. 1985. 89p.

Pittin, Renee
"Documentation and Analysis of the Invisible Work of
Invisible Women: A Nigerian Case Study." International
Labour Review. Volume 123 #4 July-August, 1984. pp.
473-490.
Pittin, Renee
"Migration of Women in Nigeria: The Hausa Case."
International Migration Review. Volume 18 #4 Winter,
1984. pp. 1293-1314.
Remy, Dorothy
"Underdevelopment and the Experience of Women: A Nigerian
Case Study." (In) Williams, Gavin (ed.). Nigeria:
Economy and Society. London: Collings. 1976. pp.
123-134.
Schildkrout, Enid
"Dependence and Autonomy: The Economic Activities of
Secluded Hausa Women in Kano, Nigeria." (In) Bay, Edna
G. (ed.). Women and Work in Africa. Boulder, Colorado:
Westview Press. Westview Special Studies in Africa.
1982. pp. 55-81.
Schildkrout, Enid
"Dependence and Autonomy: The Economic Activities of
Secluded Hausa Women in Kano." (In) Oppong, Christine
(ed.). Female and Male in West Africa. London: George
Allen and Unwin. 1983. pp. 107-126.
Sheehan, Glen and Standing, Guy
"A Note on Economic Activity of Women in Nigeria."
Pakistan Development Review. Volume 17 #2 Summer, 1978.
pp. 253-261.
Simmons, Emmy
Economic Research on Women in Rural Development in
Northern Nigeria. Washington, D.C.: American Council on
Education. Overseas Liaison Committee. OLC Paper #10.
September, 1976. 26p.
Spiro, Heather M.
The Fifth World: Women's Rural Activities and Time
Budgets in Nigeria. London: University of London. Queen
Mary College. Department of Geography. Occasional Paper
#19. 1981. 59p.
Spiro, Heather M.
The Ilora Farm Settlement in Nigeria. West Hartford,
Connecticut: Kumarian Press. Women's Roles and Gender
Differences in Development. Cases for Planners. Volume
Five. 1985. 89p.
Spiro, Heather M.
The Role of Women in Farming in Oyo State, Nigeria: A
Case Study in Two Rural Communities. Ibadan, Nigeria:
International Institute of Tropical Agriculture:
Agricultural Economics Discussion Paper #7. 1980. 36p.
Standing, Guy and Sheehan, Glen (eds.)
"Economic Activity of Women in Nigeria." (In) Standing,
G. and Sheehan, G. (eds.). Labour Force Participation in

Low Income Countries. Geneva: International Labour
Organization. 1978. pp. 129-136.
Sudarkasa, Niara
"Women and Migration in Contemporary West Africa." (In)
Wellesley Editorial Committee. Women and National
Development: The Complexities of Change. Chicago:
University of Chicago Press. 1977. pp. 178-189.
Sudarkasa, Niara
"Women and Migration in Contemporary West Africa."
Signs. Volume 3 #1 Autumn, 1977. pp. 178-189.
Trager, Lillian
"Market Women in the Urban Economy: The Role of Yoruba
Intermediaries in a Medium Sized City." African Urban
Notes. Volume 2 #3 Fall/Winter, 1976. pp. 1-10.
Trager, Lillian
"New Economic Structures and Women's Trade Activities:
Ilesa, Nigeria." Paper Presented at the Annual Meeting
of the African Studies Association. Paper #117. Boston,
Massachusetts. 1976. 12p.
United Nations Economic Commission for Africa (UNECA)
Women and Agriculture in Nigeria. Addis Ababa, Ethiopia:
UNECA. Research Series. 1981.
United Nations Educational, Scientific and Cultural Organ.
Women and Development: Indicators of Their Changing
Role. Paris: UNESCO. Socio-Economic Studies #3. 1981.
112p.
Uyanga, Joseph T.
"Family Size and the Participation of Women in the Labor
Force: A Nigerian Case Study." African Urban Notes.
Volume 2 #2 Spring, 1976. pp. 59-72.
Uyanga, Joseph T.
"Family Size, Family Income and Working Mothers in the
Jos Plateau Area." Savanna. Volume 6 #1 June, 1977.
pp. 25-29.
Uyanga, Joseph T.
"Socio-Economic Values in the Fertility Behavior of
Nigerians." Social Action. #4 October-December, 1977.
pp. 379-398.
Watts, Susan J.
"Rural Women as Food Processors and Traders: Eko Making
in the Ilorin Area of Nigeria." Journal of Developing
Areas. Volume 19 October, 1984. pp. 71-82.
Zack-Williams, A.B.
"Female Labour and Exploitation Within African Social
Formations." (In) Women in Nigeria Today. London: Zed
Press. 1985. pp. 61-67.

EDUCATION AND TRAINING

Aborampah, Osei-Mensah
"Determinants of Breast-Feeding and Post-Partum Sexual
Abstinence: Analysis of a Sample of Yoruba Women, Western

Nigeria." Journal of Biosocial Science. Volume 17 #4
October, 1985. pp. 461-469.
Achebe, Christie C.
  "Social Limitations of the Academic Woman to the Pursuit
  of Education." Nigerian Journal of Education. Volume 2
  #1 1979.
Adeleye, J.A.
  "Contraceptives and the Female Undergraduates in Ibadan,
  Nigeria." East Africa Medical Journal. Volume 58 #8
  August, 1981. pp. 616-621.
Agheyisi, R.U.
  "The Labour Market Implications of the Access of Women to
  Higher Education in Nigeria." (In) Women in Nigeria
  Today. London: Zed Press. 1985. pp. 143-156.
Awosika, K.
  "Women's Education and Participation in the Labour Force:
  The Case of Nigeria." (In) Rendel, M. (ed.). Women,
  Power and Political Systems. London: Croom Helm. 1981.
  262p.
Ayangade, Okun
  Preliminary Observations on Sex Education and
  Contraceptive Practice Among Nigerian Female
  Under-Graduates. Proceedings of the Meeting on
  Contraceptive Delivery Systems. University of Ife. Ife,
  Nigeria. 1983.
Ballay, Ute B.
  "Women in Nigeria: Aspects of Social Transformation."
  Africana Marburgensia. Volume 16 #2 1983. pp. 33-59.
Beckett, Paul A. and O'Connell, James O.
  "Education and the Situation of Women: Background and
  Atttitudes of Christian and Muslim Female Students at a
  Nigerian University." Cultures et Developpement. Volume
  8 #2 1976. pp. 242-265.
Bray, T.M.
  "Universal Primary Education in Kano State: The First
  Year." Savanna. Volume 6 #1 1977. pp. 3-14.
Bray, T.M.
  "Universal Primary Education in Kano State: The Second
  Year." Savanna. Volume 7 #2 1978. pp. 176-178.
Caldwell, John C.
  "Education as a Factor in Mortality Decline: An
  Examination of Nigerian Data." Population Studies.
  Volume 33 #3 November, 1979. pp. 395-413.
Coker, E. Joyce
  "Training Women for Scientific and Technical Careers."
  Paper Presented at the National Workshop on Women in the
  Modern Sector Labour Force in Nigeria. Lagos, Nigeria:
  University of Lagos. March, 1985.
Csapo, Marg
  "Religious, Social and Economic Factors Hindering the
  Education of Girls in Northern Nigeria." Comparative
  Education. Volume 17 #3 1981. pp. 311-319.

David, Sarah
"Women and Industrial Training: Personal Experiences."
Paper Presented at the Third Annual Conference on Women
in Nigeria. Port Harcourt, Nigeria: University of Port
Harcourt. April, 1984.

Ejiogu, Aloy M.
"Sex Differences in the Leader Behavior of Nigerian
College Principals." Journal of Education Administration
and History. Volume 14 #1 1982. pp. 55-61.

Ekam, Anna G.
"The Contributions of the Holy Child Sisters to Women's
Education in the Cross River State of Nigeria, From
1930-1967." Ph.D Dissertation: Catholic University of
America. Washington, D.C. 1980. 196p.

Enabulele, A.B.
"The Role of Women's Associations in Nigeria's
Development: Social Welfare Aspect." (In) Women in
Nigeria Today. London: Zed Press. 1985. pp. 187-194.

Fadayomi, T.O. and Adelola, I.O. and Oni, B. and Omogbehin,
V.A. and Egbunike, N.A.
The Role of Working Mothers in Early Childhood Education:
A Nigerian Case Study. Paris: UNESCO. Nigerian
Institute of Social and Economic Research. February,
1978. 68p.

Fapohunda, Eleanor R.
Male and Female Career Ladders in Nigerian Academia.
East Lansing, Michigan: Michigan State University.
Office of Women in International Development. Working
Paper #17. 1983. 19p.

Greene, P.A.
Innovative Approaches in Rural Women's Programmes in
Three African Countries: Kenya, Nigeria, Sierra Leone:
Case Studies. Rome: United Nations Food and Agriculture
Organization. 1985. 148p.

Harrington, Judith A.
"Education, Female Status and Fertility in Nigeria."
Paper Presented to the Population Association of America.
Atlanta, Georgia. 1978.

Harrington, Judith A.
Education, Female Status and Fertility in Nigeria. Ann
Arbor, Michigan: University of Michigan. School of
Public Health. Department of Population Planning. 1978.

Hundung, Martha and Igoche, George
"Integrating Conscientization Into a Program for
Illiteracy, Women in Nigeria." Convergence. Volume 13
#1/2 January-February, 1980. pp. 110-117.

Iweriebor, Ifeyinwa
"On Becoming a Person--Proposals for Using Education for
the Humanisation of Womankind." Paper Presented at the
Third Annual Conference on Women in Nigeria. Port
Harcourt, Nigeria: University of Port Harcourt. April,
1984.

Kisekka, Mere N.
"The Identification and Use of Indicators of Women's
Participation in Socio-Economic Development in the
Context of Nigeria and Uganda." Paper Presented at the
Meeting of Experts on the Indicators of Women's
Participation in Socio-Economic Development. Paris:
United Nations Educational, Scientific and Cultural
Organization. 1980. 52p.

Ladipo, Patricia A. and Adegoke, M.O.
"An Assessment of Rural Women's Agricultural Roles and
Needs: Implications for Home Economics Extension
Curriculum." Paper Presented at the Workshop on the Role
of Women and Home Economics in Rural Development in
Africa. Rome: United Nations Food and Agricultural
Organization. Alexandria, Egypt. October 17, 1983. 12p.

LeVine, Robert A.
"Influences of Women's Schooling on Maternal Behavior in
the Third World." Comparative Education Review. Volume
24 #2 Part Two June, 1980. pp. S78-S105.

Longhurst, Richard
The Provision of Basic Needs for Women: A Case Study of a
Hausa Village in Nigeria. Geneva: International Labour
Organization. Draft Report. 1977.

Mangvwat, Joyce A.
"Home Economics in Northern Nigeria: An Historical Study,
1842-1980." Ph.D Dissertation: University of
Wisconsin-Madison. Madison, Wisconsin. 1981. 150p.

Martin, Carol M.
"Skill-Building or Unskilled Labour for Female Youth: A
Bauchi Case." (In) Oppong, Christine (ed.). Female and
Male in West Africa. London: George Allen and Unwin.
1983. pp. 223-235.

Martin, Carol M.
"Women Job Seekers in Bauchi State, Nigeria: Policy
Options for Employment and Training." Ed.D Thesis:
University of Massachusetts. Amherst, Massachusetts.
1981. 312p.

Martin, Carol M.
"Women Job Seekers--Unskilled Labor or Skill-Building
Alternatives? Case of Bauchi State, Nigeria." Paper
Presented at the Annual Meeting of the African Studies
Association. Paper #81. Bloomington, Indiana. October
21-24, 1981.

Musa, Ayuba Z.
"Assessment of Societal Perceptions and Attitudes Toward
Marriage and Educated Hausa Women in the Northern States
of Nigeria." Ph.D Dissertation: Ohio State University.
Columbus, Ohio. 1981. 178p.

Mustapha, A.R.
"On Combating Women's Exploitation and Oppression in
Nigeria." (In) Women in Nigeria Today. London: Zed
Press. 1985. pp. 241-246.

Nevadomsky, J.
"Motivations of Married Women to Higher Education in Nigeria." International Journal of Women's Studies. Volume 4 #5 1981.

Odu, Dorcus B.
"A Conceptual Programme Planning Model for Adult Education Programmes for Women in Rural Areas of Nigeria Through Extension Home Economics." Ph.D Dissertation: University of Nebraska. Lincoln, Nebraska. 1978. 133p.

Oduyoye, Mercy A.
"Standing on Both Feet: Education and Leadership Training of Women in the Methodist Church, Nigeria." Ecumenical Review. Volume 33 #1 January, 1981. pp. 60-71.

Oni, Gbolahan A.
"Effects of Women's Education on Postpartum Practices and Fertility in Urban Nigeria." Studies in Family Planning. Volume 16 #6 Part One November-December, 1985. pp. 321-331.

Oni, Gbolahan A.
"The Effects of Women's Education on Postpartum Nonsusceptible Period in Ilorin, an Urban Community in Nigeria." Ph.D Dissertation: Johns Hopkins University. Baltimore, Maryland. 1985. 374p.

Pittin, Renee
"Marriage and Alternative Strategies: Career Patterns of Hausa Women in Katsina City." Ph.D Dissertation: University of London. School of Oriental and African Studies. London, England. 1979.

Pittin, Renee
"Organizing for the Future." (In) Women in Nigeria Today. London: Zed Press. 1985. pp. 231-240.

Roberts, G.B.
"Parental Attitude Towards Education of Female Children: A Survey of Gokana in Borno Local Government Area." Paper Presented at the Third Annual Conference of Women in Nigeria. Port Harcourt, Nigeria: University of Port Harcourt. April, 1984.

Schildkrout, Enid
"Schooling or Seclusion: Choices for Northern Nigerian Women." Cultural Survival Quarterly. Volume 8 #2 Summer, 1984. pp. 46-48.

Sembajwe, Israel S.
"Education and Accuracy of Age Reporting Among Yoruba Females in Western Nigeria." Social Biology. Volume 27 #4 Winter, 1980. pp. 294-303.

Tibenderana, Peter K.
"The Beginnings of Girl's Education in the Native Administration Schools in Northern Nigeria, 1930-1945." Journal of African History. Volume 26 #1 1985. pp. 93-109.

Ugwuegbu, D.C.E.
"Educational Orientation and Nigerian Students' Attitudes

to Husband-Wife Relations." Journal of Social
Psychology. Volume 106 October, 1978. pp. 121-122.
Zack-Williams, A.B.
"Female Urban Unemployment." (In) Women in Nigeria
Today. London: Zed Press. 1985. pp. 104-113.

EMPLOYMENT AND LABOR

Adekanye, Tomilayo O.
"Rural Fish Marketing in Africa: Some Empirical
Considerations From Nigeria." Journal of Rural
Development. Volume 6 #1 June, 1983. pp. 77-85.
Adekanye-Adeyokunnu, T.
Women in Nigerian Agriculture. Ibadan, Nigeria:
University of Ibadan. Department of Agricultural
Economics. 1982.
Adekoya, M.A.
"Barriers to an Effective Organization of Women's Work.
The Women's Programme Section in Nigeria." Assignment
Children. Volume 38 #2 April-June, 1977. pp. 80-83.
Adepoju, Aderanti
"Migration and Fertility: A Case Study in South-West
Nigeria." (In) Oppong, C. and Adaba, G. and
Bekombo-Priso, M. and Mogey, J. (eds.). Marriage,
Fertility and Parenthood in West Africa. Canberra,
Australia: Australian National University. Department of
Demography. Volume Two. 1978. pp. 491-506.
Adepoju, Aderanti
"Migration, Employment and Fertility: A Case Study in
South-West Nigeria." Paper Presented to the 15th
International Seminar on Family Research. Lome, Togo.
1976.
Adeyeye, V.A.
"Women in Traditional Agriculture: Oyo State of Nigeria
Experience." MSc Thesis: University of Ibadan.
Department of Agricultural Economics. Ibadan, Nigeria.
1977.
Adeyokunnu (Adekanye), Tomilayo O.
Women and Agriculture in Nigeria. Addis Ababa, Ethiopia:
United Nations Economic Commission for Africa. African
Training and Research Centre for Women. 1980.
Afonja, Simi A.
"Changing Modes of Production and the Sexual Division of
Labor Among the Yoruba." Signs. Volume 7 #2 Winter,
1981. pp. 299-313.
Afonja, Simi A.
"The Historical Evolution of the Sexual Division of Labor
in Nigeria." Paper Presented at the Meeting of Experts
on the Theoretical Frameworks and Methodological
Approaches to Studies on the Role of Women in History as
Actors in Economic, Social, Political and Ideological
Processes. Paris: United Nations Educational, Scientific
and Cultural Organization. 1984. 20p.

Akande, Jadesola O.
"Participation of Women in Rural Development." (In)
International Labour Organization (ILO). Rural
Development and Women in Africa. Geneva: ILO. 1984.
pp. 129-135.

Arinola, O.A.N.
"The Implications of Female Labour Force Participation on
the Family: A Case Study of Some Factory Workers." B.Sc
Dissertation: University of Ibadan. Department of
Sociology. Ibadan, Nigeria. 1978.

Arowolo, Oladele O.
"Female Labour Force Participation and Fertility: The
Case of Ibadan City in the Western State of Nigeria."
(In) Oppong, C. and Adaba, G. and Bekombo-Priso, M. and
Mogey, J. (eds.). Marriage, Fertility and Parenthood in
West Africa. Canberra, Australia: Australian National
University. Department of Demography. Volume Two.
1978. pp. 533-564.

Arowolo, Oladele O.
"Female Labour Force Participation and Fertility: The
Case of Ibadan City in the Western State of Nigeria."
Paper Presented at the Conference on Marriage, Parenthood
and Fertility in West Africa. 25th International Seminar
of the International Sociological Association. Lome,
Togo. January 3-9, 1976.

Awosika, K.
"Nigerian Women in the Informal Labour Market." Paper
Presented at the Wellesley Conference on Women and
Development. Wellesley, Massachusetts: Wellesley
College. Wellesley Center for Research on Women. June,
1976.

Awosika, K.
"Women's Education and Participation in the Labour Force:
The Case of Nigeria." (In) Rendel, M. (ed.). Women,
Power and Political Systems. London: Croom Helm. 1981.
262p.

Benson, Susan and Duffield, Mark
"Women's Work and Economic Change: The Hausa in Sudan and
in Nigeria." I.D.S. Bulletin. Volume 10 #9 June, 1979.
pp. 13-19.

Brown, C.K.
The Participation of Women in Rural Development in Kaduna
State of Nigeria. Zaria, Nigeria: Centre for Social and
Economic Research. ABU Research Paper #5. 1979. 20p.

Coker, E. Joyce
"Training Women for Scientific and Technical Careers."
Paper Presented at the National Workshop on Women in the
Modern Sector Labour Force in Nigeria. Lagos, Nigeria:
University of Lagos. March, 1985.

Dangugo, H.S.
"Women in Electronic Media." (In) Women in Nigeria
Today. London: Zed Press. 1985. pp. 208-211.

NIGERIA

David, Sarah
  "Women and Industrial Training: Personal Experiences."
  Paper Presented at the Third Annual Conference on Women
  in Nigeria. Port Harcourt, Nigeria: University of Port
  Harcourt. April, 1984.
DeLargy, Pamela and Bilsborrow, Richard E.
  A Comparative Assessment of the Fertility Impact of Rural
  Development Projects. Chapel Hill, North Carolina:
  University of North Carolina. Carolina Population
  Center. 1983.
Dennis, Carolyne
  "Capitalist Development and Women's Work: A Nigerian Case
  Study." Review of African Political Economy. #27/28
  1983. pp. 103-119.
Dennis, Carolyne
  "Women and Development: What Kind of Development?" Paper
  Presented at the National Conference on Nigerian Women
  and Development in Relation to Changing Family Structure.
  Ibadan, Nigeria. University of Ibadan. 1976.
Di Domenico, Catherine M. and Asuni, Judy and Scott,
Jacqueline
  "Changing Status of African Women: An Exploratory Study
  of Working Mothers in Ibadan, Nigeria." (In)
  International Planned Parenthood Federation (IPPF).
  Proceedings of the IPPF Africa Regional Conference.
  London: IPPF. 1977. pp. 283-284.
Di Domenico, Catherine M. and Majuetan, L. Lacey
  "Female Industrial Recruits: Women Workers at the
  Nigerian Tobacco Company Factory at Ibadan." Paper
  Presented at the National Conference on Nigerian Women
  and Development in Relation to Changing Family Structure.
  Ibadan, Nigeria: University of Ibadan. April 26-30,
  1976.
Di Domenico, Catherine M.
  "Male and Female Factory Workers in Ibadan." (In)
  Oppong, Christine (ed.). Female and Male in West Africa.
  London: George Allen and Unwin. 1983. pp. 256-265.
Di Domenico, Catherine M. and Lacey-Mojuetan, Linda
  "Occupational Status of Women in Nigeria: A Comparison of
  Two Urban Centres." Paper Presented at the Conference on
  Nigerian Women and Development in Relation to Changing
  Family Structure. Ibadan, Nigeria: University of Ibadan.
  Department of Sociology. April 26-30, 1976. 13p.
Di Domenico, Catherine M. and Lacey-Mojuetan, Linda
  "Occupational Status of Women in Nigeria: A Comparison of
  Two Urban Centres." Africana Marburgensia. Volume 10 #2
  1977. pp. 62-79.
Emeagwali, G.T.
  "Women in Pre-Capitalistic Socio-Economic Formations in
  Nigeria." (In) Women in Nigeria. London: Zed Press.
  1985. pp. 52-55.
Enabulele, A.B.
  "The Role of Women's Associations in Nigeria's

Development: Social Welfare Aspect." (In) Women in
Nigeria Today. London: Zed Press. 1985. pp. 187-194.
Enahoro, Diane S.
"Constraints to Women Entering Mid-Level Technical
Occupations in Nigeria." Paper Presented at the Third
Annual Women in Nigeria Conference. Port Harcourt,
Nigeria: University of Port Harcourt. April, 1984.
Essien, Ruth A.
"Perceptions of Nigerian College Students Toward the Role
of Women in Nigerian Development." Ph.D Dissertation:
University of Southern California. Los Angeles,
California. 1981. 214p.
Fadayomi, T.O. and Adelola, I.O. and Oni, B. and Omogbehin,
V.A. and Egbunike, N.A.
The Role of Working Mothers in Early Childhood Education:
A Nigerian Case Study. Paris: UNESCO. Nigerian
Institute of Social and Economic Research. February,
1978. 68p.
Fagbemi, S.
"Occupational and Familial Role Conflicts of Working
Women: A Case Study of the Lafia Canning Factory,
Ibadan." BSc Dissertation: University of Ibadan,
Department of Sociology. Ibadan, Nigeria. 1978.
Fapohunda, Eleanor R.
"Characteristics of Women Workers in Lagos: Data for
Reconsideration by Labour Market Theorists." Labour and
Society. Volume 3 #2 April, 1978. pp. 158-171.
Fapohunda, Eleanor R.
"Characteristics of Women Workers in Lagos: Data for
Reconsideration by Labour Market Theorists." Paper
Presented at the Annual Conference of the Western
Economic Association. Anaheim, California. June 20-30,
1977.
Fapohunda, Eleanor R.
Male and Female Career Ladders in Nigerian Academia.
East Lansing, Michigan: Michigan State University.
Office of Women in International Development. Working
Paper #17. 1983. 19p.
Fapohunda, Eleanor R.
"The Child-Care Dilemma of Working Mothers in African
Cities: The Case of Lagos, Nigeria." (In) Bay, Edna G.
(ed.). Women and Work in Africa. Boulder, Colorado:
Westview Press. Westview Special Studies in Africa.
1982. pp. 277-288.
Fapohunda, Eleanor R.
Urban Women's Labour Force Participation Rate Patterns in
Nigeria. Lagos, Nigeria: University of Lagos. 1976.
Fapohunda, Eleanor R.
"Women at Work in Nigeria: Factors Affecting Modern
Sector Employment." (In) Damachi, U.G. and Diejomaoh,
V.P. (eds.). Human Resources and African Development.
New York: Praeger Publishers. 1978. pp. 225-238.

Fapohunda, Olanrewaju J. and Fapohunda, Eleanor R.
   The Working Mothers of Lagos. Washington, D.C.:
   Smithsonian Institution. Interdisciplinary
   Communications Committee. Report of a Study. 1976.
Favi, F.
   Women's Role in Economic Development: A Case Study of
   Villages in Oyo State. Ibadan, Nigeria: University of
   Ibadan. Department of Agricultural Extension. Ibadan,
   Nigeria. 1977.
Feyisetan, Bamikale J.
   "Fertility and Female Employment in Lagos, Nigeria."
   Genus. Volume 41 #1/2 January-June, 1985. pp. 57-76.
Guyer, Jane I.
   "Food, Cocoa, and the Division of Labour by Sex in Two
   West African Societies." Comparative Studies in Society
   and History. Volume 22 #3 July, 1980. pp. 355-370.
Ipaye, Babatunde
   "A Psycho-Demographic View of the Changing Family Within
   the African Context." Paper Presented at the Seminar on
   the Changing Family in the African Context, 1983. Paris:
   United Nations Educational, Scientific and Cultural
   Organization. Maseru, Lesotho. 1984. 26p.
Iro, M.I.
   "The Main Features of a Working Life Table of the Female
   Labour Force in Nigeria, 1965." Journal of the Royal
   Statistical Society, Series A. Volume 139 #2 1976. pp.
   258-265.
Jackson, C.
   "Hausa Women and Agricultural Change on the Kano River
   Project, Nigeria." (In) Adams, W.M. and Grove, A.T.
   (eds.). Irrigation in Tropical Africa: Problems and
   Problem Solving. Cambridge, England: Cambridge
   University. African Studies Center. 1984. pp. 67-74.
Jackson, S.
   "Hausa Women on Strike." Review of African Political
   Economy. #13 1978. pp. 21-36.
Jones, Gavin and Lucas, David W.
   "Some Sociocultural Factors Affecting Female Labour Force
   Participation in Jakarta and Lagos." Labour Capital and
   Society. Volume 12 #2 November, 1979. pp. 19-52.
Kisekka, Mere N.
   "The Identification and Use of Indicators of Women's
   Participation in Socio-Economic Development in the
   Context of Nigeria and Uganda." Paper Presented at the
   Meeting of Experts on the Indicators of Women's
   Participation in Socio-Economic Development. Paris:
   United Nations Educational, Scientific and Cultural
   Organization. 1980. 52p.
Lacey, Linda
   "Interurban Flows of Population and Occupational Skills
   to Three Cities in Nigeria." International Migration
   Review. Volume 19 #4 Winter, 1985. pp. 686-707.

Lacey, Linda and Di Domenico, Catherine M.
"Occupational Status of Women in Nigeria: A Comparison of
Two Urban Centres." Ithaca, New York: Cornell
University. Department of City and Regional Planning and
the Program in Urban and Regional Studies. Working
Papers in Planning #27. 1979. 17p.
Ladipo, Patricia A. and Adegoke, M.O.
"An Assessment of Rural Women's Agricultural Roles and
Needs: Implications for Home Economics Extension
Curriculum." Paper Presented at the Workshop on the Role
of Women and Home Economics in Rural Development in
Africa. Rome: United Nations Food and Agricultural
Organization. Alexandria, Egypt. October 17, 1983.
12p.
Ladipo, Patricia A.
"Developing Women's Cooperatives: An Experiment in Rural
Nigeria." Journal of Development Studies. Volume 17 #3
April, 1981. pp. 123-136.
Ladipo, Patricia A.
Developing Women's Cooperatives: An Experiment in Rural
Nigeria. Totowa, New Jersey: Frank Cass. 1981. pp.
123-136.
Longhurst, Richard
"Resource Allocation and the Sexual Division of Labor: A
Case Study of a Moslem Hausa Village in Northern
Nigeria." (In) Beneria, Lourdes (ed.). Women and
Development: The Sexual Division of Labor in Rural
Societies: A Study. New York: Praeger Publishers.
Praeger Special Studies. 1982. pp. 95-117.
Longhurst, Richard
"Rural Development Planning and the Sexual Division of
Labour: A Case Study of a Moslem Hausa Village in
Northern Nigeria." (In) International Labour
Organization (ILO). Rural Development and Women in
Africa. Geneva: ILO. 1984. pp. 117-122.
Longhurst, Richard
Rural Development Planning and the Sexual Division of
Labour: A Case Study of a Moslem Village in Northern
Nigeria. Geneva: International Labour Organization.
World Employment Programme Research Working Paper.
Mimeograph #10. 1980.
Longhurst, Richard
The Provision of Basic Needs for Women: A Case Study of a
Hausa Village in Nigeria. Geneva: International Labour
Organization. Draft Report. 1977.
Madunagu, B.E.
"Contemporary Positions and Experiences of Women." (In)
Women in Nigeria Today. London: Zed Press. 1985. pp.
132-137.
Martin, Carol M.
"Skill-Building or Unskilled Labour for Female Youth: A
Bauchi Case." (In) Oppong, Christine (ed.). Female and

Male in West Africa.   London: George Allen and Unwin.
1983.   pp. 223-235.

Martin, Carol M.
"Women Job Seekers in Bauchi State, Nigeria: Policy
Options for Employment and Training."   Ed.D Thesis:
University of Massachusetts.   Amherst, Massachusetts.
1981.   312p.

Martin, Carol M.
"Women Job Seekers--Unskilled Labor or Skill-Building
Alternatives?   Case of Bauchi State, Nigeria."   Paper
Presented at the Annual Meeting of the African Studies
Association.   Paper #81.   Bloomington, Indiana.   October
21-24, 1981.

Mba, Nina E.
"Women and Work in Nigeria: An Historical Perspective."
(In) Sanabary, Nagat E. (ed.).   Women and World in the
Third World: The Impact of Industrialization and Global
Economic Interdependence.   Berkeley, California:
University of California.   Center for the Study,
Education and Advancement of Women.   1983.

Meldrum, Brenda and Di Domenico, Catherine M.
"Production and Reproduction: Women and Breastfeeding:
Some Nigerian Examples."   Social Science and Medicine.
Volume 16 #13 1982.   pp. 1247-1251.

Mickelwait, Donald R. and Riegelman, Mary Ann and Sweet,
Charles F.
Women in Rural Development: A Survey of the Roles of
Women in Ghana, Lesotho, Kenya, Nigeria...   Boulder,
Colorado: Westview Press.   1976.   224p.

Morgan, Robert W.
"Yoruban Modernization and Fertility in Lagos."   (In)
Morgan, Robert W. New Perspectives on the Demographic
Transition.   Washington, D.C.: Smithsonian Institution.
Interdisciplinary Communications Program.   Occasional
Monograph #4.   1976.   pp. 1-51.

Nevadomsky, J.
"Motivations of Married Women to Higher Education in
Nigeria."   International Journal of Women's Studies.
Volume 4 #5 1981.

Ntamere, C.C.
"Choice of Career and the Effect on Income Differences
Between Men and Women."   Paper Presented at the Third
Annual Conference on Women in Nigeria.   Port Harcourt,
Nigeria: University of Port Harcourt.   April, 1984.

Nweke, T.
"The Role of Women in Nigerian Society: The Media."   (In)
Women in Nigeria Today.   London: Zed Press.   1985.   pp.
210-207.

Ogundipe-Leslie, Molara
"Women in Nigeria."   (In) Women in Nigeria Today.
London: Zed Press.   1985.   pp. 119-131.

Ogunsheye, F. Aetowun and Awosika, Keziah and Dennis,
Carolyn and Didomenko, Catherine and Akinkoye, O.
   Nigerian Women and Development. Ibadan, Nigeria:
   University of Nigeria. 1982.
Okojie, Christiana E.E.
   "An Economic Analysis of Labour Supply of Women in Benin
   City." Ph.D. Dissertation: University of Ibadan.
   Ibadan, Nigeria. 1981.
Okojie, Christiana E.E.
   "Determinants of Labour Force Participation of Urban
   Women in Nigeria: A Case Study of Benin City." Nigerian
   Journal of Economic and Social Studies. Volume 25 #1
   1983. pp. 39-59.
Okojie, Christiana E.E.
   "Female Migrants in the Urban Labour Market: Benin City,
   Nigeria." Canadian Journal of African Studies. Volume
   18 #3 1984. pp. 547-562.
Okpala, Amon O.
   "Female Labor Force Participation and Fertility in
   Nigeria: A Study of Lagos." Ph.D Dissertation: Louisiana
   State University and Agricultural and Mechanical College.
   Baton Rouge, Louisiana. 1984. 158p.
Olajumoke, Cecy M.
   "Women's Participation in Trade Unions." Paper Presented
   at the National Workshop on Women in the Modern Sector
   Labour Force in Nigeria. Lagos, Nigeria: University of
   Lagos. March, 1985.
Onibokun, O.
   "Female Labour-Force Participation in Nigeria." (In)
   Ogbue, R.M. Experiments in Integration: The Nigerian
   Experience. Paris: UNESCO. Educafrica Special Issue,
   1981. Regional Office for Education in Africa. 1981.
   pp. 161-167.
Osuntogun, A.
   "Rural Women in Agricultural Development: A Nigerian Case
   Study." Paper Presented at the Conference on Nigerian
   Women and Development in Relation to Changing Family
   Structure. Ibadan, Nigeria: University of Ibadan. 1976.
Owuamanam, Donatus O.
   "Marriage and Aspiration to Professional Leadership of
   Women Student Teachers in Nigeria." Journal of
   Psychology. Volume 115 #1 September, 1983. pp.
   103-106.
Palmer, Ingrid
   Impact of Male Out-Migration on Women in Farming. West
   Hartford, Connecticut: Kumarian Press. Women's Roles and
   Gender Differences in Development. Volume Seven. Cases
   for Planners. 1985. 89p.
Palmer, Ingrid
   The Impact of Agrarian Reform on Women. West Hartford,
   Connecticut: Kumarian Press. Women's Roles and Gender
   Differences in Development. Volume Six. Cases for
   Planners. 1985. 89p.

Peil, Margaret
    "Urban Contacts: A Comparison of Women and Men." (In)
    Oppong, Christine (ed.). Female and Male in West Africa.
    London: George Allen and Unwin. 1983. pp. 275-282.
Pittin, Renee
    "Documentation and Analysis of the Invisible Work of
    Invisible Women: A Nigerian Case Study." International
    Labour Review. Volume 123 #4 July-August, 1984. pp.
    473-490.
Pittin, Renee
    "Marriage and Alternative Strategies: Career Patterns of
    Hausa Women in Katsina City." Ph.D Dissertation:
    University of London. School of Oriental and African
    Studies. London, England. 1979.
Pittin, Renee
    "Organizing for the Future." (In) Women in Nigeria
    Today. London: Zed Press. 1985. pp. 231-240.
Pittin, Renee
    Documentation of Women's Work in Nigeria: Problems and
    Solutions. Geneva: International Labour Organization.
    World Employment Programme Research Working Papers, #125.
    Restricted Mimeograph. 1982. 49p.
Schildkrout, Enid
    "Dependence and Autonomy: The Economic Activities of
    Secluded Hausa Women in Kano, Nigeria." (In) Bay, Edna
    G. (ed.). Women and Work in Africa. Boulder, Colorado:
    Westview Press. Westview Special Studies in Africa.
    1982. pp. 55-81.
Schildkrout, Enid
    "Dependence and Autonomy: The Economic Activities of
    Secluded Hausa Women in Kano." (In) Oppong, Christine
    (ed.). Female and Male in West Africa. London: George
    Allen and Unwin. 1983. pp. 107-126.
Schildkrout, Enid
    "Schooling or Seclusion: Choices for Northern Nigerian
    Women." Cultural Survival Quarterly. Volume 8 #2
    Summer, 1984. pp. 46-48.
Schildkrout, Enid
    "Women's Work and Children's Work: Variations Among
    Moslems of Kano." (In) Wallman, S. (ed.). Social
    Anthropology of Work. New York: Academic Press. ASA
    Monograph #19. 1979. pp. 69-85.
Sheehan, Glen and Standing, Guy
    "A Note on Economic Activity of Women in Nigeria."
    Pakistan Development Review. Volume 17 #2 Summer, 1978.
    pp. 253-261.
Simmons, Emmy
    Economic Research on Women in Rural Development in
    Northern Nigeria. Washington, D.C.: American Council on
    Education. Overseas Liaison Committee. OLC Paper #10.
    September, 1976. 26p.
Standing, Guy and Sheehan Glen (eds.)
    "Economic Activity of Women in Nigeria." (In) Standing,
    G. and Sheehan, G. (eds.). Labour Force Participation in

Low Income Countries. Geneva: International Labour
Organization. 1978. pp. 129-136.
Sudarkasa, Niara
"Women and Migration in Contemporary West Africa." (In)
Wellesley Editorial Committee. Women and National
Development: The Complexities of Change. Chicago:
University of Chicago Press. 1977. pp. 178-189.
Sudarkasa, Niara
"Women and Migration in Contemporary West Africa."
Signs. Volume 3 #1 Autumn, 1977. pp. 178-189.
Trager, Lillian
"Market Women in the Urban Economy: The Role of Yoruba
Intermediaries in a Medium Sized City." African Urban
Notes. Volume 2 #3 Fall/Winter, 1976. pp. 1-10.
Trager, Lillian
"New Economic Structures and Women's Trade Activities:
Ilesa, Nigeria." Paper Presented at the Annual Meeting
of the African Studies Association. Paper #117. Boston,
Massachusetts. 1976. 12p.
United Nations Economic Commission for Africa (UNECA)
Women and Agriculture in Nigeria. Addis Ababa, Ethiopia:
UNECA. Research Series. 1981.
United Nations Educational, Scientific and Cultural Organ.
Women and Development: Indicators of Their Changing
Role. Paris: UNESCO. Socio-Economic Studies #3. 1981.
112p.
Uyanga, Joseph T.
"Family Size and the Participation of Women in the Labor
Force: A Nigerian Case Study." African Urban Notes.
Volume 2 #2 Spring, 1976. pp. 59-72.
Uyanga, Joseph T.
"Family Size, Family Income and Working Mothers in the
Jos Plateau Area." Savanna. Volume 6 #1 June, 1977.
pp. 25-29.
Zack-Williams, A.B.
"Female Labour and Exploitation Within African Social
Formations." (In) Women in Nigeria Today. London: Zed
Press. 1985. pp. 61-67.
Zack-Williams, A.B.
"Female Urban Unemployment." (In) Women in Nigeria
Today. London: Zed Press. 1985. pp. 104-113.

EQUALITY AND LIBERATION

Afonja, Simi A.
"Current Explanations of Sex-Inequality: A
Reconsideration." Nigerian Journal of Economic and
Social Studies. Volume 21 #2 1981.
Agheyisi, R.U.
"The Labour Market Implications of the Access of Women to
Higher Education in Nigeria." (In) Women in Nigeria
Today. London: Zed Press. 1985. pp. 143-156.

Mustapha, A.R.
"On Combating Women's Exploitation and Oppression in Nigeria." (In) Women in Nigeria Today. London: Zed Press. 1985. pp. 241-246.

Obadina, E.
"How Relevant is the Western Women's Liberation Movement for Nigeria?" (In) Women in Nigeria Today. London: Zed Press. 1985. pp. 138-142.

FAMILY LIFE

Achebe, Christie C.
"Continuities, Changes and Challenges: Women's Roles in Nigerian Society." Presence Africaine. # 120 1981. pp. 3-16.

Achike, Okay
"Problems of Creation and Dissolution of Customary Marriages in Nigeria." (In) Roberts, Simon (ed.). Law and the Family in Nigeria. Hague, Netherlands: Mouton. 1977. pp. 145-158.

Adekoya, M.A.
"Barriers to an Effective Organization of Women's Work. The Women's Programme Section in Nigeria." Assignment Children. Volume 38 #2 April-June, 1977. pp. 80-83.

Adeniyi, E.O.
"Population Growth and Fertility Among the Nupe of Nigeria." (In) Oppong, C. and Adaba, G. and Bekombo-Priso, M. and Mogey, J. (eds.). Marriage, Fertility and Parenthood in West Africa. Canberra, Australia: Australian National University. Department of Demography. Volume Two. 1978. pp. 435-451.

Adeokun, Lawrence A.
"Fertility Inhibiting Effects of the Intermediate Fertility Variables in Two Nigerian Sub-Groups." Genus. Volume 41 #3-4 July-December, 1984. pp. 89-106.

Adeokun, Lawrence A.
"Lactation Abstinence in Family Building Among the Ekitis of South-West Nigeria." Paper Presented at the National Workshop on Population and Economic Development in Nigeria in the 1980's. Lagos, Nigeria: University of Lagos. Human Resource Unit. September 12-14, 1979.

Adeokun, Lawrence A.
"Lactation Abstinence in Family Building Among the Ekitis of Southwest Nigeria." (In) Chojnacka, H. and Olusanya, P.O. and Folayan, Ojo (eds.). Population and Economic Development in Nigeria in the 1980's. New York: United Nations. 1981. pp. 41-57.

Akinkoye, Olu
"Attitude to Child-Bearing by Single Nigerian Women." Nigerian Journal of Economic and Social Studies. Volume 26 #1 March, 1984.

Aluko, G.B. and Alfa, M.O.
    "Marriage and Family." (In) Women in Nigeria Today.
    London: Zed Press. 1985. pp. 163-173.
Arinola, O.A.N.
    "The Implications of Female Labour Force Participation on
    the Family: A Case Study of Some Factory Workers." B.Sc
    Dissertation: University of Ibadan. Department of
    Sociology. Ibadan, Nigeria. 1978.
Ballay, Ute B.
    "Women in Nigeria: Aspects of Social Transformation."
    Africana Marburgensia. Volume 16 #2 1983. pp. 33-59.
Benson, Susan and Duffield, Mark
    "Women's Work and Economic Change: The Hausa in Sudan and
    in Nigeria." I.D.S. Bulletin. Volume 10 #9 June, 1979.
    pp. 13-19.
Burfisher, Mary E. and Horenstein, Nadine R.
    "Sex Roles and Development Effects on the Nigerian Tiv
    Farm Household." Rural Africana. #21 Winter, 1985.
    pp. 31-50.
Burfisher, Mary E. and Horenstein, Nadine R.
    Sex Roles in the Nigerian Tiv Farm Household and the
    Differential Impacts of Development Projects. Washington
    D.C.: U.S. Department of Agriculture. International
    Economics Division. 1982.
Caldwell, John C.
    Fertility and Household Economy in Nigeria. Calgary,
    Canada: University of Calgary. 1976. 77p.
Caldwell, John C.
    "Fertility and the Household Economy in Nigeria."
    Journal of Comparative Family Studies. Volume 7 #2
    Summer, 1976. pp. 193-253.
Caldwell, John C.
    "Marriage, the Family and Fertility in Sub-Saharan Africa
    With Special Reference to Research Programmes in Ghana
    and Nigeria." (In) Huzayyin, S.A. and Acsadi, G.T.
    (eds.). Family and Marriage in Some African and Asian
    Countries. Cairo: Cairo Demographic Centre. CDC
    Research Monograph #6. 1976. pp. 359-371.
Caldwell, John C.
    The Changing African Family Project: A Report With
    Special Reference to the Nigerian Segment. Canberra,
    Australia: Australian National University. 1976. 26p.
Callaway, Barbara J.
    "Ambiguous Consequences of the Socialization and
    Seclusion of Hausa Women." Journal of Modern African
    Studies. Volume 22 #3 September, 1984. pp. 429-450.
Callaway, Barbara J. and Kleeman, Katherine E.
    "Women in Nigeria: Three Women of Kano: Modern Women and
    Traditional Life." Africa Report. Volume 30 #2
    March-April, 1985. pp. 26-29.
Chalifoux, Jean-Jacques
    "Secondary Marriage and Levels of Seniority Among the

Abisi (Pitti) Nigeria." Journal of Comparative Family
Studies. Volume 11 #3 Special Issue 1980. pp. 325-334.
Cohen, Ronald
"How to Grow Feet Out of Your Ears When You Land on Your
Head: Validity in African Survey." (In) Marshall, John
F. and Polgar, Steven (eds.). Culture, Natality and
Family Planning. Chapel Hill, North Carolina: University
of North Carolina. Carolina Population Center. 1976.
pp. 288-301.
Coles, Catherine M.
"Muslim Women in Town: Social Change Among the Hausa of
Northern Nigeria." Ph.D Dissertation: University of
Wisconsin-Madison. Madison, Wisconsin. 1983. 556p.
Coles, Catherine M.
"Urban Muslim Women and Social Change in Northern
Nigeria." Paper Presented at the Annual Meeting of the
African Studies Association. Paper #20. Washington,
D.C. November 4-7, 1982.
Coles, Catherine M.
Urban Muslim Women and Social Change in Northern
Nigeria. East Lansing, Michigan: Michigan State
University. Office of Women in International
Development. Working Paper #19. March, 1983. 28p.
Copley, Anthony
"The Debate on Widow Remarriage and Polygamy: Aspects of
Moral Change in 19th Century Bengal and Yorubaland."
Journal of Imperial and Commonwealth History. Volume 7
#2 January, 1979. pp. 128-148.
Dennis, Carolyne
"Women and Development: What Kind of Development?" Paper
Presented at the National Conference on Nigerian Women
and Development in Relation to Changing Family Structure.
Ibadan, Nigeria. University of Ibadan. 1976.
Di Domenico, Catherine M. and Asuni, Judy and Scott,
Jacqueline
"Changing Status of African Women: An Exploratory Study
of Working Mothers in Ibadan, Nigeria." (In)
International Planned Parenthood Federation (IPPF).
Proceedings of the IPPF Africa Regional Conference.
London: IPPF. 1977. pp. 283-284.
Di Domenico, Catherine M. and Majuetan, L. Lacey
"Female Industrial Recruits: Women Workers at the
Nigerian Tobacco Company Factory at Ibadan." Paper
Presented at the National Conference on Nigerian Women
and Development in Relation to Changing Family Structure.
Ibadan, Nigeria: University of Ibadan. April 26-30,
1976.
Durojaiye, Michael O.
"The Changing Family in the Nigerian Context." Paper
Presented at the Seminar on the Changing Family in the
African Context. Paris: United Nations Educational,
Scientific and Cultural Organization. Maseru, Lesotho.
1984. 7p.

Ekejiuba, Felicia
"Contemporary Households and Major Socioeconomic
Transitions in Eastern Nigeria: Towards a
Reconceptualization of the Household." Paper Presented
at the Conferemce on Conceptualizing the Household.
Cambridge, Massachusetts: Harvard University. November,
1984.

Ekpere, J.A. and Oyedipe, F.P. and Adegboye, R.O.
"Family Role Differentiation Within the Kwara Nomadic
Fulani." (In) Oppong, C. and Adaba, G. and
Bekombo-Priso, M. and Mogey, J. (eds.). Marriage,
Fertility and Parenthood in West Africa. Canberra,
Australia: Australian National University. Department of
Demography. Volume One. 1978. pp. 55-67.

Fagbemi, S.
"Occupational and Familial Role Conflicts of Working
Women: A Case Study of the Lafia Canning Factory,
Ibadan." BSc Dissertation: University of Ibadan,
Department of Sociology. Ibadan, Nigeria. 1978.

Fapohunda, Eleanor R.
"Women at Work in Nigeria: Factors Affecting Modern
Sector Employment." (In) Damachi, U.G. and Diejomaoh,
V.P. (eds.). Human Resources and African Development.
New York: Praeger Publishers. 1978. pp. 225-238.

Fapohunda, Olanrewaju J. and Fapohunda, Eleanor R.
The Working Mothers of Lagos. Washington, D.C.:
Smithsonian Institution. Interdisciplinary
Communications Committee. Report of a Study. 1976.

Farooq, Ghazi M. and Ekanem, Ita I. and Ojelade, M.A.
Family Size Preferences and Fertility in South-Western
Nigeria. Geneva: International Labour Office. World
Employment Programme Research. Population and Employment
Working Paper #54. May, 1977. 33p.

Farooq, Ghazi M. and Ojelade, Mukaila A. and Ekanem, Ita I.
"Family Size Preferences and Fertility in Southern
Nigeria." Pula. Volume 2 #2 February, 1983. pp.
83-111.

Farooq, Ghazi M.
Household Fertility Decision-Making in Nigeria. Geneva:
International Labour Organization. Population and Labour
Policies Branch. Employment and Development Working
Paper #75A. 1980.

Farooq, Ghazi M.
"Household Fertility Decision-Making in Nigeria." (In)
Farooq, Ghazi M. and Simmons, George B. (eds.).
Fertility in Developing Countries: An Economic
Perspective on Research and Policy Issues. New York: St.
Martin's Press. 1985. pp. 312-350.

Farooq, Ghazi M. and Adeokun, Lawrence A.
"Impact of Rural Family Planning Program in Ishan,
Nigeria, 1969-1972." Studies in Family Planning. Volume
7 #6 June, 1976. pp. 158-169.

Grossbard, Amyra
   "An Economic Analysis of Polygyny: The Case of
   Maiduguri." Current Anthropology. Volume 17 #4
   December, 1976. pp. 701-707.
Harrington, Judith A.
   "Education, Female Status and Fertility in Nigeria."
   Paper Presented to the Population Association of America.
   Atlanta, Georgia. 1978.
Harrington, Judith A.
   "Some Micro-Socioeconomics of Female Status in Nigeria."
   Paper Presented at the Conference: Women in Poverty: What
   do We Know?. Washington, D.C.: International Centre for
   Research on Women. 1978.
Harrington, Judith A.
   Education, Female Status and Fertility in Nigeria. Ann
   Arbor, Michigan: University of Michigan. School of
   Public Health. Department of Population Planning. 1978.
Hill, Polly
   "Women's House Trade." (In) Hill, Polly. Population,
   Prosperity and Poverty: Rural Kano, 1900 and 1970.
   Cambridge, New York: Cambridge University Press. 1977.
   240p.
Ipaye, Babatunde
   "A Psycho-Demographic View of the Changing Family Within
   the African Context." Paper Presented at the Seminar on
   the Changing Family in the African Context, 1983."
   Paris: United Nations Educational, Scientific and
   Cultural Organization. Maseru, Lesotho. 1984. 26p.
Iro, M.I.
   "Social Correlates of Divorce Among Lagos Elites Who
   Married in Nigeria." (In) Oppong, C. and Adaba, G. and
   Bekombo-Priso, M. and Mogey, J. (eds.). Marriage,
   Fertility and Parenthood in West Africa. Canberra,
   Australia: Australian National University. Department of
   Demography. Volume One. 1978. pp. 399-406.
Iro, M.I.
   "The Pattern of Elite Divorce in Lagos: 1961-1973."
   Journal of Marriage and the Family. Volume 38 #1
   February, 1976. pp. 177-182.
LeVine, Robert A.
   "Influences of Women's Schooling on Maternal Behavior in
   the Third World." Comparative Education Review. Volume
   24 #2 Part Two June, 1980. pp. S78-S105.
Lucas, David W. and Ukaegbu, Alfred O.
   "Other Limits of Acceptable Family Size in Southern
   Nigeria." Journal of Biosocial Science. Volume 9 #1
   January, 1977. pp. 73-82.
Mack, Delores E.
   "Husbands and Wives in Lagos: The Effects of
   Socioeconomic Status on the Patterns of Family Living."
   Journal of Marriage and the Family. Volume 40 #4
   November, 1978. pp. 807-816.
Martin, S.
   "Gender and Innovation--Farming, Cooking and Palm
   Processing in the Ngwa Region, Southeastern Nigeria,

1900-1930." Journal of African History. Volume 25 #4
1984. pp. 411-427.
Meldrum, Brenda
"Traditional Child-Rearing Practices of the Oje Market
Women of Ibadan." (In) Curran, H. Valerie (ed.).
Nigerian Children: Developmental Perspectives. Boston:
Routledge and Kegan Paul. 1984. pp. 174-196.
Morton-Williams, Peter
"Family Structures in an Egbado Yoruba Community." (In)
Oppong, C. and Adaba, G. and Bekombo-Priso, M. and Mogey,
J. (eds.). Marriage, Fertility and Parenthood in West
Africa. Canberra, Australia: Australian National
University. Department of Demography. Volume One.
1978. pp. 69-102.
Mudambi, Sumati
"Interrelationships Between Family Structure and Family
Resources in Eastern Nigeria." Journal of Family
Welfare. Volume 26 #3 March, 1980. pp. 13-26.
Muller, Jean-Claude
"On the Relevance of Having Two Husbands: Contribution to
the Study of Polygynous/Polyandrous Marital Forms of the
Jos Plateau." Journal of Comparative Family Studies.
Volume 11 #3 Special Iss. Summer, 1980. pp. 359-369.
Okediji, Frances O. and Caldwell, John C. and Caldwell, Pat
and Ware, Helen
"The Changing African Family Project: A Report With
Special Reference to the Nigerian Segment." Studies in
Family Planning. Volume 7 #5 May, 1976. pp. 126-136.
Okediji, Francis O. and Caldwell, John C. and Caldwell, Pat
and Ware, Helen
"The Changing African Family Project: A Report With
Special Reference to the Nigerian Segment." (In) Oppong,
C. and Adaba, G. and Bekombo-Priso, M. and Mogey, J.
(eds.). Marriage, Fertility and Parenthood in West
Africa. Canberra, Australia: Australian National
University. Department of Demography. 1978. pp.
717-746.
Orubbuloye, Tunji
"High Fertility and the Rural Economy: A Study of Yoruba
Society in Western Nigeria." (In) Caldwell, John C.
(ed.). The Persistence of High Fertility: Population
Prospects in the Third World. Canberra, Australia:
Australian National University. Department of
Demography. Volume One. 1977. pp. 361-392.
Orubuloye, I.O.
"Family Obligations and Fertility in Nigeria: The Case of
the Yoruba of Western Nigeria." (In) Ruzicka, Lado T.
(ed.). The Economic and Social Supports for High
Fertility: Proceedings of the Conference. Canberra,
Australia: Australian National University. Development
Studies Center. November 16-18, 1977. pp. 203-217.
Osuntogun, A.
"Rural Women in Agricultural Development: A Nigerian Case
Study." Paper Presented at the Conference on Nigerian

Women and Development in Relation to Changing Family
Structure. Ibadan, Nigeria: University of Ibadan. 1976.
Palmer, Ingrid
Impact of Male Out-Migration on Women in Farming. West
Hartford, Connecticut: Kumarian Press. Women's Roles and
Gender Differences in Development. Volume Seven. Cases
for Planners. 1985. 89p.
Pittin, Renee
"Migration of Women in Nigeria: The Hausa Case."
International Migration Review. Volume 18 #4 Winter,
1984. pp. 1293-1314.
Sangree, Walter H.
"The Persistence of Polyandry in Irigwe, Nigeria."
Journal of Comparative Family Studies. Volume 11 #3
Special Iss. Summer, 1980. pp. 335-343.
Schildkrout, Enid
"Dependence and Autonomy: The Economic Activities of
Secluded Hausa Women in Kano, Nigeria." (In) Bay, Edna
G. (ed.). Women and Work in Africa. Boulder, Colorado:
Westview Press. Westview Special Studies in Africa.
1982. pp. 55-81.
Schildkrout, Enid
"Dependence and Autonomy: The Economic Activities of
Secluded Hausa Women in Kano." (In) Oppong, Christine
(ed.). Female and Male in West Africa. London: George
Allen and Unwin. 1983. pp. 107-126.
Smedley, Audrey
"The Implications of Birom Cicisbeism." Journal of
Comparative Family Studies. Volume 11 #3 Special Issue.
Summer, 1980. pp. 345-357.
Sudarkasa, Niara
"Women and Migration in Contemporary West Africa." (In)
Wellesley Editorial Committee. Women and National
Development: The Complexities of Change. Chicago:
University of Chicago Press. 1977. pp. 178-189.
Sudarkasa, Niara
"Women and Migration in Contemporary West Africa."
Signs. Volume 3 #1 Autumn, 1977. pp. 178-189.
Temuru, S.
"Mother and Child in the Lagos Metropolis." Nigeria
Magazine. #132/133 1980. pp. 3-22.
Uchendu, Patrick K.
"The Changing Cultural Role of Igbo Women in Nigeria,
1914-1975." Ph.D Dissertation: New York University. New
York, New York. 1980. 339p.
Ukaegbu, Alfred O.
"Family Size Preference of Spouses in Rural Eastern
Nigeria." Journal of Development Studies. Volume 14 #4
July, 1978. pp. 150-164.
Ukaegbu, Alfred O.
"Fertility of Women in Polynous Unions in Rural Eastern
Nigeria." Journal of Marriage and Family. Volume 39 #2
May, 1977. pp. 397-404.

United Nations Educational, Scientific and Cultural Organ.
   Women and Development: Indicators of Their Changing
   Role. Paris: UNESCO. Socio-Economic Studies #3. 1981.
   112p.
Uyanga, Joseph T.
   "Correlates of Population Pressure on Rural Households: A
   Nigerian Case Study." Journal of Comparative Family
   Studies. Volume 12 #2 Spring, 1981. pp. 219-232.
Uyanga, Joseph T.
   "Family Size and the Participation of Women in the Labor
   Force: A Nigerian Case Study." African Urban Notes.
   Volume 2 #2 Spring, 1976. pp. 59-72.
Uyanga, Joseph T.
   "Family Size, Family Income and Working Mothers in the
   Jos Plateau Area." Savanna. Volume 6 #1 June, 1977.
   pp. 25-29.
Uyanga, Joseph T.
   "The Value of Children and Childbearing in Rural
   Southeastern Nigeria." Rural Africana. #7 Spring,
   1980. pp. 37-53.
Ware, Helen
   "Polygyny: Women's Views in a Transitional Society,
   Nigeria, 1975." Journal of Marriage and Family. Volume
   41 #1 February, 1979. pp. 185-195.

FAMILY PLANNING AND CONTRACEPTION

Aborampah, Osei-Mensah
   "Determinants of Breast-Feeding and Post-Partum Sexual
   Abstinence: Analysis of a Sample of Yoruba Women, Western
   Nigeria." Journal of Biosocial Science. Volume 17 #4
   October, 1985. pp. 461-469.
Acsadi, Gyorgy
   "Traditional Birth Control Methods in Yorubaland." (In)
   Marshall, John F. and Polgar, Steven (eds.). Culture,
   Natality, and Family Planning. Chapel Hill, North
   Carolina: University of North Carolina. Carolina
   Population Center. 1976. pp. 126-155.
Adaba, Gemma
   "Rationality and Responsibility in Family Planning in
   Traditional African Society." (In) Oppong, C. and Adaba,
   G. and Bekombo-Priso, M. and Mogey, J. (eds.). Marriage,
   Fertility and Parenthood in West Africa. Canberra,
   Australia: Australian National University. Department of
   Demography. Volume Two. 1978. pp. 655-672.
Adegbola, O. and Page, Hilary J. and Lesthaeghe, Ron J.
   Breast-Feeding and Post-Partum Abstinence in Metropolitan
   Lagos. Lagos, Nigeria: University of Lagos. Human
   Resources Research Unit. Faculty of Social Sciences.
   Research Bulletin. #80-3. 1980. 38p.
Adeleye, J.A.
   "Contraceptives and the Female Undergraduates in Ibadan,

Nigeria." East Africa Medical Journal. Volume 58 #8 August, 1981. pp. 616-621.

Adeniyi, E.O.
"Population Growth and Fertility Among the Nupe of Nigeria." (In) Oppong, C. and Adaba, G. and Bekombo-Priso, M. and Mogey, J. (eds.). Marriage, Fertility and Parenthood in West Africa. Canberra, Australia: Australian National University. Department of Demography. Volume Two. 1978. pp. 435-451.

Adeokun, Lawrence A.
"Family Planning in Southwest Nigeria: Levels and Determinants of 'KAP'." (In) Adeokun, L.A. (ed.). 1971-1975 National Survey of Fertility, Family and Family Planning, Phase I: Southwest Nigeria. Ife, Nigeria: University of Ife. Department of Demography and Social Statistics. Monograph #1. 1979. pp. 62-104.

Adeokun, Lawrence A.
"Fertility Inhibiting Effects of the Intermediate Fertility Variables in Two Nigerian Sub-Groups." Genus. Volume 41 #3-4 July-December, 1984. pp. 89-106.

Adeokun, Lawrence A.
"Marital Sexual Relationships and Birth Spacing Among Two Yoruba Sub-Groups." Africa. Volume 52 #4 1982. pp. 1-14.

Adeokun, Lawrence A.
"Marital Sexuality and Birth Spacing Among the Yoruba." (In) Oppong, Christine (ed.). Female and Male in West Africa. London: George Allen and Unwin. 1983. pp. 127-137.

Adeokun, Lawrence A.
The Next Child: Spacing Strategies in Yorubaland. Philadelphia, Pennsylvania: University of Pennsylvania. Population Studies Center. African Demography Program. Working Paper #8. September, 1981. 81p.

Adepoju, Aderanti
"Rationality and Fertility in the Traditional Yoruba Society, Southwest, Nigeria." (In) Caldwell, J.C. (ed.). The Persistence of High Fertility: Population Prospects in the Third World. Canberra, Australia: Australian National University. Volume One. 1977. pp. 123-151.

Ajobor, L.N.
"Contraceptives and Abortions in Nigeria." Nigerian Medical Journal. Volume 6 July, 1976. pp. 367+.

Aluko, G.B. and Alfa, M.O.
"Marriage and Family." (In) Women in Nigeria Today. London: Zed Press. 1985. pp. 163-173.

Arowolo, Oladele O.
"Determinants of Fertility Among Yorubas of Nigeria." (In) Hyo-Chai, Lee. Recent Empirical Findings on Fertility: Korea, Nigeria, Tunisia, Venezuala, Philippines. Washington, D.C.: Smithsonian Institution. Interdisciplinary Communications Program. Occasional Monograph #7. 1976. pp. 27-45.

Arowolo, Oladele O.
"Female Labour Force Participation and Fertility: The Case of Ibadan City in the Western State of Nigeria." (In) Oppong, C. and Adaba, G. and Bekombo-Priso, M. and Mogey, J. (eds.). Marriage, Fertility and Parenthood in West Africa. Canberra, Australia: Australian National University. Department of Demography. Volume Two. 1978. pp. 533-564.

Arowolo, Oladele O.
"Female Labour Force Participation and Fertility: The Case of Ibadan City in the Western State of Nigeria." Paper Presented at the Conference on Marriage, Parenthood and Fertility in West Africa. 25th International Seminar of the International Sociological Association. Lome, Togo. January 3-9, 1976.

Arowolo, Oladele O.
"Fertility of Urban Yoruba Working Women: A Case Study of Ibadan City." Nigerian Journal of Economic and Social Studies. Volume 19 #1 March, 1977. pp. 37-66.

Ayangade, Okun
"Characteristics of Contraceptive Acceptors in an Urban Nigerian Setting." International Journal of Gynaecology and Obstetrics. Volume 22 1984. pp. 59-66.

Ayangade, Okun
"Integrated Family Planning Services: A Nigerian Example." East African Medical Journal. Volume 61 #5 May, 1984. pp. 412-419.

Ayangade, Okun
"Preliminary Observations on Sex Education and Contraceptive Practice Among Nigerian Female Under-Graduates." Proceedings of the Meeting on Contraceptive Delivery Systems. University of Ife. Ife, Nigeria. 1983.

Bamisaiye, Anne and De Sweemer, Cecile and Ransome-Kuti, Olikoye
"Developing a Clinic Strategy Appropriate to Community Family Planning Needs and Practices." Studies in Family Planning. Volume 9 #2-3 February-March, 1978. pp. 44-48.

Bongaarts, John
The Fertility Impact of Traditional and Changing Childspacing Practices in Tropical Africa. New York: Population Council. Center for Policy Studies. Working Paper #42. May, 1979. 27p.

Caldwell, John C. and Caldwell, Pat
"Cause and Sequence in the Reduction of Postnatal Abstinence in Ibadan City, Nigeria." (In) Page, Hilary J, and Lesthaeghe, Ron (eds.). Child-Spacing in Tropical Africa: Traditions and Change. New York: Acadenmic Press. 1981. pp. 181-199.

Caldwell, John C.
Fertility and Household Economy in Nigeria. Calgary, Canada: University of Calgary. 1976. 77p.

Caldwell, John C.
  "Fertility and the Household Economy in Nigeria."
  Journal of Comparative Family Studies. Volume 7 #2
  Summer, 1976. pp. 193-253.
Caldwell, John C.
  "Marriage, the Family and Fertility in Sub-Saharan Africa
  With Special Reference to Research Programmes in Ghana
  and Nigeria." (In) Huzayyin, S.A. and Acsadi, G.T.
  (eds.). Family and Marriage in Some African and Asian
  Countries. Cairo: Cairo Demographic Centre. CDC
  Research Monograph #6. 1976. pp. 359-371.
Caldwell, John C.
  The Changing African Family Project: A Report With
  Special Reference to the Nigerian Segment. Canberra,
  Australia: Australian National University. 1976. 26p.
Caldwell, John C.
  "The Economic Rationality of High Fertility: An
  Investigation Illustrated With Nigerian Survey Data.
  Population Studies (London). Volume 31 #1 March, 1977.
  pp. 5-27.
Caldwell, John C. and Ware, Helen
  "The Evolution of Family Planning in an African City:
  Ibadan, Nigeria." Population Studies. Volume 31 #3
  November, 1977. pp. 487-508.
Caldwell, John C. and Caldwell, Pat
  "The Role of Marital Sexual Abstinence in Determining
  Fertility: A Study of the Yoruba of Nigeria." Population
  Studies. Volume 31 #2 July, 1977. pp. 193-217.
Caldwell, John C.
  The Socio-Economic Explanation of High Fertility: Papers
  on the Yoruba Society of Nigeria. Canberra, Australia:
  Australian National University. Department of
  Demography. Changing African Family Project. Series #1.
  1976.
Caldwell, John C.
  Theory of Fertility Decline. New York: Academic Press.
  1982. 385p.
Caldwell, John C.
  "Variations in the Incidence of Sexual Abstinence and the
  Duration of Postnatal Abstinence Among the Yoruba of
  Nigeria." (In) Leridon, Henri and Menken, Jane (eds.).
  Natural Fertility. Patterns and Determinants of Natural
  Fertility: Proceedings of a Seminar on Natural Fertility.
  Liege, Belgium: International Union for the Scientific
  Study of Population. 1979. pp. 397-407.
Cohen, Ronald
  "How to Grow Feet Out of Your Ears When You Land on Your
  Head: Validity in African Survey." (In) Marshall, John
  F. and Polgar, Steven (eds.). Culture, Natality and
  Family Planning. Chapel Hill, North Carolina: University
  of North Carolina. Carolina Population Center. 1976.
  pp. 288-301.

DeLargy, Pamela and Bilsborrow, Richard E.
A Comparative Assessment of the Fertility Impact of Rural
Development Projects. Chapel Hill, North Carolina:
University of North Carolina. Carolina Population
Center. 1983.

Dow, Thomas E.
"Breast Feeding and Abstinence Among the Yoruba."
Studies in Family Planning. Volume 8 #8 August, 1977.
pp. 208-214.

Dow, Thomas E.
Breast-Feeding, Abstinence, and Family Planning Among the
Yoruba and Other Sub-Saharan Groups: Patterns and Policy
Implications. Purchase, New York: State University of
New York. Department of Sociology. 1978.

Doyle, Pat and Morley, David and Woodland, Margaret and
Cole, Jane J.
"Birth Intervals, Survival and Growth in a Nigerian
Village." Journal of Biosocial Science. Volume 10 #1
January, 1978. pp. 81-94.

Edigbo, P.O. and Chukudebelu, W.O.
"Child Spacing and Child Mortality Among Nigerian Ibos."
International Journal of Gynaecology and Obstetrics.
Volume 18 #5 1980. pp. 372-374.

Ekanem, Ita I. and Uche, Chukwudum
"Knowledge, Attitude and Practice of Family Planning in
Eastern Nigeria: Implications and Prospects." Odu.
Volume 17 #1 1978. pp. 36-63.

Ekanem, Ita I. and Farooq, Ghazi M.
"The Dynamics of Population Change in Southern Nigeria."
Genus. Volume 33 #1/2 1977. pp. 119-140.

Ekanem, Ita I.
"Ways of Controlling Family Size: A Case Study of Eastern
Nigeria." (In) Oppong, C. and Adaba, G. and
Bekombo-Priso, M. and Mogey, J. (eds.). Marriage,
Fertility and Parenthood in West Africa. Canberra,
Australia: Australian National University. Department of
Demography. Volume Two. 1978. pp. 691-715.

Ezimokhai, M. and Ajabor, L.N. and Jackson, M. and Izilien,
M.I.
"Response of Unmarried Adolescents to Contraceptive
Advice and Service in Nigeria." International Journal of
Gynaecology and Obstetrics. Volume 19 #6 December,
1981. pp. 481-485.

Fajumi, James O.
"Alterations in Blood Lipids and Side Effects Induced by
Depo-Provera in Nigerian Women." Contraception. Volume
27 #2 February, 1983. pp. 161-175.

Farooq, Ghazi M. and Ekanem, Ita I. and Ojelade, M.A.
Family Size Preferences and Fertility in South-Western
Nigeria. Geneva: International Labour Office. World
Employment Programme Research. Population and Employment
Working Paper #54. May, 1977. 33p.

Farooq, Ghazi M. and Ojelade, Mukaila A. and Ekanem, Ita I.
"Family Size Preferences and Fertility in Southern
Nigeria." Pula. Volume 2 #2 February, 1983. pp.
83-111.

Farooq, Ghazi M.
Household Fertility Decision-Making in Nigeria. Geneva:
International Labour Organization. Population and Labour
Policies Branch. Employment and Development Working
Paper #75A. 1980.

Farooq, Ghazi M.
"Household Fertility Decision-Making in Nigeria." (In)
Farooq, Ghazi M. and Simmons, George B. (eds.).
Fertility in Developing Countries: An Economic
Perspective on Research and Policy Issues. New York: St.
Martin's Press. 1985. pp. 312-350.

Farooq, Ghazi M. and Adeokun, Lawrence A.
"Impact of Rural Family Planning Program in Ishan,
Nigeria, 1969-1972." Studies in Family Planning. Volume
7 #6 June, 1976. pp. 158-169.

Ilori, Felicia
Factors Determining Rural-Urban Fertility Differentials
in Western Nigeria: A Case Study of Ife, Ilesha and
Selected Rural Areas in Oyo Province. Ife, Nigeria:
University of Ife. 1976.

Ipaye, Babatunde
"A Psycho-Demographic View of the Changing Family Within
the African Context." Paper Presented at the Seminar on
the Changing Family in the African Context, 1983. Paris:
United Nations Educational, Scientific and Cultural
Organization. Maseru, Lesotho. 1984. 26p.

Lesthaeghe, Ron J. and Page, Hilary J. and Adegbola, O.
"Child-Spacing and Fertility in Lagos." (In) Page,
Hilary J. and Lesthaeghe, Ron (eds.). Child-Spacing in
Tropical Africa: Traditions and Change. New York:
Academic Press. 1981. pp. 147-179.

Lucas, David W. and Ukaegbu, Alfred O.
"Other Limits of Acceptable Family Size in Southern
Nigeria." Journal of Biosocial Science. Volume 9 #1
January, 1977. pp. 73-82.

Lucas, David W.
"Urban and Rural Fertility in Southern Nigeria." (In)
Ruzicka, Lado T. (ed.). The Economic and Social Supports
for High Fertility: Proceedings of the Conference. 1976.
Canberra, Australia: Australian National University.
Development Studies Center. Canberra, Australia.
November 16-19, 1977. pp. 409-435.

Mack, Delores E.
"Husbands and Wives in Lagos: The Effects of
Socioeconomic Status on the Patterns of Family Living."
Journal of Marriage and the Family. Volume 40 #4
November, 1978. pp. 807-816.

Morgan, Robert W.
"Yoruban Modernization and Fertility in Lagos." (In)
Morgan, Robert W. New Perspectives on the Demographic

Transition. Washington, D.C.: Smithsonian Institution.
Interdisciplinary Communications Program. Occasional
Monograph #4. 1976. pp. 1-51.
Morton-Williams, Peter
    "Family Structures in an Egbado Yoruba Community." (In)
    Oppong, C. and Adaba, G. and Bekombo-Priso, M. and Mogey,
    J. (eds.). Marriage, Fertility and Parenthood in West
    Africa. Canberra, Australia: Australian National
    University. Department of Demography. Volume One.
    1978. pp. 69-102.
Mott, Frank L. and Mott, Susan H. (eds.)
    "Household Fertility Decisions in West Africa--A
    Comparison of Male and Female Survey Results." Studies
    in Family Planning. Volume 16 #2 March-April, 1985.
    pp. 88-99.
Mudambi, Sumati
    "Interrelationships Between Family Structure and Family
    Resources in Eastern Nigeria." Journal of Family
    Welfare. Volume 26 #3 March, 1980. pp. 13-26.
Naghma, E. Rehan and McFarlane, Hildegarde P. and Sani, Sule
    "Profile of Contraceptive Clients in Katsina, Northern
    Nigeria." Journal of Biosocial Science. Volume 16 #4
    October, 1984. pp. 427-436.
Ogbeide, D.O. and Edebiri, A.A.
    "A Two Year Study of Organised Family Planning Services
    in a Developing Country: Experiences in Bendel State of
    Nigeria." East African Medical Journal. Volume 61 #6
    June, 1984. pp. 470-476.
Ogbuagu, Philip A.
    "Depo-Provera--A Choice or an Imposition on the African
    Woman: A Case Study of Depo Proversa Usage in Maiduguri."
    African Review. Volume 10 #2 1983. pp. 39-51.
Ogbuagu, Stella
    "Women and Depo-Provera Usage in Nigeria: Chosen or
    Imposed Forms of Birth Control?" Rural Africana. #21
    Winter, 1985. pp. 81-90.
Ogum, G.E.O. and Okorafor, A.E.
    "Seasonality of Births in South-Eastern Nigeria."
    Journal of Biosocial Science. Volume 11 #2 April, 1979.
    pp. 209-218.
Ojelade, Mukaila A.
    "The Socioeconomic Determinants of Fertility Behavior and
    Attitude in Southwest Nigeria, 1971-1973." Ph.D
    Dissertation: University of Pennsylvania. Philadelphia,
    Pennsylvania. 1982. 273p.
Okediji, Frances O. and Caldwell, John C. and Caldwell, Pat
and Ware, Helen
    "The Changing African Family Project: A Report With
    Special Reference to the Nigerian Segment." Studies in
    Family Planning. Volume 7 #5 May, 1976. pp. 126-136.
Okonjo, K.
    "Rural Women's Credit Systems: A Nigerian Example."

Studies in Family Planning. Volume 10 #11/12.
November-December, 1979. pp. 326-331.
Okonjo, Kamene
    "Rural Women's Credit Systems: A Nigerian Example."
    Studies in Family Planning. Volume 10 #11/12
    November-December, 1979. pp. 326-331.
Okore, Augustine O.
    "Rural-Urban Fertility Differentials in Southern Nigeria:
    An Assessment of Some Available Evidence." Population
    Studies. Volume 34 #1 March, 1980. pp. 171-179.
Okore, Augustine O.
    "The Ibos of Arochukwu in the Imo State, Nigeria." (In)
    Caldwell, John C. (ed.). The Persistence of High
    Fertility: Population Prospects in the Third World.
    Canberra, Australia: Australian National University.
    Volume One. 1977. pp. 313-330.
Okore, Augustine O.
    "The Rationale of High Fertility in Rural Nigeria: The
    Case of Ibos in Arochukwu in Iwo State." (In) Ruzicka,
    Lado T. (ed.). The Economic and Social Supports for High
    Fertility: Proceedings of the Conference. Canberra,
    Australia: Australian National University. Development
    Studies Center. November 16-18, 1977. pp. 253-274.
Okpala, Amon O.
    "Female Labor Force Participation and Fertility in
    Nigeria: A Study of Lagos." Ph.D Dissertation: Louisiana
    State University and Agricultural and Mechanical College.
    Baton Rouge, Louisiana. 1984. 158p.
Omideyi, Adekunbi K.
    "Age at Marriage and Marital Fertility in Eastern
    Nigeria." Genus. Volume 39 #1-4 January-December,
    1983. pp. 141-154.
Omideyi, Adekunbi K.
    "The Persistence of High Fertility in Eastern Nigeria: An
    Analysis Based Upon a Sample Survey of Married Women in
    1971-72." Ph.D Dissertation: University of London.
    London School of Economics. London, England. 1983.
    403p.
Omu, A.E. and Oronsaye, A.U. and Faal, M.K. and Asuquo, E.E.
    "Adolescent Induced Abortion in Benin City, Nigeria."
    International Journal of Gynaecology and Obstetrics.
    Volume 19 #6 December, 1981. pp. 495-499.
Oni, Gbolahan A.
    "Effects of Women's Education on Postpartum Practices and
    Fertility in Urban Nigeria." Studies in Family Planning.
    Volume 16 #6 Part One November-December, 1985. pp.
    321-331.
Oni, Gbolahan A.
    "The Effects of Women's Education on Postpartum
    Nonsusceptible Period in Ilorin, an Urban Community in
    Nigeria." Ph.D Dissertation: Johns Hopkins University.
    Baltimore, Maryland. 1985. 374p.

Onwuazor, Sammy N.
"Continuity and Change: Abortion and Family Size in a
Nigerian Village." (In) Epstein, T. Scarlett and
Jackson, Darrell (eds.). The Feasibility of Fertility
Planning: Micro Perspectives. Oxford, England: Pergamon
Press. 1977. pp. 67-96.
Oronsaye, A.U. and Odiase, G.I.
"Attitudes Toward Abortion and Contraception Among
Nigerian Secondary School Girls." International Journal
of Gynaecology and Obstetrics. Volume 21 #5 October,
1983. pp. 423-426.
Orubuloye, I.O.
"Child-Spacing Among Rural Yoruba Women: Ekiti and Ibadan
Divisions in Nigeria." (In) Page, Hilary J. and
Lesthaeghe, Ron (eds.). Child-Spacing in Tropical
Africa: Traditions and Change. New York: Academic Press.
1981. pp. 225-236.
Orubuloye, I.O.
"Family Obligations and Fertility in Nigeria: The Case of
the Yoruba of Western Nigeria." (In) Ruzicka, Lado T.
(ed.). The Economic and Social Supports for High
Fertility: Proceedings of the Conference. Canberra,
Australia: Australian National University. Development
Studies Center. November 16-18, 1977. pp. 203-217.
Orubuloye, I.O.
"Fertility, Sexual Abstinence and Contraception Among the
Yoruba of Western Nigeria: A Study of Selected Rural
Communities in Ekiti and Ibadan Divisions." Ph.D
Dissertation: Australian National University. Department
of Demography. Canberra, Australia. 1977.
Orubuloye, I.O.
"Sexual Abstinence Patterns in Rural Western Nigeria:
Evidence From a Survey of Yoruba Women." Social Science
and Medicine. Volume 13A #6 November, 1979. pp.
667-672.
Orubuloye, I.O.
"Sexual Abstinence Patterns in Rural Western Nigeria:
Evidence From a Survey of Yoruba Women." Social Science
and Medicine. Volume 13a #6 November, 1979. pp.
667-672.
Orubuloye, I.O.
Abstinence as a Method of Birth Control: Fertility and
Child-Spacing Practice Amid Rural Yoruba Women in
Nigeria. Canberra, Australia: Australian National
University. Department of Demography. Changing African
Family Project. Monograph #8. 1981. 116p.
Ottong, Joseph G.
"Population Dynamics, Fertility and Family Planning in a
Rural Community: A Study in Manchol, Southern Nigeria."
(In) Oppong, C. and Adaba, G. and Bekomba-Priso, M. and
Mogey, J. (eds.). Marriage, Fertility and Parenthood in
West Africa. Canberra, Australia: Australian National
University. Department of Demography. Volume Two.
1978.

Owie, Ikponmwosa
"Religious Identity and Attitudes Toward Contraceptives
Among University Students in Nigeria." Social Biology.
Volume 30 #1 Spring, 1983. pp. 101-105.
Oyemade, Adefunke and Ogunmuyiwa, Taiwo A.
"Sociocultural Factors and Fertility in A Rural Nigerian
Community." Studies in Family Planning. Volume 12 #3
March, 1981. pp. 109-111.
Rehan, Naghma E. and Abashiya, Aubu K.
"Breastfeeding and Abstinence Among Hausa Women."
Studies in Family Planning. Volume 12 #5 May, 1981.
pp. 233-237.
Rehan, Naghma E.
"Knowledge, Attitude and Practice of Family Planning in
Hausa Women." Social Sciences and Medicine. Volume 18
#10 October, 1984. pp. 839-844.
Rehan, Naghma E.
"Profile of Contraceptive Clients in Katsina, Northern
Nigeria." Journal of Biosocial Science. Volume 16 #4
1984. pp. 427-436.
Santow, G. and Bracher, M.
"Patterns of Postpartum Sexual Abstinence and Their
Implications for Fertility in Ibadan, Nigeria." (In)
Page, Hilary J. and Lesthaeghe, Ron (eds.).
Child-Spacing in Tropical Africa: Traditions and Change.
New York: Academic Press. 1981. pp. 201-223.
U.S. Agency for International Development (U.S. AID)
U.S. AID Operations Research Project Summary: Community
Based Distribution of Low Cost Family Planning and
Maternal Child Health Services in Rural Nigeria.
Washington, D.C.: U.S. Department of State. U.S. AID.
Unpublished. February, 1981.
Uche, Chukwudum and Ekanem, Ita I.
"Knowledge, Attitude and Practice of Family Planning in
Eastern Nigeria: Implications, Prospects and
Suggestions." Sociologus. Volume 32 #2 1982. pp.
97-126.
Udjo, E.O.
"Obstacles to Successful Fertility Control in Nigeria."
Social Science and Medicine. Volume 19 #11 1984. pp.
1167-1171.
Ukaegbu, Alfred O.
"Family Planning Attitudes and Practices in Rural Eastern
Nigeria." Studies in Family Planning. Volume 8 #7
July, 1977. pp. 177-183.
Ukaegbu, Alfred O.
"Family Size Preference of Spouses in Rural Eastern
Nigeria." Journal of Development Studies. Volume 14 #4
July, 1978. pp. 150-164.
Ukaegbu, Alfred O.
"Socio-Cultural Determination of Fertility: A Case Study
of Rural Eastern Nigeria." Journal of Comparative Family
Studies. Volume 8 #1 Spring, 1977. pp. 99-115.

Uyanga, Joseph T.
"Child Mortality and Contraception Usage: A Study of
Rural Acceptors in Nigeria." Rural Africana. #14 Fall,
1982. pp. 61-68.
Uyanga, Joseph T.
"Correlates of Population Pressure on Rural Households: A
Nigerian Case Study." Journal of Comparative Family
Studies. Volume 12 #2 Spring, 1981. pp. 219-232.
Uyanga, Joseph T.
"Is Overcrowded Urban Living a Factor in Fertility
Decisions? A Case Study of Metropolitan Calabar."
Social Action. Volume 29 #2 April-June, 1979. pp.
150-162.
Uyanga, Joseph T.
"Socio-Economic Values in the Fertility Behavior of
Nigerians." Social Action. #4 October-December, 1977.
pp. 379-398.
Verma, O.P. and Singha, P.
"Fertility Pattern of Muslim Hausa Women in Northern
Nigeria." Nigerian Journal of Economic and Social
Studies. Volume 24 #2 July, 1982. pp. 185-198.
Weidemann, Wesley C.
"Attitudes Toward Family Planning in Southern Nigeria."
(In) International Planned Parenthood Federation (IPPF).
Proceedings of the IPPF Africa Regional Conference.
London: IPPF. 1977. pp. 66-73.
Weiss, Eugene and Udo, A.A.
The Calabar Rural MCH/FP Project: What We Have Learned
About Family Planning. New York: Population Council.
1980.
Weiss, Eugene and Udo, A.A.
"The Calabar Rural Maternal and Child Health/Family
Planning Project." Studies in Family Planning. Volume
12 #2 February, 1981. pp. 47-57.
Weiss, Eugene and Ayeni, Olasola and Ladipo, O.A.
The Role of Modern Family Planning on Southwestern Rural
Nigeria. New York: Columbia University. Center for
Population and Family Health. 1985.
Wien, E.M.
"Vitamin B6 Status of Nigerian Women Using Various
Methods of Contraception." American Journal of Clinical
Nutrition. Volume 31 #8 August, 1978. pp. 1392-1396.

FERTILITY AND INFERTILITY

Aborampah, Osei-Mensah
"Plural Marriage, Post-Partum Abstinence and Fertility
Among the Yoruba of Western Nigeria." Ph.D Dissertation:
University of Wisconsin-Madison. Madison, Wisconsin.
1981. 214p.
Adegbola, O. and Page, Hilary J.
"Nuptiality and Fertility in Metropolitan Lagos:
Components and Compensating Mechanisms." (In) Ruzicka,

L.T. (ed.). Nuptiality and Fertility: Proceedings of a
Seminar. Liege, Belgium: International Union for the
Scientific Study of Population. Bruges, Belgium.
January 8-11, 1982. pp. 337-362.
Adeniyi, E.O.
"Population Growth and Fertility Among the Nupe of
Nigeria." (In) Oppong, C. and Adaba, G. and
Bekombo-Priso, M. and Mogey, J. (eds.). Marriage,
Fertility and Parenthood in West Africa. Canberra,
Australia: Australian National University. Department of
Demography. Volume Two. 1978. pp. 435-451.
Adeokun, Lawrence A.
"Family Planning in Southwest Nigeria: Levels and
Determinants of 'KAP'." (In) Adeokun, L.A. (ed.).
1971-1975 National Survey of Fertility, Family and Family
Planning, Phase I: Southwest Nigeria. Ife, Nigeria:
University of Ife. Department of Demography and Social
Statistics. Monograph #1. 1979. pp. 62-104.
Adeokun, Lawrence A.
"Fertility Inhibiting Effects of the Intermediate
Fertility Variables in Two Nigerian Sub-Groups." Genus.
Volume 41 #3/4 July-December, 1984. pp. 89-106.
Adepoju, Aderanti
"Migration and Fertility: A Case Study in South-West
Nigeria." (In) Oppong, C. and Adaba, G. and
Bekombo-Priso, M. and Mogey, J. (eds.). Marriage,
Fertility and Parenthood in West Africa. Canberra,
Australia: Australian National University. Department of
Demography. Volume Two. 1978. pp. 491-506.
Adepoju, Aderanti
"Migration, Employment and Fertility: A Case Study in
South-West Nigeria." Paper Presented to the 15th
International Seminar on Family Research. Lome, Togo.
1976.
Adepoju, Aderanti
"Rationality and Fertility in the Traditional Yoruba
Society, Southwest, Nigeria." (In) Caldwell, J.C. (ed.).
The Persistence of High Fertility: Population Prospects
in the Third World. Canberra, Australia: Australian
National University. Volume One. 1977. pp. 123-151.
Arowolo, Oladele O.
"Determinants of Fertility Among Yorubas of Nigeria."
(In) Hyo-Chai, Lee. Recent Empirical Findings on
Fertility: Korea, Nigeria, Tunisia, Venezuala,
Philippines. Washington, D.C.: Smithsonian Institution.
Interdisciplinary Communications Program. Occasional
Monograph #7. 1976. pp. 27-45.
Arowolo, Oladele O.
"Female Labour Force Participation and Fertility: The
Case of Ibadan City in the Western State of Nigeria."
(In) Oppong, C. and Adaba, G. and Bekombo-Priso, M. and
Mogey, J. (eds.). Marriage, Fertility and Parenthood in
West Africa. Canberra, Australia: Australian National

University. Department of Demography. Volume Two.
1978. pp. 533-564.
Arowolo, Oladele O.
"Female Labour Force Participation and Fertility: The
Case of Ibadan City in the Western State of Nigeria."
Paper Presented at the Conference on Marriage, Parenthood
and Fertility in West Africa. 25th International Seminar
of the International Sociological Association. Lome,
Togo. January 3-9, 1976.
Arowolo, Oladele O.
"Fertility of Urban Yoruba Working Women: A Case Study of
Ibadan City." Nigerian Journal of Economic and Social
Studies. Volume 19 #1 March, 1977. pp. 37-66.
Basumallik, M.K. and Sengupta, J.K.
"Infertility in Borno Women." Annals of Borno. #1 1983.
pp. 195-200.
Bongaarts, John
The Fertility Impact of Traditional and Changing
Childspacing Practices in Tropical Africa. New York:
Population Council. Center for Policy Studies. Working
Paper #42. May, 1979. 27p.
Caldwell, John C. and Caldwell, Pat
"Cause and Sequence in the Reduction of Postnatal
Abstinence in Ibadan City, Nigeria." (In) Page, Hilary
J. and Lesthaeghe, Ron (eds.). Child-Spacing in Tropical
Africa: Traditions and Change. New York: Acadenmic
Press. 1981. pp. 181-199.
Caldwell, John C.
Fertility and Household Economy in Nigeria. Calgary,
Canada: University of Calgary. 1976. 77p.
Caldwell, John C.
"Fertility and the Household Economy in Nigeria."
Journal of Comparative Family Studies. Volume 7 #2
Summer, 1976. pp. 193-253.
Caldwell, John C.
"Marriage, the Family and Fertility in Sub-Saharan Africa
With Special Reference to Research Programmes in Ghana
and Nigeria." (In) Huzayyin, S.A. and Acsadi, G.T.
(eds.). Family and Marriage in Some African and Asian
Countries. Cairo: Cairo Demographic Centre. CDC
Research Monograph #6. 1976. pp. 359-371.
Caldwell, John C.
The Changing African Family Project: A Report With
Special Reference to the Nigerian Segment. Canberra,
Australia: Australian National University. 1976. 26p.
Caldwell, John C.
"The Economic Rationality of High Fertility: An
Investigation Illustrated With Nigerian Survey Data.
Population Studies (London). Volume 31 #1 March, 1977.
pp. 5-27.
Caldwell, John C. and Caldwell, Pat
"The Role of Marital Sexual Abstinence in Determining

Fertility: A Study of the Yoruba of Nigeria." Population
Studies. Volume 31 #2 July, 1977. pp. 193-217.
Caldwell, John C.
The Socio-Economic Explanation of High Fertility: Papers
on the Yoruba Society of Nigeria. Canberra, Australia:
Australian National University. Department of
Demography. Changing African Family Project. Series #1.
1976.
Caldwell, John C.
Theory of Fertility Decline. New York: Academic Press.
1982. 385p.
Chukudebelu, W.O. and Esege, N. and Megafu, U.
"Etiological Factors in Infertility in Enugu, Nigeria."
Infertility. Volume 2 #2 1979. pp. 193-200.
DeLargy, Pamela and Bilsborrow, Richard E.
A Comparative Assessment of the Fertility Impact of Rural
Development Projects. Chapel Hill, North Carolina:
University of North Carolina. Carolina Population
Center. 1983.
Ekanem, Ita I. and Farooq, Ghazi M.
"The Dynamics of Population Change in Southern Nigeria."
Genus. Volume 33 #1/2 1977. pp. 119-140.
Ekanem, Ita I.
"Ways of Controlling Family Size: A Case Study of Eastern
Nigeria." (In) Oppong, C. and Adaba, G. and
Bekombo-Priso, M. and Mogey, J. (eds.). Marriage,
Fertility and Parenthood in West Africa. Canberra,
Australia: Australian National University. Department of
Demography. Volume Two. 1978. pp. 691-715.
Farooq, Ghazi M. and Ekanem, Ita I. and Ojelade, M.A.
Family Size Preferences and Fertility in South-Western
Nigeria. Geneva: International Labour Office. World
Employment Programme Research. Population and Employment
Working Paper #54. May, 1977. 33p.
Feyisetan, Bamikale J.
"Fertility and Female Employment in Lagos, Nigeria."
Genus. Volume 41 #1/2 January-June, 1985. pp. 57-76.
Gyepi-Garbrah, Benjamin
Adolescent Fertility in Nigeria. Boston: Pathfinder
Fund. 1985. 69p.
Harrington, Judith A.
"Education, Female Status and Fertility in Nigeria."
Paper Presented to the Population Association of America.
Atlanta, Georgia. 1978.
Harrington, Judith A.
Education, Female Status and Fertility in Nigeria. Ann
Arbor, Michigan: University of Michigan. School of
Public Health. Department of Population Planning. 1978.
Hyo-Chai, Lee and Hyoung, Cho and Arowolo, Oladele O. and
Popkin, Barry M.
Recent Empirical Findings on Fertility: Korea, Nigeria,
Tunisia... Washington, D.C.: Smithsonian Institution.
Interdisciplinary Communications Program. Occasional
Monograph Series #7. December, 1976. 144p.

Ilori, Felicia
    Factors Determining Rural-Urban Fertility Differentials
    in Western Nigeria: A Case Study of Ife, Ilesha and
    Selected Rural Areas in Oyo Province. Ife, Nigeria:
    University of Ife. 1976.
International Statistical Institute (ISI)
    The Nigeria Fertility Survey, 1981-82: A Summary of
    Findings. London: ISI. World Fertility Survey Summary
    of Country Report #49. September, 1984. 18p.
Lesthaeghe, Ron J. and Page, Hilary J. and Adegbola, O.
    "Child-Spacing and Fertility in Lagos." (In) Page,
    Hilary J. and Lesthaeghe, Ron (eds.). Child-Spacing in
    Tropical Africa: Traditions and Change. New York:
    Academic Press. 1981. pp. 147-179.
Lucas, David W.
    "Urban and Rural Fertility in Southern Nigeria." (In)
    Ruzicka, Lado T. (ed.). The Economic and Social Supports
    for High Fertility: Proceedings of the Conference. 1976.
    Canberra, Australia: Australian National University.
    Development Studies Center. Canberra, Australia.
    November 16-19, 1977. pp. 409-435.
MacLean, Una
    "Folk Medicine and Fertility: Aspects of Yoruba Medical
    Practice Affecting Women." (In) MacCormack, C.P. (ed.).
    Ethnography of Fertility and Birth. London: Academic
    Press. 1982. pp. 161-179.
Morgan, Robert W.
    "Yoruban Modernization and Fertility in Lagos." (In)
    Morgan, Robert W. New Perspectives on the Demographic
    Transition. Washington, D.C.: Smithsonian Institution.
    Interdisciplinary Communications Program. Occasional
    Monograph #4. 1976. pp. 1-51.
Morton-Williams, Peter
    "Family Structures in an Egbado Yoruba Community." (In)
    Oppong, C. and Adaba, G. and Bekombo-Priso, M. and Mogey,
    J. (eds.). Marriage, Fertility and Parenthood in West
    Africa. Canberra, Australia: Australian National
    University. Department of Demography. Volume One.
    1978. pp. 69-102.
Mott, Frank L. and Mott, Susan H. (eds.)
    "Household Fertility Decisions in West Africa--A
    Comparison of Male and Female Survey Results." Studies
    in Family Planning. Volume 16 #2 March-April, 1985.
    pp. 88-99.
Nigeria. National Population Bureau
    The Nigeria Fertility Survey, 1981/82. Lagos, Nigeria:
    National Population Bureau. Two Volumes. 1984. 664p.
Ogum, G.E.O.
    "Fertility Differentials in Nigeria." Genus. Volume 36
    #3/4 July-December, 1980. pp. 203-213.
Ojelade, Mukaila A.
    "The Socioeconomic Determinants of Fertility Behavior and
    Attitude in Southwest Nigeria, 1971-1973." Ph.D

Dissertation: University of Pennsylvania. Philadelphia, Pennsylvania. 1982. 273p.

Okediji, Frances O. and Caldwell, John C. and Caldwell, Pat and Ware, Helen
"The Changing African Family Project: A Report With Special Reference to the Nigerian Segment." Studies in Family Planning. Volume 7 #5 May, 1976. pp. 126-136.

Okediji, Francis O. and Caldwell, John C. and Caldwell, Pat and Ware, Helen
"The Changing African Family Project: A Report With Special Reference to the Nigerian Segment." (In) Oppong, C. and Adaba, G. and Bekombo-Priso, M. and Mogey, J. (eds.). Marriage, Fertility and Parenthood in West Africa. Canberra, Australia: Australian National University. Department of Demography. 1978. pp. 717-746.

Okore, Augustine O.
"Rural-Urban Fertility Differentials in Southern Nigeria: An Assessment of Some Available Evidence." Population Studies. Volume 34 #1 March, 1980. pp. 171-179.

Okore, Augustine O.
"The Ibos of Arochukwu in the Imo State, Nigeria." (In) Caldwell, John C. (ed.). The Persistence of High Fertility: Population Prospects in the Third World. Canberra, Australia: Australian National University. Volume One. 1977. pp. 313-330.

Okore, Augustine O.
"The Rationale of High Fertility in Rural Nigeria: The Case of Ibos in Arochukwu in Iwo State." (In) Ruzicka, Lado T. (ed.). The Economic and Social Supports for High Fertility: Proceedings of the Conference. Canberra, Australia: Australian National University. Development Studies Center. November 16-18, 1977. pp. 253-274.

Okpala, Amon O.
"Female Labor Force Participation and Fertility in Nigeria: A Study of Lagos." Ph.D Dissertation: Louisiana State University and Agricultural and Mechanical College. Baton Rouge, Louisiana. 1984. 158p.

Omideyi, Adekunbi K.
"Age at Marriage and Marital Fertility in Eastern Nigeria." Genus. Volume 39 #1-4 January-December, 1983. pp. 141-154.

Omideyi, Adekunbi K.
"The Persistence of High Fertility in Eastern Nigeria: An Analysis Based Upon a Sample Survey of Married Women in 1971-72." Ph.D Dissertation: University of London. London School of Economics. London, England. 1983. 403p.

Oni, Gbolahan A.
"The Effects of Women's Education on Postpartum Nonsusceptible Period in Ilorin, an Urban Community in Nigeria." Ph.D Dissertation: Johns Hopkins University. Baltimore, Maryland. 1985. 374p.

NIGERIA

Orubbuloye, Tunji
"High Fertility and the Rural Economy: A Study of Yoruba Society in Western Nigeria." (In) Caldwell, John C. (ed.). The Persistence of High Fertility: Population Prospects in the Third World. Canberra, Australia: Australian National University. Department of Demography. Volume One. 1977. pp. 361-392.

Orubuloye, I.O.
"Family Obligations and Fertility in Nigeria: The Case of the Yoruba of Western Nigeria." (In) Ruzicka, Lado T. (ed.). The Economic and Social Supports for High Fertility: Proceedings of the Conference. Canberra, Australia: Australian National University. Development Studies Center. November 16-18, 1977. pp. 203-217.

Orubuloye, I.O.
"Fertility, Sexual Abstinence and Contraception Among the Yoruba of Western Nigeria: A Study of Selected Rural Communities in Ekiti and Ibadan Divisions." Ph.D Dissertation: Australian National University. Department of Demography. Canberra, Australia. 1977.

Orubuloye, I.O.
Abstinence as a Method of Birth Control: Fertility and Child-Spacing Practice Amid Rural Yoruba Women in Nigeria. Canberra, Australia: Australian National University. Department of Demography. Changing African Family Project. Monograph #8. 1981. 116p.

Otolorin, E.O.
"Reproductive Performance Following Active Management of Diabetic Pregnancies at the University College Hospital, Ibadan, Nigeria." African Journal of Medicine and Medical Sciences. Volume 14 #3-4. September-December, 1985. pp. 155-160.

Ottong, Joseph G.
"Population Dynamics, Fertility and Family Planning in a Rural Community: A Study in Manchol, Southern Nigeria." (In) Oppong, C. and Adaba, G. and Bekomba-Priso, M. and Mogey, J. (eds.). Marriage, Fertility and Parenthood in West Africa. Canberra, Australia: Australian National University. Department of Demography. Volume Two. 1978.

Oyemade, Adefunke and Ogunmuyiwa, Taiwo A.
"Sociocultural Factors and Fertility in A Rural Nigerian Community." Studies in Family Planning. Volume 12 #3 March, 1981. pp. 109-111.

Santow, G.
"A Microsimulation Model of Human Fertility: Theory and Applications to the Yoruba of Western Nigeria." Ph.D Dissertation: Australian National University. Canberra, Australia. 1979.

Santow, G. and Bracher, M.
"Patterns of Postpartum Sexual Abstinence and Their Implications for Fertility in Ibadan, Nigeria." (In) Page, Hilary J. and Lesthaeghe, Ron (eds.).

403

Child-Spacing in Tropical Africa: Traditions and Change. New York: Academic Press. 1981. pp. 201-223.

Santow, M.G.
"A Microsimulation of Yoruba Fertility." Mathematical Biosciences. Volume 42 #1/2 1978. pp. 93-117.

Sembajwe, I.S.L.
"Religious Fertility Differentials Among the Yoruba of Western Nigeria." Journal of Biosocial Science. Volume 12 #2 April, 1980. pp. 153-164.

Sembajwe, Israel S.
Fertility and Infant Mortality Amongst the Yoruba in Western Nigeria. Canberra, Australia: Australian National University. Department of Demography. Changing African Family Project Monograph #6. 1981. 144p.

Sembajwe, Israel S.
"Religious Fertility Differentials Among the Yoruba of Western Nigeria." Journal of Biosocial Science. Volume 12 #2 April, 1980. pp. 153-164.

Tshinyongolo, Mulunda
"Fertility Differentials in Urban Nigeria." Ph.D Dissertation: University of Michigan. Ann Arbor, Michigan. 1981. 356p.

Ukaegbu, Alfred O.
"Fertility of Women in Polynous Unions in Rural Eastern Nigeria." Journal of Marriage and Family. Volume 39 #2 May, 1977. pp. 397-404.

Ukaegbu, Alfred O.
"Socio-Cultural Determination of Fertility: A Case Study of Rural Eastern Nigeria." Journal of Comparative Family Studies. Volume 8 #1 Spring, 1977. pp. 99-115.

Uyanga, Joseph T.
"Is Overcrowded Urban Living a Factor in Fertility Decisions? A Case Study of Metropolitan Calabar." Social Action. Volume 29 #2 April-June, 1979. pp. 150-162.

Uyanga, Joseph T.
"Socio-Economic Values in the Fertility Behavior of Nigerians." Social Action. #4 October-December, 1977. pp. 379-398.

Verma, O.P. and Singha, P.
"Fertility Pattern of Muslim Hausa Women in Northern Nigeria." Nigerian Journal of Economic and Social Studies. Volume 24 #2 July, 1982. pp. 185-198.

HEALTH, NUTRITION AND MEDICINE

Aborampah, Osei-Mensah
"Determinants of Breast-Feeding and Post-Partum Sexual Abstinence: Analysis of a Sample of Yoruba Women, Western Nigeria." Journal of Biosocial Science. Volume 17 #4 October, 1985. pp. 461-469.

Aborampah, Osei-Mensah
"Plural Marriage, Post-Partum Abstinence and Fertility
Among the Yoruba of Western Nigeria." Ph.D Dissertation:
University of Wisconsin-Madison. Madison, Wisconsin.
1981. 214p.

Abudu, O. and Akinkugbe, A.
"Clinical Causes and Classification of Perinatal
Mortality in Lagos." International Journal of
Gynaecology and Obstetrics. Volume 20 #6 December,
1982. pp. 443-448.

Acsadi, Gyorgy
"Traditional Birth Control Methods in Yorubaland." (In)
Marshall, John F. and Polgar, Steven (eds.). Culture,
Natality, and Family Planning. Chapel Hill, North
Carolina: University of North Carolina. Carolina
Population Center. 1976. pp. 126-155.

Adegbola, O. and Page, Hilary J. and Lesthaeghe, Ron J.
Breast-Feeding and Post-Partum Abstinence in Metropolitan
Lagos. Lagos, Nigeria: University of Lagos. Human
Resources Research Unit. Faculty of Social Sciences.
Research Bulletin. #80-3. 1980. 38p.

Adegboye, D.S.
"Cultural Examination of Female Outpatients in Zaria,
Nigeria for Genital Mycoplasmas." Nigerian Medical
Journal. Volume 9 #7-8 July-August, 1979. pp. 675-678.

Adeleye, J.A.
"Contraceptives and the Female Undergraduates in Ibadan,
Nigeria." East Africa Medical Journal. Volume 58 #8
August, 1981. pp. 616-621.

Adeokun, Lawrence A.
"Lactation Abstinence in Family Building Among the Ekitis
of South-West Nigeria." Paper Presented at the National
Workshop on Population and Economic Development in
Nigeria in the 1980's. Lagos, Nigeria: University of
Lagos. Human Resource Unit. September 12-14, 1979.

Adeokun, Lawrence A.
"Lactation Abstinence in Family Building Among the Ekitis
of Southwest Nigeria." In) Chojnacka, H. and Olusanya,
P.O. and Folayan, Ojo (eds.). Population and Economic
Development in Nigeria in the 1980's. New York: United
Nations. 1981. pp. 41-57.

Ajobor, L.N.
"Contraceptives and Abortions in Nigeria." Nigerian
Medical Journal. Volume 6 July, 1976. pp. 367+.

Akingba, J.B.
"Abortion, Maternity and the Other Health Problems in
Nigeria." Nigerian Medical Journal. Volume 7 #4
October, 1977. pp. 465-471.

Alakija, Wole
"Method of Child Delivery in Benin City and its
Environs." Journal of Tropical Pediatrics. Volume 30 #1
1984. pp. 48-49.

Arowolo, Oladele O.
"Determinants of Fertility Among Yorubas of Nigeria."
(In) Hyo-Chai, Lee. Recent Empirical Findings on
Fertility: Korea, Nigeria, Tunisia, Venezuala,
Philippines. Washington, D.C.: Smithsonian Institution.
Interdisciplinary Communications Program. Occasional
Monograph #7. 1976. pp. 27-45.
Arowolo, Oladele O.
"Female Labour Force Participation and Fertility: The
Case of Ibadan City in the Western State of Nigeria."
(In) Oppong, C. and Adaba, G. and Bekombo-Priso, M. and
Mogey, J. (eds.). Marriage, Fertility and Parenthood in
West Africa. Canberra, Australia: Australian National
University. Department of Demography. Volume Two.
1978. pp. 533-564.
Arowolo, Oladele O.
"Female Labour Force Participation and Fertility: The
Case of Ibadan City in the Western State of Nigeria."
Paper Presented at the Conference on Marriage, Parenthood
and Fertility in West Africa. 25th International Seminar
of the International Sociological Association. Lome,
Togo. January 3-9, 1976.
Arowolo, Oladele O.
"Fertility of Urban Yoruba Working Women: A Case Study of
Ibadan City." Nigerian Journal of Economic and Social
Studies. Volume 19 #1 March, 1977. pp. 37-66.
Awaritefe, A.
"Anxiety and Menstrual Bleeding in Nigerian Females."
Mental Health and Society. Volume 5 #5-6 1978. pp.
257-265.
Ayangade, O.
"Characteristics and Significance of the Latent Phase in
the Outcome of Labor Among Nigerian Parturients."
Journal of the National Medical Association. Volume 76
#6 June, 1984. pp. 609-613.
Ayangade, Okun
"Characteristics of Contraceptive Acceptors in an Urban
Nigerian Setting." International Journal of Gynaecology
and Obstetrics. Volume 22 1984. pp. 59-66.
Ayangade, Okun
"Integrated Family Planning Services: A Nigerian
Example." East African Medical Journal. Volume 61 #5
May, 1984. pp. 412-419.
Ayangade, Okun
"Preliminary Observations on Sex Education and
Contraceptive Practice Among Nigerian Female
Under-Graduates." Proceedings of the Meeting on
Contraceptive Delivery Systems. University of Ife. Ife,
Nigeria. 1983.
Ayangade, Samuel O.
"Maternal Mortality in a Semi-Urban Nigerian Community."
Journal of the National Medical Association. Volume 73
#2 February, 1981. pp. 137-140.

Bakare, Christopher G.
"Medical and Parmedical Opinion in Nigeria." (In) David,
Henry P. and Friedman, Herbert L. and Van Der Tak, Jean
and Sevilla, Marylis J. (eds.). Abortion in
Psychological Research. New York: Springer Publishing.
Transnational Family Research Institute Monographs.
1978. pp. 259-283.
Bamisaiye, Anne and Oyediran, M.A.
"Breast-Feeding Among Female Employees at a Major Health
Institution in Lagos, Nigeria." Social Science and
Medicine. Volume 17 #23 1983. pp. 1867-1871.
Bamisaiye, Anne and De Sweemer, Cecile and Ransome-Kuti,
Olikoye
"Developing a Clinic Strategy Appropriate to Community
Family Planning Needs and Practices." Studies in Family
Planning. Volume 9 #2-3 February-March, 1978. pp.
44-48.
Basumallik, M.K. and Sengupta, J.K.
"Infertility in Borno Women." Annals of Borno. #1 1983.
pp. 195-200.
Caffrey, K.T.
"Maternal Mortality - A Continuing Challenge in Tropical
Practice. A Report From Kaduna, Northern Nigeria." East
African Medical Journal. Volume 56 #6 June, 1979. pp.
274-277.
Caldwell, John C.
"Education as a Factor in Mortality Decline: An
Examination of Nigerian Data." Population Studies.
Volume 33 #3 November, 1979. pp. 395-413.
Caldwell, John C. and Ware, Helen
"The Evolution of Family Planning in an African City:
Ibadan, Nigeria." Population Studies. Volume 31 #3
November, 1977. pp. 487-508.
Chiedozi, L.C.
"Breast Carcinoma in Young Nigerian Women." Tropical and
Geographical Medicine. Volume 36 #3 September, 1984.
pp. 249-253.
Chukudebelu, W.O. and Esege, N. and Megafu, U.
"Etiological Factors in Infertility in Enugu, Nigeria."
Infertility. Volume 2 #2 1979. pp. 193-200.
Darougar, S.
"Chlamydial Genital Infection in Ibadan, Nigeria. A
Seroepidemiological Survey." British Journal of Venereal
Diseases. Volume 58 #6 December, 1982. pp. 366-369.
Demehin, Ade O.
"Sexual Attitudes in Traditional and Modern Yoruba
Society." International Quarterly of Community Health
and Education. Volume 4 #3 1983. pp. 231-238.
Di Domenico, Catherine M. and Burdin, J.M.
"Breastfeeding Practices Among Urban Women in Ibadan,
Nigeria." (In) Raphael, D. (ed.). Breastfeeding and
Food Policy in a Hungry World. New York: Academic Press.
1979.

Dopamu, P.A.
   "Obstetrics and Gynaecology Among the Yoruba."   Orita.
   Volume 14 #1   June, 1982.   pp.34-42.
Dow, Thomas E.
   "Breast Feeding and Abstinence Among the Yoruba."
   Studies in Family Planning.   Volume 8 #8   August, 1977.
   pp. 208-214.
Dow, Thomas E.
   Breast-Feeding, Abstinence, and Family Planning Among the
   Yoruba and Other Sub-Saharan Groups: Patterns and Policy
   Implications.   Purchase, New York: State University of
   New York. Department of Sociology. 1978.
Doyle, Pat and Morley, David and Woodland, Margaret and
Cole, Jane J.
   "Birth Intervals, Survival and Growth in a Nigerian
   Village." Journal of Biosocial Science. Volume 10 #1
   January, 1978. pp. 81-94.
Edeh, J.
   "Abortion and the Law in Nigeria: A Psychiatrists View."
   Nigerian Medical Journal. Volume 9 #5/6 1979. pp.
   631-634.
Edigbo, P.O. and Chukudebelu, W.O.
   "Child Spacing and Child Mortality Among Nigerian Ibos."
   International Journal of Gynaecology and Obstetrics.
   Volume 18 #5 1980. pp. 372-374.
Egwuatu, V.E.
   "Complications of Female Circumcision in Nigerian Igbos."
   British Journal of Obstetrics and Gynaecology. Volume 88
   #11 November, 1981. pp. 1090-1093.
Ekpo, M.
   "Menstrual Pattern of College Students." Nigerian
   Medical Journal. Volume 9 #7-8 July-August, 1979. pp.
   669-674.
Ekwempu, C.C.
   "Maternal Mortality in Eclampsia in the Guinea Savannah
   Region of Nigeria." Clinical and Experimental
   Hypertension (B) Volume 1 #4 1982. pp. 531-537.
Elegbe, Isaac A. and Elegbe, Iyabode
   "Quantitive Relationships of Candida Albicans Infections
   and Dressing Patterns in Nigerian Women." American
   Journal of Public Health. Volume 73 April, 1983. pp.
   450-452.
Enabulele, A.B.
   "The Role of Women's Associations in Nigeria's
   Development: Social Welfare Aspect." (In) Women in
   Nigeria Today. London: Zed Press. 1985. pp. 187-194.
Ezimokhai, M. and Ajabor, L.N. and Jackson, M. and Izilien,
M.I.
   "Response of Unmarried Adolescents to Contraceptive
   Advice and Service in Nigeria." International Journal of
   Gynaecology and Obstetrics. Volume 19 #6 December,
   1981. pp. 481-485.

Fajumi, James O.
"Alterations in Blood Lipids and Side Effects Induced by Depo-Provera in Nigerian Women." Contraception. Volume 27 #2 February, 1983. pp. 161-175.

Fakeye, O.
"The Interrelationships Between Age, Physical Measurements and Body Composition at Menarche in Schoolgirls at Ibadan, Nigeria." International Journal of Gynaecology and Obstetrics. Volume 23 #1 February, 1985. pp. 55-58.

Fapohunda, Eleanor R.
"The Child-Care Dilemma of Working Mothers in African Cities: The Case of Lagos, Nigeria." (In) Bay, Edna G. (ed.). Women and Work in Africa. Boulder, Colorado: Westview Press. Westview Special Studies in Africa. 1982. pp. 277-288.

Feyisetan, Bamikale J.
"Fertility and Female Employment in Lagos, Nigeria." Genus. Volume 41 #1/2 January-June, 1985. pp. 57-76.

Goyea, H.
"Age of Menarche and Pre-Menarcheal Awareness of Some Benin City School Girls." East African Medical Journal. Volume 59 #9 September, 1982. pp. 610-616.

Gyepi-Garbrah, Benjamin
Adolescent Fertility in Nigeria. Boston: Pathfinder Fund. 1985. 69p.

Harrington, Judith A.
"Nutritional Stress and Economic Responsibility: A Study of Nigerian Women." (In) Buvinic, Mayra and Lycette, Margaret A. and McGreevey, William P. (eds.). Women and Poverty in the Third World. Baltimore, Maryland: Johns Hopkins University. 1983. pp. 130-156.

Harrison, Kelsey
"Child-Bearing, Health and Social Priorities: A Survey of 22,744 Consecutive Hospital Births in Zaria, Northern Nigeria." British Journal of Obstetrics and Gynaecology, Supplement. Volume 92 #5 October, 1985. 119p.

Hartfield, V.J.
"Maternal Mortality in Nigeria Compared With Earlier International Experience." International Journal of Gynaecology and Obstetrics. Volume 18 #1 July-August, 1980. pp. 70-75.

Hartfield, V.J.
"Prevention of Maternal Death in a Nigerian Village." International Journal of Gynaecology and Obstetrics. Volume 18 #2 September-October, 1980. pp. 150-152.

Ilori, Felicia
Factors Determining Rural-Urban Fertility Differentials in Western Nigeria: A Case Study of Ife, Ilesha and Selected Rural Areas in Oyo Province. Ife, Nigeria: University of Ife. 1976.

Iregbulem, L.M.
"Post-Circumcision Vulval Adhesions in Nigerians."

British Journal of Plastic Surgery. Volume 33 #1
January, 1980. pp. 83-86.
Ityavar, Dennis A.
"A Traditional Midwife Practice, Sokoto State, Nigeria."
Social Science and Medicine. Volume 18 #6 1984. pp.
497-501.
Johnson, B.C.
"Female Circumcision in Nigeria." Paper Presented at the
Seminar on Traditional Practices Affecting the Health of
Women and Children: Female Circumcision, Childhood
Marriage, Nutritional Taboos, etc. Alexandria, Egypt:
World Health Organization. Eastern Mediterranean
Regional Office. Khartoum, Sudan. February 10-15, 1979.
Ladipo, Patricia A. and Ojo, A.O. and James, S. and Stewart,
K.R.
"Menstrual Regulation in Ibadan, Nigeria." International
Journal of Gynaecology and Obstetrics. Volume 15 #5
1978. pp. 428-432.
MacLean, Una
"Folk Medicine and Fertility: Aspects of Yoruba Medical
Practice Affecting Women." (In) MacCormack, C.P. (ed.).
Ethnography of Fertility and Birth. London: Academic
Press. 1982. pp. 161-179.
Mathur, D.N.
"Age at Menarche in Nigerian Athletes." British Journal
of Sports Medicine. Volume 16 #4 December, 1982. pp.
250-252.
Mbofung, C.M. and Omololu, A.
"Dietary Fibre in the Diets of Urban and Rural Yoruba
Nigerian Women." Nutritional Research. Volume 4 #2
March-April, 1984. pp. 225-235.
Mbofung, C.M.
"Zinc, Copper and Iron Concentrations in the Plasma and
Diets of Lactating Nigerian Women." British Journal of
Nutrition. Volume 53 #3 May, 1985. pp. 427-439.
Megafu, U.
"Factors Influencing the Outcome of Labour in the
Nigerian Primigravidae." East African Medical Journal.
Volume 59 #11 November, 1982. pp. 726-732.
Megafu, U.
"Female Ritual Circumcision in Africa: An Investigation
of the Presumed Benefits Among the Ibos of Nigeria."
East African Medical Journal. Volume 60 #11 1983. pp.
793-800.
Meldrum, Brenda and Di Domenico, Catherine M.
"Production and Reproduction: Women and Breastfeeding:
Some Nigerian Examples." Social Science and Medicine.
Volume 16 #13 1982. pp. 1247-1251.
Myers, Robert A.
"Circumcision: Its Nature and Practice Among Some Ethnic
Groups in Southern Nigeria." Social Science and
Medicine. Volume 21 #5 1985. pp. 581-588.

Obayemi, T.O.
"Maternal Mortality in Rupture of the Uterus." Nigerian
Medical Journal. Volume 8 #5 September, 1978. pp.
433-437.

Ogbeide, D.O. and Edebiri, A.A.
"A Two Year Study of Organised Family Planning Services
in a Developing Country: Experiences in Bendel State of
Nigeria." East African Medical Journal. Volume 61 #6
June, 1984. pp. 470-476.

Ogbuagu, Philip A.
"Depo-Provera--A Choice or an Imposition on the African
Woman: A Case Study of Depo Proversa Usage in Maiduguri."
African Review. Volume 10 #2 1983. pp. 39-51.

Ogbuagu, Stella
"Women and Depo-Provera Usage in Nigeria: Chosen or
Imposed Forms of Birth Control?" Rural Africana. #21
Winter, 1985. pp. 81-90.

Ogum, G.E.O.
"Fertility Differentials in Nigeria." Genus. Volume 36
#3/4 July-December, 1980. pp. 203-213.

Ogum, G.E.O. and Okorafor, A.E.
"Seasonality of Births in South-Eastern Nigeria."
Journal of Biosocial Science. Volume 11 #2 April, 1979.
pp. 209-218.

Ogunbanjo, B.O. and Osoba, A.O.
"Trichomonal Vaginitis in Nigerian Women." Tropical and
Geographical Medicine. Volume 36 #1 March, 1984. pp.
67-70.

Ojofeitimi, E.O.
"Assessment of the Nutritional Status of Nigerian Rural
Children and Mothers Perceptions of Quality of Life."
Child Care Health and Development. Volume 10 #6 1984.
pp. 349-358.

Okoisor, A.T.
"Maternal Mortality in the Lagos University Teaching
Hospital. A Five Year Survey--1970-1974." Nigerian
Medical Journal. Volume 8 #4 July, 1978. pp. 349-354.

Okojie, S.E.
"Induced Illegal Abortions in Benin City, Nigeria."
International Journal of Gynaecology and Obstetrics.
Volume 14 #6 1976. pp. 517-521.

Olatunbosun, D.A.
"Effect of the Sickle-Cell Gene on the Age of the
Menarche in Nigerian Girls." Nigerian Medical Journal.
Volume 8 #5 September, 1978. pp. 443-445.

Omu, A.E. and Oronsaye, A.U. and Faal, M.K. and Asuquo, E.E.
"Adolescent Induced Abortion in Benin City, Nigeria."
International Journal of Gynaecology and Obstetrics.
Volume 19 #6 December, 1981. pp. 495-499.

Omu, A.E. and Ogbimi, A.O. and Ihongbe, J.
"Trypsin Inhibitory Capacity in Serum of Women With
Carcinoma of the Cervix in Benin City, Nigeria." Journal

of Obstetrics and Gynaecology. Volume 5 #1 1984. pp. 53-55.

Onadeko, M.O.
"Female Circumcision in Nigeria: A Fact or a Farce?" Journal of Tropical Pediatrics. Volume 31 #4 August, 1981. pp. 180-184.

Oni, Gbolahan A.
"Effects of Women's Education on Postpartum Practices and Fertility in Urban Nigeria." Studies in Family Planning. Volume 16 #6 Part One November-December, 1985. pp. 321-331.

Oni, Gbolahan A.
"The Effects of Women's Education on Postpartum Nonsusceptible Period in Ilorin, an Urban Community in Nigeria." Ph.D Dissertation: Johns Hopkins University. Baltimore, Maryland. 1985. 374p.

Onuorah, J.U. and Ajayi, O.A.
"Riboflavin Content of Breast-Milk in Lactating Nigerian Women: Its Implications for Child-Welfare in Developing Countries." Nutrition Reports International. Volume 31 #6 1985. pp. 1211-1217.

Oronsaye, A.U. and Odiase, G.I.
"Attitudes Toward Abortion and Contraception Among Nigerian Secondary School Girls." International Journal of Gynaecology and Obstetrics. Volume 21 #5 October, 1983. pp. 423-426.

Osotimehin, B.
"Sequential Hormone Measurements After Menstrual Regulation in Normal Nigerian Women." African Journal of Medicine and Medical Sciences. Volume 14 #1-2 March-June, 1985. pp. 105-109.

Osuhor, P.C.
"Stillbirths in a Savannah District of Northern Nigeria: The Socio-Economic Socio-Cultural Factors." Nigerian Medical Journal. Volume 9 #4 April, 1979. pp. 481-485.

Otolorin, E.O.
"Reproductive Performance Following Active Management of Diabetic Pregnancies at the University College Hospital, Ibadan, Nigeria." African Journal of Medicine and Medical Sciences. Volume 14 #3-4. September-December, 1985. pp. 155-160.

Ottong, Joseph G.
"Population Dynamics, Fertility and Family Planning in a Rural Community: A Study in Manchol, Southern Nigeria." (In) Oppong, C. and Adaba, G. and Bekomba-Priso, M. and Mogey, J. (eds.). Marriage, Fertility and Parenthood in West Africa. Canberra, Australia: Australian National University. Department of Demography. Volume Two. 1978.

Oyakhire, G.K.
"Environmental Factors Influencing Maternal Mortality in Zaria, Nigeria." Royal Society of Health Journal. Volume 100 #2 April, 1980. pp. 72-74.

Page, Hilary J. and Lesthaeghe, Ron J. and Adegbola, O.
    Breast-Feeding and Abstinence: Socioeconomic
    Differentials in Metropolitan Lagos. Brussels, Belgium:
    Vrije Universiteit Brussel. Centrum Sociologie. 1977.
Rehan, Naghma E. and Abashiya, Aubu K.
    "Breastfeeding and Abstinence Among Hausa Women."
    Studies in Family Planning. Volume 12 #5 May, 1981.
    pp. 233-237.
Rehan, Naghma E.
    "Profile of Contraceptive Clients in Katsina, Northern
    Nigeria." Journal of Biosocial Science. Volume 16 #4
    1984. pp. 427-436.
Santow, G. and Bracher, M.
    "Patterns of Postpartum Sexual Abstinence and Their
    Implications for Fertility in Ibadan, Nigeria." (In)
    Page, Hilary J. and Lesthaeghe, Ron (eds.).
    Child-Spacing in Tropical Africa: Traditions and Change.
    New York: Academic Press. 1981. pp. 201-223.
Sembajwe, Israel S.
    "Education and Accuracy of Age Reporting Among Yoruba
    Females in Western Nigeria." Social Biology. Volume 27
    #4 Winter, 1980. pp. 294-303.
Sembajwe, Israel S.
    "Fertility and Infant Mortality Amongst the Yoruba in
    Western Nigeria." Canberra, Australia: Australian
    National University. Department of Demography. Changing
    African Family Project Monograph #6. 1981. 144p.
Sogbanmu, M.O. and Aregbesola, Y.A.
    "Menarchal Age in Nigerian School-Girls: Its Relationship
    to the Height, Weight and Menstrul Profile."
    International Journal of Gynaecology and Obstetrics.
    Volume 16 1979. pp. 339-340.
Sogbanmu, M.O.
    "Perinatal Mortality and Maternal Mortality in General
    Hospital, Ondo, Nigeria. Use of High Risk Pregnancy
    Predictive Scoring Index." Nigerian Medical Journal.
    Volume 9 #4 April, 1979. pp. 475-479.
Sogbanmu, M.O.
    "Perinatal Mortality and Maternal Mortality in General
    Hospital, Ondo, Nigeria. Use of High Risk Pregnancy
    Predictive Scoring Index." Nigerian Medical Journal.
    Volume 9 #1 January, 1979. pp. 123-127.
Soyinka, Femi
    "Sexual Behavior Among University Students in Nigeria."
    Archives of Sexual Behavior. Volume 8 January, 1979.
    pp. 15-26.
Temuru, S.
    "Mother and Child in the Lagos Metropolis." Nigeria
    Magazine. #132/133 1980. pp. 3-22.
U.S. Agency for International Development (U.S. AID)
    U.S. AID Operations Research Project Summary: Community
    Based Distribution of Low Cost Family Planning and
    Maternal Child Health Services in Rural Nigeria.

Washington, D.C.: U.S. Department of State. U.S. AID.
Unpublished. February, 1981.
Uche, Chukwudum
The Environment of Infant and Child Mortality: The Case
of Nigerian Villages. Providence, Rhode Island: Brown
University. Population Studies Center. 1985.
Uche, G.O.
"The Age of Menarche in Nigerian Urban School Girls."
Annals of Human Biology. Volume 6 #4 July-August, 1979.
pp. 395-398.
Udjo, E.O.
"Obstacles to Successful Fertility Control in Nigeria."
Social Science and Medicine. Volume 19 #11 1984. pp.
1167-1171.
Uyanga, Joseph T.
"Child Mortality and Contraception Usage: A Study of
Rural Acceptors in Nigeria." Rural Africana. #14 Fall,
1982. pp. 61-68.
Uyanga, Joseph T.
"Rural-Urban Differences in Child Care and Breastfeeding
Behavior in South Eastern Nigeria." Social Science and
Medicine. Volume 14D #1 March, 1980. pp. 23-29.
Weiss, Eugene and Udo, A.A.
The Calabar Rural MCH/FP Project: What We Have Learned
About Family Planning. New York: Population Council.
1980.
Weiss, Eugene and Udo, A.A.
"The Calabar Rural Maternal and Child Health/Family
Planning Project." Studies in Family Planning. Volume
12 #2 February, 1981. pp. 47-57.
Weiss, Eugene and Ayeni, Olasola and Ladipo, O.A.
The Role of Modern Family Planning on Southwestern Rural
Nigeria. New York: Columbia University. Center for
Population and Family Health. 1985.
Wien, E.M.
"Vitamin B6 Status of Nigerian Women Using Various
Methods of Contraception." American Journal of Clinical
Nutrition. Volume 31 #8 August, 1978. pp. 1392-1396.
Zaidi, S.M.H.
"Perception of Parental Sex Preference by Nigerian
Children." Journal of Social Psychology. Volume 108 2nd
Half August, 1979. pp. 267-268.

HISTORY

Afonja, Simi A.
"The Historical Evolution of the Sexual Division of Labor
in Nigeria." Paper Presented at the Meeting of Experts
on the Theoretical Frameworks and Methodological
Approaches to Studies on the Role of Women in History as
Actors in Economic, Social, Political and Ideological
Processes. Paris: United Nations Educational, Scientific
and Cultural Organization. 1984. 20p.

Copley, Anthony
  "The Debate on Widow Remarriage and Polygamy: Aspects of
  Moral Change in 19th Century Bengal and Yorubaland."
  Journal of Imperial and Commonwealth History. Volume 7
  #2 January, 1979. pp. 128-148.
Fieloux, M.
  "Bibliographic Chronicle: Invisible and Mute
  Women--Concerning Ibo Riots of 1929." Cahiers d'Etudes
  Africaines. Volume 17 #1 1977. pp. 189+.
Hill, Polly
  "Women's House Trade." (In) Hill, Polly. Population,
  Prosperity and Poverty: Rural Kano, 1900 and 1970.
  Cambridge, New York: Cambridge University Press. 1977.
  240p.
Ifeka-Moller, Caroline
  "Female Militancy and Colonial Revolt: The Women's War of
  1929, Eastern Nigeria." (In) Ardener, S. (ed.).
  Perceiving Women. New York: Halsted Press. 1977. pp.
  127-157.
Ifeka-Moller, Caroline
  "Racial Categories and Sexual Images in Colonial
  Nigeria." Paper Presented at the Meeting of the African
  Studies Association of the United Kingdom. 1978. 16p.
Johnson, Cheryl J.
  "Grass Roots Organizing: Women in Anticolonial Activity
  on South-Western Nigeria." African Studies Review.
  Volume 25 #2/3 July-September, 1982. pp. 137-158.
Johnson, Cheryl J.
  "Madam Alimotu Pelewuru and the Lagos Market Women."
  Tarikh. Volume 7 #1 1981. pp. 1-10.
Johnson, Cheryl J.
  "Nigerian Women and British Colonialism: The Yoruba
  Example With Selected Biographies." Ph.D Dissertation:
  Northwestern University. Evanston, Illinois. 1978.
  314p.
Mangvwat, Joyce A.
  "Home Economics in Northern Nigeria: An Historical Study,
  1842-1980." Ph.D Dissertation: University of
  Wisconsin-Madison. Madison, Wisconsin. 1981. 150p.
Mann, Kristin
  "Marriage Choices Among the Educated African Elite in
  Lagos Colony, 1880-1915." International Journal of
  African Historical Studies. Volume 14 #2 1981. pp.
  210-228.
Mann, Kristin
  "The Dangers of Dependence: Chrisitian Marriage Among the
  Elite Women in Lagos Colony, 1880-1915." Journal of
  African History. Volume 24 #1 1983. pp. 37-56.
Mann, Kristin
  "The Dangers of Dependence: The Response of Educated
  Christian Women in Lagos Colony to Western Marriage."
  Paper Presented at the Annual Meeting of the African

Studies Association. Los Angeles, California. October,
1979.

Mann, Kristin
"Women's Rights in Law and Practice: Marriage and Dispute
Settlement in Colonial Lagos." (In) Hay, Margaret J. and
Wright, Marcia (eds.). African Women and the Law:
Historical Perspectives. Boston: Boston University.
African Studies Center. Boston University Papers on
Africa. Volume 7. 1982. pp. 151-171.

Martin, S.
"Gender and Innovation--Farming, Cooking and Palm
Processing in the Ngwa Region, Southeastern Nigeria,
1900-1930." Journal of African History. Volume 25 #4
1984. pp. 411-427.

Mba, Nina E.
Nigerian Women Mobilized: Women's Political Activity in
Southern Nigeria, 1900-1965. Berkeley, California:
University of California. Institute of International
Studies. Research Series #48. 1982. 348p.

Mba, Nina E.
"Women in Southern Nigerian Political History,
1900-1965." Ph.D. Dissertation: University of Ibadan.
Ibadan, Nigeria. 1978.

Mohammed, H.D.
"Women in Nigerian History: Examples From Borno Empire,
Nupeland, and Igboland." (In) Women in Nigeria Today.
London: Zed Press. 1985. pp. 45-51.

Okonjo, Kamene
"The Dual-Sex Political System in Operation: Igbo Women
and Community Politics in Midwestern Nigeria." (In)
Hafkin, N.J. and Bay, Edna G. (eds.). Women in Africa:
Studies in Social and Economic Change. Stanford,
California: Stanford University Press. 1976. pp. 45-58.

Omojayowo, Akin
"Mother in Israel: Chridtianah Olatunrinle in Ondo (c.
1855-1941)." (In) Isichei, Elizabeth (ed.). Varieties
of Christian Experience in Nigeria. London: MacMillan
Press Ltd. 1982. pp. 141-148.

Tibenderana, Peter K.
"The Beginnings of Girl's Education in the Native
Administration Schools in Northern Nigeria, 1930-1945."
Journal of African History. Volume 26 #1 1985. pp.
93-109.

Van Allen, Judith
"'Aba Riots' or Igbo 'Women's Work'? Ideology,
Stratification and the Invisibility of Women." (In)
Hafkin, N.J. and Bay, E.G. (eds.). Women in Africa.
Stanford, California: Stanford University Press. 1976.
pp. 59-85.

Van Allen, Judith
"'Sitting on a Man': Colonialism and the Lost Political
Institutions of Igbo Women." (In) Tiffany, Sharon W.

(ed.). Women and Society: An Anthropological Reader.
St. Albans, Vermont: Eden Press. 1979. pp. 163-187.
Van Allen, Judith
   "Aba Riots or Igbo Women's War." Ufahamu. Volume 6 #1
   1976.

LAW AND LEGAL ISSUES

Achike, Okay
   "Problems of Creation and Dissolution of Customary
   Marriages in Nigeria." (In) Roberts, Simon (ed.). Law
   and the Family in Nigeria. Hague, Netherlands: Mouton.
   1977. pp. 145-158.
Akande, Jadesola O.
   Law and the Status of Women in Nigeria. Addis Ababa,
   Ethiopia: United Nations Economic Commission for Africa.
   African Training and Research Centre for Women. 1979.
   77p.
Amechi, E.E.
   "Woman-to-Woman Marriage: Its Legal Significance." Aman.
   Volume 1 #1 1981. pp. 20-35.
Edeh, J.
   "Abortion and the Law in Nigeria: A Psychiatrists View."
   Nigerian Medical Journal. Volume 9 #5/6 1979. pp.
   631-634.
Kasunmu, A.B.
   "Economic Consequences of Divorce: A Case Study of Some
   Judicial Decisions in Lagos." (In) Roberts, Simon (ed.).
   Law and the Family in Africa. Hague, Netherlands:
   Mouton. 1977. pp. 129-143.
Mann, Kristin
   "Women's Rights in Law and Practice: Marriage and Dispute
   Settlement in Colonial Lagos." (In) Hay, Margaret J. and
   Wright, Marcia (eds.). African Women and the Law:
   Historical Perspectives. Boston: Boston University.
   African Studies Center. Boston University Papers on
   Africa. Volume 7. 1982. pp. 151-171.
Perchonock, N.
   "Double Oppression: Women and Land Matters in Kaduna
   State." (In) Women in Nigeria Today. London: Zed Press.
   1985. pp. 82-103.
Pittin, Renee
   "Hausa Women and Islamic Law: Is Reform Necessary."
   Paper Presented at the Annual Meeting of the African
   Studies Association. Paper #75. 1979. 19p.
Spaulding, J.
   "The Misfortunes of Some: The Advantages of Others: Land
   Sales by Women in Sinnar." (In) Hay, M.J. and Wright, M.
   (eds.). African Women and the Law: Historical
   Perspectives. Boston: Boston University. African
   Studies Center. 1978. pp. 3-18.

United Nations Economic Commission for Africa (UNECA)
    Law and the Status of Women in Nigeria. Addis Ababa,
    Ethiopia: UNECA. 1979.

LITERATURE

Adetokunbo, Pearse
    "Symbolic Characterization of Women in the Plays and
    Prose of Wole Soyinka." Ba Shiru. Volume 9 #12 1978.
    pp. 39-46.
Azuonye, Chukwma
    "Women's Folklore in the Novels of Flora Nwapa: Its
    Relevance to the Realistic Portrayal of the Igbo Woman."
    Paper Presented at the 1981 African Literature
    Association Conference. Baltimore, Maryland: University
    of Maryland. African-American Studies Department. 1981.
Berrian, Brenda F.
    "African Women as Seen in the Works of Flora Nwapa and
    Ama Ata Aidoo." CLA Journal. Volume 25 #3 March, 1982.
    pp. 331-339.
Davies, Carole B.
    "Maidens, Mistresses and Matrons: Feminine Images in
    Selected Soyinka Works." (In) Anyidoho, Kofi and Porter,
    Abioseh M. and Racine, Daniel and Spleth, Janice (eds.).
    Interdisciplinary Dimensions of African Literature.
    Washington, D.C.: Three Continents Press. 1985. pp.
    89-99.
Emecheta, Buchi
    "It's Me Who's Changed (Interview)." Connexions. #4
    Spring, 1982.
Frank, Katherine
    "The Death of a Slave Girl: African Womanhood in the
    Novels of Buchi Emecheta." World Literature Written in
    English. Volume 21 #3 1982. pp. 476-496.
Frank, Katherine
    "The Death of the Slave Girl: African Womanhood in the
    Novels of Buchi Emecheta." World Literature Written in
    English. Volume 21 #3 1982. pp. 476-497.
Haynes, J.
    "Some Notes on the Image of 'Women' in Some African
    Poems." (In) Women in Nigeria Today. London: Zed Press.
    1985. pp. 217-225.
Ikonne, Chidi
    "The Society and Women's Quest for Selfhood in Flora
    Nwapa's Early Novels." Kunapipi. Volume 6 #1 1984. pp.
    68-72.
Ikonne, Chidi
    "Women in Igbo Folktales." Paper Presented at the 1982
    African Literature Association Conference. Baltimore,
    Maryland: Univerisity of Maryland. African-American
    Studies Department. 1982.

Mack, Beverly B.
  "'Waka Daya Ba Ta Kare Nika" One Song Will Not Finish the
  Grinding: Hausa Women's Oral Literature." Paper
  Presented at the 1981 African Literature Association
  Conference. Baltimore, Maryland: University of Maryland.
  African-American Studies Department. 1981.
Mack, Beverly B.
  "Waka Daya Ba Ta Kare Nika'--One Song Will Not Finish the
  Grinding: Hausa Women's Oral Literature." (In) Wylie,
  Hal (ed.). Contemporary African Literature. Washington,
  D.C.: Three Continents. 1983. pp. 15-46.
Mack, Beverly B.
  "Wakokin Mata: Huasa Women's Oral Poetry." Ph.D
  Dissertation: University of Wisconsin-Madison. Madison,
  Wisconsin. 1981. 328p.
McCaffrey, Kathleen M.
  "Image of the Mother in the Stories of Ama Ata Aidoo."
  Africa Women. #23 1979. pp. 40-41.
Nasser, Merun
  "Achebe and His Women: A Social Science Perspective."
  Africa Today. Volume 27 #3 Third Quarter, 1980. pp.
  21-28.
Nicholson, Mary N.
  "Two Perspectives of African Womanhood: Flora Nwapa's
  'Efuru' and Elechi Amadi's 'The Concubine'." Paper
  Presented at the 1984 African Literature Association
  Conference. Baltimore, Maryland: University of Maryland.
  African-American Studies Department. 1984.
Nwankwo, Chimalum
  "The Feminist Impulse and Social Realism in Ama Aidoo's
  'No Sweetness Here' and 'Sister Killjoy'." Paper
  Presented at the 1983 African Literature Association
  Conference. Baltimore, Maryland: University of Maryland.
  African-American Studies Department. 1983.
Ojoade, J.O.
  "African Sexual Proverbs--Some Yoruba Examples."
  Folklore. Volume 94 #2 1983. pp. 201-213.
Oysakin, Ade
  "The Image of Women in Ifa Literary Corpus." Nigeria
  Magazine. #141 1982. pp. 16-23.
Palmer, E.T.
  "The Feminine Point of View: Buchi Emecheta's 'The Joys
  of Motherhood'." African Literature Today. # 13 1983.
  pp. 38-55.
Pearse, Adetukunbo
  "Symbolic Characterization of Women in the Plays and
  Prose of Wole Soyinka." Ba Shiru. Volume 9 #1-2 1978.
  pp. 39-46.
Purisch, C.
  "Soyinka's Superwomen." Paper Presented at the First
  Annual Ibadan African Literature Conference. Ibadan,
  Nigeria: University of Ibadan. July, 1976.
Schmidt, Nancy J.
  "African Women Writers of Literature for Children."

World Literature Written in English. Volume 17 1978.
pp. 18-21.
St. Peter, Christine
"Changing Worlds: The Nigerian Novels of Buchi Emecheta."
Atlantis. Volume 11 Fall, 1985. pp. 134-146.
Staudt, Kathleen A.
"The Characterization of Women in Soyinka and Armah." Ba
Shiru. Volume 8 #2 1977. pp. 63-69.

MARITAL RELATIONS AND NUPTIALITY

Aborampah, Osei-Mensah
"Determinants of Breast-Feeding and Post-Partum Sexual
Abstinence: Analysis of a Sample of Yoruba Women, Western
Nigeria." Journal of Biosocial Science. Volume 17 #4
October, 1985. pp. 461-469.
Aborampah, Osei-Mensah
"Plural Marriage, Post-Partum Abstinence and Fertility
Among the Yoruba of Western Nigeria." Ph.D Dissertation:
University of Wisconsin-Madison. Madison, Wisconsin.
1981. 214p.
Achebe, Christie C.
"Continuities, Changes and Challenges: Women's Roles in
Nigerian Society." Presence Africaine. # 120 1981. pp.
3-16.
Achike, Okay
"Problems of Creation and Dissolution of Customary
Marriages in Nigeria." (In) Roberts, Simon (ed.). Law
and the Family in Nigeria. Hague, Netherlands: Mouton.
1977. pp. 145-158.
Acsadi, Gyorgy
"Traditional Birth Control Methods in Yorubaland." (In)
Marshall, John F. and Polgar, Steven (eds.). Culture,
Natality, and Family Planning. Chapel Hill, North
Carolina: University of North Carolina. Carolina
Population Center. 1976. pp. 126-155.
Adaba, Gemma
"Rationality and Responsibility in Family Planning in
Traditional African Society." (In) Oppong, C. and Adaba,
G. and Bekombo-Priso, M. and Mogey, J. (eds.). Marriage,
Fertility and Parenthood in West Africa. Canberra,
Australia: Australian National University. Department of
Demography. Volume Two. 1978. pp. 655-672.
Adegbola, O. and Page, Hilary J.
"Nuptiality and Fertility in Metropolitan Lagos:
Components and Compensating Mechanisms." (In) Ruzicka,
L.T. (ed.). Nuptiality and Fertility: Proceedings of a
Seminar. Liege, Belgium: International Union for the
Scientific Study of Population. Bruges, Belgium.
January 8-11, 1982. pp. 337-362.
Adegbola, O. and Page, Hilary J. and Lesthaeghe, Ron J.
Breast-Feeding and Post-Partum Abstinence in Metropolitan
Lagos. Lagos, Nigeria: University of Lagos. Human

Resources Research Unit. Faculty of Social Sciences. Research Bulletin. #80-3. 1980. 38p.

Adelowo, E.D.
"Islamic Marriage System and the Extents of its Adoption by Yoruba Muslims of Nigeria." Orita. Volume 14 #1 June, 1982. pp. 16-33.

Ademola, Ade
"Changes in the Patterns of Marriage and Divorce in a Yoruba Town." Rural Africana. #14 Fall, 1982. pp. 1-24.

Adeokun, Lawrence A.
"Family Planning in Southwest Nigeria: Levels and Determinants of 'KAP'." (In) Adeokun, L.A. (ed.). 1971-1975 National Survey of Fertility, Family and Family Planning, Phase I: Southwest Nigeria. Ife, Nigeria: University of Ife. Department of Demography and Social Statistics. Monograph #1. 1979. pp. 62-104.

Adeokun, Lawrence A.
"Marital Sexual Relationships and Birth Spacing Among Two Yoruba Sub-Groups." Africa. Volume 52 #4 1982. pp. 1-14.

Adeokun, Lawrence A.
"Marital Sexuality and Birth Spacing Among the Yoruba." (In) Oppong, Christine (ed.). Female and Male in West Africa. London: George Allen and Unwin. 1983. pp. 127-137.

Adeokun, Lawrence A.
The Next Child: Spacing Strategies in Yorubaland. Philadelphia, Pennsylvania: University of Pennsylvania. Population Studies Center. African Demography Program. Working Paper #8. September, 1981. 81p.

Adepoju, Aderanti
"Migration and Fertility: A Case Study in South-West Nigeria." (In) Oppong, C. and Adaba, G. and Bekombo-Priso, M. and Mogey, J. (eds.). Marriage, Fertility and Parenthood in West Africa. Canberra, Australia: Australian National University. Department of Demography. Volume Two. 1978. pp. 491-506.

Adepoju, Aderanti
"Migration, Employment and Fertility: A Case Study in South-West Nigeria." Paper Presented to the 15th International Seminar on Family Research. Lome, Togo. 1976.

Adepoju, Aderanti
"Rationality and Fertility in the Traditional Yoruba Society, Southwest, Nigeria." (In) Caldwell, J.C. (ed.). The Persistence of High Fertility: Population Prospects in the Third World. Canberra, Australia: Australian National University. Volume One. 1977. pp. 123-151.

Agbamuche, Josephine N.
Customary Marriage in Akwukwu-Igbo. Lagos, Nigeria: Unicorn Enterprises. 1981. 14p.

Aluko, G.B. and Alfa, M.O.
    "Marriage and Family."   (In) Women in Nigeria Today.
    London: Zed Press. 1985. pp. 163-173.
Amechi, E.E.
    "Woman-to-Woman Marriage: Its Legal Significance."   Aman.
    Volume 1 #1 1981. pp. 20-35.
Arinola, O.A.N.
    "The Implications of Female Labour Force Participation on
    the Family: A Case Study of Some Factory Workers." B.Sc
    Dissertation: University of Ibadan.   Department of
    Sociology. Ibadan, Nigeria. 1978.
Arowolo, Oladele O.
    "Determinants of Fertility Among Yorubas of Nigeria."
    (In) Hyo-Chai, Lee. Recent Empirical Findings on
    Fertility: Korea, Nigeria, Tunisia, Venezuala,
    Philippines. Washington, D.C.: Smithsonian Institution.
    Interdisciplinary Communications Program. Occasional
    Monograph #7. 1976. pp. 27-45.
Bamisaiye, Anne and De Sweemer, Cecile and Ransome-Kuti,
Olikoye
    "Developing a Clinic Strategy Appropriate to Community
    Family Planning Needs and Practices." Studies in Family
    Planning. Volume 9 #2-3 February-March, 1978. pp.
    44-48.
Bongaarts, John
    The Fertility Impact of Traditional and Changing
    Childspacing Practices in Tropical Africa. New York:
    Population Council. Center for Policy Studies. Working
    Paper #42. May, 1979. 27p.
Burfisher, Mary E. and Horenstein, Nadine R.
    "Sex Roles and Development Effects on the Nigerian Tiv
    Farm Household." Rural Africana. #21 Winter, 1985.
    pp. 31-50.
Burfisher, Mary E. and Horenstein, Nadine R.
    Sex Roles in the Nigerian Tiv Farm Household and the
    Differential Impacts of Development Projects. Washington
    D.C.: U.S. Department of Agriculture. International
    Economics Division. 1982.
Caldwell, John C. and Caldwell, Pat
    "Cause and Sequence in the Reduction of Postnatal
    Abstinence in Ibadan City, Nigeria." (In) Page, Hilary
    J. and Lesthaeghe, Ron (eds.). Child-Spacing in Tropical
    Africa: Traditions and Change. New York: Acadenmic
    Press. 1981. pp. 181-199.
Caldwell, John C.
    "Marriage, the Family and Fertility in Sub-Saharan Africa
    With Special Reference to Research Programmes in Ghana
    and Nigeria." (In) Huzayyin, S.A. and Acsadi, G.T.
    (eds.). Family and Marriage in Some African and Asian
    Countries. Cairo: Cairo Demographic Centre. CDC
    Research Monograph #6. 1976. pp. 359-371.
Caldwell, John C. and Ware, Helen
    "The Evolution of Family Planning in an African City:

Ibadan, Nigeria." Population Studies. Volume 31 #3
November, 1977. pp. 487-508.

Caldwell, John C. and Caldwell, Pat
"The Role of Marital Sexual Abstinence in Determining
Fertility: A Study of the Yoruba of Nigeria." Population
Studies. Volume 31 #2 July, 1977. pp. 193-217.

Caldwell, John C.
The Socio-Economic Explanation of High Fertility: Papers
on the Yoruba Society of Nigeria. Canberra, Australia:
Australian National University. Department of
Demography. Changing African Family Project. Series #1.
1976.

Caldwell, John C.
"Variations in the Incidence of Sexual Abstinence and the
Duration of Postnatal Abstinence Among the Yoruba of
Nigeria." (In) Leridon, Henri and Menken, Jane (eds.).
Natural Fertility. Patterns and Determinants of Natural
Fertility: Proceedings of a Seminar on Natural Fertility.
Liege, Belgium: International Union for the Scientific
Study of Population. 1979. pp. 397-407.

Chalifoux, Jean-Jacques
"Secondary Marriage and Levels of Seniority Among the
Abisi (Pitti) Nigeria." Journal of Comparative Family
Studies. Volume 11 #3 Special Issue 1980. pp. 325-334.

Copley, Anthony
"The Debate on Widow Remarriage and Polygamy: Aspects of
Moral Change in 19th Century Bengal and Yorubaland."
Journal of Imperial and Commonwealth History. Volume 7
#2 January, 1979. pp. 128-148.

Demehin, Ade O.
"Sexual Attitudes in Traditional and Modern Yoruba
Society." International Quarterly of Community Health
and Education. Volume 4 #3 1983. pp. 231-238.

Denga, Daniel I.
"Childlessness and Marital Adjustment in Northern
Nigeria." Journal of Marriage and Family. Volume 44 #3
August, 1979. pp. 799-802.

Dow, Thomas E.
"Breast Feeding and Abstinence Among the Yoruba."
Studies in Family Planning. Volume 8 #8 August, 1977.
pp. 208-214.

Dow, Thomas E.
Breast-Feeding, Abstinence, and Family Planning Among the
Yoruba and Other Sub-Saharan Groups: Patterns and Policy
Implications. Purchase, New York: State University of
New York. Department of Sociology. 1978.

Doyle, Pat and Morley, David and Woodland, Margaret and
Cole, Jane J.
"Birth Intervals, Survival and Growth in a Nigerian
Village." Journal of Biosocial Science. Volume 10 #1
January, 1978. pp. 81-94.

Durojaiye, Michael O.
"The Changing Family in the Nigerian Context." Paper

Presented at the Seminar on the Changing Family in the
African Context. Paris: United Nations Educational,
Scientific and Cultural Organization. Maseru, Lesotho.
1984. 7p.
Edigbo, P.O. and Chukudebelu, W.O.
"Child Spacing and Child Mortality Among Nigerian Ibos."
International Journal of Gynaecology and Obstetrics.
Volume 18 #5 1980. pp. 372-374.
Ekanem, Ita I. and Uche, Chukwudum
"Knowledge, Attitude and Practice of Family Planning in
Eastern Nigeria: Implications and Prospects." Odu.
Volume 17 #1 1978. pp. 36-63.
Ekanem, Ita I.
"Ways of Controlling Family Size: A Case Study of Eastern
Nigeria." (In) Oppong, C. and Adaba, G. and
Bekombo-Priso, M. and Mogey, J. (eds.). Marriage,
Fertility and Parenthood in West Africa. Canberra,
Australia: Australian National University. Department of
Demography. Volume Two. 1978. pp. 691-715.
Fagbemi, S.
"Occupational and Familial Role Conflicts of Working
Women: A Case Study of the Lafia Canning Factory,
Ibadan." BSc Dissertation: University of Ibadan,
Department of Sociology. Ibadan, Nigeria. 1978.
Fardon, Richard
"Sisters, Wives, Wards and Daughters: A Transformational
Analysis of the Political Organization of the Tiv and
Their Neighbors." Part One. Africa. Volume 54 #4 1984.
pp. 2-21.
Fardon, Richard
"Sisters, Wives, Wards and Daughters: A Transformational
Analysis of the Political Organization of the Tiv and
Their Neighbors." Part Two. Africa. Volume 55 #1 1985.
pp. 77-91.
Farooq, Ghazi M. and Ojelade, Mukaila A. and Ekanem, Ita I.
"Family Size Preferences and Fertility in Southern
Nigeria." Pula. Volume 2 #2 February, 1983. pp.
83-111.
Farooq, Ghazi M.
Household Fertility Decision-Making in Nigeria. Geneva:
International Labour Organization. Population and Labour
Policies Branch. Employment and Development Working
Paper #75A. 1980.
Farooq, Ghazi M.
"Household Fertility Decision-Making in Nigeria." (In)
Farooq, Ghazi M. and Simmons, George B. (eds.).
Fertility in Developing Countries: An Economic
Perspective on Research and Policy Issues. New York: St.
Martin's Press. 1985. pp. 312-350.
Grossbard, Amyra
"An Economic Analysis of Polygyny: The Case of
Maiduguri." Current Anthropology. Volume 17 #4
December, 1976. pp. 701-707.

424

Harrington, Judith A.
    "Education, Female Status and Fertility in Nigeria."
    Paper Presented to the Population Association of America.
    Atlanta, Georgia. 1978.
Harrington, Judith A.
    Education, Female Status and Fertility in Nigeria. Ann
    Arbor, Michigan: University of Michigan. School of
    Public Health. Department of Population Planning. 1978.
Ilori, Felicia
    Factors Determining Rural-Urban Fertility Differentials
    in Western Nigeria: A Case Study of Ife, Ilesha and
    Selected Rural Areas in Oyo Province. Ife, Nigeria:
    University of Ife. 1976.
Ipaye, Babatunde
    "A Psycho-Demographic View of the Changing Family Within
    the African Context." Paper Presented at the Seminar on
    the Changing Family in the African Context, 1983."
    Paris: United Nations Educational, Scientific and
    Cultural Organization. Maseru, Lesotho. 1984. 26p.
Iro, M.I.
    "Social Correlates of Divorce Among Lagos Elites Who
    Married in Nigeria." (In) Oppong, C. and Adaba, G. and
    Bekombo-Priso, M. and Mogey, J. (eds.). Marriage,
    Fertility and Parenthood in West Africa. Canberra,
    Australia: Australian National University. Department of
    Demography. Volume One. 1978. pp. 399-406.
Iro, M.I.
    "The Pattern of Elite Divorce in Lagos: 1961-1973."
    Journal of Marriage and the Family. Volume 38 #1
    February, 1976. pp. 177-182.
Karanja, Wambui W.
    "Conjugal Decision-Making: Some Data From Lagos." (In)
    Oppong, Christine (ed.). Female and Male in West Africa.
    London: George Allen and Unwin. 1983. pp. 236-241.
Kasunmu, A.B.
    "Economic Consequences of Divorce: A Case Study of Some
    Judicial Decisions in Lagos." (In) Roberts, Simon (ed.).
    Law and the Family in Africa. Hague, Netherlands:
    Mouton. 1977. pp. 129-143.
LeVine, Robert A.
    "Influences of Women's Schooling on Maternal Behavior in
    the Third World." Comparative Education Review. Volume
    24 #2 Part Two June, 1980. pp. S78-S105.
Lesthaeghe, Ron J. and Page, Hilary J. and Adegbola, O.
    "Child-Spacing and Fertility in Lagos." (In) Page,
    Hilary J. and Lesthaeghe, Ron (eds.). Child-Spacing in
    Tropical Africa: Traditions and Change. New York:
    Academic Press. 1981. pp. 147-179.
Lucas, David W.
    "Urban and Rural Fertility in Southern Nigeria." (In)
    Ruzicka, Lado T. (ed.). The Economic and Social Supports
    for High Fertility: Proceedings of the Conference. 1976.
    Canberra, Australia: Australian National University.

Development Studies Center. Canberra, Australia. November 16-19, 1977. pp. 409-435.

Mack, Delores E.
"Husbands and Wives in Lagos: The Effects of Socioeconomic Status on the Patterns of Family Living." Journal of Marriage and the Family. Volume 40 #4 November, 1978. pp. 807-816.

Mann, Kristin
"Marriage Choices Among the Educated African Elite in Lagos Colony, 1880-1915." International Journal of African Historical Studies. Volume 14 #2 1981. pp. 210-228.

Mann, Kristin
Marrying Well: Status and Social Change Among the Educated Elite in Colonial Lagos. Cambridge, England: Cambridge University Press. African Studies Series #47. 1985. 194p.

Mann, Kristin
"The Dangers of Dependence: Chrisitian Marriage Among the Elite Women in Lagos Colony, 1880-1915." Journal of African History. Volume 24 #1 1983. pp. 37-56.

Mann, Kristin
"The Dangers of Dependence: The Response of Educated Christian Women in Lagos Colony to Western Marriage." Paper Presented at the Annual Meeting of the African Studies Association. Los Angeles, California. October, 1979.

Mann, Kristin
"Women's Rights in Law and Practice: Marriage and Dispute Settlement in Colonial Lagos." (In) Hay, Margaret J. and Wright, Marcia (eds.). African Women and the Law: Historical Perspectives. Boston: Boston University. African Studies Center. Boston University Papers on Africa. Volume 7. 1982. pp. 151-171.

Morton-Williams, Peter
"Family Structures in an Egbado Yoruba Community." (In) Oppong, C. and Adaba, G. and Bekombo-Priso, M. and Mogey, J. (eds.). Marriage, Fertility and Parenthood in West Africa. Canberra, Australia: Australian National University. Department of Demography. Volume One. 1978. pp. 69-102.

Mott, Frank L. and Mott, Susan H. (eds.)
"Household Fertility Decisions in West Africa--A Comparison of Male and Female Survey Results." Studies in Family Planning. Volume 16 #2 March-April, 1985. pp. 88-99.

Mudambi, Sumati
"Interrelationships Between Family Structure and Family Resources in Eastern Nigeria." Journal of Family Welfare. Volume 26 #3 March, 1980. pp. 13-26.

Muller, Jean-Claude
"On Bridewealth and Meaning Among the Rukuba, Plateau State, Nigeria." Africa. Volume 48 #2 1978. pp. 161-175.

Muller, Jean-Claude
"On the Relevance of Having Two Husbands: Contribution to
the Study of Polygynous/Polyandrous Marital Forms of the
Jos Plateau." Journal of Comparative Family Studies.
Volume 11 #3 Special Issue. Summer, 1980. pp. 359-369.
Musa, Ayuba Z.
"Assessment of Societal Perceptions and Attitudes Toward
Marriage and Educated Hausa Women in the Northern States
of Nigeria." Ph.D Dissertation: Ohio State University.
Columbus, Ohio. 1981. 178p.
Nevadomsky, J.
"Motivations of Married Women to Higher Education in
Nigeria." International Journal of Women's Studies.
Volume 4 #5 1981.
Nwankwo, Joyce N.
"A Comparison of Responses of Unmarried Nigerian Final
Year University Male and Female Students to Factors That
Affect Mate Selection." Ph.D Dissertation: University of
Iowa. Iowa City, Iowa. 1981. 139p.
Ogbeide, D.O. and Edebiri, A.A.
"A Two Year Study of Organised Family Planning Services
in a Developing Country: Experiences in Bendel State of
Nigeria." East African Medical Journal. Volume 61 #6
June, 1984. pp. 470-476.
Omideyi, Adekunbi K.
"Age at Marriage and Marital Fertility in Eastern
Nigeria." Genus. Volume 39 #1-4 January-December,
1983. pp. 141-154.
Omideyi, Adekunbi K.
"The Persistence of High Fertility in Eastern Nigeria: An
Analysis Based Upon a Sample Survey of Married Women in
1971-72." Ph.D Dissertation: University of London.
London School of Economics. London, England. 1983.
403p.
Onwuazor, Sammy N.
"Continuity and Change: Abortion and Family Size in a
Nigerian Village." (In) Epstein, T. Scarlett and
Jackson, Darrell (eds.). The Feasibility of Fertility
Planning: Micro Perspectives. Oxford, England: Pergamon
Press. 1977. pp. 67-96.
Orubuloye, I.O.
"Child-Spacing Among Rural Yoruba Women: Ekiti and Ibadan
Divisions in Nigeria." (In) Page, Hilary J. and
Lesthaeghe, Ron (eds.). Child-Spacing in Tropical
Africa: Traditions and Change. New York: Academic Press.
1981. pp. 225-236.
Orubuloye, I.O.
"Family Obligations and Fertility in Nigeria: The Case of
the Yoruba of Western Nigeria." (In) Ruzicka, Lado T.
(ed.). The Economic and Social Supports for High
Fertility: Proceedings of the Conference. Canberra,
Australia: Australian National University. Development
Studies Center. November 16-18, 1977. pp. 203-217.

NIGERIA

Orubuloye, I.O.
   "Fertility, Sexual Abstinence and Contraception Among the
   Yoruba of Western Nigeria: A Study of Selected Rural
   Communities in Ekiti and Ibadan Divisions." Ph.D
   Dissertation: Australian National University. Department
   of Demography. Canberra, Australia. 1977.
Orubuloye, I.O.
   "Sexual Abstinence Patterns in Rural Western Nigeria:
   Evidence From a Survey of Yoruba Women." Social Science
   and Medicine. Volume 13A #6 November, 1979. pp.
   667-672.
Orubuloye, I.O.
   "Sexual Abstinence Patterns in Rural Western Nigeria:
   Evidence From a Survey of Yoruba Women." Social Science
   and Medicine. Volume 13a #6 November, 1979. pp.
   667-672.
Orubuloye, I.O.
   Abstinence as a Method of Birth Control: Fertility and
   Child-Spacing Practice Amid Rural Yoruba Women in
   Nigeria. Canberra, Australia: Australian National
   University. Department of Demography. Changing African
   Family Project. Monograph #8. 1981. 116p.
Ottong, Joseph G.
   "Population Dynamics, Fertility and Family Planning in a
   Rural Community: A Study in Manchol, Southern Nigeria."
   (In) Oppong, C. and Adaba, G. and Bekomba-Priso, M. and
   Mogey, J. (eds.). Marriage, Fertility and Parenthood in
   West Africa. Canberra, Australia: Australian National
   University. Department of Demography. Volume Two.
   1978.
Owuamanam, Donatus O.
   "Marriage and Aspiration to Professional Leadership of
   Women Student Teachers in Nigeria." Journal of
   Psychology. Volume 115 #1 September, 1983. pp.
   103-106.
Oyemade, Adefunke and Ogunmuyiwa, Taiwo A.
   "Sociocultural Factors and Fertility in A Rural Nigerian
   Community." Studies in Family Planning. Volume 12 #3
   March, 1981. pp. 109-111.
Page, Hilary J. and Lesthaeghe, Ron J. and Adegbola, O.
   Breast-Feeding and Abstinence: Socioeconomic
   Differentials in Metropolitan Lagos. Brussels, Belgium:
   Vrije Universiteit Brussel. Centrum Sociologie. 1977.
Peil, Margaret
   "Urban Contacts: A Comparison of Women and Men." (In)
   Oppong, Christine (ed.). Female and Male in West Africa.
   London: George Allen and Unwin. 1983. pp. 275-282.
Pittin, Renee
   "Marriage and Alternative Strategies: Career Patterns of
   Hausa Women in Katsina City." Ph.D Dissertation:
   University of London. School of Oriental and African
   Studies. London, England. 1979.

Rehan, Naghma E. and Abashiya, Aubu K.
"Breastfeeding and Abstinence Among Hausa Women."
Studies in Family Planning. Volume 12 #5 May, 1981.
pp. 233-237.
Rehan, Naghma E.
"Knowledge, Attitude and Practice of Family Planning in
Hausa Women." Social Sciences and Medicine. Volume 18
#10 October, 1984. pp. 839-844.
Salamone, Frank A.
"Levirate, Widows and Types of Marriage Among the Dukawa
of Northern Nigeria." Afrika und Ubersee. Volume 64 #1
1981. pp. 129-136.
Salamone, Frank A.
"The Arrow and the Bird: Proverbs in the Solution of
Hausa Conjugal Conflicts." Journal of Anthropological
Research. Volume 32 #4 Winter, 1976. pp. 358-371.
Sangree, Walter H.
"Going Home to Mother: Traditional Marriage Among the
Irigwe of Benue-Plateau State, Nigeria." (In) Tiffany,
Sharon W. (ed.). Women and Society: An Anthropological
Reader. St. Albans, Vermont: Eden Press. 1979. pp.
189-207.
Sangree, Walter H.
"The Persistence of Polyandry in Irigwe, Nigeria."
Journal of Comparative Family Studies. Volume 11 #3
Special Issue. Summer, 1980. pp. 335-343.
Santow, G. and Bracher, M.
"Patterns of Postpartum Sexual Abstinence and Their
Implications for Fertility in Ibadan, Nigeria." (In)
Page, Hilary J. and Lesthaeghe, Ron (eds.).
Child-Spacing in Tropical Africa: Traditions and Change.
New York: Academic Press. 1981. pp. 201-223.
Sembajwe, I.S.L.
"Religious Fertility Differentials Among the Yoruba of
Western Nigeria." Journal of Biosocial Science. Volume
12 #2 April, 1980. pp. 153-164.
Sembajwe, Israel S.
"Effect of Age at First Marriage, Number of Wives, and
Type of Marital Union on Fertility." Journal of
Biosocial Science. Volume 11 #3 July, 1979. pp.
341-351.
Smedley, Audrey
"The Implications of Birom Cicisbeism." Journal of
Comparative Family Studies. Volume 11 #3 Special Issue.
Summer, 1980. pp. 345-357.
Uche, Chukwudum and Ekanem, Ita I.
"Knowledge, Attitude and Practice of Family Planning in
Eastern Nigeria: Implications, Prospects and
Suggestions." Sociologus. Volume 32 #2 1982. pp.
97-126.
Uchendu, Patrick K.
"The Changing Cultural Role of Igbo Women in Nigeria,
1914-1975." Ph.D Dissertation: New York University. New
York, New York. 1980. 339p.

Udjo, E.O.
   "Obstacles to Successful Fertility Control in Nigeria."
   Social Science and Medicine. Volume 19 #11 1984. pp.
   1167-1171.
Ugwuegbu, D.C.E.
   "Educational Orientation and Nigerian Students' Attitudes
   to Husband-Wife Relations." Journal of Social
   Psychology. Volume 106 October, 1978. pp. 121-122.
Ukaegbu, Alfred O.
   "Family Planning Attitudes and Practices in Rural Eastern
   Nigeria." Studies in Family Planning. Volume 8 #7
   July, 1977. pp. 177-183.
Ukaegbu, Alfred O.
   "Family Size Preference of Spouses in Rural Eastern
   Nigeria." Journal of Development Studies. Volume 14 #4
   July, 1978. pp. 150-164.
Ukaegbu, Alfred O.
   "Fertility of Women in Polynous Unions in Rural Eastern
   Nigeria." Journal of Marriage and Family. Volume 39 #2
   May, 1977. pp. 397-404.
Ukaegbu, Alfred O.
   "Socio-Cultural Determination of Fertility: A Case Study
   of Rural Eastern Nigeria." Journal of Comparative Family
   Studies. Volume 8 #1 Spring, 1977. pp. 99-115.
Ukaegbu, Alfred O.
   "The Role of Traditional Marriage Habits in Population
   Growth: The Case of Rural Eastern Nigeria." Africa.
   Volume 46 #4 1976. pp. 390-398.
Uyanga, Joseph T.
   "Is Overcrowded Urban Living a Factor in Fertility
   Decisions? A Case Study of Metropolitan Calabar."
   Social Action. Volume 29 #2 April-June, 1979. pp.
   150-162.
Uyanga, Joseph T.
   "Socio-Economic Values in the Fertility Behavior of
   Nigerians." Social Action. #4 October-December, 1977.
   pp. 379-398.
Ware, Helen
   "Polygyny: Women's Views in a Transitional Society,
   Nigeria, 1975." Journal of Marriage and Family. Volume
   41 #1 February, 1979. pp. 185-195.
Watts, Susan J.
   "Marriage, Migration, A Neglected Form of Long-Term
   Mobility: A Case Study From Iborin, Nigeria."
   International Migration Review. Volume 17 #4 Winter,
   1983. pp. 682-698.
Weidemann, Wesley C.
   "Attitudes Toward Family Planning in Southern Nigeria."
   (In) International Planned Parenthood Federation (IPPF).
   Proceedings of the IPPF Africa Regional Conference.
   London: IPPF. 1977. pp. 66-73.

NIGERIA

MASS NEDIA

Adeogun, Modupe F.
  "Attitude of Nigerian Mass Media Towards Women." Paper
  Presented at the Women and Education Conference. Port
  Harcourt, Nigeria: University of Port Harcourt. April,
  1984.
Akpan, Emmanuel D.
  "News Photos and Stories: Men's and Women's Roles in Two
  Nigerian Newspapers." Ph.D Dissertation: Ohio State
  University. Columbus, Ohio. 1979. 144p.
Dangugo, H.S.
  "Women in Electronic Media." (In) Women in Nigeria
  Today. London: Zed Press. 1985. pp. 208-211.
Nweke, T.
  "The Role of Women in Nigerian Society: The Media." (In)
  Women in Nigeria Today. London: Zed Press. 1985. pp.
  210-207.

MIGRATION

Adepoju, Aderanti
  "Migration and Fertility: A Case Study in South-West
  Nigeria." (In) Oppong, C. and Adaba, G. and
  Bekombo-Priso, M. and Mogey, J. (eds.). Marriage,
  Fertility and Parenthood in West Africa. Canberra,
  Australia: Australian National University. Department of
  Demography. Volume Two. 1978. pp. 491-506.
Adepoju, Aderanti
  "Migration, Employment and Fertility: A Case Study in
  South-West Nigeria." Paper Presented to the 15th
  International Seminar on Family Research. Lome, Togo.
  1976.
Lacey, Linda
  "Interurban Flows of Population and Occupational Skills
  to Three Cities in Nigeria." International Migration
  Review. Volume 19 #4 Winter, 1985. pp. 686-707.
Mustapha, A.R.
  "On Combating Women's Exploitation and Oppression in
  Nigeria." (In) Women in Nigeria Today. London: Zed
  Press. 1985. pp. 241-246.
Okojie, Christiana E.E.
  "Female Migrants in the Urban Labour Market: Benin City,
  Nigeria." Canadian Journal of African Studies. Volume
  18 #3 1984. pp. 547-562.
Palmer, Ingrid
  Impact of Male Out-Migration on Women in Farming. West
  Hartford, Connecticut: Kumarian Press. Women's Roles and
  Gender Differences in Development. Volume Seven. Cases
  for Planners. 1985. 89p.
Pittin, Renee
  Migration of Women in Nigeria: The Hausa Case.
431

International Migration Review. Volume 18 #4 Winter, 1984. pp. 1293-1314.

Sudarkasa, Niara
"Women and Migration in Contemporary West Africa." (In) Wellesley Editorial Committee. Women and National Development: The Complexities of Change. Chicago: University of Chicago Press. 1977. pp. 178-189.

Sudarkasa, Niara
"Women and Migration in Contemporary West Africa." Signs. Volume 3 #1 Autumn, 1977. pp. 178-189.

Watts, Susan J.
"Marriage, Migration, A Neglected Form of Long-Term Mobility: A Case Study From Iborin, Nigeria." International Migration Review. Volume 17 #4 Winter, 1983. pp. 682-698.

MISCELLANEOUS

Adedeji, John A.
"The Acceptance of Nigerian Women in Sport." International Review of Sport Sociology. Volume 13 #1 1978. pp. 39-47.

Anyanwu, S.U.
"Issues in and Patterns of Women's Participation of Sports in Nigeria." International Review of Sport Sociology. Volume 15 #1 1980. pp. 85-95.

Hoch-Smith, Judith
"Radical Yoruba Female Sexuality: The Witch and the Prostitute." (In) Hoch-Smith, Judith and Spring, Anita (eds.). Women in Ritual and Symbolic Roles. New York: Plenum Press. 1978. pp. 245-267.

Mohammed, A.
'Home Outside the Home' (A Sociological Conception of Prostitution Am ong the Hausa). Kano, Nigeria: Bayero University. Department of Sociology. Seminar Paper. 1980.

NATIONALISM

Johnson, Cheryl J.
"Grass Roots Organizing: Women in Anticolonial Activity on South-Western Nigeria." African Studies Review. Volume 25 #2/3 July-September, 1982. pp. 137-158.

Johnson, Cheryl J.
"Madam Alimotu Pelewuru and the Lagos Market Women." Tarikh. Volume 7 #1 1981. pp. 1-10.

Johnson, Cheryl J.
"Nigerian Women and British Colonialism: The Yoruba Example With Selected Biographies." Ph.D Dissertation: Northwestern University. Evanston, Illinois. 1978. 314p.

ORGANIZATIONS

Anyanwu, S.U.
"Issues in and Patterns of Women's Participation of Sports in Nigeria." International Review of Sport Sociology. Volume 15 #1 1980. pp. 85-95.

Ejiogu, Aloy M.
"Sex Differences in the Leader Behavior of Nigerian College Principals." Journal of Education Administration and History. Volume 14 #1 1982. pp. 55-61.

Enabulele, A.B.
"The Role of Women's Associations in Nigeria's Development: Social Welfare Aspect." (In) Women in Nigeria Today. London: Zed Press. 1985. pp. 187-194.

Johnson, Cheryl J.
"Grass Roots Organizing: Women in Anticolonial Activity on South-Western Nigeria." African Studies Review. Volume 25 #2/3 July-September, 1982. pp. 137-158.

Ladipo, Patricia A.
"Developing Women's Cooperatives: An Experiment in Rural Nigeria." Journal of Development Studies. Volume 17 #3 April, 1981. pp. 123-136.

Ladipo, Patricia A.
Developing Women's Cooperatives: An Experiment in Rural Nigeria. Totowa, New Jersey: Frank Cass. 1981. pp. 123-136.

Olajumoke, Cecy M.
"Women's Participation in Trade Unions." Paper Presented at the National Workshop on Women in the Modern Sector Labour Force in Nigeria. Lagos, Nigeria: University of Lagos. March, 1985.

Pittin, Rene
"Organizing for the Future." (In) Women in Nigeria Today. London: Zed Press. 1985. pp. 231-240.

Pittin, Renee
"Organizing for the Future." (In) Women in Nigeria Today. London: Zed Press. 1985. pp. 231-240.

Sangree, Walter H.
"Traditional Coalitions Among Women of Irigwe, Nigeria: From Co-Wife to Possession Cult Ties." Paper Presented at the Annual Meeting of the African Studies Association. Paper #112. Bloomington, Indiana. October 21-24, 1981.

Yusuf, B.
"Nigerian Women in Politics: Problems and Prospects." (In) Women in Nigeria Today. London: Zed Press. 1985. pp. 212-216.

POLITICS AND GOVERNMENT

Awosika, K.
"Women's Education and Participation in the Labour Force: The Case of Nigeria." (In) Rendel, M. (ed.). Women,

Power and Political Systems. London: Croom Helm. 1981. 262p.

Dennis, Carolyne
"Capitalist Development and Women's Work: A Nigerian Case Study." Review of African Political Economy. #27/28 1983. pp. 103-119.

Jackson, S.
"Hausa Women on Strike." Review of African Political Economy. #13 1978. pp. 21-36.

Johnson, Cheryl J.
"Grass Roots Organizing: Women in Anticolonial Activity on South-Western Nigeria." African Studies Review. Volume 25 #2/3 July-September, 1982. pp. 137-158.

Johnson, Cheryl J.
"Madam Alimotu Pelewuru and the Lagos Market Women." Tarikh. Volume 7 #1 1981. pp. 1-10.

Madunagu, B.E.
"Contemporary Positions and Experiences of Women." (In) Women in Nigeria Today. London: Zed Press. 1985. pp. 132-137.

Mba, Nina E.
"Funmilayo Ransome-Kuti: Continuity and Change in Yoruba Women's Political Action." Paper Presented at the Annual Meeting of the African Studies Association. Paper #56. Washington, D.C. November 4-7, 1982.

Mba, Nina E.
Nigerian Women Mobilized: Women's Political Activity in Southern Nigeria, 1900-1965. Berkeley, California: University of California. Institute of International Studies. Research Series #48. 1982. 348p.

Mba, Nina E.
"Women in Southern Nigerian Political History, 1900-1965." Ph.D. Dissertation: University of Ibadan. Ibadan, Nigeria. 1978.

Mustapha, A.R.
"On Combating Women's Exploitation and Oppression in Nigeria." (In) Women in Nigeria Today. London: Zed Press. 1985. pp. 241-246.

Ogundipe-Leslie, Molara
"Women in Nigeria." (In) Women in Nigeria Today. London: Zed Press. 1985. pp. 119-131.

Okonjo, Kamene
"Sex Roles in Nigerian Politics." (In) Oppong, Christine (ed.). Female and Male in West Africa. London: George Allen and Unwin. 1983. pp. 211-222.

Okonjo, Kamene
"The Dual-Sex Political System in Operation: Igbo Women and Community Politics in Midwestern Nigeria." (In) Hafkin, N.J. and Bay, Edna G. (eds.). Women in Africa: Studies in Social and Economic Change. Stanford, California: Stanford University Press. 1976. pp. 45-58.

Okonjo, Kamene
"Women's Political Participation in Nigeria." (In)

Steady, Filomina C. (ed.).   The Black Woman
Cross-Culturally.   Cambridge, Massachusetts: Schenkman
Publishing.   1981.   pp. 79-106.
Perchonock, N.
   "Double Oppression: Women and Land Matters in Kaduna
   State."   (In) Women in Nigeria Today.   London: Zed Press.
   1985.   pp. 82-103.
Pittin, Renee
   "Organizing for the Future."   (In) Women in Nigeria
   Today.   London: Zed Press.   1985.   pp. 231-240.
Yusuf, B.
   "Nigerian Women in Politics: Problems and Prospects."
   (In) Women in Nigeria Today.   London: Zed Press.   1985.
   pp. 212-216.

RELIGION AND WITCHCRAFT

Adelowo, E.D.
   "Islamic Marriage System and the Extents of its Adoption
   by Yoruba Muslims of Nigeria."   Orita.   Volume 14 #1
   June, 1982.   pp. 16-33.
Ademola, Ade
   "Changes in the Patterns of Marriage and Divorce in a
   Yoruba Town."   Rural Africana.   #14   Fall, 1982.   pp.
   1-24.
Adeney, Miriam
   "A Woman Liberated--For What?"   Christianity Today.
   Volume 28   January 13, 1984.   pp. 28-30.
Beckett, Paul A. and O'Connell, James O.
   "Education and the Situation of Women: Background and
   Atttitudes of Christian and Muslim Female Students at a
   Nigerian University."   Cultures et Developpement.   Volume
   8 #2 1976.   pp. 242-265.
Boyd, J.
   "The Role of Women as Agents Religieux in Sokoto,"
   Canadian Journal of African Studies.   Volume 19 #2 1985.
Callaway, Helen
   "Women in Yoruba Tradition and in the Cherubim and
   Seraphim Society."   (In) Kalu, O.U. (ed.).   The History
   of Christianity in West Africa.   New York: Longman.
   1980.   pp. 321-332.
Clarke, Peter
   "Birom Women Evangelist, Vo Gyang of Forum (FL.
   1927-1929)."   (In) Isichei, Elizabeth (ed.).   Varieties
   of Chrisitan Experience in Nigeria.   London: MacMillan
   Press Ltd.   1982.   pp. 163-176.
Cobbald, Elizabeth
   "Muslim Hausa Women in Northern Nigeria: An Annotated
   Bibliography."   African Research and Documentation.
   Volume 32 1983.   pp. 22-29.
Coles, Catherine M.
   "Muslim Women in Town: Social Change Among the Hausa of

Northern Nigeria." Ph.D Dissertation: University of
Wisconsin-Madison. Madison, Wisconsin. 1983. 556p.
Coles, Catherine M.
"Urban Muslim Women and Social Change in Northern
Nigeria." Paper Presented at the Annual Meeting of the
African Studies Association. Paper #20. Washington,
D.C. November 4-7, 1982.
Coles, Catherine M.
Urban Muslim Women and Social Change in Northern
Nigeria. East Lansing, Michigan: Michigan State
University. Office of Women in International
Development. Working Paper #19. March, 1983. 28p.
Csapo, Marg
"Religious, Social and Economic Factors Hindering the
Education of Girls in Northern Nigeria." Comparative
Education. Volume 17 #3 1981. pp. 311-319.
Daly, Catherine
"On Display: Prescribed Aesthetics Among Kalabari
Females." Paper Presented at the Annual Meeting of the
African Studies Association. Paper #28. Bloomington,
Indiana. October 21-24, 1981.
Daly, Mary C.
"Kalabari Female Appearance and the Tradition of Iria."
Ph.D Dissertation: University of Minnesota. Minneapolis,
Minnesota. 1984. 204p.
Drewal, Henry J.
"Art and Perception of Women in Yoruba Culture." Cahiers
d'Etudes Africaines. Volume 17 #4 1977. pp. 545-567.
Drewal, Henry J. and Drewal, Margaret T.
G.EL.ED.E: Art and Female Power Among the Yoruba.
Bloomington, Indiana: Indiana University Press.
Traditional Arts of Africa Series. 1983. 306p.
Ekam, Anna G.
"The Contributions of the Holy Child Sisters to Women's
Education in the Cross River State of Nigeria, From
1930-1967." Ph.D Dissertation: Catholic University of
America. Washington, D.C. 1980. 196p.
Hendrixson, Joyce
"Islam and the Changing Position of Women in Sokoto:
Appearance and Reality." Paper Presented at the Annual
Meeting of the African Studies Association. Paper #42.
Philadelphia, Pennsylvania. 1980.
Hoch-Smith, Judith
"Radical Yoruba Female Sexuality: The Witch and the
Prostitute." (In) Hoch-Smith, Judith and Spring, Anita
(eds.). Women in Ritual and Symbolic Roles. New York:
Plenum Press. 1978. pp. 245-267.
Mann, Kristin
"The Dangers of Dependence: Chrisitian Marriage Among the
Elite Women in Lagos Colony, 1880-1915." Journal of
African History. Volume 24 #1 1983. pp. 37-56.
Oduyoye, Mercy A.
"Standing on Both Feet: Education and Leadership Training

of Women in the Methodist Church, Nigeria." Ecumenical
Review. Volume 33 #1 January, 1981. pp. 60-71.
Offiong, Daniel A.
    "Social Relations and Witch Beliefs Among the Ibibio of
    Nigeria." Journal of Anthropological Research. Volume
    39 #1 1983. pp. 81-95.
Offiong, Daniel A.
    "Social Relations and Witch Beliefs Among the Ibibio."
    Africa. Volume 53 #3 1983. pp. 73-82.
Offiong, Daniel A.
    "The 1978-79 Akpan Ekwong Anti-Witchcraft Crusade in
    Nigeria." Anthropologica. Volume 24 #1 1982. pp.
    27-42.
Offiong, Daniel A.
    "Witchcraft Among the Ibibio of Nigeria." African
    Studies Review. Volume 26 #1 March, 1983. pp. 91-106.
Omojayowo, Akin
    "Mother in Israel: Chridtianah Olatunrinle in Ondo (c.
    1855-1941)." (In) Isichei, Elizabeth (ed.). Varieties
    of Christian Experience in Nigeria. London: MacMillan
    Press Ltd. 1982. pp. 141-148.
Owie, Ikponmwosa
    "Religious Identity and Attitudes Toward Contraceptives
    Among University Students in Nigeria." Social Biology.
    Volume 30 #1 Spring, 1983. pp. 101-105.
Pittin, Renee
    "Hausa Women and Islamic Law: Is Reform Necessary."
    Paper Presented at the Annual Meeting of the African
    Studies Association. Paper #75. 1979. 19p.
Schildkrout, Enid
    "Dependence and Autonomy: The Economic Activities of
    Secluded Hausa Women in Kano, Nigeria." (In) Bay, Edna
    G. (ed.). Women and Work in Africa. Boulder, Colorado:
    Westview Press. Westview Special Studies in Africa.
    1982. pp. 55-81.
Schildkrout, Enid
    "Dependence and Autonomy: The Economic Activities of
    Secluded Hausa Women in Kano." (In) Oppong, Christine
    (ed.). Female and Male in West Africa. London: George
    Allen and Unwin. 1983. pp. 107-126.
Sembajwe, I.S.L.
    "Religious Fertility Differentials Among the Yoruba of
    Western Nigeria." Journal of Biosocial Science. Volume
    12 #2 April, 1980. pp. 153-164.
Sembajwe, Israel S.
    "Religious Fertility Differentials Among the Yoruba of
    Western Nigeria." Journal of Biosocial Science. Volume
    12 #2 April, 1980. pp. 153-164.
Smith, Mary F.
    Baba of Karo: A Woman of the Muslim Hausa. New Haven,
    Connecticut: Yale University Press. 1981. 304p.
Udjo, E.O.
    "Obstacles to Successful Fertility Control in Nigeria."

Social Science and Medicine. Volume 19 #11 1984. pp.
1167-1171.
Verma, O.P. and Singha, P.
"Fertility Pattern of Muslim Hausa Women in Northern
Nigeria." Nigerian Journal of Economic and Social
Studies. Volume 24 #2 July, 1982. pp. 185-198.

RESEARCH

Cobbald, Elizabeth
"Muslim Hausa Women in Northern Nigeria: An Annotated
Bibliography." African Research and Documentation.
Volume 32 1983. pp. 22-29.
Fieloux, M.
"Bibliographic Chronicle: Invisible and Mute
Women--Concerning Ibo Riots of 1929." Cahiers d'Etudes
Africaines. Volume 17 #1 1977. pp. 189+.
Kisekka, Mere N.
Women and Development in Nigeria: A Bibliography. Addis
Ababa, Ethiopia: United Nations Economic Commission for
Africa. African Training and Research Centre for Women.
Bibliography Series #4. 1981. 122p.
Pittin, Renee
Documentation of Women's Work in Nigeria: Problems and
Solutions. Geneva: International Labour Organization.
World Employment Programme Research Working Papers, #125.
Restricted Mimeograph. 1982. 49p.
Sharpe, B.
"Social Knowledge and Farming Systems Research:
Ethnicity, Power and the Invisible Farmers of North
Central Nigeria." African Social Research. #38 1985.
Simmons, Emmy
Economic Research on Women in Rural Development in
Northern Nigeria. Washington, D.C.: American Council on
Education. Overseas Liaison Committee. OLC Paper #10.
September, 1976. 26p.

SEX ROLES

Achebe, Christie C.
"Continuities, Changes and Challenges: Women's Roles in
Nigerian Society." Presence Africaine. # 120 1981. pp.
3-16.
Achike, Okay
"Problems of Creation and Dissolution of Customary
Marriages in Nigeria." (In) Roberts, Simon (ed.). Law
and the Family in Nigeria. Hague, Netherlands: Mouton.
1977. pp. 145-158.
Adekanye, Tomilayo O.
"Innovation and Rural Women in Nigeria: Cassava
Processing and Food Production." (In) Ahmed, Iftikhar

(ed.). Technology and Rural Women: Conceptual and
Empirical Issues. Boston: George Allen and Unwin. 1985.
pp. 252-283.

Adekanye, Tomilayo O.
"Women in Agriculture in Nigeria: Problems and Policies
for Development." Women's Studies International. Volume
7 #6 1984. pp. 423-431.

Adekanye-Adeyokunnu, T.
Women in Nigerian Agriculture. Ibadan, Nigeria:
University of Ibadan. Department of Agricultural
Economics. 1982.

Adekoya, M.A.
"Barriers to an Effective Organization of Women's Work.
The Women's Programme Section in Nigeria." Assignment
Children. Volume 38 #2 April-June, 1977. pp. 80-83.

Adeyemo, Remi
"Women in Rural Areas: A Case Study of Southwestern
Nigeria." Canadian Journal of African Studies. Volume
18 #3 1984. pp. 563-572.

Adeyeye, V.A.
"Women in Traditional Agriculture: Oyo State of Nigeria
Experience." MSc Thesis: University of Ibadan.
Department of Agricultural Economics. Ibadan, Nigeria.
1977.

Adeyokunnu (Adekanye), Tomilayo O.
Women and Agriculture in Nigeria. Addis Ababa, Ethiopia:
United Nations Economic Commission for Africa. African
Training and Research Centre for Women. 1980.

Adeyokunnu, Tomilayo O.
"Rural Development and the Position of Women in Africa:
Problems and Policies." Paper Presented at the Meeting
of the Experts on Research on the Status of Women,
Development and Population Trends: Evaluation and
Prospects. Paris: United Nations Educational, Scientific
and Cultural Organization. 1980. 32p.

Afonja, Simi A.
"Changing Modes of Production and the Sexual Division of
Labor Among the Yoruba." Signs. Volume 7 #2 Winter,
1981. pp. 299-313.

Afonja, Simi A.
"Current Explanations of Sex-Inequality: A
Reconsideration." Nigerian Journal of Economic and
Social Studies. Volume 21 #2 1981.

Afonja, Simi A.
"The Historical Evolution of the Sexual Division of Labor
in Nigeria." Paper Presented at the Meeting of Experts
on the Theoretical Frameworks and Methodological
Approaches to Studies on the Role of Women in History as
Actors in Economic, Social, Political and Ideological
Processes. Paris: United Nations Educational, Scientific
and Cultural Organization. 1984. 20p.

Afonja, Simi A.
"Women, Power and Authority in Traditional Yoruba

Society." (In) Dupe, Leela and Leacock, Eleanor and
Ardener, Shirley (eds.). Viaibility and Power: Essays on
Women in Society and Development. Delhi, India: Oxford
University Press. 1983.

Akande, Jadesola O.
Law and the Status of Women in Nigeria. Addis Ababa,
Ethiopia: United Nations Economic Commission for Africa.
African Training and Research Centre for Women. 1979.
77p.

Aluko, G.B. and Alfa, M.O.
"Marriage and Family." (In) Women in Nigeria Today.
London: Zed Press. 1985. pp. 163-173.

Arinola, O.A.N.
"The Implications of Female Labour Force Participation on
the Family: A Case Study of Some Factory Workers." B.Sc
Dissertation: University of Ibadan. Department of
Sociology. Ibadan, Nigeria. 1978.

Awe, B.
"The Iyalode in the Traditional Yoruba Political System."
(In) Schlegel, Alice E. (ed.). Sexual Stratification: A
Cross-Cultural View. New York: Columbia University
Press. 1977. pp. 144-160.

Babatunde, E.D.
"Ketu Myths and the Status of Women: A Structural
Interpretation of Some Yoruba Myths of Origin." Journal
of the Anthropological Society of Oxford. Volume 14 #3
1983. pp. 301-306.

Ballay, Ute B.
"Women in Nigeria: Aspects of Social Transformation."
Africana Marburgensia. Volume 16 #2 1983. pp. 33-59.

Burfisher, Mary E. and Horenstein, Nadine R.
"Sex Roles and Development Effects on the Nigerian Tiv
Farm Household." Rural Africana. #21 Winter, 1985.
pp. 31-50.

Burfisher, Mary E. and Horenstein, Nadine R.
Sex Roles in the Nigerian Tiv Farm Household and the
Differential Impacts of Development Projects. Washington
D.C.: U.S. Department of Agriculture. International
Economics Division. 1982.

Burfisher, Mary E. and Horenstein, Nadine R.
Sex Roles in the Nigerian Tiv Farm Household. West
Hartford, Connecticut: Kumarian Press. Women's Roles and
Gender Differences in Development, Cases for Planners.
Volume 2. 1985. 62p.

Caldwell, John C.
The Socio-Economic Explanation of High Fertility: Papers
on the Yoruba Society of Nigeria. Canberra, Australia:
Australian National University. Department of
Demography. Changing African Family Project. Series #1.
1976.

Callaway, Barbara J. and Kleeman, Katherine E.
"Women in Nigeria: Three Women of Kano: Modern Women and

Traditional Life." Africa Report. Volume 30 #2
March-April, 1985. pp. 26-29.

Callaway, Helen
"Women in Yoruba Tradition and in the Cherubim and
Seraphim Society." (In) Kalu, O.U. (ed.). The History
of Christianity in West Africa. New York: Longman.
1980. pp. 321-332.

Chalifoux, Jean-Jacques
"Secondary Marriage and Levels of Seniority Among the
Abisi (Pitti) Nigeria." Journal of Comparative Family
Studies. Volume 11 #3 Special Issue 1980. pp. 325-334.

Coles, Catherine M.
"Muslim Women in Town: Social Change Among the Hausa of
Northern Nigeria." Ph.D Dissertation: University of
Wisconsin-Madison. Madison, Wisconsin. 1983. 556p.

Coles, Catherine M.
"Urban Muslim Women and Social Change in Northern
Nigeria." Paper Presented at the Annual Meeting of the
African Studies Association. Paper #20. Washington,
D.C. November 4-7, 1982.

Coles, Catherine M.
Urban Muslim Women and Social Change in Northern
Nigeria. East Lansing, Michigan: Michigan State
University. Office of Women in International
Development. Working Paper #19. March, 1983. 28p.

Csapo, Marg
"Religious, Social and Economic Factors Hindering the
Education of Girls in Northern Nigeria." Comparative
Education. Volume 17 #3 1981. pp. 311-319.

Daly, Catherine
"On Display: Prescribed Aesthetics Among Kalabari
Females." Paper Presented at the Annual Meeting of the
African Studies Association. Paper #28. Bloomington,
Indiana. October 21-24, 1981.

Daly, Mary C.
"Kalabari Female Appearance and the Tradition of Iria."
Ph.D Dissertation: University of Minnesota. Minneapolis,
Minnesota. 1984. 204p.

Demehin, Ade O.
"Sexual Attitudes in Traditional and Modern Yoruba
Society." International Quarterly of Community Health
and Education. Volume 4 #3 1983. pp. 231-238.

Di Domenico, Catherine M. and Asuni, Judy and Scott,
Jacqueline
"Changing Status of African Women: An Exploratory Study
of Working Mothers in Ibadan, Nigeria." (In)
International Planned Parenthood Federation (IPPF).
Proceedings of the IPPF Africa Regional Conference.
London: IPPF. 1977. pp. 283-284.

Drewal, Henry J. and Drewal, Margaret T.
G.EL.ED.E: Art and Female Power Among the Yoruba.
Bloomington, Indiana: Indiana University Press.
Traditional Arts of Africa Series. 1983. 306p.

Durojaiye, Michael O.
    "The Changing Family in the Nigerian Context." Paper
    Presented at the Seminar on the Changing Family in the
    African Context. Paris: United Nations Educational,
    Scientific and Cultural Organization. Maseru, Lesotho.
    1984. 7p.
Ejiogu, Aloy M.
    "Sex Differences in the Leader Behavior of Nigerian
    College Principals." Journal of Education Administration
    and History. Volume 14 #1 1982. pp. 55-61.
Ekejiuba, Felicia
    "Contemporary Households and Major Socioeconomic
    Transitions in Eastern Nigeria: Towards a
    Reconceptualization of the Household." Paper Presented
    at the Conference on Conceptualizing the Household.
    Cambridge, Massachusetts: Harvard University. November,
    1984.
Ekpere, J.A. and Oyedipe, F.P. and Adegboye, R.O.
    "Family Role Differentiation Within the Kwara Nomadic
    Fulani." (In) Oppong, C. and Adaba, G. and
    Bekombo-Priso, M. and Mogey, J. (eds.). Marriage,
    Fertility and Parenthood in West Africa. Canberra,
    Australia: Australian National University. Department of
    Demography. Volume One. 1978. pp. 55-67.
Emeagwali, G.T.
    "Women in Pre-Capitalistic Socio-Economic Formations in
    Nigeria." (In) Women in Nigeria. London: Zed Press.
    1985. pp. 52-55.
Enahoro, Diane S.
    "Constraints to Women Entering Mid-Level Technical
    Occupations in Nigeria." Paper Presented at the Third
    Annual Women in Nigeria Conference. Port Harcourt,
    Nigeria: University of Port Harcourt. April, 1984.
Essien, Ruth A.
    "Perceptions of Nigerian College Students Toward the Role
    of Women in Nigerian Development." Ph.D Dissertation:
    University of Southern California. Los Angeles,
    California. 1981. 214p.
Fadayomi, T.O. and Adelola, I.O. and Oni, B. and Omogbehin,
V.A. and Egbunike, N.A.
    The Role of Working Mothers in Early Childhood Education:
    A Nigerian Case Study. Paris: UNESCO. Nigerian Institute
    of Social and Economic Research. February, 1978. 68p.
Fagbemi, S.
    "Occupational and Familial Role Conflicts of Working
    Women: A Case Study of the Lafia Canning Factory,
    Ibadan." BSc Dissertation: University of Ibadan,
    Department of Sociology. Ibadan, Nigeria. 1978.
Guyer, Jane I.
    "Food, Cocoa, and the Division of Labour by Sex in Two
    West African Societies." Comparative Studies in Society
    and History. Volume 22 #3 July, 1980. pp. 355-370.

Harrington, Judith A.
   "Nutritional Stress and Economic Responsibility: A Study
   of Nigerian Women." (In) Buvinic, Mayra and Lycette,
   Margaret A. and McGreevey, William P. (eds.). Women and
   Poverty in the Third World. Baltimore, Maryland: Johns
   Hopkins University. 1983. pp. 130-156.
Harrington, Judith A.
   "Some Micro-Socioeconomics of Female Status in Nigeria."
   Paper Presented at the Conference: Women in Poverty: What
   do We Know?. Washington, D.C.: International Centre for
   Research on Women. 1978.
Haynes, J.
   "Some Notes on the Image of 'Women' in Some African
   Poems." (In) Women in Nigeria Today. London: Zed Press.
   1985. pp. 217-225.
Hendrixson, Joyce
   "Islam and the Changing Position of Women in Sokoto:
   Appearance and Reality." Paper Presented at the Annual
   Meeting of the African Studies Association. Paper #42.
   Philadelphia, Pennsylvania. 1980.
Hendrixson, Joyce
   "Women and Class Structures in Sokoto." Paper Presented
   at the Annual Meeting of the African Studies Association.
   Paper #51. Bloomington, Indiana. October 21-24, 1981.
Ifeka-Moller, Caroline
   "Racial Categories and Sexual Images in Colonial
   Nigeria." Paper Presented at the Meeting of the African
   Studies Association of the United Kingdom. 1978. 16p.
Ilori, Felicia
   Factors Determining Rural-Urban Fertility Differentials
   in Western Nigeria: A Case Study of Ife, Ilesha and
   Selected Rural Areas in Oyo Province. Ife, Nigeria:
   University of Ife. 1976.
Jackson, C.
   "Hausa Women and Agricultural Change on the Kano River
   Project, Nigeria." (In) Adams, W.M. and Grove, A.T.
   (eds.). Irrigation in Tropical Africa: Problems and
   Problem Solving. Cambridge, England: Cambridge
   University. African Studies Center. 1984. pp. 67-74.
Jones, Gavin and Lucas, David W.
   "Some Sociocultural Factors Affecting Female Labour Force
   Participation in Jakarta and Lagos." Labour Capital and
   Society. Volume 12 #2 November, 1979. pp. 19-52.
Knowles, C.
   "Women Under Development: Some Preliminary Remarks."
   (In) Women in Nigeria Today. London: Zed Press. 1985.
   pp. 68-81.
Ladipo, Patricia A. and Adegoke, M.O.
   "An Assessment of Rural Women's Agricultural Roles and
   Needs: Implications for Home Economics Extension
   Curriculum." Paper Presented at the Workshop on the Role
   of Women and Home Economics in Rural Development in
   Africa. Rome: United Nations Food and Agricultural

Organization. Alexandria, Egypt. October 17, 1983.
12p.

Longhurst, Richard
"Resource Allocation and the Sexual Division of Labor: A
Case Study of a Moslem Hausa Village in Northern
Nigeria." (In) Beneria, Lourdes (ed.). Women and
Development: The Sexual Division of Labor in Rural
Societies: A Study. New York: Praeger Publishers.
Praeger Special Studies. 1982. pp. 95-117.

Longhurst, Richard
"Rural Development Planning and the Sexual Division of
Labour: A Case Study of a Moslem Hausa Village in
Northern Nigeria." (In) International Labour
Organization (ILO). Rural Development and Women in
Africa. Geneva: ILO. 1984. pp. 117-122.

Longhurst, Richard
Rural Development Planning and the Sexual Division of
Labour: A Case Study of a Moslem Village in Northern
Nigeria. Geneva: International Labour Organization.
World Employment Programme Research Working Paper.
Mimeograph #10. 1980.

Longhurst, Richard
The Provision of Basic Needs for Women: A Case Study of a
Hausa Village in Nigeria. Geneva: International Labour
Organization. Draft Report. 1977.

Mack, Delores E.
"Husbands and Wives in Lagos: The Effects of
Socioeconomic Status on the Patterns of Family Living."
Journal of Marriage and the Family. Volume 40 #4
November, 1978. pp. 807-816.

Madunagu, B.E.
"Contemporary Positions and Experiences of Women." (In)
Women in Nigeria Today. London: Zed Press. 1985. pp.
132-137.

Mann, Kristin
"Women's Rights in Law and Practice: Marriage and Dispute
Settlement in Colonial Lagos." (In) Hay, Margaret J. and
Wright, Marcia (eds.). African Women and the Law:
Historical Perspectives. Boston: Boston University.
African Studies Center. Boston University Papers on
Africa. Volume 7. 1982. pp. 151-171.

Martin, S.
"Gender and Innovation--Farming, Cooking and Palm
Processing in the Ngwa Region, Southeastern Nigeria,
1900-1930." Journal of African History. Volume 25 #4
1984. pp. 411-427.

Mba, Nina E.
"Women and Work in Nigeria: An Historical Perspective."
(In) Sanabary, Nagat E. (ed.). Women and World in the
Third World: The Impact of Industrialization and Global
Economic Interdependence. Berkeley, California:
University of California. Center for the Study,
Education and Advancement of Women. 1983.

Mohammed, A.
'Home Outside the Home' (A Sociological Conception of Prostitution Am ong the Hausa). Kano, Nigeria: Bayero University. Department of Sociology. Seminar Paper. 1980.

Mohammed, H.D.
"Women in Nigerian History: Examples From Borno Empire, Nupeland, and Igboland." (In) Women in Nigeria Today. London: Zed Press. 1985. pp. 45-51.

Musa, Ayuba Z.
"Assessment of Societal Perceptions and Attitudes Toward Marriage and Educated Hausa Women in the Northern States of Nigeria." Ph.D Dissertation: Ohio State University. Columbus, Ohio. 1981. 178p.

Mustapha, A.R.
"On Combating Women's Exploitation and Oppression in Nigeria." (In) Women in Nigeria Today. London: Zed Press. 1985. pp. 241-246.

Obadina, E.
"How Relevant is the Western Women's Liberation Movement for Nigeria?" (In) Women in Nigeria Today. London: Zed Press. 1985. pp. 138-142.

Ogundipe-Leslie, Molara
"Nigeria: Not Spinning on the Axis." (In) Morgan, Robin (ed.). Sisterhood is Global. Garden City, New York: Anchor Books. 1984. pp. 494-504.

Ogundipe-Leslie, Molara
"Women in Nigeria." (In) Women in Nigeria Today. London: Zed Press. 1985. pp. 119-131.

Ogunsheye, F. Aetowun and Awosika, Keziah and Dennis, Carolyn and Didomenko, Catherine and Akinkoye, O.
Nigerian Women and Development. Ibadan, Nigeria: University of Nigeria. 1982.

Okonjo, Isabel K.
"The Role of Women in Social Change Among The Igbo of Southeastern Nigeria Living West of the River Niger." Ph.D Dissertation: Boston University. Boston, Massachusetts. 1976. 220p.

Okonjo, Kamene
"Sex Roles in Nigerian Politics." (In) Oppong, Christine (ed.). Female and Male in West Africa. London: George Allen and Unwin. 1983. pp. 211-222.

Okonjo, Kamene
"The Dual-Sex Political System in Operation: Igbo Women and Community Politics in Midwestern Nigeria." (In) Hafkin, N.J. and Bay, Edna G. (eds.). Women in Africa: Studies in Social and Economic Change. Stanford, California: Stanford University Press. 1976. pp. 45-58.

Omu, Fred I.A. and Makinwa, P. and Ozo, A.O.
Proceedings of the National Conference on Integrated Rural Development and Women in Development. Benin City, Nigeria: University of Benin. Center for Social,

Cultural and Environmental Research. September 22-26, 1980.

Osuntogun, A.
"Rural Women in Agricultural Development: A Nigerian Case Study." Paper Presented at the Conference on Nigerian Women and Development in Relation to Changing Family Structure. Ibadan, Nigeria: University of Ibadan. 1976.

Palmer, Ingrid
Impact of Male Out-Migration on Women in Farming. West Hartford, Connecticut: Kumarian Press. Women's Roles and Gender Differences in Development. Volume Seven. Cases for Planners. 1985. 89p.

Palmer, Ingrid
The Impact of Agrarian Reform on Women. West Hartford, Connecticut: Kumarian Press. Women's Roles and Gender Differences in Development. Volume Six. Cases for Planners. 1985. 89p.

Perchonock, N.
"Double Oppression: Women and Land Matters in Kaduna State." (In) Women in Nigeria Today. London: Zed Press. 1985. pp. 82-103.

Pittin, Rene
"Gender and Class in Nigeria." Review of African Political Economy. #31 December, 1984. pp. 71-81.

Pittin, Renee
"Documentation and Analysis of the Invisible Work of Invisible Women: A Nigerian Case Study." International Labour Review. Volume 123 #4 July-August, 1984. pp. 473-490.

Pittin, Renee
"Hausa Women and Islamic Law: Is Reform Necessary." Paper Presented at the Annual Meeting of the African Studies Association. Paper #75. 1979. 19p.

Roberts, G.B.
"Parental Attitude Towards Education of Female Children: A Survey of Gokana in Borno Local Government Area." Paper Presented at the Third Annual Conference of Women in Nigeria. Port Harcourt, Nigeria: University of Port Harcourt. April, 1984.

Salamone, Frank A.
"The Arrow and the Bird: Proverbs in the Solution of Hausa Conjugal Conflicts." Journal of Anthropological Research. Volume 32 #4 Winter, 1976. pp. 358-371.

Sangree, Walter H.
"Going Home to Mother: Traditional Marriage Among the Irigwe of Benue-Plateau State, Nigeria." (In) Tiffany, Sharon W. (ed.). Women and Society: An Anthropological Reader. St. Albans, Vermont: Eden Press. 1979. pp. 189-207.

Sangree, Walter H.
"The Persistence of Polyandry in Irigwe, Nigeria." Journal of Comparative Family Studies. Volume 11 #3 Special Iss. Summer, 1980. pp. 335-343.

Sangree, Walter H.
"Traditional Coalitions Among Women of Irigwe, Nigeria: From Co-Wife to Possession Cult Ties." Paper Presented at the Annual Meeting of the African Studies Association. Paper #112. Bloomington, Indiana. October 21-24, 1981.

Schildkrout, Enid
"Age and Gender in Hausa Society: Socio-Economic Roles of Children in Urban Kano." (In) LaFontaine, J.S. (ed.). Sex and Age as Principles of Social Differentiation. New York: Academic Press. 1978. pp. 109-137.

Schildkrout, Enid
"Women's Work and Children's Work: Variations Among Moslems of Kano." (In) Wallman, S. (ed.). Social Anthropology of Work. New York: Academic Press. ASA Monograph #19. 1979. pp. 69-85.

Sembajwe, Israel S.
"Effect of Age at First Marriage, Number of Wives, and Type of Marital Union on Fertility." Journal of Biosocial Science. Volume 11 #3 July, 1979. pp. 341-351.

Sharpe, B.
"Social Knowledge and Farming Systems Research: Ethnicity, Power and the Invisible Farmers of North Central Nigeria." African Social Research. #38 1985.

Smedley, Audrey
"The Implications of Birom Cicisbeism." Journal of Comparative Family Studies. Volume 11 #3 Special Issue. Summer, 1980. pp. 345-357.

Spaulding, J.
"The Misfortunes of Some: The Advantages of Others: Land Sales by Women in Sinnar." (In) Hay, M.J. and Wright, M. (eds.). African Women and the Law: Historical Perspectives. Boston: Boston University. African Studies Center. 1978. pp. 3-18.

Spiro, Heather M.
The Fifth World: Women's Rural Activities and Time Budgets in Nigeria. London: University of London. Queen Mary College. Department of Geography. Occasional Paper #19. 1981. 59p.

Spiro, Heather M.
The Ilora Farm Settlement in Nigeria. West Hartford, Connecticut: Kumarian Press. Women's Roles and Gender Differences in Development. Cases for Planners. Volume Five. 1985. 89p.

Spiro, Heather M.
"The Role of Women in Farming in Oyo State, Nigeria: A Case Study in Two Rural Communities." Ibadan, Nigeria: International Institute of Tropical Agriculture: Agricultural Economics Discussion Paper #7. 1980. 36p.

Uchendu, Patrick K.
"The Changing Cultural Role of Igbo Women in Nigeria, 1914-1975." Ph.D Dissertation: New York University. New York, New York. 1980. 339p.

Ugwuegbu, D.C.E.
    "Educational Orientation and Nigerian Students' Attitudes
    to Husband-Wife Relations." Journal of Social
    Psychology. Volume 106 October, 1978. pp. 121-122.
Ukaegbu, Alfred O.
    "Fertility of Women in Polynous Unions in Rural Eastern
    Nigeria." Journal of Marriage and Family. Volume 39 #2
    May, 1977. pp. 397-404.
Ukaegbu, Alfred O.
    "The Role of Traditional Marriage Habits in Population
    Growth: The Case of Rural Eastern Nigeria." Africa.
    Volume 46 #4 1976. pp. 390-398.
United Nations Economic Commission for Africa (UNECA)
    Law and the Status of Women in Nigeria. Addis Ababa,
    Ethiopia: UNECA. 1979.
United Nations Educational, Scientific and Cultural Organ.
    Women and Development: Indicators of Their Changing
    Role. Paris: UNESCO. Socio-Economic Studies #3. 1981.
    112p.
Van Allen, Judith
    "'Aba Riots' or Igbo 'Women's Work'? Ideology,
    Stratification and the Invisibility of Women." (In)
    Hafkin, N.J. and Bay, E.G. (eds.). Women in Africa.
    Stanford, California: Stanford University Press. 1976.
    pp. 59-85.
Van Allen, Judith
    "Aba Riots or Igbo Women's War." Ufahamu. Volume 6 #1
    1976.
Ware, Helen
    "Polygyny: Women's Views in a Transitional Society,
    Nigeria, 1975." Journal of Marriage and Family. Volume
    41 #1 February, 1979. pp. 185-195.
Watts, Susan J.
    "Rural Women as Food Processors and Traders: Eko Making
    in the Ilorin Area of Nigeria." Journal of Developing
    Areas. Volume 19 October, 1984. pp. 71-82.
Yusuf, B.
    "Nigerian Women in Politics: Problems and Prospects."
    (In) Women in Nigeria Today. London: Zed Press. 1985.
    pp. 212-216.
Zack-Williams, A.B.
    "Female Labour and Exploitation Within African Social
    Formations." (In) Women in Nigeria Today. London: Zed
    Press. 1985. pp. 61-67.

SEXUAL MUTILATION/CIRCUMCISION

Egwuatu, V.E.
    "Complications of Female Circumcision in Nigerian Igbos."
    British Journal of Obstetrics and Gynaecology. Volume 88
    #11 November, 1981. pp. 1090-1093.

NIGERIA

Iregbulem, L.M.
"Post-Circumcision Vulval Adhesions in Nigerians."
British Journal of Plastic Surgery. Volume 33 #1
January, 1980. pp. 83-86.
Johnson, B.C.
"Female Circumcision in Nigeria." Paper Presented at the
Seminar on Traditional Practices Affecting the Health of
Women and Children: Female Circumcision, Childhood
Marriage, Nutritional Taboos, etc. Alexandria, Egypt:
World Health Organization. Eastern Mediterranean
Regional Office. Khartoum, Sudan. February 10-15, 1979.
Megafu, U.
"Female Ritual Circumcision in Africa: An Investigation
of the Presumed Benefits Among the Ibos of Nigeria."
East African Medical Journal. Volume 60 #11 1983. pp.
793-800.
Myers, Robert A.
"Circumcision: Its Nature and Practice Among Some Ethnic
Groups in Southern Nigeria." Social Science and
Medicine. Volume 21 #5 1985. pp. 581-588.
Onadeko, M.O.
"Female Circumcision in Nigeria: A Fact or a Farce?"
Journal of Tropical Pediatrics. Volume 31 #4 August,
1981. pp. 180-184.

STATUS OF WOMEN

Adeogun, Modupe F.
"Attitude of Nigerian Mass Media Towards Women." Paper
Presented at the Women and Education Conference. Port
Harcourt, Nigeria: University of Port Harcourt. April,
1984.
Adeyokunnu, Tomilayo O.
"Rural Development and the Position of Women in Africa:
Problems and Policies." Paper Presented at the Meeting
of the Experts on Research on the Status of Women,
Development and Population Trends: Evaluation and
Prospects. Paris: United Nations Educational, Scientific
and Cultural Organization. 1980. 32p.
Afonja, Simi A.
"Current Explanations of Sex-Inequality: A
Reconsideration." Nigerian Journal of Economic and
Social Studies. Volume 21 #2 1981.
Agheyisi, R.U.
"The Labour Market Implications of the Access of Women to
Higher Education in Nigeria." (In) Women in Nigeria
Today. London: Zed Press. 1985. pp. 143-156.
Akande, Jadesola O.
Law and the Status of Women in Nigeria. Addis Ababa,
Ethiopia: United Nations Economic Commission for Africa.
African Training and Research Centre for Women. 1979.
77p.

449

Akinkoye, Olu
   "Attitude to Child-Bearing by Single Nigerian Women."
   Nigerian Journal of Economic and Social Studies. Volume
   26 #1 March, 1984.
Babatunde, E.D.
   "Ketu Myths and the Status of Women: A Structural
   Interpretation of Some Yoruba Myths of Origin." Journal
   of the Anthropological Society of Oxford. Volume 14 #3
   1983. pp. 301-306.
Beckett, Paul A. and O'Connell, James O.
   "Education and the Situation of Women: Background and
   Atttitudes of Christian and Muslim Female Students at a
   Nigerian University." Cultures et Developpement. Volume
   8 #2 1976. pp. 242-265.
Di Domenico, Catherine M. and Asuni, Judy and Scott,
Jacqueline
   "Changing Status of African Women: An Exploratory Study
   of Working Mothers in Ibadan, Nigeria." (In)
   International Planned Parenthood Federation (IPPF).
   Proceedings of the IPPF Africa Regional Conference.
   London: IPPF. 1977. pp. 283-284.
Harrington, Judith A.
   "Education, Female Status and Fertility in Nigeria."
   Paper Presented to the Population Association of America.
   Atlanta, Georgia. 1978.
Harrington, Judith A.
   "Some Micro-Socioeconomics of Female Status in Nigeria."
   Paper Presented at the Conference: Women in Poverty: What
   do We Know?. Washington, D.C.: International Centre for
   Research on Women. 1978.
Harrington, Judith A.
   Education, Female Status and Fertility in Nigeria. Ann
   Arbor, Michigan: University of Michigan. School of
   Public Health. Department of Population Planning. 1978.
Kisekka, Mere N.
   "The Identification and Use of Indicators of Women's
   Participation in Socio-Economic Development in the
   Context of Nigeria and Uganda." Paper Presented at the
   Meeting of Experts on the Indicators of Women's
   Participation in Socio-Economic Development. Paris:
   United Nations Educational, Scientific and Cultural
   Organization. 1980. 52p.
Lacey, Linda and Di Domenico, Catherine M.
   Occupational Status of Women in Nigeria: A Comparison of
   Two Urban Centres. Ithaca, New York: Cornell University.
   Department of City and Regional Planning and the Program
   in Urban and Regional Studies. Working Papers in
   Planning #27. 1979. 17p.
Mann, Kristin
   Marrying Well: Status and Social Change Among the
   Educated Elite in Colonial Lagos. Cambridge, England:
   Cambridge University Press. African Studies Series #47.
   1985. 194p.

Mustapha, A.R.
   "On Combating Women's Exploitation and Oppression in
   Nigeria." (In) Women in Nigeria Today. London: Zed
   Press. 1985. pp. 241-246.
Obadina, E.
   "How Relevant is the Western Women's Liberation Movement
   for Nigeria?" (In) Women in Nigeria Today. London: Zed
   Press. 1985. pp. 138-142.
Ogundipe-Leslie, Molara
   "Nigeria: Not Spinning on the Axis." (In) Morgan, Robin
   (ed.). Sisterhood is Global. Garden City, New York:
   Anchor Books. 1984. pp. 494-504.
Ogundipe-Leslie, Molara
   "Women in Nigeria." (In) Women in Nigeria Today.
   London: Zed Press. 1985. pp. 119-131.
Owuamanam, Donatus O.
   "Marriage and Aspiration to Professional Leadership of
   Women Student Teachers in Nigeria." Journal of
   Psychology. Volume 115 #1 September, 1983. pp.
   103-106.
Perchonock, N.
   "Double Oppression: Women and Land Matters in Kaduna
   State." (In) Women in Nigeria Today. London: Zed Press.
   1985. pp. 82-103.
Pittin, Renee
   "Organizing for the Future." (In) Women in Nigeria
   Today. London: Zed Press. 1985. pp. 231-240.
St. Peter, Christine
   "Changing Worlds: The Nigerian Novels of Buchi Emecheta."
   Atlantis. Volume 11 Fall, 1985. pp. 134-146.
Uchendu, Patrick K.
   "The Changing Cultural Role of Igbo Women in Nigeria,
   1914-1975." Ph.D Dissertation: New York University. New
   York, New York. 1980. 339p.
United Nations Economic Commission for Africa (UNECA)
   Law and the Status of Women in Nigeria. Addis Ababa,
   Ethiopia: UNECA. 1979.

URBANIZATION

Arowolo, Oladele O.
   "Fertility of Urban Yoruba Working Women: A Case Study of
   Ibadan City." Nigerian Journal of Economic and Social
   Studies. Volume 19 #1 March, 1977. pp. 37-66.
Ayangade, Okun
   "Characteristics of Contraceptive Acceptors in an Urban
   Nigerian Setting." International Journal of Gynaecology
   and Obstetrics. Volume 22 1984. pp. 59-66.
Ayangade, Samuel O.
   "Maternal Mortality in a Semi-Urban Nigerian Community."
   Journal of the National Medical Association. Volume 73
   #2 February, 1981. pp. 137-140.

Coles, Catherine M.
"Urban Muslim Women and Social Change in Northern
Nigeria." Paper Presented at the Annual Meeting of the
African Studies Association. Paper #20. Washington,
D.C. November 4-7, 1982.

Coles, Catherine M.
Urban Muslim Women and Social Change in Northern
Nigeria. East Lansing, Michigan: Michigan State
University. Office of Women in International
Development. Working Paper #19. March, 1983. 28p.

Di Domenico, Catherine M. and Lacey-Mojuetan, Linda
"Occupational Status of Women in Nigeria: A Comparison of
Two Urban Centres." Paper Presented at the Conference on
Nigerian Women and Development in Relation to Changing
Family Structure. Ibadan, Nigeria: University of Ibadan.
Department of Sociology. April 26-30, 1976. 13p.

Di Domenico, Catherine M. and Lacey-Mojuetan, Linda
"Occupational Status of Women in Nigeria: A Comparison of
Two Urban Centres." Africana Marburgensia. Volume 10 #2
1977. pp. 62-79.

Lacey, Linda
"Interurban Flows of Population and Occupational Skills
to Three Cities in Nigeria." International Migration
Review. Volume 19 #4 Winter, 1985. pp. 686-707.

Lacey, Linda and Di Domenico, Catherine M.
Occupational Status of Women in Nigeria: A Comparison of
Two Urban Centres. Ithaca, New York: Cornell University.
Department of City and Regional Planning and the Program
in Urban and Regional Studies. Working Papers in
Planning #27. 1979. 17p.

Lucas, David W.
"Urban and Rural Fertility in Southern Nigeria." (In)
Ruzicka, Lado T. (ed.). The Economic and Social Supports
for High Fertility: Proceedings of the Conference. 1976.
Canberra, Australia: Australian National University.
Development Studies Center. Canberra, Australia.
November 16-19, 1977. pp. 409-435.

Mbofung, C.M. and Omololu, A.
"Dietary Fibre in the Diets of Urban and Rural Yoruba
Nigerian Women." Nutritional Research. Volume 4 #2
March-April, 1984. pp. 225-235.

Okojie, Christiana E.E.
"Determinants of Labour Force Participation of Urban
Women in Nigeria: A Case Study of Benin City." Nigerian
Journal of Economic and Social Studies. Volume 25 #1
1983. pp. 39-59.

Okore, Augustine O.
"Rural-Urban Fertility Differentials in Southern Nigeria:
An Assessment of Some Available Evidence." Population
Studies. Volume 34 #1 March, 1980. pp. 171-179.

Oni, Gbolahan A.
"Effects of Women's Education on Postpartum Practices and
Fertility in Urban Nigeria." Studies in Family Planning.

Volume 16 #6 Part One November-December, 1985. pp.
321-331.
Peil, Margaret
    "Urban Contacts: A Comparison of Women and Men." (In)
    Oppong, Christine (ed.). Female and Male in West Africa.
    London: George Allen and Unwin. 1983. pp. 275-282.
Schildkrout, Enid
    "Age and Gender in Hausa Society: Socio-Economic Roles of
    Children in Urban Kano." (In) LaFontaine, J.S. (ed.).
    Sex and Age as Principles of Social Differentiation. New
    York: Academic Press. 1978. pp. 109-137.
Trager, Lillian
    "Market Women in the Urban Economy: The Role of Yoruba
    Intermediaries in a Medium Sized City." African Urban
    Notes. Volume 2 #3 Fall/Winter, 1976. pp. 1-10.
Tshinyongolo, Mulunda
    "Fertility Differentials in Urban Nigeria." Ph.D
    Dissertation: University of Michigan. Ann Arbor,
    Michigan. 1981. 356p.
Zack-Williams, A.B.
    "Female Urban Unemployment." (In) Women in Nigeria
    Today. London: Zed Press. 1985. pp. 104-113.

WOMEN AND THEIR CHILDREN

Akinkoye, Olu
    "Attitude to Child-Bearing by Single Nigerian Women."
    Nigerian Journal of Economic and Social Studies. Volume
    26 #1 March, 1984.
Aluko, G.B. and Alfa, M.O.
    "Marriage and Family." (In) Women in Nigeria Today.
    London: Zed Press. 1985. pp. 163-173.
Bamisaiye, Anne and Oyediran, M.A.
    "Breast-Feeding Among Female Employees at a Major Health
    Institution in Lagos, Nigeria." Social Science and
    Medicine. Volume 17 #23 1983. pp. 1867-1871.
Fadayomi, T.O. and Adelola, I.O. and Oni, B. and Omogbehin,
V.A. and Egbunike, N.A.
    The Role of Working Mothers in Early Childhood Education:
    A Nigerian Case Study. Paris: UNESCO. Nigerian
    Institute of Social and Economic Research. February,
    1978. 68p.
Fapohunda, Eleanor R.
    "The Child-Care Dilemma of Working Mothers in African
    Cities: The Case of Lagos, Nigeria." (In) Bay, Edna G.
    (ed.). Women and Work in Africa. Boulder, Colorado:
    Westview Press. Westview Special Studies in Africa.
    1982. pp. 277-288.
Fapohunda, Olanrewaju J. and Fapohunda, Eleanor R.
    The Working Mothers of Lagos. Washington, D.C.:
    Smithsonian Institution. Interdisciplinary
    Communications Committee. Report of a Study. 1976.

NIGERIA

Meldrum, Brenda
    "Traditional Child-Rearing Practices of the Oje Market
    Women of Ibadan." (In) Curran, H. Valerie (ed.).
    Nigerian Children: Developmental Perspectives. Boston:
    Routledge and Kegan Paul. 1984. pp. 174-196.
Ojofeitimi, E.O.
    "Assessment of the Nutritional Status of Nigerian Rural
    Children and Mothers Perceptions of Quality of Life."
    Child Care Health and Development. Volume 10 #6 1984.
    pp. 349-358.
Schildkrout, Enid
    "Age and Gender in Hausa Society: Socio-Economic Roles of
    Children in Urban Kano." (In) LaFontaine, J.S. (ed.).
    Sex and Age as Principles of Social Differentiation. New
    York: Academic Press. 1978. pp. 109-137.
Temuru, S.
    "Mother and Child in the Lagos Metropolis." Nigeria
    Magazine. #132/133 1980. pp. 3-22.
Uyanga, Joseph T.
    "Rural-Urban Differences in Child Care and Breastfeeding
    Behavior in South Eastern Nigeria." Social Science and
    Medicine. Volume 14D #1 March, 1980. pp. 23-29.
Uyanga, Joseph T.
    "The Value of Children and Childbearing in Rural
    Southeastern Nigeria." Rural Africana. #7 Spring,
    1980. pp. 37-53.

Senegal

AGRICULTURE

Ba, Fama H. and Ndiaye, Aminata M. and Savane,
Marie-Angelique and Thiongane, Awe
    "The Impact of Territorial Administration Reform on the
    Situation of Women in Senegal." (In) International
    Labour Organization (ILO). Rural Development and Women
    in Africa. Geneva: ILO. 1984. pp. 107-115.
Basse, M.T.
    "Women, Food and Nutrition in Africa: Perspective From
    Senegal." Food and Nutrition. Volume 10 #1 1984. pp.
    65-71.
Carr, Marilyn
    Women in Rural Senegal: Some Implications Proposed Food
    and Nutrition Interventions. Washington, D.C.: U.S.
    Department of State. U.S. Agency for International
    Development. U.S. AID Consultants Report. IBRD. Mimeo.
    June, 1978.
Cloud, Kathleen
    Women and Irrigation in the Senegal River Basin: A
    Problem in the Intensification of African Agriculture.
    Boston: Harvard Graduate School of Education. Draft
    Paper. 1982.
Dinnerstein, Myra and Cloud, Kathleen
    Report of a Fact-Finding Trip to Niger, Mali, Senegal and
    Upper Volta. Washington, D.C.: U.S. Department of State.
    U.S. Agency for International Development. 1976. 10p.
Jeffalyn Johnson and Associates Inc.
    African Women in Development. Falls Church, Virginia:
    Jeffalyn Johnson and Associates Inc. 1980. 125p.
Kane, F.
    "Female Proletariat in Senegal, Town and Country."
    Cahiers d'Etudes Africaines. Volume 17 #1 1977. pp.
    77-94.
Koehring, John
    Women in Development--Memorandum on Senegal Cereals

Production-Phase II. Washington, D.C.: U.S. Department
of State. U.S. Agency for International Development.
AFR/DR. December 3, 1979.
Lewis, Barbara C.
"The Impact of Development Policies on Women." (In) Hay,
Margaret J. and Stichter, Sharon (eds.). African Women
South of the Sahara. New York: Longman. 1984. pp.
170-187.
Loose, Edna E.
"Women in Rural Senegal: Some Economic and Social
Observations." (In) Purdue University. Workshop on
Sahelian Agriculture. Lafayette, Indiana: Purdue
University. Department of Agricultural Economics.
February 1-2, 1979. 25p.
M'Baye, Fatou
"Maisons Familiales Rurales, Senegal." (In) Blair,
Patricia W. (ed.). Health Needs of the World's Poor
Women. Washington, D.C.: Equity Policy Center. 1981.
pp. 137-138.
Mackintosh, Maureen
"Domestic Labour: Production and Reproduction." (In)
Allen, C. and Williams, G. (eds.). Subsaharan Africa.
London: Macmillan. Sociology of Developing Societies
Series. 1982. pp. 46-52.
Thomson, Martha E.
"Nonformal Education for Rural Development: The Women's
Training Center in Senegal." Ph.D Dissertation:
University of Illinois-Urbana-Champaign. Urbana,
Illinois. 1981. 301p.
Venema, Bernhard
"Male and Female Farming Systems and Agricultural
Intensification in West Africa: The Case of the Wolof,
Senegal." (In) Presvelov, C. and Spijkers-Zwart, S.
(eds.). The Household, Women and Agricultural
Development. Wageningen, Netherlands: H. Veenman en
Zonen. 1980. pp. 27-34.
Yaciuk, Gordon
"The Role of Women in Post-Harvest Technology in
Senegal." Paper Presented at a Seminar on a Challenge
for Change in Third World Agriculture. Alberta, Canada:
Alberta Institute of Agrologists and Canada's
International Development Research Center. September,
1978.

ARTS

Brooks, George E.
"Artists' Depictions of Senegalese Signares: Insights
Concerning French Racist and Sexist Attitudes in the 19th
Century." Geneve-Afrique. Volume 18 #1 1980. pp.
75-89.

Johnson, Marian
  "Black Gold: Goldsmiths, Jewelry and Women in Senegal."
  Ph.D Dissertation: Stanford University. Stanford,
  California. 1980. 668p.

BIBLIOGRAPHIES

Cham, Mbye
  "The Female Condition in Africa: A Literary Exploration
  by Mariama Ba." Current Bibliography on African Affairs.
  Volume 17 #1 1984. pp. 29+.

CULTURAL ROLES

Anderson, John E. and Goldberg, Howard I. and M'bodji, Fara
G. and Abdel-Aziz, Abdallah
  Postpartum Practices and Child Spacing in Senegal and
  Jordan. Atlanta, Georgia: U.S. Centers for Disease
  Control. Family Planning Evaluation Division. 1984.
Ben, Geloune M.
  Patterns of First Marriage and its Disruption for
  Senegalese Women. Cairo: Cairo Demographic Centre. CDC
  Research Monograph Series #12. 1981. pp. 423-447.
Braun, Armelle
  "Escape From the Passive Past: A New Role for Women in
  Senegal." Ceres. Volume 11 #4 July-August, 1978.
Brooks, George E.
  "The Signares of Saint-Louis and Goree: Women
  Entrepreneurs in 18th Century Senegal." (In) Hafkin,
  N.J. and Bay, Edna (eds.). Women in Africa: Studies in
  Social and Economic Change. Stanford, California:
  Stanford University Press. 1976. pp. 19-44.
Brooks, George E.
  "Artists' Depictions of Senegalese Signares: Insights
  Concerning French Racist and Sexist Attitudes in the 19th
  Century." Geneve-Afrique. Volume 18 #1 1980. pp.
  75-89.
Cantrelle, Pierre and Ferry, Benoit
  "The Influence of Nutrition on Fertility: The Case of
  Senegal." (In) Mosley, W. Henry (ed.). Nutrition and
  Human Reproduction. New York: Plenum Press. 1978. pp.
  353-363.
Cantrelle, Pierre and Leridon, Henri
  "Fertility, Breast-Feeding and Infant Mortality.
  Inter-Ethnic Differences in One and the Same Region:
  Salum (Senegal)." Population. Volume 35 #3 May-June,
  1980. pp. 623-648.
Case, F.I.
  "The Socio-Cultural Functions of Women in the Senegalese
  Novel." Cultures et Developpement. Volume 9 #4 1977.
  pp. 601-629.

Colvin, Lucie G.
    The Uprooted of the Western Sahel: Migrants' Quest for
    Cash in Senegambia. New York: Praeger Publishers. 1981.
    385p.
Colvin, Lucie G.
    The Uprooted in the Western Sahel: Migrants' Quest for
    Cash in the Senegambia: Final Report of the Senegambia
    Migration Study. Washington, D.C.: U.S. Department of
    State. U.S. Agency for International Development. 1980.
    307p.
Ferry, Benoit
    "The Senegalese Survey." (In) Page, Hilary J. and
    Lesthaeghe, Ron (eds.). Child-Spacing in Tropical
    Africa: Traditions and Change. New York: Academic Press.
    1981. pp 265-273.
Goldberg, Howard I. and M'bodji, Fara G. and Friedman, Jay
S.
    Fertility and Family Planning in the Sine-Saloum Region
    of Senegal. Atlanta, Georgia: Centers for Disease
    Control. Division of Reproductive Health. 1985.
Hamer, Alice J.
    "Tradition and Change: A Social History of Diola Women in
    the 20th Century." Ph.D Dissertation: University of
    Michigan. Ann Arbor, Michigan. 1983. 340p.
Hamer, Alice J.
    "Diola Women and Migration: A Case Study." (In) Colvin,
    Lucie G. The Uprooted in the Sahel: Migrant's Quest for
    Cash in the Senegambia. Final Report on the Senegambia
    Migration Study. Washington, D.C.: U.S. Department of
    State. U.S. Agency for International Development. 1979.
Hammond, Thomas N.
    "The Image of Women in Senegalese Fiction." Ph.D
    Dissertation: University of New York. Buffalo, New York.
    1976.
Johnson, Marian
    "Black Gold: Goldsmiths, Jewelry and Women in Senegal."
    Ph.D Dissertation: Stanford University. Stanford,
    California. 1980. 668p.
Kane, F.
    "Female Proletariat in Senegal, Town and Country."
    Cahiers d'Etudes Africaines. Volume 17 #1 1977. pp.
    77-94.
Lesthaeghe, Ron J. and Eelens, Frank
    Social Organization and Reproductive Regimes: Lessons
    From Sub-Saharan Africa and Historical Western Europe.
    Brussels, Belgium: Vrije Universiteit Brussel.
    Interuniversity Programme in Demography. IDP Working
    Paper #1985-1. 1985. 64p.
Loose, Edna E.
    "Women in Rural Senegal: Some Economic and Social
    Observations." (In) Purdue University. Workshop on
    Sahelian Agriculture. Lafayette, Indiana: Purdue

University.   Department of Agricultural Economics.
February 1-2, 1979.   25p.
Mackintosh, Maureen
    "Domestic Labour: Production and Reproduction."   (In)
    Allen, C. and Williams, G. (eds.).   Subsaharan Africa.
    London: Macmillan.   Sociology of Developing Societies
    Series.   1982.   pp. 46-52.
McCaffrey, Kathleen M.
    Images of Women in the Literatures of Selected Developing
    Countries.   Washington, D.C.: U.S. Department of State.
    U.S. Agency for International Development.   Office of
    Women in Development.   1981.   229p.
Messer, Ellen and Bloch, Marianne N.
    Women's and Children's Activity Profiles in Senegal and
    Mexico: A Comparison of Time Allocation and Time
    Allocation Methods.   East Lansing, Michigan: Michigan
    State University.   Office of Women in International
    Development.   1983.   15p.
Mondot-Bernard, Jacqueline M.
    "Fertility and Breast-Feeding in Africa."   African
    Environment.   #14-16 1981.   pp. 131-150.
Nichols, Douglas and Ndiaye, Salif and Burton, Nadine and
Janowitz, Barbara and Gueye, Lamine and Gueye, Mouhamadou
    "Vanguard Family Planning Acceptors in Senegal."   Studies
    in Family Planning.   Volume 16 #5   September-October,
    1985.   pp. 271-278.
Savane, Marie-Angelique
    "Senegal: Elegance Amid the Phallocracy."   (In) Morgan,
    Robin (ed.).   Sisterhood is Global.   Garden City, New
    York: Anchor Books.   1984.   pp. 589-599.
Smyley, Karen M.
    "The African Woman: Interpretations of Senegalese
    Novelists Aboulaye Sadji and Ousman Sembene."   Thesis:
    City University of New York.   New York, New York.   1977.
    275p.
Tinker, Irene and Cohen, M.
    "Street Food as a Source of Income for Women."   Ekistics.
    Volume 52 #310 1985.   pp. 83-89.
United Nations Economic Commission for Africa (UNECA)
    Nuptiality and Fertility (A Comparative Analysis of WFS
    Data).   Addis Ababa, Ethiopia: UNECA.   African Population
    Studies Series #5.   1983.   96p.
Vandewiele, Michel
    "How Senegalese Secondary School Students Feel About
    Euro-African Mixed Marriage."   Psychological Reports.
    Volume 46 #1   June, 1980.   pp. 789-790.
Vandewiele, Michel
    "Wolof Adolescents' Attitudes Towards Old People."
    Adolescence.   Volume 17 #68   Winter, 1982.   pp. 863-869.
Vandewiele, Michel
    "Perception of Women's Religious Status by Senegalese
    Adolescents."   Psychological Reports.   Volume 53 #3 Part
    One   December, 1983.   pp. 757-758.

Venema, Bernhard
    "Male and Female Farming Systems and Agricultural
    Intensification in West Africa: The Case of the Wolof,
    Senegal." (In) Presvelov, C. and Spijkers-Zwart, S.
    (eds.). The Household, Women and Agricultural
    Development. Wageningen, Netherlands: H. Veenman en
    Zonen. 1980. pp. 27-34.

DEVELOPMENT AND TECHNOLOGY

Ba, Fama H. and Ndiaye, Aminata M. and Savane,
Marie-Angelique and Thiongane, Awe
    "The Impact of Territorial Administration Reform on the
    Situation of Women in Senegal." (In) International
    Labour Organization (ILO). Rural Development and Women
    in Africa. Geneva: ILO. 1984. pp. 107-115.
Basse, M.T.
    "Women, Food and Nutrition in Africa: Perspective From
    Senegal." Food and Nutrition. Volume 10 #1 1984. pp.
    65-71.
Braun, Armelle
    "Escape From the Passive Past: A New Role for Women in
    Senegal." Ceres. Volume 11 #4 July-August, 1978.
Carr, Marilyn
    Women in Rural Senegal: Some Implications Proposed Food
    and Nutrition Interventions. Washington, D.C.: U.S.
    Department of State. U.S. Agency for International
    Development. U.S. AID Consultants Report. IBRD. Mimeo.
    June, 1978.
Cloud, Kathleen
    Women and Irrigation in the Senegal River Basin: A
    Problem in the Intensification of African Agriculture.
    Boston: Harvard Graduate School of Education. Draft
    Paper. 1982.
Dinnerstein, Myra and Cloud, Kathleen
    Report of a Fact-Finding Trip to Niger, Mali, Senegal and
    Upper Volta. Washington, D.C.: U.S. Department of State.
    U.S. Agency for International Development. 1976. 10p.
Jeffalyn Johnson and Associates Inc.
    African Women in Development. Falls Church, Virginia:
    Jeffalyn Johnson and Associates Inc. 1980. 125p.
Kane, F.
    "Female Proletariat in Senegal, Town and Country."
    Cahiers d'Etudes Africaines. Volume 17 #1 1977. pp.
    77-94.
Koehring, John
    Women in Development--Memorandum on Senegal Cereals
    Production-Phase II. Washington, D.C.: U.S. Department
    of State. U.S. Agency for International Development.
    AFR/DR. December 3, 1979.
Lewis, Barbara C.
    "The Impact of Development Policies on Women." (In) Hay,
    Margaret J. and Stichter, Sharon (eds.). African Women

South of the Sahara. New York: Longman. 1984. pp.
170-187.
Loose, Edna E.
  "Women in Rural Senegal: Some Economic and Social
  Observations." (In) Purdue University. Workshop on
  Sahelian Agriculture. Lafayette, Indiana: Purdue
  University. Department of Agricultural Economics.
  February 1-2, 1979. 25p.
National Asso. of Negro Business and Prof. Women's Clubs
  African Women Small Entrepreneurs in Senegal, The Gambia,
  Sierra Leone, Cameroon and Malawi: Prefeasibility Study
  for Providing Assistance. Washington, D.C.: NANBPA.
  1977. 82p.
Thomson, Martha E.
  "Nonformal Education for Rural Development: The Women's
  Training Center in Senegal." Ph.D Dissertation:
  University of Illinois-Urbana-Champaign. Urbana,
  Illinois. 1981. 301p.
U.S. Department of Commerce. Bureau of the Census
  Illustrative Statistics on Women in Development in
  Selected Developing Countries. Washington, D.C.: U.S.
  Department of Commerce. 1982. 24p.
Venema, Bernhard
  "Male and Female Farming Systems and Agricultural
  Intensification in West Africa: The Case of the Wolof,
  Senegal." (In) Presvelov, C. and Spijkers-Zwart, S.
  (eds.). The Household, Women and Agricultural
  Development. Wageningen, Netherlands: H. Veenman en
  Zonen. 1980. pp. 27-34.
Yaciuk, Gordon
  "The Role of Women in Post-Harvest Technology in
  Senegal." Paper Presented at a Seminar on a Challenge
  for Change in Third World Agriculture. Alberta, Canada:
  Alberta Institute of Agrologists and Canada's
  International Development Research Center. September,
  1978.

ECONOMICS

Ba, Fama H. and Ndiaye, Aminata M. and Savane,
Marie-Angelique and Thiongane, Awe
  "The Impact of Territorial Administration Reform on the
  Situation of Women in Senegal." (In) International
  Labour Organization (ILO). Rural Development and Women
  in Africa. Geneva: ILO. 1984. pp. 107-115.
Basse, M.T.
  "Women, Food and Nutrition in Africa: Perspective From
  Senegal." Food and Nutrition. Volume 10 #1 1984. pp.
  65-71.
Braun, Armelle
  "Escape From the Passive Past: A New Role for Women in
  Senegal." Ceres. Volume 11 #4 July-August, 1978.

Brooks, George E.
    "The Signares of Saint-Louis and Goree: Women
    Entrepreneurs in 18th Century Senegal." (In) Hafkin,
    N.J. and Bay, Edna (eds.). Women in Africa: Studies in
    Social and Economic Change. Stanford, California:
    Stanford University Press. 1976. pp. 19-44.
Carr, Marilyn
    Women in Rural Senegal: Some Implications Proposed Food
    and Nutrition Interventions. Washington, D.C.: U.S.
    Department of State. U.S. Agency for International
    Development. U.S. AID Consultants Report. IBRD. Mimeo.
    June, 1978.
Cloud, Kathleen
    Women and Irrigation in the Senegal River Basin: A
    Problem in the Intensification of African Agriculture.
    Boston: Harvard Graduate School of Education. Draft
    Paper. 1982.
Colvin, Lucie G.
    The Uprooted of the Western Sahel: Migrants' Quest for
    Cash in Senegambia. New York: Praeger Publishers. 1981.
    385p.
Colvin, Lucie G.
    The Uprooted in the Western Sahel: Migrants' Quest for
    Cash in the Senegambia: Final Report of the Senegambia
    Migration Study. Washington, D.C.: U.S. Department of
    State. U.S. Agency for International Development. 1980.
    307p.
Hamer, Alice J.
    "Diola Women and Migration: A Case Study." (In) Colvin,
    Lucie G. The Uprooted in the Sahel: Migrant's Quest for
    Cash in the Senegambia. Final Report on the Senegambia
    Migration Study. Washington, D.C.: U.S. Department of
    State. U.S. Agency for International Development. 1979.
Jeffalyn Johnson and Associates Inc.
    African Women in Development. Falls Church, Virginia:
    Jeffalyn Johnson and Associates Inc. 1980. 125p.
Johnson, Marian
    "Black Gold: Goldsmiths, Jewelry and Women in Senegal."
    Ph.D Dissertation: Stanford University. Stanford,
    California. 1980. 668p.
Lewis, Barbara C.
    "The Impact of Development Policies on Women." (In) Hay,
    Margaret J. and Stichter, Sharon (eds.). African Women
    South of the Sahara. New York: Longman. 1984. pp.
    170-187.
Loose, Edna E.
    "Women in Rural Senegal: Some Economic and Social
    Observations." (In) Purdue University. Workshop on
    Sahelian Agriculture. Lafayette, Indiana: Purdue
    University. Department of Agricultural Economics.
    February 1-2, 1979. 25p.
M'Baye, Fatou
    "Maisons Familiales Rurales, Senegal." (In) Blair,
    Patricia W. (ed.). Health Needs of the World's Poor

462

Women. Washington, D.C.: Equity Policy Center. 1981.
pp. 137-138.
Mackintosh, Maureen
"Domestic Labour: Production and Reproduction." (In)
Allen, C. and Williams, G. (eds.). Subsaharan Africa.
London: Macmillan. Sociology of Developing Societies
Series. 1982. pp. 46-52.
National Asso. of Negro Business and Prof. Women's Clubs
African Women Small Entrepreneurs in Senegal, The Gambia,
Sierra Leone, Cameroon and Malawi: Prefeasibility Study
for Providing Assistance. Washington, D.C.: NANBPA.
1977. 82p.
Tinker, Irene and Cohen, M.
"Street Food as a Source of Income for Women." Ekistics.
Volume 52 #310 1985. pp. 83-89.

EDUCATION AND TRAINING

M'Baye, Fatou
"Maisons Familiales Rurales, Senegal." (In) Blair,
Patricia W. (ed.). Health Needs of the World's Poor
Women. Washington, D.C.: Equity Policy Center. 1981.
pp. 137-138.
Thomson, Martha E.
"Nonformal Education for Rural Development: The Women's
Training Center in Senegal." Ph.D Dissertation:
University of Illinois-Urbana-Champaign. Urbana,
Illinois. 1981. 301p.

EMPLOYMENT AND LABOR

Ba, Fama H. and Ndiaye, Aminata M. and Savane,
Marie-Angelique and Thiongane, Awe
"The Impact of Territorial Administration Reform on the
Situation of Women in Senegal." (In) International
Labour Organization (ILO). Rural Development and Women
in Africa. Geneva: ILO. 1984. pp. 107-115.
Bashizi, Bashige
"Day-Care Centers in Senegal: A Women's Initiative."
Assignment Children. Volume 49/50 Spring, 1980. pp.
63-80.
Carr, Marilyn
Women in Rural Senegal: Some Implications Proposed Food
and Nutrition Interventions. Washington, D.C.: U.S.
Department of State. U.S. Agency for International
Development. U.S. AID Consultants Report. IBRD. Mimeo.
June, 1978.
Cloud, Kathleen
Women and Irrigation in the Senegal River Basin: A
Problem in the Intensification of African Agriculture.
Boston: Harvard Graduate School of Education. Draft
Paper. 1982.

Colvin, Lucie G.
   The Uprooted of the Western Sahel: Migrants' Quest for
   Cash in Senegambia. New York: Praeger Publishers. 1981.
   385p.
Colvin, Lucie G.
   The Uprooted in the Western Sahel: Migrants' Quest for
   Cash in the Senegambia: Final Report of the Senegambia
   Migration Study. Washington, D.C.: U.S. Department of
   State. U.S. Agency for International Development. 1980.
   307p.
Johnson, Marian
   "Black Gold: Goldsmiths, Jewelry and Women in Senegal."
   Ph.D Dissertation: Stanford University. Stanford,
   California. 1980. 668p.
Kane, F.
   "Female Proletariat in Senegal, Town and Country."
   Cahiers d'Etudes Africaines. Volume 17 #1 1977. pp.
   77-94.
Lewis, Barbara C.
   "The Impact of Development Policies on Women." (In) Hay,
   Margaret J. and Stichter, Sharon (eds.). African Women
   South of the Sahara. New York: Longman. 1984. pp.
   170-187.
Loose, Edna E.
   "Women in Rural Senegal: Some Economic and Social
   Observations." (In) Purdue University. Workshop on
   Sahelian Agriculture. Lafayette, Indiana: Purdue
   University. Department of Agricultural Economics.
   February 1-2, 1979. 25p.
Mackintosh, Maureen
   "Domestic Labour: Production and Reproduction." (In)
   Allen, C. and Williams, G. (eds.). Subsaharan Africa.
   London: Macmillan. Sociology of Developing Societies
   Series. 1982. pp. 46-52.
Thomson, Martha E.
   "Nonformal Education for Rural Development: The Women's
   Training Center in Senegal." Ph.D Dissertation:
   University of Illinois-Urbana-Champaign. Urbana,
   Illinois. 1981. 301p.
Tinker, Irene and Cohen, M.
   "Street Food as a Source of Income for Women." Ekistics.
   Volume 52 #310 1985. pp. 83-89.
Yaciuk, Gordon
   "The Role of Women in Post-Harvest Technology in
   Senegal." Paper Presented at a Seminar on a Challenge
   for Change in Third World Agriculture. Alberta, Canada:
   Alberta Institute of Agrologists and Canada's
   International Development Research Center. September,
   1978.

FAMILY LIFE

Colvin, Lucie G.
    The Uprooted of the Western Sahel: Migrants' Quest for
    Cash in Senegambia. New York: Praeger Publishers. 1981.
    385p.
Colvin, Lucie G.
    The Uprooted in the Western Sahel: Migrants' Quest for
    Cash in the Senegambia: Final Report of the Senegambia
    Migration Study. Washington, D.C.: U.S. Department of
    State. U.S. Agency for International Development. 1980.
    307p.
Hamer, Alice J.
    "Tradition and Change: A Social History of Diola Women in
    the 20th Century." Ph.D Dissertation: University of
    Michigan. Ann Arbor, Michigan. 1983. 340p.
Hamer, Alice J.
    "Diola Women and Migration: A Case Study." (In) Colvin,
    Lucie G. The Uprooted in the Sahel: Migrant's Quest for
    Cash in the Senegambia. Final Report on the Senegambia
    Migration Study. Washington, D.C.: U.S. Department of
    State. U.S. Agency for International Development. 1979.
Messer, Ellen and Bloch, Marianne N.
    Women's and Children's Activity Profiles in Senegal and
    Mexico: A Comparison of Time Allocation and Time
    Allocation Methods. East Lansing, Michigan: Michigan
    State University. Office of Women in International
    Development. 1983. 15p.
Snyder, Francis G. and Savane, Marie-Angelique
    Law and Population in Senegal: A Survey of Legislation.
    Leiden, Netherlands: Afrika-Studiecentrum. 1977. 242p.
Tinker, Irene and Cohen, M.
    "Street Food as a Source of Income for Women." Ekistics.
    Volume 52 #310 1985. pp. 83-89.
Venema, Bernhard
    "Male and Female Farming Systems and Agricultural
    Intensification in West Africa: The Case of the Wolof,
    Senegal." (In) Presvelov, C. and Spijkers-Zwart, S.
    (eds.). The Household, Women and Agricultural
    Development. Wageningen, Netherlands: H. Veenman en
    Zonen. 1980. pp. 27-34.

FAMILY PLANNING AND CONTRACEPTION

Anderson, John E. and Goldberg, Howard I. and M'bodji, Fara
G. and Abdel-Aziz, Abdallah
    Postpartum Practices and Child Spacing in Senegal and
    Jordan. Atlanta, Georgia: U.S. Centers for Disease
    Control. Family Planning Evaluation Division. 1984.
Ferry, Benoit
    "The Senegalese Survey." (In) Page, Hilary J. and
    Lesthaeghe, Ron (eds.). Child-Spacing in Tropical

Africa: Traditions and Change. New York: Academic Press.
1981. pp 265-273.
Goldberg, Howard I. and M'bodji, Fara G. and Friedman, Jay
S.
    Fertility and Family Planning in the Sine-Saloum Region
    of Senegal. Atlanta, Georgia: Centers for Disease
    Control. Division of Reproductive Health. 1985.
Lesthaeghe, Ron J. and Eelens, Frank
    Social Organization and Reproductive Regimes: Lessons
    From Sub-Saharan Africa and Historical Western Europe.
    Brussels, Belgium: Vrije Universiteit Brussel.
    Interuniversity Programme in Demography. IDP Working
    Paper #1985-1. 1985. 64p.
Nichols, Douglas and Ndiaye, Salif and Burton, Nadine and
Janowitz, Barbara and Gueye, Lamine and Gueye, Mouhamadou
    "Vanguard Family Planning Acceptors in Senegal." Studies
    in Family Planning. Volume 16 #5 September-October,
    1985. pp. 271-278.
Snyder, Francis G. and Savane, Marie-Angelique
    Law and Population in Senegal: A Survey of Legislation.
    Leiden, Netherlands: Afrika-Studiecentrum. 1977. 242p.

FERTILITY AND INFERTILITY

Ben, Geloune M.
    Patterns of First Marriage and its Disruption for
    Senegalese Women. Cairo: Cairo Demographic Centre. CDC
    Research Monograph Series #12. 1981. pp. 423-447.
Cantrelle, Pierre and Ferry, Benoit
    "The Influence of Nutrition on Fertility: The Case of
    Senegal." (In) Mosley, W. Henry (ed.). Nutrition and
    Human Reproduction. New York: Plenum Press. 1978. pp.
    353-363.
Cantrelle, Pierre and Leridon, Henri
    "Fertility, Breast-Feeding and Infant Mortality.
    Inter-Ethnic Differences in One and the Same Region:
    Salum (Senegal)." Population. Volume 35 #3 May-June,
    1980. pp. 623-648.
Ferry, Benoit
    "The Senegalese Survey." (In) Page, Hilary J. and
    Lesthaeghe, Ron (eds.). Child-Spacing in Tropical
    Africa: Traditions and Change. New York: Academic Press.
    1981. pp 265-273.
Goldberg, Howard I. and M'bodji, Fara G. and Friedman, Jay
S.
    Fertility and Family Planning in the Sine-Saloum Region
    of Senegal. Atlanta, Georgia: Centers for Disease
    Control. Division of Reproductive Health. 1985.
International Statistical Institute (ISI)
    The Senegal Fertility Survey: A Summary of Findings.
    Voorburg, Netherlands: ISI. World Fertility Survey
    Report #31. 1981. 18p.

International Statistical Institute (ISI)
    The Senegal Fertility Survey: A Summary of Findings.
    Voorburg, Netherlands: ISI. World Fertility Survey
    Report #31. 1981. 18p.
Lesthaeghe, Ron J. and Eelens, Frank
    Social Organization and Reproductive Regimes: Lessons
    From Sub-Saharan Africa and Historical Western Europe.
    Brussels, Belgium: Vrije Universiteit Brussel.
    Interuniversity Programme in Demography. IDP Working
    Paper #1985-1. 1985. 64p.
Mondot-Bernard, Jacqueline M.
    "Fertility and Breast-Feeding in Africa." African
    Environment. #14-16 1981. pp. 131-150.
United Nations Economic Commission for Africa (UNECA)
    Nuptiality and Fertility (A Comparative Analysis of WFS
    Data). Addis Ababa, Ethiopia: UNECA. African Population
    Studies Series #5. 1983. 96p.

HEALTH, NUTRITION AND MEDICINE

Anderson, John E. and Goldberg, Howard I. and M'bodji, Fara
G. and Abdel-Aziz, Abdallah
    Postpartum Practices and Child Spacing in Senegal and
    Jordan. Atlanta, Georgia: U.S. Centers for Disease
    Control. Family Planning Evaluation Division. 1984.
Bashizi, Bashige
    "Day-Care Centers in Senegal: A Women's Initiative."
    Assignment Children. Volume 49/50 Spring, 1980. pp.
    63-80.
Basse, M.T.
    "Women, Food and Nutrition in Africa: Perspective From
    Senegal." Food and Nutrition. Volume 10 #1 1984. pp.
    65-71.
Cantrelle, Pierre and Ferry, Benoit
    "The Influence of Nutrition on Fertility: The Case of
    Senegal." (In) Mosley, W. Henry (ed.). Nutrition and
    Human Reproduction. New York: Plenum Press. 1978. pp.
    353-363.
Cantrelle, Pierre and Leridon, Henri
    "Fertility, Breast-Feeding and Infant Mortality.
    Inter-Ethnic Differences in One and the Same Region:
    Salum (Senegal)." Population. Volume 35 #3 May-June,
    1980. pp. 623-648.
Ferry, Benoit
    "The Senegalese Survey." (In) Page, Hilary J. and
    Lesthaeghe, Ron (eds.). Child-Spacing in Tropical
    Africa: Traditions and Change. New York: Academic Press.
    1981. pp 265-273.
Goldberg, Howard I. and M'bodji, Fara G. and Friedman, Jay
S.
    Fertility and Family Planning in the Sine-Saloum Region

of Senegal. Atlanta, Georgia: Centers for Disease
Control. Division of Reproductive Health. 1985.

M'Baye, Fatou
"Maisons Familiales Rurales, Senegal." (In) Blair,
Patricia W. (ed.). Health Needs of the World's Poor
Women. Washington, D.C.: Equity Policy Center. 1981.
pp. 137-138.

Mondot-Bernard, Jacqueline M.
"Fertility and Breast-Feeding in Africa." African
Environment. #14-16 1981. pp. 131-150.

Nichols, Douglas and Ndiaye, Salif and Burton, Nadine and
Janowitz, Barbara and Gueye, Lamine and Gueye, Mouhamadou
"Vanguard Family Planning Acceptors in Senegal." Studies
in Family Planning. Volume 16 #5 September-October,
1985. pp. 271-278.

Rougereau, A.
"Ferritin and Iron Status in Senegalese Women." American
Journal of Clinical Nutrition. Volume 36 August, 1982.
pp. 314-318.

Vandewiele, Michel
"How Senegalese Secondary School Students Feel About
Euro-African Mixed Marriage." Psychological Reports.
Volume 46 #1 June, 1980. pp. 789-790.

HISTORY

Brooks, George E.
"The Signares of Saint-Louis and Goree: Women
Entrepreneurs in 18th Century Senegal." (In) Hafkin,
N.J. and Bay, Edna (eds.). Women in Africa: Studies in
Social and Economic Change. Stanford, California:
Stanford University Press. 1976. pp. 19-44.

Brooks, George E.
"Artists' Depictions of Senegalese Signares: Insights
Concerning French Racist and Sexist Attitudes in the 19th
Century." Geneve-Afrique. Volume 18 #1 1980. pp.
75-89.

LAW AND LEGAL ISSUES

Snyder, Francis G. and Savane, Marie-Angelique
Law and Population in Senegal: A Survey of Legislation.
Leiden, Netherlands: Afrika-Studiecentrum. 1977. 242p.

LITERATURE

Case, F.I.
"The Socio-Cultural Functions of Women in the Senegalese
Novel." Cultures et Developpement. Volume 9 #4 1977.
pp. 601-629.

Cham, Mbye
"The Female Condition in Africa: A Literary Exploration
by Mariama Ba." Current Bibliography on African Affairs.
Volume 17 #1 1984. pp. 29+.
Hammond, Thomas N.
"The Image of Women in Senegalese Fiction." Ph.D
Dissertation: University of New York. Buffalo, New York.
1976.
Lee Sonia
"The Awakening of the Self in the Heroines of Ousmane
Sembene." (In) Bell, Roseann P. and Parker, Bettye J.
and Guy-Sheftall, Beverly (eds.). Sturdy Black Bridges:
Visions of Black Women in Literature. Garden City, New
York: Anchor Books. 1979. pp. 52-60.
McCaffrey, Kathleen M.
Images of Women in the Literatures of Selected Developing
Countries. Washington, D.C.: U.S. Department of State.
U.S. Agency for International Development. Office of
Women in Development. 1981. 229p.
Sacks, Karen
"Women and Class Struggle in Sembene's God's Bits of
Wood." Signs. Volume 4 #2 Winter, 1978. pp. 363-370.
Smyley, Karen M.
"Ousmane Sembene: Portraitist of the African Woman in the
Novel." New England Journal of Black Studies. 1981. pp.
23-29.
Smyley, Karen M.
"The African Woman: Interpretations of Senegalese
Novelists Aboulaye Sadji and Ousman Sembene." Thesis:
City University of New York. New York, New York. 1977.
275p.
Smyley-Wallace, Karen M.
"Les Boutsede Bois de Oiue' and 'Xala': A Camparative
Analysis of Female Roles in Sembene's Novels." Current
Bibliography on African Affairs. Volume 17 #2 1985. pp.
129-136.

MARITAL RELATIONS AND NUPTIALITY

Anderson, John E. and Goldberg, Howard I. and M'bodji, Fara
G. and Abdel-Aziz, Abdallah
Postpartum Practices and Child Spacing in Senegal and
Jordan. Atlanta, Georgia: U.S. Centers for Disease
Control. Family Planning Evaluation Division. 1984.
Ben, Geloune M.
Patterns of First Marriage and its Disruption for
Senegalese Women. Cairo: Cairo Demographic Centre. CDC
Research Monograph Series #12. 1981. pp. 423-447.
Cantrelle, Pierre and Leridon, Henri
"Fertility, Breast-Feeding and Infant Mortality.
Inter-Ethnic Differences in One and the Same Region:
Salum (Senegal)." Population. Volume 35 #3 May-June,
1980. pp. 623-648.

Colvin, Lucie G.
   The Uprooted of the Western Sahel: Migrants' Quest for
   Cash in Senegambia. New York: Praeger Publishers. 1981.
   385p.
Colvin, Lucie G.
   The Uprooted in the Western Sahel: Migrants' Quest for
   Cash in the Senegambia: Final Report of the Senegambia
   Migration Study. Washington, D.C.: U.S. Department of
   State. U.S. Agency for International Development. 1980.
   307p.
Ferry, Benoit
   "The Senegalese Survey." (In) Page, Hilary J. and
   Lesthaeghe, Ron (eds.). Child-Spacing in Tropical
   Africa: Traditions and Change. New York: Academic Press.
   1981. pp 265-273.
Goldberg, Howard I. and M'bodji, Fara G. and Friedman, Jay
S.
   Fertility and Family Planning in the Sine-Saloum Region
   of Senegal. Atlanta, Georgia: Centers for Disease
   Control. Division of Reproductive Health. 1985.
Snyder, Francis G. and Savane, Marie-Angelique
   Law and Population in Senegal: A Survey of Legislation.
   Leiden, Netherlands: Afrika-Studiecentrum. 1977. 242p.
United Nations Economic Commission for Africa (UNECA)
   Nuptiality and Fertility (A Comparative Analysis of WFS
   Data). Addis Ababa, Ethiopia: UNECA. African Population
   Studies Series #5. 1983. 96p.
Vandewiele, Michel
   "How Senegalese Secondary School Students Feel About
   Euro-African Mixed Marriage." Psychological Reports.
   Volume 46 #1 June, 1980. pp. 789-790.

MIGRATION

Colvin, Lucie G.
   The Uprooted of the Western Sahel: Migrants' Quest for
   Cash in Senegambia. New York: Praeger Publishers. 1981.
   385p.
Colvin, Lucie G.
   The Uprooted in the Western Sahel: Migrants' Quest for
   Cash in the Senegambia: Final Report of the Senegambia
   Migration Study. Washington, D.C.: U.S. Department of
   State. U.S. Agency for International Development. 1980.
   307p.
Hamer, Alice J.
   "Diola Women and Migration: A Case Study." (In) Colvin,
   Lucie G. The Uprooted in the Sahel: Migrant's Quest for
   Cash in the Senegambia. Final Report on the Senegambia
   Migration Study. Washington, D.C.: U.S. Department of
   State. U.S. Agency for International Development. 1979.

ORGANIZATIONS

Bashizi, Bashige
  "Day-Care Centers in Senegal: A Women's Initiative."
  Assignment Children. Volume 49/50 Spring, 1980. pp.
  63-80.
M'Baye, Fatou
  "Maisons Familiales Rurales, Senegal." (In) Blair,
  Patricia W. (ed.). Health Needs of the World's Poor
  Women. Washington, D.C.: Equity Policy Center. 1981.
  pp. 137-138.
Savane, Marie-Angelique
  "Senegal: Elegance Amid the Phallocracy." (In) Morgan,
  Robin (ed.). Sisterhood is Global. Garden City, New
  York: Anchor Books. 1984. pp. 589-599.

POLITICS AND GOVERNMENT

Ba, Fama H. and Ndiaye, Aminata M. and Savane,
Marie-Angelique and Thiongane, Awe
  "The Impact of Territorial Administration Reform on the
  Situation of Women in Senegal." (In) International
  Labour Organization (ILO). Rural Development and Women
  in Africa. Geneva: ILO. 1984. pp. 107-115.

RELIGION AND WITCHCRAFT

Vandewiele, Michel
  "Perception of Women's Religious Status by Senegalese
  Adolescents." Psychological Reports. Volume 53 #3 Part
  One December, 1983. pp. 757-758.

RESEARCH

Cham, Mbye
  "The Female Condition in Africa: A Literary Exploration
  by Mariama Ba." Current Bibliography on African Affairs.
  Volume 17 #1 1984. pp. 29+.
Messer, Ellen and Bloch, Marianne N.
  Women's and Children's Activity Profiles in Senegal and
  Mexico: A Comparison of Time Allocation and Time
  Allocation Methods. East Lansing, Michigan: Michigan
  State University. Office of Women in International
  Development. 1983. 15p.
U.S. Department of Commerce. Bureau of the Census
  Illustrative Statistics on Women in Development in
  Selected Developing Countries. Washington, D.C.: U.S.
  Department of Commerce. 1982. 24p.

SEX ROLES

Braun, Armelle
    "Escape From the Passive Past: A New Role for Women in
    Senegal." Ceres. Volume 11 #4 July-August, 1978.
Hamer, Alice J.
    "Tradition and Change: A Social History of Diola Women in
    the 20th Century." Ph.D Dissertation: University of
    Michigan. Ann Arbor, Michigan. 1983. 340p.
Hamer, Alice J.
    "Diola Women and Migration: A Case Study." (In) Colvin,
    Lucie G. The Uprooted in the Sahel: Migrant's Quest for
    Cash in the Senegambia. Final Report on the Senegambia
    Migration Study. Washington, D.C.: U.S. Department of
    State. U.S. Agency for International Development. 1979.
Loose, Edna E.
    "Women in Rural Senegal: Some Economic and Social
    Observations." (In) Purdue University. Workshop on
    Sahelian Agriculture. Lafayette, Indiana: Purdue
    University. Department of Agricultural Economics.
    February 1-2, 1979. 25p.
Mackintosh, Maureen
    "Domestic Labour: Production and Reproduction." (In)
    Allen, C. and Williams, G. (eds.). Subsaharan Africa.
    London: Macmillan. Sociology of Developing Societies
    Series. 1982. pp. 46-52.
Messer, Ellen and Bloch, Marianne N.
    Women's and Children's Activity Profiles in Senegal and
    Mexico: A Comparison of Time Allocation and Time
    Allocation Methods. East Lansing, Michigan: Michigan
    State University. Office of Women in International
    Development. 1983. 15p.
Savane, Marie-Angelique
    "Senegal: Elegance Amid the Phallocracy." (In) Morgan,
    Robin (ed.). Sisterhood is Global. Garden City, New
    York: Anchor Books. 1984. pp. 589-599.
Venema, Bernhard
    "Male and Female Farming Systems and Agricultural
    Intensification in West Africa: The Case of the Wolof,
    Senegal." (In) Presvelov, C. and Spijkers-Zwart, S.
    (eds.). The Household, Women and Agricultural
    Development. Wageningen, Netherlands: H. Veenman en
    Zonen. 1980. pp. 27-34.
Yaciuk, Gordon
    "The Role of Women in Post-Harvest Technology in
    Senegal." Paper Presented at a Seminar on a Challenge
    for Change in Third World Agriculture. Alberta, Canada:
    Alberta Institute of Agrologists and Canada's
    International Development Research Center. September,
    1978.

STATUS OF WOMEN

Snyder, Francis G. and Savane, Marie-Angelique
Law and Population in Senegal: A Survey of Legislation.
Leiden, Netherlands: Afrika-Studiecentrum. 1977. 242p.

WOMEN AND THEIR CHILDREN

Bashizi, Bashige
"Day-Care Centers in Senegal: A Women's Initiative."
Assignment Children. Volume 49/50 Spring, 1980. pp.
63-80.
Messer, Ellen and Bloch, Marianne N.
Women's and Children's Activity Profiles in Senegal and
Mexico: A Comparison of Time Allocation and Time
Allocation Methods. East Lansing, Michigan: Michigan
State University. Office of Women in International
Development. 1983. 15p.

Sierra Leone

AGRICULTURE

Greene, P.A.
    Innovative Approaches in Rural Women's Programmes in
    Three African Countries: Kenya, Nigeria, Sierra Leone:
    Case Studies. Rome: United Nations Food and Agriculture
    Organization. 1985. 148p.
Jeffalyn Johnson and Associates Inc.
    African Women in Development. Falls Church, Virginia:
    Jeffalyn Johnson and Associates Inc. 1980. 125p.
King-Akerele, Olubanke
    Traditional Palm Oil Processing: Women's Role and the
    Applications of Appropriate Technology: Ivory Coast,
    Sierra Leone, Cameroons. Addis Ababa, Ethiopia: United
    Nations Economic Commission for Africa. African Training
    and Research Center for Women. 1983. 52p.
MacCormack, Carol P.
    "Control of Land, Labour and Capital in Rural Southern
    Sierra Leone." Africana Research Bulletin. Volume 6 #4
    1976.
MacCormack, Carol P.
    "Control of Land, Labor and Capital in Rural Southern
    Sierra Leone." (In) Bay, Edna G. (ed.). Women and Work
    in Africa. Boulder, Colorado: Westview Press. Westview
    Special Studies in Africa. 1982. pp. 35-53.
Rosen, David M.
    "Peasant Context of Feminist Revolt in West Africa."
    Anthropological Quarterly. Volume 56 #1 January, 1983.
    pp. 35-43.
Safilios-Rothschild, Constantina
    The Persistence of Women's Invisibility in Agriculture:
    Theoretical and Policy Lessons From Lesotho and Sierra
    Leone. New York: Population Council. Center for Policy
    Studies. Working Paper #88. September, 1982. 31p.

Safilios-Rothschild, Constantina
   "The Persistence of Women's Invisibility in Agriculture:
   Theoretical and Policy Lessons From Lesotho and Sierra
   Leone." Economic Development and Cultural Change.
   Volume 33 #2 January, 1985. pp. 299-317.
Spencer, Dunstan S.C.
   African Women in Agricultural Development: A Case Study
   in Sierra Leone. East Lansing, Michigan: Michigan State
   University. Department of Agricultural Economics.
   Njala, Sierra Leone: Njala University College.
   Department of Agricultural Economics. 1976. 36p.
Spencer, Dunstan S.C.
   African Women in Agricultural Development: A Case Study
   in Sierra Leone. Washington, D.C.: American Council on
   Education. Overseas Liaison Committee. OLC Paper #9.
   June, 1976.
Stevens, Yvette
   "Improved Technologies for Rural Women: Problems and
   Prospects in Sierra Leone." (In) Ahmed, Iftikhar (ed.).
   Technology and Rural Women. Boston: George Allen and
   Unwin. 1985. pp. 284-326.
Stevens, Yvette
   "Technologies and Rural Women's Activities: Problems and
   Prospects in Sierra Leone." (In) International Labour
   Organization (ILO). Rural Development and Women in
   Africa. Geneva: ILO. 1984. pp. 79-88.
Tommy, Joseph L.
   The Role of Women in Paddy Production: A Comparative
   Study of Decision-Making Aspects of Women in Agricultural
   Production in Moyamba District, Sierra Leone. Njala,
   Sierra Leone: Njala University College. Department of
   Agricultural Economics and Extension. December, 1980.

ARTS

Chuta, Enyinn A.
   Economics of Gara (Tie Dye) Production in Sierra Leone.
   East Lansing, Michigan: Michigan State University.
   African Rural Economy Programme. Working Paper #25.
   1978.
Ottenberg, Simon
   "Artistic and Sex Roles in a Limba Chiefdom." (In)
   Oppong, Christine (ed.). Female and Male in West Africa.
   London: George Allen and Unwin. 1983. pp. 79-90.

CULTURAL ROLES

Bailey, Mohamed S. and Weller, Robert H.
   "A Path Analysis of Fertility Differentials in Rural
   Sierra Leone." Paper Presented at the 1985 Annual
   Meeting of the American Sociological Association. 1985.
   43p.

Bailey, Mohamed S.
   Female Education and Fertility in Rural Sierra Leone: A
   Test of the Threshold Hypothesis. Tallahassee, Florida:
   Florida State University. Center for the Study. Working
   Paper #85-24. 1985. 21p.
Beoku-Betts, J.
   "Western Perceptions of African Women in the 19th Century
   and 20th Centuries." African Research Bulletin
   (Institute of African Studies, University of Sierra
   Leone). Volume 6 #4 1976.
Bledsoe, Caroline H.
   "The Political Use of Sande Ideology and Symbolism."
   American Ethnologist. Volume 11 #3 August, 1984. pp.
   455-472.
Bledsoe, Caroline H. and Isiugo-Abanihe, Uche
   Strategies of Child Fosterage Among Rural Mende
   'Grannies'. Philadelphia, Pennsylvania: University of
   Pennsylvania. Population Studies Center. 1985.
Chuta, Enyinn A.
   Economics of Gara (Tie Dye) Production in Sierra Leone.
   East Lansing, Michigan: Michigan State University.
   African Rural Economy Programme. Working Paper #25.
   1978.
Cosentino, Donald
   Defiant Maids and Stubborn Farmers: Tradition and
   Invention in Mende Story Performance. Cambridge, New
   York: Cambridge University Press. 1982. 226p.
Getaweh, S. Momolu
   "The Conceptualization of Family-Size Goals Among the
   Mende in Sierra Leone and the Vai in Liberia." Ph.D
   Dissertation: Boston University. Graduate School.
   Boston, Massachusetts. 1984. 419p.
Harrell-Bond, Barbara E.
   "Stereotypes of Western and African Patterns of Marriage
   and Family Life." Journal of Marriage and the Family.
   Volume 38 #2 1976. pp. 387-396.
Harrell-Bond, Barbara E. and Rijnsdorp, Ulrica
   "The Emergence of the 'Stranger Permit Marriage' and
   Other New Forms of Conjugal Union in Rural Sierra Leone."
   Africana Research Bulletin. Volume 6 #4 1976.
Harrell-Bond, Barbara E.
   "The Influence of the Family Case-Worker on the Struggle
   of the Family: The Sierra Leone Case." Social Research.
   Volume 44 #2 Summer, 1977. pp. 193-215.
Harrell-Bond, Barbara E. and Rijnsdorp, Ulrica
   "The Emergence of the 'Stranger-Permit' Marriage and
   Other New Forms of Conjugal Union in Rural Sierra Leone."
   (In) Roberts, Simon (ed.). Law and the Family in Africa.
   Hague, Netherlands: Mouton. 1977. pp. 205-223.
Hosken, Fran P.
   "Female Mutilation in Somalia Tests 'Human Rights
   Doctrine'." Politics and Other Human Interests. #14
   May 9, 1978. pp. 21-22.

International Labour Organization (ILO)
    National Symposium on Cooperative Education and Family
    Welfare and Rural Development. Conference Report.
    October 25-November 4, 1976. Mogadishu: Somalia: ILO
    Regional Office. 1976. 182p.
Isaac, Barry L
    "Female Fertility and Marital Form Among the Mende of
    Rural Upper Bambara Chiefdom, Sierra Leone." Ethnology.
    Volume 19 #3 July, 1980. pp. 297-314.
Isaac, Barry L. and Feinberg, W.E.
    "Marital Form and Infant Survival Among the Mende of
    Rural Upper Bambara Chiefdom, Sierra Leone." Human
    Biology. Volume 54 #3 September, 1982. pp. 627-634.
Kamara, Allieu I.
    "The Changing Family in the Sierra Leone Context." Paper
    Presented at the Seminar on the Changing Family in the
    African Context. 1983. Paris: United Nations
    Educational, Scientific and Cultural Organization.
    Maseru, Lesotho. 1984. 15p.
Kandeh, Herbert B.
    Infant and Child Mortality in the Bo District of Sierra
    Leone. Philadelphia, Pennsylvania: University of
    Pennsylvania. Population Studies Center. 1979.
Ketkar, Suhas L. and Singh, B.
    "Fertility and Household Characteristics: Some Evidence
    From Sierra Leone." Journal of African Studies. Volume
    7 #4 Winter, 1980. pp. 204-212.
Ketkar, Suhas L.
    "Socioeconomic Determinants of Family Size in Sierra
    Leone." Rural Africana. #6 Winter, 1979. pp. 25-45.
Ketkar, Suhas L.
    "Determinants of Fertility in a Developing Society: The
    Case of Sierra Leone." Population Studies. Volume 33 #3
    November, 1979. pp. 479-488.
King-Akerele, Olubanke
    Traditional Palm Oil Processing: Women's Role and the
    Applications of Appropriate Technology: Ivory Coast,
    Sierra Leone, Cameroons. Addis Ababa, Ethiopia: United
    Nations Economic Commission for Africa. African Training
    and Research Center for Women. 1983. 52p.
Liedholm, Carl and Chuta, Enyinn A.
    The Economics of Rural and Urban Small-Scale Industries
    in Sierra Leone. East Lansing, Michigan: Michigan State
    University. African Rural Economy Program. Paper #14.
    1976.
MacCormack, Carol P.
    "The Compound Head: Structure and Strategies." Africana
    Research Bulletin. Volume 6 #4 1976. pp. 44-64.
MacCormack, Carol P.
    "Control of Land, Labour and Capital in Rural Southern
    Sierra Leone." Africana Research Bulletin. Volume 6 #4
    1976.

MacCormack, Carol P.
  "Sande: The Public Face of a Secret Society." (In)
  Jules-Rosette, Bennetta (ed.). The New Religions of
  Africa. Norwood, New Jersey: Ablex Publishing Corp.
  1979. pp. 27-37.
MacCormack, Carol P.
  "Health, Fertility and Birth in Moyamba District, Sierra
  Leone." (In) MacCormack, Carol P. (ed.). Ethnography of
  Fertility and Birth. New York: Academic Press. 1982.
  pp. 115-139.
MacCormack, Carol P.
  "Slaves, Slave Owners and Slave Dealers: Sherbro Coast
  and Hinterland." (In) Robertson, Claire C. and Klein,
  Martin A. (eds,). Women and Slavery in Africa. Madison,
  Wisconsin: University of Wisconsin Press. 1983. pp.
  271-294.
MacCormack, Carol P.
  "The Cultural Ecology of Production: Sherbro Coast and
  Hinterland." (In) Green, D. (ed.). Social Organization
  and Settlement. Oxford, England: British Archaeological
  Reports. 1978.
MacCormack, Carol P.
  "Wono: Institutionalized Dependency in Sherbro Descent
  Groups." (In) Miers, S. and Kopytoff, I. (eds.).
  Slavery in Africa: Historical and Anthropological
  Perspectives. Madison, Wisconsin: University of
  Wisconsin-Madison. 1977.
MacCormack, Carol P.
  "Control of Land, Labor and Capital in Rural Southern
  Sierra Leone." (In) Bay, Edna G. (ed.). Women and Work
  in Africa. Boulder, Colorado: Westview Press. Westview
  Special Studies in Africa. 1982. pp. 35-53.
Mansaray, K.
  "Womenfolk in the Northern and Southern Provinces of
  Sierra Leone: A Note." (In) Mitchell, P.K. and Jones, A.
  (eds.). Sierra Leone Studies at Birmingham: Proceedings
  of the Third Birmingham Sierra Leone Studies Symposium,
  15-17 July, 1983. Birmingham, England: Birmingham
  University. Centre of West African Studies. 1984. pp.
  219-220.
Okoye, C.S.
  Fertility Levels and Differentials in Sierra Leone: An
  Analysis of the Fertility Data From the 1974 Population
  Census of Sierra Leone. Freetown, Sierra Leone: Central
  Statistics Office. Census Analysis Project. Volume
  Three. September, 1980. 53p.
Ottenberg, Simon
  "Artistic and Sex Roles in a Limba Chiefdom." (In)
  Oppong, Christine (ed.). Female and Male in West Africa.
  London: George Allen and Unwin. 1983. pp. 79-90.
Rosen, David M.
  "Dangerous Women: Ideology, Knowledge and Ritual Among
  the Kono of Eastern Sierra Leone." Dialectical
  Anthropology. Volume 6 #2 December, 1981. pp. 151-163.

Rosen, David M.
    "Peasant Context of Feminist Revolt in West Africa."
    Anthropological Quarterly. Volume 56 #1   January, 1983.
    pp. 35-43.
Safilios-Rothschild, Constantina
    The Persistence of Women's Invisibility in Agriculture:
    Theoretical and Policy Lessons From Lesotho and Sierra
    Leone. New York: Population Council. Center for Policy
    Studies. Working Paper #88. September, 1982. 31p.
Safilios-Rothschild, Constantina
    "The Persistence of Women's Invisibility in Agriculture:
    Theoretical and Policy Lessons From Lesotho and Sierra
    Leone." Economic Development and Cultural Change.
    Volume 33 #2   January, 1985. pp. 299-317.
Shaw, Rosalind
    "Gender and the Structuring of Reality in Temne
    Divination: An Interactive Study." Africa. Volume 55 #3
    1985. pp. 286-303.
Sierra Leone. Ministry of Health
    Infant and Early Childhood Mortality in Relation to
    Fertility Patterns: Report on an Ad-Hoc Survey in Greater
    Freetown, the Western Area and Makeni in the Northern
    Province, Sierra Leone, 1973-1975. Freetown, Sierra
    Leone: Ministry of Health. 1980. 182p.
Smith, A.H.
    "Social and Cultural Factors in Child Mortality Among the
    Temne of Magburaka, Sierra Leone." Ph.D Dissertation:
    University of Oregon. Eugene, Oregon. 1981. 382p.
Steady, Filomina C.
    "Protestant Women's Associations in Freetown, Sierra
    Leone." (In) Hafkin, N.J. and Bay, E.G. (eds.). Women
    in Africa: Studies in Social and Economic Change.
    Stanford, California: Stanford University Press. 1976.
    pp. 213-237.
Steady, Filomina C.
    "The Role of Women in the Churches in Freetown, Sierra
    Leone." (In) Fashole-Luke, Edward. Christianity in
    Independent Africa. London: R. Collings. 1978. pp.
    151-163.
Steady, Filomina C.
    "Male Roles in Fertility in Sierra Leone: The Moving
    Target." (In) Oppong, C. and Adaba, G. and
    Bekombo-Priso, M. and Mogey, J. (eds.). Marriage,
    Fertility and Parenthood in West Africa. Canberra,
    Australia: Australian National University. Department of
    Demography. Volume Two. 1978. pp. 641-653.
White, E. Frances
    "Women, Work and Ethnicity: The Sierra Leone Case." (In)
    Bay, Edna G. (ed.). Women and Work in Africa. Boulder,
    Colorado: Westview Press. Westview Special Studies in
    Africa. 1982. pp. 19-33.
White, E. Frances
    "Sierra Leonean Women and Nitida Kola: The Organization

of a 19th Century Trading Diaspora." Paper Presented at
the Annual Meeting of the African Studies Association.
Paper #116. Philadelphia, Pennsylvania. 1980.

White, E. Frances
"The Big Market in Freetown: A Case Study of Women's
Workplace." Journal of the Historical Society of Sierra
Leone. Volume 4 #1/2 1980. pp. 19-32.

White, E. Frances
"Creole Women Traders in Sierra Leone: An Economic and
Social History, 1792-1945." Ph.D Dissertation: Boston
University. Graduate School. Boston, Masachusetts.
1978. 288p.

White, E. Frances
Creole Women Traders in the 19th Century. Boston: Boston
University. African Studies Center. Working Paper #27.
1980.

White, E. Francis
"Creole Women Traders in the 19th Century."
International Journal of African Historical Studies.
Volume 14 #4 1981. pp. 601-625.

DEVELOPMENT AND TECHNOLOGY

Greene, P.A.
Innovative Approaches in Rural Women's Programmes in
Three African Countries: Kenya, Nigeria, Sierra Leone:
Case Studies. Rome: United Nations Food and Agriculture
Organization. 1985. 148p.

International Labour Organization (ILO)
National Symposium on Cooperative Education and Family
Welfare and Rural Development. Conference Report.
October 25-November 4, 1976. Mogadishu: Somalia: ILO
Regional Office. 1976. 182p.

Jeffalyn Johnson and Associates Inc.
African Women in Development. Falls Church, Virginia:
Jeffalyn Johnson and Associates Inc. 1980. 125p.

King-Akerele, Olubanke
Traditional Palm Oil Processing: Women's Role and the
Applications of Appropriate Technology: Ivory Coast,
Sierra Leone, Cameroons. Addis Ababa, Ethiopia: United
Nations Economic Commission for Africa. African Training
and Research Center for Women. 1983. 52p.

Liedholm, Carl and Chuta, Enyinn A.
The Economics of Rural and Urban Small-Scale Industries
in Sierra Leone. East Lansing, Michigan: Michigan State
University. African Rural Economy Program. Paper #14.
1976.

National Asso. of Negro Business and Prof. Women's Clubs
African Women Small Entrepreneurs in Senegal, The Gambia,
Sierra Leone, Cameroon and Malawi: Prefeasibility Study
for Providing Assistance. Washington, D.C.: NANBPA.
1977. 82p.

Rosen, David M.
"Peasant Context of Feminist Revolt in West Africa."
Anthropological Quarterly. Volume 56 #1 January, 1983.
pp. 35-43.
Safilios-Rothschild, Constantina
The Persistence of Women's Invisibility in Agriculture:
Theoretical and Policy Lessons From Lesotho and Sierra
Leone. New York: Population Council. Center for Policy
Studies. Working Paper #88. September, 1982. 31p.
Safilios-Rothschild, Constantina
"The Persistence of Women's Invisibility in Agriculture:
Theoretical and Policy Lessons From Lesotho and Sierra
Leone." Economic Development and Cultural Change.
Volume 33 #2 January, 1985. pp. 299-317.
Spencer, Dunstan S.C.
African Women in Agricultural Development: A Case Study
in Sierra Leone. East Lansing, Michigan: Michigan State
University. Department of Agricultural Economics.
Njala, Sierra Leone: Njala University College.
Department of Agricultural Economics. 1976. 36p.
Spencer, Dunstan S.C.
African Women in Agricultural Development: A Case Study
in Sierra Leone. Washington, D.C.: American Council on
Education. Overseas Liaison Committee. OLC Paper #9.
June, 1976.
Stevens, Yvette
"Improved Technologies for Rural Women: Problems and
Prospects in Sierra Leone." (In) Ahmed, Iftikhar (ed.).
Technology and Rural Women. Boston: George Allen and
Unwin. 1985. pp. 284-326.
Stevens, Yvette
"Technologies and Rural Women's Activities: Problems and
Prospects in Sierra Leone." (In) International Labour
Organization (ILO). Rural Development and Women in
Africa. Geneva: ILO. 1984. pp. 79-88.
Tommy, Joseph L.
The Role of Women in Paddy Production: A Comparative
Study of Decision-Making Aspects of Women in Agricultural
Production in Moyamba District, Sierra Leone. Njala,
Sierra Leone: Njala University College. Department of
Agricultural Economics and Extension. December, 1980.

ECONOMICS

Chuta, Enyinn A.
Economics of Gara (Tie Dye) Production in Sierra Leone.
East Lansing, Michigan: Michigan State University.
African Rural Economy Programme. Working Paper #25.
1978.
Greene, P.A.
Innovative Approaches in Rural Women's Programmes in
Three African Countries: Kenya, Nigeria, Sierra Leone:

Case Studies. Rome: United Nations Food and Agriculture
Organization. 1985. 148p.
Jeffalyn Johnson and Associates Inc.
African Women in Development. Falls Church, Virginia:
Jeffalyn Johnson and Associates Inc. 1980. 125p.
Ketkar, Suhas L.
"Socioeconomic Determinants of Family Size in Sierra
Leone." Rural Africana. #6 Winter, 1979. pp. 25-45.
Liedholm, Carl and Chuta, Enyinn A.
The Economics of Rural and Urban Small-Scale Industries
in Sierra Leone. East Lansing, Michigan: Michigan State
University. African Rural Economy Program. Paper #14.
1976.
MacCormack, Carol P.
"Control of Land, Labour and Capital in Rural Southern
Sierra Leone." Africana Research Bulletin. Volume 6 #4
1976.
MacCormack, Carol P.
"Control of Land, Labor and Capital in Rural Southern
Sierra Leone." (In) Bay, Edna G. (ed.). Women and Work
in Africa. Boulder, Colorado: Westview Press. Westview
Special Studies in Africa. 1982. pp. 35-53.
National Asso. of Negro Business and Prof. Women's Clubs
African Women Small Entrepreneurs in Senegal, The Gambia,
Sierra Leone, Cameroon and Malawi: Prefeasibility Study
for Providing Assistance. Washington, D.C.: NANBPA.
1977. 82p.
Safilios-Rothschild, Constantina
The Persistence of Women's Invisibility in Agriculture:
Theoretical and Policy Lessons From Lesotho and Sierra
Leone. New York: Population Council. Center for Policy
Studies. Working Paper #88. September, 1982. 31p.
Safilios-Rothschild, Constantina
"The Persistence of Women's Invisibility in Agriculture:
Theoretical and Policy Lessons From Lesotho and Sierra
Leone." Economic Development and Cultural Change.
Volume 33 #2 January, 1985. pp. 299-317.
Spencer, Dunstan S.C.
African Women in Agricultural Development: A Case Study
in Sierra Leone. East Lansing, Michigan: Michigan State
University. Department of Agricultural Economics.
Njala, Sierra Leone: Njala University College.
Department of Agricultural Economics. 1976. 36p.
Spencer, Dunstan S.C.
African Women in Agricultural Development: A Case Study
in Sierra Leone. Washington, D.C.: American Council on
Education. Overseas Liaison Committee. OLC Paper #9.
June, 1976.
Stevens, Yvette
"Improved Technologies for Rural Women: Problems and
Prospects in Sierra Leone." (In) Ahmed, Iftikhar (ed.).
Technology and Rural Women. Boston: George Allen and
Unwin. 1985. pp. 284-326.

Stevens, Yvette
"Technologies and Rural Women's Activities: Problems and
Prospects in Sierra Leone." (In) International Labour
Organization (ILO). Rural Development and Women in
Africa. Geneva: ILO. 1984. pp. 79-88.
White, E. Frances
"Women, Work and Ethnicity: The Sierra Leone Case." (In)
Bay, Edna G. (ed.). Women and Work in Africa. Boulder,
Colorado: Westview Press. Westview Special Studies in
Africa. 1982. pp. 19-33.
White, E. Frances
"Sierra Leonean Women and Nitida Kola: The Organization
of a 19th Century Trading Diaspora." Paper Presented at
the Annual Meeting of the African Studies Association.
Paper #116. Philadelphia, Pennsylvania. 1980.
White, E. Frances
"The Big Market in Freetown: A Case Study of Women's
Workplace." Journal of the Historical Society of Sierra
Leone. Volume 4 #1/2 1980. pp. 19-32.
White, E. Frances
"Creole Women Traders in Sierra Leone: An Economic and
Social History, 1792-1945." Ph.D Dissertation: Boston
University. Graduate School. Boston, Masachusetts.
1978. 288p.
White, E. Frances
Creole Women Traders in the 19th Century. Boston: Boston
University. African Studies Center. Working Paper #27.
1980.
White, E. Francis
"Creole Women Traders in the 19th Century."
International Journal of African Historical Studies.
Volume 14 #4 1981. pp. 601-625.

EDUCATION AND TRAINING

Bailey, Mohamed S.
Female Education and Fertility in Rural Sierra Leone: A
Test of the Threshold Hypothesis. Tallahassee, Florida:
Florida State University. Center for the Study. Working
Paper #85-24. 1985. 21p.
Greene, P.A.
Innovative Approaches in Rural Women's Programmes in
Three African Countries: Kenya, Nigeria, Sierra Leone:
Case Studies. Rome: United Nations Food and Agriculture
Organization. 1985. 148p.
International Labour Organization (ILO)
National Symposium on Cooperative Education and Family
Welfare and Rural Development. Conference Report.
October 25-November 4, 1976. Mogadishu: Somalia: ILO
Regional Office. 1976. 182p.
Ketkar, Suhas L.
"Female Education and Fertility: Some Evidence From

Sierra Leone." Journal of Developing Areas. Volume 13
#1 October, 1978. pp. 23-33.
Stevens, Yvette
"Improved Technologies for Rural Women: Problems and
Prospects in Sierra Leone." (In) Ahmed, Iftikhar (ed.).
Technology and Rural Women. Boston: George Allen and
Unwin. 1985. pp. 284-326.
Stevens, Yvette
"Technologies and Rural Women's Activities: Problems and
Prospects in Sierra Leone." (In) International Labour
Organization (ILO). Rural Development and Women in
Africa. Geneva: ILO. 1984. pp. 79-88.
United Nations Economic Commission for Africa (UNECA)
"Out-of-School Programmes for Girls and Young Women in
Sierra Leone." Paper Presented at the Expert Meeting for
English Speaking Personnel Involved in Programmes for
Out-of-School Girls. Addis Ababa, Ethiopia: UNECA.
1981.

EMPLOYMENT AND LABOR

Kamara, Allieu I.
"The Changing Family in the Sierra Leone Context." Paper
Presented at the Seminar on the Changing Family in the
African Context, Maseru, Lesotho, 1983. Paris: United
Nations Educational, Scientific and Cultural
Organization. 1984. 15p.
King-Akerele, Olubanke
Traditional Palm Oil Processing: Women's Role and the
Applications of Appropriate Technology: Ivory Coast,
Sierra Leone, Cameroons. Addis Ababa, Ethiopia: United
Nations Economic Commission for Africa. African Training
and Research Center for Women. 1983. 52p.
Liedholm, Carl and Chuta, Enyinn A.
The Economics of Rural and Urban Small-Scale Industries
in Sierra Leone. East Lansing, Michigan: Michigan State
University. African Rural Economy Program. Paper #14.
1976.
MacCormack, Carol P.
"Control of Land, Labour and Capital in Rural Southern
Sierra Leone." Africana Research Bulletin. Volume 6 #4
1976.
MacCormack, Carol P.
"The Cultural Ecology of Production: Sherbro Coast and
Hinterland." (In) Green, D. (ed.). Social Organization
and Settlement. Oxford, England: British Archaeological
Reports. 1978.
MacCormack, Carol P.
"Control of Land, Labor and Capital in Rural Southern
Sierra Leone." (In) Bay, Edna G. (ed.). Women and Work
in Africa. Boulder, Colorado: Westview Press. Westview
Special Studies in Africa. 1982. pp. 35-53.

Spencer, Dunstan S.C.
    African Women in Agricultural Development: A Case Study
    in Sierra Leone. East Lansing, Michigan: Michigan State
    University. Department of Agricultural Economics.
    Njala, Sierra Leone: Njala University College.
    Department of Agricultural Economics. 1976. 36p.
Spencer, Dunstan S.C.
    African Women in Agricultural Development: A Case Study
    in Sierra Leone. Washington, D.C.: American Council on
    Education. Overseas Liaison Committee. OLC Paper #9.
    June, 1976.
Stevens, Yvette
    "Improved Technologies for Rural Women: Problems and
    Prospects in Sierra Leone." (In) Ahmed, Iftikhar (ed.).
    Technology and Rural Women. Boston: George Allen and
    Unwin. 1985. pp. 284-326.
Stevens, Yvette
    "Technologies and Rural Women's Activities: Problems and
    Prospects in Sierra Leone." (In) International Labour
    Organization (ILO). Rural Development and Women in
    Africa. Geneva: ILO. 1984. pp. 79-88.
Tommy, Joseph L.
    The Role of Women in Paddy Production: A Comparative
    Study of Decision-Making Aspects of Women in Agricultural
    Production in Moyamba District, Sierra Leone. Njala,
    Sierra Leone: Njala University College. Department of
    Agricultural Economics and Extension. December, 1980.
United Nations Economic Commission for Africa (UNECA)
    "Out-of-School Programmes for Girls and Young Women in
    Sierra Leone." Paper Presented at the Expert Meeting for
    English Speaking Personnel Involved in Programmes for
    Out-of-School Girls. Addis Ababa, Ethiopia: UNECA.
    1981.
White, E. Frances
    "Women, Work and Ethnicity: The Sierra Leone Case." (In)
    Bay, Edna G. (ed.). Women and Work in Africa. Boulder,
    Colorado: Westview Press. Westview Special Studies in
    Africa. 1982. pp. 19-33.
White, E. Frances
    "Sierra Leonean Women and Nitida Kola: The Organization
    of a 19th Century Trading Diaspora." Paper Presented at
    the Annual Meeting of the African Studies Association.
    Paper #116. Philadelphia, Pennsylvania. 1980.
White, E. Frances
    "The Big Market in Freetown: A Case Study of Women's
    Workplace." Journal of the Historical Society of Sierra
    Leone. Volume 4 #1/2 1980. pp. 19-32.
White, E. Frances
    "Creole Women Traders in Sierra Leone: An Economic and
    Social History, 1792-1945." Ph.D Dissertation: Boston
    University. Graduate School. Boston, Masachusetts.
    1978. 288p.

White, E. Frances
    Creole Women Traders in the 19th Century. Boston: Boston
    University. African Studies Center. Working Paper #27.
    1980.
White, E. Francis
    "Creole Women Traders in the 19th Century."
    International Journal of African Historical Studies.
    Volume 14 #4 1981. pp. 601-625.

EQUALITY AND LIBERATION

Denzer, LaRay
    "Constance A. Cummings-John of Sierra Leone: Her Early
    Political Career." Tarikh. Volume 7 #1 1981. pp.
    20-32.
Okonkwo, Rina
    "Adelaide Casely Hayford: Cultural Nationalist and
    Feminist." Journal of the Historical Society of Sierra
    Leone. Volume 2 #2 1978. pp. 10-21.
Rosen, David M.
    "Peasant Context of Feminist Revolt in West Africa."
    Anthropological Quarterly. Volume 56 #1 January, 1983.
    pp. 35-43.

FAMILY LIFE

Bledsoe, Caroline H. and Isiugo-Abanihe, Uche
    Strategies of Child Fosterage Among Rural Mende
    'Grannies'. Philadelphia, Pennsylvania: University of
    Pennsylvania. Population Studies Center. 1985.
Harrell-Bond, Barbara E.
    "Stereotypes of Western and African Patterns of Marriage
    and Family Life." Journal of Marriage and the Family.
    Volume 38 #2 1976. pp. 387-396.
Harrell-Bond, Barbara E. and Rijnsdorp, Ulrica
    "The Emergence of the 'Stranger Permit Marriage' and
    Other New Forms of Conjugal Union in Rural Sierra Leone."
    Africana Research Bulletin. Volume 6 #4 1976.
Harrell-Bond, Barbara E.
    "The Influence of the Family Case-Worker on the Struggle
    of the Family: The Sierra Leone Case." Social Research.
    Volume 44 #2 Summer, 1977. pp. 193-215.
Harrell-Bond, Barbara E. and Rijnsdorp, Ulrica
    "The Emergence of the 'Stranger-Permit' Marriage and
    Other New Forms of Conjugal Union in Rural Sierra Leone."
    (In) Roberts, Simon (ed.). Law and the Family in Africa.
    Hague, Netherlands: Mouton. 1977. pp. 205-223.
International Labour Organization (ILO)
    National Symposium on Cooperative Education and Family
    Welfare and Rural Development. Conference Report.

October 25-November 4, 1976. Mogadishu: Somalia: ILO
Regional Office. 1976. 182p.
Isaac, Barry L. and Feinberg, W.E.
"Marital Form and Infant Survival Among the Mende of
Rural Upper Bambara Chiefdom, Sierra Leone." Human
Biology. Volume 54 #3 September, 1982. pp. 627-634.
Kamara, Allieu I.
"The Changing Family in the Sierra Leone Context." Paper
Presented at the Seminar on the Changing Family in the
African Context. 1983. Paris: United Nations
Educational, Scientific and Cultural Organization.
Maseru, Lesotho. 1984. 15p.
Ketkar, Suhas L. and Singh, B.
"Fertility and Household Characteristics: Some Evidence
From Sierra Leone." Journal of African Studies. Volume
7 #4 Winter, 1980. pp. 204-212.
Rosen, David M.
"Peasant Context of Feminist Revolt in West Africa."
Anthropological Quarterly. Volume 56 #1 January, 1983.
pp. 35-43.
Smith, A.H.
"Social and Cultural Factors in Child Mortality Among the
Temne of Magburaka, Sierra Leone." Ph.D Dissertation:
University of Oregon. Eugene, Oregon. 1981. 382p.

FAMILY PLANNING AND CONTRACEPTION

Bailey, Mohamed S. and Weller, Robert H.
"A Path Analysis of Fertility Differentials in Rural
Sierra Leone." Paper Presented at the 1985 Annual
Meeting of the American Sociological Association. 1985.
43p.
Bledsoe, Caroline H. and Isiugo-Abanihe, Uche
Strategies of Child Fosterage Among Rural Mende
'Grannies'. Philadelphia, Pennsylvania: University of
Pennsylvania. Population Studies Center. 1985.
Getaweh, S. Momolu
"The Conceptualization of Family-Size Goals Among the
Mende in Sierra Leone and the Vai in Liberia." Ph.D
Dissertation: Boston University. Graduate School.
Boston, Massachusetts. 1984. 419p.
Ketkar, Suhas L.
"Socioeconomic Determinants of Family Size in Sierra
Leone." Rural Africana. #6 Winter, 1979. pp. 25-45.
Ketkar, Suhas L.
"Female Education and Fertility: Some Evidence From
Sierra Leone." Journal of Developing Areas. Volume 13
#1 October, 1978. pp. 23-33.
Ketkar, Suhas L.
"Determinants of Fertility in a Developing Society: The
Case of Sierra Leone." Population Studies. Volume 33 #3
November, 1979. pp. 479-488.

Okoye, C.S.
   Fertility Levels and Differentials in Sierra Leone: An
   Analysis of the Fertility Data From the 1974 Population
   Census of Sierra Leone. Freetown, Sierra Leone: Central
   Statistics Office. Census Analysis Project. Volume
   Three. September, 1980. 53p.
Steady, Filomina C.
   "Male Roles in Fertility in Sierra Leone: The Moving
   Target." (In) Oppong, C. and Adaba, G. and
   Bekombo-Priso, M. and Mogey, J. (eds.). Marriage,
   Fertility and Parenthood in West Africa. Canberra,
   Australia: Australian National University. Department of
   Demography. Volume Two. 1978. pp. 641-653.

FERTILITY AND INFERTILITY

Bailey, Mohamed S. and Weller, Robert H.
   "A Path Analysis of Fertility Differentials in Rural
   Sierra Leone." Paper Presented at the 1985 Annual
   Meeting of the American Sociological Association. 1985.
   43p.
Bailey, Mohamed S.
   Female Education and Fertility in Rural Sierra Leone: A
   Test of the Threshold Hypothesis. Tallahassee, Florida:
   Florida State University. Center for the Study. Working
   Paper #85-24. 1985. 21p.
Bledsoe, Caroline H. and Isiugo-Abanihe, Uche
   Strategies of Child Fosterage Among Rural Mende
   'Grannies'. Philadelphia, Pennsylvania: University of
   Pennsylvania. Population Studies Center. 1985.
Dzegede, Sylvi A.
   "Urbanization and Fertility Decline in West Africa:
   Ghana, Sierra Leone and Liberia." Journal of Comparative
   Family Studies. Volume 12 #2 Spring, 1981. pp.
   233-244.
Gyepi-Garbrah, Benjamin
   Adolescent Fertility in Sierra Leone. Boston: Pathfinder
   Fund. 1985. 62p.
Isaac, Barry L
   "Female Fertility and Marital Form Among the Mende of
   Rural Upper Bambara Chiefdom, Sierra Leone." Ethnology.
   Volume 19 #3 July, 1980. pp. 297-314.
Ketkar, Suhas L. and Singh, B.
   "Fertility and Household Characteristics: Some Evidence
   From Sierra Leone." Journal of African Studies. Volume
   7 #4 Winter, 1980. pp. 204-212.
Ketkar, Suhas L.
   "Female Education and Fertility: Some Evidence From
   Sierra Leone." Journal of Developing Areas. Volume 13
   #1 October, 1978. pp. 23-33.
Ketkar, Suhas L.
   "Determinants of Fertility in a Developing Society: The

Case of Sierra Leone." Population Studies. Volume 33 #3
November, 1979. pp. 479-488.
MacCormack, Carol P.
"Health, Fertility and Birth in Moyamba District, Sierra
Leone." (In) MacCormack, Carol P. (ed.). Ethnography of
Fertility and Birth. New York: Academic Press. 1982.
pp. 115-139.
Okoye, C.S.
Fertility Levels and Differentials in Sierra Leone: An
Analysis of the Fertility Data From the 1974 Population
Census of Sierra Leone. Freetown, Sierra Leone: Central
Statistics Office. Census Analysis Project. Volume
Three. September, 1980. 53p.
Sierra Leone. Ministry of Health
Infant and Early Childhood Mortality in Relation to
Fertility Patterns: Report on an Ad-Hoc Survey in Greater
Freetown, the Western Area and Makeni in the Northern
Province, Sierra Leone, 1973-1975. Freetown, Sierra
Leone: Ministry of Health. 1980. 182p.
Steady, Filomina C.
"Male Roles in Fertility in Sierra Leone: The Moving
Target." (In) Oppong, C. and Adaba, G. and
Bekombo-Priso, M. and Mogey, J. (eds.). Marriage,
Fertility and Parenthood in West Africa. Canberra,
Australia: Australian National University. Department of
Demography. Volume Two. 1978. pp. 641-653.

HEALTH, NUTRITION AND MEDICINE

Bailey, Mohamed S. and Weller, Robert H.
"A Path Analysis of Fertility Differentials in Rural
Sierra Leone." Paper Presented at the 1985 Annual
Meeting of the American Sociological Association. 1985.
43p.
Belmont, William
Maternal Mortality in Sierra Leone. Freetown, Sierra
Leone: Sierra Leone Ministry of Health. 1978. 22p.
Gyepi-Garbrah, Benjamin
Adolescent Fertility in Sierra Leone. Boston: Pathfinder
Fund. 1985. 62p.
Hardiman, M.G.
"Planning and the Health of Mothers and Children in Rural
Areas of Sierra Leone." Journal pf Tropical Pediatrics.
Volume 27 #2 April, 1981. pp. 83-87.
Hosken, Fran P.
"Female Mutilation in Somalia Tests 'Human Rights
Doctrine'." Politics and Other Human Interests. #14
May 9, 1978. pp. 21-22.
Isaac, Barry L. and Feinberg, W.E.
"Marital Form and Infant Survival Among the Mende of
Rural Upper Bambara Chiefdom, Sierra Leone." Human
Biology. Volume 54 #3 September, 1982. pp. 627-634.

Kandeh, Herbert B.
   Infant and Child Mortality in the Bo District of Sierra
   Leone. Philadelphia, Pennsylvania: University of
   Pennsylvania. Population Studies Center. 1979.
MacCormack, Carol P.
   "Health, Fertility and Birth in Moyamba District, Sierra
   Leone." (In) MacCormack, Carol P. (ed.). Ethnography of
   Fertility and Birth. New York: Academic Press. 1982.
   pp. 115-139.
Okoye, C.S.
   Fertility Levels and Differentials in Sierra Leone: An
   Analysis of the Fertility Data From the 1974 Population
   Census of Sierra Leone. Freetown, Sierra Leone: Central
   Statistics Office. Census Analysis Project. Volume
   Three. September, 1980. 53p.
Sierra Leone. Ministry of Health
   Infant and Early Childhood Mortality in Relation to
   Fertility Patterns: Report on an Ad-Hoc Survey in Greater
   Freetown, the Western Area and Makeni in the Northern
   Province, Sierra Leone, 1973-1975. Freetown, Sierra
   Leone: Ministry of Health. 1980. 182p.
Smith, A.H.
   "Social and Cultural Factors in Child Mortality Among the
   Temne of Magburaka, Sierra Leone." Ph.D Dissertation:
   University of Oregon. Eugene, Oregon. 1981. 382p.

HISTORY

Beoku-Betts, J.
   "Western Perceptions of African Women in the 19th Century
   and 20th Centuries." African Research Bulletin
   (Institute of African Studies, University of Sierra
   Leone). Volume 6 #4 1976.
Cosentino, Donald
   Defiant Maids and Stubborn Farmers: Tradition and
   Invention in Mende Story Performance. Cambridge, New
   York: Cambridge University Press. 1982. 226p.
Cromwell, Adelaide M.
   An African Victorian Feminist: The Life and Times of
   Adelaide Smith Casely Hayford, 1868-1960. London: Frank
   Cass. 1985. 256p.
Denzer, LaRay
   "Constance A. Cummings-John of Sierra Leone: Her Early
   Political Career." Tarikh. Volume 7 #1 1981. pp.
   20-32.
MacCormack, Carol P.
   "Slaves, Slave Owners and Slave Dealers: Sherbro Coast
   and Hinterland." (In) Robertson, Claire C. and Klein,
   Martin A. (eds,). Women and Slavery in Africa. Madison,
   Wisconsin: University of Wisconsin Press. 1983. pp.
   271-294.

MacCormack, Carol P.
    "Wono: Institutionalized Dependency in Sherbro Descent
    Groups." (In) Miers, S. and Kopytoff, I. (eds.).
    Slavery in Africa: Historical and Anthropological
    Perspectives. Madison, Wisconsin: University of
    Wisconsin-Madison. 1977.
Okonkwo, Rina
    "Adelaide Casely Hayford: Cultural Nationalist and
    Feminist." Journal of the Historical Society of Sierra
    Leone. Volume 2 #2 1978. pp. 10-21.
White, E. Frances
    "Sierra Leonean Women and Nitida Kola: The Organization
    of a 19th Century Trading Diaspora." Paper Presented at
    the Annual Meeting of the African Studies Association.
    Paper #116. Philadelphia, Pennsylvania. 1980.
White, E. Frances
    "The Big Market in Freetown: A Case Study of Women's
    Workplace." Journal of the Historical Society of Sierra
    Leone. Volume 4 #1/2 1980. pp. 19-32.
White, E. Frances
    "Creole Women Traders in Sierra Leone: An Economic and
    Social History, 1792-1945." Ph.D Dissertation: Boston
    University. Graduate School. Boston, Masachusetts.
    1978. 288p.
White, E. Frances
    Creole Women Traders in the 19th Century. Boston: Boston
    University. African Studies Center. Working Paper #27.
    1980.
White, E. Francis
    "Creole Women Traders in the 19th Century."
    International Journal of African Historical Studies.
    Volume 14 #4 1981. pp. 601-625.

LAW AND LEGAL ISSUES

Harrell-Bond, Barbara E. and Rijnsdorp, Ulrica
    "The Emergence of the 'Stranger Permit Marriage' and
    Other New Forms of Conjugal Union in Rural Sierra Leone."
    Africana Research Bulletin. Volume 6 #4 1976.
Harrell-Bond, Barbara E. and Rijnsdorp, Ulrica
    "The Emergence of the 'Stranger-Permit' Marriage and
    Other New Forms of Conjugal Union in Rural Sierra Leone."
    (In) Roberts, Simon (ed.). Law and the Family in Africa.
    Hague, Netherlands: Mouton. 1977. pp. 205-223.

MARITAL RELATIONS AND NUPTIALITY

Bailey, Mohamed S. and Weller, Robert H.
    "A Path Analysis of Fertility Differentials in Rural
    Sierra Leone." Paper Presented at the 1985 Annual
    Meeting of the American Sociological Association. 1985.
    43p.

Dzegede, Sylvi A.
   "Urbanization and Fertility Decline in West Africa:
   Ghana, Sierra Leone and Liberia." Journal of Comparative
   Family Studies. Volume 12 #2 Spring, 1981. pp.
   233-244.
Getaweh, S. Momolu
   "The Conceptualization of Family-Size Goals Among the
   Mende in Sierra Leone and the Vai in Liberia." Ph.D
   Dissertation: Boston University. Graduate School.
   Boston, Massachusetts. 1984. 419p.
Harrell-Bond, Barbara E.
   "Stereotypes of Western and African Patterns of Marriage
   and Family Life." Journal of Marriage and the Family.
   Volume 38 #2 1976. pp. 387-396.
Harrell-Bond, Barbara E. and Rijnsdorp, Ulrica
   "The Emergence of the 'Stranger Permit Marriage' and
   Other New Forms of Conjugal Union in Rural Sierra Leone."
   Africana Research Bulletin. Volume 6 #4 1976.
Harrell-Bond, Barbara E. and Rijnsdorp, Ulrica
   "The Emergence of the 'Stranger-Permit' Marriage and
   Other New Forms of Conjugal Union in Rural Sierra Leone."
   (In) Roberts, Simon (ed.). Law and the Family in Africa.
   Hague, Netherlands: Mouton. 1977. pp. 205-223.
Isaac, Barry L
   "Female Fertility and Marital Form Among the Mende of
   Rural Upper Bambara Chiefdom, Sierra Leone." Ethnology.
   Volume 19 #3 July, 1980. pp. 297-314.
Isaac, Barry L. and Feinberg, W.E.
   "Marital Form and Infant Survival Among the Mende of
   Rural Upper Bambara Chiefdom, Sierra Leone." Human
   Biology. Volume 54 #3 September, 1982. pp. 627-634.
Kamara, Allieu I.
   "The Changing Family in the Sierra Leone Context." Paper
   Presented at the Seminar on the Changing Family in the
   African Context. 1983. Paris: United Nations
   Educational, Scientific and Cultural Organization.
   Maseru, Lesotho. 1984. 15p.
Ketkar, Suhas L. and Singh, B.
   "Fertility and Household Characteristics: Some Evidence
   From Sierra Leone." Journal of African Studies. Volume
   7 #4 Winter, 1980. pp. 204-212.
Ketkar, Suhas L.
   "Socioeconomic Determinants of Family Size in Sierra
   Leone." Rural Africana. #6 Winter, 1979. pp. 25-45.
Ketkar, Suhas L.
   "Determinants of Fertility in a Developing Society: The
   Case of Sierra Leone." Population Studies. Volume 33 #3
   November, 1979. pp. 479-488.
Okoye, C.S.
   Fertility Levels and Differentials in Sierra Leone: An
   Analysis of the Fertility Data From the 1974 Population
   Census of Sierra Leone. Freetown, Sierra Leone: Central

Statistics Office. Census Analysis Project. Volume
Three. September, 1980. 53p.
Sierra Leone. Ministry of Health
Infant and Early Childhood Mortality in Relation to
Fertility Patterns: Report on an Ad-Hoc Survey in Greater
Freetown, the Western Area and Makeni in the Northern
Province, Sierra Leone, 1973-1975. Freetown, Sierra
Leone: Ministry of Health. 1980. 182p.
Smith, A.H.
"Social and Cultural Factors in Child Mortality Among the
Temne of Magburaka, Sierra Leone." Ph.D Dissertation:
University of Oregon. Eugene, Oregon. 1981. 382p.
Steady, Filomina C.
"Male Roles in Fertility in Sierra Leone: The Moving
Target." (In) Oppong, C. and Adaba, G. and
Bekombo-Priso, M. and Mogey, J. (eds.). Marriage,
Fertility and Parenthood in West Africa. Canberra,
Australia: Australian National University. Department of
Demography. Volume Two. 1978. pp. 641-653.

MASS MEDIA

Anani, Elma and Keita, Alkaly M. and Rahman, Awatef A.
Women and the Mass Media in Africa: Case Studies From
Sierra Leone, the Niger and Egypt. Addis Ababa,
Ethiopia: United Nations Economic Commission for Africa.
African Training and Research Centre for Women. 1981.
38p.

MIGRATION

Dzegede, Sylvi A.
"Urbanization and Fertility Decline in West Africa:
Ghana, Sierra Leone and Liberia." Journal of Comparative
Family Studies. Volume 12 #2 Spring, 1981. pp.
233-244.

NATIONALISM

Okonkwo, Rina
"Adelaide Casely Hayford: Cultural Nationalist and
Feminist." Journal of the Historical Society of Sierra
Leone. Volume 2 #2 1978. pp. 10-21.

ORGANIZATIONS

Bledsoe, Caroline H.
"The Political Use of Sande Ideology and Symbolism."
American Ethnologist. Volume 11 #3 August, 1984. pp.
455-472.

Steady, Filomina C.
    "Protestant Women's Associations in Freetown, Sierra
    Leone." (In) Hafkin, N.J. and Bay, E.G. (eds.). Women
    in Africa: Studies in Social and Economic Change.
    Stanford, California: Stanford University Press. 1976.
    pp. 213-237.
White, E. Frances
    "Sierra Leonean Women and Nitida Kola: The Organization
    of a 19th Century Trading Diaspora." Paper Presented at
    the Annual Meeting of the African Studies Association.
    Paper #116. Philadelphia, Pennsylvania. 1980.

RELIGION AND WITCHCRAFT

MacCormack, Carol P.
    "Sande: The Public Face of a Secret Society." (In)
    Jules-Rosette, Bennetta (ed.). The New Religions of
    Africa. Norwood, New Jersey: Ablex Publishing Corp.
    1979. pp. 27-37.
Rosen, David M.
    "Dangerous Women: Ideology, Knowledge and Ritual Among
    the Kono of Eastern Sierra Leone." Dialectical
    Anthropology. Volume 6 #2 December, 1981. pp. 151-163.
Shaw, Rosalind
    "Gender and the Structuring of Reality in Temne
    Divination: An Interactive Study." Africa. Volume 55 #3
    1985. pp. 286-303.
Steady, Filomina C.
    "Protestant Women's Associations in Freetown, Sierra
    Leone." (In) Hafkin, N.J. and Bay, E.G. (eds.). Women
    in Africa: Studies in Social and Economic Change.
    Stanford, California: Stanford University Press. 1976.
    pp. 213-237.
Steady, Filomina C.
    "The Role of Women in the Churches in Freetown, Sierra
    Leone." (In) Fashole-Luke, Edward. Christianity in
    Independent Africa. London: R. Collings. 1978. pp.
    151-163.

SEX ROLES

Cosentino, Donald
    Defiant Maids and Stubborn Farmers: Tradition and
    Invention in Mende Story Performance. Cambridge, New
    York: Cambridge University Press. 1982. 226p.
Harrell-Bond, Barbara E.
    "Stereotypes of Western and African Patterns of Marriage
    and Family Life." Journal of Marriage and the Family.
    Volume 38 #2 1976. pp. 387-396.
International Labour Organization (ILO)
    National Symposium on Cooperative Education and Family

Welfare and Rural Development. Conference Report.
October 25-November 4, 1976. Mogadishu: Somalia: ILO
Regional Office. 1976. 182p.

Isaac, Barry L. and Feinberg, W.E.
"Marital Form and Infant Survival Among the Mende of
Rural Upper Bambara Chiefdom, Sierra Leone." Human
Biology. Volume 54 #3 September, 1982. pp. 627-634.

Kamara, Allieu I.
"The Changing Family in the Sierra Leone Context." Paper
Presented at the Seminar on the Changing Family in the
African Context. 1983. Paris: United Nations
Educational, Scientific and Cultural Organization.
Maseru, Lesotho. 1984. 15p.

Ketkar, Suhas L. and Singh, B.
"Fertility and Household Characteristics: Some Evidence
From Sierra Leone." Journal of African Studies. Volume
7 #4 Winter, 1980. pp. 204-212.

MacCormack, Carol P.
"The Compound Head: Structure and Strategies." Africana
Research Bulletin. Volume 6 #4 1976. pp. 44-64.

MacCormack, Carol P.
"The Cultural Ecology of Production: Sherbro Coast and
Hinterland." (In) Green, D. (ed.). Social Organization
and Settlement. Oxford, England: British Archaeological
Reports. 1978.

Mansaray, K.
"Womenfolk in the Northern and Southern Provinces of
Sierra Leone: A Note." (In) Mitchell, P.K. and Jones, A.
(eds.). Sierra Leone Studies at Birmingham: Proceedings
of the Third Birmingham Sierra Leone Studies Symposium,
15-17 July, 1983. Birmingham, England: Birmingham
University. Centre of West African Studies. 1984. pp.
219-220.

Ottenberg, Simon
"Artistic and Sex Roles in a Limba Chiefdom." (In)
Oppong, Christine (ed.). Female and Male in West Africa.
London: George Allen and Unwin. 1983. pp. 79-90.

Rosen, David M.
"Dangerous Women: Ideology, Knowledge and Ritual Among
the Kono of Eastern Sierra Leone." Dialectical
Anthropology. Volume 6 #2 December, 1981. pp. 151-163.

Safilios-Rothschild, Constantina
The Persistence of Women's Invisibility in Agriculture:
Theoretical and Policy Lessons From Lesotho and Sierra
Leone. New York: Population Council. Center for Policy
Studies. Working Paper #88. September, 1982. 31p.

Safilios-Rothschild, Constantina
"The Persistence of Women's Invisibility in Agriculture:
Theoretical and Policy Lessons From Lesotho and Sierra
Leone." Economic Development and Cultural Change.
Volume 33 #2 January, 1985. pp. 299-317.

Shaw, Rosalind
"Gender and the Structuring of Reality in Temne

Divination: An Interactive Study." Africa. Volume 55 #3
1985. pp. 286-303.

URBANIZATION

Dzegede, Sylvi A.
  "Urbanization and Fertility Decline in West Africa:
  Ghana, Sierra Leone and Liberia." Journal of Comparative
  Family Studies. Volume 12 #2 Spring, 1981. pp.
  233-244.
Liedholm, Carl and Chuta, Enyinn A.
  The Economics of Rural and Urban Small-Scale Industries
  in Sierra Leone. East Lansing, Michigan: Michigan State
  University. African Rural Economy Program. Paper #14.
  1976.

WOMEN AND THEIR CHILDREN

Bledsoe, Caroline H. and Isiugo-Abanihe, Uche
  Strategies of Child Fosterage Among Rural Mende
  'Grannies'. Philadelphia, Pennsylvania: University of
  Pennsylvania. Population Studies Center. 1985.
Hardiman, M.G.
  "Planning and the Health of Mothers and Children in Rural
  Areas of Sierra Leone." Journal pf Tropical Pediatrics.
  Volume 27 #2 April, 1981. pp. 83-87.

Togo

Biraimah, Karen C.
   "The Impact of Gender-Differentiated Education on Third
   World Women's Expectations: A Togolese Case Study." Ph.D
   Dissertation: State University of New York at Buffalo.
   Buffalo, New York. 1982. 379p.
Biraimah, Karen C.
   "The Impact of Western Schools on Girls' Expectations: A
   Togolese Case." (In) Kelly, Gail P. and Elliott, Carolyn
   M. (eds.). Women's Education in the Third World:
   Comparative Perspectives. Albany, New York: State
   University of New York Press. 1982. pp. 188-200.
Biraimah, Karen C.
   "The Impact of Western Schools on Girls' Expectations: A
   Togolese Case." Comparative Education Review. Volume 24
   #2 June, 1980. pp. S196-S208.
Dagadzi, Veronique
   "Law and the Status of Women in Togo: Discrimination
   Against Women in Togo." (In) Columbia Human Rights LAw
   Review (eds.). Law and the Status of Women: An
   International Symposium. New York: United Nations.
   Centre for Social Development and Humanitarian Affairs.
   1977. pp. 295-302.
Kiers, Eric J.
   "Madame Mercedes-Benz: Merchant of Togo." Ms. Volume 5
   April, 1977. pp. 112+.
Locoh, T. and Adaba, Gemma
   "Child-Spacing in Togo: The Southeast Togo Survey
   (EFSE)." (In) Page, Hilary J. and Lesthaeghe, Ron
   (eds.). Child-Spacing in Tropical Africa: Traditions and
   Change. New York: Academic Press. 1981. pp. 255-263.
Waife, Ronald S. and Burkhart, Marianne (eds.)
   The Nonphysician and Family Health in Sub-Saharan Africa:
   Proceedings of a Conference, Freetown, Sierra Leone,
   September 1-4, 1980. Chestnut Hill, Massachusetts:
   Pathfinder Fund. 1981. 141p.

General Subject Bibliography—
Central Africa

Alausa, O. and Osoba, A.O.
   "The Role of Sexually Transmitted Diseases in Male
   Infertility in Tropical Africa." Nigerian Medical
   Journal. Volume 8 #3 May, 1978. pp. 225-229.
Attah, E.B.
   Family Nucleation and Fertility Change in Tropical
   Africa: Background to the Demographic Transition.
   Atlanta, Georgia: Atlanta University. Department of
   Sociology. 1985.
Berger, Iris
   "Women, Religion and Social Change: East and Central
   African Perspectives." Paper Presented at the Conference
   on Women and Development. Wellesley, Massachusetts:
   Wellesley College. Wellesley College Center for Research
   on Women. June 2-6, 1976. 25p.
Bongaarts, John
   "The Impact on Fertility of Traditional and Changing
   Child-Spacing Practices." (In) Page, Hilary J. and
   Lesthaeghe, Ron (eds.). Child-Spacing in Tropical
   Africa. New York: Academic Press. 1981. pp. 111-129.
Caldwell, John C. and Caldwell, Pat
   "The Demographic Evidence for the Incidence and Cause of
   Abnormally Low Fertility in Tropical Africa." World
   Health Statistics Quarterly. Volume 36 #1 1983. pp.
   2-34.
Caldwell, John C. and Caldwell, Pat
   Cultural Forces Tending to Sustain High Fertility in
   Tropical Africa. Canberra, Australia: Australian
   National University. 1984.
Caldwell, Pat
   "Issues of Marriage and Marital Change: Tropical Africa
   and the Middle East." (In) Huzayyin, S.A. and Acsadi,
   G.T. (eds.). Family and Marriage in Some African and

Asiatic Countries. Cairo: Cairo Demographic Centre.
Research Monograph Series #6. 1976. pp. 325-335.

Cantrelle, Pierre and Ferry, Benoit and Mondot, J.
"Relationships Between Fertility and Mortality in
Tropical Africa." (In) Preston, Samuel H. (ed.). The
Effects of Infant and Child Mortality on Fertility. New
York: Academic Press. 1978. pp. 181-205.

Fields, Karen E.
"Political Contingencies of Witchcraft in Colonial
Central Africa." Canadian Journal of African Studies.
Volume 16 #3 1982. pp. 567-593.

Gray, R.H.
"Birth Intervals, Postpartum Sexual Abstinence and Child
Health." (In) Page, Hilary J. and Lesthaeghe, Ron
(eds.). Child-Spacing in Tropical Africa: Traditions and
Change. New York: Academic Press. 1981. pp. 93-109.

Igbinovia, Patrick E.
"Prostitution in Black Africa." International Journal of
Women's Studies. Volume 7 #5 November-December, 1984.
pp. 430-449.

Jett, Joyce
The Role of Traditional Midwives in the Modern Health
Sector in West and Central Africa. Washington, D.C.:
U.S. Department of State. U.S. Agency for International
Development. January, 1977. 150p.

Jett, Joyce
The Role of Traditional Midwives in the Modern Health
Sector in West and Central Africa. Washington, D.C.:
U.S. Department of State. U.S. Agency for International
Development. January, 1977. 150p.

Jewsiewicki, B.
"Lineage Mode of Production: Social Inequalities in
Equatorial Central Africa." (In) Crummey, Donald and
Steward, C.C. (eds.). Modes of Production in Africa: The
Precolonial Era. Beverly Hills, California: Sage
Publications. 1981. pp. 93-114.

Mabogunje, A.L.
"The Policy Implications of Changes in Child-Spacing
Practices in Tropical Africa." (In) Page, Hilary J. and
Lesthaeghe, Ron (eds.). Child-Spacing in Tropical
Africa: Traditions and Changes. New York: Academic
Press. 1981. pp. 303-316.

Marks, Shula and Unterhalter, Elaine
Women and the Migrant Labour System in Southern Africa.
Lusaka, Zambia: United Nations Economic Commission for
Africa. Multinational Programming and Operational Centre
for Eastern and Central Africa. 1978. 15p.

Muriuki, Margaret N.
"The Role of Women in African Librarianship: The Next 25
Years." Paper Presented at the Standing Conference of
Eastern, Central and Southern African Libraries. Lusaka,
Zambia. October 4-9, 1976.

Mushanga, Tibamanya M.
    "Wife Victimization in East and Central Africa."
    Victimology. Volume 2 #3/4 1977. pp. 479-486.
Page, Hilary J. and Lesthaeghe, Ron J. (eds.)
    Child-Spacing in Tropical Africa: Traditions and Change.
    New York: Academic Press. Studies in Population Series.
    1981. 332p.
Pagezy, Helen
    "Some Aspects of Daily Work of Women Oto and Twa Living
    in Equatorial Forest Middle." L'Anthropolgie. Volume 80
    #3 1976. pp. 465-906.
Sala-Diakanda, Mpembele
    "Problems of Infertility and Sub-Fertility in West and
    Central Africa." (In) International Union for the
    Scientific Study of Population (IUSSP). International
    Population Conference. Papers of the 19th General
    Conference. Liege, Belgium: IUSSP. Volume Three. 1981.
    pp. 643-666.
Schoenmaeckers, Ronald C. and Shah, I.H. and Lesthaeghe, Ron
J. and Tambashe, O.
    "The Child-Spacing Tradition and the Postpartum Taboo in
    Tropical Africa: Anthropological Evidence." (In) Page,
    Hilary J. and Lesthaeghe, Ron (eds.). Child-Spacing in
    Tropical Africa: Traditions and Change. New York:
    Academic Press. 1981. pp. 25-71.
Schoenmaeckers, Ronald C.
    The Child-Spacing Tradition and the Postpartum Taboo in
    Tropical Africa: Anthropological Evidence. Paper
    Prepared for the IUSSP Workshop on Child-Spacing in
    Tropical Africa: Tradition and Change. Brussels,
    Belgium: International Union for the Scientific Study of
    Population. April, 17-19, 1979.
Turner, Edith
    "Girl Into Woman." Anthropology and Humanism Quarterly.
    Volume 10 #2 1985. pp. 27-32.
Ukaegbu, Alfred O.
    "Marriage Habits and Fertility of Women in Tropical
    Africa: A Socio-Cultural Perspective." (In) Dupaquier,
    J. and Helin, E. and Laslett, P. and Livi-Bacci, M.
    (eds.). Marriage and Remarriage in Populations of the
    Past. New York: Academic Press. Population and Social
    Structure: Advances in Historical Demography Series.
    1981. pp. 127-137.
United Nations Economic Commission for Africa (UNECA)
    Establishment of Sub-Regional Machinery to Enhance the
    Role of Women in the Progress of Economic and Social
    Development in the Central African Sub-Region and to
    Promote and Guide the Activities of the ECA's Training
    and Research Centre for Women. Yaounde, Cameroon: MULPOC
    (Multi-National Operations Center for Central African
    Library). March, 1978.
Wright, Marcia
    "Bwanikwa: Consciousness and Protest Among Slave Women in
    Central Africa, 1886-1911." (In) Robertson, Claire C.

and Klein, Martin A. (eds.). Women and Slavery in
Africa. Madison, Wisconsin: University of Wisconsin
Press. 1983. pp. 246-267.
Wright, Marcia
"Technology and Women's Control Over Production: Three
Case Studies From East-Central Africa and Their
Implications for Esther Boserup's Thesis About the
Displacement of Women." Paper Presented at the
Rockefeller Foundation Workshop on Women, Household and
Human Capital Development in Low Income Countries. New
York: Rockefeller Foundation. July, 1982.

NATIONS OF CENTRAL AFRICA

Burundi

NO CITATIONS

Cameroon

ABORTION

Gwan Achu, Emmanuel
  "Origins and Elements of the Population Policies of the
  Cameroon Republic." Science and Technology Review:
  Social Sciences Series. Volume 3 #1/2 January-June,
  1985. pp. 116-128.

AGRICULTURE

Bryson Judy C.
  "Women and Agriculture in Sub-Saharan Africa:
  Implications for Development." Journal of Development
  Studies. Volume 17 #3 April, 1981. pp. 29-46.
Bryson, Judy C.
  Women and Economic Development in Cameroon. Washington,
  D.C.: U.S. Department of State. U.S. Agency for
  International Development. Office of Women in
  Development. January, 1979. 153p.
DeLancey, Mark W.
  "Women's Palm Oil Cooperatives, Fako Division, Cameroon:
  A Microstudy in the Problems of Development." Paper
  Presented at the Annual Meeting of the African Studies
  Association. Paper #24. Washington, D.C. November 4-7,
  1982.
DeLancey, Virginia H.
  "The Relationship Between Female Labor Force
  Participation and Fertility: Compatibility of Roles on a
  Cameroon Plantation." Paper Presented at the Annual
  Meeting of the African Studies Association. Paper #21.
  Baltimore, Maryland. 1978. 20p.
Ebot, Moses T.
  "Effects of Access to Social Services on Differential

Fertility in Three Types of Agriculture." Ph.D
Dissertation: University of Iowa. Iowa City, Iowa.
1978. 248p.

Endeley, J.B.
"Agricultural Extension and the Economic Development of
Women: Case Study of Cameroon." Paper Presented at the
Workshop on the Role of Women and Home Economics in Rural
Development in Africa. Rome: United Nations Food and
Agriculture Organization. Alexandria, Egypt. October
17, 1983. 8p.

Ferguson, Anne and Horn, Nancy
"Resource Guide: Women in Agriculture in the Cameroons."
East Lansing, Michigan: Bean/Cowpea CRSP (Collaborative
Research Support Program). 1984.

Guyer, Jane I.
Family and Farm in Southern Cameroon. Boston: Boston
University. African Studies Center. African Research
Studies #15. 1984. 154p.

Guyer, Jane I.
"Female Farming and the Evolution of Food Production
Patterns Amongst the Beti of South-Central Cameroon."
Africa. Volume 50 #4 1980. pp. 341-356.

Guyer, Jane I.
"Food, Cocoa, and the Division of Labour by Sex in Two
West African Societies." Comparative Studies in Society
and History. Volume 22 #3 July, 1980. pp. 355-370.

Guyer, Jane I.
The Women's Farming System, the Lekie Southern Cameroon.
Yaounde, Cameroon: ENSA (National Advanced School of
Agriculture Library). 1977.

Guyer, Jane I.
"Women in the Rural Economy: Contemporary Variations."
(In) Hay, Margaret J. and Stichter, Sharon (eds.).
African Women South of the Sahara. New York: Longman.
1984. pp. 19-32.

Henn, Jeanne K.
"Peasants, State and Capital: The Political Economy of
Rural Incomes in Cameroon." Ph.D Dissertation: Harvard
University. Cambridge, Massachusetts. 1978. 396p.

Ifeanyichikwu Okafor, Theresa
The Role of Women in Village Developmemt: Income Earning
and Participation in Massaka, S.W. Cameroon. Buea,
Cameroon: Regional Pan African Institute for
Development/West Africa. 1981. 33p.

Jones, C.
"Women's Labour Allocation and Irrigated Rice Production
in North Cameroon." (In) Greenshields, B.L. and Bellamy,
M.A. (eds.). Rural Development:Growth and Inequity.
London: Aldershot, Gower. 1983. pp.172-177.

Jones, Christine W.
"The Mobilization of Women's Labor for Cash Crop
Production: A Game Theoretic Approach to Rice Production

in North Cameroon." American Journal of Agricultural
Economics. Volume 65 December, 1983. pp. 1049-1054.

Jones, Christine W.
"The Mobilization of Women's Labor for Cash Crop
Production: A Game Theoretical Approach." Ph.D
Dissertation: Harvard University. Cambridge,
Massachusetts. 1983. 194p.

Jones, Christine W.
"Women's Labour Allocation and Irrigated Rice Production
in North Cameroon." Paper Presented for the
International Association of Agricultural Economists.
Jakarta, Indonesia. August, 1982.

King-Akerele, Olubanke
Traditional Palm Oil Processing: Women's Role and the
Applications of Appropriate Technology: Ivory Coast,
Sierra Leone, Cameroons. Addis Ababa, Ethiopia: United
Nations Economic Commission for Africa. African Training
and Research Center for Women. 1983. 52p.

Koenig, Dolores B.
"Why Women Migrate, Agricultural Workers in Africa."
Paper Presented at the Annual Meeting of the American
Anthropological Association. Washington, D.C. November
21, 1976.

Miriti, Enid J.
Case Study on the Role of Women in Rural Development,
Barombi New Town. Buea, Cameroon: Regional Pan-African
Institute for Development/West Africa. 1980. 40p.

Monde, Caroline S.
Appropriate Technology for Rural Women: A Case Study of
Bai Bikom Village. Buea, Cameroon: Regional Pan-African
Institute for Development/West Africa. 1980. 27p.

Ouden, J.H.B. den
"Incorporation and Changes in the Composite Household:
The Effects of Coffee Introduction and Food Crop
Commercialization in Two Bamileke Chiefdoms, Cameroon."
(In) Presvelou, C. and Spijkers-Zwart, S. (eds.). The
Household, Women and Agricultural Development.
Wageninger, Netherlands: H. Veenman En Zonen. 1980. pp.
41-67.

Walker, Sheila S. and Brazier, Ellen
"Women, Education and Rural Development in Cameroon: The
Fulbe of the Garoua Region." African American Scholar.
Volume 1 #5 June, 1977.

Zeryehoun, Tayye
The Role of Rural Women in Development--A Case Study in
Massaka Village. Buea, Cameroon: Regional Pan-African
Institute for Development/West Africa. 1980. 21p.

BIBLIOGRAPHIES

Ferguson, Anne and Horn, Nancy
Resource Guide: Women in Agriculture in the Cameroons.

East Lansing, Michigan: Bean/Cowpea CRSP (Collaborative
Research Support Program). 1984.

CULTURAL ROLES

Bryson Judy C.
    "Women and Agriculture in Sub-Saharan Africa:
    Implications for Development." Journal of Development
    Studies. Volume 17 #3 April, 1981. pp. 29-46.
Clignet, Remi and Sween, Joyce A.
    "Interaction Between Historical and Sociological Times in
    the Analysis of Fertility in West Cameroon." Paper
    Presented at the 15th Annual Seminar on Family Research.
    Lome, Togo. January, 1976.
Clignet, Remi and Sween, Joyce A.
    "Plural Marriage and Family Planning in West Cameroon."
    Washinton, D.C.: U.S. Department of State. Foreign
    Affairs Research Documentation Center. 1978. 76p.
Clignet, Remi
    "Social Change and Sexual Differentiation in the Cameroon
    and the Ivory Coast." Signs. Volume 3 #1 Autumn, 1977.
    pp. 244-266.
Clignet, Remi
    "Social Change and Sexual Differentiation in the Cameroon
    and the Ivory Coast." (In) Wellesley Editorial
    Committee. Women in National Development. Chicago:
    University of Chicago Press. 1977. pp. 244-260.
Cooksey, B.
    "Education and Sexual Inequality in Cameroon." Journal
    of Modern African Studies. Volume 20 #1 March, 1982.
    pp. 167-177.
David, N. and Voas, David
    "Societal Causes of Infertility and Population Decline
    Among the Settled Fulani of North Cameroon." Man.
    Volume 16 #4 December, 1981. pp. 644-664.
Ebot, Moses T.
    "Effects of Access to Social Services on Differential
    Fertility in Three Types of Agriculture." Ph.D
    Dissertation: University of Iowa. Iowa City, Iowa.
    1978. 248p.
Guimera, L.M.
    "Witchcraft Illness in the Evuzok Nosological System."
    Culture, Medicine and Psychiatry. Volume 2 #4 December,
    1978. pp. 373-396.
Guyer, Jane I.
    Family and Farm in Southern Cameroon. Boston: Boston
    University. African Studies Center. African Research
    Studies #15. 1984. 154p.
Guyer, Jane I.
    "Female Farming and the Evolution of Food Production
    Patterns Amongst the Beti of South-Central Cameroon."
    Africa. Volume 50 #4 1980. pp. 341-356.

Guyer, Jane I.
   "Food, Cocoa, and the Division of Labour by Sex in Two
   West African Societies." Comparative Studies in Society
   and History. Volume 22 #3 July, 1980. pp. 355-370.
Guyer, Jane I.
   Household Budgets and Women's Incomes. Brookline,
   Massachusetts: Boston University. African Studies
   Center. Working Papers #28. 1980. 24p.
Guyer, Jane I.
   "The Economic Position of Beti Widows, Past and Present."
   (In) Barbier, J.C. and Moutome, J. (eds.). Femmes Du
   Cameroun: Meres Pacifiques Femmes Rebelles. Paris:
   Karthala. 1985.
Guyer, Jane I.
   "The Economic Position of Beti Widows: Past and Present."
   Boston: Boston University. African Studies Center.
   Working Paper #22. 1979. 19p.
Guyer, Jane I.
   The Women's Farming System, the Lekie Southern Cameroon.
   Yaounde, Cameroon: ENSA (National Advanced School of
   Agriculture Library). 1977.
Jones, C.
   "Women's Labour Allocation and Irrigated Rice Production
   in North Cameroon." (In) Greenshields, B.L. and Bellamy,
   M.A. (eds.). Rural Development:Growth and Inequity.
   London: Aldershot, Gower. 1983. pp.172-177.
King-Akerele, Olubanke
   Traditional Palm Oil Processing: Women's Role and the
   Applications of Appropriate Technology: Ivory Coast,
   Sierra Leone, Cameroons. Addis Ababa, Ethiopia: United
   Nations Economic Commission for Africa. African Training
   and Research Center for Women. 1983. 52p.
Koenig, Dolores B.
   "Sex, Work and Social Class in Cameroon." Ph.D
   Dissertation: Northwestern University. Evanston,
   Illinois. August, 1977. 359p.
Lantum, Dan N.
   Fertility and Some Factors Affecting it: Divorce in
   Cameroon. Yaounde, Cameroon: University of Yaounde.
   1978. 11p.
Lee, Bun S.
   Fertility Adaptations by Rural-Urban Migrants in
   Cameroon. Omaha, Nebraska: University of Nebraska-Omaha.
   Department of Economics, College of Business. 1985.
Lesthaeghe, Ron J. and Eelens, Frank
   Social Organization and Reproductive Regimes: Lessons
   From Sub-Saharan Africa and Historical Western Europe.
   Brussels, Belgium: Vrije Universiteit Brussel.
   Interuniversity Programme in Demography. IDP Working
   Paper #1985-1. 1985. 64p.
Martin, Jean Y.
   "Unequal Access to School Education in Northern
   Cameroon." African Environment. #14-16 1980. pp.
   61-88.

Mbinde, T.N.
    A Survey of Prostitutes in Victoria Town, South West
    Province. Buea, Cameroon 1976. 31p.
Miriti, Enid J.
    Case Study on the Role of Women in Rural Development,
    Barombi New Town. Buea, Cameroon: Regional Pan-African
    Institute for Development/West Africa. 1980. 40p.
Monde, Caroline S.
    Appropriate Technology for Rural Women: A Case Study of
    Bai Bikom Village. Buea, Cameroon: Regional Pan-African
    Institute for Development/West Africa. 1980. 27p.
Mutinta, Barnabas M.
    Women in Development: A Case Study of Women in
    Development in Mofako Bekondo New Town. Buea, Cameroon:
    Regional Pan-African Institute for Development/West
    Africa. 1980. 38p.
Okafor, Theresa I.
    A Case Study on the Role of Massaka Village Women in the
    Development of Massaka Village--Consequences of
    Income-Earning Activities and Participati on in Local
    Organizations. Buea, Cameroon: Regional Pan African
    Institute for Development/West Africa. 1980. 32p.
Ouden, J.H.B. den
    "Incorporation and Changes in the Composite Household:
    The Effects of Coffee Introduction and Food Crop
    Commercialization in Two Bamileke Chiefdoms, Cameroon."
    (In) Presvelou, C. and Spijkers-Zwart, S. (eds.). The
    Household, Women and Agricultural Development.
    Wageninger, Netherlands: H. Veenman En Zonen. 1980. pp.
    41-67.
Sween, Joyce A. and Clignet, Remi
    "Female Matrimonial Roles and Fertility in Africa." (In)
    Oppong, C. and Adaba, G. and Bekombo-Priso, M. and Mogey,
    J. (eds.). Marriage, Fertility and Parenthood in West
    Africa. Canberra, Australia: Australian National
    University. Department of Demography. Volume Two.
    1978. pp. 565-600.
Walker, Sheila S.
    "From Cattle Camp to City: Changing Roles of Fulbe Women
    in Northern Cameroon." Journal of African Studies.
    Volume 7 Spring, 1980. pp. 54-69.
Weekes-Vagliani, Winifred and Bekombo-Priso, Manga
    Family Life and Structure in Southern Cameroon. Paris:
    Organization of Economic Cooperation and Development.
    Development Centre. Technical Papers. 1976. 87p.
Weekes-Vagliani, Winifred
    "Some Explanations of High Fertility Among Rural Women in
    Southern Cameroon." (In) Caldwell, John C. (ed.). The
    Persistence of High Fertility: Population Prospects in
    the Third World. Canberra, Australia: Australian
    National University. Department of Demography. Volume
    One. 1977. pp. 451-468.

Zoe-Obianga, Rose
   "The Role of Women in Present Day Africa." (In)
   Appiah-Kubi, Kofi and Torres, Sergio (eds.). African
   Theology en Route: Papers From the Pan-African Conference
   of Third World Theologians, December 17-23, 1977, Accra,
   Ghana. Maryknoll, New York: Orbis Books. 1979. pp.
   145-149.

DEVELOPMENT AND TECHNOLOGY

Bryson Judy C.
   "Women and Agriculture in Sub-Saharan Africa:
   Implications for Development." Journal of Development
   Studies. Volume 17 #3 April, 1981. pp. 29-46.
Bryson, Judy C.
   Women and Economic Development in Cameroon. Washington,
   D.C.: U.S. Department of State. U.S. Agency for
   International Development. Office of Women in
   Development. January, 1979. 153p.
DeLancey, Mark W.
   "Women's Palm Oil Cooperatives, Fako Division, Cameroon:
   A Microstudy in the Problems of Development." Paper
   Presented at the Annual Meeting of the African Studies
   Association. Paper #24. Washington, D.C. November 4-7,
   1982.
DeLancey, Virginia H.
   "Women at the Cameroon Development Corporation: How Their
   Money Works: A Study of Small-Scale Accumulation of
   Capital by Women in Cameroon." Paper Presented at the
   Annual Meeting of the African Studies Association. Paper
   #20. Houston, Texas. 1977. 23p.
Endeley, J.B.
   "Agricultural Extension and the Economic Development of
   Women: Case Study of Cameroon." Paper Presented at the
   Workshop on the Role of Women and Home Economics in Rural
   Development in Africa. Rome: United Nations Food and
   Agriculture Organization. Alexandria, Egypt. October
   17, 1983. 8p.
Guyer, Jane I.
   "Female Farming and the Evolution of Food Production
   Patterns Amongst the Beti of South-Central Cameroon."
   Africa. Volume 50 #4 1980. pp. 341-356.
Guyer, Jane I.
   "Women in the Rural Economy: Contemporary Variations."
   (In) Hay, Margaret J. and Stichter, Sharon (eds.).
   African Women South of the Sahara. New York: Longman.
   1984. pp. 19-32.
Henn, Jeanne K.
   "Peasants, State and Capital: The Political Economy of
   Rural Incomes in Cameroon." Ph.D Dissertation: Harvard
   University. Cambridge, Massachusetts. 1978. 396p.

Ifeanyichikwu Okafor, Theresa
   The Role of Women in Village Developmemt: Income Earning
   and Participation in Massaka, S.W. Cameroon. Buea,
   Cameroon: Regional Pan African Institute for
   Development/West Africa. 1981. 33p.
Jamanka, Mamadou B.
   Ekona Mbenge Women's Role in Development: Case Study
   Report. Buea, Cameroon: Regional Pan-African Institute
   for Development/West Africa. 1980. 39p.
Jones, C.
   "Women's Labour Allocation and Irrigated Rice Production
   in North Cameroon." (In) Greenshields, B.L. and Bellamy,
   M.A. (eds.). Rural Development:Growth and Inequity.
   London: Aldershot, Gower. 1983. pp.172-177.
Jones, Christine W.
   "The Mobilization of Women's Labor for Cash Crop
   Production: A Game Theoretic Approach to Rice Production
   in North Cameroon." American Journal of Agricultural
   Economics. Volume 65 December, 1983. pp. 1049-1054.
Jones, Christine W.
   "The Mobilization of Women's Labor for Cash Crop
   Production: A Game Theoretical Approach." Ph.D
   Dissertation: Harvard University. Cambridge,
   Massachusetts. 1983. 194p.
Jones, Christine W.
   "Women's Labour Allocation and Irrigated Rice Production
   in North Cameroon." Paper Presented for the
   International Association of Agricultural Economists.
   Jakarta, Indonesia. August, 1982.
Kibuka, E.P.
   Evaluation of Community Development: Women's Work in the
   South West and North West Provinces of the United
   Republic of Cameroon. Geneva: International Labour
   Organization. Pan African Institute for Development.
   1979. 68p.
King-Akerele, Olubanke
   Traditional Palm Oil Processing: Women's Role and the
   Applications of Appropriate Technology: Ivory Coast,
   Sierra Leone, Cameroons. Addis Ababa, Ethiopia: United
   Nations Economic Commission for Africa. African Training
   and Research Center for Women. 1983. 52p.
Miriti, Enid J.
   Case Study on the Role of Women in Rural Development,
   Barombi New Town. Buea, Cameroon: Regional Pan-African
   Institute for Development/West Africa. 1980. 40p.
Monde, Caroline S.
   Appropriate Technology for Rural Women: A Case Study of
   Bai Bikom Village. Buea, Cameroon: Regional Pan-African
   Institute for Development/West Africa. 1980. 27p.
Mutinta, Barnabas M.
   Women in Development: A Case Study of Women in
   Development in Mofako Bekondo New Town. Buea, Cameroon:

Regional Pan-African Institute for Development/West
    Africa. 1980. 38p.
National Asso. of Negro Business and Prof. Women's Clubs
    African Women Small Entrepreneurs in Senegal, The Gambia,
    Sierra Leone, Cameroon and Malawi: Prefeasibility Study
    for Providing Assistance. Washington, D.C.: NANBPA.
    1977. 82p.
Nwigwe, Nkuku
    "Nchifua Kangkolo and the Co-Operative Movement." Africa
    Women. #21 1979. pp. 39-40.
Okafor, Theresa I.
    A Case Study on the Role of Massaka Village Women in the
    Development of Massaka Village--Consequences of
    Income-Earning Activities and Participati on in Local
    Organizations. Buea, Cameroon: Regional Pan African
    Institute for Development/West Africa. 1980. 32p.
Ouden, J.H.B. den
    "Incorporation and Changes in the Composite Household:
    The Effects of Coffee Introduction and Food Crop
    Commercialization in Two Bamileke Chiefdoms, Cameroon."
    (In) Presvelou, C. and Spijkers-Zwart, S. (eds.). The
    Household, Women and Agricultural Development.
    Wageninger, Netherlands: H. Veenman En Zonen. 1980. pp.
    41-67.
U.S. Department of Commerce. Bureau of the Census
    Illustrative Statistics on Women in Development in
    Selected Developing Countries. Washington, D.C.: U.S.
    Department of Commerce. 1982. 24p.
Walker, Sheila S. and Brazier, Ellen
    "Women, Education and Rural Development in Cameroon: The
    Fulbe of the Garoua Region." African American Scholar.
    Volume 1 #5 June, 1977.
Zeryehoun, Tayye
    The Role of Rural Women in Development--A Case Study in
    Massaka Village. Buea, Cameroon: Regional Pan-African
    Institute for Development/West Africa. 1980. 21p.

DIVORCE

Lantum, Dan N.
    Fertility and Some Factors Affecting it: Divorce in
    Cameroon. Yaounde, Cameroon: University of Yaounde.
    1978. 11p.

ECONOMICS

Bryson Judy C.
    "Women and Agriculture in Sub-Saharan Africa:
    Implications for Development." Journal of Development
    Studies. Volume 17 #3 April, 1981. pp. 29-46.

Bryson, Judy C.
   Women and Economic Development in Cameroon. Washington,
   D.C.: U.S. Department of State. U.S. Agency for
   International Development. Office of Women in
   Development. January, 1979. 153p.
DeLancey, Mark W.
   "Women's Palm Oil Cooperatives, Fako Division, Cameroon:
   A Microstudy in the Problems of Development." Paper
   Presented at the Annual Meeting of the African Studies
   Association. Paper #24. Washington, D.C. November 4-7,
   1982.
DeLancey, Virginia H.
   "Women at the Cameroon Development Corporation: How Their
   Money Works: A Study of Small-Scale Accumulation of
   Capital by Women in Cameroon." Paper Presented at the
   Annual Meeting of the African Studies Association. Paper
   #20. Houston, Texas. 1977. 23p.
Endeley, J.B.
   "Agricultural Extension and the Economic Development of
   Women: Case Study of Cameroon." Paper Presented at the
   Workshop on the Role of Women and Home Economics in Rural
   Development in Africa. Rome: United Nations Food and
   Agriculture Organization. Alexandria, Egypt. October
   17, 1983. 8p.
Guyer, Jane I.
   "Female Farming and the Evolution of Food Production
   Patterns Amongst the Beti of South-Central Cameroon."
   Africa. Volume 50 #4 1980. pp. 341-356.
Guyer, Jane I.
   "Food, Cocoa, and the Division of Labour by Sex in Two
   West African Societies." Comparative Studies in Society
   and History. Volume 22 #3 July, 1980. pp. 355-370.
Guyer, Jane I.
   Household Budgets and Women's Incomes. Brookline,
   Massachusetts: Boston University. African Studies
   Center. Working Papers #28. 1980. 24p.
Guyer, Jane I.
   "The Economic Position of Beti Widows, Past and Present."
   (In) Barbier, J.C. and Moutome, J. (eds.). Femmes Du
   Cameroun: Meres Pacifiques Femmes Rebelles. Paris:
   Karthala. 1985.
Guyer, Jane I.
   The Economic Position of Beti Widows: Past and Present.
   Boston: Boston University. African Studies Center.
   Working Paper #22. 1979. 19p.
Guyer, Jane I.
   The Women's Farming System, the Lekie Southern Cameroon.
   Yaounde, Cameroon: ENSA (National Advanced School of
   Agriculture Library). 1977.
Guyer, Jane I.
   "Women in the Rural Economy: Contemporary Variations."
   (In) Hay, Margaret J. and Stichter, Sharon (eds.).

African Women South of the Sahara. New York: Longman.
1984. pp. 19-32.
Henn, Jeanne K.
"Peasants, State and Capital: The Political Economy of
Rural Incomes in Cameroon." Ph.D Dissertation: Harvard
University. Cambridge, Massachusetts. 1978. 396p.
Ifeanyichikwu Okafor, Theresa
The Role of Women in Village Developmemt: Income Earning
and Participation in Massaka, S.W. Cameroon. Buea,
Cameroon: Regional Pan African Institute for
Development/West Africa. 1981. 33p.
Jamanka, Mamadou B.
Ekona Mbenge Women's Role in Development: Case Study
Report. Buea, Cameroon: Regional Pan-African Institute
for Development/West Africa. 1980. 39p.
Jones, Christine W.
"The Mobilization of Women's Labor for Cash Crop
Production: A Game Theoretic Approach to Rice Production
in North Cameroon." American Journal of Agricultural
Economics. Volume 65 December, 1983. pp. 1049-1054.
Jones, Christine W.
"The Mobilization of Women's Labor for Cash Crop
Production: A Game Theoretical Approach." Ph.D
Dissertation: Harvard University. Cambridge,
Massachusetts. 1983. 194p.
Jones, Christine W.
"Women's Labour Allocation and Irrigated Rice Production
in North Cameroon." Paper Presented for the
International Association of Agricultural Economists.
Jakarta, Indonesia. August, 1982.
Kibuka, E.P.
Evaluation of Community Development: Women's Work in the
South West and North West Provinces of the United
Republic of Cameroon. Geneva: International Labour
Organization. Pan African Institute for Development.
1979. 68p.
Koenig, Dolores B.
"Why Women Migrate, Agricultural Workers in Africa."
Paper Presented at the Annual Meeting of the American
Anthropological Association. Washington, D.C. November
21, 1976.
Mutinta, Barnabas M.
Women in Development: A Case Study of Women in
Development in Mofako Bekondo New Town. Buea, Cameroon:
Regional Pan-African Institute for Development/West
Africa. 1980. 38p.
National Asso. of Negro Business and Prof. Women's Clubs
African Women Small Entrepreneurs in Senegal, The Gambia,
Sierra Leone, Cameroon and Malawi: Prefeasibility Study
for Providing Assistance. Washington, D.C.: NANBPA.
1977. 82p.
Okafor, Theresa I.
A Case Study on the Role of Massaka Village Women in the

Development of Massaka Village--Consequences of
Income-Earning Activities and Participati on in Local
Organizations. Buea, Cameroon: Regional Pan African
Institute for Development/West Africa. 1980. 32p.
Ouden, J.H.B. den
"Incorporation and Changes in the Composite Household:
The Effects of Coffee Introduction and Food Crop
Commercialization in Two Bamileke Chiefdoms, Cameroon."
(In) Presvelou, C. and Spijkers-Zwart, S. (eds.). The
Household, Women and Agricultural Development.
Wageninger, Netherlands: H. Veenman En Zonen. 1980. pp.
41-67.
Walker, Sheila S. and Brazier, Ellen
"Women, Education and Rural Development in Cameroon: The
Fulbe of the Garoua Region." African American Scholar.
Volume 1 #5 June, 1977.
Zeryehoun, Tayye
The Role of Rural Women in Development--A Case Study in
Massaka Village. Buea, Cameroon: Regional Pan-African
Institute for Development/West Africa. 1980. 21p.

EDUCATION AND TRAINING

Cooksey, B.
"Education and Sexual Inequality in Cameroon." Journal
of Modern African Studies. Volume 20 #1 March, 1982.
pp. 167-177.
Endeley, J.B.
"Agricultural Extension and the Economic Development of
Women: Case Study of Cameroon." Paper Presented at the
Workshop on the Role of Women and Home Economics in Rural
Development in Africa. Rome: United Nations Food and
Agriculture Organization. Alexandria, Egypt. October
17, 1983. 8p.
Martin, Jean Y.
"Unequal Access to School Education in Northern
Cameroon." African Environment. #14-16 1980. pp.
61-88.
Walker, Sheila S. and Brazier, Ellen
"Women, Education and Rural Development in Cameroon: The
Fulbe of the Garoua Region." African American Scholar.
Volume 1 #5 June, 1977.

EMPLOYMENT AND LABOR

Bryson Judy C.
"Women and Agriculture in Sub-Saharan Africa:
Implications for Development." Journal of Development
Studies. Volume 17 #3 April, 1981. pp. 29-46.

DeLancey, Virginia H.
"The Relationship Between Female Labor Force
Participation and Fertility: Compatibility of Roles on a
Cameroon Plantation." Paper Presented at the Annual
Meeting of the African Studies Association. Paper #21.
Baltimore, Maryland. 1978. 20p.
DeLancey, Virginia H.
"The Relationship Between Female Wage Employment and
Fertility in Africa: An Example From Cameroon." Ph.D
Dissertation: University of South Carolina. Columbia,
South Carolina. 1980. 393p.
Endeley, J.B.
"Agricultural Extension and the Economic Development of
Women: Case Study of Cameroon." Paper Presented at the
Workshop on the Role of Women and Home Economics in Rural
Development in Africa. Rome: United Nations Food and
Agriculture Organization. Alexandria, Egypt. October
17, 1983. 8p.
Ferguson, Anne and Horn, Nancy
Resource Guide: Women in Agriculture in the Cameroons.
East Lansing, Michigan: Bean/Cowpea CRSP (Collaborative
Research Support Program). 1984.
Guyer, Jane I.
"Food, Cocoa, and the Division of Labour by Sex in Two
West African Societies." Comparative Studies in Society
and History. Volume 22 #3 July, 1980. pp. 355-370.
Guyer, Jane I.
Household Budgets and Women's Incomes. Brookline,
Massachusetts: Boston University. African Studies
Center. Working Papers #28. 1980. 24p.
Guyer, Jane I.
The Women's Farming System, the Lekie Southern Cameroon.
Yaounde, Cameroon: ENSA (National Advanced School of
Agriculture Library). 1977.
Guyer, Jane I.
"Women in the Rural Economy: Contemporary Variations."
(In) Hay, Margaret J. and Stichter, Sharon (eds.).
African Women South of the Sahara. New York: Longman.
1984. pp. 19-32.
Jamanka, Mamadou B.
Ekona Mbenge Women's Role in Development: Case Study
Report. Buea, Cameroon: Regional Pan-African Institute
for Development/West Africa. 1980. 39p.
Jones, C.
"Women's Labour Allocation and Irrigated Rice Production
in North Cameroon." (In) Greenshields, B.L. and Bellamy,
M.A. (eds.). Rural Development:Growth and Inequity.
London: Aldershot, Gower. 1983. pp.172-177.
Jones, Christine W.
"The Mobilization of Women's Labor for Cash Crop
Production: A Game Theoretic Approach to Rice Production
in North Cameroon." American Journal of Agricultural
Economics. Volume 65 December, 1983. pp. 1049-1054.

Jones, Christine W.
  "The Mobilization of Women's Labor for Cash Crop
  Production: A Game Theoretical Approach." Ph.D
  Dissertation: Harvard University. Cambridge,
  Massachusetts. 1983. 194p.
Jones, Christine W.
  "Women's Labour Allocation and Irrigated Rice Production
  in North Cameroon." Paper Presented for the
  International Association of Agricultural Economists.
  Jakarta, Indonesia. August, 1982.
Kibuka, E.P.
  Evaluation of Community Development: Women's Work in the
  South West and North West Provinces of the United
  Republic of Cameroon. Geneva: International Labour
  Organization. Pan African Institute for Development.
  1979. 68p.
King-Akerele, Olubanke
  Traditional Palm Oil Processing: Women's Role and the
  Applications of Appropriate Technology: Ivory Coast,
  Sierra Leone, Cameroons. Addis Ababa, Ethiopia: United
  Nations Economic Commission for Africa. African Training
  and Research Center for Women. 1983. 52p.
Koenig, Dolores B.
  "Sex, Work and Social Class in Cameroon." Ph.D
  Dissertation: Northwestern University. Evanston,
  Illinois. August, 1977. 359p.
Koenig, Dolores B.
  "Why Women Migrate, Agricultural Workers in Africa."
  Paper Presented at the Annual Meeting of the American
  Anthropological Association. Washington, D.C. November
  21, 1976.
Ouden, J.H.B. den
  "Incorporation and Changes in the Composite Household:
  The Effects of Coffee Introduction and Food Crop
  Commercialization in Two Bamileke Chiefdoms, Cameroon."
  (In) Presvelou, C. and Spijkers-Zwart, S. (eds.). The
  Household, Women and Agricultural Development.
  Wageninger, Netherlands: H. Veenman En Zonen. 1980. pp.
  41-67.

EQUALITY AND LIBERATION

Smith, Robert P.
  "Mongo Beti: The Novelist Looks at Independence and the
  Status of African Women." CLA Journal. Volume 19
  March, 1976. pp. 301-311.

FAMILY LIFE

Guyer, Jane I.
  Family and Farm in Southern Cameroon. Boston: Boston

University. African Studies Center. African Research
Studies #15. 1984. 154p.
Koenig, Dolores B.
"Why Women Migrate, Agricultural Workers in Africa."
Paper Presented at the Annual Meeting of the American
Anthropological Association. Washington, D.C. November
21, 1976.
Ouden, J.H.B. den
"Incorporation and Changes in the Composite Household:
The Effects of Coffee Introduction and Food Crop
Commercialization in Two Bamileke Chiefdoms, Cameroon."
(In) Presvelou, C. and Spijkers-Zwart, S. (eds.). The
Household, Women and Agricultural Development.
Wageninger, Netherlands: H. Veenman En Zonen. 1980. pp.
41-67.
Weekes-Vagliani, Winifred and Bekombo-Priso, Manga
Family Life and Structure in Southern Cameroon. Paris:
Organization of Economic Cooperation and Development.
Development Centre. Technical Papers. 1976. 87p.

FAMILY PLANNING AND CONTRACEPTION

Clignet, Remi and Sween, Joyce A.
Plural Marriage and Family Planning in West Cameroon.
Washinton, D.C.: U.S. Department of State. Foreign
Affairs Research Documentation Center. 1978. 76p.
David, N. and Voas, David
"Societal Causes of Infertility and Population Decline
Among the Settled Fulani of North Cameroon." Man.
Volume 16 #4 December, 1981. pp. 644-664.
DeLancey, Virginia H.
"The Relationship Between Female Wage Employment and
Fertility in Africa: An Example From Cameroon." Ph.D
Dissertation: University of South Carolina. Columbia,
South Carolina. 1980. 393p.
Ebot, Moses T.
"Effects of Access to Social Services on Differential
Fertility in Three Types of Agriculture." Ph.D
Dissertation: University of Iowa. Iowa City, Iowa.
1978. 248p.
Gwan Achu, Emmanuel
"Origins and Elements of the Population Policies of the
Cameroon Republic." Science and Technology Review:
Social Sciences Series. Volume 3 #1/2 January-June,
1985. pp. 116-128.
Lee, Bun S.
Fertility Adaptations by Rural-Urban Migrants in
Cameroon. Omaha, Nebraska: University of Nebraska-Omaha.
Department of Economics, College of Business. 1985.
Lesthaeghe, Ron J. and Eelens, Frank
Social Organization and Reproductive Regimes: Lessons
From Sub-Saharan Africa and Historical Western Europe.

Brussels, Belgium: Vrije Universiteit Brussel.
Interuniversity Programme in Demography. IDP Working
Paper #1985-1. 1985. 64p.
Mitchell, Joseph R. and Helfenbein, Saul
Project Design for a Reproductive Health Program in
Cameroon. Washington, D.C.: American Public Health
Association. 1978. 111p.
Sween, Joyce A. and Clignet, Remi
"Historical Changes in the Influence of the Status of
Women on Fertility--West Cameroon." Paper Presented at
the Meeting of the International Sociological
Association. Uppsala, Sweden. August, 1978.
Weekes-Vagliani, Winifred
"Some Explanations of High Fertility Among Rural Women in
Southern Cameroon." (In) Caldwell, John C. (ed.). The
Persistence of High Fertility: Population Prospects in
the Third World. Canberra, Australia: Australian
National University. Department of Demography. Volume
One. 1977. pp. 451-468.

FERTILITY AND INFERTILITY

Clignet, Remi and Sween, Joyce A.
"Interaction Between Historical and Sociological Times in
the Analysis of Fertility in West Cameroon." Paper
Presented at the 15th Annual Seminar on Family Research.
Lome, Togo. January, 1976.
David, N. and Voas, David
"Societal Causes of Infertility and Population Decline
Among the Settled Fulani of North Cameroon." Man.
Volume 16 #4 December, 1981. pp. 644-664.
DeLancey, Virginia H.
"The Relationship Between Female Labor Force
Participation and Fertility: Compatibility of Roles on a
Cameroon Plantation." Paper Presented at the Annual
Meeting of the African Studies Association. Paper #21.
Baltimore, Maryland. 1978. 20p.
DeLancey, Virginia H.
"The Relationship Between Female Wage Employment and
Fertility in Africa: An Example From Cameroon." Ph.D
Dissertation: University of South Carolina. Columbia,
South Carolina. 1980. 393p.
Ebot, Moses T.
"Effects of Access to Social Services on Differential
Fertility in Three Types of Agriculture." Ph.D
Dissertation: University of Iowa. Iowa City, Iowa.
1978. 248p.
Eelens, Frank and Donne, L.
The Proximate Determinants of Fertility in Sub-Saharan
Africa: A Factbook Based on the Results of the World
Fertility Survey. Brussels, Belgium: Vrije Universiteit

Brussel. Interuniversity Programme in Demography. IDP
Working Paper #1985-3. 1985. 122p.

International Statistical Institute (ISI)
The Cameroon Fertility Survey, 1978: A Summary of
Findings. Voorburg, Netherlands: ISI. World Fertility
Survey Report #41. October, 1983. 14p.

Lantum, Dan N.
Fertility and Some Factors Affecting it: Divorce in
Cameroon. Yaounde, Cameroon: University of Yaounde.
1978. 11p.

Larsen, Ulla
A Comparative Study of the Levels and the Covariates of
Sterility in Cameroon, Kenya and Sudan. Princeton, New
Jersey: Princeton University. Office of Population
Research. 1985.

Lee, Bun S.
Fertility Adaptations by Rural-Urban Migrants in
Cameroon. Omaha, Nebraska: University of Nebraska-Omaha.
Department of Economics, College of Business. 1985.

Lesthaeghe, Ron J. and Eelens, Frank
Social Organization and Reproductive Regimes: Lessons
From Sub-Saharan Africa and Historical Western Europe.
Brussels, Belgium: Vrije Universiteit Brussel.
Interuniversity Programme in Demography. IDP Working
Paper #1985-1. 1985. 64p.

Nasah, B.T.
"Aetiology of Infertility in Cameroon." Nigerian Medical
Journal. Volume 9 #5/6 May-June, 1979. pp. 601-605.

Sween, Joyce A. and Clignet, Remi
"Female Matrimonial Roles and Fertility in Africa." (In)
Oppong, C. and Adaba, G. and Bekombo-Priso, M. and Mogey,
J. (eds.). Marriage, Fertility and Parenthood in West
Africa. Canberra, Australia: Australian National
University. Department of Demography. Volume Two.
1978. pp. 565-600.

Sween, Joyce A. and Clignet, Remi
"Historical Changes in the Influence of the Status of
Women on Fertility--West Cameroon." Paper Presented at
the Meeting of the International Sociological
Association. Uppsala, Sweden. August, 1978.

Weekes-Vagliani, Winifred
"Some Explanations of High Fertility Among Rural Women in
Southern Cameroon." (In) Caldwell, John C. (ed.). The
Persistence of High Fertility: Population Prospects in
the Third World. Canberra, Australia: Australian
National University. Department of Demography. Volume
One. 1977. pp. 451-468.

HEALTH, NUTRITION AND MEDICINE

Clignet, Remi and Sween, Joyce A.
"Interaction Between Historical and Sociological Times in

the Analysis of Fertility in West Cameroon." Paper
Presented at the 15th Annual Seminar on Family Research.
Lome, Togo. January, 1976.
Ebot, Moses T.
"Effects of Access to Social Services on Differential
Fertility in Three Types of Agriculture." Ph.D
Dissertation: University of Iowa. Iowa City, Iowa.
1978. 248p.
Guimera, L.M.
"Witchcraft Illness in the Evuzok Nosological System."
Culture, Medicine and Psychiatry. Volume 2 #4 December,
1978. pp. 373-396.
Gwan Achu, Emmanuel
"Origins and Elements of the Population Policies of the
Cameroon Republic." Science and Technology Review:
Social Sciences Series. Volume 3 #1/2 January-June,
1985. pp. 116-128.
Lantum, Dan N.
Fertility and Some Factors Affecting it: Divorce in
Cameroon. Yaounde, Cameroon: University of Yaounde.
1978. 11p.
Larsen, Ulla
A Comparative Study of the Levels and the Covariates of
Sterility in Cameroon, Kenya and Sudan. Princeton, New
Jersey: Princeton University. Office of Population
Research. 1985.
Mitchell, Joseph R. and Helfenbein, Saul
Project Design for a Reproductive Health Program in
Cameroon. Washington, D.C.: American Public Health
Association. 1978. 111p.
Nasah, B.T.
"Aetiology of Infertility in Cameroon." Nigerian Medical
Journal. Volume 9 #5/6 May-June, 1979. pp. 601-605.

HISTORY

Sweet, Joyce A. and Clignet, Remi
"Historical Changes in the Influence of the Status of
Women on Fertility--West Cameroon." Paper Presented at
the Meeting of the International Sociological
Association. Uppsala, Sweden. August, 1978.

LAW AND LEGAL ISSUES

Zollner, Joy
"Women's Rights in Africa and the United States." Africa
Report. Volume 22 #1 January-February, 1977. pp. 6-9.

LITERATURE

Smith, Robert P.
"Mongo Beti: The Novelist Looks at Independence and the
Status of African Women." CLA Journal. Volume 19
March, 1976. pp. 301-311.
Tala, Kashim I.
"Some Images of Women in Cameroon Fiction." New
Horizons. Volume 3 #1 1983. pp. 1-14.

MARITAL RELATIONS AND NUPTIALITY

Clignet, Remi and Sween, Joyce A.
Plural Marriage and Family Planning in West Cameroon.
Washinton, D.C.: U.S. Department of State. Foreign
Affairs Research Documentation Center. 1978. 76p.
David, N. and Voas, David
"Societal Causes of Infertility and Population Decline
Among the Settled Fulani of North Cameroon." Man.
Volume 16 #4 December, 1981. pp. 644-664.
Lantum, Dan N.
Fertility and Some Factors Affecting it: Divorce in
Cameroon. Yaounde, Cameroon: University of Yaounde.
1978. 11p.
Lee, Bun S.
Fertility Adaptations by Rural-Urban Migrants in
Cameroon. Omaha, Nebraska: University of Nebraska-Omaha.
Department of Economics, College of Business. 1985.
Sween, Joyce A. and Clignet, Remi
"Female Matrimonial Roles and Fertility in Africa." (In)
Oppong, C. and Adaba, G. and Bekombo-Priso, M. and Mogey,
J. (eds.). Marriage, Fertility and Parenthood in West
Africa. Canberra, Australia: Australian National
University. Department of Demography. Volume Two.
1978. pp. 565-600.

MIGRATION

Koenig, Dolores B.
"Why Women Migrate, Agricultural Workers in Africa."
Paper Presented at the Annual Meeting of the American
Anthropological Association. Washington, D.C. November
21, 1976.
Lee, Bun S.
Fertility Adaptations by Rural-Urban Migrants in
Cameroon. Omaha, Nebraska: University of Nebraska-Omaha.
Department of Economics, College of Business. 1985.

MISCELLANEOUS

Mbinde, T.N.
   A Survey of Prostitutes in Victoria Town, South West
   Province. Buea, Cameroon. 1976. 31p.

ORGANIZATIONS

DeLancey, Mark W.
   "Women's Palm Oil Cooperatives, Fako Division, Cameroon:
   A Microstudy in the Problems of Development." Paper
   Presented at the Annual Meeting of the African Studies
   Association. Paper #24. Washington, D.C. November 4-7,
   1982.
DeLancey, Virginia H.
   "Women at the Cameroon Development Corporation: How Their
   Money Works: A Study of Small-Scale Accumulation of
   Capital by Women in Cameroon." Paper Presented at the
   Annual Meeting of the African Studies Association. Paper
   #20. Houston, Texas. 1977. 23p.
Nwigwe, Nkuku
   "Nchifua Kangkolo and the Co-Operative Movement." Africa
   Women. #21 1979. pp. 39-40.
Okafor, Theresa I.
   A Case Study on the Role of Massaka Village Women in the
   Development of Massaka Village--Consequences of
   Income-Earning Activities and Participati on in Local
   Organizations. Buea, Cameroon: Regional Pan African
   Institute for Development/West Africa. 1980. 32p.

POLITICS AND GOVERNMENT

Gwan Achu, Emmanuel
   "Origins and Elements of the Population Policies of the
   Cameroon Republic." Science and Technology Review:
   Social Sciences Series. Volume 3 #1/2 January-June,
   1985. pp. 116-128.
Henn, Jeanne K.
   "Peasants, State and Capital: The Political Economy of
   Rural Incomes in Cameroon." Ph.D Dissertation: Harvard
   University. Cambridge, Massachusetts. 1978. 396p.

RELIGION AND WITCHCRAFT

Guimera, L.M.
   "Witchcraft Illness in the Evuzok Nosological System."
   Culture, Medicine and Psychiatry. Volume 2 #4 December,
   1978. pp. 373-396.
Zoe-Obianga, Rose
   "The Role of Women in Present Day Africa." (In)

Appiah-Kubi, Kofi and Torres, Sergio (eds.). African
Theology en Route: Papers From the Pan-African Conference
of Third World Theologians, December 17-23, 1977, Accra,
Ghana. Maryknoll, New York: Orbis Books. 1979. pp.
145-149.

RESEARCH

Ferguson, Anne and Horn, Nancy
    Resource Guide: Women in Agriculture in the Cameroons.
    East Lansing, Michigan: Bean/Cowpea CRSP (Collaborative
    Research Support Program). 1984.
U.S. Department of Commerce. Bureau of the Census
    Illustrative Statistics on Women in Development in
    Selected Developing Countries. Washington, D.C.: U.S.
    Department of Commerce. 1982. 24p.

SEX ROLES

Bryson Judy C.
    "Women and Agriculture in Sub-Saharan Africa:
    Implications for Development." Journal of Development
    Studies. Volume 17 #3 April, 1981. pp. 29-46.
Clignet, Remi
    "Social Change and Sexual Differentiation in the Cameroon
    and the Ivory Coast." Signs. Volume 3 #1 Autumn, 1977.
    pp. 244-266.
Clignet, Remi
    "Social Change and Sexual Differentiation in the Cameroon
    and the Ivory Coast." (In) Wellesley Editorial
    Committee. Women in National Development. Chicago:
    University of Chicago Press. 1977. pp. 244-260.
Guyer, Jane I.
    "Female Farming and the Evolution of Food Production
    Patterns Amongst the Beti of South-Central Cameroon."
    Africa. Volume 50 #4 1980. pp. 341-356.
Guyer, Jane I.
    "Food, Cocoa, and the Division of Labour by Sex in Two
    West African Societies." Comparative Studies in Society
    and History. Volume 22 #3 July, 1980. pp. 355-370.
Jones, C.
    "Women's Labour Allocation and Irrigated Rice Production
    in North Cameroon." (In) Greenshields, B.L. and Bellamy,
    M.A. (eds.). Rural Development:Growth and Inequity.
    London: Aldershot, Gower. 1983. pp.172-177.
Koenig, Dolores B.
    "Sex, Work and Social Class in Cameroon." Ph.D
    Dissertation: Northwestern University. Evanston,
    Illinois. August, 1977. 359p.
Mbinde, T.N.
    A Survey of Prostitutes in Victoria Town, South West
    Province. Buea, Cameroon. 1976. 31p.

Ouden, J.H.B. den
  "Incorporation and Changes in the Composite Household:
  The Effects of Coffee Introduction and Food Crop
  Commercialization in Two Bamileke Chiefdoms, Cameroon."
  (In) Presvelou, C. and Spijkers-Zwart, S. (eds.). The
  Household, Women and Agricultural Development.
  Wageninger, Netherlands: H. Veenman En Zonen. 1980. pp.
  41-67.
Sween, Joyce A. and Clignet, Remi
  "Female Matrimonial Roles and Fertility in Africa." (In)
  Oppong, C. and Adaba, G. and Bekombo-Priso, M. and Mogey,
  J. (eds.). Marriage, Fertility and Parenthood in West
  Africa. Canberra, Australia: Australian National
  University. Department of Demography. Volume Two.
  1978. pp. 565-600.
Walker, Sheila S.
  "From Cattle Camp to City: Changing Roles of Fulbe Women
  in Northern Cameroon." Journal of African Studies.
  Volme 7 Spring, 1980. pp. 54-69.

STATUS OF WOMEN

Clignet, Remi
  "Social Change and Sexual Differentiation in the Cameroon
  and the Ivory Coast." Signs. Volume 3 #1 Autumn, 1977.
  pp. 244-266.
Smith, Robert P.
  "Mongo Beti: The Novelist Looks at Independence and the
  Status of African Women." CLA Journal. Volume 19
  March, 1976. pp. 301-311.
Sween, Joyce A. and Clignet, Remi
  "Historical Changes in the Influence of the Status of
  Women on Fertility--West Cameroon." Paper Presented at
  the Meeting of the International Sociological
  Association. Uppsala, Sweden. August, 1978.

URBANIZATION

Lee, Bun S.
  Fertility Adaptations by Rural-Urban Migrants in
  Cameroon. Omaha, Nebraska: University of Nebraska-Omaha.
  Department of Economics, College of Business. 1985.

Central African Republic

NO CITATIONS

Congo

South West Africa People's Organization (SWAPO)
    Study Tours of Namibian Women to Mozambique and the Congo
    and the SWAPO Women's Council Workshop: Namibia. Paris:
    United Nations Educational, Scientific and Cultural
    Organization. Lusaka, Zambia. November 26, 1981. 34p.

Equatorial Guinea

Wingert, Peter
"Under a Tropical Sun: Women and the Old Traditions in
Equatorial Guinea." Other Side. #159 December, 1984.
pp. 14-17.

Gabon

NO CITATIONS

Rwanda

Boyton, W.H.
    A Report on Assistance to Develop a National Maternal and
    Child Healt and Family Planning Program in Rwanda.
    Washington D.C.: American Public Health Association.
    1981. 234p.
Lepage, Philippe and Munyakazi, Christophe and Hennart,
Philippe
    "Breastfeeding and Hospital Mortality in Children in
    Rwanda." Lancet. #8243 August 22, 1981. pp. 409-411.
Ueda, Fiyuiko
    "Ukvu Ritual: Death and Sexuality Among the Kambu."
    Senri Ethnological Studies. #15 1984. pp. 109-129.
United Nations
    Rural Women's Participation in Development. New York:
    United Nations. Development Programme. Evaluation Study
    #3. June, 1980. 226p.
United Nations Food and Agriculture Organization (FAO)
    Profile of Women in Agriculture and Rural Development in
    Rwanda. Rome: United Nations FAO. Home Economics and
    Social Programmes Service. June, 1979. 26p.
Vandersypen, M.
    "Free Women in Kigali." Cahiers d'Etudes Africaines.
    Volume 17 #1 1977. pp. 95-120.

Sao Tome

Silva, Andrade E.
"Women in the Cape Verde Islands: The National Liberation
Struggle, National Reconstruction and Prospects." Paper
Presented at the Meeting of Experts on the History of
Women's Contribution to National Liberation Struggles and
Their Roles and Needs During Reconstruction in Newly
Independent Countries in Africa. Paris: United Nations
Educational, Scientific andCultural Organization.
Bissau, Guinea-Bissau. 1983. 21p.

Zaire

AGRICULTURE

Barnes, Virginia L.
  Changes in Crop Mixtures and Their Relationship to Gender
  Role Changes Among the Lugbara. Cambridge,
  Massachusetts: Harvard University. Joint Harvard/MIT
  Group. Working Paper #2. 1984.
Blain, Daniele
  "A Farming System for Women: The Case of Cassava
  Production in Zaire." Ceres. Volume 18 May-June, 1985.
  pp. 43-46.
Klingshirn, A.
  Investment of Women in Co-Operatives in Zaire and Ghana.
  Rome: United Nations Food and Agriculture Organization.
  UNFPA/FAO Study. 1978.
Mitchnik, David A.
  The Role of Women in Rural Zaire and Upper Volta:
  Improving Methods of Skill Acquisition. Oxford, England:
  OXFAM. OXFAM Working Paper #2. 1978. 36p.
Peacock, Nadine R.
  "The Mbuti of Northeast Zaire: Women and Subsistence
  Exchange." Cultural Survival Quarterly. Volume 8 #2
  Summer, 1984. pp. 15-17.
Wilson, Francille R.
  "Reinventing the Past and Circumscribing the Future:
  Authenticite' and the Negative Image of Women's Work in
  Zaire." (In) Bay, Edna G. (ed.). Women and Work in
  Africa. Boulder, Colorado: Westview Press. Westview
  Special Studies in Africa. 1982. pp. 153-170.

CULTURAL ROLES

Adams, Lois
    "Women in Zaire: Disparate Status and Roles." (In)
    Lindsay, Beverly (ed.). Comparative Perspectives of
    Third World Women: The Impact of Race, Sex and Class.
    New York: Praeger Publishers. 1980. pp. 55-77.
Anderson, Barbara A. and McCabe, James L.
    Nutrition and the Fertility of Younger Women in Kinshasa,
    Zaire. New Haven, Connecticut: Yale University Press.
    Economic Growth Center. Center Discussion Paper #248.
    May, 1976. 22p.
Anderson, Barbara A. and McCabe, James L.
    "Nutrition and the Fertility of Younger Women in
    Kinshasa, Zaire." Journal of Development Economics.
    Volume 4 #4 December, 1977. pp. 343-364.
Barnes, Virginia L.
    Changes in Crop Mixtures and Their Relationship to Gender
    Role Changes Among the Lugbara. Cambridge,
    Massachusetts: Harvard University. Joint Harvard/MIT
    Group. Working Paper #2. 1984.
Bertrand, Jane T. and Mangani, Nlandu and Mansilu, Matondo
and Landry, Evelyn
    "Factors Influencing the Use of Traditional Versus Modern
    Family Planning Methods in Bas Zaire." Studies in Family
    Planning. Volume 16 #6 Part One November-December,
    1985. pp. 332-341.
Bertrand, Jane T. and Mangani, Nlandu and Mansilu, Matondo
    "The Acceptability of Household Distribution of
    Contraceptives in Zaire." International Family Planning
    Perspectives. Volume 10 #1 March, 1984. pp. 21-26.
Bertrand, Jane T. and Bertrand, W.E. and Malonga, Miatudila
    "The Use of Traditional and Modern Methods of Fertility
    Control in Kinshasa, Zaire." Population Studies. Volume
    37 #1 March, 1983. pp. 129-136.
Blain, Daniele
    "A Farming System for Women: The Case of Cassava
    Production in Zaire." Ceres. Volume 18 May-June, 1985.
    pp. 43-46.
Broadhead, Susan H.
    "Slave Wives, Free Sisters: Bakongo Women and Slavery c.
    1700-1850." (In) Robertson, Claire C. and Klein, Martin
    A. (eds.). Women and Slavery in Africa. Madison,
    Wisconsin: University of Wisconsin Press. 1983. pp.
    160-181.
Brown, Judith E. and Brown, Richard C.
    "Characteristics of Contraceptive Acceptors in Rural
    Zaire." Studies in Family Planning. Volume 11 #12
    December, 1980. pp. 378-384.
Carael, M.
    "Child-Spacing, Ecology and Nutrition in the Kivu
    Province of Zaire." (In) Page, Hilary J. and Lesthaeghe,
    Ron (eds.). Child-Spacing in Tropical Africa: Traditions

and Change. New York: Academic Press. 1981. pp.
275-286.

Carael, M. and Stanbury, John B.
"Promotion of Birth Spacing on Idjwi Island, Zaire."
Studies in Family Planning. Volume 14 #5 May, 1983.
pp. 134-142.

Carael, M.
"Relations Between Birth Intervals and Nutrition in Three
Central African Populations." (In) Mosley, W.H. (ed.).
Nutrition and Human Reproduction. New York: Plenum
Press. 1978. pp. 365-384.

Cavalli-Sforza, L.L.
"Exploration and Mating Range in African Pygmies."
Annals of Human Genetics. Volume 46 Part 3 July, 1982.
pp. 257-270.

Diakanda, M. Sala and Ngondo, A. Pitshandenge and Tabutin,
Dominique and Vilquin, E.
"Fertility and Child-Spacing in Western Zaire." (In)
Page, Hilary J. and Lesthaeghe, Ron (eds.).
Child-Spacing in Tropical Africa: Traditions and Change.
New York: Academic Press. 1981. pp. 287-299.

Erasto, Muga
Studies in Prostitution: East, West and South Africa,
Zaire and Nevada. Nairobi: Kenya Literature Bureau.
1980.

Fabian, Johannes
"Man and Woman in the Teachings of the Jamaa Movement in
Shaba." Bulletin de Theologie Africaine. Volume 2 #4
July-December, 1980. pp. 257-276.

Fabian, Johannes
"Man and Women in the Teachings of the Jamaa Movement."
(In) Jules-Rosette, Bennetta (ed.). The New Religions of
Africa. Norwood, New Jersey: Ablex Publishing Corp.
1979. pp. 169-183.

Gould, Terri F.
"A New Class of Professional Zairian Women." African
Review. Volume 7 #3/4 1977. pp. 92-105.

Gould, Terri F.
"The Educated Woman in a Developing Country: Professional
Zairian Women in Lumumbashi." Ph.D Dissertation: Union
Graduate School. 1976.

Gould, Terri F.
"The Educated Women and Social Change: A Sociological
Study of Women Students at the National University of
Zaire." (In) University of Dar-es-Salaam. Papers in
Education and Development. Dar-es-Salaam, Tanzania:
University of Dar-es-Salaam. 1976.

Gould, Terri F.
"Value Conflict and Development: The Struggle of the
Professional Zairian Woman." Journal of Modern African
Studies. Volume 16 #1 March, 1978. pp. 133-140.

Harms, Robert
"Sustaining the System: Trading Towns Along the Middle

Zaire." (In) Robertson, Claire C. and Klein, Martin A. (eds.). Women and Slavery in Africa. Madison, Wisconsin: University of Wisconsin Press. 1983. pp. 95-110.

Hennart, Philippe and Vis, H.L.
"Breast-Feeding and Post Partum Amenorrhoea in Central Africa. One: Milk Production in Rural Areas." Journal of Tropical Pediatrics. Volume 26 #5 October, 1980. pp. 177-183.

Hennart, Philippe and Vis, H.L. and Ruchababisha, M.
"Breast-Feeding and Post-Partum Amenorrhoea in Central Africa." Journal of Tropical Pediatrics. Volume 29 #3 June, 1983. pp. 185-189.

Heymer, A.
"Bayaka Pygmies: Mother-Child Relationship and Behavior Patterns Between Small Children and Different Other Women Group Members." Homo. Volume 32 #2 1981. pp. 130-139.

Heymer, A.
"Bayaka Pygmies: Social Grooming in Women and Girls and Grooming Rivalry." Homo. Volume 30 #3 1979. pp. 196-202.

Hilton, Anne
"Family and Kinship Among the Kongo South of the Zaire River From the 16th to the 19th Centuries." Journal of African History. Volume 24 #2 1983. pp. 189-206.

Kerkhofs, Jan
"Religious Life for Women in Zaire." Pro Mundi Vita Dossier Africa. #14 May, 1980. pp. 1-31.

Lunganga, K.M. and Sarma, R.S.
"Infertility in Zaire." (In) Cairo Demographic Centre (CDC). Determinants of Fertility in Some African and Asian Countries. Cairo: CDC. CDC Research Monograph Series #10. 1982. pp. 375-390.

MacGaffey, Janet
"Class Relations in a Dependent Economy: Businessmen and Businesswomen in Kisangani, Zaire." Ph.D Dissertation: Bryn Mawr College. Bryn Mawr, Pennsylvania. 1981. 328p.

MacGaffey, Janet
"Class Relations in a Dependent Economy: Businessmen and Businesswomen in Kisangani, Zaire." Paper Presented at the Annual Meeting of the African Studies Association. Paper #82. Bloomington, Indiana. 1981.

MacGaffey, Janet
"The Effect of Rural-Urban Ties, Kinship and Marriage on Household Structure in a Kongo Village." Canadian Journal of African Studies. Volume 17 #1 1983. pp. 69-84.

McCabe, James L.
Differential Fertility and Infant Mortality in Urban Zaire. New Haven, Connecticut: Yale University Press. Economic Growth Center. 1977.

McFalls, Joseph A.
  "Population Subfecundity." Intercom. Volume 6 #4
  April, 1978. pp. 7-9.
Mitchnik, David A.
  The Role of Women in Rural Zaire and Upper Volta:
  Improving Methods of Skill Acquisition. Oxford, England:
  OXFAM. OXFAM Working Paper #2. 1978. 36p.
Mock, N.B. and Bertrand, Jane T. and Mangani, Nlandu
  Correlates and Implications of Breastfeeding Practices in
  Bas Zaire. New Orleans, Louisiana: Tulane University.
  Unpublished Manuscript. 1984.
Newbury, M. Catharine
  "Ebutumwa Bw'Emiogo: The Tyranny of Cassava: A Women's
  Tax Revolt in Eastern Zaire." Canadian Journal of
  African Studies. Volume 18 #1 1984. pp. 35-54.
Packard, Randall M.
  "Social Change and the History of Misfortune Among the
  Bashu of Eastern Zaire." (In) Karp, Ivan and Bird,
  Charles S. (eds.). Explorations in African Systems of
  Thought. Bloomington, Indiana: Indiana University Press.
  1980. pp. 237-267.
Pagezy, Helen
  "Attitude of Ntomba Society Towards the Primiparous Women
  and Its Biological Effects." Journal of Biosocial
  Science. Volume 15 #3 August, 1983. pp. 235-246.
Peacock, Nadine R.
  "The Mbuti of Northeast Zaire: Women and Subsistence
  Exchange." Cultural Survival Quarterly. Volume 8 #2
  Summer, 1984. pp. 15-17.
Peacock, Nadine R.
  "Time Allocation, Work and Fertility Among Efe Pygmy
  Women of Northeast Zaire." Ph.D Dissertation: Harvard
  University. Cambridge, Massachusetts. 1985. 210p.
Romaniuk, A.
  "Increase in Natural Fertility During the Early Stages of
  Modernization: Evidence From an African Case Study,
  Zaire." Population Studies. Volume 34 #2 July, 1980.
  pp. 292-310.
Sala-Diakanda, Mpembele and Pitshandenge, N.A. and Tabutin,
Dominique and Vilquin, E.
  "Fertility and Child-Spacing in Western Zaire." (In)
  Page, Hilary J. and Lesthaeghe, Ron (eds.).
  Child-Spacing in Tropical Africa. New York: Academic
  Press. 1981. 332p.
Sala-Diakanda, Mpembele and Lohle-Tart, Louis
  Social Science Research for Population Policy Design:
  Case Study of Zaire. Liege, Belgium: International Union
  for the Scientific Study of Population. IUSSP Paper #24.
  1982. 55p.
Schoepf, Brooke G.
  The 'Wild,' the 'Lazy' and the 'Matriarchal': Nutrition
  and Cultural Survival in the Zairian Copperbelt. East

Lansing, Michigan: Michigan State University. Women in
International Development. Working Paper #96.
September, 1985. 22p.

Seetharam, K.S. and Samba-Batumba, Nyuwa
"Selected Aspects of Household Structure and Marriage
Patterns in Kintambo, Kinshasa." (In) Huzayyin, S.A. and
Acsadi, G.T. (eds.). Family and Marriage in Some African
and Asiatic Countries. Cairo: Cairo Demographic Centre.
CDC Research Monograph Series #6. 1976. pp. 223-242.

Sosne, Elinor
"Of Biases and Queens: The Shi Past Through an
Androgynous Looking Glass." History in Africa. Volume 6
1979. pp. 225-252.

Turnbull, Colin M.
"Mbuti Womanhood." (In) Dahlberg, Frances (ed.). Woman
the Gatherer. New Haven, Connecticut: Yale University
Press. 1981. pp. 205-219.

Turnbull, Colin M.
"The Ritualization of Potential Conflict Between the
Sexes Among the Mbuti." (In) Leacock, Eleanor and Lee,
Richard. Politics and History in Band Societies.
Cambridge, England: Cambridge University Press. 1982.
pp. 133-155.

Voas, David
"Subfertility and Disruption in the Congo Basin." (In)
University of Edinburgh. African Historical Demography.
Edinburgh, Scotland: University of Edinburgh. Centre of
African Studies. 1981. pp. 777-802.

Waife, Ronald S.
Traditional Methods of Birth Control in Zaire. Chestnut
Hill, Massachusetts: Pathfinder Fund. Pathpapers #4.
December, 1978. 19p.

Wilson, Alton E.
An Assessment of Population/Family Planning Program
Activities in Zaire. Washington, D.C.: American Public
Health Association. 1979. 31p.

Wilson, Francille R.
"Reinventing the Past and Circumscribing the Future:
Authenticite' and the Negative Image of Women's Work in
Zaire." (In) Bay, Edna G. (ed.). Women and Work in
Africa. Boulder, Colorado: Westview Press. Westview
Special Studies in Africa. 1982. pp. 153-170.

Wrzesinska, Alicja
"Contemporaneousness of Young African Girls' Attitudes."
Africa. (Italy) Volume 36 #2 1981. pp. 183-208.

Wrzesinska, Alicja
"Women, the Family and Modernisation in Zaire." (In)
Bandt, Jacques De and M'andi, Peter. European Studies in
Development: New Trends in European Development Studies.
London: MacMillan. 1980. pp. 259-268.

Yates, Barbara A.
"Church, State and Education in Belgian Africa:
Implications for Contemporary Third World Women." (In)

Kelly, Gail P. and Elliott, Carolyn M. (eds.). Women's
Education in the Third World: Comparative Perspectives.
Albany, New York: State University of New York Press.
1982. pp. 127-151.
Yates, Barbara A.
"Colonialism, Education and Work: Sex Differentiation in
Colonial Zaire." (In) Bay, Edna G. (ed.). Women and
Work in Africa. Boulder, Colorado: Westview Press.
Westview Special Studies in Africa. 1982. pp. 127-152.
Yates, Barbara A.
"Sex Differences in Career Opportunities and Education in
the Belgian Congo." Paper Presented at the Meetings of
the American Educational Research Association. New
Orleans, Louisiana. 1978.

DEVELOPMENT AND TECHNOLOGY

Blain, Daniele
"A Farming System for Women: The Case of Cassava
Production in Zaire." Ceres. Volume 18 May-June, 1985.
pp. 43-46.
Gould, Terri F.
"Value Conflict and Development: The Struggle of the
Professional Zairian Woman." Journal of Modern African
Studies. Volume 16 #1 March, 1978. pp. 133-140.
Klingshirn, A.
Investment of Women in Co-Operatives in Zaire and Ghana.
Rome: United Nations Food and Agriculture Organization.
UNFPA/FAO Study. 1978.
MacGaffey, Janet
"Class Relations in a Dependent Economy: Businessmen and
Businesswomen in Kisangani, Zaire." Ph.D Dissertation:
Bryn Mawr College. Bryn Mawr, Pennsylvania. 1981.
328p.
MacGaffey, Janet
"Class Relations in a Dependent Economy: Businessmen and
Businesswomen in Kisangani, Zaire." Paper Presented at
the Annual Meeting of the African Studies Association.
Paper #82. Bloomington, Indiana. 1981.
Mitchnik, David A.
The Role of Women in Rural Zaire and Upper Volta:
Improving Methods of Skill Acquisition. Oxford, England:
OXFAM. OXFAM Working Paper #2. 1978. 36p.
Schoepf, Brooke G.
The 'Wild,' the 'Lazy' and the 'Matriarchal': Nutrition
and Cultural Survival in the Zairian Copperbelt. East
Lansing, Michigan: Michigan State University. Women in
International Development. Working Paper #96.
September, 1985. 22p.
Wrzesinska, Alicja
"Women, the Family and Modernisation in Zaire." (In)

Bandt, Jacques De and M'andi, Peter. European Studies in
Development: New Trends in European Development Studies.
London: MacMillan. 1980. pp. 259-268.

ECONOMICS

Blain, Daniele
    "A Farming System for Women: The Case of Cassava
    Production in Zaire." Ceres. Volume 18 May-June, 1985.
    pp. 43-46.
Gould, Terri F.
    "A New Class of Professional Zairian Women." African
    Review. Volume 7 #3/4 1977. pp. 92-105.
Gould, Terri F.
    "The Educated Woman in a Developing Country: Professional
    Zairian Women in Lumumbashi." Ph.D Dissertation: Union
    Graduate School. 1976.
Gould, Terri F.
    "Value Conflict and Development: The Struggle of the
    Professional Zairian Woman." Journal of Modern African
    Studies. Volume 16 #1 March, 1978. pp. 133-140.
Klingshirn, A.
    Investment of Women in Co-Operatives in Zaire and Ghana.
    Rome: United Nations Food and Agriculture Organization.
    UNFPA/FAO Study. 1978.
MacGaffey, Janet
    "Class Relations in a Dependent Economy: Businessmen and
    Businesswomen in Kisangani, Zaire." Ph.D Dissertation:
    Bryn Mawr College. Bryn Mawr, Pennsylvania. 1981.
    328p.
MacGaffey, Janet
    "Class Relations in a Dependent Economy: Businessmen and
    Businesswomen in Kisangani, Zaire." Paper Presented at
    the Annual Meeting of the African Studies Association.
    Paper #82. Bloomington, Indiana. 1981.
Newbury, M. Catharine
    "Ebutumwa Bw'Emiogo: The Tyranny of Cassava: A Women's
    Tax Revolt in Eastern Zaire." Canadian Journal of
    African Studies. Volume 18 #1 1984. pp. 35-54.
Peacock, Nadine R.
    "The Mbuti of Northeast Zaire: Women and Subsistence
    Exchange." Cultural Survival Quarterly. Volume 8 #2
    Summer, 1984. pp. 15-17.
Wilson, Francille R.
    "Reinventing the Past and Circumscribing the Future:
    Authenticite' and the Negative Image of Women's Work in
    Zaire." (In) Bay, Edna G. (ed.). Women and Work in
    Africa. Boulder, Colorado: Westview Press. Westview
    Special Studies in Africa. 1982. pp. 153-170.

EDUCATION AND TRAINING

Galloway, R.K.
    "Training Traditional Birth Attendants in Rural Zaire."
    Public Health Reviews. Volume 12 #3/4 1984. pp.
    311-315.
Gould, Terri F.
    "A New Class of Professional Zairian Women." African
    Review. Volume 7 #3/4 1977. pp. 92-105.
Gould, Terri F.
    "The Educated Woman in a Developing Country: Professional
    Zairian Women in Lumumbashi." Ph.D Dissertation: Union
    Graduate School. 1976.
Gould, Terri F.
    "The Educated Women and Social Change: A Sociological
    Study of Women Students at the National University of
    Zaire." (In) University of Dar-es-Salaam. Papers in
    Education and Development. Dar-es-Salaam, Tanzania:
    University of Dar-es-Salaam. 1976.
Mitchnik, David A.
    The Role of Women in Rural Zaire and Upper Volta:
    Improving Methods of Skill Acquisition. Oxford, England:
    OXFAM. OXFAM Working Paper #2. 1978. 36p.
Wrzesinska, Alicja
    "Contemporaneousness of Young African Girls' Attitudes."
    Africa. (Italy) Volume 36 #2 1981. pp. 183-208.
Yates, Barbara A.
    "Church, State and Education in Belgian Africa:
    Implications for Contemporary Third World Women." (In)
    Kelly, Gail P. and Elliott, Carolyn M. (eds.). Women's
    Education in the Third World: Comparative Perspectives.
    Albany, New York: State University of New York Press.
    1982. pp. 127-151.
Yates, Barbara A.
    "Colonialism, Education and Work: Sex Differentiation in
    Colonial Zaire." (In) Bay, Edna G. (ed.). Women and
    Work in Africa. Boulder, Colorado: Westview Press.
    Westview Special Studies in Africa. 1982. pp. 127-152.
Yates, Barbara A.
    "Sex Differences in Career Opportunities and Education in
    the Belgian Congo." Paper Presented at the Meetings of
    the American Educational Research Association. New
    Orleans, Louisiana. 1978.

EMPLOYMENT AND LABOR

Blain, Daniele
    "A Farming System for Women: The Case of Cassava
    Production in Zaire." Ceres. Volume 18 May-June, 1985.
    pp. 43-46.

Gould, Terri F.
  "A New Class of Professional Zairian Women." African
  Review. Volume 7 #3/4 1977. pp. 92-105.
Gould, Terri F.
  "The Educated Woman in a Developing Country: Professional
  Zairian Women in Lumumbashi." Ph.D Dissertation: Union
  Graduate School. 1976.
Gould, Terri F.
  "The Educated Women and Social Change: A Sociological
  Study of Women Students at the National University of
  Zaire." (In) University of Dar-es-Salaam. Papers in
  Education and Development. Dar-es-Salaam, Tanzania:
  University of Dar-es-Salaam. 1976.
Gould, Terri F.
  "Value Conflict and Development: The Struggle of the
  Professional Zairian Woman." Journal of Modern African
  Studies. Volume 16 #1 March, 1978. pp. 133-140.
Klingshirn, A.
  Investment of Women in Co-Operatives in Zaire and Ghana.
  Rome: United Nations Food and Agriculture Organization.
  UNFPA/FAO Study. 1978.
Wilson, Francille R.
  "Reinventing the Past and Circumscribing the Future:
  Authenticite' and the Negative Image of Women's Work in
  Zaire." (In) Bay, Edna G. (ed.). Women and Work in
  Africa. Boulder, Colorado: Westview Press. Westview
  Special Studies in Africa. 1982. pp. 153-170.
Yates, Barbara A.
  "Colonialism, Education and Work: Sex Differentiation in
  Colonial Zaire." (In) Bay, Edna G. (ed.). Women and
  Work in Africa. Boulder, Colorado: Westview Press.
  Westview Special Studies in Africa. 1982. pp. 127-152.

EQUALITY AND LIBERATION

Gould, Terri F.
  "The Educated Women and Social Change: A Sociological
  Study of Women Students at the National University of
  Zaire." (In) University of Dar-es-Salaam. Papers in
  Education and Development. Dar-es-Salaam, Tanzania:
  University of Dar-es-Salaam. 1976.

FAMILY LIFE

Adams, Lois
  "Women in Zaire: Disparate Status and Roles." (In)
  Lindsay, Beverly (ed.). Comparative Perspectives of
  Third World Women: The Impact of Race, Sex and Class.
  New York: Praeger Publishers. 1980. pp. 55-77.
Carael, M.
  "Child-Spacing, Ecology and Nutrition in the Kivu
  Province of Zaire." (In) Page, Hilary J. and Lesthaeghe,

Ron (eds.). Child-Spacing in Tropical Africa: Traditions
and Change. New York: Academic Press. 1981. pp.
275-286.

Diakanda, M. Sala and Ngondo, A. Pitshandenge and Tabutin,
Dominique and Vilquin, E.
   "Fertility and Child-Spacing in Western Zaire." (In)
   Page, Hilary J. and Lesthaeghe, Ron (eds.).
   Child-Spacing in Tropical Africa: Traditions and Change.
   New York: Academic Press. 1981. pp. 287-299.

Hilton, Anne
   "Family and Kinship Among the Kongo South of the Zaire
   River From the 16th to the 19th Centuries." Journal of
   African History. Volume 24 #2 1983. pp. 189-206.

MacGaffey, Janet
   "The Effect of Rural-Urban Ties, Kinship and Marriage on
   Household Structure in a Kongo Village." Canadian
   Journal of African Studies. Volume 17 #1 1983. pp.
   69-84.

Peacock, Nadine R.
   "Time Allocation, Work and Fertility Among Efe Pygmy
   Women of Northeast Zaire." Ph.D Dissertation: Harvard
   University. Cambridge, Massachusetts. 1985. 210p.

Seetharam, K.S. and Samba-Batumba, Nyuwa
   "Selected Aspects of Household Structure and Marriage
   Patterns in Kintambo, Kinshasa." (In) Huzayyin, S.A. and
   Acsadi, G.T. (eds.). Family and Marriage in Some African
   and Asiatic Countries. Cairo: Cairo Demographic Centre.
   CDC Research Monograph Series #6. 1976. pp. 223-242.

Wrzesinska, Alicja
   "Contemporaneousness of Young African Girls' Attitudes."
   Africa. (Italy) Volume 36 #2 1981. pp. 183-208.

Wrzesinska, Alicja
   "Women, the Family and Modernisation in Zaire." (In)
   Bandt, Jacques De and M'andi, Peter. European Studies in
   Development: New Trends in European Development Studies.
   London: MacMillan. 1980. pp. 259-268.

FAMILY PLANNING AND CONTRACEPTION

Bertrand, Jane T. and Mangani, Nlandu and Mansilu, Matondo
and Landry, Evelyn
   "Factors Influencing the Use of Traditional Versus Modern
   Family Planning Methods in Bas Zaire." Studies in Family
   Planning. Volume 16 #6 Part One November-December,
   1985. pp. 332-341.

Bertrand, Jane T. and Mangani, Nlandu and Mansilu, Matondo
   "The Acceptability of Household Distribution of
   Contraceptives in Zaire." International Family Planning
   Perspectives. Volume 10 #1 March, 1984. pp. 21-26.

Bertrand, Jane T. and Bertrand, W.E. and Malonga, Miatudila
   "The Use of Traditional and Modern Methods of Fertility
   Control in Kinshasa, Zaire." Population Studies. Volume
   37 #1 March, 1983. pp. 129-136.

Brown, Judith E. and Brown, Richard C.
"Characteristics of Contraceptive Acceptors in Rural
Zaire." Studies in Family Planning. Volume 11 #12
December, 1980. pp. 378-384.

Carael, M.
"Child-Spacing, Ecology and Nutrition in the Kivu
Province of Zaire." (In) Page, Hilary J. and Lesthaeghe,
Ron (eds.). Child-Spacing in Tropical Africa: Traditions
and Change. New York: Academic Press. 1981. pp.
275-286.

Carael, M. and Stanbury, John B.
"Promotion of Birth Spacing on Idjwi Island, Zaire."
Studies in Family Planning. Volume 14 #5 May, 1983.
pp. 134-142.

Diakanda, M. Sala and Ngondo, A. Pitshandenge and Tabutin,
Dominique and Vilquin, E.
"Fertility and Child-Spacing in Western Zaire." (In)
Page, Hilary J. and Lesthaeghe, Ron (eds.).
Child-Spacing in Tropical Africa: Traditions and Change.
New York: Academic Press. 1981. pp. 287-299.

Romaniuk, A.
"Increase in Natural Fertility During the Early Stages of
Modernization: Evidence From an African Case Study,
Zaire." Population Studies. Volume 34 #2 July, 1980.
pp. 292-310.

Sala-Diakanda, Mpembele and Pitshandenge, N.A. and Tabutin,
Dominique and Vilquin, E.
"Fertility and Child-Spacing in Western Zaire." (In)
Page, Hilary J. and Lesthaeghe, Ron (eds.).
Child-Spacing in Tropical Africa. New York: Academic
Press. 1981. 332p.

Sala-Diakanda, Mpembele and Lohle-Tart, Louis
"Social Science Research for Population Policy Design:
Case Study of Zaire." Liege, Belgium: International
Union for the Scientific Study of Population. IUSSP
Paper #24. 1982. 55p.

U.S. Agency for International Development (U.S. AID)
U.S. AID Operations Research Project Summary: Increasing
the Availability of Contraceptives Through
Community-Based Outreach in the Region of Bas, Zaire.
Washington, D.C.: U.S. Department of State. U.S. AID.
1981.

Voas, David
"Subfertility and Disruption in the Congo Basin." (In)
University of Edinburgh. African Historical Demography.
Edinburgh, Scotland: University of Edinburgh. Centre of
African Studies. 1981. pp. 777-802.

Waife, Ronald S.
Traditional Methods of Birth Control in Zaire. Chestnut
Hill, Massachusetts: Pathfinder Fund. Pathpapers #4.
December, 1978. 19p.

Wilson, Alton E.
An Assessment of Population/Family Planning Program

Activities in Zaire. Washington, D.C.: American Public
Health Association. 1979. 31p.

FERTILITY AND INFERTILITY

Anderson, Barbara A. and McCabe, James L.
    Nutrition and the Fertility of Younger Women in Kinshasa,
    Zaire. New Haven, Connecticut: Yale University Press.
    Economic Growth Center. Center Discussion Paper #248.
    May, 1976. 22p.
Anderson, Barbara A. and McCabe, James L.
    "Nutrition and the Fertility of Younger Women in
    Kinshasa, Zaire." Journal of Development Economics.
    Volume 4 #4 December, 1977. pp. 343-364.
Bertrand, Jane T. and Bertrand, W.E. and Malonga, Miatudila
    "The Use of Traditional and Modern Methods of Fertility
    Control in Kinshasa, Zaire." Population Studies. Volume
    37 #1 March, 1983. pp. 129-136.
Carael, M. and Stanbury, John B.
    "Promotion of Birth Spacing on Idjwi Island, Zaire."
    Studies in Family Planning. Volume 14 #5 May, 1983.
    pp. 134-142.
Diakanda, M. Sala and Ngondo, A. Pitshandenge and Tabutin,
Dominique and Vilquin, E.
    "Fertility and Child-Spacing in Western Zaire." (In)
    Page, Hilary J. and Lesthaeghe, Ron (eds.).
    Child-Spacing in Tropical Africa: Traditions and Change.
    New York: Academic Press. 1981. pp. 287-299.
Lunganga, K.M. and Sarma, R.S.
    "Infertility in Zaire." (In) Cairo Demographic Centre
    (CDC). Determinants of Fertility in Some African and
    Asian Countries. Cairo: CDC. CDC Research Monograph
    Series #10. 1982. pp. 375-390.
McCabe, James L.
    Differential Fertility and Infant Mortality in Urban
    Zaire. New Haven, Connecticut: Yale University Press.
    Economic Growth Center. 1977.
McFalls, Joseph A.
    "Population Subfecundity." Intercom. Volume 6 #4
    April, 1978. pp. 7-9.
Peacock, Nadine R.
    "Time Allocation, Work and Fertility Among Efe Pygmy
    Women of Northeast Zaire." Ph.D Dissertation: Harvard
    University. Cambridge, Massachusetts. 1985. 210p.
Romaniuk, A.
    "Increase in Natural Fertility During the Early Stages of
    Modernization: Evidence From an African Case Study,
    Zaire." Population Studies. Volume 34 #2 July, 1980.
    pp. 292-310.
Sala-Diakanda, Mpembele and Pitshandenge, N.A. and Tabutin,
Dominique and Vilquin, E.
    "Fertility and Child-Spacing in Western Zaire." (In)

Page, Hilary J. and Lesthaeghe, Ron (eds.).
Child-Spacing in Tropical Africa. New York: Academic
Press. 1981. 332p.

Sala-Diakanda, Mpembele and Lohle-Tart, Louis
Social Science Research for Population Policy Design:
Case Study of Zaire. Liege, Belgium: International Union
for the Scientific Study of Population. IUSSP Paper #24.
1982. 55p.

Voas, David
"Subfertility and Disruption in the Congo Basin." (In)
University of Edinburgh. African Historical Demography.
Edinburgh, Scotland: University of Edinburgh. Centre of
African Studies. 1981. pp. 777-802.

HEALTH, NUTRITION AND MEDICINE

Anderson, Barbara A. and McCabe, James L.
Nutrition and the Fertility of Younger Women in Kinshasa,
Zaire. New Haven, Connecticut: Yale University Press.
Economic Growth Center. Center Discussion Paper #248.
May, 1976. 22p.

Anderson, Barbara A. and McCabe, James L.
"Nutrition and the Fertility of Younger Women in
Kinshasa, Zaire." Journal of Development Economics.
Volume 4 #4 December, 1977. pp. 343-364.

Bertrand, Jane T. and Mangani, Nlandu and Mansilu, Matondo
"The Acceptability of Household Distribution of
Contraceptives in Zaire." International Family Planning
Perspectives. Volume 10 #1 March, 1984. pp. 21-26.

Bertrand, Jane T. and Bertrand, W.E. and Malonga, Miatudila
"The Use of Traditional and Modern Methods of Fertility
Control in Kinshasa, Zaire." Population Studies. Volume
37 #1 March, 1983. pp. 129-136.

Caraël, M.
"Child-Spacing, Ecology and Nutrition in the Kivu
Province of Zaire." (In) Page, Hilary J. and Lesthaeghe,
Ron (eds.). Child-Spacing in Tropical Africa: Traditions
and Change. New York: Academic Press. 1981. pp.
275-286.

Caraël, M.
"Relations Between Birth Intervals and Nutrition in Three
Central African Populations." (In) Mosley, W.H. (ed.).
Nutrition and Human Reproduction. New York: Plenum
Press. 1978. pp. 365-384.

Ellison, P.T.
"Endocrine Studies of Female Gonadal Function in the
Northern Ituri Forest, Zaire." American Journal of
Physical Anthropology. Volume 63 #2 1984. pp. 202-203.

Galloway, R.K.
"Training Traditional Birth Attendants in Rural Zaire."
Public Health Reviews. Volume 12 #3/4 1984. pp.
311-315.

Hennart, Philippe
   "Comparative Study of Nursing Mothers in Africa (Zaire)
   and in Europe (Sweden): Breastfeeding Behavior,
   Nutritional Status, Lactational Hyperprolactinaemia and
   Status of the Menstrual Role." Clinical Endocrinology.
   Volume 22 #2 February, 1985. pp. 179-187.
Hennart, Philippe and Vis, H.L.
   "Breast-Feeding and Post Partum Amenorrhoea in Central
   Africa. One: Milk Production in Rural Areas." Journal
   of Tropical Pediatrics. Volume 26 #5 October, 1980.
   pp. 177-183.
Hennart, Philippe and Vis, H.L. and Ruchababisha, M.
   "Breast-Feeding and Post-Partum Amenorrhoea in Central
   Africa." Journal of Tropical Pediatrics. Volume 29 #3
   June, 1983. pp. 185-189.
Lunganga, K.M. and Sarma, R.S.
   "Infertility in Zaire." (In) Cairo Demographic Centre
   (CDC). Determinants of Fertility in Some African and
   Asian Countries. Cairo: CDC. CDC Research Monograph
   Series #10. 1982. pp. 375-390.
McCabe, James L.
   Differential Fertility and Infant Mortality in Urban
   Zaire. New Haven, Connecticut: Yale University Press.
   Economic Growth Center. 1977.
Mock, N.B. and Bertrand, Jane T. and Mangani, Nlandu
   Correlates and Implications of Breastfeeding Practices in
   Bas Zaire. New Orleans, Louisiana: Tulane University.
   Unpublished Manuscript. 1984.
Romaniuk, A.
   "Increase in Natural Fertility During the Early Stages of
   Modernization: Evidence From an African Case Study,
   Zaire." Population Studies. Volume 34 #2 July, 1980.
   pp. 292-310.
Schoepf, Brooke G.
   The 'Wild,' the 'Lazy' and the 'Matriarchal': Nutrition
   and Cultural Survival in the Zairian Copperbelt. East
   Lansing, Michigan: Michigan State University. Women in
   International Development. Working Paper #96.
   September, 1985. 22p.
U.S. Agency for International Development (U.S. AID)
   U.S. AID Operations Research Project Summary: Increasing
   the Availability of Contraceptives Through
   Community-Based Outreach in the Region of Bas, Zaire.
   Washington, D.C.: U.S. Department of State. U.S. AID.
   1981.
Waife, Ronald S.
   Traditional Methods of Birth Control in Zaire. Chestnut
   Hill, Massachusetts: Pathfinder Fund. Pathpapers #4.
   December, 1978. 19p.
Wilson, Alton E.
   An Assessment of Population/Family Planning Program
   Activities in Zaire. Washington, D.C.: American Public
   Health Association. 1979. 31p.

HISTORY

Broadhead, Susan H.
"Slave Wives, Free Sisters: Bakongo Women and Slavery c.
1700-1850." (In) Robertson, Claire C. and Klein, Martin
A. (eds.). Women and Slavery in Africa. Madison,
Wisconsin: University of Wisconsin Press. 1983. pp.
160-181.
Harms, Robert
"Sustaining the System: Trading Towns Along the Middle
Zaire." (In) Robertson, Claire C. and Klein, Martin A.
(eds.). Women and Slavery in Africa. Madison,
Wisconsin: University of Wisconsin Press. 1983. pp.
95-110.
Hilton, Anne
"Family and Kinship Among the Kongo South of the Zaire
River From the 16th to the 19th Centuries." Journal of
African History. Volume 24 #2 1983. pp. 189-206.
Jacobs, Sylvia M.
"Their 'Special Mission': Afro-American Women as
Missionaries in the Congo, 1894-1937." (In) Jacobs,
Sylvia M. (ed.). Black Americans and the Missionary
Movement in Africa. Westport, Connecticut: Greenwood
Press. 1982. pp. 157-159.
Newbury, M. Catharine
"Ebutumwa Bw'Emiogo: The Tyranny of Cassava: A Women's
Tax Revolt in Eastern Zaire." Canadian Journal of
African Studies. Volume 18 #1 1984. pp. 35-54.
Sosne, Elinor
"Of Biases and Queens: The Shi Past Through an
Androgynous Looking Glass." History in Africa. Volume 6
1979. pp. 225-252.
Voas, David
"Subfertility and Disruption in the Congo Basin." (In)
University of Edinburgh. African Historical Demography.
Edinburgh, Scotland: University of Edinburgh. Centre of
African Studies. 1981. pp. 777-802.
Yates, Barbara A.
"Church, State and Education in Belgian Africa:
Implications for Contemporary Third World Women." (In)
Kelly, Gail P. and Elliott, Carolyn M. (eds.). Women's
Education in the Third World: Comparative Perspectives.
Albany, New York: State University of New York Press.
1982. pp. 127-151.
Yates, Barbara A.
"Colonialism, Education and Work: Sex Differentiation in
Colonial Zaire." (In) Bay, Edna G. (ed.). Women and
Work in Africa. Boulder, Colorado: Westview Press.
Westview Special Studies in Africa. 1982. pp. 127-152.
Yates, Barbara A.
"Sex Differences in Career Opportunities and Education in
the Belgian Congo." Paper Presented at the Meetings of

the American Educational Research Association. New
Orleans, Louisiana. 1978.

LAW AND LEGAL ISSUES

Adams, Lois
    "Women in Zaire: Disparate Status and Roles." (In)
    Lindsay, Beverly (ed.). Comparative Perspectives of
    Third World Women: The Impact of Race, Sex and Class.
    New York: Praeger Publishers. 1980. pp. 55-77.

MARITAL RELATIONS AND NUPTIALITY

Adams, Lois
    "Women in Zaire: Disparate Status and Roles." (In)
    Lindsay, Beverly (ed.). Comparative Perspectives of
    Third World Women: The Impact of Race, Sex and Class.
    New York: Praeger Publishers. 1980. pp. 55-77.
Bertrand, Jane T. and Mangani, Nlandu and Mansilu, Matondo
and Landry, Evelyn
    "Factors Influencing the Use of Traditional Versus Modern
    Family Planning Methods in Bas Zaire." Studies in Family
    Planning. Volume 16 #6 Part One November-December,
    1985. pp. 332-341.
Bertrand, Jane T. and Mangani, Nlandu and Mansilu, Matondo
    "The Acceptability of Household Distribution of
    Contraceptives in Zaire." International Family Planning
    Perspectives. Volume 10 #1 March, 1984. pp. 21-26.
Bertrand, Jane T. and Bertrand, W.E. and Malonga, Miatudila
    "The Use of Traditional and Modern Methods of Fertility
    Control in Kinshasa, Zaire." Population Studies. Volume
    37 #1 March, 1983. pp. 129-136.
Brown, Judith E. and Brown, Richard C.
    "Characteristics of Contraceptive Acceptors in Rural
    Zaire." Studies in Family Planning. Volume 11 #12
    December, 1980. pp. 378-384.
Carael, M.
    "Child-Spacing, Ecology and Nutrition in the Kivu
    Province of Zaire." (In) Page, Hilary J. and Lesthaeghe,
    Ron (eds.). Child-Spacing in Tropical Africa: Traditions
    and Change. New York: Academic Press. 1981. pp.
    275-286.
Carael, M. and Stanbury, John B.
    "Promotion of Birth Spacing on Idjwi Island, Zaire."
    Studies in Family Planning. Volume 14 #5 May, 1983.
    pp. 134-142.
Diakanda, M. Sala and Ngondo, A. Pitshandenge and Tabutin,
Dominique and Vilquin, E.
    "Fertility and Child-Spacing in Western Zaire." (In)
    Page, Hilary J. and Lesthaeghe, Ron (eds.).
    Child-Spacing in Tropical Africa: Traditions and Change.
    New York: Academic Press. 1981. pp. 287-299.

Fabian, Johannes
    "Man and Woman in the Teachings of the Jamaa Movement in
    Shaba." Bulletin de Theologie Africaine. Volume 2 #4
    July-December, 1980. pp. 257-276.
Fabian, Johannes
    "Man and Women in the Teachings of the Jamaa Movement."
    (In) Jules-Rosette, Bennetta (ed.). The New Religions of
    Africa. Norwood, New Jersey: Ablex Publishing Corp.
    1979. pp. 169-183.
MacGaffey, Janet
    "The Effect of Rural-Urban Ties, Kinship and Marriage on
    Household Structure in a Kongo Village." Canadian
    Journal of African Studies. Volume 17 #1 1983. pp.
    69-84.
Peacock, Nadine R.
    "Time Allocation, Work and Fertility Among Efe Pygmy
    Women of Northeast Zaire." Ph.D Dissertation: Harvard
    University. Cambridge, Massachusetts. 1985. 210p.
Sala-Diakanda, Mpembele and Pitshandenge, N.A. and Tabutin,
Dominique and Vilquin, E.
    "Fertility and Child-Spacing in Western Zaire." (In)
    Page, Hilary J. and Lesthaeghe, Ron (eds.).
    Child-Spacing in Tropical Africa. New York: Academic
    Press. 1981. 332p.
Seetharam, K.S. and Samba-Batumba, Nyuwa
    "Selected Aspects of Household Structure and Marriage
    Patterns in Kintambo, Kinshasa." (In) Huzayyin, S.A. and
    Acsadi, G.T. (eds.). Family and Marriage in Some African
    and Asiatic Countries. Cairo: Cairo Demographic Centre.
    CDC Research Monograph Series #6. 1976. pp. 223-242.
Wrzesinska, Alicja
    "Contemporaneousness of Young African Girls' Attitudes."
    Africa. (Italy) Volume 36 #2 1981. pp. 183-208.
Wrzesinska, Alicja
    "Women, the Family and Modernisation in Zaire." (In)
    Bandt, Jacques De and M'andi, Peter. European Studies in
    Development: New Trends in European Development Studies.
    London: MacMillan. 1980. pp. 259-268.

MISCELLANEOUS

Erasto, Muga
    Studies in Prostitution: East, West and South Africa,
    Zaire and Nevada. Nairobi: Kenya Literature Bureau.
    1980.

ORGANIZATIONS

Klingshirn, A.
    Investment of Women in Co-Operatives in Zaire and Ghana.
    Rome: United Nations Food and Agriculture Organization.
    UNFPA/FAO Study. 1978.

Newbury, M. Catharine
"Ebutumwa Bw'Emiogo: The Tyranny of Cassava: A Women's
Tax Revolt in Eastern Zaire." Canadian Journal of
African Studies. Volume 18 #1 1984. pp. 35-54.

RELIGION AND WITCHCRAFT

Fabian, Johannes
"Man and Woman in the Teachings of the Jamaa Movement in
Shaba." Bulletin de Theologie Africaine. Volume 2 #4
July-December, 1980. pp. 257-276.
Fabian, Johannes
"Man and Women in the Teachings of the Jamaa Movement."
(In) Jules-Rosette, Bennetta (ed.). The New Religions of
Africa. Norwood, New Jersey: Ablex Publishing Corp.
1979. pp. 169-183.
Jacobs, Sylvia M.
"Their 'Special Mission': Afro-American Women as
Missionaries in the Congo, 1894-1937." (In) Jacobs,
Sylvia M. (ed.). Black Americans and the Missionary
Movement in Africa. Westport, Connecticut: Greenwood
Press. 1982. pp. 157-159.
Kerkhofs, Jan
"Religious Life for Women in Zaire." Pro Mundi Vita
Dossier Africa. #14 May, 1980. pp. 1-31.
Yates, Barbara A.
"Church, State and Education in Belgian Africa:
Implications for Contemporary Third World Women." (In)
Kelly, Gail P. and Elliott, Carolyn M. (eds.). Women's
Education in the Third World: Comparative Perspectives.
Albany, New York: State University of New York Press.
1982. pp. 127-151.

RESEARCH

Sala-Diakanda, Mpembele and Lohle-Tart, Louis
Social Science Research for Population Policy Design:
Case Study of Zaire. Liege, Belgium: International Union
for the Scientific Study of Population. IUSSP Paper #24.
1982. 55p.

SEX ROLES

Adams, Lois
"Women in Zaire: Disparate Status and Roles." (In)
Lindsay, Beverly (ed.). Comparative Perspectives of
Third World Women: The Impact of Race, Sex and Class.
New York: Praeger Publishers. 1980. pp. 55-77.
Barnes, Virginia L.
Changes in Crop Mixtures and Their Relationship to Gender

Role Changes Among the Lugbara. Cambridge,
Massachusetts: Harvard University. Joint Harvard/MIT
Group. Working Paper #2. 1984.

Diakanda, M. Sala and Ngondo, A. Pitshandenge and Tabutin,
Dominique and Vilquin, E.
"Fertility and Child-Spacing in Western Zaire." (In)
Page, Hilary J. and Lesthaeghe, Ron (eds.).
Child-Spacing in Tropical Africa: Traditions and Change.
New York: Academic Press. 1981. pp. 287-299.

Fabian, Johannes
"Man and Woman in the Teachings of the Jamaa Movement in
Shaba." Bulletin de Theologie Africaine. Volume 2 #4
July-December, 1980. pp. 257-276.

Fabian, Johannes
"Man and Women in the Teachings of the Jamaa Movement."
(In) Jules-Rosette, Bennetta (ed.). The New Religions of
Africa. Norwood, New Jersey: Ablex Publishing Corp.
1979. pp. 169-183.

Mitchnik, David A.
The Role of Women in Rural Zaire and Upper Volta:
Improving Methods of Skill Acquisition. Oxford, England:
OXFAM. OXFAM Working Paper #2. 1978. 36p.

Pagezy, Helen
"Attitude of Ntomba Society Towards the Primiparous Women
and Its Biological Effects." Journal of Biosocial
Science. Volume 15 #3 August, 1983. pp. 235-246.

Peacock, Nadine R.
"The Mbuti of Northeast Zaire: Women and Subsistence
Exchange." Cultural Survival Quarterly. Volume 8 #2
Summer, 1984. pp. 15-17.

Peacock, Nadine R.
"Time Allocation, Work and Fertility Among Efe Pygmy
Women of Northeast Zaire." Ph.D Dissertation: Harvard
University. Cambridge, Massachusetts. 1985. 210p.

Sala-Diakanda, Mpembele and Pitshandenge, N.A. and Tabutin,
Dominique and Vilquin, E.
"Fertility and Child-Spacing in Western Zaire." (In)
Page, Hilary J. and Lesthaeghe, Ron (eds.).
Child-Spacing in Tropical Africa. New York: Academic
Press. 1981. 332p.

Schoepf, Brooke G.
The 'Wild,' the 'Lazy' and the 'Matriarchal': Nutrition
and Cultural Survival in the Zairian Copperbelt. East
Lansing, Michigan: Michigan State University. Women in
International Development. Working Paper #96.
September, 1985. 22p.

Seetharam, K.S. and Samba-Batumba, Nyuwa
"Selected Aspects of Household Structure and Marriage
Patterns in Kintambo, Kinshasa." (In) Huzayyin, S.A. and
Acsadi, G.T. (eds.). Family and Marriage in Some African
and Asiatic Countries. Cairo: Cairo Demographic Centre.
CDC Research Monograph Series #6. 1976. pp. 223-242.

Turnbull, Colin M.
   "Mbuti Womanhood." (In) Dahlberg, Frances (ed.). Woman
   the Gatherer. New Haven, Connecticut: Yale University
   Press. 1981. pp. 205-219.
Turnbull, Colin M.
   "The Ritualization of Potential Conflict Between the
   Sexes Among the Mbuti." (In) Leacock, Eleanor and Lee,
   Richard. Politics and History in Band Societies.
   Cambridge, England: Cambridge University Press. 1982.
   pp. 133-155.
Wilson, Francille R.
   "Reinventing the Past and Circumscribing the Future:
   Authenticite' and the Negative Image of Women's Work in
   Zaire." (In) Bay, Edna G. (ed.). Women and Work in
   Africa. Boulder, Colorado: Westview Press. Westview
   Special Studies in Africa. 1982. pp. 153-170.
Wrzesinska, Alicja
   "Women, the Family and Modernisation in Zaire." (In)
   Bandt, Jacques De and M'andi, Peter. European Studies in
   Development: New Trends in European Development Studies.
   London: MacMillan. 1980. pp. 259-268.
Yates, Barbara A.
   "Colonialism, Education and Work: Sex Differentiation in
   Colonial Zaire." (In) Bay, Edna G. (ed.). Women and
   Work in Africa. Boulder, Colorado: Westview Press.
   Westview Special Studies in Africa. 1982. pp. 127-152.
Yates, Barbara A.
   "Sex Differences in Career Opportunities and Education in
   the Belgian Congo." Paper Presented at the Meetings of
   the American Educational Research Association. New
   Orleans, Louisiana. 1978.

SLAVERY

Broadhead, Susan H.
   "Slave Wives, Free Sisters: Bakongo Women and Slavery c.
   1700-1850." (In) Robertson, Claire C. and Klein, Martin
   A. (eds.). Women and Slavery in Africa. Madison,
   Wisconsin: University of Wisconsin Press. 1983. pp.
   160-181.
Harms, Robert
   "Sustaining the System: Trading Towns Along the Middle
   Zaire." (In) Robertson, Claire C. and Klein, Martin A.
   (eds.). Women and Slavery in Africa. Madison,
   Wisconsin: University of Wisconsin Press. 1983. pp.
   95-110.

STATUS OF WOMEN

Adams, Lois
   "Women in Zaire: Disparate Status and Roles." (In)
   Lindsay, Beverly (ed.). Comparative Perspectives of

Third World Women: The Impact of Race, Sex and Class.
New York: Praeger Publishers. 1980. pp. 55-77.

WOMEN AND THEIR CHILDREN

Heymer, A.
    "Bayaka Pygmies: Mother-Child Relationship and Behavior
    Patterns Between Small Children and Different Other Women
    Group Members." Homo.   Volume 32 #2 1981. pp. 130-139.
Heymer, A.
    "Bayaka Pygmies: Social Grooming in Women and Girls and
    Grooming Rivalry." Homo.   Volume 30 #3 1979. pp.
    196-202.

General Subject Bibliography— Sub-Saharan Africa

ABORTION

Cook, Rebecca J. and Dickens, Bernard N.
    "Abortion Law in African Commonwealth Countries."
    Journal of African Law. Volume 25 #2 1981. pp. 60-79.

AGRICULTURE

Bryson Judy C.
    "Women and Agriculture in Sub-Saharan Africa:
    Implications for Development." Journal of Development
    Studies. Volume 17 #3 April, 1981. pp. 29-46.
Dey, Jennie M.
    Women in Rice Farming Systems, Focus: Subsaharan Africa.
    Rome: United Nations Food and Agriculture Organization.
    Women in Agriculture Series #2. 1984. 106p.
Henn, Jeanne K.
    "Women in the Rural Economy: Past, Present and Future."
    (In) Hay, Margaret J. and Stichter, Sharon (eds.).
    African Women South of the Sahara. New York: Longman.
    1984. pp. 1-18.
Lancaster, Chet S.
    "Women, Horticulture and Society in Sub-Saharan Africa."
    American Anthropologist. Volume 78 #3 September, 1976.
    pp. 539-564.
Ritchie, Jean A.
    The Integration of Women in Agrarian Reform and Rural
    Development in English Speaking Countries of the African
    Region. Rome: United Nations Food and Agriculture
    Organization. March, 1978. 95p.
United Nations Food and Agriculture Organization (FAO)
    The State of Food and Agriculture; 1983: World Review:

The Situation in Sub-Saharan Africa; Women in Developing
Agriculture. New York: FAO. FAO Agriculture Series #16.
1984. 221p.
Wipper, Audrey
"Women's Voluntary Associations." (In) Hay, Margaret J.
and Stichter, Sharon (eds.). African Women South of the
Sahara. New York: Longman. 1984. pp. 69-86.
World Bank
Rural Development Projects: A Retrospective View of Bank
Experience in Sub-Saharan Africa. Washington, D.C.:
World Bank. Report #2242. October 13, 1978.

BIBLIOGRAPHIES

Saulniers, Suzanne S. and Rakowski, Cathy A.
Women in the Development Process: A Select Bibliography
on Women in Sub-Saharan Africa and Latin America.
Austin, Texas: University of Texas Press. Institute of
Latin American Studies. 1977. 287p.

CULTURAL ROLES

Bingham, Marjorie W. and Gross, Susan H.
Women in Africa of the Sub-Sahara. Hudson, Wisconsin:
Gem Publishers. Volume One: Ancient Times to the
Twentieth Century. Volume Two: The Twentieth Century.
1982. 260p.
Bongaarts, John and Frank, Odile and Lesthaeghe, Ron J.
"The Proximate Determinants of Fertility in Sub-Saharan
Africa." Population and Developement Review. Volume 10
#3 September, 1984. pp. 511-538+.
Boserup, Ester
"Economic and Demographic Interrelationships in
Sub-Saharan Africa." Population and Development Review.
Volume 11 #3 September, 1985. pp. 383-397+.
Brown, Judith E.
"Polygyny and Family Planning in Sub-Saharan Africa."
Studies in Family Planning. Volume 12 #8-9
August-September, 1981. pp. 322-326.
Bryson Judy C.
"Women and Agriculture in Sub-Saharan Africa:
Implications for Development." Journal of Development
Studies. Volume 17 #3 April, 1981. pp. 29-46.
Caldwell, John C.
"Marriage, the Family and Fertility in Sub-Saharan Africa
With Special Reference to Research Programmes in Ghana
and Nigeria." (In) Huzayyin, S.A. and Acsadi, G.T.
(eds.). Family and Marriage in Some African and Asian
Countries. Cairo: Cairo Demographic Centre. CDC
Research Monograph #6. 1976. pp. 359-371.

Cook, Rebecca J. and Dickens, Bernard N.
"Abortion Law in African Commonwealth Countries."
Journal of African Law. Volume 25 #2 1981. pp. 60-79.
Dow, Thomas E.
Breast-Feeding, Abstinence, and Family Planning Among the
Yoruba and Other Sub-Saharan Groups: Patterns and Policy
Implications. Purchase, New York: State University of
New York. Department of Sociology. 1978.
Dunbar, Roberta
"Legislative Reform and Muslim Family Law: Effects Upon
Women's Rights in Africa South of the Sahara." Paper
Presented at the Annual Meeting of the African Studies
Association. Paper #25. Philadelphia, Pennsylvania.
October 15-18, 1980.
Frank, Odile
Child Fostering in Sub-Saharan Africa. New York:
Population Council. Center for Policy Studies. 1984.
Frank, Odile
The Demand for Fertility Control in Sub-Saharan Africa.
New York: Population Council. Center for Policy Studies.
Working Paper #117. November, 1985. 50p.
Gyepi-Garbrah, Benjamin and Nichols, Douglas J. and
Kpedekpo, Gottlieb M.
Adolescent Fertility in Sub-Saharan Africa: An Overview.
Boston: Pathfinder Fund. 1985. 51p.
Hay, Margaret J. and Stichter, Sharon B. (eds.)
African Women South of the Sahara. New York: Longman.
1984.
Henn, Jeanne K.
"Women in the Rural Economy: Past, Present and Future."
(In) Hay, Margaret J. and Stichter, Sharon (eds.).
African Women South of the Sahara. New York: Longman.
1984. pp. 1-18.
Howard, R.
"Women's Rights in English-Speaking Sub-Saharan Africa."
(In) Welch, Claude E. and Meltzer, Ronald I. (eds.).
Human Rights and Development in Africa. Albany, New
York: State University of New York Press. 1984.
Kamanga, Kawaye
"The Dilemma of High Fertility in Sub-Saharan Africa."
Ph.D Dissertation: University of Pittsburgh. Pittsburgh,
Pennsylvania. 1985. 140p.
Kamanga, Kawaye
"The Dilemma of High Fertility in Sub-Saharan Africa."
Ph.D Dissertation: University of Pittsburgh. Pittsburgh,
Pennsylvania. 1985. 140p.
Lancaster, Chet S.
"Women, Horticulture and Society in Sub-Saharan Africa."
American Anthropologist. Volume 78 #3 September, 1976.
pp. 539-564.
Lee, S.
"The Image of the Woman in the African Folktale From the
Sub-Saharan Francophone Area." Yale French Studies. #53
1976. pp. 19-28.

Lesthaeghe, Ron J. and Ohadike, Patrick O. and Kocher, James
E. and Page, Hilary J.
    "Child-Spacing and Fertility in Sub-Saharan Africa: An
    Overview of Issues." (In) Page, Hilary J. and
    Lesthaeghe, Ron (eds.). Child-Spacing in Tropical
    Africa: Traditions and Change. New York: Academic Press.
    1981. pp. 3-23.
Lesthaeghe, Ron J.
    Fertility and its Proximate Determinants in Sub-Saharan
    Africa: The Record of the 1960's and 70's. Brussels,
    Belgium: Vrije Universiteit Brussel. Interuniversity
    Programme in Demography. IPD Working Paper #1984-2.
    1984. 117p.
Lesthaeghe, Ron J. and Eelens, Frank
    Social Organization and Reproductive Regimes: Lessons
    From Sub-Saharan Africa and Historical Western Europe.
    Brussels, Belgium: Vrije Universiteit Brussel.
    Interuniversity Programme in Demography. IDP Working
    Paper #1985-1. 1985. 64p.
Morris, H.F.
    "The Development of Statutory Marriage Law in 20th
    Century British Colonial Africa." Journal of African
    Law. Volume 23 #1 1979. pp. 37-64.
Mwaniki, N. and Marasha, M. and Mati, J.K.G. and Mwaniki,
M.K. (eds.)
    Surgical Contraception in Sub-Saharan Africa:
    Proceedings. Nairobi: University of Nairobi. Paper
    Presented at a Conference May 8-13, 1977. Sponsored by
    the Pathfinder Fund. Chestnut Hill, Massachusetts.
    1979. 182p.
Newman, Jeanne S.
    Women of the World: Sub-Saharan Africa. Washington,
    D.C.: U.S. Department of Commerce. U.S. Agency for
    International Development. Office of Women in
    Development. August, 1984. 200p.
O'Barr, Jean F.
    African Women in Politics. (In) Hay, Margaret J. and
    Stichter, Sharon (eds.). African Women South of the
    Sahara. New York: Longman. 1984. pp. 140-155.
Ritchie, Jean A.
    The Integration of Women in Agrarian Reform and Rural
    Development in English Speaking Countries of the African
    Region. Rome: United Nations Food and Agriculture
    Organization. March, 1978. 95p.
Staudt, Kathleen A.
    "Victorian Womanhood in British Colonial Africa." Paper
    Presented to the Conference on the History of Women. St.
    Paul, Minnesota: College of St. Catherine. October
    21-23, 1977.
Staudt, Kathleen A.
    Women's Politics and Capitalist Transformation in
    Subsaharan Africa. East Lansing, Michigan: Michigan

State University. Office of Women in International
Development. Working Paper #54. April, 1984.
Strobel, Margaret A.
    "Women in Religion and in Secular Ideology." (In) Hay,
    Margaret J. and Stichter, Sharon (eds.). African Women
    South of the Sahara. New York: Longman. 1984. pp.
    87-101.
United Nations
    Impact on Women of Socioeconomic Changes in Africa South
    of the Sahara: Project Proposal. Geneva: United Nations
    Research Institute for Social Development. Reference
    Center. 1979. 56p.
Valentine, C.H. and Revson, J.E.
    "Cultural Traditions, Social Change, and Fertility in
    Sub-Saharan Africa." Journal of Modern African Studies.
    Volume 17 #3 September, 1979. pp. 453-472.
Waife, Ronald S. and Burkhart, Marianne (eds.)
    The Nonphysician and Family Health in Sub-Saharan Africa:
    Proceedings of a Conference, Freetown, Sierra Leone,
    September 1-4, 1980. Chestnut Hill, Massachusetts:
    Pathfinder Fund. 1981. 141p.
White, Luise S.
    "Women in the Changing African Family." (In) Hay,
    Margaret J. and Stichter, Sharon (eds.). African Women
    South of the Sahara. New York: Longman. 1984. pp.
    53-68.
Wipper, Audrey
    "Women's Voluntary Associations." (In) Hay, Margaret J.
    and Stichter, Sharon (eds.). African Women South of the
    Sahara. New York: Longman. 1984. pp. 69-86.
Wulf, Deirdre
    "The Future of Family Planning in Sub-Saharan Africa."
    International Family Planning Perspectives. Volume 11 #1
    March, 1985. pp. 1-8.

DEVELOPMENT AND TECHNOLOGY

Bryson Judy C.
    "Women and Agriculture in Sub-Saharan Africa:
    Implications for Development." Journal of Development
    Studies. Volume 17 #3 April, 1981. pp. 29-46.
Dey, Jennie M.
    Women in Rice Farming Systems, Focus: Subsaharan Africa.
    Rome: United Nations Food and Agriculture Organization.
    Women in Agriculture Series #2. 1984. 106p.
Lancaster, Chet S.
    "Women, Horticulture and Society in Sub-Saharan Africa."
    American Anthropologist. Volume 78 #3 September, 1976.
    pp. 539-564.
Newman, Jeanne S.
    "Some Indicators of Women's Economic Roles in Sub-Saharan
    Africa." Paper Presented at the Annual Meeting of the
    American Statistical Association. Toronto, Ontario,
    Canada. August, 1983.

Newman, Jeanne S.
  Women of the World: Sub-Saharan Africa. Washington,
  D.C.: U.S. Department of Commerce. U.S. Agency for
  International Development. Office of Women in
  Development. August, 1984. 200p.
Ritchie, Jean A.
  The Integration of Women in Agrarian Reform and Rural
  Development in English Speaking Countries of the African
  Region. Rome: United Nations Food and Agriculture
  Organization. March, 1978. 95p.
Saulniers, Suzanne S. and Rakowski, Cathy A.
  Women in the Development Process: A Select Bibliography
  on Women in Sub-Saharan Africa and Latin America.
  Austin, Texas: University of Texas Press. Institute of
  Latin American Studies. 1977. 287p.
Staudt, Kathleen A.
  Women's Politics and Capitalist Transformation in
  Subsaharan Africa. East Lansing, Michigan: Michigan
  State University. Office of Women in International
  Development. Working Paper #54. April, 1984.
United Nations
  Impact on Women of Socioeconomic Changes in Africa South
  of the Sahara: Project Proposal. Geneva: United Nations
  Research Institute for Social Development. Reference
  Center. 1979. 56p.
United Nations Economic Commission for Africa (UNECA)
  "National Machinery for the Integration of Women in
  Development in African Countries." Paper Presented to
  the Regional Conference on the Implementation of the
  National Regional and Worlds Plans of Action for the
  Integration of Women in Development. Addis Ababa,
  Ethiopia: UNECA. Nouakchott, Mauritania. 1977. 54p.
United Nations Food and Agriculture Organization (FAO)
  The State of Food and Agriculture; 1983: World Review:
  The Situation in Sub-Saharan Africa; Women in Developing
  Agriculture. New York: FAO. FAO Agriculture Series #16.
  1984. 221p.
United Nations Fund for Population Activities
  Forum on Population and Development for Women Leaders
  From Sub-Saharan African Countries. New York: United
  Nations Fund for Population Activities. May 15-18, 1984.
  39p.
World Bank
  Rural Development Projects: A Retrospective View of Bank
  Experience in Sub-Saharan Africa. Washington, D.C.:
  World Bank. Report #2242. October 13, 1978.

ECONOMICS

Boserup, Ester
  "Economic and Demographic Interrelationships in

Sub-Saharan Africa." Population and Development Review.
Volume 11 #3 September, 1985. pp. 383-397+.
Brown, Judith E.
"Polygyny and Family Planning in Sub-Saharan Africa."
Studies in Family Planning. Volume 12 #8-9
August-September, 1981. pp. 322-326.
Bryson Judy C.
"Women and Agriculture in Sub-Saharan Africa:
Implications for Development." Journal of Development
Studies. Volume 17 #3 April, 1981. pp. 29-46.
Dey, Jennie M.
Women in Rice Farming Systems, Focus: Subsaharan Africa.
Rome: United Nations Food and Agriculture Organization.
Women in Agriculture Series #2. 1984. 106p.
Henn, Jeanne K.
"Women in the Rural Economy: Past, Present and Future."
(In) Hay, Margaret J. and Stichter, Sharon (eds.).
African Women South of the Sahara. New York: Longman.
1984. pp. 1-18.
Newman, Jeanne S.
"Some Indicators of Women's Economic Roles in Sub-Saharan
Africa." Paper Presented at the Annual Meeting of the
American Statistical Association. Toronto, Ontario,
Canada. August, 1983.
Newman, Jeanne S.
Women of the World: Sub-Saharan Africa. Washington,
D.C.: U.S. Department of Commerce. U.S. Agency for
International Development. Office of Women in
Development. August, 1984. 200p.
Robertson, Claire C.
"Women in the Urban Economy." (In) Hay, Margaret J. and
Stichter, Sharon (eds.). African Women South of the
Sahara. New York: Longman. 1984. pp. 33-50.
Staudt, Kathleen A.
Women's Politics and Capitalist Transformation in
Subsaharan Africa. East Lansing, Michigan: Michigan
State University. Office of Women in International
Development. Working Paper #54. April, 1984.
United Nations Food and Agriculture Organization (FAO)
The State of Food and Agriculture; 1983: World Review:
The Situation in Sub-Saharan Africa; Women in Developing
Agriculture. New York: FAO. FAO Agriculture Series #16.
1984. 221p.
Wipper, Audrey
"Women's Voluntary Associations." (In) Hay, Margaret J.
and Stichter, Sharon (eds.). African Women South of the
Sahara. New York: Longman. 1984. pp. 69-86.
World Bank
Rural Development Projects: A Retrospective View of Bank
Experience in Sub-Saharan Africa. Washington, D.C.:
World Bank. Report #2242. October 13, 1978.

EDUCATION AND TRAINING

Robertson, Claire C.
"Women in the Urban Economy." (In) Hay, Margaret J. and
Stichter, Sharon (eds.). African Women South of the
Sahara. New York: Longman. 1984. pp. 33-50.
United Nations Economic Commission for Africa (UNECA)
"National Machinery for the Integration of Women in
Development in African Countries." Paper Presented to
the Regional Conference on the Implementation of the
National Regional and Worlds Plans of Action for the
Integration of Women in Development. Addis Ababa,
Ethiopia: UNECA. Nouakchott, Mauritania. 1977. 54p.

EMPLOYMENT AND LABOR

Bryson Judy C.
"Women and Agriculture in Sub-Saharan Africa:
Implications for Development." Journal of Development
Studies. Volume 17 #3 April, 1981. pp. 29-46.
Dey, Jennie M.
Women in Rice Farming Systems, Focus: Subsaharan Africa.
Rome: United Nations Food and Agriculture Organization.
Women in Agriculture Series #2. 1984. 106p.
Newman, Jeanne S.
"Some Indicators of Women's Economic Roles in Sub-Saharan
Africa." Paper Presented at the Annual Meeting of the
American Statistical Association. Toronto, Ontario,
Canada. August, 1983.
Robertson, Claire C.
"Women in the Urban Economy." (In) Hay, Margaret J. and
Stichter, Sharon (eds.). African Women South of the
Sahara. New York: Longman. 1984. pp. 33-50.
United Nations
Impact on Women of Socioeconomic Changes in Africa South
of the Sahara: Project Proposal. Geneva: United Nations
Research Institute for Social Development. Reference
Center. 1979. 56p.
White, Luise S.
"Women in the Changing African Family." (In) Hay,
Margaret J. and Stichter, Sharon (eds.). African Women
South of the Sahara. New York: Longman. 1984. pp.
53-68.

EQUALITY AND LIBERATION

Howard, R.
"Women's Rights in English-Speaking Sub-Saharan Africa."
(In) Welch, Claude E. and Meltzer, Ronald I. (eds.).
Human Rights and Development in Africa. Albany, New
York: State University of New York Press. 1984.

Urdang, Stephanie
"Women in National Liberation Movements."   (In) Hay,
Margaret J. and Stichter, Sharon (eds.).   African Women
South of the Sahara. New York: Longman. 1984. pp.
156-169.

FAMILY LIFE

Bingham, Marjorie W. and Gross, Susan H.
Women in Africa of the Sub-Sahara. Hudson, Wisconsin:
Gem Publishers. Volume One: Ancient Times to the
Twentieth Century. Volume Two: The Twentieth Century.
1982. 260p.
Boserup, Ester
"Economic and Demographic Interrelationships in
Sub-Saharan Africa." Population and Development Review.
Volume 11 #3 September, 1985. pp. 383-397+.
Brown, Judith E.
"Polygyny and Family Planning in Sub-Saharan Africa."
Studies in Family Planning. Volume 12 #8-9
August-September, 1981. pp. 322-326.
Caldwell, John C.
"Marriage, the Family and Fertility in Sub-Saharan Africa
With Special Reference to Research Programmes in Ghana
and Nigeria." (In) Huzayyin, S.A. and Acsadi, G.T.
(eds.). Family and Marriage in Some African and Asian
Countries. Cairo: Cairo Demographic Centre. CDC
Research Monograph #6. 1976. pp. 359-371.
Lancaster, Chet S.
"Women, Horticulture and Society in Sub-Saharan Africa."
American Anthropologist. Volume 78 #3 September, 1976.
pp. 539-564.
United Nations
Impact on Women of Socioeconomic Changes in Africa South
of the Sahara: Project Proposal. Geneva: United Nations
Research Institute for Social Development. Reference
Center. 1979. 56p.
Valentine, C.H. and Revson, J.E.
"Cultural Traditions, Social Change, and Fertility in
Sub-Saharan Africa." Journal of Modern African Studies.
Volume 17 #3 September, 1979. pp. 453-472.
White, Luise S.
"Women in the Changing African Family." (In) Hay,
Margaret J. and Stichter, Sharon (eds.). African Women
South of the Sahara. New York: Longman. 1984. pp.
53-68.

FAMILY PLANNING AND CONTRACEPTION

Boserup, Ester
"Economic and Demographic Interrelationships in

Sub-Saharan Africa." Population and Development Review.
Volume 11 #3 September, 1985. pp. 383-397+.
Brown, Judith E.
"Polygyny and Family Planning in Sub-Saharan Africa."
Studies in Family Planning. Volume 12 #8-9
August-September, 1981. pp. 322-326.
Caldwell, John C.
"Marriage, the Family and Fertility in Sub-Saharan Africa
With Special Reference to Research Programmes in Ghana
and Nigeria." (In) Huzayyin, S.A. and Acsadi, G.T.
(eds.). Family and Marriage in Some African and Asian
Countries. Cairo: Cairo Demographic Centre. CDC
Research Monograph #6. 1976. pp. 359-371.
Dow, Thomas E.
Breast-Feeding, Abstinence, and Family Planning Among the
Yoruba and Other Sub-Saharan Groups: Patterns and Policy
Implications. Purchase, New York: State University of
New York. Department of Sociology. 1978.
Frank, Odile
Child Fostering in Sub-Saharan Africa. New York:
Population Council. Center for Policy Studies. 1984.
Frank, Odile
The Demand for Fertility Control in Sub-Saharan Africa.
New York: Population Council. Center for Policy Studies.
Working Paper #117. November, 1985. 50p.
Kamanga, Kawaye
"The Dilemma of High Fertility in Sub-Saharan Africa."
Ph.D Dissertation: University of Pittsburgh. Pittsburgh,
Pennsylvania. 1985. 140p.
Kamanga, Kawaye
"The Dilemma of High Fertility in Sub-Saharan Africa."
Ph.D Dissertation: University of Pittsburgh. Pittsburgh,
Pennsylvania. 1985. 140p.
Lesthaeghe, Ron J. and Ohadike, Patrick O. and Kocher, James
E. and Page, Hilary J.
"Child-Spacing and Fertility in Sub-Saharan Africa: An
Overview of Issues." (In) Page, Hilary J. and
Lesthaeghe, Ron (eds.). Child-Spacing in Tropical
Africa: Traditions and Change. New York: Academic Press.
1981. pp. 3-23.
Lesthaeghe, Ron J. and Eelens, Frank
Social Organization and Reproductive Regimes: Lessons
From Sub-Saharan Africa and Historical Western Europe.
Brussels, Belgium: Vrije Universiteit Brussel.
Interuniversity Programme in Demography. IDP Working
Paper #1985-1. 1985. 64p.
Mwaniki, N. and Marasha, M. and Mati, J.K.G. and Mwaniki,
M.K. (eds.)
Surgical Contraception in Sub-Saharan Africa:
Proceedings. Nairobi: University of Nairobi. Paper
Presented at a Conference May 8-13, 1977. Sponsored by
the Pathfinder Fund. Chestnut Hill, Massachusetts.
1979. 182p.

Wulf, Deirdre
    "The Future of Family Planning in Sub-Saharan Africa."
    International Family Planning Perspectives. Volume 11 #1
    March, 1985. pp. 1-8.

FERTILITY AND INFERTILITY

Adegbola, O.
    "New Estimates of Fertility and Child Mortality in
    Africa, South of the Sahara." Population
    Studies(London). Volume 31 #3 1977. pp. 467-486.
Belsey, Mark A.
    Biological Factors Other Than Nutrition and Lactation
    Which May Influence Natural Fertility: Additional Notes
    With Particular Reference to Sub-Saharan Africa. Paper
    Presented at the International Union for the Scientific
    Study of Population Seminar on Natural Fertility. Leige,
    Belgium: IUSSP. Paris, France. 1977.
Belsey, Mark A.
    "Biological Factors Other Than Nutrition and Lactation
    Which May Influence Natural Fertility: Additional Notes
    With Particular Reference to Sub-Saharan Africa." (In)
    Leridon, Henri and Menken, Jane (eds.). Natural
    Fertility: Patterns and Determinants of Natural
    Fertility. Liege, Belgium: International Union for the
    Scientific Study of Population. 1979. pp. 253-272.
Belsey. Mark A.
    "The Epidemiology of Infertility: A Review With
    Particular Reference to Sub-Saharan Africa." Bulletin of
    the World Health Organization. Volume 54 #3 1976. pp.
    319-341.
Bongaarts, John and Frank, Odile and Lesthaeghe, Ron J.
    "The Proximate Determinants of Fertility in Sub-Saharan
    Africa." Population and Developement Review. Volume 10
    #3 September, 1984. pp. 511-538+.
Boserup, Ester
    "Economic and Demographic Interrelationships in
    Sub-Saharan Africa." Population and Development Review.
    Volume 11 #3 September, 1985. pp. 383-397+.
Caldwell, John C.
    "Marriage, the Family and Fertility in Sub-Saharan Africa
    With Special Reference to Research Programmes in Ghana
    and Nigeria." (In) Huzayyin, S.A. and Acsadi, G.T.
    (eds.). Family and Marriage in Some African and Asian
    Countries. Cairo: Cairo Demographic Centre. CDC
    Research Monograph #6. 1976. pp. 359-371.
Eelens, Frank and Donne, L.
    The Proximate Determinants of Fertility in Sub-Saharan
    Africa: A Factbook Based on the Results of the World
    Fertility Survey. Brussels, Belgium: Vrije Universiteit
    Brussel. Interuniversity Programme in Demography. IDP
    Working Paper #1985-3. 1985. 122p.

Ekanem, Ita I.
"Prospects of Fertility Decline in Sub-Saharan Africa."
Population Studies. #67 1979. pp. 174-196.
Frank, Odile
"Infertility in Sub-Saharan Africa: Estimates and
Implications." Population and Development Review.
Volume 9 #1 March, 1983. pp. 137-144+.
Frank, Odile
Infertility in Sub-Saharan Africa. New York: Population
Council. Center for Population Studies. Working Working
Paper #97. June, 1983. 107p.
Frank, Odile
The Demand for Fertility Control in Sub-Saharan Africa.
New York: Population Council. Center for Policy Studies.
Working Paper #117. November, 1985. 50p.
Gyepi-Garbrah, Benjamin and Nichols, Douglas J. and
Kpedekpo, Gottlieb M.
Adolescent Fertility in Sub-Saharan Africa: An Overview.
Boston: Pathfinder Fund. 1985. 51p.
Kamanga, Kawaye
"The Dilemma of High Fertility in Sub-Saharan Africa."
Ph.D Dissertation: University of Pittsburgh. Pittsburgh,
Pennsylvania. 1985. 140p.
Kamanga, Kawaye
"The Dilemma of High Fertility in Sub-Saharan Africa."
Ph.D Dissertation: University of Pittsburgh. Pittsburgh,
Pennsylvania. 1985. 140p.
Lesthaeghe, Ron J. and Ohadike, Patrick O. and Kocher, James
E. and Page, Hilary J.
"Child-Spacing and Fertility in Sub-Saharan Africa: An
Overview of Issues." (In) Page, Hilary J. and
Lesthaeghe, Ron (eds.). Child-Spacing in Tropical
Africa: Traditions and Change. New York: Academic Press.
1981. pp. 3-23.
Lesthaeghe, Ron J.
Fertility and its Proximate Determinants in Sub-Saharan
Africa: The Record of the 1960's and 70's. Brussels,
Belgium: Vrije Universiteit Brussel. Interuniversity
Programme in Demography. IPD Working Paper #1984-2.
1984. 117p.
Lesthaeghe, Ron J. and Eelens, Frank
Social Organization and Reproductive Regimes: Lessons
From Sub-Saharan Africa and Historical Western Europe.
Brussels, Belgium: Vrije Universiteit Brussel.
Interuniversity Programme in Demography. IDP Working
Paper #1985-1. 1985. 64p.
Valentine, C.H. and Revson, J.E.
"Cultural Traditions, Social Change, and Fertility in
Sub-Saharan Africa." Journal of Modern African Studies.
Volume 17 #3 September, 1979. pp. 453-472.

HEALTH, NUTRITION AND MEDICINE

Adegbola, O.
    "New Estimates of Fertility and Child Mortality in
    Africa, South of the Sahara." Population
    Studies(London). Volume 31 #3 1977. pp. 467-486.
Belsey, Mark A.
    Biological Factors Other Than Nutrition and Lactation
    Which May Influence Natural Fertility: Additional Notes
    With Particular Reference to Sub-Saharan Africa. Paper
    Presented at the International Union for the Scientific
    Study of Population Seminar on Natural Fertility. Leige,
    Belgium: IUSSP. Paris, France. 1977.
Belsey, Mark A.
    "Biological Factors Other Than Nutrition and Lactation
    Which May Influence Natural Fertility: Additional Notes
    With Particular Reference to Sub-Saharan Africa." (In)
    Leridon, Henri and Menken, Jane (eds.). Natural
    Fertility: Patterns and Determinants of Natural
    Fertility. Liege, Belgium: International Union for the
    Scientific Study of Population. 1979. pp. 253-272.
Belsey. Mark A.
    "The Epidemiology of Infertility: A Review With
    Particular Reference to Sub-Saharan Africa." Bulletin of
    the World Health Organization. Volume 54 #3 1976. pp.
    319-341.
Bongaarts, John and Frank, Odile and Lesthaeghe, Ron J.
    "The Proximate Determinants of Fertility in Sub-Saharan
    Africa." Population and Developement Review. Volume 10
    #3 September, 1984. pp. 511-538+.
Dow, Thomas E.
    Breast-Feeding, Abstinence, and Family Planning Among the
    Yoruba and Other Sub-Saharan Groups: Patterns and Policy
    Implications. Purchase, New York: State University of
    New York. Department of Sociology. 1978.
Ekanem, Ita I.
    "Prospects of Fertility Decline in Sub-Saharan Africa."
    Population Studies. #67 1979. pp. 174-196.
Frank, Odile
    "Infertility in Sub-Saharan Africa: Estimates and
    Implications." Population and Development Review.
    Volume 9 #1 March, 1983. pp. 137-144+.
Frank, Odile
    Infertility in Sub-Saharan Africa. New York: Population
    Council. Center for Population Studies. Working Working
    Paper #97. June, 1983. 107p.
Frank, Odile
    The Demand for Fertility Control in Sub-Saharan Africa.
    New York: Population Council. Center for Policy Studies.
    Working Paper #117. November, 1985. 50p.
Gyepi-Garbrah, Benjamin and Nichols, Douglas J. and
Kpedekpo, Gottlieb M.

Adolescent Fertility in Sub-Saharan Africa: An Overview.
Boston: Pathfinder Fund. 1985. 51p.
Kamanga, Kawaye
"The Dilemma of High Fertility in Sub-Saharan Africa."
Ph.D Dissertation: University of Pittsburgh. Pittsburgh,
Pennsylvania. 1985. 140p.
Kamanga, Kawaye
"The Dilemma of High Fertility in Sub-Saharan Africa."
Ph.D Dissertation: University of Pittsburgh. Pittsburgh,
Pennsylvania. 1985. 140p.
Lesthaeghe, Ron J.
Fertility and its Proximate Determinants in Sub-Saharan
Africa: The Record of the 1960's and 70's. Brussels,
Belgium: Vrije Universiteit Brussel. Interuniversity
Programme in Demography. IPD Working Paper #1984-2.
1984. 117p.
Ramachandran, K.V. and Venkatacharya, K. and Teklu, Tesfay
Fertility and Mortality Levels, Patterns and Trends in
Some Anglophone African Countries. Legon, Ghana: United
Nations Regional Institute for Population Studies. 1979.
78p.
Waife, Ronald S. and Burkhart, Marianne (eds.)
The Nonphysician and Family Health in Sub-Saharan Africa:
Proceedings of a Conference, Freetown, Sierra Leone,
September 1-4, 1980. Chestnut Hill, Massachusetts:
Pathfinder Fund. 1981. 141p.
Wulf, Deirdre
"The Future of Family Planning in Sub-Saharan Africa."
International Family Planning Perspectives. Volume 11 #1
March, 1985. pp. 1-8.

HISTORY

Bingham, Marjorie W. and Gross, Susan H.
Women in Africa of the Sub-Sahara. Hudson, Wisconsin:
Gem Publishers. Volume One: Ancient Times to the
Twentieth Century. Volume Two: The Twentieth Century.
1982. 260p.
Henn, Jeanne K.
"Women in the Rural Economy: Past, Present and Future."
(In) Hay, Margaret J. and Stichter, Sharon (eds.).
African Women South of the Sahara. New York: Longman.
1984. pp. 1-18.
Morris, H.F.
"The Development of Statutory Marriage Law in 20th
Century British Colonial Africa." Journal of African
Law. Volume 23 #1 1979. pp. 37-64.
O'Barr, Jean F.
African Women in Politics. (In) Hay, Margaret J. and
Stichter, Sharon (eds.). African Women South of the
Sahara. New York: Longman. 1984. pp. 140-155.
Ramachandran, K.V. and Venkatacharya, K. and Teklu, Tesfay
Fertility and Mortality Levels, Patterns and Trends in
Some Anglophone African Countries. Legon, Ghana: United

Nations Regional Institute for Population Studies.   1979.
78p.
Staudt, Kathleen A.
    "Victorian Womanhood in British Colonial Africa."   Paper
    Presented to the Conference on the History of Women.   St.
    Paul, Minnesota: College of St. Catherine.   October
    21-23, 1977.

LAW AND LEGAL ISSUES

Cook, Rebecca J. and Dickens, Bernard N.
    "Abortion Law in African Commonwealth Countries."
    Journal of African Law.   Volume 25 #2 1981.   pp. 60-79.
Dunbar, Roberta
    "Legislative Reform and Muslim Family Law: Effects Upon
    Women's Rights in Africa South of the Sahara."   Paper
    Presented at the Annual Meeting of the African Studies
    Association.   Paper #25.   Philadelphia, Pennsylvania.
    October 15-18, 1980.
Howard, R.
    "Women's Rights in English-Speaking Sub-Saharan Africa."
    (In) Welch, Claude E. and Meltzer, Ronald I. (eds.).
    Human Rights and Development in Africa.   Albany, New
    York: State University of New York Press.   1984.
Morris, H.F.
    "The Development of Statutory Marriage Law in 20th
    Century British Colonial Africa."   Journal of African
    Law.   Volume 23 #1 1979.   pp. 37-64.

LITERATURE

LaPin, Deidre
    "Women in African Literature."   (In) Hay, Margaret J. and
    Stichter, Sharon (eds.).   African Women South of the
    Sahara.   New York: Longman.   1984.   pp. 102-118.
Lee, S.
    "The Image of the Woman in the African Folktale From the
    Sub-Saharan Francophone Area."   Yale French Studies.   #53
    1976.   pp. 19-28.

MARITAL RELATIONS AND NUPTIALITY

Bongaarts, John and Frank, Odile and Lesthaeghe, Ron J.
    "The Proximate Determinants of Fertility in Sub-Saharan
    Africa."   Population and Developement Review.   Volume 10
    #3 September, 1984.   pp. 511-538+.
Boserup, Ester
    "Economic and Demographic Interrelationships in
    Sub-Saharan Africa."   Population and Development Review.
    Volume 11 #3 September, 1985.   pp. 383-397+.
Brown, Judith E.
    "Polygyny and Family Planning in Sub-Saharan Africa."

Studies in Family Planning. Volume 12 #8-9
August-September, 1981. pp. 322-326.
Caldwell, John C.
    "Marriage, the Family and Fertility in Sub-Saharan Africa
    With Special Reference to Research Programmes in Ghana
    and Nigeria." (In) Huzayyin, S.A. and Acsadi, G.T.
    (eds.). Family and Marriage in Some African and Asian
    Countries. Cairo: Cairo Demographic Centre. CDC
    Research Monograph #6. 1976. pp. 359-371.
Dow, Thomas E.
    Breast-Feeding, Abstinence, and Family Planning Among the
    Yoruba and Other Sub-Saharan Groups: Patterns and Policy
    Implications. Purchase, New York: State University of
    New York. Department of Sociology. 1978.
Dunbar, Roberta
    "Legislative Reform and Muslim Family Law: Effects Upon
    Women's Rights in Africa South of the Sahara." Paper
    Presented at the Annual Meeting of the African Studies
    Association. Paper #25. Philadelphia, Pennsylvania.
    October 15-18, 1980.
Frank, Odile
    Child Fostering in Sub-Saharan Africa. New York:
    Population Council. Center for Policy Studies. 1984.
Lesthaeghe, Ron J. and Ohadike, Patrick O. and Kocher, James
E. and Page, Hilary J.
    "Child-Spacing and Fertility in Sub-Saharan Africa: An
    Overview of Issues." (In) Page, Hilary J. and
    Lesthaeghe, Ron (eds.). Child-Spacing in Tropical
    Africa: Traditions and Change. New York: Academic Press.
    1981. pp. 3-23.
Lesthaeghe, Ron J.
    Fertility and its Proximate Determinants in Sub-Saharan
    Africa: The Record of the 1960's and 70's. Brussels,
    Belgium: Vrije Universiteit Brussel. Interuniversity
    Programme in Demography. IPD Working Paper #1984-2.
    1984. 117p.
Morris, H.F.
    "The Development of Statutory Marriage Law in 20th
    Century British Colonial Africa." Journal of African
    Law. Volume 23 #1 1979. pp. 37-64.
Valentine, C.H. and Revson, J.E.
    "Cultural Traditions, Social Change, and Fertility in
    Sub-Saharan Africa." Journal of Modern African Studies.
    Volume 17 #3 September, 1979. pp. 453-472.
White, Luise S.
    "Women in the Changing African Family." (In) Hay,
    Margaret J. and Stichter, Sharon (eds.). African Women
    South of the Sahara. New York: Longman. 1984. pp.
    53-68.

MIGRATION

Robertson, Claire C.
    "Women in the Urban Economy." (In) Hay, Margaret J. and

Stichter, Sharon (eds.). African Women South of the
Sahara. New York: Longman. 1984. pp. 33-50.

MISCELLANEOUS

United Nations Fund for Population Activities
    Forum on Population and Development for Women Leaders
    From Sub-Saharan African Countries. New York: United
    Nations Fund for Population Activities. May 15-18, 1984.
    39p.

NATIONALISM

O'Barr, Jean F.
    African Women in Politics. (In) Hay, Margaret J. and
    Stichter, Sharon (eds.). African Women South of the
    Sahara. New York: Longman. 1984. pp. 140-155.
Urdang, Stephanie
    "Women in National Liberation Movements." (In) Hay,
    Margaret J. and Stichter, Sharon (eds.). African Women
    South of the Sahara. New York: Longman. 1984. pp.
    156-169.

ORGANIZATIONS

United Nations Economic Commission for Africa (UNECA)
    "National Machinery for the Integration of Women in
    Development in African Countries." Paper Presented to
    the Regional Conference on the Implementation of the
    National Regional and Worlds Plans of Action for the
    Integration of Women in Development. Addis Ababa,
    Ethiopia: UNECA. Nouakchott, Mauritania. 1977. 54p.
Wipper, Audrey
    "Women's Voluntary Associations." (In) Hay, Margaret J.
    and Stichter, Sharon (eds.). African Women South of the
    Sahara. New York: Longman. 1984. pp. 69-86.

POLITICS AND GOVERNMENT

Dunbar, Roberta
    "Legislative Reform and Muslim Family Law: Effects Upon
    Women's Rights in Africa South of the Sahara." Paper
    Presented at the Annual Meeting of the African Studies
    Association. Paper #25. Philadelphia, Pennsylvania.
    October 15-18, 1980.
O'Barr, Jean F.
    African Women in Politics. (In) Hay, Margaret J. and
    Stichter, Sharon (eds.). African Women South of the
    Sahara. New York: Longman. 1984. pp. 140-155.
Staudt, Kathleen A.
    Women's Politics and Capitalist Transformation in

Subsaharan Africa. East Lansing, Michigan: Michigan
State University. Office of Women in International
Development. Working Paper #54. April, 1984.
United Nations Economic Commission for Africa (UNECA)
"National Machinery for the Integration of Women in
Development in African Countries." Paper Presented to
the Regional Conference on the Implementation of the
National Regional and Worlds Plans of Action for the
Integration of Women in Development. Addis Ababa,
Ethiopia: UNECA. Nouakchott, Mauritania. 1977. 54p.
Urdang, Stephanie
"Women in National Liberation Movements." (In) Hay,
Margaret J. and Stichter, Sharon (eds.). African Women
South of the Sahara. New York: Longman. 1984. pp.
156-169.

RELIGION AND WITCHCRAFT

Dunbar, Roberta
"Legislative Reform and Muslim Family Law: Effects Upon
Women's Rights in Africa South of the Sahara." Paper
Presented at the Annual Meeting of the African Studies
Association. Paper #25. Philadelphia, Pennsylvania.
October 15-18, 1980.
Strobel, Margaret A.
"Women in Religion and in Secular Ideology." (In) Hay,
Margaret J. and Stichter, Sharon (eds.). African Women
South of the Sahara. New York: Longman. 1984. pp.
87-101.

RESEARCH

Saulniers, Suzanne S. and Rakowski, Cathy A.
Women in the Development Process: A Select Bibliography
on Women in Sub-Saharan Africa and Latin America.
Austin, Texas: University of Texas Press. Institute of
Latin American Studies. 1977. 287p.
Stichter, Sharon B.
"Some Selected Statistics on African Women." (In) Hay,
Margaret J. and Stichter, Sharon (eds.). African Women
South of the Sahara. New York: Longman. 1984. pp.
188-194.
Tadesse, Zenebework
"Research Trends on Women in Sub-Saharan Africa." Paper
Presented at the Meeting of Experts on Research and
Teaching Related to Women: Evaluation and Prospects.
Paris: United Nations Educational, Scientific and
Cultural Organization. May, 1980. 12p.
Tadesse, Zenebeworke
Survey of Principal Social Science Research on Women in
Sub-Saharan Africa. Unpublished Manuscript. 1979.
United Nations Economic Commission for Africa (UNECA)
An Inventory of Social Science Research on Women's Roles

and Status in Sub-Saharan Africa Since 1960. (Draft)
Addis Ababa, Ethiopia: UNECA. 1982.

SEX ROLES

Bryson Judy C.
   "Women and Agriculture in Sub-Saharan Africa:
   Implications for Development." Journal of Development
   Studies. Volume 17 #3 April, 1981. pp. 29-46.
Dey, Jennie M.
   Women in Rice Farming Systems, Focus: Subsaharan Africa.
   Rome: United Nations Food and Agriculture Organization.
   Women in Agriculture Series #2. 1984. 106p.
Dunbar, Roberta
   "Legislative Reform and Muslim Family Law: Effects Upon
   Women's Rights in Africa South of the Sahara." Paper
   Presented at the Annual Meeting of the African Studies
   Association. Paper #25. Philadelphia, Pennsylvania.
   October 15-18, 1980.
Henn, Jeanne K.
   "Women in the Rural Economy: Past, Present and Future."
   (In) Hay, Margaret J. and Stichter, Sharon (eds.).
   African Women South of the Sahara. New York: Longman.
   1984. pp. 1-18.
Howard, R.
   "Women's Rights in English-Speaking Sub-Saharan Africa."
   (In) Welch, Claude E. and Meltzer, Ronald I. (eds.).
   Human Rights and Development in Africa. Albany, New
   York: State University of New York Press. 1984.
Lancaster, Chet S.
   "Women, Horticulture and Society in Sub-Saharan Africa."
   American Anthropologist. Volume 78 #3 September, 1976.
   pp. 539-564.
Lesthaeghe, Ron J. and Ohadike, Patrick O. and Kocher, James
E. and Page, Hilary J.
   "Child-Spacing and Fertility in Sub-Saharan Africa: An
   Overview of Issues." (In) Page, Hilary J. and
   Lesthaeghe, Ron (eds.). Child-Spacing in Tropical
   Africa: Traditions and Change. New York: Academic Press.
   1981. pp. 3-23.
United Nations Economic Commission for Africa (UNECA)
   An Inventory of Social Science Research on Women's Roles
   and Status in Sub-Saharan Africa Since 1960. (Draft)
   Addis Ababa, Ethiopia: UNECA. 1982.
Valentine, C.H. and Revson, J.E.
   "Cultural Traditions, Social Change, and Fertility in
   Sub-Saharan Africa." Journal of Modern African Studies.
   Volume 17 #3 September, 1979. pp. 453-472.

STATUS OF WOMEN

Dunbar, Roberta
   "Legislative Reform and Muslim Family Law: Effects Upon

Women's Rights in Africa South of the Sahara." Paper
Presented at the Annual Meeting of the African Studies
Association. Paper #25. Philadelphia, Pennsylvania.
October 15-18, 1980.
Ritchie, Jean A.
The Integration of Women in Agrarian Reform and Rural
Development in English Speaking Countries of the African
Region. Rome: United Nations Food and Agriculture
Organization. March, 1978. 95p.
United Nations Economic Commission for Africa (UNECA)
An Inventory of Social Science Research on Women's Roles
and Status in Sub-Saharan Africa Since 1960. (Draft)
Addis Ababa, Ethiopia: UNECA. 1982.
Urdang, Stephanie
"Women in National Liberation Movements." (In) Hay,
Margaret J. and Stichter, Sharon (eds.). African Women
South of the Sahara. New York: Longman. 1984. pp.
156-169.

Author Index

Denga, Daniel I. 330,423
Dennis, Carolyne 318,330,341,353(2),355,359(2),362,372(2),
  377,382,434,445
Denzer, LaRay 188,191,192,486,490
Deshen, Shlomo 123,132,138
Dettwyler, Katherine A. 310
Development Alternatives Inc. 202,206,208,209
Dey, Jennie M. 221(4),554,558,560,561,572
Di Domenico, Catherine M. 167,174,178,184,193,330(5),338,
  355,359,361,362,372(5),375,376,382(2),407,410,441,450(2),
  452(3)
Diakanda, M. Sala 534,542,543,544,548,551
  See also: Sala-Diakanda, Mpembele
Dickens, Bernard N. 554,556,568
Didomenko, Catherine 318,341,362,377,445
Diepenhorst, M.J. 78,85
Dinan, Carmel 232,247(2),255(3),277,285
Dinnerstein, Myra 202,206,310,313,455,460
Donne, L. 200,268,300,564
Dopamu, P.A. 408
Dorph, K.J. 35,39,42,117,128,135,138,148,157,160
Doucet, Marie-Jo 313
Dow, Thomas E. 330,331,391(2),408(2),423(2),556,563,566,569
Doyle, Pat 331,391,408,423
Drewal, Henry J. 320(2),331(2),436(2),441
Drewal, Margaret T. 320,331,436,441
Duffield, Mark 327,359,371,381
Dugbaza, Tetteh 225,232,242,247,285
Dulansey, Maryanne L. 1,4,9,11,165,167,174,176
Duly, Colin 234,277
Dumor, Ernest K. 225,232,233,242,247(3),250,255(3),258,281,
  289
Dunayevskaya, Raya 123,131,135
Dunbar, Roberta 556,568,569,570,571,572(2)
Duquette, D.G. 291
Durojaiye, Michael O. 331,382,423,442
Durrani, Lorna H. 144,149,150,162
Duza, A. 60,78,91
Duza, M. Badrud 4,5,13,20(2),26(2),51,74,144,158,161,290
Dwyer, Daisy H. 123(5),132,135(2),138(2),140(3)
Dzegede, Sylvi A. 268,277,280,288,307,488,492,493,496
Dzidzienyo, Stella 233,256,285

Early, Evelyn A. 48,51(4),61,64,69,74,75,91,109
Ebin, Victoria 233,268,271
Ebot, Moses T. 504,507,518,519,521
Edebiri, A.A. 340,393,411,427
Edeh, J. 315,331,408,417
Edigbo, P.O. 331,391,408,424
Eelens, Frank 200(2),234,266,268,269,295,299,300(2),458,
  508,518,519,520,557,563,564,565
Egan, Susan 2,5,16,27,166,168,184,192,195
Egbunike, N.A. 332,367,373,442,453
Egwuatu, V.E. 408,448
Egypt. Central Agency for Public Mobilisation and

AUTHOR INDEX

Statisitics 66,69,85,91,104
Egypt. National Commission for UNESCO 51,67,69,109,115
Egypt. Population and Family Planning Board 51,75,78,85, 108
Egypt. State Information Service 52,61,109,113
Egyptian Ministry of Information 64,69
Ehtewish, Omran S. 119
Eid, E.E. 85,89
Ejiogu, Aloy M. 367,433,442
Ekam, Anna G. 367,436
Ekanem, Ita I. 331(3),333(2),348,383(2),391(4),392,396, 400(3),424(3),429,565,566
Ekejiuba, Felicia 331,383,442
Ekpere, J.A. 332,383,442
Ekpo, M. 408
Ekwempu, C.C. 408
El Baymoumi, Soheir 52,91,100,113
El Belghiti, Malika 123,127(2),129(2),131(2),140
El Guindi, Fadwa 52(2),73(2),107(2),109(2)
El Hakim, Ahmed S. 52(3),91(3),112(3)
El Kalla, Hassan H. 78,91
El Saadawi, Nawal 5,13,26,27,52(2),67,73(2),98(2),109(2), 113
El-Atoum, Shafik 78,84,100
El-Badry, M.A. 84
El-Badry, Samia M. 62,82,95
El-Bahy, M. 95
El-Deeb, Bothaina M. 52(2),78(2),85(2),100
El-Guenedi, Mervat M. 77,89,99
El-Guenedi, Moushera M. 77,89,99
El-Guindy M. 53,63,85
El-Huni, Ali M. 119
El-Karamani, Yussuf I. 53,79,107
El-Kharboutly, Maitre A. 53,75,98,100,107,114
El-Khorazaty, Mohamed Nabil E. 80(2),81,87,88(2),101,102, 103
El-Maaddawi, Y. 60,83,96,104
El-Masry, G. 60,83,96,104
El-Messiri, Sawsan 53,114
El-Nagar, M. 85,90
El-Nomrosi, M.M. 85
El-Rafie, M. 79,85,91,100
El-Sherbini, A.F. 85,90
Elegbe, Isaac A. 332,408
Elegbe, Iyabode 332,408
Eliraz, Giora 73,96,114
Elkins, T.E. 271
Ellison, P.T. 545
Ellovich, Risa S. 293,294(3),301(2),304(3)
Elwert, Georg 167,179,189,192,193
Emeagwali, G.T. 317,332,359,372,442,
Emecheta, Buchi 418
Enabulele, A.B. 353,367,372,408,433
Enahoro, Diane S. 353,373,442
Endeley, J.B. 505,510,513,515,516

582

297,298,317,333,360,374,442,505(5),507(2),508(5),510(2),
513(7),516(3),517,524(2)
Gwan Achu, Emmanuel 504,518,521,523
Gyeke, L. 225,241,246
Gyepi-Garbrah, Benjamin 307,400,409,489,556,565,566

Hagaman, Barbara L. 234,248,262,277,282,285
Hagan, A.L. 1,9,11,12
Hagan, George P. 234(2),245(2),262(2),277(2)
Hakem, Ahmed M. 53,97
Hakiki, Fatiha 33(2),34(2),37(2),43(2)
Halila, Souad 145,151,157
Hall, Marjorie J. 53,98
Hall, Richard 18
Hamer, Alice J. 221,458(2),470,472(2)
Hammam, Mona 64(3),69(2)
Hammam, Nabila M. 49,74,99
Hammond, Thomas N. 274,458,469
Hamzawi, Riad 53,69,79,86(2),92,101
Hanbel, Ibrahim 70,75,92,115
Handem, Diana 291
Handwerker, W. Penn 307(2)
Hardiman, M.G. 489,496
Harfoush, Samira 124,130
Harms, Robert 534,547,552
Harrell-Bond, Barbara E. 168,174,192,198,248,273,281,282,
476(4),486(4),491,492(3),494
Harrington, Judith A. 333,334(3),367(2),384(3),400(2),409,
425(2),443(2),450(3)
Harrison, Graham 234,277
Harrison, Kelsey 409
Harrow, K. 33,40,44,45,119,124,135,140,141,145,157,161,162
Hartfield, V.J. 409(2)
Hassan, Ezzeldin O. 79,86
Hassan, Shafick S. 61,64,70,79,86
Hassouna, Mary T. 80(3),92(3),101
Hay, Margaret J. 556
Hayani, Ibrahim 5,14,20,22,26
Haynes, J. 334,418,443
Hefnawi, F.G. 80,89,92(2),93,95,115
Helfenbein, Saul 519,521
Helmy, Hussein A. 81,87
Hemmings-Gapihan, Grace S. 203(2),204(2),206,208(2),210,
211,214
Henderson, Helen K. 203,204,214
Hendrixson, Joyce 334(2),436,443(2)
Henn, Jeanne K. 505,510,514,523,554,556,560,567,572
Hennart, Philippe 530,535(2),546(3)
Hershman, Paul 234,277,285
Hevi-Yiboe, L.A. 234,262,277,285
Heymer, A. 535(2),553(2)
Hill, Allan G. 17,21,184,191,310
Hill, Polly 321,334,384,415
Hilton, Anne 535,542,547
Hirschmann, David 121,124,127,129,137,140

About the Compiler

Native Californian Davis A. Bullwinkle was raised in the San Francisco Bay area. Early interest in Black history and African Studies led to undergraduate degrees in History and Anthropology from California State University-Chico. Under the guidance of professors in History and Anthropology, Mr. Bullwinkle specialized in African Studies. He received a Masters of Library Science degree from Emporia State University in Kansas.

Mr. Bullwinkle has published bibliographic articles on Drought and Desertification in Africa, Nomadism and Pastoralism in Africa, and Women in Africa during the 1970's. All were published in the former Washington, D.C., African Bibliographic Center's "Current Bibliography on African Affairs." He is presently employed by the Arkansas State Library in Little Rock, Arkansas, where he is the Senior Reference Librarian. He recently married and has three stepchildren.